ADVANCE PRAISE FOR *AMERICA IN THE 21ST CENTURY*

"In *America in the 21st Century*, Larry continues where he left off with *Patriot's History*, detailing the War on Terror, the rise of the Democrat Party under Barack Obama and its subsequent fall. He chronicles with a critical, but unbiased eye, the era of 'wokeness' and its accompanying pathologies, the transformational realignment of the major political parties in the Trump era, and the Covid debacle. This book is thorough, informative, and enlightening, and most of all optimistic, reflecting Larry's refreshingly positive spirit, as contrasted with so many other historians, political commentators, and so-called influencers. In these pages you'll find both the truth and abundant evidence to believe that America is on a path to surpass its historically unparalleled greatness. This work is highly readable and is essential for your library, your friends, and your kids."

–David Limbaugh, Author of *Guilty by Reason of Insanity* and *Jesus Is Risen*

ALSO BY THE AUTHOR

A Patriot's History of the United States
48 Liberal Lies About American History
Reagan: The American President
Dragonslayers: Six Presidents and Their War with the Swamp

AMERICA IN THE 21ST CENTURY

LARRY SCHWEIKART

Published by Bombardier Books
An Imprint of Post Hill Press
ISBN: 979-8-89565-329-6
ISBN (eBook): 979-8-89565-330-2

America in the 21st Century:
A History of the Past Quarter Century

Cover Design by Conroy Accord

This book, as well as any other Bombardier Books publications, may be purchased in bulk quantities at a special discounted rate. Contact orders@bombardierbooks.com for more information.

This is a work of nonfiction. All people, locations, events, and situations are portrayed to the best of the author's memory.

Post Hill Press
New York • Nashville
posthillpress.com

Published in the United States of America
1 2 3 4 5 6 7 8 9 10

To those whom I love…don't make me say it.

CONTENTS

INTRODUCTION
THE DISASTER THAT WASN'T

It was approaching midnight in Canberra, Australia. Around the world people anxiously watched their computer screens—or *anything* digital for that matter. Over the previous two years, industry insiders had been concerned about the biggest computer glitch of all time, something called the "Y2K bug."[1] Outgoing President Bill Clinton, not wishing any more tarnish on his already-stained reputation, had sent his "czar" on the bug to be in the air when the clock turned to the witching hour. It was a symbolic goat tethering: If John Koskinen—Clinton's digital specialist—was wrong, there was a good chance his airplane would crash out of the sky with him in it.

Only four or five years earlier, no one (except a few serious IT nerds) even knew of a "millennium bug," as the Y2K issue was called, let alone were concerned about it. Insiders started to notice that the computer programs and formatting of calendar data had all been set to just two-digit changes. For example, the year 1996 on the computer would just read "96." But the flip over to a new century had, at least in many cases, never been considered, let alone programmed. Over a relatively short period, it dawned on those in the tech industry that the shift at midnight to the year 2000 could cause catastrophic damage if computers tried to reset to 1900, thus possibly causing them to spectacularly crash. No one knew the dangers. Some insisted that everything from computer-controlled gas pumps to water treatment plants could experience complete failure. Others warned that electronically controlled (and thus computer-reliant) prison doors would fly open, provoking images of the murder rampage scenes in the movie *Natural Born Killers*.

Warning signs first appeared when grocery store credit card readers began rejecting cards with expiration dates after 2000.[2] JavaScript, Microsoft Excel, and even some programming languages such as Perl and Java experienced glitches.[3] Since no one knew exactly what the ramifications of the bug were, people grew concerned that anything digital, including Social Security checks or Individual Retirement Account disbursements automatically dispatched by computers, would cease.

IT departments that foresaw a problem quickly made inroads with corporations to address it, but even those possessing robust systems supposedly with rewritten codes still had no idea what midnight going into the year 2000 would bring. One grocery store IT director kept mum about his company's success, afraid that if they missed something it would generate embarrassing headlines. "Better to be an anonymous success than a public failure," he reasoned.[4] The potential of a nuclear power plant going berserk—with Chernobyl still fresh in peoples' minds—instilled sobriety into the tech departments of corporations around the world. By 1998 most had major efforts under way to prevent a meltdown. That year, Congress formed an oversight committee.[5]

The companies were successful. As one Stanford professor claimed, "the Y2K crisis didn't happen precisely because people started preparing for it over a decade in advance."[6] While some may have thought it a hoax or a waste of time, the event was a good illustration of how, if America's business sector perceives something to be problem, it could take measures to correct it.

Just a quarter century earlier, Americans would have been mystified if you had spoken of a nationwide shutdown caused by computers. To

Americans of the 1970s, most of the computing devices—really little more than advanced calculators at that time—were found in big businesses, and the overwhelming majority of them came marked "IBM." "Big Blue," as Tom Watson Jr.'s company was nicknamed, had controlled 85 percent of the world computer market in the late 1960s. No one thought any other company could even challenge its dominance.

While computers had been necessary to landing a man on the moon (with what then was a programming capability that today would fit in a single iPhone), by the mid-1970s the machines had worked their way into almost every major business by performing payroll, keeping personnel records, scheduling airline flights, and a myriad of other functions. (In 1952, CBS had used a computer to predict the outcome of the election.) IBM and its massive mainframe systems dominated the market and, with a few exceptions, defined what a computer was. That changed with the arrival of the Apple 1 in 1976. Even then, home or "desktop" computers were hardly a rage, and certainly not a necessity. Most industry executives thought them a toy with little sales potential.

A host of other companies were already producing personal computers before Apple, and after Steve Jobs and Steve Wozniak sprang their device on the world, dozens more joined the competition. The most successful of those, Bill Gates's IBM Personal Computer (PC), soon surpassed Apple in sales, but at the time, picking a winner still remained anybody's guess. What all but a few futurists such as George Gilder missed, however, was that the PC would soon become the essence of modern computing, relegating mainframes to only the most massive of government and business headquarters. And then the PC would be replaced by even smaller devices, such as laptops and even phones.

With the birth of the internet in 1991, the value of a personal computer soared even more as the world was opened up to any individual connected to the World Wide Web ("www"). The predicted transformation of economics and culture began shortly after that, much as Gilder predicted in his series of books. Far more than any time in the previous one hundred years, people could be connected in unexpected and unpredictable ways. Consumers could literally shop the globe, and personal information began to seep out despite layers of preventative protocols.

In retrospect, it appeared that the "happy age" of economist John Maynard Keynes had come to pass. His 1920 book *The Economic Consequences of the Peace* celebrated the world that had existed just a few years earlier when

> the inhabitant of London could order by telephone, sipping his morning tea in bed, the various products of the whole earth, in such quantity as he might see fit, and reasonably expect their early delivery upon his doorstep; he could at the same moment and by the same means adventure his wealth in the natural resources and new enterprises of any quarter of the world, and share, without exertion or even trouble, in their prospective fruits and advantages; or he could decide to couple the security of his fortunes with the good faith of the townspeople of any substantial municipality in any continent that fancy or information might recommend. He could secure forthwith, if he wished it, cheap and comfortable means of transit to any country or climate without passport or other formality, could despatch [sic] his servant to the neighboring office of a bank for such supply of the precious metals as might seem convenient, and could then proceed abroad to foreign quarters, without knowledge of their religion, language, or customs.[7]

Except what took days, weeks, or months in Keynes's time now could take seconds with the internet, especially when it came to the transmission of information.

Until the internet itself became the leading source of news, the major newspapers and television outlets remained secure as gatekeepers. That also changed in June 1980 with the founding of Cable News Network (CNN) by Ted Turner in Atlanta. Broadcasting news unceasingly, CNN made news a twenty-four-hour business. CNN opened the door for numerous forms of news competition that would soon, in turn, relegate it to a lower status and ultimately shrinking viewership. More important, since real news (i.e., events that had a significant impact on the lives of a majority of the population) did not occur every hour, let alone every minute, the very concept of news changed. It took a back seat to an endless deluge of filler, quasi-news, gossip, rumor, and above all entertainment or advertising disguised as "news." News transformed from information that people could "access" to a product for corporations to sell. (It's worth noting that the "news division" of major networks was never viewed as a profit center.) The epitome of what CNN started came with Operation Desert Storm in 1991, where the United States and its allies crushed an Iraqi army that, on paper at least, seemed formidable—all of which occurred under the watchful eye of the camera. It was the first war in history that was broadcasted in real time, with a modicum of censorship.

Nothing spoke to the drama or titillation of this new definition of news as did the scandal involving President Clinton. His dalliances with Monica Lewinsky, a young intern in the Oval Office—and his subsequent criminal acts of lying to federal authorities, forgery, and attempting to coerce witnesses—gripped the public. For several years leading up to his 1998 impeachment for lying under oath and obstruction of justice, Clinton's sex life (and associated lies) dominated the twenty-four-hour news media. Television lawyers and legal experts babbled ceaselessly about his predicament—though, of course, nothing on the scale of the O. J. Simpson trial in 1995, which produced a cottage industry of lawyer-celebrities on the cable channels.

Clinton was impeached on two counts of "high crimes and misdemeanors" in 1998 but was acquitted on both by the Senate trial in 1999, all under the full-time glare of cameras and, by then, relentless analyses by AM radio hosts such as Rush Limbaugh. Clinton's acquittal was entirely derived from his high-performing economy, itself largely based on policies from an earlier era, that of Ronald Reagan. Clinton, when discussing with his inner circle how best to keep up his poll numbers, heeded the advice of his adviser James Carville ("It's the economy, stupid") and wisely left most of those policies in place. He also owed his survival to a new type of politics that surpassed even Franklin D. Roosevelt's "brains trust," a "war room" of loyalists who sent out faxed "talking points" daily to a slavish media that repeated them, often verbatim and often universally.

Still, the Lewinsky affair left Americans gravely distressed about Clinton's behavior and the declining decorum he brought to the Oval Office. Equally significant, the acquittal—for which most Americans expressed approval—nevertheless left them with a growing cynicism of the political process. They knew in their hearts Clinton should have been removed, but his policies paid too well.

Perhaps the most cataclysmic development to come out of the Lewinsky affair occurred not in the Oval Office, but in a small office that housed a new internet news source run by a Walter Duranty–wannabe, Matt Drudge. Matt Drudge and Andrew Breitbart had created a news aggregator site run on less than $3,500 a day that reached into newsrooms from *The Washington Post* and *The New York Times* to dozens of political, business, and cultural magazines around the country to hundreds of smaller papers. Able to see headlines—and stories—before they were published, *The Drudge Report* simply provided a web link (or, in the vernacular, "linked") to the original stories. But understanding the market, Drudge recast the headlines in a more shocking, muckraker style, such as "Newsweek Kills Story on White House Intern," which was his blockbuster headline that first revealed the presence of Monica Lewinsky.[8] Drudge only broke the story because part of the story itself was the fact that the so-called mainstream media of the day—*Newsweek*—already had the details and planned to kill it. Or, the liberal media was lying by omission to protect Clinton. For the first time in the history of journalism, the journalists themselves became the object of reporting.

Once it became clear that stories could be previewed and that links to them could be provided to the public, it was game over for editors with an agenda. (That led, in 2008, to the UK's *The Daily Telegraph* labeling Drudge the "world's most powerful journalist.")[9] Someone would have information somewhere. It only needed to be found, and internet sleuths soon figured out how to expose it to the public. Indeed, their business model depended on getting it out sooner rather than later, accuracy be damned, which produced yet another transformation in journalism.

That strategy had already been forced on television news by CNN. At first, CNN held to a certain degree of objectivity, but by the early 1990s, its liberal bias had caught up to it. Indeed, during the years of Reagan's presidency, virtually all of the somewhat-objective news shows had drifted farther left in their effort to diminish or dilute the impact of Reagan's success. A decade later, when CNN joined them, there was a gaping hole for an alternative, conservative (or, some would say, honest) news service. That hole was filled in 1996 by Fox News.

With the increasingly partisan, liberally biased news and the twenty-four-hour news cycle, stories could no longer be kept secret. They could only be "spun," as political insiders called it. That is, partisans could put their own interpretation on a story while claiming the same "facts" as their opponents. Control of stories became critical, especially when it came to life-and-death situations such as the FBI raid at David Koresh's Waco compound in 1993 or the wave of Islamic terrorist attacks (commencing that same year with the World Trade Center truck bombing). It was here, in this new Wild West arena of news, that Drudge and the new open media came face to face with Clinton's sexual escapades.

By itself, Clinton's sex life would not have generated as much concern (presuming he had never lied under oath or engaged in a half dozen other illegal cover-ups) except that they seemed to taint his job performance in other ways. He had been on the phone discussing troop deployments related to the Yugoslav War in 1995 while receiving oral sex from Monica Lewinsky. On at least one occasion, according to the report investigating President Donald Trump for "Russian collusion," the Russians actually taped Clinton having phone sex with Lewinsky.[10] Fortunately, no disastrous consequences stemmed from his distractions. Later, however, Clinton would exhibit a similar lack of focus over the terrorist Osama bin Laden, and America would pay a heavy—and still ongoing—price for that. But that was still in the future.

Just a month after the newly elected Clinton had been sworn in, Islamic radicals attacked the New York World Trade Center in 1993 with a car bomb in an effort to collapse one of the towers into the other. It failed, but revealed the sheer audacity of the conspirators, including the main funder, Khalid Sheikh Mohammed (though he went by at least fifty pseudonyms). A Pakistani raised in Kuwait, Mohammed (there were multiple spellings) was a member of the radical Muslim Brotherhood and studied in the US, receiving a BS degree in 1986 from North Carolina Agricultural and Technical State University.[11] He quit the Muslim Brotherhood because they were not violent enough.

Relocating to Peshawar, Pakistan, Mohammed joined the jihad or "holy war" against the Soviets in Afghanistan. After receiving an advanced degree from Punjab University, he moved to Qatar. During that time, he funded a group of like-minded killers that included Ramzi Yousef, Mahmud Abouhalima, and Mohammad Salameh who plotted to blow up one of the support structures in the World Trade Center tower so that it would collapse into the other. When that failed, he relocated to the Philippines where he conceived of Operation Bojinka. This Manila-based plot involved terrorists boarding a total of twelve flights, leaving bombs with timers, and then leaving to board other planes. All explosions were set to go off at the same time, which, they hoped, would kill at least five thousand people. Mohammed had assumed most of the passengers would be Americans. However, a different sort of explosion caused the plot to fail. An accidental fire in the apartment the bomb makers were using led Philippine authorities to find a laptop computer with detailed plans to the scheme. At that time, Col. Rodolfo Mendoza, a counterterrorism expert for the Philippine police, warned that Mohammed and the others who escaped the dragnet had a plan to fly a plane into CIA headquarters in Langley, Virginia. Mendoza said the tip was "not taken seriously."[12] Mendoza's story would be repeated endlessly until 9/11. Routinely, the CIA and FBI dismiss claims by foreign intelligence officers or police as unreliable.

Mohammed, though, was just getting started. He returned to Qatar and obtained a government job in the ministry of electricity and water. On a trip to Sudan in 1995, he met the son of a Saudi millionaire named Osama bin Laden. A dedicated hater who had fought Russians in Afghanistan, Bin Laden now transferred his venom to Israel and the US, known by the terms the "near enemy" and the "far enemy," respectively. Mohammed then popped up on the radar of the US, which asked Qatar to arrest him in 1996. He fled to Afghanistan and, within a year, was reunited with Bin Laden who also had his terrorist group, al-Qaeda ("the Base"), operating there. Bin Laden failed to recruit Mohammed to al-Qaeda until after the terrorist organization proved itself in the 1998 bombings of American embassies in Nairobi, Kenya, and Dar Es Salaam, Tanzania, that killed more than two hundred people.

For the first time, Bin Laden and al-Qaeda came under scrutiny from the FBI. Under Clinton and his Attorney General Janet Reno, the US fought terrorism with a "law enforcement" approach (as opposed to war) and indicted twenty-one people for various roles in the bombings. Lawrence Wright, a journalist and expert on al-Qaeda, concluded that initially Bin Laden used the embassies as targets to lure the US into Afghanistan. But Clinton only took half measures, ordering a series of missile strikes on Sudan and Bin Laden's Afghan bases. Those did minimal damage to the terror organization. (In Sudan, the US apparently bombed an aspirin factory.) Before long, information surfaced that in an effort to get the "most favorable nation" trading status, Sudan had offered Clinton Bin Ladin alive or dead six separate times. Clinton refused, citing the likelihood that convicting him in a courtroom would be difficult—again, a function of the law enforcement response to terrorism. Although the 9/11 Commission—which many claim was an effort to whitewash any specific culpability—claimed there was "no credible evidence" that the Sudanese Minister of Defense, Elfatih Erwa, had offered up Bin Laden, journalist/historian Lawrence Wright stated that in his interviews with Erwa such an offer was made.[13]

Clinton's weakness, and the futility of the law enforcement approach, worked to the detriment of Clinton's vice president, Al Gore, who became the Democratic nominee for the presidency in 2000. Even as Gore prepared to take on Clinton's mantle, al-Qaeda formulated new plots. The next attack involved a terror bombing of four tourist sites in Jordan, a bomb planted at Los Angeles International Airport (LAX), the use of a suicide boat-bomb to strike the USS *The Sullivans*, and the hijacking of Indian Airlines Flight 814 to occur on or near January 1, 2000. Collectively, those were known as the "millennium plots." They were broken up almost by accident when, on December 14, 1999, a border guard in Washington state stopped an Algerian man, Ahmed Ressam, who was bringing in explosives about the size of those used to destroy the Murrah Federal Building in Oklahoma City in 1995. Authorities learned that Ressam's target was LAX. Ressam was more of a freelance murderer—not a regular, throat-slashing, al-Qaeda true believer (though he learned his trade at one of the camps Bin Laden financed). Other millennium plots were foiled as well: Jordanian forces broke up the attack there, and the attempted bombing of *The Sullivans* unraveled when the boat carrying the explosives sank before detonating. The Indian Airlines flight was taken hostage, then all prisoners released in exchange for captive militants.

Even with all that carnage, there was no indication Clinton took al-Qaeda or Islamic terrorists as seriously as he should have. America soon paid a heavy price. Al-Qaeda struck again on the water in Yemen's Aden harbor, using similar tactics to *The Sullivans* attack, when a bomb-laden terrorist craft blew up alongside the USS *Cole*, a guided missile destroyer, punching a gash in the ship's side. Seventeen sailors were killed and another thirty-seven injured, and as Clinton again failed to respond, Bin Laden grew even more angry that he had failed to provoke the "far enemy."

Those repeated attacks on America remained largely concealed by a US media focused on Clinton's struggle with (to them) evil Republicans trying to oust a popular president. Moreover, for the first time since the administration of John F. Kennedy, when news sources concealed Jack's multiple affairs and serious health issues, the Clinton-era media engaged in cover-up mode to protect the president from criticism. Nothing Clinton did—or didn't do—to stop al-Qaeda during his presidency came in for scrutiny from the major news sources.

A further troublesome development within journalism involved the way the major outlets were rapidly consolidating in ways that would have prompted a trustbuster like Teddy Roosevelt to vigorously prosecute them. Smaller newspapers around the country were gobbled up by larger corporations, while even the largest papers were being folded into larger non-news corporate entities. In 2000, the *Times Mirror* merged with the Tribune Company, publisher of the *Chicago Tribune*, and bringing into the company the *Baltimore Sun*. By 2018, Gannett, publisher of the popular *USA Today*, acquired a total of 216 papers, including 107 dailies; New Media/GateHouse owned 451 papers (mostly smaller, local papers), including 153 dailies; and Digital First Media controlled the *Denver Post*, the *Boston Herald*, the *Orange County Register*, and San Jose's *The Mercury News*, among 155 other papers.[14] To be sure, as of 2000, these giants had not acquired all of these papers, but the trend was shocking: Locally owned papers with regional viewpoints were extinguished, replaced by large corporations mostly headquartered in large cities and run, not by locals, but by liberal elites of the "ruling class." By the turn of the century, it was difficult to cite a single large-city newspaper that could be considered in any way conservative in its outlook or editorials.

That meant that a narrow, uniform, almost identical "party line" of news was transmitted on a steady basis. While the television monopoly of the "Big Three" (ABC, NBC, and CBS) had been broken by CNN and, later, Fox Television, still only Fox offered truly different views on politics and the economy. For that reason, Limbaugh's revolutionary radio show retained a powerful audience of twenty million, with roughly four to five million tuning in at a given time. Limbaugh sustained his audience through both Republican and Democratic presidencies and warded off a constant stream of attacks on his sponsors and radio stations. Early in the 2000s, Democrats tried to mimic Limbaugh's success in talk radio with liberal hosts, but all attempts failed. None had his wit, his humor, but most importantly, none had his political analysis skills.

With few exceptions, Limbaugh proved accurate in his predictions of shifts in the political winds. He had, for example, early in the life of his show identified a war against SUVs (sport utility vehicles, which had found a niche between vans and the more obsolete station wagons) as the vanguard of the then-labeled "global warming" movement. Limbaugh warned that the attack on SUVs was the first shot in a war by environmentalists to eliminate the auto—long a desire of leftists as they pined for an America more like Europe with its mass transportation. SUVs constituted freedom, independence, and, above all, divisions of wealth, as only more affluent members of the middle class could afford them. The left, on the other hand, wanted mass transportation systems it could monitor and control and sought to force populations onto buses, subways, and trains. Limbaugh brilliantly noted that he could "read the stitches on a fastball"[15] (i.e., the intent of liberals and/or their policies) and correctly observed that "they (i.e., liberals) will tell you who they fear"[16] by their attacks.

What made Limbaugh's voice so powerful and attractive was the fact that he stood almost alone in such warnings. With the exception of *The Washington Times*, then dismissed as a newspaper of the "Moonies" because of its ownership by the Korean Unification Church, Sun Myung Moon, and Fox News (which remained mainline conservative, not populist, in its reporting), viewpoints such as those Limbaugh held couldn't be found in any major national forum. Most important, Limbaugh had access to ordinary Americans—truckers on the road listening to him, housewives at home, people on lunch breaks. One actor, who wished to remain anonymous, once told me that even in liberal Hollywood, "All the guys in the trucks [meaning set builders, lighting, and sound people] listen to Rush on their lunch hour. You can hear them."

Another destructive side effect of the twenty-four-hour news cycle emerged: Outlets demanded "news," even if there was none to be had. Events such as the arrest and trial of former football star O. J. Simpson in 1994–95 took on televised lives of their own as armies of "legal analysts" bombarded viewers with the intricacies of courtroom maneuvers and the reliability of DNA evidence. When it came to Clinton, however, inside reporting was off limits. Senate rules kept the proceedings secret—and the impeachment trial itself sped by quickly as Democrats and a handful of timid Republicans who feared voter backlash against them due to Clinton's polling numbers hastened the trial to an early acquittal on both counts.

As the 1990s wore down and the nation prepared to enter the twenty-first century, all surrounded by the Y2K disaster that wasn't, it was apparent that while people willingly allowed Clinton to stay in office, they had had enough of "Clintonism." Indeed, in many ways with the Soviets beaten, Saddam Hussein supposedly contained by sanctions and no-fly zones, and the central problem of former Yugoslavia neatly wrapped up through the Dayton Accords, the central conflict and most pressing problem seemed to be the domestic politics. After several years' worth of investigations, special counsels, impeachment, and stained dresses, it seemed to many that now America's battles would only be at home. The election of 2000 with its confusions, claims, counterclaims, counts, recounts, and "dimpled" and hanging chads only confirmed that view. In so many ways, it was that election and its concomitant complacency, imposed by a peaceful world that launched the US into fifteen years of cronyism, misjudgments, corruption, and decline, only to be perched on the precipice of greatness again.

That is how America started the twenty-first century.

CHAPTER 1
A RAZOR-THIN ELECTION

The Republicans' failure to remove Bill Clinton via impeachment bore long-term dyspeptic effects for the nation. Clinton's tarnished image could not be repaired, which was bad news for the Democratic presidential candidate in the 2000 election, his vice president Al Gore. Yet at the same time, Clinton introduced a level of sleaze and disrespect into the Oval Office that has never effectively been purged and hence could never again be an effective tool for attacking incumbents.

Accepting the vice presidency from Clinton in 1992 had been a bitter pill for the arrogant and perpetually pious Tennessean, Albert Gore Jr. was "the golden boy," the one intended to run against George H. W. Bush in 1992, and it still grated on him that Clinton had claimed the nomination by employing the party's internal leadership.

Gore's path originated in the late 1980s, when a group of Democratic strategists grew alarmed at the shellacking the party got at the hands of Ronald Reagan in 1984. They formed a planning committee called the Democratic Leadership Council (DLC).[17] Founded in 1985 by Al From, the DLC's goal was to reorient the party away from radical leftism and more toward issues—and candidates—who could occupy the center. Often going by the label "New Democrats" or "Third Way," the DLC's most immediate goal was to win back white middle-class voters. Candidates such as George McGovern, Walter Mondale, and Michael Dukakis had been white enough, but their positions stood far to the left of the mainstream of American society. Mondale had even gone so far in 1984 as to promise that he would raise taxes. At the same time, radicals such as Jesse Jackson swam along as power brokers while Northeastern liberals such as Dukakis or Ted Kennedy were the preferred front men. Jackson had personally entered the 1983 race on the heels of his "Rainbow Coalition" with his own race-driven views that troubled and repelled middle-class voters. The only exception between the McGovern loss in 1972 and Mondale's crushing defeat in 1984 was Jimmy Carter, who sold himself as a centrist veteran businessman. Once in office, he promptly swung far left with the rest of them.[18]

Political scientist Donald Critchlow and historian William Rorabaugh detailed how the radical left used a quest for "social justice" to take over 1960s liberalism.[19] George McGovern marked that shift. He openly ran as a "progressive"—the name by which the radical liberals increasingly wanted to go by because of the stain associated with the word "liberal." Despite McGovern's disastrous defeat at the hands of the hated Richard Nixon, the party kept all of the "McGovern rules" within the party that had been implemented to get him elected. At the same time, radicals had moved into the Democratic Party in the 1960s and came from three main directions: first were the veterans of the Civil Rights Movement; a second group arrived as children of white, middle-class liberals who rejected the Cold War; and the third comprised the famed "red diaper babies" described by former communist David Horowitz.[20] Born into a family of communists, Horowitz became a '60s radical and friend of all the far-left icons, including Tom Hayden and Huey Newton. He knew those of whom he wrote.

Collectively, this new core of far-left Democrats had been crushed by the assassination of Robert F. Kennedy and the subsequent trouncing in the primaries of the anti-war fallback candidate Eugene McCarthy. It only deepened their resolve to force an unpopular radical into power by "burrow[ing] deep inside existing institutions [the Democratic Party]."[21] Yet despite dominating protest marches and vocal caucuses, the progressives stood helpless as the mainstream liberal Hubert Humphrey, viewed by radicals as one of the establishment (and thus someone to defeat), easily won the nomination in 1968. A mythology developed that if RFK had just lived, he would have defeated the Minnesotan. In fact, all of the mainstream magazines of the day, including *Time*, *Newsweek*, and *U.S. News & World Report*, a week before RFK's death all agreed that Humphrey already had the nomination secured.[22] It also went largely ignored that Republican up-and-comer Ronald Reagan, then governor of California, had debated Bobby Kennedy in 1967 and so thoroughly whipped him that Kennedy reportedly told his staff never to put him opposite Reagan again. Despite Kennedy's appeal to the young and the anti-war left, those groups still remained a distinct minority in the party, especially when it came to the power brokers capable of mischief to ensure their candidate won.

As a result of Humphrey's expected nomination victory, the progressives threw the most massive temper tantrum since the Confederate States of America left the Union. Some ten thousand to twenty thousand far-left protesters descended on Chicago, seat of the Democratic National Convention, hoping to somehow prevent Humphrey's ascension. Democratic Mayor Richard Daley had just seen his city racked by race riots and had no intention of letting a few thousand drug-infused hippies take it over. He dispatched the twelve thousand–strong Chicago Police Department, supported by over 7,500 United States Army troops and augmented with hundreds of FBI and, likely, CIA agents to quell violence. On August 25, 1968, police charged into Lincoln Park with few rules, even to the point that they had been urged to "get newsmen."[23] A natural alliance between the radicals and the news media, which would only grow over the next five decades, developed, and as British historian Paul Johnson wrote in his monumental book *Modern Times*, the leftists "won the media contest in that they succeeded in branding Daley's law-enforcement as a 'police riot.'"[24] The most trusted man in America, CBS News anchor Walter Cronkite, observing the images of students and delegates being beaten in the streets outside, snapped, "It makes us…want to just turn off the cameras…and get the devil out of here and leave the Democrats to their agony."[25]

In fact, Daley had already infiltrated radical groups, "sabotaging their schemes to acquire buses, and giving out false information at phone banks."[26] He assembled "Daley Dozers," which were Jeeps outfitted with barbed wire on the front to clear the streets. Demonstrators, in a harbinger of the twenty-first century, learned to play to the cameras. If mobs saw reporters, they turned up the violence levels. This was noted in the subsequent report by the National Commission on the Causes and Prevention of Violence.[27]

In a sense, the "battle of Chicago" was fought after the war was won. Protesters never got their desire of ending the Vietnam War, at least as they envisioned it. Years later, the man they most hated, Richard Nixon, did what two Democratic presidents had failed to do and withdrew all troops from Vietnam, ensuring the communist takeover there. But what the protesters did accomplish was to introduce the notion that governments could be intimidated (or, they hoped, even removed) by vocal minorities. Admittedly, the anti-war forces in America eventually exceeded the 50 percent mark in the polls, but that came quite late. Applying the tactics from the civil rights marchers (who possessed a much more powerful moral component than the anti-war or other student protesters), students and the left as a whole believed their own hype and grew furious when institutions didn't act in a manner that showed that they believed it as well.

Then came *Rules for Radicals*. When Saul Alinsky's book came out in 1971, it was first turned on *Democrats* as a manual for how to take over the party.[28] One of those who was influenced by *Rules* was a community organizer in Chicago, Barack Obama. Radicals embraced its concepts of an internal takeover as liberals pushed out anyone who resisted, frightening and intimidating mainstream voters. Their efforts led to the creation of a "reform" commission that would change the way delegates were selected. After all, Humphrey had won the nomination without even competing in the primaries. Delegates from the McCarthy camp allied with those of McGovern, the anti-war candidate from South Dakota, and succeeded in winning just enough of a majority at the convention in 1968 to form the commission. It would fundamentally reshape the Democratic Party.

In the wake of McGovern's shocking defeat, Democrats had to reorient to a "centrist-appearing" party—even if they in fact were as radical as ever. That meant finding new candidates who did not seem extreme or threatening, especially white men from Southern states. This constituted a 180-degree inversion of the original Democratic Party as founded by Martin Van Buren.[29] The "Little Magician," as Van Buren was known, was deeply troubled by the implications of the Missouri Compromise. To him, this presaged a steady expansion of anti-slave states that, in the near future, would legislate against slavery, triggering a civil war. Van Buren's solution involved creating a new political party—the Democrats—who would be rewarded with jobs in return for party loyalty, regardless of their personal position on slavery. In other words, Van Buren intended to bribe them. But there was a little more to the Magician's plan. One component involved the presidency. He concluded that even in 1826 no Deep South slaveholder would ever again be elected president, but at the same time, he reasoned, neither would a Northern anti-slave politician. The solution was to have a "northern man of southern principles," as historian Richard Brown termed it, who would simply not act on slavery.[30] Without going into too much detail, the system had massive weaknesses, not the least of which was if the wrong "northern man" came into the presidency, which was exactly what happened in 1860.

As we fast forward 110 years, we see the Democrats become increasingly viewed as a party of—or at the very least controlled by—extreme Northeastern liberals. To be sure, many of the Democratic power brokers and leading candidates came from California, Illinois, and middle-America places such as Iowa or the West in states such as Colorado. Yet the image of the party seemed Northeastern in character, with politicians such as Chris Dodd, Paul Tsongas, Ed Boland, Jim Florio, Bella Abzug, Liz Holtzman, Stephen Solarz, Charles Rangel, Michael Dukakis, Ted Kennedy, and later Ed Koch, John Kerry, and Hillary Clinton (who identified with New York, not Bill's Arkansas) leading the parade. New York black activists such as Al Sharpton, who could not win an elective office, remained a powerful influence. There were also Northeastern influencers, such as academics Michael Harrington, Richard Cloward, Frances Fox Piven, and Howard Zinn; law professors such as Laurence Tribe, whose book *God Save This Honorable Court* were frequently consulted by Democrats; Alan Dershowitz, also a liberal favorite, gained fame for defending Claus von Bulow; Drew Days III, who headed Carter's civil rights division; and then there were clergymen such as Fr. Robert Drinan, all tinged with the Northeastern liberal chic.

This spectrum of sooty players, far from the rainbow they would eventually affix as their label (when at the time it had nothing to do with homosexuals and everything to do with different races), descended like a gray cloud over the Democrats. Almost every issue bore their smudge, from the radical racism of Sharpton and Rangel to the anti-birth bellowing of the Zero Population Growth movement founded by Yale biologist Charles Remington and Connecticut lawyer Richard Bowers. Remington and Bowers received no small degree of help from Stanford's Paul Ehrlich who, over the two decades after he published the highly influential *The Population Bomb* in 1968, would prove stupendously wrong in almost every prophetic utterance he wrote.[31]

None of those individuals made the Democrats look like a party of the common people or middle America. Hence, the first out of the gate to challenge this mold was Georgia's Jimmy Carter. Indeed, Carter became the first true Southerner (as opposed to a Texas Westerner like Lyndon B. Johnson) to win the presidency as a Southerner since Tennessee's James K. Polk in 1844, proving the prescience of Van Buren. Soon, Carter was followed by Virginia's Chuck Robb, Arkansas's Bill Clinton, and Tennessee's Al Gore (and still later, John Edwards and Jim

Webb). In essence, they had rewritten Van Buren's maxim of needing a "northern man of southern principles" to finding a "southern man of midwestern principles." They knew how to speak in moderate tones with their southern accents, softening their abrasive content. Clinton had come from the governorship in his state, Gore from a Senate seat in his. In reality, though, it was Gore for whom the DLC was originally created. Clinton—and his Arkansas base—was considered second tier.

Gore had a pedigree as his father was a US senator, but when 1988 rolled around and he entered the race, it was clear he was just too young and inexperienced. Clinton possessed a charm advantage, energized by a highly refined sense of reading people that derived from his childhood with an alcoholic father. More importantly, he quickly grasped the potential for employing the machinery of the DLC itself to elevate his name nationally. As head of the National Governors Association, Clinton spoke on its behalf endlessly around the country and became the face of the organization. In short order, Clinton made himself Gore's equal. His schmoozy charm contrasted with Gore's arrogance and stiffness to put him over the top.

Nominated in 1992, Clinton benefited from a third-party candidate, Ross Perot, who was in-again, out-again in the race. Perot stayed just long enough to muddy the waters but focused almost all his criticism on the Republican, George H. W. Bush. Accordingly, Clinton won with a shockingly low 43 percent of the vote—the least since Woodrow Wilson won the presidency with only 41.8 percent in 1912. He wisely listened to his advisers who told him, "It's the economy stupid" and when he asked if his election depended on an (expletive-deleted) bunch of bond traders, they answered in the affirmative. Clinton heard and obeyed.

He had benefited from Reagan's energy and taxation policies and did little to change them. From Reagan, Clinton still had low marginal tax rates and lower corporate rates. From Bush, he had low energy prices, thanks to Bush's war to liberate Kuwait. From a half dozen previous presidents, Clinton inherited the end of the Cold War. While certainly it would have been possible to mess that up, Clinton rode the policies for two terms.

Now, eight years later, it was finally Gore's turn. By then, Gore had an impressive résumé. Although he opposed the Vietnam War, he served with the engineers in country as a journalist. His superior, Brigadier General Ken Cooper, described his trips into the field with Gore as situations where "I could have worn a tuxedo."[32] Surprisingly, Gore returned from the war still opposed to it but much more sympathetic to the local Vietnamese who struggled against communism. As he told journalist Myra MacPherson in 1988, his experience in Southeast Asia "gave me a tolerance for complexity that I don't think I had before.... [I] really didn't take into account the fact that there were an awful lot of South Vietnamese who desperately wanted to hang on to what they called freedom. Coming face to face with those sentiments expressed by people who did the laundry and ran the restaurants and worked in the fields was something I was naively unprepared for."[33]

After a stint as a journalist at Nashville's *The Tennessean*, Gore ran for and won a House seat and then the Senate seat in Tennessee. To do so, he had to "reinvent himself as a conservative on several hot-button issues."[34] Younger Gore in 1976 had opposed gun registration laws, thought homosexuality was "abnormal," and was a reliable pro-life vote when it came to abortion. But by the time it came to consider a national office, Gore changed his tunes. According to one adviser, "what we have to do is deny, deny, deny" that the Tennessean had ever held such positions.[35]

Again, he struggled to be seen as real, swinging from suits to blue jeans and work shirts, and as before he seemed to be the wrong man at the wrong time. His 1988 campaign was dogged with questions about his student and Vietnam War use of marijuana—normally a minor issue a seasoned politician would have flicked off like a fly. But President Reagan had just nominated Douglas Ginsburg to the US Supreme Court, and the judge had to withdraw after it was learned he had used marijuana in the past. Then, as Gore positioned himself against

Massachusetts governor Michael Dukakis, Missouri Congressman Richard Gephardt gained traction. It prevented Gore from being the guy who wasn't a Northern liberal, while the Reverend Jesse Jackson secured the black vote and took several Southern primaries. And there was one other stumble awaiting Gore that would ironically sink the eventual primary winner: Dukakis, who was the first to raise Willie Horton's prison release as a campaign issue. Horton, a black inmate in Dukakis's state prison system, was granted a furlough. While out, Horton attacked a Maryland couple, raping the wife. Although Gore didn't refer to Horton by name, he slammed Dukakis as being the "principal advocate and defender that...provided weekend passes for convicted criminals, including those convicted of first-degree murder who are serving life sentences without parole."[36]

When the 1992 campaign rolled around, an enervated Gore felt bored in the Senate but didn't think he could make another presidential run. Clinton, on the other hand, needed to divert the race away from Gennifer Flowers's claims that threw light on his already shaky character. Gore, Clinton told a senior aide, "reminded him, in both intellect and temperament, of...his wife."[37] In July of 1992, Clinton brought the Tennessean onto the team. By then, Gore had published his eco-manifesto, *Earth in the Balance* (or as conservative talk show host Rush Limbaugh labeled it, "Earth in the Lurch"). It cemented Gore as a heavyweight in the new leftist religion of "climate change" and while many of his key arguments would be decimated by reality and science in the subsequent years, it served to establish him as one of the most revered thinkers on the subject.[38] Unfortunately for Gore, being Clinton's vice president required him to distance himself from the book, as Clinton did not bleed green the way Gore did.

Indeed, Gore so distrusted Clinton that he demanded a written agreement outlining the relationship and responsibilities for the vice president in the new administration. It did little good. His first two years produced little except to encourage Clinton to listen to his veep—which he did. Ultimately, that mattered little. Clinton stumbled into a string of errors, and Gore lost in his first significant attempt at inserting climate change language into a bill (the British thermal unit, or BTU tax). Clinton's fiasco in Somalia, where the infamous "Black Hawk Down" firefight left eighteen American troops dead and eighty wounded, badly tarnished the administration's foreign policy.

Gore headed a "reinventing government" initiative, the likes of which rarely reinvented anything. No Democratic administration was ever going to willingly slash government jobs or programs, no matter how irrelevant or wasteful. Gore relied on "empowering" federal bureaucracies, which meant he empowered them to further ensconce themselves into the burgeoning new "administrative state" that was entirely unresponsive to either courts or legislators. With Gore's help in a timely debate on *Larry King Live* against former presidential candidate Ross Perot, Gore effectively pitched the North American Free Trade Agreement. It looked good at the time, but Perot proved right in prophesying that it would mean an exodus of jobs to Mexico. (Perot at the time did not point out that an even greater exodus would occur from immigrants coming across the border *from* Mexico.)

It was one of the few victories in a string of scandal-plagued years in which the prudish Gore had to run interference for Clinton. Slapped with a stinging midterm election that saw the Republicans take control of the House of Representatives for the first time in forty years, Clinton was forced on defense. In contrast, Gore increasingly looked good.[39] Clinton survived through a process of "triangulation," where he placed himself above both parties' bickering in Congress. And, with the help of a surging economy, he kept his polls high enough to not only get reelected over a weak GOP candidate, Bob Dole, but to also use the economy to prevent the Senate from removing him after his impeachment. Clinton may have been a lame duck, but he was a survivor lame duck. And that left Gore in the unwelcome position of having to contrast what he would bring to the presidency over that of Clinton. Moreover, Gore had to tread carefully on the very issues that had landed Clinton only the second impeachment in American history. For example, he couldn't criticize his predecessor's moral failings too much, as that would play into the hands of the Republicans. At the same time, Gore had to make the case that he was superior in terms of character. That carried its own risk, as Gore's pious and imperious temperament could surface too easily.

Gore's only real competition in the primaries came from a Northeastern liberal, Senator Bill Bradley of New Jersey. A Princeton grad, Bradley had been a famous basketball star with the New York Knicks on their championship team, but in the national political arena, he came off as just another stiff Ivy Leaguer, aloof and indifferent to working-class concerns. If Gore was boring, Bradley was a walking Ambien. Although Gore himself suffered from perpetual condescension, his Southern accent and Tennessee background concealed his more radical leanings, especially when it came to the environment. Almost ignored was the Green Party candidate, consumer activist Ralph Nader, who ultimately would deny Gore the presidency.

When nominated at the convention, following a rousing speech by Clinton (which was mostly about himself), Gore came on stage. When he finished his acceptance speech, his wife Tipper joined him and he gave her an odd, lingering kiss that looked more about making a point that, yes, he was married than about actual affection. Part of that symbolism was that Gore knew that he had to distance himself from Clinton's sexual taint by emphasizing his healthy marriage, yet still align himself with Clinton's economic prosperity.

It was a thin tightrope. He avoided appearing with the president and selected as his own veep candidate, another snoozer, Senator Joe Lieberman. At the time, Lieberman touted himself as "pro-life" (a position he'd quickly abandon, as was necessary for any Democrat), and he had been one of the first to denounce Clinton's "sexcapades" in the White House. Although a Northeasterner from Connecticut, Lieberman was seen as honest and moderate. Nevertheless, he brought no energy to the ticket at all, possessing an almost somnambulant personality. It didn't matter: Gore had successfully pushed any other potential candidates toward the exit and won with only nine abstentions keeping the final delegate count from being unanimous. And throughout the campaign, Gore managed to keep both Clinton and Nader, a kind of yin and yang of Democratic voter groups, at arm's length.[40]

Gore had, according to *Time* magazine, an "almost primal bitterness" about the president's conduct.[41] Anxious to rebuild his image after the impeachment, Clinton made numerous public statements about Gore's campaign, including one in *The New York Times* where he urged his understudy to loosen up.[42] Clinton then followed up with a statement saying that he was only trying to help, all of which had the effect of leaving Gore looking like anything but a leader. And Gore was rattled by a poll that showed that 40 percent of those who approved of his job as vice president said they would vote for Bush.[43]

Ever since Republican Senator Bob Dole lost to Clinton in a blowout in 1996, the Republicans had pursued new blood. It came in the form of George H. W. Bush's son, George W. Bush, the governor of Texas. While a limited communicator with a fairly short track record, the Texan nevertheless swept aside Arizona Senator John McCain, who had cultivated a reputation as a "moderate." McCain had been famous in the Senate for "reaching across the aisle" to enable Democrats to pass their legislation while never demanding they do the same to reciprocate. He came under sharp attacks from Limbaugh, who asked where the monuments to "great moderates in history" were. McCain failed to tar Bush as an intolerant right-winger and only carried a few states before exiting. Bush crushed him by nearly 1,300 delegates. It should have been a warning sign for McCain, who would run again in 2006, that he could appeal only to the most liberal Republicans, not to the mainstream.

"W," as he was called, hewed to a narrow agenda on his stump speech, mostly a "No Child Left Behind" educational program that had seemed to work in Texas. Perhaps the most remarkable aspect of the campaign was Bush's criticism of Clinton's use of troops in Somalia. In a comment soon to become heavy with irony, Bush used a presidential debate to state, "I don't think troops ought to be used for what's called nation-building."[44] Otherwise, Bush ran on not being Clinton, or at least, the sleazy Clinton as opposed to the charming Clinton.

George W. Bush had run for a House seat in the Midland, Texas, area in 1978 and lost. Educated at Yale, Bush had served during the Vietnam War in the Texas Air National Guard—hardly the "war hero" image, but Bush had applied for combat duty and was turned down. In 2004, Bush's actual service would stack up against his opponent's faux heroism in Vietnam when Kerry ostensibly received a Purple Heart for injuries some claim he had caused by an accident. At any rate, Bush had a leg up on Clinton, who had fraudulently promised to enlist in Arkansas's Reserve Officers' Training Corps program, then reneged. Bush's National Guard service was only slightly eclipsed by Gore's "tuxedo" time as a journalist.

When his father, George H. W. Bush, was vice president, George W. ran into a guitar-playing political consultant named Lee Atwater who had represented numerous candidates. During a family grilling session, Atwater was asked if George W. would be trustworthy. Later, he buttonholed Jeb and George W., inviting them to join their father's campaign in DC and "keep an eye on him and his staff."[45] George W. agreed and moved to DC to work with no title, focusing on fundraising and delivering surrogate speeches to volunteers. He got his baptism of fire with the press when he arranged an interview with *Newsweek* reporter Margaret Warner, who promised to be fair, only to headline the piece, "Fighting the Wimp Factor."[46] In George W.'s mind, his father perfectly navigated the transition from loyal vice president to presidential candidate. Indeed, this author's biography of Reagan, called *Reagan: The American President*, gave the highest marks to Vice President George H. W. Bush for extreme loyalty to "the Gipper."[47] Certainly the senior Bush's tenure ranks up with Richard Nixon's extremely effective vice presidency to Dwight Eisenhower. As veep, Bush senior repeatedly stood up for Reagan in private meetings of the National Security Council, never disagreed with his boss publicly a single time, and always had Reagan's back. If there ever was a model for the office of vice president, George H. W. Bush was it.

Between watching his father and conducting his own failed House campaign, George W. took in all aspects of the American political scene. After the election in 1989, he and his wife Laura moved back to Texas, in part because he had an offer to become a part owner of the Texas Rangers baseball team in the Dallas–Fort Worth area. He cobbled together the group of investors, successfully bid for the team, and spent five seasons as general manager where, he would joke, his most important act was to trade all-star hitter Alex Rodriguez. In truth, he took a losing team and transformed it into a winner and commercial success, overseeing construction of a new stadium.

George H. W. Bush's defeat in 1992 to Clinton led the son to consider running for the governorship of Texas. Enlisting the help of strategist Karl Rove (who would later be dubbed "Bush's brain"), George W. prepared to challenge Texas Governor Ann "Ma" Richards. He pulled off a surprising upset. Two years into his governorship, he had all but made up his mind to run for president. After the nomination, he selected former Wyoming congressman, his father's secretary of defense, and Halliburton executive Dick Cheney to vet his vice presidential candidates, only to conclude Cheney himself outshone them all.[48] And he brought along Rove—who had opposed the selection of Cheney as veep—as his political adviser.

Anyone paying attention at the time would have seen that while vanquished as a candidate, McCain was a future problem for Arizona, the Republican Party, and Bush. The only reliable "conservative" position he seemed to hold was that he supported a strong military. Other than that, over time he would slather himself all over the news, cherishing the sobriquet "maverick," when in fact he was a liberal Democratic ideologically in all things except when it came to foreign military actions and balanced budgets. He claimed to be pro-life, but managed to support enough judges who would not overturn *Roe v. Wade* to ensure nothing happened.

In contrast, Bush was personally pro-life, generously promising to act on *Roe v. Wade* if it were in his ability. Already in place for nearly twenty years, *Roe v. Wade* had posed problems for the Democratic Party. It was already clashing with the Zero Population Growth movement that sought sterilization for families that already had five children. Great Society programs had already sterilized female patients—twenty thousand in 1972 alone, of whom 20 percent were black.[49] Early on—though not for long—feminists found that abortion on demand stood in conflict with women's rights around the globe, especially when it came to coercive measures that violated women's wills. Distribution of the Dalkon Shield intrauterine device by the US Agency for International Development was particularly targeted after evidence surfaced that it produced severe pelvic infections. A 1974–75 United Nations grant of $40 million paid for over one million sterilizations.[50] As with any commitment to pro-life causes, however, it always came down to the judges, and there Bush would disappoint.

Fortunately for Bush or Gore, there seemed little that would happen with *Roe* in the near future. Polls were roughly split. As in all polling, exactly how the question was asked made a major difference. For example, if a ban on abortion included a phrase about "except in cases of rape, incest, or the health of the mother," a majority was against it. Without those qualifications, a majority still supported abortion. Likewise, polls asking if abortions should be allowed in the third trimester showed nearly two-thirds opposition, while those asking if it should be legal in the first trimester had solid support.

Lacking such a polarizing and galvanizing issue, the campaign of 2000 largely swung on domestic issues related to the projected budget surplus, tax plans, and the Clinton record of immorality. Gore, though, had a problem Bush did not have: a candidate on his flank siphoning votes. Ralph Nader, a Jesuit-like activist and consumer advocate who had successfully fought General Motors, increasingly looked to peel off votes from the Democrat. Nader appealed to the ultra-purists on the left, who saw Gore as a corporate shill. Gore would find that unlike many other opponents, Nader could neither be threatened nor bought.

Finally, Gore had a personality problem: He wasn't Clinton. Bush described Gore as "stiff, serious, and aloof. It looked like he had been running for president his entire life."[51] If Bush had known the history behind the DLC, he would have realized Gore indeed *had* been running his whole life.

Bush had other advantages. He had learned from Clinton's ability to fundraise, pulling in $36 million in small donations within just three months of his announcement. He did surprisingly well in the debates, by most accounts winning all three as Gore—even according to one of his more enthusiastic biographers—"made sighs and gestures" toward Bush as he was speaking and came off stiff and programmed.[52] Nor did it hurt that Nader was left out of the debates because he was not polling the required 15 percent nationally. Bush dodged a "Perot problem" of being shot at from two sides on a debate stage. Gore's only memorable line was "lockbox," a term for which Limbaugh ridiculed him mercilessly and was a special fund set up to protect the budget surplus (which in reality was only needed because Congress repeatedly failed to do its job).

In the final seven polls, Bush had a lead that ranged from thirteen points to two but only trailed in two out of seventeen polls in October and November. Both November polls had him up by four and two points.[53] Then, in the final weekend, a Democratic operative discovered Bush had a DUI (driving under the influence of alcohol) charge on his record in 1976 when he was arrested near Kennebunkport, Maine. In his presidential memoir, *Decision Points*, Bush labeled the decision not to acknowledge the DUI as the "single costliest political mistake I ever made."[54] Above all, it seemed to suggest that Bush might not be all that ethically different from Clinton. He admitted to the infraction and the cover-up on November 2, which caused his support among evangelicals to soften. His four-point lead going into the final weekend vanished.[55]

Nevertheless, in what was a shock to Democrats, Gore lost every Southern state, except his home state of Tennessee, to Bush. Clearly, the Democratic Leadership Council strategy did not translate from Clinton to Gore. In a harbinger of elections to come, Gore took the Northeast, the Pacific coast, and most of the upper Midwest. Bush carried the Southern states, the Southern Midwestern, and West. Gore won New Mexico by only 355 votes, but as the results rolled in, it would be clear that the election would hinge on the state of Florida. Bush had 246 electoral votes and Gore 250 with 270 needed to win. Florida, with its twenty-five electoral votes, would decide the election.

For decades, the television networks waited for the actual vote tallies before "calling" a state for one candidate or another. In fact, in 1952—the first televised election coverage ever—a computer named UNIVAC "predicted" the winner. But then political experts discovered that key swing precincts around the nation seemed to be unerring predictors. (Indeed, they were...until the 2020 election when Donald Trump carried almost all of the "bellwether" counties and still lost.) Specific counties, including Wood in Ohio, Loudoun in Virginia, and Hillsborough in Florida, would usually predict the winner. This led networks to heavily sample such counties with exit polling (polls of people who had just voted) and then call an election even before voting had ended.[56] CBS anchor Dan Rather—who would later broadcast a known lie on television when he claimed Bush had attempted to get out of his Texas Air National Guard duties and was disproven within half an hour, eventually forcing his resignation—sternly assured viewers, "Let's get one thing straight right from the get-go.... If we say somebody's carried a state, you can pretty much take it to the bank. Book it!"[57] Except on this night.

Florida constituted a particularly difficult state for exit pollers because the "panhandle" region in the northwest was in a different time zone. Its votes didn't report for an hour after the rest of the state, and it tended to vote heavily Republican. Sure enough, at 7:50 p.m. on election night in November 2000, CBS (with Dan "Book it!" Rather) called Florida for Gore while votes were still coming in...with Bush ahead! There were reports of Bush supporters in the panhandle leaving the lines to vote because they thought that their votes wouldn't count—a perverse form of vote tampering.[58] At one point, Bush said he was "deflated, disappointed, and a little stunned."[59]

But before long, several networks reversed their calls. CNN changed its call at 9:55 p.m., saying that Florida was too close to assign a winner.[60] Although the lead shrank, with 100 percent of the votes counted, Bush led by 537 votes. At 2:35 a.m. Eastern time, the networks said Bush had won Florida and the Electoral College, 271 votes to 266, for the closest election in American history. Gore's campaign chairman, Bill Daley, "was pale."[61] Gore eventually won the popular vote by about 543,000.[62]

The election laws of the state of Florida required a recount that expanded Bush's lead to 950. The Secretary of State Katherine Harris certified Bush the winner at three o'clock in the morning. Gore conceded. But just forty-five minutes later, he called Bush and un-conceded. Yet then he said, things had changed. The state of Florida was in fact too close to call.[63] Bush, who just hours earlier was stunned at a loss, now was equally shocked and a little irritated: "Let me make sure I understand. You're calling me back to retract your concession?" to which Gore snippily said, "You don't have to get snippy about this." Having retracted the concession, Gore's team was convinced there were more votes "out there" and that they could find them. In one of the most audacious efforts in American election history, Gore's team decided to try to force a recount—but only of selected counties that would favor Gore! The fiasco began when Democratic operatives in Palm Beach County, which had a "butterfly ballot" (in which the names were on one side and the hole to punch through was on the other, but not perfectly aligned), claimed they had mistakenly voted for Nader because of the misalignment.[64] Unsaid was the fact that Palm Beach County was totally dominated by Democrats, who had designed and distributed the butterfly ballots in the first place.[65] As one of Gore's advisers said, "Do everything you can to put numbers on the board. Whether they're erased or chiseled in granite, get them on the board."[66] For their part, Bush's team produced T-shirts that parodied the Gore–Lieberman ticket as "Sore-Loserman."

Bush's team wisely responded to a selective recount with Fourteenth Amendment arguments that it would deprive all non-recounted Floridians of their votes. As the competing views wound their way through the legal system, three counties started recounting ballots with such absurd measurements as a "hanging chad" becoming actual legitimate grounds for admitting or rejecting a ballot. (A "hanging chad" is when a voter punched the ballot through with a stylus, but the chad was not separated from the ballot—not to be confused with a "dimpled chad," in which the voter did not make a full hole with the stylus, only an indentation.) In all of these ballot examinations, an election official was put in the position of having to decipher a voter's *intention* without, of course, actually knowing it. Meanwhile, Secretary of State Harris had a constitutional requirement to certify a result seven days after the election, and it was clear none of the recounts would come close to meeting that deadline. The Florida Supreme Court, in a unanimous decision, directed the hand recounts continue and extended Harris's deadline to certify until November 26. This was clearly a violation of Florida's own law. But it meant that suddenly Gore had a route to the Oval Office. James Baker, Bush's spokesman, called it a "judicial coup."[67] Without question, the Florida Supreme Court had virtually rewritten Florida's election laws *after the fact*, ignoring the will of the people.

Except the Florida Supreme Court screwed up. Even with this extended timetable, two counties (including Democrat-heavy Miami-Dade) realized they couldn't get through all of the ballots by the newly established deadline. Instead, the canvassing board abandoned the full recount—*precisely what the Florida Supreme Court had bent the law to enable it to do!*—and now went with counting only the "undervotes," where there were votes for other candidates but no clear vote for the president. Republican operatives, now copying the Democrats, stormed the canvassing board as observers, forcing the board to meet again and unanimously vote to discontinue the recount. It seems that if they could not cheat in secret, they preferred not to cheat at all, and the boards pleaded to end the process, citing time constraints. Many saw the implications of this decision: Gore couldn't win without "new" votes from the Democrat-heavy Miami-Dade. While he had gained a few votes, it wasn't enough.

On November 26, which was the extended deadline ordered by the Florida Supreme Court, Secretary of State Harris again certified George Bush the winner, this time by 537 votes. Overseas ballots actually slightly increased Bush's tenuous lead, while the newly discovered Gore votes in the incomplete Miami-Dade recount were not counted (because the recount was never finished).

Once again Gore resisted. This should have been the end of it, but the Gore team immediately began referring to "the process" as if there was still an ongoing series of steps to be worked out. Gore's lawyers said they would "contest" the election, meaning it would be mid-December before anything became final. Gore's team now wanted a full recount of Miami-Dade County's "undervote." Jesse Jackson appeared, predictably claiming the discrepancies showed racial profiling. Reluctantly, the US Supreme Court was brought into the fray on December 4 in *Bush v. Palm Beach County Canvassing Board*. Not only did the Supreme Court deliver a legal verdict, but it also provided extremely strong guidance to the Florida Supreme Court to end the charade.

In this unanimous decision, the Supreme Court asked the Florida Supreme Court to clarify the basis of its decision. This was a polite legal way of saying, "This won't stand up. It's unconstitutional." For example, the justices told the Florida court that it was *not* operating by normal Florida voting law, but by the US Constitution, Article II, Section 1, where the power was vested not in state courts but in the state legislature. Then the US Supreme Court vacated the decision (negated it by returning it to the Florida Supreme Court for review and clarification).

Florida's legislature then immediately stepped up on December 8 in a special session to name Florida's electors. If the Florida Supreme Court misbehaved again, two sets of electors (note—not "fake electors") would go to Congress and, constitutionally, the set named by the legislature would be the only one recognized. Meanwhile, a Florida circuit court judge, N. Samuel Sauls (a Democrat) who took himself to be a sort of backwoods Solomon, heard a witness on rubber, a political scientist, and two statisticians rule that there was "no credible statistical evidence" that would produce a reasonable probability that Gore won. Sauls delivered his decision on December 4, hours after the Supreme Court had vacated the Florida Supreme Court's ruling. While this should have been "the end" for the third time, it actually opened the door for Gore to appeal to the Florida Supreme Court on December 8.

Yet once again, the Florida justices (this time by a 4–3 vote) opened the door for Gore by saying that every undervote in Florida needed to be counted immediately. (Again, "counting" an undervote involved actually ascribing the voter's intent—why did the voter *not* vote for the president? Did he or she mean to vote but the vote wasn't registered?) Moreover, the Florida Supreme Court handed Gore all the votes he claimed from the incomplete recounts that were already started. Just as the US Supreme Court had sent the case back to Florida, now it was the Florida justices' turn to send the case back to the circuit court—except now Sauls had recused himself and a new justice, Terry Lewis, concocted a system for counting the votes in short order.

Lewis's solution was not only impossible but was also a direct violation of the US Supreme Court's rather clear warning. Obviously miffed, on December 12, just a day after the Florida Supreme Court ruled, the US justices issued an order to stop counting. That meant that at least five justices, a majority, agreed that there was a substantial likelihood that the plaintiff (Bush) would win the case. Practically speaking, it killed Gore's hopes of "finding" new votes through more delays. Two hours before the "safe harbor" deadline for certifying electors and with a 7–2 decision, the court ruled that the recount order by the Florida Supreme Court was unconstitutional and violated equal protection (because all votes in Florida were not recounted). Five Republican justices also said there was no way to recount the votes under the constitutional deadline. Three Democratic justices plus Republican David Souter dissented, claiming that the statutes in question did not define a "legal vote."[68]

Some argued that the Supreme Court "selected" Bush, that he wasn't "elected." The authors of *The Perfect Tie*, while noting legal concerns of the case, pointed to political and social realities. "Would the consequences of [the Supreme Court] not acting have on balance been worse?" The end was "likely to be more legitimate than any other end now on the horizon." The court, which had a "reservoir of respect," was "perhaps the only institution at that point in a position to [end the saga]. If not the Supreme Court, then who?"[69] Moreover, as will be seen in the presidency of Trump, attempts at forcing elected and appointed officials to fulfill their constitutional duties fail. Trump would repeatedly challenge Congress to pass legislation, only to be met by inaction, whereupon he would issue executive orders to achieve the mission. In 2017, when it came to local violence spread by the fascist "antifa" groups, Trump urged governors and mayors to crack down rather than sending in federal troops. Again, they whiffed. So it was in Florida, where, given not one, but *two* opportunities to employ constitutional law and principles, the state supreme court took the partisan approach.

Others complained that the US Supreme Court had gotten politicized. One could ask, "What the heck was happening in the Florida Supreme Court?" But the simple fact is—as would become incredibly obvious in the subsequent two decades—the court (indeed all courts) was *always* a political institution since the time of John Marshall, who reserved for himself and his fellow justices the right to determine what the Constitution said in *Marbury v. Madison*. How political a decision was *Dred Scott v. Sandford*? Many forgot that Congress itself had become fully embroiled in the electoral process in the election of 1876, wherein the Republican-dominated Congress stepped into three states' elections and deemed them flawed. Overriding the ostensibly fair elections in Louisiana, Florida, and South Carolina, Congress via a commission concluded that there was electoral fraud and disenfranchisement of black people. By a series of 8–7 votes, the Electoral Commission awarded the three states in question to Republican Rutherford B. Hayes, giving him a single electoral vote victory in the Electoral College and making him president. There was no disturbance at his inauguration. But behind the scenes, Democrats and Southerners had fought hard and implied that without major concessions, violence would occur and perhaps even the

Civil War would start again. As a result, the Republicans gave in to three major demands from the Democrats: a number of federal cabinet appointees who were Southerners, the removal of all federal troops from states that were still occupied, and federal subsidies for the Southern Pacific Railroad.[70]

At least Gore, with a weak case, had the good sense not to pursue the challenges any further, as Hillary Clinton would do (with no evidence) in 2016. Trump's claims had substantial evidence, on the other hand, and he issued a number of challenges in 2020. Many thought that Nixon should have challenged the results of the 1960 election. Regardless, after December 12, 2000, the election was over, and Bush had won what two political scientists called "the perfect tie."[71] Not only was the presidential election close, but each side also won fifty senators (meaning the Republicans, with Vice President Cheney voting, would have the tie breaker), and the House had the fourth lowest differential in history. America was indeed a house divided.

A different picture emerged from the postmortem of voter analysis, which showed how much Gore had slipped with Clinton voters in 1996. He won 7 percent fewer Hispanics, 5 percent fewer eighteen to twenty-nine-year-olds, 4 percent fewer Catholics, 5 percent fewer Republicans, and 5 percent fewer "moderates." [72] The only area in which Gore gained any ground over Clinton from four years earlier was among black people (6 percent) and sixty-year-olds and older (3 percent). He also did better with the poor and with large population areas, though he and Bush split evenly on the suburbs.[73] In short, Gore the technocrat, did well in big cities that gravitated toward technocrats, and predictably he lost badly in rural areas. As the authors of *The Perfect Tie* concluded, "Al Gore did indeed lose [the race] in the campaign.... George W. Bush ran a better campaign."[74] The outcome differed from many political scientists' computer models, which had Gore as the clear winner with a victory margin of between four and twenty points, but the political scientists who wrote *The Perfect Tie* admitted that a "concern for the moral state" of the nation played a large role in voters' minds—a factor that was not adequately captured in the models.

As Mike Allen and I noted in *A Patriot's History of the United States*, Clinton had left a destructive legacy to his party. When he was elected in 1992, Democrats had held both the House and the Senate and the governorship of New York, as well as the mayorships of both New York and Los Angeles. Within a decade, Republicans took the governorships of California, New Jersey, Michigan, New York, and Wisconsin as well as held the House and Senate (with Republican senators elected in New Jersey, Pennsylvania, and Michigan). In states where there was a pure two-party legislature after 2002, Republicans held twenty-five seats and Democrats held twenty-two. Two were tied. Despite perceptions that Bill Clinton was good for the Democratic Party, it turned out he was only good for Bill Clinton. Bill's only shining light was that Hillary Clinton had won the US Senate seat in New York.[75] In retrospect, both popular Democratic presidents of the period 1990–2015, Clinton and Obama, had almost no coattails with Democratic voters.

Other oddities of the campaign stood out: Bush's running mate was Cheney, a hawkish former congressman from Wyoming. During the campaign, virtually every news outlet used *exactly* the same word to describe Cheney's addition to the ticket: "gravitas." Limbaugh ran audio clips of at least a dozen anchors and reporters using that precise word. The implication was that Bush was too inexperienced to actually be president and needed someone with Cheney's experience. The real message, of course, was that the media had begun reading from an identical script, which many suspected was faxed daily to them by the Democratic National Convention.

Over the long haul of Bush's presidency, Cheney, instead of adding intellectual heft, came to taint the administration with his connections to military defense contractor Halliburton. When Bush ordered the invasion of Iraq, Halliburton promised to be a major beneficiary.

But in the spring and summer of 2000, there were few thoughts of war. The Cold War had ended. The Soviet Union had been badly fragmented as Belarus, Estonia, Latvia, Lithuania, Georgia, the "'Stans" (Kazakhstan, Uzbekistan, Turkmenistan), and Ukraine had all become independent nations. Boris Yeltsin, who had guided Russia out of its communist stage, had yielded power to a new president, Vladimir Putin. With the exception of a four-year span from 2008 to 2012, Putin had served as Russia's president. He ostensibly did not want a new Cold War. Thus, with the exception of a few "hot spots" that had gotten Clinton drawn in, there were no more wars to fight...or so it seemed.

CHAPTER 2
THE GREAT SATAN

How much does a narrow election matter? It somewhat depends on the definition of "narrow." In 2018, the Republicans lost the House when Democrats carried nearly thirty seats in which the final margin was around two points. It was a very, very close election despite the fact that virtually all of the seats broke in the same direction, in favor of the Democrats. Did the Democrats treat it as such? Of course not. They acted as though they had a mandate. In 2001, clearly President George W. Bush would have trouble arguing that with a nine hundred–vote final margin in a single state (while losing the popular vote), a fifty-fifty Senate, and a mere nine-vote difference in the House where he had a national mandate. It was therefore expected that he would nibble around the edges of policy rather than seek serious change.

With peace at hand, he anticipated his term to be dominated by education. His "No Child Left Behind" program promised to address an American educational system that had steadily fallen behind that of the rest of the world. American students were woefully behind in math and science, not to mention history and literature skills. To his surprise, then, one of the first issues that dominated his time and attention was that of stem cells.

Bush had been lobbied to provide federal medical assistance for Alzheimer's disease—all the more strongly so since former president Ronald Reagan had been diagnosed with it in 1994.[76] On Bush's ninth day in office, he held a meeting with his domestic policy team. "Chief briefer," Margaret Spellings, reviewed a number of topics when she came to the "Dickey Amendment" to permit federal funding for embryonic stem cell research. Bush stopped her and asked, "What exactly is a stem cell?" Spellings explained the different possible uses of stem cells, but the only way to extract embryonic stem cells was to kill the embryo. In other words, one life had to be destroyed to save another. Bush had to decide whether to allow the grants approved under Clinton to proceed, and the issue was a minefield. Were frozen embryos human life? Bioethicist Dr. Louis Guenin had argued in *Science* magazine that allowing embryonic stem cell research would not endanger the life of any babies, but others claimed that the practice would transform the perceptions of human life as a marketable resource, indeed as a commodity.[77]

Both arguments resonated with Bush, who had lost a sister to childhood leukemia, but he also knew that permitting the destruction of human embryos for research would open the door to human engineering. And the stem cell debate was intricately intertwined with the abortion issue. Ultimately, Bush felt called to lead the nation toward a culture of life. He had reinstituted the "Mexico City policy," canceled by Clinton, which prevented federal funding of overseas abortions. Bush called in scientists, ethics professors, religious leaders, and others to discuss the issue. One argument in favor was that most of the stem cells that would be used would be discarded anyway. Many groups pointed out the research potential of such stem cell lines. At the same time, it was inarguable that any particular stem cell line could become a person. Ultimately, the debate boiled down to this: Regardless of whether an embryo would die, did that allow society to use it as a natural resource? And to what degree did marketing and profiting from doomed tissue constitute ghoulishness over science? Bush finally decided to let the government fund research on stem cell lines from embryos that had already been destroyed but urged Congress to increase federal funding for alternative sources of stem cells.

It was in the stem cell debate that Bush learned of what he saw as a new dynamic in American politics—highly personal criticism: "Partisan opponents and commentators questioned my legitimacy, my intelligence, and my sincerity. They mocked my appearance, my accent, and my religious beliefs. I was labeled a Nazi, a war criminal, and Satan himself.... One lawmaker called me both a loser and a liar. He became majority leader of the US Senate."[78]

Even for the time, Bush's view was ferociously naive. Had not Bush witnessed the "politics of personal destruction" against the innocent women who had come forward to claim Bill Clinton sexually harassed them? Had he not seen a man once revered in Washington, DC, Kenneth Starr, demonized with character assassination by James Carville and the Clinton team? Had he not seen Carville go on national media, repeatedly, to term women who were sexually harassed (or, in the case of Juanita Broaddrick, allegedly raped) by Clinton as "nuts and sluts?" Had he not seen Vice President Dan Quayle's intellect questioned repeatedly because he misspelled a word?

It was even worse, though. Bush admitted that he knew Abraham Lincoln was likened to a tyrant and a baboon and that papers had called for the assassination of both George Washington and John Adams. He surely knew Franklin Roosevelt had been labeled a "dictator" by major newspapers. Nevertheless, Bush's apparent lack of understanding about the nature of politics in America, not to mention American history itself, was shocking. He referred to it as a "death spiral of decency during my time in office."[79]

What differentiated Bush was that he and his political adviser Karl Rove made a conscious decision *not* to respond to such attacks, thereby ceding the accusations to the enemy. Historian Paul Johnson, writing about America's restraint in the Vietnam War, nevertheless made an analogous point: "The experience of the twentieth century indicates that self-imposed restraints by a civilized power are worse than useless. They are interpreted by friend and foe alike as evidence, not of humanity, but of guilt and lack of righteous conviction."[80] Rush Limbaugh lamented Bush's weakness when it came to pushing back, noting that it allowed his opponents to get away with larger slanders because they first got away with smaller lies. When he pressed Bush for the reasons he didn't defend himself, Bush responded: "I have way too much respect for this office to drag it down into the gutter of modern-day politics. I am not gonna respond to these obviously political attacks, personal attacks. [I] have too much respect for the office to turn it into that."[81]

Another development that changed since the 1970s that made politics more bitter was the birth of a new, genuinely alternative conservative media. First, this was led by *The Washington Times* and then joined and the conservative reach expanded by Limbaugh. The *Times*, while offering alternative interpretations of news and producing its own research, nevertheless could be dismissed as a "Moonie Paper" (referring to the fact that it was owned by the Unification Church of Rev. Sun Myung Moon in Korea).[82]

Limbaugh's emergence as a national figure in 1988 could be considered miraculous. He single-handedly revived AM talk radio, which was dying as a medium. Limbaugh's show appeared nationally from noon till 3:00 p.m. Eastern time Monday through Friday—right in the middle of the workday, so not during "drive time," a slot industry officials considered the "death valley" of radio. Limbaugh saw it as an opportunity to have a monopoly on that time. Before long, he built an audience of up to twenty million listeners weekly, with three to five million listening at any given time. In other words, he had a loyal and large audience that easily challenged the viewers of traditional evening news from only three sources: the ABC, NBC, and CBS television networks.

Limbaugh's vault to dominance nationally as a conservative icon showed how America had begun to ignore elitists' standards (of others), particularly those of the traditional conservative elites. By the time he became a national presence, Limbaugh had already gone through two divorces: Roxy McNeely (divorced 1980) and Michelle Sixta (divorced 1990). Both maintained strict confidence about their relationship. He also had not served in the military, being diagnosed with bone spurs. In short, the Moral Majority organization of Jerry Falwell, or other Christian leaders, might have shunned him under different circumstances.

But Limbaugh struck a national chord, not just because he had a good voice, a great sense of comedy, and excellent political instincts, but because he was a self-made man who admitted all he ever wanted to do was be a radio host. He dropped out of college. He boasted that he had been fired seven times. Yet he connected with millions of Americans precisely *because* of those failures. Limbaugh did not pretend to be a war hero (whose valor was later questioned, such as John Kerry, or nonexistent, such as Richard Blumenthal), and he never presented himself as a moral paragon or military strategist. His hometown of Cape Girardeau, Missouri, was farther conceptually from Hollywood or New York than it was in sheer milage. He was, as it were, "one of us." Through it all, he remained a steadfast advocate of the "average" American, of America, and of life. And he proved a spectacular businessman. As he always said, the purpose of his show was to attract an audience large enough to charge high rates to advertisers.

In his three hours, Limbaugh always began with the major news items of the day, adding deep analysis. He was particularly attuned to interpreting the left-leaning news organizations' stories and headlines. (One could often determine what was likely actually happening from the opposite of their headlines in *The New York Times* or *The Washington Post* in many cases.) But "Rush," as he was generally known, didn't limit himself to politics: He also ventured into economics, culture, and sports. Nor did he have guests: He was the show, and when he took callers—as he fondly said—it was for the purpose of "making the host look good." At times, he even indulged long, diatribe calls from black Muslims (officially called the Nation of Islam), such as "Rita X," to show how extreme and detached from reality they were. He had his team prepare parodies, including songs "sung" by current politicians. When the World Wide Web appeared, and all other show hosts and writers raced to start their own websites, Limbaugh patiently waited until he could come up with a model that actually showed a profit.

Despite controlling almost all other media outlets, the left in America nevertheless deeply feared Limbaugh, realizing that he could expose their intentions and motivations faster than any politician, including a president. When the Republicans gained control of Congress in January 1995, they designated Limbaugh an honorary member of the freshman class and invited him to speak to the caucus. He warned them of the media and of the siren-like allure of wanting their attention and love. His political acumen was exceedingly accurate. In thirty years of broadcasting, he only made a few major errors in his predictions (saying, for example, that Hillary Clinton would never run for office because she could never survive losing or that Joe Biden would never finish the 2020 Democratic primaries).

He gained such influence that a few comments from him could catapult the mainstream media into apoplectic fits. After Barack Obama's election victory, Limbaugh was asked to write a four hundred–word essay as to his reaction to an Obama presidency. Limbaugh replied, "I only need four: I hope he fails." Although even Fox News and other so-called conservative media joined the chorus of criticisms, over eight years after Obama left the office, the wake of destruction he had inflicted on the country made Limbaugh's words look Olympian in their wisdom.

The Washington Times in print and Limbaugh on the radio were followed in 1996 by an alternative conservative television news outlet, Fox News, founded by Australian Rupert Murdoch.[83] Roger Ailes, who headed the news division, chose to populate his broadcast team with beautiful women, a feature that also set Fox apart from other networks. Ailes also pushed Fox to be more Hollywood and showbiz in its presentation, further differentiating it from the stodgy networks.

Even though Bush now possessed the conservative outlets to respond to his nasty critics, he maintained his strategy of taking the "high road."[84] And historian Johnson's assessment proved accurate. The absence of countering the attacks only made Bush appear weaker and less convinced. And in what would become all the most shocking and, ultimately, revolting was when Bush—having not uttered a single criticism of the Obama administration—frequently commented negatively on the administration of Donald Trump. Indeed, Bush would criticize Trump far more viciously than he ever did the Democrats.

But that lay in the future. For Bush, as he noted in his presidential memoir, *Decision Points*, his day on September 11 began like most other days—reading the Bible, then while it was still dark, a jog with the Secret Service agents in tow. He was in Florida for an education event at a local school near Sarasota. He went to the Emma E. Booker Elementary School to tout his education policies. Just earlier, an ABC/*Washington Post* poll gave Bush 61 percent approval on the issue. Now, he was going to listen to a group of elementary school kids read. He met with the school principal, Gwendolyn Tose-Rigell, a Democrat who considered Bush a "phony."[85]

He went into a class of second graders to observe a reading lesson. Earlier, as always, he had the President's Daily Brief from the CIA, which noted issues in Russia, China, and Palestine. Nothing was included about Afghanistan or a terrorist named Osama bin Laden. Rove mentioned to him a strange development in New York City, where a plane had crashed into the North Tower of the World Trade Center. Bush "envisioned a little propeller plane horribly lost."[86] Little did he know the world had just changed, and America's place in it was to be adrift ever since.

His national security adviser, Condoleezza Rice, called: It wasn't a small prop plane—it was a commercial jetliner. Bush thought that the plane must have had the "worst pilot in the world," but then he sat down and went in front of the second grade readers. He could hear pagers going off—strictly forbidden when with the president. Then his Chief of Staff, Andrew Card, interrupted him (an act that is unheard of) and whispered in his ear, "A second plane has hit the second tower." Suddenly, the president couldn't remember anything the teacher was saying from that point on. He kept thinking, "America is under attack."[87] Bush wrote that his first reaction was outrage, but when he looked at the faces of the children, he realized that they would be counting on him to protect them. He was determined not to frighten the class, so he completed the reading drill, then calmly left. The principal, who had viewed him just an hour earlier as a phony, said, "He was very, very composed.... All I can say is he looked very presidential."[88] Video showed when the president's mind immediately left the classroom as he ran through a catalog of thoughts about who did it, why, and what the right response would be. Clinton's failure to capture or kill Osama bin Laden now came home to roost.

The initial reports of hijacked planes expected that these would result in hostage situations. No one, as of yet, had taken over a jetliner to turn it into a flying bomb. The first plane hit the North Tower of the World Trade Center, generating temperatures of 1,800 degrees. The 110-story tower turned into an inferno, and no one above the hundredth floor made it out alive. A French documentary film company caught the impact by accident. Emergency teams responded, but firefighters knew there was no way to pump water up one hundred stories. Steel, glass, and even human remains fell on the police below. Then came the jumpers: people trapped above the hundredth floor, facing death by fire or smoke inhalation, jumped. One of them, known as the "Falling Man," who was captured in a photo almost diving head down, was finally identified years later.[89]

As bystanders watched in horror, a second jetliner, United Airlines Flight 175 flying from Boston to Los Angeles, blasted into the South Tower of the World Trade Center. There, many employees had been assured that it was safe to return to work and had reentered the building.

At the time Andrew Card gave Bush the news, he had already concluded America was under attack and "we were going to war."[90] CIA Director George Tenet already drew his own conclusion: "This has [Osama] bin Laden all over it."[91] Soon, another disaster unfolded as an American Airlines flight reversed course and flew into the Pentagon, while a fourth—its passengers alerted by phones to the news of the suicide planes—went down in a Pennsylvania field as the heroes aboard stormed the cockpit and prevented the jihadists from crashing it into its target (which subsequent evidence suggested was Congress).

Then, before anyone could process these attacks, the two burning World Trade Center towers collapsed, pancaking down in giant clouds of dust and rubble. Subsequent conspiracy theorists tried to claim that there were no people aboard the planes (clearly there were—many phoned relatives, including the wife of the solicitor general, Barbara Olson, who was on the plane that plowed into the Pentagon). Some tried to claim that invisible operatives had planted hundreds of tons of bombs that detonated the towers (but still couldn't explain the airplanes slamming into them). Still others tried to claim that jet fuel couldn't reach temperatures high enough to bring down the steel—claims later disproven by multiple engineers.[92] A mystery remains, however, about the collapse of the adjacent Building 7, which has yet to be fully explained.

Americans watched in horror at the second plane's impact, which many people saw on live television. They shuddered as America's two tallest buildings collapsed. And they recoiled at the zombie-like images of dust-drenched New Yorkers staggering out of the rubble and clouds, evacuating their city. Not seen were the hundreds of firefighters and police who were crushed in the collapse and the hundreds of others who suffered smoke inhalation damage to their lungs. Almost immediately, armies of volunteers descended on the city from all over the country, ordinary people just picking up and clearing rubble or give blood. Future President Trump raced to the scene to lend aid. Rescue dogs were used to search for survivors. There were almost none in the rubble. Two steel girders had been molded by the heat into a cross, which rescue workers raised up. Three firemen hoisted an American flag, Iwo Jima–style, above the trade site. New York City immediately committed to building one or more new structures on the site and solicited designs. (The winning design, the "Freedom Tower," while technically taller than either of the two World Trade Center towers, would not have the same striking silhouette on the skyline of the city.)

No such images of a foreign attack on the American mainland existed in the nation's collective memory. The British burning of Washington, DC occurred almost two hundred years earlier, before photographs. The Oklahoma City bombing was an act of a domestic terrorist. But an enemy attack on America's most powerful city producing casualties exceeding those at Pearl Harbor? It was beyond imagination for much of the country.

Except for a few references on the news during the bombings of United States embassies in Africa in 1998, the terrorist group "al-Qaeda" was known to only a handful of people, almost all of them in the military or intelligence agencies in Washington.[i] Throughout the war of the mujahideen against the Soviets under President Reagan, Bin Laden was a virtual unknown figure who had mostly been learning the terror craft while financing mostly anti-Soviet operations. His father was a wealthy contractor in Saudi Arabia; he had become radicalized, obsessed with the "near enemy" (Israel) and the "far enemy" (the US, whom many Islamic radicals called "The Great Satan"). After the Soviets were driven from Afghanistan, Bin Laden turned his attention to forcing America entirely out of the Middle East. Holed up for a time in Sudan, eventually he hightailed it to Afghanistan, where he was welcomed by the Taliban's ultra-fundamentalist Islamic government. Soon allied with his uncle, Khalid Sheikh Mohammed—the brains behind many of the more audacious al-Qaeda attacks—Bin Laden began work on the "planes" plot.

Once protected by the Taliban in Afghanistan, Bin Laden formed al-Qaeda or "the base." Even on the threshold of 9/11, however, Bin Laden and al-Qaeda were relegated to low-level threats until the summer of 2001. It would not be long before President Bush was all too tired of hearing about them.

---

i As with many foreign names and terms, "al-Qaeda" can also be spelled "al Qa'ida," "al Qaeda," and so on. Osama bin Laden likewise is often spelled "Usama" and/or with a capital "B" in "bin." My style here is "al-Qaeda" and "Osama bin Laden."

As 9/11 unfolded, Bush received a briefing—all information was still incomplete—and at the time some four thousand aircrafts were still in the skies over the US. Within the next few hours, the Federal Aviation Administration would land them all. A press gaggle gathered as Bush made a statement to the nation, using odd language: The US would "conduct a full-scale investigation and to hunt down and find those folks who committed this act."[93] His use of the term "those folks" to describe bloodthirsty monsters who had just killed three thousand people seemed disconnected. He was then hustled aboard Air Force One, where he spoke by phone with Vice President Dick Cheney in the secure bunker at the White House. Cheney noted that jet fighters had been scrambled to intercept any other airliners that refused to be deterred from their path or which did not respond. He needed an order from the commander in chief as to whether to authorize the military jets to shoot down such aircrafts, possibly full of civilians. Bush didn't hesitate. "You bet," he replied. He realized, "We're under attack. This is a war. And it took me no time to realize this was a war."[94] In his memoir, *Decision Points*, Bush recalled thinking about his time as a pilot and told his chief of staff, "I cannot imagine what it would be like to receive this order."[95]

A subsequent documentary film called *Clear the Skies* revealed that on 9/11 there were only *four* total jet fighters on alert for "combat air patrol" on the entire Northeastern coast. Two of the jets that were scrambled that day did not even have missiles or operational guns—they had not been outfitted with any ammunition. Interviewed for the film, the pilots understood that their orders were to ram the jetliners if they didn't respond, killing themselves in the process.[96]

For a moment the nation was united. Bush, in his finest hour, had two signature moments. In the first, he delivered a speech in the National Cathedral in Washington, DC, in which he designated a national day of prayer. Without a doubt, it was the finest speech of Bush's presidency:

> On Tuesday, our country was attacked with deliberate and massive cruelty. We have seen the images of fire and ashes,

> and bent steel. Now come the names, the list of casualties we are only beginning [to read].... They are the names of people who faced death and in their last moments called home to say, be brave, and I love you.... War has been waged against us by stealth and deceit and murder.... This conflict was begun on the timing and terms of others; it will end in a way and at an hour of our choosing.[97]

From there, Bush went to an equally memorable appearance in New York City, where, in a tan windbreaker and armed with a megaphone, he climbed atop a pile of rubble to address the rescue workers. He began to speak to the crowd when the bullhorn cut out. Someone shouted, "We can't hear you." Bush turned, with his bullhorn now working, and said, "I can hear *you*! The rest of the world hears you," and pointing to the spot where the World Trade Center had stood, shouted "and the people who knocked these buildings down will hear *all* of us soon!"[98] Bush later told a joint session of Congress, "Either you are with us, or you are with the terrorists," producing another memorable line."[99]

A month later, Bush threw out the first pitch of game three of the 2001 World Series between the Arizona Diamondbacks and the New York Yankees.[100] The Secret Service had strongly urged against the president standing alone on the pitcher's mound with the high expectation of assassination attempts. But Bush donned body armor underneath his windbreaker. He met with Yankee captain Derek Jeter, who asked, "Are you going to throw it from the mound or in front of the mound?" and Bush said, "I was going to throw it from in front of the mound." Jeter said, "I wouldn't do that. They'll boo ya." Bush replied, "Ok, I'll throw it from the mound." Then as Bush walked to the mound, Jeter added, "Don't bounce it; they'll boo ya." Jeter's words summed up Yankees baseball: Even such a historically important event as a presidential first pitch needed to respect the game. Bush had warmed up in a hitting area but now said "the pressures mounted." He gave a thumbs up to the crowd, then threw a perfect strike.[101]

Few moments could have galvanized the country, even if only for a short period, in the way that Bush's rubble/bullhorn speech and his first pitch did. And, perhaps fittingly, in the quintessential American event in the spring, football's Super Bowl, the New England Patriots won.

Speaking to a crowd of construction workers was one thing, but Bush needed to finally, and formally, address the nation and Congress, which he did on September 20 to a joint session. Vice President Cheney was not at his normal position next to the Speaker of the House, Dennis Hastert, because he was at a secure location out of concerns that al-Qaeda wasn't finished.

Bush opened by saying, "Mr. Speaker…in the normal course of events, Presidents come to this chamber to report on the state of the Union. Tonight, no such report is needed. It has already been delivered by the American people."[102] "Americans are asking," he said, "How will we fight and win this war?" He answered that the US would use "every means of diplomacy, every tool of intelligence, every instrument of law enforcement, every financial influence, and every necessary weapon of war" to topple al-Qaeda's global network. But he warned, "Americans should not expect one battle, but a lengthy campaign, unlike any other we have ever seen. It may include dramatic strikes, visible on TV, and covert operations, secret even in success."[103] He then issued what became the "with us or against us" dictum that "Every nation…now has a decision to make: Either you are with us, or you are with the terrorists." That would play a significant role in getting Pakistan off the dime when it came to rendering tacit support to terrorists while pretending to be a US ally.

As always, the devil was in the details. While the president spoke with his bullhorn on the rubble mound or from the bully pulpit to Congress, the CIA and the Pentagon were developing plans to get Osama bin Laden, which everyone knew would almost certainly involve invading the "graveyard of empires," Afghanistan. Less a nation and more a collection of mountain tribes whose hatred for each other was legendary, Afghanistan had daunting terrain in which tanks and heavy-tracked vehicles were not as effective as they had been in Kuwait and Iraq. Getting into Afghanistan was easy. Getting out was always the problem.

In the days following the 9/11 attacks, it appeared that Bush was doing nothing. Editorials criticized him for being slow to retaliate. But against whom? Where? Bin Laden was almost certainly in the Tora Bora mountains in caves, impervious to missiles or bombs. Like the Japanese on Iwo Jima, al-Qaeda would have to be rooted out, stronghold by stronghold. Both Rumsfeld and Bush were acutely aware that Afghanistan was viewed as the graveyard of empires, having beaten the British Empire and the USSR in the last 150 years. But there was some good news. The Northern Alliance of Afghan tribes had been an ally to the US since the Russian invasion. Indeed, a clear alert that something big was planned for America was ignored when al-Qaeda assassinated the Northern Alliance leader Ahmad Massoud on September 9. Massoud, a Pashtun military genius, had led the resistance against the Taliban. He was known as the "Lion of Panjshir," and his assassination should have alerted everyone in intelligence that al-Qaeda was preparing a very big attack on America.[104] Indeed, just the previous April, Massoud had personally warned European and American authorities that a large-scale imminent attack was coming.

Massoud's greatest champion in Washington was Richard Clarke, the national coordinator for counterterrorism who had been watching Bin Laden for some time. Formally, he headed the Counterterrorism Security Group that once included, immediately after the 1993 World Trade Center bombing, John O'Neill, chief of the FBI's counterterrorism section. O'Neill was in the North Tower when it fell. Clarke briefed Bush's National Security Advisor Condoleezza Rice in January when the Bush team came into office. She gave him the impression that she had never heard of al-Qaeda and downgraded Clarke's position so that he reported to deputies, not principals. Undaunted, Clarke continued to press the strategy of arming Massoud and the Northern Alliance throughout the summer.

There was another major obstacle that had prevented the US intelligence agencies from stopping 9/11: The Clinton administration had put up a "wall" between the information that could be shared between the FBI and the CIA, courtesy of a memo written by Jamie Gorelick, the deputy attorney general.[105] Bush's Attorney General John Ashcroft, in particular, criticized the lack of cooperation and quoted an FBI investigator complaining that "whatever has happened to this, someday somebody will die."[106] The CIA used the "wall" as an excuse to refuse to share the identities of terrorists in photographs with the FBI.[107] Lawrence Wright, the historian of al-Qaeda's activities at this time, described the process as "bizarre."[108]

Indeed, as the military and intelligence forces were marshaled to attack al-Qaeda, a stream of information poured in about the incompetence and missed opportunities to stop the attacks in the first place. Over the summer, for example, a Phoenix FBI field agent, Kenneth Williams, sent an electronic communication to FBI headquarters and agents in New York advising them of "the possibility of a coordinated effort by Osama bin Laden to send students to the US to attend civil aviation universities and colleges." He urged the FBI to make a record of the flight schools and compile a list of Muslim students.[109]

Nothing came of those requests, but in August, a flight school contacted the FBI field office to report a student named Zacarias Moussaoui, who had asked suspicious questions about flight patterns around New York City and the cockpit doors. The FBI was unable to get a search warrant for Moussaoui's computer, causing the Minneapolis supervisor to explode that he was "trying to keep someone from taking a plane and crashing it into the World Trade Center."[110] This was just one of dozens of alerts that were lost in the system.

Former CIA Director Tenet, in his memoir *At the Center of the Storm*, recounted many of these incidents, including one involving bombers from the USS *Cole* who were found at a meeting in Malaysia in March 2001. "Once we had learned [their] names," he wrote, the "CIA should have placed them on a watchlist that might have prevented their entering the United States."[111] "Officers in the field, where primary responsibility for watchlisting resided, thought headquarters would do it, and vice versa." Second, when information was delivered to headquarters in Langley, Virginia, the cable was marked "information" rather than "action." But they had a photo of the person, whom FBI agent John O'Neill recognized as one of the *Cole* bombers. But the photo wasn't confirmed until June, when agents were sure of the identities in the photos and had to ship them "over the wall" (of separation) to the CIA. By the time of the 9/11 attacks (in *September*), the photos hadn't yet arrived.[112]

Nine months after 9/11, *Time* magazine, obviously using CIA leaks, ran an article called "How the FBI Blew the Case" against the al-Qaeda terrorists in an issue called "The Bombshell Memo." This story focused on FBI agent Coleen Rowley who had sent a letter to FBI Director Robert Mueller (later to be the special counsel in the illegitimate investigation of Trump for "Russian collusion"), reviewing requests from her Minneapolis office to obtain a search warrant for Zacarias Moussaoui. That French-born al-Qaeda operative who had flight training was originally to be one of the hijackers but was arrested in Minnesota on an immigration violation. But even with the Minnesota office sending up to seventy emails a week begging to search his laptop, Washington headquarters rejected them all.[113] When information from French intelligence came to the FBI that Moussaoui was planning to use an aircraft as a terror weapon, "They felt the information did not meet the threshold of the FISA [Foreign Intelligence Surveillance Act] statute," and the FBI did not search his luggage.[114]

The FBI's response to the story? Rather than admit error, the bureau leaked a counternarrative to *Newsweek* called "The 9/11 Terrorists the CIA Should have Caught," describing the botched Malaysia meeting.[115] Certainly the FBI was awash in failures, and within the period from the Atlanta Centennial Olympic Park bombing, with its false arrest of Richard Jewell, to the government's settlement of a $5.8 million lawsuit filed by Steven Hatfill over the FBI's false arrest of him in the 2001 anthrax attacks, the FBI stumbled through a decade of the utmost incompetence.[116]

But the CIA was hardly effective, either. As Tenet revealed in his book, the same decade produced one massive intelligence failure after another at the CIA. Tenet presented a list of incompetence that should have forced the complete dissolution of the agency. The CIA missed opportunities to add terrorists Nawaf al-Hazmi and Khalid al-Mihdhar to the watch list ("we missed them all"), failed to get information to Langley on these two ("Clearly, a communication breakdown occurred"), and many more.[117] It should be recalled that the CIA, prior to 9/11, had also bungled the removal of the shah of Iran and allowed the Ayatollah Ruhollah Khomeini to come to power there, badly *overestimated* the economic power of the USSR in the 1970s, and failed to stop either of the African embassy bombings, the attack on the *Cole*, or even the 1993 World Trade Center truck bombing.

Now, the Bush administration had to ponder an offensive in Afghanistan but with Massoud, America's best native ally, gone. Even working with the Northern Alliance became more difficult: None of his successors possessed his skill or military prowess. Although Tenet promised that "we need to go in fast, hard and light," and that al-Qaeda would "believe [that] we will withdraw in the face of casualties and never engage them in hand-to-hand combat," over time the response differed little from that of the Soviets' big footprint in Afghanistan.[118] Bush and his team also erroneously bought into the premise that the US could invade a primitive, backward, and completely tribal (and *Muslim*) nation, yet do so as a modern liberator bringing democracy and women's rights. In his public speeches, the president insisted it was about helping Afghans rid their country of a foreign menace. At home, he and his spokespeople clumsily referred to "women of cover"[119] in hopes of portraying Islam in a more favorable light.

Certainly, Bush's strategy differed from the foot-dragging of Clinton. He didn't seek legal protections; he just declared war, though with the now-common "joint resolution" of Congress rather than a formal declaration. And initially, it appeared much would be different on the ground. Tenet told the president, "I want the CIA to be the first on the ground," then he issued a memo commanding all of his divisions to fully share information. "There can be no bureaucratic impediments to success."[120] And because of the giant logistic apparatus of the military, Tenet got his wish: On October 17, just a month after 9/11, when the first Special Forces units arrived, they were met by the CIA officers, who had been in country for some time. By then, the assessment of the situation was that the Northern Alliance forces on their own could not overcome the Taliban (particularly in Mazar-i-Sharif) and that no viable Pashtun alternative government currently existed to the Taliban. (The Northern Alliance were Tajiks, while the majority of the Southern tribes were Pashtuns, and the two tribes were archenemies.)

Just six weeks after the towers collapsed, *The New York Times* predicted a "quagmire" in Afghanistan. Neither the Pentagon nor the CIA saw it that way. The very next day, the key Taliban center of Mazar-i-Sharif fell in a major victory for the Northern Alliance and a handful of American Special Forces. Before long, a new leader, Hamid Karzai, who had broader support in the central part of the country, arose to lead the resistance to the Taliban. Afghanistan settled into a grind, but one that the US and its allies were steadily winning militarily. Outside of military progress, however, Bush's goal of "changing hearts and minds" was only coming true superficially. In January 2004, the nation held a presidential election in which women voted and displayed the evidence of it with the "purple finger" in which they made their mark. America's media mostly ignored a significant breakthrough for Muslim women—and supposedly a victory for feminism—in the country out of their disdain for Bush.

Meanwhile, al-Qaeda (at least temporarily) had vanquished from Afghanistan and headed into the remote northern areas of Pakistan. There, Pakistan as an ally could not be invaded, and Pakistan had a working relationship with al-Qaeda. President Pervez Musharraf had no intention of invading the al-Qaeda–dominated northern areas—it could mean his entire government could collapse in the backlash. Later, it was also learned that Pakistani intelligence had been compromised by al-Qaeda.

Bush's team turned its attention to Saddam Hussein's Iraq. Saddam still possessed various chemical and biological weapons and/or weapons *capabilities* (later broadly referred to as "weapons of mass destruction" or WMDs). Because the "WMDs in Iraq" mantra would affect US politics, foreign policy, and even affect the "lessons" of Bush's actions, it behooves this text to get the record straight. In doing so, it must remain at the forefront that while the documents, speeches, and record to some degree speak for themselves, the motivations, understandings, and rationalizations (many after the fact) do not. The web of interrelationships, intelligence assessments, assumptions, and above all the long history of Saddam's record cannot be discarded without altering the arguments for war at the time. It would be akin to quoting the "War Hawks" in 1812 and disregarding an entire decade of British naval depredations that led up to war.

Deputy director of the CIA, Michael Morell admitted[ii] "the bottom line for the intelligence community and the [CIA] was that we got the vast majority of the judgments on Iraq and WMD wrong."[121] To properly assess the situation in 2002 and 2003 as it informed Bush's decision making, two circumstances are absolutely fundamental. First, having just experienced the most horrifying and deadly attack on American soil since Pearl Harbor and the first attack on the American homeland since the War of 1812, Bush had moved the risk-avoidance meter nearly off the chart. No president of either party, and probably even some of

ii As with all history, sources are everything. After the Iraq War debacle, a number of policy and elected officials, generals, and former spies all surged forth to explain their decisions—mostly in support of the war. I reject the notion that "everyone" who worked for the CIA, FBI, National Security Council, or any other government organization was entirely corrupt or disingenuous. Moreover, it seems that while the "Deep State" certainly existed (and has existed well back into the 1800s), it had not become nearly as politicized in the early 2000s as it became later, especially after President Trump threatened its very existence. Therefore, unless otherwise noted, I take these sources at their word when they say they believed the evidence. Similarly, I reject (for the most part—there are exceptions) the view that all publishing houses are merely "fronts" for the CIA. Some were and are. Some were not.

the handful of the more-isolationist politicians thrust into the Oval Office, would have dared disregard the avalanche of intelligence reports that insisted Saddam Hussein had WMDs. Bush received reports from foreign nations across the alliance and ideological spectrum: Israel, the United Kingdom, Russia, Germany, Egypt, and Jordan, plus the United Nations itself unanimously agreed that Saddam had WMDs. The UN had gone so far as to pass more than a dozen resolutions to that effect. Muslim and Jewish nations, former communist and Western states all were in agreement. Later, it was learned that Germany did not trust its sources but *did not inform the CIA of its skepticism.*[122] Could that have been a "turning point"? Two of the four streams of information on the mobile poison labs Saddam supposedly possessed were weak.

Morell expressed his position as follows: "I believed Saddam had chemical and biological weapons, was restarting his nuclear weapons program, and was working on missiles of various ranges.... I worried less about Saddam's giving these weapons to al Qa'ida than I did about his eventually using them himself."[123]

CIA Director Tenet said that the case against Saddam started with the National Security Council. By the time Tenet met with Bush and delivered the two words that would haunt him and the administration for over a decade—it's a "slam dunk"[124] he told the president—the case for a war to remove Saddam was signed, sealed, and delivered.

Douglas Feith, undersecretary for defense for policy, argued that "the problem of Saddam Hussein predated 9/11."[125] Having voluntarily limited the US to merely repelling the Iraqis out of Kuwait in 1991 and preventing the removal Saddam, he remained a constant irritant in the region until the time of the invasion in 2003. He had shut down UN weapons inspectors in 1998, leading then (under President Clinton) to the Iraq Liberation Act, which called for the policy of the US to remove Saddam. Prominent Democrats, such as Senator Carl Levin of Michigan, Tom Daschle of South Dakota, and John Kerry of Massachusetts, sent a letter to Clinton at that time urging him to "take necessary actions" to respond to Saddam's WMD programs (that they then believed existed).

Levin said in October 1998, "I believe we must carefully consider other actions [if Saddam doesn't comply] *including, if necessary, the use of force to destroy suspect sites* [italics added]."[126]

After Operation Desert Storm, when the US and her allies had the ability to utterly eradicate the entire Iraqi military and to drive into Baghdad to remove Saddam—but rejected those measures—Saddam's aggressions required the imposition of a no-fly zone over the northern part of the country where Saddam had used helicopter gunships to kill rival Kurds.[127] He proceeded to harbor terrorists from Abu Nidal (a Palestinian bomber) to Abu Abbas (the leader of the *Achille Lauro* takeover in 1985). He also hosted an al-Qaeda terrorist named Abu Musab al-Zarqawi, who later emerged as a major target when the war started.[128] To say "harbored" does not quite capture the extent of the support Saddam provided, which included permitting training camps with full American passenger liners to train in seizing aircraft and allowing the terrorists access to the Iraqi Intelligence Service that directed the bioweapons programs. Even to the most skeptical observer, it should have been obvious that Saddam *could* have not only been aiding and abetting al-Qaeda terrorists but also supplying them with the expertise to make bioweapons—*if not the actual bioweapons themselves.* And while people such as Morell and Feith could differ over whether or not Saddam actually was engaging in such close cooperation, the possibility clearly existed.

To reiterate, *no* American president less than two years after 9/11 could have stood by and allowed such a festering ulcer to grow.

Then there was the UN, whose own WMD inspectors discovered that the Iraqi WMD program had advanced considerably since they supposedly halted it in the wake of Operation Iraqi Freedom. A 1995 UN Special Commission on Iraq learned from a defector, Hussein Kamil, Saddam's brother-in-law and the head of the WMD program, that Iraq itself admitted it had an "offensive BW [biological weapons] programme, but still denied any weaponization."[129] (Astonishingly Kamil returned to Iraq with a pledge of a pardon from Saddam: Family members, not

Saddam himself, killed him immediately upon his return.) In the case of a bioweapon called "camel pox," Iraq not only had worked on this before Desert Storm but also had actually *accelerated* the research after the war.

For brutal dictators such as Idi Amin, Muammar Gaddafi, and Saddam Hussein, terror was merely another tool in their belt for maintaining control. Other ruthless so-called leaders, from Fidel Castro to the ayatollahs in Iran, routinely used similar methods. Iraq stood out because of the previous Kuwait invasion, because of the UN sanctions, and most important of all, *because it was immediately post-9/11*. All policy made in the immediate aftermath of 9/11 took on a different hue that, perhaps, ten years later would not produce the same responses, even from a George W. Bush.

Two groups inside Iraq added particular nuances to Saddam's terror tendencies. The Kurds in the North had desired their own "Kurdistan" for decades. Saddam had ruthlessly suppressed them, including using chemical weapons on them, triggering another UN sanction.[130] In the South, the Shiite Muslims (Saddam was a Sunni) also constituted a threat as the dictator saw it. The UN Security Council's Iraq Survey Group in 2006 reported that Saddam not only hid his WMD programs inside his intelligence apparatus but also concealed production under "dual-use" facilities that he could plausibly claim served civilian needs.[131]

Assessing the existence and extent of WMDs in Iraq at the time relied on two other major sources of information. Actual American spies in Iraq were nonexistent. But emigrant groups and those seeking political amnesty were plentiful. Unfortunately, such individuals always had an axe to grind. Discerning their reliability constituted an art, which is precisely why over the years people have referred to the "art of spy craft" and "tradecraft." Sources such as Alawi Chalabi, a secular Shiite Muslim, had crossed Saddam and fled to England where he founded an opposition group, the Iraqi National Congress. To what degree was Chalabi's information reliable? He had been consulting with the CIA since 1991. But there were at least a dozen similar individuals providing information, despite questionable motivations and timeliness. Many had left

Iraq a decade earlier. Another major source, Ayad Allawi (who headed the Iraqi National Accord), left for London in 1971. What remained for actual spying operations? Satellite information (or signals intelligence, SIGINT), which would be late, proved to be similarly questionable. Was someone moving a barrel containing a bioweapon or a fifty-gallon drum of oil? Later, those kinds of SIGINT would generate drastically different conclusions than were reached at the time. Again, given Saddam's history, it was completely understandable to assume the worst.

A Washington, DC, think tank called the Project for the New American Century published an open letter to President Clinton bearing over 1,800 names of former national security officials calling for "the only acceptable strategy" that would mean "a willingness to undertake military action…[including] removing Saddam Hussein and his regime from power."[132] Bush's team had actually started to debate the Iraq policy before 9/11, specifically the US interest in maintaining respect for the UN resolutions and the Security Council. President Harry Truman had been the first to appeal to "international authority" over purely American national security interests when he unadvisedly sought UN support in the Korean War, launched by a "succession of blunders."[133] Truman had full authority under the Potsdam Agreement to boot the North Koreans out of South Korea but instead sought to cloak the operation in the "moral authority" of the UN. (In historian Johnson's eyes, this undermined the concept of the "UN as a useful, but limited body, and set it on a course which transformed it into an instrument of ideological propaganda.")[134] Unlike Truman, Bush at least sought congressional approval of the "War on Terror" first—but not in the form of a declaration of war, rather more of an easily obtained joint resolution.

Now, a half century after Korea, Bush found himself again trying to wrap American action in the mantle of a broader coalition sanctioned by the UN and at the same time endeavoring to keep the UN Security Council from being exposed as ineffective. Gone were the Security Council's own constraints from 1991. Weapons inspectors had been booted out of Iraq, sanctions (as they almost always do) were backfiring with world condemnation, and now the cease-fire provisions had deteriorated.[135] Speaking to the UN itself, Bush warned that "the conduct of the Iraqi regime is a threat to the authority of the United Nations.... Will the United Nations serve the purpose of its founding, or will it be irrelevant?"[136] Saddam had blatantly violated sixteen Security Council resolutions. Bush, whether right on WMDs or any other claim about the war, was deadly accurate in laying the cause of war at the very feet of the UN for being unwilling to enforce any of them when it was possible to do so without war.

While the UN remained largely superfluous, wholly corrupt, and overly dominated by leftist ideologues of the Bandung generation (so termed by historian Johnson to refer to the post–World War II third-world leaders), it also suffered from a sclerosis that afflicted many modern institutions. A tendency toward inaction characterized almost all large bodies. Feith, the former undersecretary of defense for policy, noted that "when one government office proposes an initiative, the other agencies typically point out how it might go wrong." Thus, "officials tend to prefer the predictability of the status quo."[137] When it came to Iraq, the debate about the dangers of removing Saddam versus leaving him in place were pervasive. But Feith's observation only goes so far and assumes entirely rational actors seeking America's (or the world's) best interest (even if by their own definition). A decade later, under President Trump, the entire bureaucracy would become so infused by the threat posed to the "uni-party" and the Deep State as a whole that it acted in an accord never before seen in American history.

For now, though, contentious differences remained over how to deal with Iraq, even if virtually all of those varied views agreed on the basic assumption that Saddam was an immediate threat who had to be addressed in some way. Retired General Colin Powell, Bush's secretary of state who had played a key role in calling off the dogs when General Norman Schwarzkopf stood on the brink of toppling Saddam in 1991, led the "sanctions" group. His chief ally was his deputy, Richard Armitage. Both believed in sanctions for sanctions sake. Neither had a long-term explanation for why they would work (which, historically, they almost never did except when employed against tiny, easily blockaded nations). Like the UN's policy of threaten-but-don't-act, sanctions joined another widely discussed solution that amounted to nothing: an internal coup. Did the Bush administration genuinely believe that it could topple Saddam internally? The record suggests that this was the brainchild of Condoleezza Rice, who sought to find a common ground among the different factions within the administration.

Gradually, the idealistic and unobtainable argument for spreading liberty and "freeing the Iraqi people" was forced into the two genuinely strategic objectives of removing Saddam's WMDs and eliminating al-Qaeda bases in Iraq. It stemmed in part from Bush's obsession with casting a larger cloak of morality over military operations that had emerged during the invasion of Afghanistan. There, attempts to include the liberation of women became a staple of US propaganda, and one that leftist media organs completely ignored.

"Women's rights" were an important issue only until it left American shores (or those of our allies). An unwritten rule was that American liberals could never condemn intense, pervasive, and often brutal Islamic oppression of women because that would entail criticizing *Islam* while adding potentially positive arguments for the imperialism that had restrained it. Bush had even gone so far after 9/11 to downplay the terrorists as Muslims, pressed by his staff to show concern for retaliation against Muslims in America. (As noted earlier, in his October 11, 2001, press conference he would lament that "women of cover" were "afraid of going out of their homes alone.")[138] Of course, in major American cities that was true in times of peace for women of any faith—or no faith.

Central to understanding the invasion of Iraq is that *plans were already well developed* prior to 9/11 based on Saddam's behavior over the previous ten years. As the saying goes, "If you're a hammer, every problem looks like a nail." In the very first strategy meeting after the World Trade Center attacks, all focus was on Afghanistan. Iraq was deferred.[139] Gradually, as al-Qaeda and the Taliban were subdued in

Afghanistan (though hardly defeated), the administration turned its sights back to Iraq. Immediately after launching Operation Enduring Freedom, Secretary of Defense Donald Rumsfeld called in his team to evaluate how to neutralize the WMD threat and terrorism in Iraq. He was presented with options for a "short war" (again using the largely fictional "internal resistance"), then a few weeks later developed a war plan with strategic guidance for General Tommy Franks, who would head any military action there. Rumsfeld insisted on a wide range of options, not just invasion. He strongly argued for keeping any conflict as small as possible to focus entirely on WMDs and terrorism. The wider it got, he reasoned, the more likelihood a rogue group or al-Qaeda cell would obtain weapons from unguarded facilities.[140] Indeed, had Rumsfeld's strategy been followed, the Iraq War would have concluded in less than a year with a US withdrawal and a report showing no actual WMDs could be found (but plenty of evidence of the previous existence of WMDs). Bush's legacy might have been much different.

Britain stood by the US in the Iraq planning. War hawk British Prime Minister Tony Blair visited Washington in February 2001, and Bush took an immediate liking to him. In his memoir, Bush recalled that they agreed that "if we had to remove Saddam from power, Tony and I would have an obligation to help the Iraqi people replace Saddam's tyranny with a democracy."[141] This was a deeply flawed and monumentally bad decision. It suggested that a liberator had an "obligation" to go beyond liberation, that "democracy" was to be imposed (whether desired or not), and that any exit strategy would be enormously difficult to pin down. In part, it was imposed on Bush by the press, who harped on the slogan, "If you break it, you own it." Certainly seldom prior to World War II had the US felt obligated to install a new government over a defeated foe. It had not occurred in the Mexican War, in Cuba after the Spanish-American War, or in Germany after World War I, except for the condition that the kaiser had to abdicate. When, for example, was a country sufficiently "democratic?" After one election? Two? Bush and Blair's incomprehensible commitment to "nation building" was shaky on its surface and full of potholes in a westernized nation, such as Greece or Italy after World War II. But in Islamic states that had no concept whatsoever of the rule of law, checks and balances, or even (usually) basic human rights, the goal was unobtainable from the start. At a second visit by the Blairs to Crawford, Texas, in April 2002, Blair pushed an ultimatum involving a UN resolution backed by "serious consequences."[142]

A month after Mazar-i-Sharif fell to American Special Forces and the Northern Alliance in Afghanistan, Bush made a decision to remove Saddam's regime. A growing concern was that Saddam's wanton violation of UN resolutions and the no-fly zones meant that war was inevitable: To Bush, the only questions were when and on whose terms. He thought it too dangerous to allow Saddam to control the answer to those questions. It was not enough to believe that Saddam destroyed the WMDs; it was not enough to even have proof he had destroyed the WMDs. For the threat to disappear, Saddam's factories would have to be eliminated, or he could easily ramp up again. In other words, the weapons themselves constituted only a part of the WMD issues; the capability was a larger component. After the war, only the stockpiles were missing—a subject to address later. But no one questioned the intent or capability to make the weapons. Later, Feith would argue that "the decision to feature the CIA's badly crafted assessments of Iraqi WMD stockpiles...was unfortunate, because the existence of those stockpiles was not a cornerstone of our rationale for going to war."[143]

A much different picture developed at the CIA, where one agent said "no one pushed us [to believe Saddam had WMDs]—we were already there," meaning they already believed WMDs existed in Iraq.[144] Further, "to go to war knowing you are soon going to be proven wrong would be insane."[145] And while agents such as Morell would attempt to distinguish "assumptions" from "judgments," to the public it looked like splitting hairs. Later, excuses included the fact that the information was dated, as much as four years, the sources from the Iraqi defectors and/or ex-patriots was highly slanted, the satellite or photo analysis failed to include qualifiers, or plain, old "analytic creep." At any rate, when pressed by

Bush to sharpen the arguments for a *public* presentation, including a UN speech, CIA Director Tenet was asked if he had better information to add to the debate, and he replied affirmatively. "I thought it would be possible," he said, "to declassify enough additional information—communications intercepts, satellite reconnaissance photos, sanitized human intelligence reports and so forth—to help the public understand what *we believed to be true*."[146] Tenet later claimed in his book *At the Center of the Storm* that it was this question he was answering when he used the two words that haunted him the rest of his life, it's a "slam dunk."[147]

It is historically critical to restate that what led to the "WMDs in Iraq" was a series of shadings or imprecision in language given to Bush. This devolved almost entirely from the fact that at every occasion, CIA briefers, especially John McLaughlin and Tenet, never strongly suggested that there was a possibility no WMDs existed because *every one of them believed such weapons did exist*, and it would only be a matter of dragging them out before cameras. In other words, an invasion would prove what they already "knew." Subsequently, another layer of requiring a level of confidence in judgments would be added—but this hardly solved the problem if those doing the assessments had convinced themselves that a high level of confidence existed. As Charles Duelfer, who led the weapons hunt, put it, Saddam continued the charade to deter Iran, not the US, and gambled that US intelligence was good enough to determine the real story. Morrell summed this up as "even Saddam turned out to be overconfident in US intelligence capabilities."[148]

One final possibility must therefore be considered, which is that the WMDs were there all along and got moved. The CIA and others in the intelligence community, it could be argued, became so desperate to make excuses that they bought into an entirely new—but false—story that complied with subsequent news organizations' views. Trying to deflect the claim that they had deliberately pushed the nation into war with false information, they adopted the position that they were merely incompetent. Duelfer, therefore, might have told the truth—that he found no such WMDs—and yet not discovered a deeper truth, namely that they indeed existed and were moved.

A powerful voice for this argument came from former Iraqi General Georges Sada, part of Saddam's inner circle. In his book *Saddam's Secrets*, published after the invasion, Sada personally attested to the regime using WMDs in attacks. Sada's story relied on multiple discussions with Iraqi "captains" (presumably pilots) who said that in 1981 the dictator used such weapons against Iraqis and that these "friends" told him that the WMDs had been moved to Syria, while the remaining nuclear weapons were destroyed.[149] In the "Duelfer Report," this claim was only called "unlikely" but could not be discounted. Syria indeed later showed evidence of having such weapons. In the debate over another WMD ingredient, yellowcake—a uranium concentrate—the US found over 550 tons in Iraq.[150]

Defense Secretary Rumsfeld, in his book *Known and Unknown*, noted that the "intelligence community reported near total confidence in their conclusions" and the assessments were "unusually consistent."[151] He also admitted that "in the run-up to the war in Iraq, we heard a great deal about what our intelligence community knew or thought they knew, but not enough about what they knew they didn't know."[152] It was a recurring postwar rationale that the evidence—whether WMDs or al-Qaeda having a major presence in Iraq—did not receive sufficient scrutiny. Especially troubling for Bush, however, came a report that an al-Qaeda general named Abu al-Zarqawi was in Iraq and operating a weapons lab. (Later, the first part was confirmed—Zarqawi indeed was there—but the latter part was not true. He did not have a weapons lab.)[153]

At any rate, the die was cast. Informed with a consistent message from the CIA and reinforced by the meetings General Franks, the Middle Eastern–area commander, had with Egypt's president Hosni Mubarak and Jordan's King Hussein (who both believed Saddam had WMDs), Bush took his case public.

In October 2002, the House of Representatives passed a resolution authorizing force against Iraq by a strong margin of 297–133 (a larger margin of 47 votes than what the 1991 joint resolution received in the House). The Senate followed with a vote of 77–23. None of the Iraq War supporters left any room to run from their votes:

- Senator Joe Biden said, "We have no choice but to eliminate the threat."
- Senator Hillary Clinton said, "Intelligence reports show that Saddam Hussein has worked to rebuild his chemical and biological weapons…[and] has given aid, comfort, and sanctuary to terrorists, including al-Qaeda members."[154]
- Former Vice President Al Gore said that the West had been unable to deter Saddam with other measures and that "we should assume that [the search for WMDs] will continue as long as Saddam is in power."
- Senator John Kerry said, "When I vote to give the President… the authority to use force, if necessary, to disarm Saddam Hussein, it is because I believe that a deadly arsenal of weapons of mass destruction in his hands is a threat."[155]

A unanimous 15–0 vote at the UN Security Council followed on November 8 offering Saddam "one final opportunity to comply" or face "serious consequences." What the Iraqi dictator submitted to the UN on December 7 was reams of "irrelevant paperwork clearly designed to deceive."[156] Even Hans Blix, the milquetoast UN Swede who led the inspections team, was underwhelmed. Senator Joe Lieberman called it a "twelve-thousand-page, one-hundred-pound lie."[157] It was at that moment, a few days before Christmas 2002, that Bush hesitated once more and called in CIA Director Tenet to be sure. Tenet delivered his "slam dunk" assessment at that time. Bush recalled, "I believed him.… If anything, we worried that the CIA was *underestimating* Saddam, as it had before the Gulf War [emphasis mine]."[158]

Democratic support for the war should not have been surprising, as just two weeks later voters would weigh in—and they still stood behind Bush and, as they saw it, his efforts to keep them safe. That November,

Republicans slightly increased their House margin by eight (229–204) and in the Senate gained two to hold a two-seat majority. Some of the Republican momentum in the Senate had come from the betrayal of "Jumpin'" Jim Jeffords of Vermont, who had given the GOP a single-seat advantage in 2000, only to change party affiliation immediately after the election to "independent" and deny the Republicans a popularly elected Senate majority. At any rate, the 2002 gains for Republicans bucked the trend of the party gaining power in non-presidential elections.

British Prime Minister Blair strongly recommended obtaining a new UN resolution. Bush decided to have Powell make a presentation to the UN. Three major themes developed in the war pitch: WMDs, removal of al-Qaeda in Iraq, and liberation of the Iraqi people. Secretary of State Powell took the case to the Security Council of the UN on February 5, 2003. He presented evidence for mobile production vans designed to evade detection by inspectors; showed evidence of Scud missiles capable of carrying chem/bio weapons; produced testimony that Saddam's son Qusay had ordered the removal of WMDs from Saddam's palaces and was dispersing rocket launchers and warheads to western Iraq; and repeatedly reminded the UN that all of these actions were in violation of various resolutions the Security Council had passed.[159] A new resolution was out of the question. Mexico, Chile, and other allies would not support one. To Bush, the path to war seemed anything but rushed: He had a UN resolution. It had been six years since Saddam kicked out weapons inspectors, six months since Bush issued his ultimatum, and four months since the UN resolution. To Bush, diplomacy did not feel rushed—"It felt like it was taking forever."[160]

At his State of the Union address in January 2002, Bush invoked the term "axis of evil" that he insisted described a "link between the governments that pursued WMD and the terrorist who could use those weapons."[161] Specifically, he named Iraq, Iran, and North Korea. Bush had been discussing strategies with German Chancellor Gerhard Schroeder, who he claimed privately supported military action, saying that "if you make it fast and make it decisive, I will be with you."[162]

Thus, Bush believed he had unconditional support from both Great Britain and Germany and assumed the UN would back him as well. In September, he addressed the UN Security Council. Then in February, Powell addressed the UN General Assembly.

On March 17, 2003, Bush demanded that Saddam and his two sons surrender and leave Iraq and that all weapons inspectors be allowed in immediately. He gave the dictator forty-eight hours to comply.

Differences between the approach to military actions in Iraq and Afghanistan arose. Afghanistan resisted a major, traditional invasion due to its mountainous nature and the absence of a formal military enemy. Another critical factor surfaced in that unlike Afghanistan where early on Massoud had provided a local leader to rally around (and after his death, other acceptable, though less effective, men stepped forward), in Iraq, no Sunni of such standing could be found.

Beginning after Christmas in 2001, Bush began a series of meetings with General Franks. As commander of the US Central Command in the Middle East, Franks would lead any invasion. Like Napoleon, Franks was an artilleryman by training. But he more resembled the former star of Middle East combat, General Norman Schwarzkopf, in his approach to military action. Both were traditionalists, uncomfortable in the new areas of cyber warfare, financial warfare, and guerrilla asymmetry. During the battle of the Tora Bora mountains in Afghanistan from December 6 to 17, 2001, Franks came under heated criticism for his failure to deploy eight hundred troops from the army's mountain division to capture Osama bin Laden who was supposedly held up in the caves. Both the general and Bush questioned the evidence Bin Laden was there, but they also feared if he was, the terrorist would simply retreat across the border to Pakistan. There, he would have been held—if not outright harbored—by the vacillating Pakistani government.[163]

Bin Laden was in fact there. He did escape. Whether adding more troops would have been successful is one of the what-ifs of history. While it certainly would have been a major public relations coup for the administration, the very nature of al-Qaeda (as the US would soon learn in Iraq) was hydra-like with numerous cells and active leaders.

Now, in preparation for the invasion of Iraq, Franks and Secretary of Defense Rumsfeld perpetually butted heads. Rumsfeld lacked the understanding of some military demands, but far better than Franks's more traditional view. Rumsfeld believed the imperative was that the war be a quick one. Although in the media Rumsfeld was depicted as pressing for a "smaller footprint," fewer troops, and rapid "Pattonesque" movement, in fact the force was substantial. Over 450,000 troops were available in theater at the outset of war. Franks was steeped in the army "way of war": overwhelming firepower, delivered unceasingly and only then sending in live American troops when the enemy had been as reduced as possible. In short, Franks envisioned an Iraq invasion as resembling Operation Desert Storm—but with a key missing ingredient. The Iraq operation would have no giant surprise envelopment move.

Rumsfeld and the Pentagon war planners were entirely correct in their assessment that most of Saddam's troops would, as they had in 1991, run. What they had not planned on was that absent a procedure to bring them back as American allies in a new Iraqi army, most would turn into guerrillas fighting for warlords. Rumsfeld badly misjudged their numbers, referring to them as "dead enders." A second major difference between the Kuwait war and Iraq was that in Operation Desert Storm, Saddam had relied on his manpower and artillery superiority to protect dug-in troops and defeat the coalition. Those were eviscerated by allied air, pinned in place by deception, and then encircled by the so-called Hail Mary. Saddam's new fighters were ordered to disperse, refrain from offering coalition air power any high-value targets, and take up guerilla warfare and terror attacks, if necessary, as suicide bombers.

On March 20, 2003, the missiles flew, and the coalition forces surged across the border. A total of over 370,000 US, British, Australian, Polish, and Kurdish troops invaded from Kuwait in the South or from Kurdish zones in the North. (Rumsfeld had warned that including specifics in Powell's UN speech about the Khurmal facility would lead to its immediate destruction by the Iraqis and to the flight of most of the operatives there—which it did.) But even at that, when coalition forces arrived, they found "clear signs of chemical weapons production," chemical hazard suits, and Arabic manuals to make chemical weapons, as well as traces of cyanide, ricin, and other toxins.[164]

What followed the initial missile strikes, which had been characterized by Franks as "shock and awe," indeed shocked almost everybody. American forces, moving up two long pincers, bypassed strong points and rocketed to Baghdad, initially taking the airport in a "thunder run" blitz of armor, followed shortly by a second "thunder run" into Baghdad itself. That armored action rewrote military history, for it was the first time unsupported armor not only took a major city but also held it against infantry counterattacks.[165] "Thunder run" was an operation recommended at the time by Colonel Steve Hummer. And regardless of whatever else one thought of the US military performance, it is noteworthy that colonels in the field were sending tactical suggestions upwards to generals or that they adopted new tactics in the field without requesting permission or fearing reprisals. Their actions constituted a level of autonomy unseen in almost any other military force in history.

When US forces in Firdos Square toppled Saddam's statue on April 9, 2003, it seemed to indicate that the war was over. Coalition forces swept northward in twenty days to capture the enemy's capital—a remarkable military success in any age. In fact, America's troubles and the combat that went with it had only started with the commitment to "nation building." Powell, in one of the rare moments when his judgment proved sound, warned Bush that if they removed Saddam, they "owned" Iraq.[166] In other words, "nation building" might not be an option.

Military planners found that Saddam's top lieutenants had organized fierce terrorist resistance in the north and west of Iraq. Their objective? Civil war. They sought to incite the Southern Shiites to rise up against the Sunni majority in the North. Using IEDs (improvised explosive devices) in roads and narrow city streets, the insurgents exacted a fearful toll, not just on American troops but on civilians as well. Indeed, both Sunni and Shiite extremists, seeing their opportunity to control the nation, attacked each other and civilian targets with venom. On August 19, a truck bomber blew up the UN building in Baghdad, forcing the UN to pull out.[167] Just ten days later, radicals used car bombs to blow up the Imam Ali mosque in Najaf, killing nearly one hundred civilians. Terrorists staged bombings in Baghdad (the Red Cross and four Iraqi police stations on October 27), killing 34 and injuring 224; in Nasiriya (the Italian military headquarters on November 12), killing 18 Italians and 9 Iraqis; and in Karbala (four suicide attacks on coalition barracks on December 27), killing 19 and injuring 200. Just in the first six months of 2004, terrorists struck Erbil, the capital of Iraqi Kurdistan (the offices of the Kurdish political parties on February 1), killing 117 and injuring 133; Karbala and Baghdad (massacres on the holy day of Ashura, March 2), killing over 80 and injuring 200 Shiite Muslims; Basra (car bombings on April 21), killing 74 and injuring 100; and Mosul (car bombings on June 24), killing 62 and injuring 220.[168] From 2003 through 2011, there were nearly eighty *major* suicide bomber attacks reported: The number from IEDs and smaller, less-reported attacks were vastly higher. A RAND study in 2008 confirmed that in 2003, the terrorists switched from attacking coalition forces to targeting civilians in a bid to incite a civil war and to encourage locals to demand the withdrawal of foreign troops.[169]

Nevertheless, Bush delivered a positive speech to the UN in September 2003, arguing that the war had come down to "those who seek order, and those who spread chaos," a struggle in which there was "no neutral ground." He attempted to flatter the UN by saying the "international coalition in Iraq is meeting its responsibilities," that the coalition was "helping to improve the daily lives of the Iraqi people," and that Iraq had a "truly representative" governing council. He continued to press for an effort to stop "the proliferation of weapons of mass destruction," and for the first time, highlighted the genuine problem of human trafficking, calling it a "special evil in the abuse and exploitation of the most innocent and vulnerable."[170]

Al-Qaeda and its Iraqi allies exported terrorism beyond Iraq in an effort to shatter the coalition. In March 2004, al-Qaeda bombed the Cercanías commuter train system in Madrid, Spain, killing one hundred ninety-three and injuring nearly two thousand. The event so rattled the Spanish government that Bush's ally, the incumbent José María Aznar, saw his party defeated in the elections three days later. By the end of April, Spain had withdrawn all troops from Iraq. Clearly, the terrorists' message was received. A year later, suicide bombers hit three London subways, killing 56 and injuring 700. England, however, hung tough in the coalition, though Blair suffered a loss of support, and by 2007 he resigned.

Bush had first appointed Jay Garner, a former military officer, as the head of the Coalition Provisional Authority to get the country back on its feet, but he lasted just over two weeks until Paul Bremer took over and issued an order prohibiting members of the Baathist Party of Saddam Hussein from holding government positions. In principle, it was similar to the "denazification" of Germany after World War II. In practice, it had much different effects. Germans never resorted to suicide bombing simply because they didn't have jobs in the army or government. The Iraqis did. Chief among the implications of the policy was that the Iraqi army would be disbanded rather than brought into the ranks seeking to stabilize the country.

Seeking to find the WMDs that virtually everyone thought existed, the Iraq Survey Group was formed. It issued a report in 2004 (the "Duelfer Report"), stating that Iraq did not have a viable WMD program but did find trace elements of WMDs in multiple locations.[171] A simultaneous effort involved the manhunt for Saddam and his various lieutenants. In a July 22, 2003, raid, members of the 101st Airborne killed Saddam's sons, Uday and Qusay. Saddam hid until December when he was turned in by family members. A lull followed after Saddam's capture. Coalition forces refocused on training a new Iraqi security force and physically rebuilding the damaged infrastructure.

But the peace was temporary. New hotbeds of insurgents appeared, most notably Fallujah in the west. There, al-Qaeda had taken over the town and commanded the countryside with the support of local warlords. A revived insurgency in 2004 targeted the new Iraqi security forces and civilians. Four US civilian contractors were ambushed in Fallujah, their bodies Mogadishu-style dragged through the streets (as occurred in 1993 when the bodies of killed Americans were dragged through the Somali city). Bush was prepared to retake the Fallujah no matter what the cost but was dissuaded both by Blair and by Iraqi supporters who warned it would make it difficult to form an interim government. Bush acceded to the request and instead deployed a legion of snipers around the city who eviscerated al-Qaeda fighters one at a time. With Blair safely reelected, the Second Battle of Fallujah—now against a vastly weakened enemy—concluded in November.

A much different problem arose when news of US soldiers and officers committing prisoner abuse at Abu Ghraib prison broke. In truth, the abuse was little more than minor humiliation and came nowhere close to the torture and bloodletting unleashed on coalition troops by al-Qaeda. But opponents of the war seized on it as a means to impugn Bush's moral justifications for the war. (*The New York Times* alone had more than twenty front-page articles on the prisoner abuse, which included making male prisoners wear women's underwear and pose with a dog collar.)[172] No major outlet asked whether an Islamic culture based on shame and honor actually may have been more attuned to such images than Western societies.

An Iraqi transitional government was elected in January 2005, including eligible Kurds and Shiite Muslims. Slowly, violence appeared to be abetting, and some fifteen thousand American forces were withdrawn, but in May, new rounds of suicide-bombing terror hit targets across Iraq. Indeed, in 2005, the number of terror-related incidents rose by almost ten thousand.

The manhunt for the last major al-Qaeda leader in Iraq, Zarqawi, ended in June 2006 when American forces destroyed him in a building. Just a few weeks before, the formal government of Iraq took office. Following a year-long trial, the Iraqis hanged Saddam on December 30, 2006. It changed little. Neither Bush nor the Congress, which was increasingly seeing an opportunity to hammer a weakened Bush, found much to be optimistic about in Iraq. Under pressure from Congress, and particularly Arizona "maverick" Senator John McCain, Bush agreed to an independent review of the military situation, conducted by the Iraq Survey Group. It reported that the situation in Iraq was "deteriorating" and that no exit was in sight. Terrorists were launching just under one thousand attacks *a week*, the Western part of the country seemed lost, and there did not seem to be enough "boots on the ground" to secure the peace.[173]

With the war as a background, Bush had run for reelection in 2004. His opponent, Massachusetts Senator John Kerry, hoped his Vietnam War record and commendations would provide him sufficient cover as a "hawk" to pull out of Iraq. Bush, like his father after Desert Storm, had gained approval ratings above 90 percent following 9/11, but Iraq steadily eroded those. Nevertheless, as late as May 2003, his approval hovered in the 60 percent range. The war, clearly, would be the major campaign issue, and Democrats thought that by nominating a decorated veteran in Kerry, they could short-circuit concerns he might be weak on terrorism. Kerry had easily dispatched challenger Howard Dean, the governor of Vermont who was caught in a live video after a campaign stop yelling maniacally, "Yeaaaaahhhh!" What came to be known as the "Dean scream" cost the governor, whose campaign crashed immediately thereafter. Kerry also beat South Carolina Senator John Edwards, eventually making him his vice president.

Two scandals, one real and one phony, emerged during the campaign. First, a group called Swift Boat Vets and POWs for Truth attacked Kerry's exaggerated claims about his Vietnam service and his swift boat operations.[174] The "Swift Vets," as they were called, not only produced a book of detailed testimony but also produced a powerful video featuring at least a half dozen Medal of Honor recipients who questioned Kerry's claims of gallantry in the war. Some went so far as to say Kerry's wounds were caused by an explosion he himself caused

through clumsiness. It proved enough to damage him.

A second scandal—a phony one—unfolded with a new hit piece from CBS's Dan Rather on Bush over his Texas Air National Guard service during Vietnam.[175] The episode illustrated the remarkable new power of the internet. A group of "Freepers" (users of the website www.freerepublic.com), within a mere thirty minutes, had proved that the typewriter—which was used to make the document, rather than used to prove Bush's negligence—was not produced yet. Rather had to resign in disgrace, as did others on the *60 Minutes* CBS team that concocted the hoax. Ironically, then, two different lingering stories from Vietnam helped decide the 2004 election.

Even so, it was close. Bush won 50.7 percent of the popular vote but only gathered 286 electoral votes, being put over the top in Ohio by a narrow 118,000 votes. He carried New Mexico, as well as all the rest of the non–Pacific Rim West; all of the South, including Virginia; and Midwestern state Indiana. Kerry, in an ominous note for Republicans, took the Rust Belt Midwest of Minnesota, Wisconsin, Michigan, and Pennsylvania, as well as New Hampshire (which had narrowly gone for Bush in 2000). The new electoral map made the Rust Belt a necessity for Republicans in the future, as Virginia, New Mexico, and Colorado would soon slip away. The message was mixed: Americans still had some confidence in Bush but clearly wanted him to wrap up Iraq and Afghanistan with a genuine "mission accomplished." It would not prove that easy.

Using the findings of the Iraq Survey Group to pound away at Bush, the Democrats and their Republican allies such as McCain got their desired troop increase. McCain and other Republican "hawks" genuinely thought the US needed more men, particularly combat soldiers; Democrats feigned support as a means to further criticize Bush's handling of the war. Under pressure, Bush announced in his 2007 State of the Union address that he would deploy an additional twenty thousand combat troops to the war-torn regions of Iraq under the new "surge strategy." Thus, instead of reducing troops in Iraq, Bush now was increasing them. It raised memories among some of Vietnam, with its web of lies.

And it was too late. Having voted for the war, many Democrats ran against it. They also recruited dozens of military veterans to run for House and Senate seats to deflect charges of being "soft on terror." Battered and defensive Republicans also had to defend Bush's handling of Hurricane Katrina relief, which was viewed as inept, and three major Republican scandals (the Jack Abramoff lobbying scandal, Congressman Mark Foley soliciting sexually suggestive messages and emails to congressional pages, and Congressman Duke Cunningham's bribery case). That perfect storm led to Democratic control of the Senate by gaining five seats and the House by gaining thirty-one seats, as well as picking up six governorships. The public had given Bush time and now concluded that he had failed to deliver. Even before Katrina, Bush's job approval was rarely above 40 percent by late 2006. His situation was not improved by the developments in the western province of Anbar.

Tribes there had been coerced into supporting the insurrection. Al-Qaeda often completely moved in or, at the very least, intimidated local tribal leaders. They co-opted the al-Salmani tribe, sparking a reaction known as the "Anbar Awakening," in which Western Sunni tribes joined with the US military in an alliance that took control of Fallujah and Ramadi.

Some questioned the effectiveness of the "surge," claiming that improved spying on Iraqi insurgent leadership accounted for higher success rates.[176] Regardless of the cause—spying, the additional combat infantrymen, or the Anbar Awakening, American troop deaths began to fall and overall violence against the coalition fell to the lowest levels since the invasion.[177] Claims that "friendly" deaths had decreased or that enemy deaths increased were themselves in question because of the practice of Iraqi morgues using a nebulous category to separate civilians from official Iraqi military deaths. Far from exaggerating the numbers of militants killed (as had happened in Vietnam), the real body count *underestimated* them. For example, on July 26 and June 7, 2006, *USA Today* and *The New York Times* both cited a statistic of 3,149 "civilians" killed in Iraq in a month. Yet the "Iraq Coalition Casualty Count" put the number of "Iraqi Security Forces and Civilian Deaths" at 870. Who were the other 2,879 if they weren't civilians? The answer was clear: likely insurgents. Battlefield reality meant that over ninety terrorists were being removed per day, and since 2003 when hostilities started, coalition forces had eliminated over one hundred thousand and perhaps as many as 120,000.[178]

These may appear as just statistics, but they contained a colossal reality for al-Qaeda. They simply ran out of bodies. American troops historically have had a killed-in-action-to-wounded ratio of 13 percent (i.e., 13 percent of battlefield wounds are fatal, though in the case of Americans in Iraq, an astonishing 55 percent of the wounded returned to action in seventy-two hours!).[179] Employing a very generous 8:1 wounded/killed ratio to the terrorists, those numbers suggest that in addition to the known dead, wounded numbers may have ranged from 288,000 to 960,000! And that only counted those whose bodies were recovered by coalition forces, meaning the real count might have been even higher. In other words, in a shocking statistic few cared to mention, whatever else Bush's invasion of Iraq did, it removed between *a quarter of a million and three quarters of a million terrorists* from the map.

In addition, slowly the US military adapted to terrorist tactics. This analysis was borne out in reports of IED attacks, where from January to June of 2006, despite more actual explosions, new methods of dealing with IEDs reduced American casualties by 15 percent. And as horrific as IED detonations were, battlefield reports showed that one of the major sources of casualties from the attacks was drivers who lost control of their vehicles. When the Marines implemented new "difficult driving" training at Camp Lejeune, the ratio of American death-per-attack fell to the point where it took nearly one hundred IEDs to kill a single US soldier. For comparison, a pilot in World War I only stood a 50 percent chance of returning from a mission.[180]

In December 2008, the Department of Defense reported that the overall level of violence had dropped by nearly 80 percent since the "surge," and American casualties had fallen by two-thirds. The Brookings Institution agreed with those assessments, noting that civilian deaths and the number of attacks had fallen fivefold since the summer of 2007.[181] Nevertheless, General David Petraeus, who had assumed Franks's old position as commander of US Central Command, said in congressional testimony in early 2008 that "we haven't turned any corners, we haven't seen any lights at the end of the tunnel."[182] Nor would Bush.

By the time he left office, no withdrawal date had been set. When Bush's successor, Obama, came into the presidency, having run against the Iraq War, he promptly announced that the US mission would end in August 2010. A "transitional force" of fifty thousand troops trained Iraqi security forces and engaged in leading the counterterrorism operations. Iraq's Prime Minister Nouri al-Maliki supported the withdrawal.[183]

The remaining American forces in Iraq left in 2011 after the US and Iraq failed to negotiate a status-of-forces agreement. American forces remained in Afghanistan until 2021, when President Biden abruptly and incompetently removed them, leaving millions of dollars' worth of US military equipment in Taliban hands—the Taliban had returned to power in Afghanistan—and stranding numerous Afghan allies and interpreters to their fates. Thirteen Americans died in the botched and incoherent withdrawal.

Bush had succeeded in eliminating al-Qaeda at the cost of his presidency. But a new terrorist group, the "Islamic State of Iraq and Syria," or ISIS, filled the void in 2014. Obama would prove inept in handling ISIS, leaving it to yet another Republican, Trump, to end the threat. The "Great Satan" may have been pushed out of Afghanistan and Iraq, but Bush's "War on Terror" took generations of terrorists with him.

CHAPTER 3
LENT DECLIN

It would have been hard to match again the "golden accident" of prosperity brought by the period of 1946–1965 under any circumstances. Following World War II, the United States simultaneously held the position of the world's largest producer and world's largest consumer. Aside from the attack on Pearl Harbor and the invasion of some territorial islands, the American mainland had not suffered any significant damage. (A few incendiary balloon bombs were released with no effect, and a Japanese submarine fired rounds at the American coast.) Thus, the US's economic engine revved undisturbed for four years, reaching unimaginable heights of productivity. At the same time, consumption was limited via rationing, so Americans piled up savings.

All that pent-up demand exploded after 1945 in a tidal wave of home and auto buying, accelerated by the needs of millions of newly created families. The resulting "baby boom" started an economic force that affected the nation for the remainder of the century. By the 1990s, even with the computer revolution, productivity began to slow as people increasingly took more leisure time and spent their accumulated earnings.

American dominance stemmed from not only this "golden accident" of being untouched by war while becoming the "arsenal of democracy" but also from the postwar structure of the Bretton Woods agreement. The rebuilt free nations of the world agreed to use the US dollar as the "reserve currency," meaning all transactions ultimately were denominated in dollars, regardless of what national currencies were in use. Under Bretton Woods, the US and virtually the rest of the noncommunist world agreed to operate on the basis of free trade. That meant that American goods (at first) would flow into foreign nations. As "futurist" Peter Zeihan noted, "Everything that makes the global economy tick—from reliable access to global energy supplies to the ability to sell into the American market to the free movement of capital—is a direct outcome of the ongoing American commitment to Bretton Woods."[184]

Then something virtually none of the overpopulation alarmists thought could happen, happened: The "demographic inversion," in which falling birth rates in Japan, Germany, China, the United Kingdom, Canada, and virtually everywhere except the Islamic world struck. (By 2023, India surpassed China not only in population growth but also in actual population!)[185] Indeed, by 2014, the US was the *only* nation still on a trajectory to have a growing capital market based on a steady population.[186] And astoundingly, by 2030, the US is projected to be, on average, *younger* than China!

From 1955 to the 1980s, as the war-torn European and Asian countries rebuilt their economies with considerable help from Uncle Sam, they began to export heavily to America. This dynamic was accelerated by the fact that the US began to hamstring itself economically through high union wages, managerial stagnation, the dominance of "finance men" over production specialists, and the explosion of the regulatory bureaucracy. In the 1950s, American prosperity was such that steel, autos, electronics, textiles, and other businesses could afford to pay higher wages rather than suffer a strike. Sweetheart deals for unions resulted in the highest-paid workforces in the world, with a typical 1960s-era union worker owning two cars and a vacation home, sometimes even a boat.

Without realizing it, those highly paid employees had sent their own jobs overseas to cheaper labor, although they certainly had some help.

Within corporate management, a different—but no less destructive—development had occurred: The "production men" from the 1920s, 1930s, and 1940s who had come up "from the line" and knew how to build the products they managed were replaced by "finance men," managers who had come in from newly formed business schools and who specialized in accounting ("bean counting," as most referred to it). Alfred Chandler Jr., in his 1977 classic *The Visible Hand*, documented the history of the professional managers and the disproportionate composition of the "finance men," noting that a powerful motivation to ensure steady gains for stock prices led to a risk-averse climate in all major "big business" (as defined by Chandler as any business in which management was separated from ownership). Between 1865 and 1965, virtually all major businesses in America came to be dominated by professional managers with boards of directors, *not* by the owners. While those who came up through production could explain in common sense terms why certain systems would or would not work, the "finance men" always had mastery of the numbers and could defeat any real-world argument.

David Halberstam, in his classic book about Ford and Nissan, *The Reckoning*, related an incident at Ford where the "production men" wanted new paint ovens because the newer cars and trucks were too big for the existing facilities. "Finance men" countered that they could just paint cars in a two-stage process, half at a time. (Of course, this would have resulted in uneven paint that would dry at different rates.) Halberstam found that by the mid-1960s, "Detroit" (meaning top management) determined what parts every plant needed. Shipments of parts arrived, even if they were wrong. A manager who had leftover parts at the end of the month would be scrutinized and even punished, so it became common practice to dump excess parts in the rivers. A common joke was that a person could walk across some Michigan rivers on the discarded auto parts.[187]

Over the span of two decades, dominance by the "finance men" led to a stagnation of development or adaptation of new technologies in American autos, including slowness in deploying disc brakes, fuel injection, front-wheel drive, and other breakthroughs seen in the Japanese-made vehicles. By the 1980s, when Chrysler needed a federal bailout and when General Motors and Ford had seen Toyota take the lead in units sold, the process of climbing back was difficult. Certainly as of the present, Detroit has never recovered.

At the same time, Japan and the European nations began building brand-new, state-of-the-art factories with more compliant unions (but a wider social net) that outperformed the older, World War II–era American factories. As British historian Paul Johnson noted, "West Germany acquired the most effective union structure of any leading industrial nation, with no rival federations (as in the US), no religious-Marxist divisions (as in Italy and France) no political unions (as in Britain), and, above all, no craft unions."[188] Japan, especially, had moved into electronics and autos, so much so that by the 1990s "Japan, Inc." had become a major concern among American economic theorists. Japan's economy crashed in short order, replaced by a new threat, that of Communist China.

Bretton Woods remained the economic governing paradigm for most of the world, however. To some degree, this committed the US to ensure, for example, the free flow of oil at market prices. While there were definitely principles about international aggression to acquire oil in the Iraq War in 1991 (Operation Desert Storm), there remained an underlying agreement that the US had replaced England and the Royal Navy in the position of "world policeman." This rationale brought the US into "brush fire" conflicts in not only Iraq but also Serbia, Somalia, Syria, Libya, and other hotspots. For the most part, except for the invasion of Afghanistan and Iraq due to 9/11 or ancillary concerns about WMDs, these were air wars conducted with very few American ground troops.

The structure of Bretton Woods began unraveling at least by 2010, if not earlier. After Iraq and Afghanistan, Americans were no longer eager to spend treasure or blood in remote locations where America's immediate national interests were not obvious. One of the few things still tying the US to a "stable" Middle East was oil. After President Donald Trump swept away all the restrictions on building refineries, drilling, and fracking, the US surged to be self-sufficient in energy—something it had not been for almost a century. America, which had been the world's largest energy importer for thirty years, started to "simply fall off the global energy map" because of domestic production, especially shale.[189] While Joe Biden reversed much of that, especially shale and laying pipelines, the energy infrastructure lurked, ready to end any remaining energy dependence at all. Moreover, the US became the leading exporter of certain types of energy, including liquefied natural gas. The upshot of this energy independence under Trump was that America could refuse to participate in foreign conflicts where our interests were not at stake. And once reelected in 2024, Trump turned on the oil and liquefied natural gas spigots again.

Still other factors pointed to American global economic superiority for the far-distant future. For example, America remained the world's largest consumer market, triple that of any other country and larger than the next six countries combined. In addition, the US still had untapped prime lands that could be improved where most of the world had none. In comparison, not a single Middle Eastern country was self-sufficient in foodstuffs. The 2022 invasion of Ukraine by Russia shut down the "breadbasket of Europe," Ukraine, and led to sharply rising food prices there, although Russia continued to have sufficient food.

CLASS CHASM

Many, nevertheless, saw a rising income gap, a sort of class chasm, in America not seen since the Reagan years. Thomas Piketty and Joseph Stiglitz, among others, concluded that the US's top income shares had increased significantly since the 1980s.[190] Others, however, have claimed that income inequality actually declined because economists had missed other income sources Americans enjoyed.[191] While it is possible that lower-income groups may have fared slightly better than previously thought, they only did so from income that people did not report. In other words, they participated in "hidden income" from a black-market economy that could prove highly inconsistent, unreliable, and often even illegal. It appeared that no matter what estimates economists used, it was hard to deny that especially after 1970 the rich got richer.

But there is little question that America's economy changed significantly for lower classes under President Trump. Black unemployment fell, energy production soared, and savings rose. Then, when Trump was out, his reforms went with him as did any hope of fixing the serious structural issues facing the American economy and workplace. A class chasm reappeared.

From 1960–2010, a "ruling class," or the "new upper class" as sociologist Charles Murray called it, came into greater concentrations of wealth and power than ever before in history. Murray tracked a markedly growing canyon between the upper class of the last thirty years and the middle class. For example, in the 1960s, an upper-class home might have four bedrooms instead of two or three, might have an extra bathroom, and might have a two-car (instead of one-car) garage. But "it seldom bore any resemblance to a mansion."[192] Extremely wealthy people had few options when it came to autos to distinguish themselves from other groups, as not many Mercedes-Benz or Jaguar dealers existed. More importantly, "people who were not wealthy could get access to the top of the line for a lot less in 1963 than in 2010."[193] Staples such as chicken, eggs, and steak or orders at a restaurant from a chef's salad to a hot fudge sundae even at expensive restaurants were within reach. The image of luxury in most Americans' minds at the time was a Cadillac. "The supreme emblem of wealth in 2010," as Murray noted, "didn't even exist in 1963," i.e., the private jet.[194]

A personal example should suffice. Growing up in a suburb of Phoenix in the 1960s, from the savings left by a ranch manager, my mother and I lived in a three-bedroom, two-bath, two-car garage house with air conditioning. In that, we resembled *most* of the houses around us. Yet diagonally across the street live one of the wealthier families in the entire town. They owned two lots—the second lot was for their pool, to which I was invited many times. I played with the kids; we went to school together. Behind us was another family, not quite as wealthy, but well off. Wherever one went in our little suburb, the "classes" mixed in almost every way. We shopped together, attended ball games together, and went to church together. That slowly changed as the social groups separated since the 1980s.

Other critical, non-wealth gaps between the two groups also appeared. An increasingly distinctive intellectual culture emanating from the Ivy League and a handful of other uber-elite schools, such as Duke, Massachusetts Institute of Technology, Stanford, and Northwestern University, controlled most of the government, finance, and the media. Matthew Whitaker, President Trump's acting attorney general, found when he came into the Trump administration that "the first thing coastal elites want to know about you is where you went to school.... They perk up if your answer includes an Ivy League school or...Stanford, Chicago, Duke, Georgetown, William & Mary, or the University of Virginia."[195] He added, Americans who "went to a state college or an agricultural school...are nobodies to the coastal elite."[196] Instead, Trump stocked his administration with graduates of Central Washington, Texas A&M, Calvin University, Wheaton College, University of Georgia, University of Wisconsin-Eau Claire, and other non-elite schools. (And shockingly, many of those, including John Kelly, Jeff Sessions, James Mattis, and Dan Coats, to one degree or another identified entirely with the "ruling class" and stabbed Trump in the back during their tenure.)

One could see the new culture deriving from these institutions in parking lots (where foreign cars, not American brands except for Tesla, were de rigueur). Americans in the middle and lower classes drove Honda Civics, Honda Accords, Toyota Camrys, and a potpourri of SUVs. And trucks. Armies of trucks, especially outside the East Coast, commanded American highways.

But even in terms of how different classes looked, there were noticeable traits. Elites generally were thinner, lighter, and healthier. They could afford expensive gym memberships, manicures, massages, and medical care, including that of the cosmetic variety. Commuters of the upper classes listened to National Public Radio, for the middle classes, pop/rock music or Rush Limbaugh. When it came to entertainment, average Americans watched television, often smoked, and ate at a handful of national chain restaurants by 2010. Upper classes rarely watched the most popular television shows and dared not set foot in a Chili's or Outback Steakhouse. Indeed, when now–US Senator and vice-presidential candidate but then-writer J. D. Vance of Ohio first invited some of his new upper-class friends to a Cracker Barrel restaurant, they were horrified.[197]

Overall, two separate worlds had emerged in white America—one of elites from top universities who in some cases *would not even interact* with someone outside their intellectual/financial strata and...everyone else. As the government was increasingly staffed with members from the upper classes, the already yawning divisions between the ruling class and the country class grew even more astounding.

People "who were not wealthy could get access to the top of the line for a lot less in 1963 than in 2010."[198] Staples such as chicken, eggs, steak, or orders at a restaurant from chef's salad to a hot fudge sundae even at expensive restaurants were within reach. As increasingly government was staffed with members from the upper classes, the already yawning divisions between the ruling class and the country class grew even more astounding. For almost sixty years, middle-class and working-class wealth grew at almost the same pace as that of the top 10 percent.[199] That was achieved largely through the persistent increase in housing prices.

Then, suddenly, it ended. In 2007, the housing crash caused the bottom 50 percent of wealth holders to fall off a statistical cliff, putting their relative wealth *below that of 1950*![200] But it hardly took any of the ultrawealthy along. A new financial crisis would emerge that would drive a farther wedge into American society.

FRAGILE BY DESIGN

Understanding the origins of the 2007–2008 "subprime mortgage crisis," as it came to be known, involves unwinding several threads. Even today, as banking experts Charles Calomiris and Stephen Haber noted, "While there is broad agreement about [the] basic facts, there is no consensus as to the fundamental causes of the subprime crisis."[201] It is worth noting that this crisis came within a hair of spreading to the entire economy and recreating the Great Depression.

While differing over the respective weight that various factors played in the crisis, it boiled down to two major weaknesses located entirely in the finance-government nexus. First, bank loan portfolios, particularly those related to housing and home mortgages, became critically risky. Second, that risk was not offset by voluntary or mandated new infusions of shareholder capital to guarantee that losses would remain private. Two other lesser tier problems added fuel to the conflagration: first, "derivative securities," which did not represent *a* piece of property or even *a* loan but represented the equivalent of loans on loans. It constituted little less than gambling on the performance of a package of loans. Second, banks started lending into capital markets through other new financial instruments called "tranches" (groups of usually less-than-optimal bonds).[202]

Nevertheless, the president of the New York Federal Reserve Bank (and future treasury secretary) Timothy Geithner, in 2007, insisted that any problems were the result of "a large increase in savings" (harkening back to the discredited Keynesian "sumps of wealth" claims for the cause of the stock market crash of 1929) and that it produced a boom. The "larger the boom, the greater the potential risk of damage when it deflates."[203] Ignoring the carnage imposed on the finances and lives of ordinary people, Geithner celebrated the "wave of financial innovation," and in a "repair [and] then reform" process that would take time,

Geithner argued for a "comprehensive reassessment of...regulation."[204] His statement constituted as sterile a response to the breakdown of the US economy as could be imagined.

When the initial fires subsided, some of the largest financial institutions in America—Citibank, American International Group (AIG), Merrill Lynch, Bear Stearns, Lehman Brothers, Wachovia, Washington Mutual, and Countrywide Financial—would either fail or have to be bailed out by the federal government. Two public-private enterprises, Fannie Mae (the Federal National Mortgage Association) and Freddie Mac (the Federal Home Loan Mortgage Corporation), "two of the largest holders of American mortgage debt, collapse[d] under a sea of bad loans."[205] This new conflagration would cause the Treasury to spend $431 billion in 2008 to save the banking system, and Congress followed with a $787 billion emergency spending bill.

Economists Calomiris and Haber concluded that "the subprime crisis was notable not just for the spectacular magnitude of the economic collapse it caused but also for the unprecedented steps that the Federal Reserve and the US government took to head off" an economic collapse.[206] Attempts to contain the contagion, while successful in the short term, led to fundamental long-term economic insanity of low growth and high interest rates, reviving the Ford/Carter "stagflation" all over again. For example, when both the Fed's and the government's initial steps proved inadequate to rekindle growth—the Fed had dropped rates to "zero bound" nominal interest rates—the Fed instigated "quantitative easing," or essentially printing money in order to buy government debt. Then, to change the expectations of investors, the Fed took the unprecedented step of committing to a long-term policy of low interest rates. At the end of these manipulations, the government ended up owning Fannie Mae and Freddie Mac, as well as the Federal Housing Administration, meaning that "the Fed and the treasury account[ed] for the vast majority of American mortgage funding."[207] And the national debt soared by another trillion dollars.

BIG BANKS, BAD ACTIVISTS

One could tell the story of the collapse from two perspectives: that of the increasing consolidation of banks and that of activists. Both pressured legislators to cut regulative corners, both encouraged exceedingly risky behavior with little concern for ordinary people, and both came together to forge a coalition that consolidated America's banks into a gaggle of megabanks that everyone claimed—or at least, hoped—were too big to fail.

To fully appreciate how a financial catastrophe developed, a short history of American banking and finance is essential, for the weakness had very long and deep roots.

America from its earliest days had a banking system unique in the world, with dozens of small unit (often called "country") banks. These represented a structure that catered to strong lobbying by local interests. In contrast, almost every country in the world had a single, powerful central bank. The US didn't have such an institution until the First Bank of the United States, or BUS, whose charter lasted from 1791 to 1811. A Second Bank of the United States was chartered in 1816, but its charter also expired in 1836 after President Andrew Jackson's famous Bank War. However, technically speaking, neither was a "central bank." Both were four-fifths privately owned and neither had "lender of last resort" capabilities, but both did have banknote creation authority (as did *every chartered bank in the US*). After the Second BUS died, the US entered a unique period of "free banking," meaning state-incorporated banks that did not require a vote of the legislature. Remarkably, this period proved relatively stable for banking with few failures.[208] Only one major exception occurred, the Panic of 1857, which Calomiris and I showed in 1991 was entirely due to political—not financial—forces: The *Dred Scott* decision caused the bonds of Western-oriented railroads to crash and took down the New York banking system with it.[209]

After the Civil War, a long period of competition existed between "national" banks that received a charter from the federal government in return for buying bonds that the government held as reserves and state-chartered banks that held traditional gold and silver (or other bonds) as capital. A key difference, though, was that *only* national banks could print banknotes (the National Banking Acts of 1863 and 1864 had placed a 10 percent tax on all non-national bank notes). There was a consistent shortage of money, especially in times of high demand and especially in the West and South. Local unit bankers began to lobby for reform, which eventually came with the Federal Reserve Act in 1913. It is important to understand that contrary to the conspiracy claims of a group at Jekyll Island, the Federal Reserve Act represented over twenty years of lobbying *by small, local unit bankers across the country* for an institution with the power of "lender of last resort." Still, well into the latter parts of the twentieth century, the US had thousands of small, unit banks, many with low capitalizations.

This system, while remarkably democratic, was also remarkably unstable. America had financial panics in 1819, 1837, 1857 (caused by politics), 1873, 1893, 1907, 1930–33, 1987, and 2007–08. "Reform" and more regulation did not address the structural problems. In fact, new large banks formed an unlikely alliance with activist groups bent on extending credit to those with little ability to repay. Big banks won approval from Congress to form "megabanks," while activist groups received an astonishing $850 billion in credit that was disbursed from 1992 and 2007.[210] More bribe money was paid through fees for administering direct-credit programs/contributions to those groups. ACORN (the Association of Community Organizations for Reform Now) received over $13 million from Bank of America, $9.5 million from JPMorgan Chase, $8 million from Citibank, over $7 million from HSBC, and another $1.4 million from Capital One. The total fees—essentially bribe money to keep the activists off their back—came to $9.5 billion by 2000.[211]

Some of this money came through the 1977 Community Reinvestment Act, or CRA, a response to pressure from Jessie Jackson and other civil rights activists over what they claimed was a practice of redlining. Although banks denied redlining existed, structurally it could not help but develop when aspiring homebuyers in poor parts of town, with little credit and low income, sought a mortgage. Activists claimed banks ceased looking at individual applications and drew a "red line" around certain residential areas, refusing to lend there due to extremely high default rates. Activists claimed redlining was racially motivated because a higher proportion of black people lived in the redlined areas. Bankers and most economists argued the practice was common sense lending. George Gilder, in *Wealth and Poverty*, noted that the central factor in real estate prices was the distance from the poor. Either way, the "CRA would have been inconsequential had there not been a merger movement.... [And] total CRA commitments represented only a trivial percentage of total American mortgage lending."[212] When CRA came into contact with the bank merger movement, however, fireworks started. Large banks submitted to new high-risk lending standards to secure support for their mergers.

Activists did not stop with purported redlining policies, or, more accurately, they infected other large institutions with them, which did, in fact, become a problem. They set their sights on Fannie Mae and Freddy Mac. In 1938, the US government established Fannie Mae as a "government-sponsored enterprise," or GSE, owned and controlled by the US government, to provide local banks with government money to finance home loans. In 1968, Fannie Mae went private and was owned by stockholders. Freddie Mac was created in 1970 as a stockholder-owned GSE to buy a large number of loans from mortgage lenders. The government imposed targets for lending to (basically unqualified) borrowers to meet racial and other quotas in the 1990s and early 2000s. To illustrate how risky and dangerous the forced lending was, the banks agreed to purchase mortgages with down payments of 3 percent as opposed to the industry standard of 20 percent! Here is where the toxic CRA mortgages came in. Fannie and Freddie had to meet government-required targets for "underserved" areas (i.e., very high-risk neighborhoods). Thus, the government forced those GSEs to weaken their underwriting standards and, to justify lending to redlined areas, chopped the supports out from *all* standards for all borrowers. (As Calomiris and Haber explained, that is why damage hit both low-income urban areas such as Detroit and solid middle-class communities such as Hemet, California.)

NINJA (NO INCOME, NO JOB, AND NO ASSETS)

By 2004, Fannie and Freddie were purchasing "vast amounts of risky mortgage loans, including so called Alt-A loans with little or no documentation of income."[213] (In the film *The Big Short*, hedge fund managers who went to Florida to research these loans met with realtors who touted their "NINJA" loans: "no income, no job, and no assets." To the realtors, those people represented *good* clients because they were easy to lend to.)[214]

In retrospect, as foolish as the CRA was, it only affected a trivial percentage of overall mortgage lending. And far from being strong-armed, the GSEs, such as Fannie and Freddie, enthusiastically joined the megabanks to generate new mortgages. The rigor with which the CRA regulations were enforced depended to some extent on the administration holding power: Republicans tended to demand fewer of these loans. Thus, the impact of the CRA was not immediate for the housing market until 1995 when, for the first time, regulators established quotas to ensure banks met the CRA standards. Two years earlier, the Department of Housing and Urban Development under Bill Clinton had begun bringing legal actions against mortgage bankers who declined a higher percentage of minority applicants over white applicants. Clinton directed still more energy at CRA enforcement when his then–Department of Housing and Urban Development changed the regulations to allow another $2.4 trillion in mortgages for "affordable housing."[215] (At that time, the median home price was $163,000.) Fannie Mae then announced an additional $2 billion purchase of CRA mortgages.

But there was still more instability to be built into the system. Fannie and Freddie, plus another new creation, the Federal Home Loan Bank Board, took on massive toxic debt by 2007. By 2009, the three "backstopped" 90 percent of the new mortgages.[216] The die was already then cast.[217]

There were still more weaknesses in the stock and bond markets that undergirded the coming disaster. Clinton's Commodity Futures Modernization Act, passed in 2000, enabled over-the-counter financial "derivatives" to remain unregulated. (Derivatives were new financial instruments that were based, not on a specific product like a house or a car, but on the performance of a trend, such as an index or interest rate. Those indices included "hedges" or bets against price increases or decreases.) In other words, the new financial instruments were conglomerations of existing conglomerations that included "bets" placed on how those conglomerations' prices would perform!

From 2001 to June 2008, the derivatives market skyrocketed, going from $900 billion to $62 trillion outstanding.[218] As Michael Lewis, author of *The Big Short* noted, "In 2000 there had been $130 billion in subprime mortgage lending and $55 billion [*sic*]...had been repackaged in mortgage bonds."[219] But by 2005, those amounts had skyrocketed to $625 billion in subprime mortgage loans, $507 billion of which were in bonds. And worst of all, three-fourths of all subprime loans had some form of floating—not fixed—interest rate. This dwarfed the stock market, which mortgage trader Steve Eisman called a "zit" compared with the size of the bond market.[220] When Clinton said his administration would be decided by "a bunch of f**king bond traders," he was right. Only it had gotten worse. Much, much worse.

One analyst who saw the weakness, Sy Jacobs, stated the obvious: "Any business where you can sell a product and make money without having to worry how the product performs is going to attract sleazy people."[221] With the new derivatives, such as "credit default swaps"—essentially a contracted insurance policy against an asset defaulting or failing—a new form of making money without any concern for how the product performed now turned the mortgage market into a virtual casino. It led to the practice of betting on the stock market or housing market to fail. So those "conglomerations" we discussed? Now a form of betting on them via default insurance policies was introduced. Worse, outsiders with no interest in the actual assets, or housing, or mortgages whatsoever, with a possibility of defaulting, could participate in this form of gambling on housing.[222] By 2007, credit default swaps totaled over $62 trillion, little of it transparent to regulators. In essence, the US housing market had turned into a giant casino with speculators betting on the likelihood of defaults going up or down.

THE HOUSE YOU WANT

On top of all those existing weaknesses, further pressure to reduce housing prices came from the media, which emphasized luxurious homes in shows such as *Cribs*. Ignored was the real price of such mansions, while the phrase "affordable housing" came to mean "housing people wanted at a price they wanted" as opposed to housing people could not afford with their income. In fact, economist Thomas Sowell noted that "affordable housing, by common standards, [had] been the norm across most of the country, but with glaring exceptions" where housing prices were vastly higher than the nation as a whole.[223] And in the "cribs" they didn't show, they often had no furniture inside because their owners could barely afford the mortgage payments themselves.

Banks had already stepped in with an instrument called an "ARM," or "adjustable-rate mortgage," whereby the homebuyer had a flexible rate that could move up if interest rates rose. Homebuyers who were fine with an interest rate of 3 percent jumped in—but they would default if that rate doubled. That proved disastrous for those who guessed wrong on the direction of interest rates. Then there came the "balloon" mortgage, in which rates remained lower than normal for seven years, whereupon the buyer owed a gigantic onetime "balloon" payment. Both of these instruments targeted buyers who, under normal conditions, would not be able to afford a home loan.

But that did not seem to matter either to the bankers or to the politicians. Federal Housing Commissioner John Weicher said in 2004, "the White House [i.e., George W. Bush] doesn't think that those who can afford the monthly payment but have been unable to save for a down payment should be deprived of owning a home," adding, "we do not anticipate any costs to taxpayers."[224] Saving for a home, apparently, was old fashioned. Although the recommended down payment for a home in the post–World War II era had fallen from 50 percent to (depending on the bank) 10 or 15 percent, virtually no lenders thought that a person who could not amass 10 percent of the home cost was a good credit risk. This was borne out by a study by *The Economist* in February 2009 that found "…of 73,000 loans modified [downward in payment requirements], 43% were again delinquent eight months later."[225]

Many other voices shouted warnings: Peter Wallison of the American Enterprise Institute said in 2005 that, barring a congressional restriction on the agencies lending, "there will be a massive default with huge losses to the taxpayers."[226] The chairman of the Federal Reserve Board warned, "We are placing the total financial system of the future at a substantial risk," although he said that (as of 2005) the risk was still negligible.[227] Leading Democrats such as Congressman Barney Frank, however, downplayed concerns, saying that critics "exaggerate a threat of safety."[228] His Senate counterpart, Chris Dodd, likewise praised Fannie Mae and Freddie Mac as "one of the great success stories of all time."[229] Debt held by the private sector soared in the years 1978 to 2007 from $3 trillion to $36 trillion.[230]

While substantially *deregulating* the lending aspects of banks to create fatal capital ratios, at the same time federal and state governments were *increasingly regulating banks*, imposing layers of environmental regulation and others on builders that continued to drive prices up. Yet these only made houses more unaffordable for lower-income people—the very ones (supposedly) the governments were trying to help. Thomas

Sowell noted that those times in which "housing markets became unaffordable closely followed the approval of state growth-management laws or restrictive local plans."[231]

On top of all those instabilities, the three major credit rating companies, Standard & Poor's, Fitch Ratings, and Moody's, all had incentives to rate securities higher than their real value because they were paid by the banks. Credit rating companies defended their actions as merely "opinions" and "free speech." They claimed if they lowered the valuations of funds too much, the banks and lending institutions would simply go to a competitor who would provide the valuation they wanted. Economist Joseph Stiglitz labeled the rating agencies one of the "key culprits" of the financial crisis.[232]

Finally, in the first five years of the 2000s, rising home prices and unreasonably easy credit combined to turn many average Americans into home speculators. They could borrow, take out a second or even third mortgage on other properties, and pay by drawing on the value of their own home until they sold. Some acquired low-money down or balloon-interest-rate loans to purchase second and third homes to resell. Until they couldn't. In the film *The Big Short*, this was driven home by the interview the fund managers had with a stripper—who at that time owned several homes for speculation and all with flexible interest rates. As early as 2005, insiders started raising alarms. One Florida real estate company said "as much as 85 percent of all condominium sales in the downtown Miami market are accounted for by investors and speculators."[233] In truth, more than four decades' worth of continually, unceasingly rising home prices convinced many of these operators that the value of houses would keep going up.[234] From that perspective—for either lenders or borrowers—were their expectations indeed "reckless" as economist Paul Samuelson claimed?[235]

Eventually, mortgage brokers and mortgage bankers would blame each other: "Who made this mess?" asked the chairman of the Mortgage Bankers Association. "The short-term folks...who get a commission when the deal happens."[236] His counterpart at the National Association of Mortgage Brokers said that blame lay with "Wall Street, federally chartered banks, state-chartered lenders and underwriters."[237] Economist Gary Gordon cast a pox on both their houses, calling the entire structure a "shadow banking system" in which financial firms conducted runs on other firms by not renewing sale and repurchasing agreements or increasing the margins (known as a "haircut").[238]

Any one of these malignant banking/credit practices would have caused disruption. Combined, in 2008 they produced the worst crash since the Great Depression with what was called the "subprime mortgage crisis." Did the regulators see it coming? Research (including internal emails) suggests that the answer is "absolutely."[239] Worse, they contributed to the collapse after it started. Once they saw the foundations quivering, "regulators and supervisors could have intervened. They could have forced the banks to recognize losses sooner and go to the market to acquire more capital."[240] For their part, banks could have issued new shares to generate a cushion of capital but did not, largely because they "believed (correctly, with the significant exception of Lehman) that they had too-big-to-fail protection."[241] However, as with Lehman Brothers, when the "too-big-to-fail" banks actually did go under, panic set in.[242]

END OF "TOO BIG TO FAIL"

Ripples appeared when there was news of the collapse of new home sales in 2007, when sales plunged by the largest amount on record. Mark Zandi, the chief economist at Moody's said, "It looks like the floor fell out of the housing market in December [2007]."[243]

The first major domino to fall was Bear Stearns, which had set up a $3.2 billion loan to bail out one of its funds in 2007, revealing that that summer two of its subprime hedge funds had lost nearly half their value. In March 2008, the company failed.

The next giant to collapse, Lehman Brothers, had held large positions in mortgage "tranches" (bundles of toxic loans packaged with a few good loans for appearances). In the second quarter of 2008, Lehman reported losses of $2.8 billion and its stock lost three-quarters of its value. Amid a deepening housing market collapse, Lehman announced yet another large loss ($3.9 billion) by the fall of 2008. Panicked bankers met at the Federal Reserve Bank of New York, hoping to prevent a global crisis, but attempted deals to find a buyer for the decaying Lehman Brothers failed, as did the company itself on September 15, 2008, when it declared bankruptcy. Those proceedings revealed that JPMorgan Chase had already provided Lehman with $138 billion in Fed-backed advances, meaning Lehman had also weakened JPMorgan Chase.

Although Merrill Lynch was heavily invested in subprime mortgages, it stayed afloat, but AIG did not: After a series of bailouts and loans, the company reported a record $62 billion loss in late 2008—then paid $165 million in bonuses to its executives.[244]

As the devastation spread, it affected ordinary Americans and their savings. From June 2007 to November 2008, Americans lost 25 percent of their net worth and the Standard & Poor's index fell by almost half. Housing prices dropped 30 percent, and home equity fell by almost $5 trillion.[245] Unemployment doubled as 8.5 million lost their jobs; real GDP contracted by 5 percent. American growth would not again regain the precrash levels until President Trump invigorated the economy in 2017. America's smoking waste spread to Europe, where debt soared, and the Europeans sank into a depression (though less substantial than that of the US). As the haze cleared, more than a million homes were in foreclosure by 2011. However, many had not learned their lessons, and as late as 2015, 17 percent of homeowners were "upside down" on mortgages, meaning their debt exceeded their home's value.

Bush met with his Secretary of the Treasury Henry Paulsen and Federal Reserve Chairman Ben Bernanke: "Is this the worst crisis since the Great Depression?" he asked. Bernanke answered: "Yes...we have not seen anything like this since the 1930s."[246] Bush's response was telling. He said, "If we're really looking at another Great Depression...you can be damn sure I'm going to be Roosevelt, not Hoover."[247] Thus, for the second time in eight years, Bush relied on nearly universal advice to act, and, in both cases, the actions proved unwise or outright wrong. An interesting contrast could be found with Winston Churchill, who repeatedly stood on principle against nearly unanimous opposition to follow a path that later turned out to be right.[248]

Bush relied on a plan by Bernanke and Paulsen's replacement at the Treasury, Tim Geithner. The Fed lowered interest rates dramatically (the Federal funds rate fell from 5.25 percent to just 2 percent) and began to issue short-term loans to member banks through "open market operations." Congress passed the Economic Stimulus Act of 2008 and the American Recovery and Reinvestment Act in 2009. Both followed the old, failed New Deal policies of "demand-side" economics, which held that by inserting money into the economy, the government could produce growth through consumer demand. On the banking side, over one hundred banks failed and were taken over by the Federal Deposit Insurance Corporation.

In the last months of the Bush administration, Bernanke and, by then, Treasury Secretary Geithner forced the major banks to accept the Troubled Asset Relief Program (TARP), a $700 billion bailout. Some big institutions, such as Citibank, insisted they didn't need a bailout and resisted until they were strong-armed into joining the program. JPMorgan Chase received $25 billion in loans, Wells Fargo $25 billion, the failing AIG $40 billion, Bank of America $45 billion, and Citigroup $50 billion. Some of the banks, including Citibank, paid their loans back quickly and in full. More troubling, however, was that much of the TARP money was used for other purposes, including bailing out the floundering General Motors, as well as other non-financial organizations.[249] Lehman Brothers was rescued, but Bear Stearns was not, leading to market confusion as to what was necessary for aid. Economist John Taylor of Stanford described TARP as "a two-and-a-half-page legislation, with no mention of oversight and few restrictions on the use" of the money.[250]

All the politicians' and bankers' legerdemain provided a convenient smoke screen for whom to blame. What it could not cover was the real-life impact on ordinary people, particularly young people entering the work force. In 2007, Matthew Kuzma had just completed a summer internship for a prominent bank in Pittsburgh, making three times the minimum wage. He planned on repeating the internship the next year and then entering the job market immediately upon graduation. "Then," he said, "the bottom fell out.... I graduated, but there were no jobs." He doubled down on the old standby, more education. "Twelve months later, I had two degrees but no job.... I ended up waiting tables, and was in good company. It seemed my whole graduating class was in a funk." To this day, Kuzma recalled comments of his classmates: "It's like my entire life is on pause." "I don't know what I'm doing wrong." He found that the subprime crisis cost him several years: "There was a five-year delay to get things started."[251]

Another person had a narrow escape from financial destitution. "Winter" (a pseudonym), who had advanced hepatitis, could no longer work in late 2006 and had to sell his house in New Jersey and move to a Catskills cottage he had purchased two years earlier. The market was still hot, and Winter got out in May 2007—just as the housing market collapsed. Within a few months, that New Jersey house was valued at less than half what Winter sold it for. Having survived hepatitis, the crash, and a new bout of non-Hodgkin's lymphoma, Winter "lived in my $30,000 cottage with 8 birds and a dog until 2013" and sold the cottage for four times what he had purchased it for. As he noted, "timing is everything."[252]

Thousands echoed those stories on both sides—some fortunate, others not. A litany of regrets and laments from elder millennials who suffered through the recession could be found: "I was 27 and just getting started." But the recession changed their financial habits so that this millennial said, "I'll never buy a condo again.... They appreciate slowly and drop like a rock in value when there is a housing downturn.... Never be loyal to a company. They'll drop you like a bad habit."[253] Unemployment rose from 4.7 percent in November 2007 to 10 percent in October 2009, and as one millennial recalled, "People used to full blown congratulate you for getting a job in a shop."[254] Another recalled that "it was also a time when any workplace grievance you had was shut down by 'be grateful you have a job.'"[255]

Politically, a serious side effect of the financial crisis was the demolition of the Republican Party's brand. Bush's support, already low, collapsed. Arizona Senator John McCain, running for president against Democratic Senator Barack Obama, suspended his campaign on September 24 to seek a solution to the crisis. Obama didn't. (In reality, McCain played almost no role in the negotiations: It was purely for show.) McCain had led in many polls prior to suspending and never recovered. Worse, the traditional, eroding Republican Party, which was swamped in the 2006 and 2008 elections, did not know it at the time but was in the process of a massive transformation to the point where it would almost be unrecognizable in fourteen years. And while the Democrats were on top for the time being, the 2007–2008 subprime crisis produced the seeds of their loss of Congress in 2010, then the Senate, and then the presidency itself in 2016. In a sense, neither party survived the Great Recession of 2007.

One individual, however, whose name is synonymous with tech—Steve Jobs—had not only survived the Y2K bug and the subprime crisis but had also grown his computer company, Apple, to become one of the most identifiable companies in the world. Fittingly, Apple waded through the financial maelstrom with few problems (although some members of its board were sued because of alleged securities fraud during the housing bust.)[256]

If political leaders and industrial icons typified the heroes of previous ages, Jobs personified his. Slight, wiry, with a pointy nose, he epitomized the twenty-first century "nerd." Born in San Francisco in 1955 to a Catholic American mother and a Muslim Syrian father, Jobs had been put up for adoption when Joanne Schieble's parents opposed her husband's faith. She traveled to the West Coast for the birth and insisted that the adoptive parents be college graduates. Paul and Clara Jobs did not fit the bill: Paul was a machinist, a repossession agent, and car salesman. Joanne Schieble only relented when the adoptive parents promised to pay for their baby's college education.[257] A child so difficult his parents thought about returning him, Jobs became a "socially awkward loner," a prankster, and misbehaved constantly. He drove his parents to remove him from his public school and relocate to Cupertino School District, which the family could barely afford.

He had closely watched his father, however, absorbing his craftsmanship and mechanical skills: "He knew how to build anything."[258] At one point, he witnessed a non-electronic amplifier that disproved everything about amplifiers his father had taught him. "It was a very big moment that's burned into my mind," he recalled. It was the moment "when I realized that I was smarter than my parents."[259] Yet the experience only left him feeling more detached from his family and the world.

Studying electronics in high school, he met his future business partner Steve Wozniak. The two concocted an illegal scheme to sell "blue boxes" that allowed free-long distance calls when attached to traditional phone lines. The electronic bootlegging formed the seed that later became the Apple tree. He entered Reed College in 1972.

Without telling his parents—because he deemed the overall education worthless and didn't want them to pay for it—Jobs dropped out while nevertheless auditing classes, including one on calligraphy that influenced his Macintosh computer fonts. Then Jobs's life began to resemble that of another general troublemaker, Sam Colt, famous for his revolver. As Colt did, Jobs traveled to India (though his journey was voluntary), where he dabbled in Indian spirituality and eventually became a Buddhist. He donned Indian clothing when he returned to America, still without direction or money.

He was inspired by a video game company Atari to reunite with Wozniak to develop a chip for the machine. Wozniak proved the conceptual genius, while Jobs mastered sales and schmoozing deals (which was odd, given his personality). What happened next epitomized the phrase "necessity is the mother of invention." Both men wanted a personal computer, but one did not exist. As Jobs put it, he sought to build a "Volkswagen" of computing. Wozniak, as usual, engaged in the production aspect, creating a basic design of the Apple 1 computer, and Jobs, as usual, insisted he could sell it. They formed Apple in April 1976.

While the original devices were primitive, Jobs's concept was artistic. He wanted beautiful perfection that would make a machine a work of near–medieval trade mastery. As they grew the company, Jobs and Wozniak's invention characterized a new phase in technology. *Time* magazine, which usually had a "Man of the Year," featured a "Machine of the Year": the computer. Jobs and Wozniak were multimillionaires. They had another breakthrough in the 1980s with the advanced Macintosh computer. By that time, however, Apple—the company—had started to trend in the direction of virtually every other large corporation, namely one run by professional managers. Sales had slowed, Jobs's personality grated, and the board forced upon him the former Pepsi CEO John Sculley, who knew nothing about computers. When Jobs's Macintosh failed to defeat the IBM Personal Computer (much of whose operating systems came from another flawed visionary, Bill Gates), Jobs planned a coup to oust Sculley that had become known, and it was Jobs who was given the heave-ho in 1985.

Before he left, Jobs had overseen the creation of a graphics group that permitted computer graphics to replace human animators. Partnering with Disney (after which he said he would never work with the company again), Pixar produced a number of box office hits such as *Toy Story* (1995), *A Bug's Life* (1998), *Finding Nemo* (2003), and *Cars* (2006). In 2005, Disney's new CEO, Bob Iger, purchased Pixar for $7.4 billion, increasing Jobs's wealth. Unlike previous partners, Iger liked Jobs and found him no trouble. "Who wouldn't want Steve Jobs to have influence over how a company is run?" Iger asked.[260]

Meanwhile, Jobs returned to Apple in 1997 after the company concluded that it needed his vision and genius. In that he broke the mold of the manager-driven company by returning it (for one of the few times in American business history) to an entrepreneur/founder-driven company. He did something else, however, that was both revolutionary and completely consistent with a virtually unbroken rule, namely that the leader in the field never makes the next big breakthrough. Jobs's interest in music had led him to conceive of a portable, wallet-sized music player made possible only by the process of digitizing music. Turning musical sounds into digits had become possible in the 1970s with the recording by Ry Cooder called *Bop Till You Drop*. Digital pulse modulation had appeared forty years earlier in Japan, but it took until the 1980s before the major record companies had embraced some form of digital recording. Sony and Phillips codeveloped a "compact disc" in 1982 and steadily music moved from vinyl and tapes to "CDs." Likewise, analog recording studios were replaced by digital recording studios (with vast implications for the very nature of music, including the personalization of playlists to such a degree that no two people on Earth have the same playlists.

While CDs became popular, they still were not portable, thus Sony's "Walkman" tape player became the dominant technology in the field of personal portable music. Jobs, along with some of his engineers, reimagined a better MP3 player than currently existed. *Fortune* labeled the device "Apple's 21st-Century Walkman," without fully understanding what it had written. Once again, the major breakthrough in the field (in this case, portable personal music consumption) did not come from Sony, but a computer company, Apple, that saw the potential of cross-pollination. Although phone technology, including Job's other breakthrough, the iPhone (unveiled in 2007), signaled the death of the stand-alone music player, it constituted another marvel milestone in Jobs's career.

And the iPhone surpassed the iPod. Unlike earlier cell phones, the iPhone combined phone capability with a digital camera, a music player, and (before long) hundreds of "apps" or applications from calculators to pedometers to weather forecasts to email. Far from sitting in his recliner after his initial success, Jobs handed the world not one, not two, but three technological breakthroughs (with the iPad, or portable computer, as his third).

He had done so while under a virtual death sentence for more than a decade. In 2003, Jobs was diagnosed with pancreatic cancer, which at the time had little chance for a cure or remission. Here, his flirtation with Eastern mystic medicine harmed him. He refused surgery for nine months and in 2009 wrote an internal memo announcing a leave of absence. That became permanent in 2011, and he died just two months after his second resignation from the company.

Jobs, never an ardent Americanist, nevertheless embodied the essence of the American entrepreneur. Often pursuing fantastic and impossible technologies, Jobs occasionally grasped them. In doing so, he never succumbed to a larger deadly disease that had started to grip America's industrial might: a spirit of decline.

MANAGING DECLINE

If the immediate effects of the subprime/housing crisis badly damaged the American economy (in particular, affecting a whole generation of youth who were trying to enter the collapsing job market at the time), the far deeper impact of half a century of regulatory and environmental controls on the industry had retarded economic growth and innovation. Some of the slowdown was inevitable as millions of baby boomers retired and productivity declined, especially since 2003.[261] Fewer people worked fewer hours. Economist Robert Gordon noted that if the pace of 1970 to 2014 had been maintained, real GDP per person would have been double what it actually was. In other words, the productivity explosion touted by the advocates of the computer may have been overstated.

However, it's also possible that such analysis failed to properly account for the productivity quotient of computerization. For example, the cost of developing an iPhone from scratch in 2020 would have priced the iPhone at between $51,000 and $51 *million*. Part of the difficulty in assessing productivity value from computerization is that the digital world encompasses everything. Where could computerization be excluded? In our iPhone example, in previous eras, economists would calculate the speed and/or cost reduction of a new rotary dial phone over the previous iteration of a phone. But such a comparison became meaningless with the introduction of cell phones, any of which has hundreds if not thousands of applications ("apps"). People could use such software to write and send mail (email), play games, follow the stock market, get their news, use a phone as a Global Positioning System (GPS) for maps and directions, or as a dictionary. They could conduct banking—including taking and paying for business transactions—pay employees, watch videos, listen to and record music, take photos, or track their daily caloric expenditure, just to name a very few. Thus, a proper calculation of the value of an iPhone over a rotary dial phone would require *a measurement calculation for each and every application on a given phone.* Using such math, the $51,000 iPhone is in fact not far off. It may be very low.

Or consider Jobs's genius invention, the iPod. It did more than make music portable: It enabled consumers to reconstruct entire albums ("playlists"), except these albums contained thousands of songs. And no one person's playlist ever was identical to another. (My own playlist, for example, contains music from bands I was in that never were produced or marketed by record companies.) In essence, the iPod created millions of "music producers." Indeed, new digital music technology even permitted "mash-ups," or one song overlaid with another in the same key and containing a similar beat. (Think The Doors' "Riders on the Storm" with Blondie's "Rapture," or Tupac Shakur's "Changes" overlaid on top of Bruce Hornsby's "The Way It Is.") How are such things accounted for in productivity statistics?

Even using more traditional productivity measurements, economist Robert Gordon found a 35 percent improvement in autos between 1967 and 2012 based on the reduction of price and increase in quality, plus another 5 percent increase in fuel efficiency—all while auto fatalities declined from 45 per million miles driven in 1909 to 1.1 in 2012. How did all those calculations factor into the value of a car?[262]

Traditional statistics had severely understated the actual price declines by as much as 4.3 *times* from 1952 to 1983, and modern-day output per hour and per person had risen faster in the postwar era than even in the previously undercounted period of 1870–1928.[263]

Does that mean the US will follow that pattern in the twenty-first century via computer-driven improvements in productivity? A heated debate still rages about whether such productivity from the internet still exists.[264] At the same time, the consumption of services has outpaced the consumption of goods for some time.[265] However, much of the optimism that the internet would continue to increase productivity was based on the shift to "work from home" introduced during the China Virus[iii] lockdowns. McKinsey & Company found that some aspects of online services, but a relatively long period of stagnation in capital formation followed.[266] "Distance education," for example, merely revealed to parents what incompetence and horrors their kids were being subjected to in public schools. It in no way enhanced productivity in education, except that it increased the number of homeschoolers who flew under the statistical radar anyway.

There are also major concerns about the nature of consumer-driven data mining that has resulted in massive invasions of privacy. Have *we* become the product? Or worse, the raw material? Prior to 2015, few raised such concerns.

There was no question, however, that the retiring baby boomers changed the American economy, and if they worked in the twenty-first century, they often did so off the books. Federal and state welfare also severely damaged work effort. It also, according to many, affected the marriage rate (and, as we have seen, married couples are more productive than two single individuals in the same job situations).[267] George Gilder observed as early as 1981 in his classic book *Wealth and Poverty* that "the only dependable route from poverty is always work, family, and faith. The first principle is that in order to move up, the poor must not only work, they must work harder than the classes above them."[268]

---

iii This is also represented as "COVID-19," "Covid," or the "China Virus." For purposes here, I will use "Covid" or "China Virus" interchangeably.

Worldwide, of course, nearly every country in the world was top heavy in its population structure (i.e., more older and fewer younger people). But of all the nations, only the US "boomers" continued to have children. As futurist Peter Zeihan noted, "There are no German [Generation] Ys or Canadian Ys or Korean Ys," and even in the younger countries such as Poland or China, "it's as if there were a line drawn between 1980 and 1985...when everyone simply stopped repopulating."[269] A depopulating world has left the US as one of the *youngest* nations on Earth, younger than every other first-world country except Australia, New Zealand, Ireland, Cyprus, and Iceland and on target to be younger than China before 2030. Many of these nations actually crossed the demographic death threshold—including some of America's major economic competitors, Germany, Belgium, Austria, and Italy—and by 2030, virtually all of Europe will be in an irrecoverable spiral without major immigration. Japan was the first major country to age past any hope of demographic recovery. Japanese people aren't having children in any sustainable ratio in the twenty-first century, yet with the rising threat of China, Japan has reinvigorated its navy to surpass that of England.

More recently, since 2000, there has been a decline in the share of college graduates working in non-routine, abstract occupations and a rise in those working manual jobs.[270] Men were slowly drawn back into the labor force after 2014—then Covid hit. America's growth rate, which recovered under Trump, again slowed.

Since 2000, far from engaging in aggressive policies that would boost productivity, encourage families, keep interest rates low, and celebrate entrepreneurship, America's leadership seemed to be satisfied with managing the decline. Many, if not most, leftist intellectuals celebrated that reality. "Decline is not a choice. It's a fact," sneered one writer at *The Week*.[271] While as president, Obama could hardly publicly state that the US was on the skids, but others not bound by the limitations of the office could, including former President Clinton, who said in 2011 that the US was no longer the world's sole superpower as it was under his administration. "Relatively speaking," he said, "in the 21st century we will have to share the position will [sic] a lot of countries."[272]

THE SLEEPING ENERGY GIANT

Lurking beneath a slowing economy, however, lay the most extensive and vast energy reserves in the world. In America, natural gas, "the most versatile industrial input in existence, the basic building block of modern society...[was] a *waste* [emphasis in original] product."[273] By 2023, almost 40 percent of all American electricity was generated by natural gas, which, as it turned out, was a by-product of a new energy source, shale oil. With pipelines from America to Canada and Mexico, shale had a final price that was close to merely the transport price of Canadian natural gas, making it a powerful option. America's energy soon became a prominent source of both Canadian and Mexican energy.

That booming energy sector by itself accounted for almost a half-million jobs in 2014, jobs which came almost entirely from expansion, as once the infrastructure for a well or pipeline is completed, there was never a need to build a second road or gathering station. Shale, or fine-grained sedimentary rock that contained organic material that could generate oil, had accounted for nearly half the jobs created in the US from 2007 to 2014, which then saved Americans an average of over $1,000 a year in energy costs.[274] By 2020, President Trump had sufficiently encouraged and motivated energy production that, for all intents and purposes, the US was energy independent. Ronald Reagan could only dream of such a state!

Indeed, the American energy revolution—even when dampened down by foolish government regulations and obstruction—rested on a fundamental fact that the US not only had the best petroleum engineers in the world but also had nearly two decades' worth of "learn by doing," for which there was no shortcut. Virtually no other countries had America's property rights, which not only meant the right to individually own land but also the potential right to own all mineral rights beneath it. Across the entire globe, only in the US can people individually own oil beneath the ground (as well as gold, silver, and precious metals). As of 2016, a landowner could obtain a permit to drill within two days of application. Most nations couldn't even comprehend shale drilling with their shallow financial resources. (China, meanwhile, which sits on an ocean of shale and has extremely inexpensive labor, has revised its shale output downward by over two-thirds. Its shale fields are vast but widespread, requiring massive capital to acquire—which China lacked.) Ultimately, "only the United States has the magic blend of geology, legal and regulatory environment, available capital, and above all the experience and know-how to make shale work on a massive scale."[275]

Keeping abreast of foreign economic developments remained crucial for the US, even if it turned briefly toward "America first" policies under Trump, only to see many reversed under Biden. China faced aggregate debt that had grown at the fastest rate in the world (a fact that, for many Americans looking at the national debt, would seem hard to believe). The Chinese embarked on a stringent program of keeping their money from leaving China, while hinting that they would try to create an alternative to the US dollar as a reserve currency. Similarly, after the Russian invasion of Ukraine and the American (and Western) economic retaliation, Russia, India, Brazil, and Saudi Arabia all joined China in suggesting that they may create their own "reserve currency." Despite massive problems at home, made worse by the Biden administration, the US dollar still remained the only practical and internationally credible store of value.

Seemingly, the dollar's position came under pressure from a new form of technological money called a "Bitcoin," or digital currency.[276] Invented conceptually in 2008, Bitcoin was a software created the following year by an anonymous user who used the concept of a "blockchain," or a public ledger that recorded all Bitcoin transactions. Each block contained cryptographic records of the previous block up to the original "genesis block." Transactions were broadcasted through one person sending a certain number of Bitcoins to another across the network.

Since all transactions were public, so to speak, there was no need for any central oversight. In theory, a Bitcoin could not be double-spent, unlike physical money, which banks use as reserves to issue additional money (a "money multiplier," or "fractional reserve banking"). Proponents considered this both more democratic and, at the same time, more secure than traditional money—even gold-backed currency.

The Bitcoin format was first tested between 2011 and 2012 on the black market, including on "Silk Road," where Bitcoins were exclusively used as payment for transactions. Over $200 million (or 9.9 billion Bitcoins) exchanged "digital hands." Contrary to the wishes of the founders, in 2013, the US government created regulatory guidelines for "decentralized and virtual currencies," subjecting the Bitcoin field to regulation. Agencies from the Drug Enforcement Administration to the FBI have raided various Bitcoin "farms," including Silk Road. That same year, the Chinese Communist government prohibited financial institutions from using Bitcoin.

Such actions only tended to make Bitcoin more popular, and by 2017, more than 2.9 million customers used (or held) Bitcoin. The actual trading "exchanges" themselves began to fracture as users differed over the processes and various hacks, the largest coming from Coincheck and Bithumb in 2018. Slowly, though, mainstream users such as Massachusetts Mutual Life and Square held Bitcoin. The price per Bitcoin soared to over $37,000 in 2021; in February of that year, the automaker Tesla announced it would accept Bitcoin in payment for vehicles, which sent the price soaring to over $44,000.

Again, Democrats—in this case led by Biden—sought to impede the free market, seeking instead to have a government-controlled digital currency. Such was the exact opposite of the currency's purpose. In 2024, to the chagrin of progressives and liberals everywhere, Trump made considerable inroads with younger voters when he endorsed private Bitcoin at a cryptocurrency convention and vowed to fire the head of the Securities and Exchange Commission who currently had throttled the use of digital currency. The crowd exploded.[277] He also announced his support for a US Bitcoin stockpile, treating it like any other currency.[278]

Still, the currency had serious drawbacks, including the difficulty of making refunds, high transaction costs, and waiting up to ten minutes to travel through the block. Although the Chicago Board Options Exchange and the Chicago Mercantile Exchange both traded Bitcoin futures, it had not been accepted by most governments, and those which did allow it did so mainly as an experiment (as with the Central Bank of Venezuela). In 2025, Argentina suffered a massive digital currency collapse, though not Bitcoin itself. El Salvador voted to make Bitcoin legal tender there, as did the Central African Republic, mainly in an attempt to boost investment. *Forbes* named Bitcoin as the best investment of 2013, but its use as a medium of transaction—the original goal of the creator—remained undetermined as of this writing in 2025. With changes in the Securities and Exchange Commission under Trump, it appeared digital currency in America was on the way toward massive acceptance as an alternative currency.

Nevertheless, Bitcoin's image as a "counter-dollar" currency struck the International Monetary Fund, which warned El Salvador to reverse the decision to use it as legal tender. Opposition by globalist institutions such as the International Monetary Fund and the left-leaning writer Paul Krugman (whose predictions have been almost entirely wrong for over thirty years) suggest that in fact Bitcoin may have a future and may indeed pose a threat to the dollar—but not in the short run.

AMERICA FIRST

Even before Trump won the presidency on a platform of "America first" and disengagement with the rest of the world in terms of outsourcing and climate treaties, the US had started to withdraw from foreign activism. As president, Trump hit the ground running, taking the US out of the Trans-Pacific Partnership and withdrew from the disastrous Paris Accords.[279] But before he could extract America from China, the pandemic hit and limited much of his ability to emphasize America first, though the fact that so much of the pharmaceutical supply chain came from China was ominous. In other words, the US remained the only nation on the planet with global reach and global power, but which no longer had global interests.[280]

Trump attempted to extricate the US from its China supply chain, but there he found the going tougher. Persuading companies to abandon multibillion-dollar facilities and investments and relocate to more expensive countries (not to mention the US itself) was something Trump could not accomplish with an executive order or a presidential decision. Instead, Trump hoped to slowly persuade American and Chinese companies to build more plants domestically, beginning with the January 2022 announcement that Foxconn, the world's largest contract electronics maker, would set up a display-making plant in Wisconsin with an investment of $7 billion.[281] The company planned to start production in 2020 with thirteen thousand new employees, even though the state of Wisconsin routinely denied any tax subsidies to Foxconn. It began production in 2021. After a year, the company scaled down its production estimates as few of the suppliers were close to Wisconsin.

Trump's efforts at implementing "America first" economic solutions were stonewalled at every turn by even the Republican Congress of 2017–19, but certainly the Democratic Congress from 2019–23. Speaker of the House Paul Ryan and Senate Majority Leader Mitch McConnell made sure that budgets had plenty of tax cuts but little else in the way of incentivizing companies to build and buy American. Instead, Trump had to try to strong-arm auto companies and others to build in the US. Again, in his very first month, he pushed the big three automakers to build more cars in the US: "I want new plants to be built here for cars sold here," he said.[282] His first secretary of state, former ExxonMobil CEO Rex Tillerson (or "T-Rex" as he was colloquially called) proved inept at persuading, given that most of his background had been in dictating policy. Trump's trade representative, Robert Lighthizer, was more capable, especially alongside Commerce Secretary Wilbur Ross. Still, the ability to force companies out of low-cost China proved difficult. Instead, Trump realized tariffs would be needed.

In January 2018, Trump imposed tariffs on solar panels and washing machines of between 30 and 50 percent, affecting about 4 percent of US imports. Those were soon extended to the European Union, Canada, and Mexico, while tariffs on Chinese goods were increased again.[283] When foreign nations retaliated, Trump activated the Commodity Credit Corporation, a New Deal program, to assist farmers. It seemed to befuddle economic "experts" that Trump *wanted* Chinese retaliation to continue to pressure American firms to leave the Communist nation. Moreover, Trump had taken a page from the Democrats' playbook, as many of them had called for tougher actions on trade, even going so far as to say Obama didn't do enough. Among those most put on the edge were senators such as socialist Bernie Sanders, who had repeatedly called for such measures, especially for singling out China.

Then, as rapidly as the nation recovered, it stopped.

"BIDENOMICS"

A blizzard of new regulations had spread like fungus throughout the economy since 1960, braking growth. Regulations, particularly under President Biden, proved powerful roadblocks to energy and manufacturing expansion. Even leftist critics such as Noah Smith warned that America was rapidly being relegated to a "build-nothing country."[284] Environmental regulations, for example, have crippled the ability to build more housing in major urban areas, especially California. By 2023, housing started to languish at 2008 levels. Infrastructure—even in those cities that touted the blessings of "mass transit"—wallowed in high costs and poor service. Again, in California, an ambitious high-speed rail project was scaled back repeatedly until it barely connected any major cities (in theory) and was consumed in massive cost overruns. Originally estimated to cost $33 billion, by 2023 the price tag was four times that amount. Similarly, so-called green energy programs stumbled with investors shying away from unreliable wind and land-consuming solar power. (A 2023 estimate of the amount of wind power needed by the year 2050 to replace oil and gas was that it would take a land mass the size of five Midwestern states covered with windmills.)[285]

In short, much of the sclerosis with which the US was dealing by the 2020s came from misguided attempts to impose climate regulations and/or replace existing energy sources with unproven and dangerous alternatives. Electric vehicles, for example, had begun to catch fire at alarming rates due to their lithium batteries. While at the same time, major lithium sources in the world, such as Chile, had nationalized their lithium deposits, meaning supply would be limited and vastly more expensive—and, in fact, Chile had even begun to negotiate with the Communist Chinese about exclusive lithium delivery!

On top of those towering issues, the US economy by the mid-2020s was still reeling from the economic fallout of the Covid lockdowns. Not only did those cause massive immediate disruption, but they produced the "largest upward transfer of wealth in history."[286] Despite the fact that America had thirty million small businesses compared with just twenty thousand big corporations, large companies were deemed "essential" and allowed to stay open during the pandemic when gyms, salons, restaurants, movie theaters, pet stores, and hundreds of other businesses were shuttered.[287] Meanwhile, seven big tech companies alone gained $3.4 trillion in market value as ordinary Americans were losing their lifelong dreams. Supposedly, to help compensate, the government instigated a monetary stimulus and provided loans: The stimulus resulted in inflation (which reached 7 percent by 2023), and getting the loans was time consuming. Even if a business qualified, it might not arrive in time to save the firm. All those horrors were accompanied by clever marketing campaigns telling viewers that "we're all in this together." Any business executive who spoke out against the lockdowns was fired, as described by Levi's executive Jennifer Sey, who resigned over the lockdown politics.

Originally rolled out on April 15, 2020, as "15 days to flatten the curve," referring to the surge in cases that authorities thought would overwhelm hospitals.[288] When two weeks came and went, President Trump was angry, suspecting that he had been misled and said, "I'm not going to preside over the funeral of the greatest country in the world."[289] In fact, quarantines were not employed in other epidemics and pandemics, including those in 1929, 1940–44, 1957–58, or 1967–68. By all measures, the lockdowns did not stop Covid in any way or even slow it down. But the pandemic spurred a massive burst of new government spending, perhaps as high as $6 trillion. Personal income, which had soared under Trump by $4.2 trillion, temporarily grew as people banked their "stimulus checks." Savings tripled in the first quarter of 2020, then crashed to one-third of the pre-panic levels under Biden. Ridiculous policies were enacted by private businesses trying to keep government off their backs so they could stay open: Walmart and other "big box" stores painted arrows on their floors indicating one-way travel, and spots six feet across were placed on the floor in front of checkout stands. Plexiglass barriers were erected, and the population was virtually forced to wear completely ineffective masks. Huddling indoors was encouraged, despite the fact that sunshine was a known killer of the virus.

The lockdowns wiped out millions of American businesses, with at least one hundred thousand restaurants closed in Manhattan alone, including well-known legacy establishments. As vaccinations were imposed on health care employees, employment in the health care sector fell by over one million in 2020 alone. Lawsuits alleging that vaccine requirements violated personal religious beliefs and other civil liberties exploded. Ultimately, the US Supreme Court sided with the government in requiring vaxxes for the armed services but found that private businesses could not force vaccinations on employees.[290]

In addition to the massive shocks brought about by the China Virus and its attendant lockdowns, a large structural change in the American economy was afoot. Baby boomers had accelerated the economy when they had entered the workforce in the early 1960s; with their retirements, a slowdown was inevitable. Sharply rising prices spurred by inflation and the supply chain snags required them to reenter the workforce. They did so at the expense of younger would-be employees.

Welfare changes since the 1960s had severely damaged the work ethic. A common practice among younger employees emerged, called "quiet quitting," in which work from home yielded the minimal effort. A similar trend, "coffee badging," met the corporate world's requirement of a certain number of hours at an office by checking in using an identification badge...just long enough to get coffee or attend one meeting, then skedaddle home.[291] Not only did the work-from-home mentality yield lower productivity, but a resumed forced attendance policy at offices had precipitated a shocking level of laziness, breeding a generation of slackers who looked for ways to avoid work rather than provide excellence.

As college enrollment stalled, more young men especially found employment in blue-collar jobs.[292] Blue-collar jobs, to the elites' surprise, not only were still necessary but also absolutely essential. Without an American-born, local workforce of such service personnel, their lives would come to a halt.

Pervading both the exodus from college and the new attraction of blue-collar work, concerns over millennials failing to reach the living standards of their parents permeated the thoughts of younger generations. Some experts suggested that millennials, especially, were not as badly off as many thought. For one thing, when comparing boomers and millennials, adjusted for their share of the population, millennials were on a similar growth trajectory to their parents.[293] Indeed, already Gen X was richer than boomers at the same age, and millennials are on track to surpass Xers. Millennials came of economic age just as the recession of 2008 hit, which set them back.[294] Moreover, millennials were only a little behind boomers' home ownership rates, and Gen Zers were tracking ahead of their parents.[295] And millennials were building wealth per capita at the same pace as their predecessors. Where they differed from earlier generations was in having children, which tended to make people more politically conservative, which millennials did not.

Otherwise, even millennials themselves, by a small majority, thought they were doing better than their parents. Nevertheless, the harrowing 2007–2008 experiences stayed with many and contributed to the mental dégringolade of younger people as well.

BACK ON THE MENU

Obama had sought to manage America's decline. Trump rejected that approach and had shown that large changes were possible in the American industry if encouraged by lower regulations and less government. Biden's controversial election in 2020, however, changed the upward dynamic immediately. Stagnation immediately set in, even if upper-tier jobs in finance and tech seemed to expand. After allowing for the China Virus damage to the economy, the engine of democracy had still not recovered by April 2023. From a high of 63.5 million participating in the labor force in 2019, three years after the China Virus the labor force participation still languished at under sixty-two million—when at normal growth rates the economy should have had more than seventy million employed.[296] The foolish Covid relief spending came back with a vengeance after Biden's election, with inflation reaching over 7.5 percent. Gas prices (at under two dollars a gallon under Trump) skyrocketed to five dollars a gallon; while meat, chicken, and egg prices soared. As of March 2023, Biden trailed only Jimmy Carter in the "Presidential Inflation Rate."[297] The public as a whole expected inflation to get worse for the next ten years, with measures of sentiment reaching all-time highs.[298]

Biden, though running as a "moderate," quickly made clear that he (or his advisors guiding him) would push for a "Green New Deal," a massive climate change plan that would destroy American industry. His team began passing regulations trying to eliminate gas stoves, to make it more difficult to use air conditioners to cool houses, and to eliminate gas-powered vehicles by 2030. The so-called American Rescue Plan Act, passed in early 2021, pushed the nation into inflation according to the Federal Reserve Bank of San Francisco.[299] (Research indicated that the previous stimulus under Trump in early 2020 had not touched off inflation.)[300]

The crashing of the economy seemed almost deliberate. Biden threw open the borders to allow in millions of illegal immigrants, overwhelming health care and municipal administrative systems. He also passed a flood of "green" regulations that layered cost after cost on American businesses. It was not that Biden merely slowed down or stopped all the growth in the Trump years but had radically reversed all growth to the point that the US suffered through twenty-five straight months of real "negative growth" (i.e., decline) after accounting for inflation. Consumer confidence plummeted to lower levels than before Covid.[301] Managed decline—if not actual destruction—was back on the menu.

BUDS OF SPRING

The American economy has always been a miraculous thing. America's character and deeply embedded foundations have proven resistant to even some of the worst administrations in history. Land values, for example, always return (as occurred after the Panic of 1837). A "fragile-by-design" banking system has been, nevertheless, flexible enough to bend with multiple depressions but survive even the worst: 1837, 1893, 1907, 1932, and 2008. Natural resource wealth and the world's wealthiest free consumer market always provides a point for a quick turnaround.

Despite the twelve out of sixteen years of bad-to-terrible economic policies, a full lost year from Covid, and "green" initiatives, the US economy has not only survived but has also seen a factory boom.[302] Trump's return in 2024 signaled the buds of spring.

CHAPTER 4
THE ROT

After leaving the presidency, Barack Obama whined that while the twentieth century may have excluded "women and people of color," it was a time of commonality, especially of information, an idyllic era (in his view) in which everyone could watch one of three approved television news programs and walked away with the same basic message. There was a shared set of facts only because tight regulation and the extremely high cost of competition made alternative views impossible.[303]

Although Obama and other liberals would complain that it was radio host Rush Limbaugh who punctured this balloon, in reality CNN, which launched in 1980, opened the door to virtually all cable news. Limbaugh followed in 1988. Later, the internet further expanded the sources from which people could seek alternate views. Well into 2024, the "big five" of CBS, ABC, NBC, CNN, and Fox News still provided most Americans with their news. But an increasing percentage of younger people went to websites like video sites such as YouTube, Rumble, or CloutHub and social media outlets such as Facebook (now Meta) or Twitter (now X), though some of the earlier social media sites, including Myspace, had virtually ceased to exist. And an even more powerful influence, that of shorter social media video sites such as Instagram and TikTok, increasingly proved the domain of the younger sets. TikTok especially appealed to teens and people in their twenties with very short videos of a few seconds to up to sixty minutes—but most were less than two minutes. By 2019, TikTok was the seventh-most downloaded application in the United States, surpassing Facebook, YouTube, and Instagram.

TikTok's algorithm was viewed as one of the most advanced in history for shaping user interactions and experiences, and the site monitored many behaviors by viewers. As a company with Chinese connections (the Chinese counterpart is Douyin), the app was heavily censored and manipulated by the Chinese to block any anti-Chinese images or news, including content related to the 1989 Tiananmen Square protests, activities of the Falun Gong group, human rights violations in Tibet, and others. Studies have shown that TikTok was a propaganda tool of the Chinese Communist government.[304]

Taken together, however, TikTok and Instagram for younger groups and Twitter/X and Facebook (Meta) for older groups, Americans had gone from a handful of highly controlled news outlets to a wide array of options. Did this harm "shared culture"? Of course, in a sense. But it also meant that a narrative favored by the media, business, military, and intelligence elites could no longer be foisted as easily on ordinary people. No dynamic transformed America more than this access to information that, in turn, helped foster the decline of shared values.

THE DISSOLUTION OF SHARED CULTURE

Access to information and entertainment online only constituted a part of the increasing divide in America between the ruling-class elites and the so-called country class. Angelo Codevilla employed this term in 2010 when he unveiled his ideas in an *American Spectator* essay.[305] Codevilla's analysis was sparked originally by the financial bailout of the major banks after the subprime crisis. He noticed that those in power seemed to represent only the elites, regardless of party affiliation. Even after the "Tea Party" revolution of 2010, many of those in the new Republican majority "did not disparage the ruling class, because most of its officials are or would like to be part of it."[306] Codevilla laid out a brilliant and seminal analysis of the shift in American society whereby an educational system combined with a normalization of the once-despised bureaucracy form a monolithic ruling class. America's modern ruling class, he wrote,

> from Boston to San Diego, was formed by an educational system that exposed them to the same ideas and gave them remarkably uniform guidance, as well as tastes and habits. These amount to a social canon of judgments about good and evil, complete with secular sacred history, sins (against minorities and the environment), and saints.... Regardless of what business or profession they are in, their road up included government channels and government money because, as government has grown, its boundary with the rest of American life has become indistinct.[307]

Wouldn't that constitute a "shared culture"? No. It only represented those at the top with access to government largesse and assistance or to elite university social cultures that empowered networking unavailable to most Americans. No longer, as Abraham Lincoln observed in the difference between the North and South in the Civil War, did the people of both sections pray to the same God. Rather, the ruling class had become its own god (or, more often, no god at all), and its members disparaged those who, as Obama said in his 2008 campaign, "cling to their guns or religion."

Politically, this separation of ordinary people and the ruling class had been building for decades. In 1968, George Wallace was one of the first to observe that "there ain't a dime's worth of difference" between the Democrats and the Republicans. As any reader of *A Patriot's History of the United States* would know, this unfolded as an inevitable result of the creation of the Democratic Party in the 1820s as a specific instrument to protect and preserve slavery. Martin Van Buren, the party's creator, had envisioned a means of excluding slavery from all political debate by rewarding party members with party, then political, jobs. His spoils system had entrenched itself well by the 1830s, when the rival Whig Party appeared. Whigs, however, found themselves unable to get off the playing field Van Buren had created. In essence, after 1828, the nature of the winner-take-all/single-member-district system guaranteed that there would be only two major parties. Others would coalesce around those who showed the greatest differences from each other, but it was focused on only the two major rivals that demonstrated the ability to win an election by garnering 50 percent of the vote.

This development, in turn, pushed both parties to the political middle. After slavery was abolished, parties still disagreed sharply over the proper solutions to America's problems, but both tempered their language in moderate, nonrevolutionary tones. After all, neither could wage war on the bureaucracy or the government itself because both needed that very government to reward loyalists with jobs. A few exceptions appeared—and usually lost elections. Those included people such as the gold-standard firebrand William Jennings Bryan, the constitutionalist Barry Goldwater, or the anti-war activist George McGovern. With the exception of Goldwater, few of these outliers proposed any serious policies that would entail a major reduction of the size or scope of government itself.

While Codevilla somewhat denigrated the notion of a bureaucratic state that rose out of a modern sociology, in fact there is something to the notion that the "Administrative Man"[308] (as blogger eugyppius termed him) is a reality and evolved from genuine business and social structures.

The appearance of the Administrative Man began in business, in the late nineteenth century, when the scale and scope of enterprises grew so large as to be unmanageable by a traditional single owner. This was especially true in the case of the railroads where their enormous scale and cost exceeded that which even one millionaire at the time could produce.

Demands put on single owners were exacerbated by the railroads' scope of operations, crossing vast territories and state lines. Finally, the very speed of the railroads challenged any single individual's control: Trains could easily get routed onto the same track, going straight at each other, before any single owner could even be alerted to the inevitable crash, let alone stop it.

As Alfred Chandler Jr. detailed in *The Visible Hand* (1977), the solution was a class of professional managers that took over almost all large-scale industries by 1900.[309] It is critical for an understanding of twenty-first century culture and the power of the ruling class to understand those managers. They tended to go to the same schools, and they developed the same attitude toward business. Managers, perhaps surprisingly, did not want shockingly high profits if they came from radical changes within the companies. Rather, they preferred a steady 2 percent annual increase for which they could plan and control.

"Planning" became a ubiquitous term throughout American society in the late 1800s and early 1900s. It embodied a sense of godlike power to control economics, society, and even war. None other than John Maynard Keynes had famously claimed that the commercial ties in place by the early 1900s made war nearly impossible, as they would disrupt trade and commerce. (It was a false claim repeated by Thomas Friedman in his "Dell Theory" nearly a century later.) Planning, advocates claimed, could not only make trains run on time or assembly lines work to near-perfection but could also take care of the indigent, run cities efficiently, and (its unstated goal) ensure that the planners themselves retained an elevated position in business, government, and culture.

Increasingly, the managerial/ruling class attended the same schools. Until the late twentieth century, they almost all went to either the Ivy League or a handful of other elite schools such as Stanford or Northwestern. There, they saw their world views reinforced and further refined, far away from the smelly, dirty, middle- and lower-class Americans who had to perform all the tasks they required but refused to do.

Another side effect of this managerial revolution of Administrative Men, the aversion to risk, embodied other fundamental changes that soon affected all of society. Anything that threatened the 2 percent annual growth or the detailed, annual city budgets constituted a problem. As a result, corporations nearly universally preferred minor tinkering on existing product lines over radical but risky breakthroughs. Think only of the threat posed by Preston Tucker and his futuristic "Tucker Torpedo" auto that, in the immediate postwar years, already featured disc brakes, fuel injection, seat belts, movable front lights, and a host of other revolutionary changes that would have cost the "Big Three" millions to match. Hence, Tucker was driven out of business after manufacturing only fifty of his cars (of which most are still roadworthy today!). Contrast that with the new models coming from Ford, Chevrolet, Oldsmobile, and other automakers in the late 1950s, where the central change was the length of a car's tail fin or the design of its rear lights.

Economist Burton Klein discovered that in the twentieth century, not a single major technological breakthrough came from the leader in the field.[310] One can go back further than that, however: In the late 1800s, the leaders in overland non-railroad transportation—the stagecoach companies of Wells Fargo and Overland—did not produce the next step in ground transportation. Instead, a Westinghouse engineer named Henry Ford, working out of his garage, invented a practical car. None of the balloon makers of the 1800s were involved in creating the first airplanes; it came from a pair of brothers in Ohio making bicycles. The premiere calculating company, Keuffel and Esser, which produced slide rules, was left in the dust by business machine companies that made the first machine calculators. IBM, which held 85 percent of the world's computer market in the 1960s, failed to invent a personal computer (which was done by Steve Jobs and Steve Wozniak) and even ridiculed the notion that it would be useful. Still later, Jobs struck again when it was his Apple *computer* company that took over the music industry with digital devices called iPods, even though the leader in the portable music player industry was Sony with its Walkman.

These were just a few of the examples of companies failing to maintain a cutting edge because of the calcification of the administrative/manager class. Risk aversion, however, had gotten far worse: Research showed that beginning in the 1990s—though for reasons having nothing to do with financial risk—science had produced fewer and fewer actually significant breakthroughs. Researchers increasingly focused on narrower and narrower areas that did not posit major changes in ideas or processes largely because of the possibility of being "canceled" by challenging existing orthodoxies.[311] In addition to generating masses of "less disruptive" papers, a growing amount of published research findings were flat-out *false*.[312] "Wokeism" definitely played a role, but the steadily deteriorating profit structure of companies and the perpetually expanding role of the Administrative Man, governed by the ruling class, ensured this long before wokeness.

By the twenty-first century, the Administrative Man lived in a city, not a town and certainly not in the country, likely to rent rather than own, and well-off but not wealthy. He was much more focused on celebrating ethnic and sexual "diversity," but not intellectual diversity. A tool of the ruling class, the Administrative Man emerged as an important cog, a subservient subordinate and capo who kept the plebes in line. In spite of the need that the members of the ruling class had for the Administrative Man, they viewed him with contempt and quietly assured each other that he cannot join their ranks.

Like their subordinate, the Administrative Man, the members of the ruling class also lived in the biggest cities where they owned, rather than rented. They dwelled in the priciest suburbs of Montgomery County, Maryland and in tony enclaves such as Buckhead, Georgia; Palo Alto, California; Beacon Hill, Massachusetts; and Boulder, Colorado. Their concentration was such that Charles Murray grouped them into "SuperZips": zip codes where the majority of the inhabitants fell above a certain wealth level *and* who had graduated from the top schools. Indeed, Murray found that unless one of the ruling class actually picked up their own dry cleaning, filled their own gas tank, or did their own food shopping, they were highly unlikely to even *interact on a casual basis* with someone outside the ruling class. They tolerated interaction with their Administrative Men but never socialized with them and certainly never interacted with those below the managerial level, if at all possible. A plumber, electrician, auto mechanic, or dry cleaner? Never. And they overwhelmingly voted Democrat and excluded people of professional prominence or position if that person did not share their politics (for example, Justice Clarence Thomas or, before him, Ronald Reagan).

The ruling-class cadre weren't that smart, either. Merely going to an Ivy League school no longer defined academic rigor—few flunked out of any colleges—and studies have shown that the so-called best colleges required the least work and yet had the highest grade point averages. Many Ivy League schools actually dropped admittance tests for a while before restoring them, reasoning that they were "racist."

And they were dishonest. Many had their work written for them by other students.[313] An epidemic of plagiarism scandals that hit Harvard and other so-called elite schools in the early 2020s merely put in public view what had been hidden—but well known—for years. Ruling-class members spent their time networking, not studying.

Once ensconced in their networks (some might say, "burrowed in"), they used their positions on state bars, regulatory agencies, councils, and boards to not only advance their fellow travelers, but also to literally persecute anyone not towing the ruling-class line. That abuse of power was in full display after the 2020 election challenges, where several lawyers, including Professor John Eastman, were disbarred merely for offering a contrary legal opinion to the ruling class.

Like Codevilla, Murray dove deep into the class divide (itself a Marxist concept, showing how far the infiltration of ordinary language had become). A number of terms were applied to the ruling class and Administrative Men including "symbolic analysts," "mind workers" (which, by the way, totally refuted the very concept of "class" Marx posited), "bourgeois bohemians," and "the creative class." Murray broke them into two groups: the "narrow elite" who wielded jobs that directly affected the nation's culture, economy, and politics and that included lawyers, judges, journalists and the top executives of corporate America. Murray estimated that, in total, the ruling class consisted of no more than a couple of hundred thousand at most and perhaps only ten thousand at minimum.

To see the impact of the "narrow elite" in action, one only has to look no further than the trials and persecutions of the January 6 ("Patriot Day") protesters or of President Donald Trump himself. Members of that "narrow elite" constituted most of the prosecutors and judges who heard those cases and the broad majority of the media reporting on them.

To understand how much the twenty-first century upper class had changed from what it was sixty years ago, one only has to look at the fact that in 1963 fewer than 10 percent of *all* Americans had a college degree. In a gathering of upper-middle or upper-class people, one would find only about one-third had graduated from college. As Murray pointed out, the cabinets of most presidents featured few people of inherited wealth at all, and (say, in the John F. Kennedy administration) most came from parents who were small farmers, one who was a sales manager of shoe company, or another who had made his living selling produce. Cultural icons of the day, such as Walt Disney and Ronald Reagan, came from small Midwestern towns and had worked in nonexecutive jobs most of their lives.

Even in the tony, wealthier suburbs of Cleveland, such as Shaker Heights, or Chevy Chase, Maryland, one did not find the "froth of castles" that the superrich of the late 1800s built in Newport, Rhode Island. A typical "upper-class" house was about twice the cost of the average home in those areas.[314] No one had a private jet, and transport by helicopter as a private, commercial, or entertainment option had not even been conceived yet. Put another way, the rich were very much "ordinary people who had more money, and in fact many considered it gauche or pompous to flaunt one's wealth by driving an inordinately expensive foreign car. (Generally, the "ladder" of social achievement dictated that the lowest classes drove Chevrolets or basic Fords, the next level up drove

Buicks or Pontiacs, the professionals had Oldsmobiles, Thunderbirds, or Chryslers, and the elites had Cadillacs and Lincoln Town Cars. Quite literally you could predict where someone was financially and socially by what they drove.)

Murray also pointed out that in elite schools, one found almost no women in their twenties with children. Large numbers of "ordinary" Americans were overweight (thanks in large part to a shift in dietary habits instituted after Dwight Eisenhower's heart attack in 1955 that led to a steady increase in carbohydrates over meat).[315] Elites were overwhelmingly thinner, to the point of being skinny by body mass metrics. Writer Tom Wolfe, in his great *Bonfire of the Vanities*, affixed the appellation "social X-rays" to elite and overwhelmingly white women. And certainly no one in the ruling class smoked!

In countless other ways, the elites or the ruling class separated themselves from the country class. Merely focusing on the top 5 percent of wealth earners, they were making about $200,000 in 2009, but the top 1 percent were making at least $440,000 that year. Those wealth percentages *were* America's upper class. Yet those in the upper regions of those wealth classes depended entirely on those at the middle and bottom of the wealth tiers for their very survival. Police, firemen, hospital employees (excluding surgeons), dry cleaners, street repair workers, and tech nerds were obviously necessary. But even academics, who might be hired at $20,000 a night to give a speech to the elites, nevertheless likely pulled in annual salaries of under $150,000. Statisticians, economists, foreign policy "experts," political scientists, and the like held high *status* in the ruling class but still struggled at the lower tier of wealth.[316]

Enabled by all the nonprofessionals who attend to their most basic needs in Maslow's hierarchy, the ruling class by the year 2000 had increasingly segregated itself politically, socially, culturally, and, of course, financially from the lower tiers of society. In Silicon Valley, the housing prices had increased so much that household help, electricians, plumbers, and car repairmen had to live more than an hour away to afford a home. Chapman University in Orange County, California, a school for lower upper class that specializes in film and business, had to purchase houses for faculty to rent at subsidized prices because young faculty were utterly priced out. (One faculty member in the business school told me of a position known as a "line" in the accounting department that had gone unfilled for years because the high salary nevertheless did not come close to covering living expenses there!)

All of this translated into two Americas, two different shared cultures instead of a single shared culture. Not only did the wealthier and uber poor vote Democrat, but the ruling class spent their leisure time entirely differently, developed different values (that embraced abortion, homosexuality, sex change, and climate ideology), and lived so as not to ever have to confront someone outside their bubble. The country class still was overwhelmingly patriotic, supported the police, held the military in high regard, attended community-oriented events such as parades and fireworks shows, watched movies, and ate at chain restaurants such as Chili's, Applebee's, or Red Lobster.

Murray encapsulated the differences in the classes in a "bubble test." It is somewhat outdated now, referencing popular movies and television shows at the time and asking about restaurant chains that have died since Covid. Nevertheless, it remains a quick identifier to separate the experiences of those in the ruling class from the country class. For example, Murray asked:

- Do you have any friends who smoke?
- How often do you eat at (then he listed popular middle-class chain restaurants such as Chili's or TGI Fridays)?
- Have you ever attended a parade that did not involve homosexual rights?
- Have you ever worked a job where you hurt at the end of the day?
- Can you name five military insignia of rank?

And many others. The upshot was that majorities of ordinary Americans do all these things, yet the ruling class would score extremely low on the bubble test. I even had one female college student at the private university where I taught score a zero, meaning she was entirely bubble-ized![317]

America had indeed become two nearly separate nations by 2020, one of rich, highly intelligent urban/suburban dwellers (whose numbers were shrinking relative to the rest of the country) and one of largely suburban, small-town, rural, noncollege working-class Americans (whose numbers were growing). Although the former controlled most of the levers of power—including courts, the legal system, and banks—their authority and status came increasingly under siege through elections and an overall collapse of public trust in their ability to govern. Politically, they held on by their fingernails. By 2024, a new populist revolution had been under way for a decade, and it was only a matter of time before the ruling class lost control of many of the institutions that allowed them to retain power. (As Elon Musk, heading President Trump's Department of Government Efficiency effort would find, many of those people received federal money from the organization US Agency for International Development as a kind of money-laundering front for the ruling class, so much so that even George Soros received the agency.)

THE GOD GAP

At the heart of the ruling class's slow loss of control lay a schism in faith. Already in the 1990s, a rift had arisen between the Republicans and Democrats over the place of God in their respective parties. In 2001, Geoffrey Layman first used the term "God gap" to refer to the growing chasm between Republicans and Democrats when it came to religion.[318] Robert Putnam, famous for his analysis of the growing class divide based on the decline of shared entertainment and civic experiences in *Bowling Alone* (2000), identified the 1960s political and social gap as fueling a religious counterrevolution that appeared in the 1970s and 1980s. That counterrevolution was identified with the Moral Majority, Family

Research Council, and the Christian Coalition of America in his book *American Grace* with David Campbell.[319]

There is little doubt, they argued, that by 2024 "the modern Republican party is a whole lot more religious than the modern Democratic party."[320] For example, by 2020, 63 percent of Republicans (the same percentage as Democrats in 1990!) believed in God with "no doubt." Another 19 percent believed with "some doubts." But Democrats had seen their faith numbers utterly crash to only 39 percent who believed with "no doubt" and only another 17 percent believed with "some doubt." A similar seventeen-point gap divided the parties on those who attended church weekly or monthly. Since the 1970s, as religious statistician and former pastor Ryan Burge noted, "the Democratic Party was a lot more Catholic compared to Republicans." Over the next fifty years, it wasn't that the Catholics became Protestants, but that both Catholics and Protestants became "nones" (no religious affiliation) at much higher levels.[321]

Young people especially had fallen away from their faith. The percentage of US teens *ever* attending a church service fell from almost 95 percent in 1975 to under 80 percent overall by 2020. Among college-aged kids, the drop-off fell even fifteen points lower to 65 percent. Only about 70 percent of youths reported any religious affiliation, and less than 75 percent believed in God.[322] When it came to younger people, high school seniors attended church weekly, even less than their older cohorts: From 1976 to 2020, the number of seniors who thought religion was important fell from 30 percent to just over 20 percent. As one authority on the religiosity of young people concluded, "What is unequivocal is the trajectory of American religion among today's young people. They are significantly less religious than high school students from decades earlier."[323] The good news? There was an inflection point in 1980 when men began attending church more than women, and both groups, slowly, returned to the halls of worship.[324] The bad news? Church attendance remained quite low, at only about 25 percent of the population.

A large-scale report in 2020 called *The State of Religion and Young People* found that 34 percent of those eighteen to thirty-four were unaffiliated with any church, half who were affiliated with a "religious tradition" had little to no trust in religious institutions, and only 13–16 percent considered themselves either "very religious" or "very spiritual."[325] Lacking any church affiliation, it was not surprising that those same young people said to an overwhelming degree that they felt isolated (60 percent), that they felt "completely alone" (24–39 percent, highest among girls), and that nearly one-third didn't think it was important to have a faith community.[326]

Within America's religious community, church growth in the Bible Belt—the South plus the swath of Sunbelt/border states—surged since 2010. Part of that obviously came from the substantial and continuing exodus from colder, Northern-tier states but also from more liberal states such as California, which lost over 750,000 people in just a few years. From East Texas through Arkansas and Tennessee and down to Florida and Arizona on the edges, the Bible Belt engulfed much of the US. Burge, one of the best analysts of modern religious trends, noted that "44% of Louisiana counties have experienced at least a ten point growth in the number of religious congregations between 2010 and 2020"; 42 % in Tennessee; and over 30% in Arizona, Mississippi, and South Dakota.[327] For the most part—except for West Virginia, whose shrinking church base reflected its economic condition—those states showing large numbers of counties with a double-digit decline in congregations were either in colder climates (Illinois, North Dakota, Iowa, and Indiana), had liberal politics (New Mexico and Oregon), or both (Oregon, Illinois, and in many populated areas of the state, New Mexico).

Reflecting a trend in American religion since the 1990s, nondenominational churches tended to make up large shares of religious bodies in states that saw gains and were sparsely represented in states showing losses. In short, the mainline Protestant (especially) and Catholic character of Illinois, Iowa, and Indiana, in particular, had tailed off. From their once-dominant position as highlighted in Paul Kleppner's classic work, *The Cross of Culture*, religious differences in those states no longer made a difference in political America.[328] Wherever one looked, religious growth had slowed. The U.S. Religion Census found 344,894 congregations across the US and by 2020 that had grown to 356,723, a rate that was far slower than the US population growth.[329] Out of nine mainline Protestant denominations, only the Assemblies of God and the Presbyterian Church in America showed any growth: The other seven main denominations, including the once seemingly bulletproof Southern Baptists, all showed significant declines.[330]

MENTAL UNHEALTH

Changes in faith, and particularly the decline in religiosity among younger people, fed a pandemic of hopelessness, depression, and loneliness. Two top-rated athletes, Naomi Osaka (tennis) and Simone Biles (gymnastics) both abruptly dropped out of their competitions for extensive periods of time because of mental health issues in the early 2020s. Biles, often considered the best gymnast in the world, said, "I have to…focus on my mental health and not jeopardize my health and well being."[331] Jean Twenge's exhaustively documented look at the responses of Gen Zers, for example, showed that their levels of loneliness had nearly doubled between 2007 and 2021, those "not satisfied with themselves" had more than doubled, and survey questions such as "can't do anything right," "do not enjoy life," and "not useful" had similarly doubled.[332] Leading popular female musicians, such as Billie Eilish and Olivia Rodrigo, frequently sang about death or suicide. Eilish's sang about burying a friend and drowning.[333] She admitted in an interview "a lot of people don't love themselves."[334] A similar lament came from Rodrigo, who predicted she would die before she got old enough to drink.[335] Others, such as Demi Lovato, battled an eating disorder and before her, Britney Spears was so mentally unstable that she spent years with her father named as her conservator.

Male singers, who tended to be older, had no fewer problems. Kanye West had such severe mental issues that he swung from embracing Christianity to parading his nearly naked consort around in public while he was covered from head to toe. Ironically, some of the biggest stars in America were Scottish-born Lewis Capaldi—whose fame triggered in him dormant Tourette's syndrome and tics—and English-born Ed Sheeran. Capaldi had mournful tunes about death, while Sheeran, who could often engage in more upbeat music, nevertheless at age thirty-three looked back to his youth and how he watched the sunrise on the "Castle on a Hill." American Post Malone admitted in song that he didn't want to sober up. In short, there was little joy in anything post-2000 that the youths heard and even less in what they thought about their life circumstances.

That depression took on other forms. By 2020, younger people expressed little interest in taking risks (note the previously referenced research to the overall reduction of risk in scientific papers and the decline in significant inventions), wanted to "stay safe," and felt threatened by words. Yet that produced an ironic reaction. Unable to validate themselves by overcoming challenges, taking (and beating) risks that developed confidence, learning how to accept criticism or even "hateful" words without letting it affect them, younger people turned on themselves. Those challenging aspects of life produced a sort of body armor, physically and mentally. Without it, twice as many teenagers in 2019 took their lives than those just twelve years earlier, and three times as many fourth through ninth graders killed themselves.[336] More American twenty-five-year olds said they were "unhappy" by 2017 than any country in the world except Canada.[337] And as the cohorts got younger, they became more pessimistic: Over 40 percent of US twelfth graders said it was hard to have hope for the world, while 30 percent said they wondered if there was any purpose to life.[338] Lacking either the confidence that came from, for want of a better term, surviving life or from a certainty of a loving God, young people in the twenty-first century acted far differently than any of their predecessors.

This was no "phase" from which they would exit, either. Between 2010 and 2015, teens sank into a relentless depressive state. More than 50 percent experienced a depressive episode in 2015 compared with 2010—and this was "clinically diagnosable major depression," not just "feeling bad."[339] Indeed, a psychiatric nurse at New York's Bellevue Hospital told *Time* magazine that every week "we have a girl who comes to the ER after some social media rumor or incident has upset her."[340] Teens discussed cutting themselves so much on social media that the hashtag #selfharm skyrocketed from 1.7 million mentions on the platform Instagram in 2014 to 2.4 million just one year later. Suicide rates also shot up, especially with girls, with three times as many twelve-to-fourteen-year-olds killing themselves in 2015 than in 2007. Especially damaging was the absence of an adult "mentor" in the lives of young people. Statistics showed a four-fold increase in the number of youths who thought they had "no purpose" or "no mission" if they lacked just one adult mentor in their lives.[341]

Several factors have been cited as contributing to an unhappy, anxious America. Liberal pundit Noah Smith, for example, claimed that a series of disasters, from the vitriolic, contested 2000 election to 9/11 to the Iraq War to Katrina, ending with the subprime crisis, all combined to make young people especially pessimistic and moribund.[342] Yet even that combination of factors could hardly compete with the period of 1860–1870, with four years of the Civil War, the first assassination of a US president, America's greatest water disaster ever with the explosion and sinking of the *Sultana*, race riots, the Ku Klux Klan and reconstruction, Indian wars and the Sand Creek massacre, and financial debacles such as the "gold corner." If anyone had a case to be made for mass depression, it would have been those who lived through that decade. Instead, they soldiered on, leading to one of the greatest growth periods in American history, from the economy to architecture to shipbuilding to invention. In fact, in the 2000s, eighth, tenth, and twelfth graders hit peak happiness; suicide was low; with the rapid expansion of "concealed carry" laws, murder rates fell from 2000 to 2020; and domestic violence had dropped, along with teen drug use and consumption of alcohol and cigarettes.[343]

Then everything flipped with the arrival of cell phones and personal electronic devices connected to social media. Not only did social media create previously unseen levels of peer pressure and the "fear of missing out" (FOMO), but it also decreased teens' sleep time: Almost half of who were surveyed reported sleeping more than seven hours (as opposed to the recommended nine hours for teens). Surprisingly, time spent watching television did not correlate much with declining sleep...but higher use of cell phones did.[344]

Filling the "God gap" with electronics, phones, and social media not only failed, but it also exacerbated other pathologies related to eating. In 2003, one study found that 4 percent of girls fifteen to nineteen were anorexic and 1–5 percent were bulimic.[345] American women had gone through a phase where anorexia was prevalent in the late 1970s and early 1980s, culminating with the billboards of Kate Moss and the death of pop star Karen Carpenter from heart failure related to anorexia. Carpenter was a mere seventy-seven pounds when she died.[346] Jennifer Sey, a former Levi's executive who broke with the company over its Covid lockdowns, admitted her own "obsessive behaviors" and credited Naomi Wolf's *The Beauty Myth* with rescuing her. "I had dropped all the bad self-harming behaviors," she wrote in a 2024 column.[347] Then it got worse. Much worse. By 2022, eating disorder visits to hospitals, doctors, and therapists doubled among kids younger than seventeen. Anorexia jumped 129 percent during that time.[348]

There is little question that the decline of religiosity and the rise of social media, particularly via the iPhone, had accelerated problems associated with eating. In particular, anorexia and bulimia were put, as it were, on steroids. But that didn't explain another dietary phenomenon that had superseded the thin-obsessed pathologies: namely that *overall* the US population was becoming obese.

BAD CALORIES, WORSE CALORIES

Few people, if any at all, in 1955 would have ever dreamed that President Eisenhower's heart attack would provoke an obesity epidemic twenty years later.[349] Yet that's precisely what happened. By the twenty-first century, it was fueled by the already morose mental state of young Americans. Eisenhower's heart attack, as I detailed in *Seven Events that Made America America*, opened a window for an anti-meat/fat zealot named Ancel Keys, a nutritionist from Minnesota, to gain control of the American Heart Association (AHA) with his false claims that fats caused cholesterol and cholesterol caused heart attacks. Thus, he began a stealthy and successful campaign to leverage the AHA to change public health. By the 1970s, he had convinced (despite nearly overwhelming evidence to the contrary) that eggs, fat, and meats were bad for Americans' health and that carbohydrates were beneficial.

Concern with obesity was nothing new in America. As early as 1952, the director for the National Institutes of Health, W. H. Sebrell Jr., had listed obesity as the "number one" nutritional problem in the US.[350] Experts agreed obesity was caused by "overeating." In 1971, with prodding by Keys and his minions, the *New England Journal of Medicine* called obesity the "most prevalent metabolic disorder of the age," and the infamous "skin-patch test" of grade-school children in 1985 found that kids were "significantly fatter" than fifteen years earlier.[351] But the true expansion of obesity—pardon the pun—came in the period of 1980–1995, when the carb revolution started by Keys set in. By 1997, some two-thirds of Americans were above their ideal weight.[352]

By 1977, thanks to unceasing lobbying by Keys, then the AHA, the government revised the famous "food pyramid" of healthy eating to reduce fats/meats by 40 percent and to increase carbohydrates by the same percentage. That ignited the obesity revolution, already undergirded by changes in exercise and work that resulted in Americans leading less physical and vigorous lives. Once the changes brought by the new emphasis on carbohydrates landed on top of the lifestyle changes, the percentage of Americans who were clinically overweight then obese exploded.

Gary Taubes's *Good Calories, Bad Calories* tracked the institutional process this war on protein took. He noted that the medical authorities were originally concerned with heart disease, not obesity. They "believe that Americans...had become gluttons. Americans ate too much of everything—particularly fat—because we could afford to."[353] Not only did a healthy diet come to be defined as a low-fat diet, but "an entire research industry arose to create palatable nonfat fat substitutes."[354] It worked. Since the 1960s, Americans consumed less red meat, fewer eggs, and more poultry and fish, and the average fat intake in total calories fell by 10 percent. Yet there was little evidence that the incidence of heart disease had fallen, and death rates related to heart disease fell mainly because of emergency medical personnel and responses. Meanwhile, the AHA admitted that between 1979 and 2003, the number of inpatient procedures for heart disease increased 470 percent, with a quarter-million Americans needing bypass surgery.[355] If heart disease didn't fall due to less meat/protein consumption, then what changed? Obesity rates shot up with increased carbohydrate-heavy diets. Whereas obesity from 1960 to 1980 had remained about 13 percent of the population, in 2004 obesity rates more than doubled. Diabetes also exploded in the population.

As late as 2005, the US Department of Agriculture's "dietary guidelines" suggested that caloric balance was the key to holding weight down and had coincided with a fifteen-year explosion in the fitness industry, accompanied by thousands of gyms, Pilates and yoga studios, and a proliferation of bike trails across America to accommodate armies of bike riders. By 2005, more than forty million Americans belonged to health clubs, continuing the "fitness revolution" that had started in 1980.[356]

Yet on average, the population got fatter. Some two in five Americans were obese, female clothing sizes were artificially increased to adjust to women's fatter bodies, "plus-size" mannequins dotted clothing stores, and a whole "fat is beautiful" movement began. Obesity (defined as having a body mass index of 30 or higher) accounted for over $173 million in medical expenditures, and there were entire cable shows dedicated to morbidly obese people (those with a body mass index of over 40), such as *My 600-lb Life*.

It wasn't just that larger numbers of Americans were clinically obese but that virtually *all* Americans had gained weight and were technically "overweight" using any number of measures. As Kelly Brownell, who headed Yale's Rudd Center for Food Policy and Obesity, noted, American culture encouraged "overeating and physical inactivity."[357] Obesity expert and surgeon Dr. Farah Husain called obesity an "epidemic," particularly childhood obesity.[358] Like other obesity surgeons, she had operated on patients as heavy as six hundred pounds. By 2016, more than half of American young adults were overweight, and within three years, one in three were clinically obese. And that number had increased in just five years!

Husain joined a growing number, including presidential candidate Robert F. Kennedy Jr., in concluding that "our food is slowly killing us" and agreed with Gary Taubes that sugar constituted one of the major health dangers.[359] (In 2024, Kennedy would run for president as a third-party candidate, then join Donald Trump's administration as Secretary of Health and Human Services where he immediately implemented many measures designed to reduce obesity and diabetes, among other maladies.)

An assault on "Big Food" started with books such as *Fast Food Nation* in 2002 and Morgan Spurlock's documentary *Super Size Me*, in which he consumed nothing but McDonald's food for thirty days and gained 24 pounds—only to be offset by an ad campaign from Subway restaurants featuring Jared Fogle who lost 245 pounds while eating only at Subway.[360] The attack on "Big Food" did not occur in a vacuum, however. Much of it was merely a continual evolution of the environmental crusade against modern society in all its manifestations: Food was just a different way to combat "global warming" or "overpopulation." For example, David and Marcia Pimentel lent academic credibility to the war on meat by claiming that meat consumption and the use of fossil fuels were inexorably intertwined and that only a vegan diet could save the planet.[361] *Scientific American* signed on to the bogus global warming theories with its own alarmist article, "How Meat Contributes to Global Warming."[362] National Public Radio insisted, "If you want to reduce emissions, it's all about beef," and that men eating meat is a problem.[363] (It's always important to blame men in particular.) A British paper, *The Sun*, ran an article called "Fatties Cause Global Warming," claiming that the process of raising just one pound of beef required ten pounds of plant protein.[364] When "greenhouse gasses" were still considered a major threat, the London School of Hygiene and Tropical Medicine said in 2009 that "food production accounts for about one fifth of greenhouse gasses" and "moving about in a heavy body is like driving a gas guzzler."[365]

Leftist concerns started to merge with more populist issues such as family farming and the threat of "Big Ag." Raj Patel, in his intro to Timothy Wise's *Eating Tomorrow*, accused "industrial agriculture" of being "an engine for the exploitation of humans."[366] In 2024, then-Democratic presidential candidate Robert F. Kennedy Jr. gained considerable attention by his attacks on industrialized agriculture and when he joined the campaign of Trump, added to Trump's MAGA ("Make America Great Again") with a new slogan, MAHA ("Make America Healthy Again"). Legal cases involving the state of Pennsylvania's campaign against small farmers markets and home-grown milk products had proceeded through the legal system.

Approved leftist positions targeting obesity, however, soon ran up against other approved leftist positions, namely "body positivity." As early as 1967, *The Saturday Evening Post* ran an article called "More People Should be Fat." Two years later, the National Association to Advance Fat Acceptance was founded, which attempted to counter virtually *all* medical evidence that too much body fat was harmful in multifarious ways. Thus, the stage was set for a war between different leftist factions in America.

Increasingly, the overwhelming number of clinically fat people brought criticism of anyone who spoke truth to the power of obesity. Retail stores and advertisers soon saw the value in "plus-sized models" that (supposedly) looked more like fatter American women. (No one worried about marketing to fat men—clothing makers just labeled clothes XXL for "extra extra large.") But although slightly larger models and mannequins had started showing up in the 1970s, a much different shape arrived in the 2000s. A broad (no pun intended) "body positivity movement" began in earnest in the 2010s. As Jennifer Sey noted, the "mere mention of weight loss being healthy was 'fat phobic.' Mention of some food being 'bad' was 'fat phobic.' No food is bad unless it is poison!"[367] Social media site Instagram fed a debate about beauty standards.[368] Why should fat women not be viewed as beautiful? They were in the past. Feminists, especially, celebrated the new fatter female bodies.

That new wave of marketing to heavier women proved nettlesome. First, so-called plus-sized mannequins in stores looked *nothing* like most obese women. This was in contrast to the "normal-sized" models which, despite having perhaps larger breasts and slightly longer legs, nevertheless did not look dramatically different from the women they sought as customers. "Plus-sized" mannequins, on the other hand, looked like they were supermodels just slightly expanded proportionally. Images of real-life obese women and the "plus-sized" models defied the imagination. *Cosmopolitan*, one of the leading female-influencer magazines, ran no fewer than three covers showing grotesquely fat women with headlines such as "This is healthy!"[369] Victoria's Secret and Abercrombie & Fitch came under criticism for continuing to show thinner people. They responded with fat ads...then the brands began to slide. Some ad agencies could not even find "plus-sized" models who actually looked good in their clothes and took to using fat suits on skinny models.[370] "As a general rule," one observer wrote, "plus-size models are defined by the fashion industry as anyone larger than a size 6."[371] (For reference, in the hit movie *The Devil Wears Prada* [2006], "Andrea," the idealistic intern who shows up to work for "Miranda," an Anna Wintour substitute, is reviled by coworkers because she is a size 6. "Andrea" was played by Anne Hathaway, who is anything but fat.)

"The model industry is filled with fatphobia," lamented one writer.[372] However, even by 2025, the fact remained that few people of either sex saw exceptionally heavy people as attractive or healthy. Entertainer Lizzo, whose obesity was on full display with tiny costumes and bikinis, nevertheless went on a diet.[373] Even while insisting she did not want to be thin, she strongly implied that she knew obesity was unhealthy. Lizzo denied using the latest weight loss wonder, a diabetes drug called Ozempic. The sudden appearance of Ozempic led some to claim that "obesity is finally falling."[374] But specialists such as Dr. Husain doubted the data, noting that one of the cited causes—the prevalence of Ozempic—was too recent to have produced such changes, too expensive, and too confined to a narrow wealthy elite.[375]

At present, not only did the "fatophiles" run counter to what a majority of women—regardless of their personal size—knew to be healthy and even "normal," they also were now in conflict with the environmental movement that insisted on reducing food intake. There was no reconciling the two.

Nor was there reconciling the growing medical practice of telling kids it was okay to be obese any more than it was acceptable to tell them that they were "born in the wrong [sexual] body." Grave confusions about what was normal, biologically sound, and overall healthy had erupted. As of 2025, no sensible medical answers had appeared.

Increasing obesity as an issue was subsumed into another concern, namely additives in mass marketing food by agribusiness companies. By the 2020s, with the presidential candidacy of Robert F. Kennedy Jr. (whose Children's Health Network had tracked the rise in obesity), many Americans turned their attention to "Big Food." Large agribusiness conglomerates over the previous half century had produced much of the packaged and processed foods found in the US diet. It was no longer just the "fast food" of *Fast Food Nation* that concerned consumers, but the endless list of additives needed to preserve and/or flavor food. When individuals sought to escape the tyranny of the additives, such as when private farmers sold direct to customers, the Deep State of the regulatory agencies came crashing down, proclaiming farmers' products as "unsafe." Pennsylvania, for example, launched attacks on Amish farmers for selling directly to customers. The state brought a lawsuit against Amos Miller, an Amish farmer, for selling raw milk directly to customers.[376] Miller's attorney, Robert Barnes, with his 1776 Law Center, conducted a poll in which over 50 percent of respondents strongly agreed or somewhat agreed that Americans should be allowed to buy food directly from farmers without government permission.[377] Even allowing for the absence of an "if...then" polling structure, Barnes's poll revealed a significant subsection of Americans who wanted direct access to food without the heavy hand of the government.

Criticisms of "Big Food" as a source of obesity, of course, were a double-edged sword: If Taubes and Kennedy were right, the environmental lobby was poised to jump in with totalitarian-level controls on all food as a threat to the environment. Ever eager to force all people in the world to submit to ridiculous and antihuman regulations, the World Economic Forum in 2021 began a campaign to convince people to eat insects.[378] World Economic Forum propaganda touted "maggots on the menu" and "insect farming." America's challenge for the remainder of the twenty-first century is to revive the family farm, reduce regulations on farm-to-consumer, dramatically cut additives, and stave off any attempts by international bodies to force Americans to eat like Third World countries. It most definitely was not to turn Americans into the human equivalent of anteaters.

BIRTH, DEATH, AND DNA

One result of the increasing spread of depression, bulimia, anorexia, and obesity was an overall discontent that caused people—mostly younger people—to question their own DNA. People lacking hope see little value in preparing today for a life in the future. Adding to the fears begun in the Cold War of nuclear warfare, or in the 1970s of overpopulation, the prosperity of the latter half of the twentieth century instilled a level of selfishness into family planning. Simply put, people began marrying later, having children later, and having fewer babies overall.

Many of the shadows cast over America in that regard were common to the rest of the world. Globally, a "birth dearth" had been underway for decades. A combination of birth control measures, rising affluence, and a nearly global resistance to large families with official national policies, such as China's "one-child" policy, had caused a steady decline in birth rates. In the West, especially in the US, the women's movement had spearheaded an effort to downplay (or even demonize) childbearing, leading the US birth rate to hit a record low in 2019. Experts warned that America faced a "demographic time bomb" that stood to be fast-tracked by the Covid pandemic.[379] States such as California by 2021 had already started to face demographic calamity with a birth rate barely half of what it was in 2000.[380]

A growing prevalence of singledom among America's rising generation of women became "the most potent political force in America," "a new republic, a new category of citizen," and, the author hoped a powerful new political force[iv,381] By 2023, only 45 percent of young adult women expressed a desire to be mothers. Perhaps surprisingly, over half of men wanted families, challenging the old notion that women had the "long horizons."[382] Many blamed the decline in families on the high cost of raising children, but even in Europe, with generous subsidies for child-rearing, fertility continued to decline. One factor affecting those attitudes was that the traditional age gap between married men and women declined to the point that, by 2024, over half had spouses who were two years younger or less.[383]

Regardless of the cause, the political fact could not be denied: Unmarried women tended to vote far to the left of the electorate and on average proved far more enamored of big government, which became a

---

iv The term "women" here always refers to biological women, not people who "felt" like a different sex.

surrogate husband. At the same time, the surging "women's rights" and homosexual movement de facto worked against traditional families. By 2023, 30 percent of women under twenty-five considered themselves lesbians (contrasted with only 5 percent of women over sixty years old).[384] This was a "sign of a deeply decadent culture…a culture that lacks the wherewithal to survive."[385] Not only were traditional, normal families under attack, but the decreasing number of stable family models also made it more difficult for young people to see what they were like.

One aspect reinforcing the decline since the 1980s came from the environmental movement. While certainly some adherents sincerely believed that the planet was in danger from human industrialization, no small number of the "green" supporters were, at heart, anti-capitalists and often pure-blood Marxists. The term for them, "watermelons" (green on the outside but red on the inside), was common. Ever since Paul Ehrlich's much-discredited *The Population Bomb* (1968), with his hysterical shrieking about the oceans drying up and mass worldwide starvation, a growing number of people had been brainwashed into believing that the world was "overpopulated."

In 2021, the population growth was the smallest in a half century, with sixty-one countries expecting declines by 2050. Virtually all of Europe saw shrinking populations since the 1970s; many, such as Russia and Spain, had near-catastrophic population collapses. This constituted a long-term demographic stagnation not "seen since the Middle Ages." That did not stop anti-populationists from arguing that "having a child…is seven times worse for the climate" than almost anything else a family could do.[386]

Nevertheless, a growing share of the American public—whether or not they actually bought into Ehrlich's "gloomsday" pronouncements—came to see larger families as a drain on their resources and lifestyle. Declining populations do not merely reflect abstract numbers: Contained within the overall declines is the threat of a rapidly aging planet, especially among the wealthiest nations such as the US, which have been the bedrock of foreign aid and development support for half a century.

At home, America's population growth was "slowing to a crawl," according to the Federal Reserve Bank of St. Louis, barely reaching six hundred thousand net births after factoring for immigration.[387] By 2023, that had already contributed to a massive public pension crisis in which American state and local pensions faced a shortfall of over $4 trillion.[388] Predictably, the worst disasters faced the most Democratic states, California and Illinois, where liabilities were at a combined $1.35 trillion in 2019. ("America's Public Pension System.") An equally dangerous trend, though, came from the reality that younger people generate more business startups and are generally responsible for more innovation within the economy.[389] As of this writing, no one was certain how much the peak in the "youth bulge" of the developing world would affect labor markets, but all agreed it was not favorable. What had become obvious was the "post-familialism" of the world's core cities, including America's largest—New York, Los Angeles, Boston, and San Francisco, among others. They had exceptionally low levels of families (let alone "traditional families") living in them, leaving them with the sobriquet, "the childless city."[390] Such cities might be "hip" or "entertaining" but became playgrounds of the rich and traps for the poor when devoid of families.

That dramatically affected school systems, which saw enrollments plummet even before Covid. The only places the population increased among those fourteen years old and under was in smaller areas with under 250,000 residents. And, as suggested by polling, residents in those larger urban areas who had families considered leaving.

In fact, since the 1960s—the era of "free love"—so-called self-expressive marriage replaced dominant family culture: Child-rearing and childbearing gave way to adult fulfillment.[391] Women, especially, delayed marriage for a career, only to find themselves biologically unable to have children (or to face a higher health risk to bear children). The media and especially Hollywood worked overtime to make nuclear families obsolete. At every turn, homosexual "marriages" were portrayed as normal and even typical.

Attempting to elevate women, colleges and universities endeavored to admit and recruit women more than men. As late as the 1970s, men had outnumbered women in college. But by 2017, the ratios shifted in favor of women, who comprised 56 percent of university students. That trend continued to grow.[392] Men increasingly saw no benefit to college, forcing even traditionally women's schools to institute men's sports programs to attract more men. Men, rightly, felt attacked and discriminated against in many classes. Women dominated already female-heavy majors such as English or sociology so much so that few men could be found in such programs. "Equal opportunity" and "equity" also entered businesses where human resources and marketing departments were dominated by women. Title IX regulations forced universities to spend exorbitant amounts on sparsely attended women's sports, even as male-dominated football and basketball paid many of the schools' bills. A new "war against men," focusing on the emasculation of Western men, was waged.[393]

By 2023, women dominated higher education. In the Ivy League, fully 75 percent of the presidents were female, and half the twenty universities rated the highest by *Forbes* magazine had a woman president, including MIT, Harvard, and Columbia. This was only a tiny component of the overall campus feminization, however: Women made up two-thirds of all college administrators that pushed the "diversity ideology."[394] Women earned 58 percent of all BAs awarded, as well as 60 percent of master's degrees and 54 percent of PhDs. Female dominance came with an ideology that said that any challenge to them, any ideas they disagreed with, or any problem they encountered was the result of an environment of fear and hate and the "persistent inequalities and discrimination, whether based on race, ethnicity, religion, sexual orientation, gender identity, ability, or other factors."[395] It was interesting that a college official would cite ability in the list of "inequalities" to be overcome.

Accompanying the position that women on campus, even in strong majorities, were discriminated against or were somehow physically unsafe, a propaganda campaign centered on notions of "offensive" ideas or "making people uncomfortable" spread rapidly, to the point that a 2018 survey of over four thousand college students found that 59 percent of women thought that promoting an "inclusive" society was more important than protecting free speech. At Barnard and Wellesley, traditionally women's schools, some 40 percent supported the use of violence against those espousing ideas they didn't like.[396]

Men simply did not sit still and wait to be abused. To some degree, they dropped out of the sexual mating and dating game altogether. A powerful countermovement started based on the writings of Rollo Tomassi (real name George Miller) in his book, *The Rational Male*.[397] In truth, Tomassi spiced up the more straightforward warnings of George Gilder in his 1986 book, *Men and Marriage*. (The original title, which the publisher recast, was *Sexual Suicide* [1975].)[398] Tomassi developed a theory of male behavior based on "hypergamy" that he claimed dominated the modern world. It constituted a strategy of women dating or marrying someone of a higher social status or economic standing in order to obtain good genes for children and security and survival benefits. An ideal man, in that theory, was someone who combined all the strong physical traits with long-term nurturing and security likelihood. Of course, in real life, Tomassi argued, the young and fit who embodied the former seldom (because of the reality that wealth came through time and experience) had little of the latter. And older, less attractive, less fit men may, on average, have had much more money and status. For that reason, he claimed, a small sliver of wealthy men at the top and a handful of sexy, handsome "Chads" (as he called them) at the bottom scooped up the majority of attractive women.

Tomassi, in his extremely successful YouTube lectures (with a following of two hundred thousand in what he called the "manosphere"), captured the attention of young men everywhere, particularly those not considered the "Chads." Though himself married, he outlined a negative view of women where he counseled men to engage in "plate spinning," namely dating multiple women at once.

No one could doubt that in an age where the institutions and the "system" were structurally aligning against average or unattractive men, by showing the only other path to attracting women, namely economic and class/cultural success, *The Rational Male* struck a huge chord. Men could (and many young men did) see themselves as displaced by women in education (true), corporations (through DEI [diversity, equity, and inclusion] hiring, also true), and even government. For a time, the military remained a bastion of resistance to non–merit-based advancement, but even that disappeared in the Obama and Biden administrations. Thus, for however extreme or misguided many found Tomassi's proscriptions, no one could deny that he spoke to millions of young American men.

One need to look no further than Morgan Stanley's touting of the "SHEconomy," where the number of female executives had increased, with women gaining ground in wage differentials and consumer power.[399] While motherhood wasn't overtly criticized, it was frequently noted how mothers who stay home usually don't earn as much as women in the workforce. By 2015, however, the male-to-female ratio of labor force participation flattened, possibly because of growing testimonies of disappointed women who missed out on having children in favor of a career. The old saw, "you can have it all" (meaning both a full-time job and children—at least children who weren't psychotic) was, in fact, a myth.

A component and major driver of the war against men was the rapid acceleration of the homosexual or "gay" movement, which by the early part of the twentieth century had been normalized through corporate advertising, product placement, entertainment, and the efforts of the Democratic Party to make the subgroup a political appendage. In the 2015 *Obergefell v. Hodges*, the Reagan-appointed Justice Anthony Kennedy joined the four liberals on the Supreme Court—Stephen Breyer, Ruth Ginsburg, Elena Kagan, and Sonia Sotomayor—to rule that same-sex couples were entitled to marry by both the due process clause and the equal protection clause of the US Constitution.[400] Under the ruling, all fifty states would be required to recognize such marriages. Opponents countered that marriage was not a purely "civil rights" matter but a fundamentally different institution existing outside the authority of government.[401]

By then, the homosexual activist movement had already moved to the next issue, that of cross-dressing and transsexualism whereby biological makes would, through surgery and chemical treatments, "become" women and women, through mastectomies and male hormones, would "become" men. (Of course, no amount of surgery or chemicals could change either their blood or their DNA.) This cultural upheaval largely started in 2016 when the Education Department under Obama threatened to cut off federal funding for any K-12 schools that did not allow students "identifying" as another sex to use the bathroom reserved for the opposite sex.[402] Just a decade earlier, such notions not only would have been considered ridiculous but also perverted. Certainly, none would ever receive actual government support.

After Obama's Justice Department threatened to sue the state of North Carolina for a law requiring people to use their bathrooms corresponding to the sex on their birth certificates, a host of virtue-signaling organizations, from the National Basketball Association to companies such as PayPal, threatened boycotts—over an issue that just five years earlier they never would have touched! People in growing numbers disregarded their own biology and "felt" like they were of a different sex; the liberal culture then took over the job of promoting and propagandizing that practice. Individuals no longer merely "cross-dressed" or role-played, but at alarming rates began undergoing radical surgeries (mastectomies for women wishing to look like men, removal of male genitals for men seeking to "become" women). By 2018, such surgeries were on the rise, with thirty-seven thousand such operations identified in a single study alone. The number of such transsexual surgeries rose threefold from 2012 to 2014.[403]

One researcher found that large numbers of teens, especially girls, had their understanding of their sexual identity influenced by peer groups, even though they displayed no other typical patterns of abnormal identity issues.[404] College students viewing themselves as a different sex shot up between 2009 and 2016, a twelve-fold increase. The "rush to destigmatize, support, and affirm those with gender dysphoria and gender identity issues, combined with social media, has created incentives to mimic these issues," wrote one analyst.[405]

In particular, differences in social styles and sensitivities to relationship inequalities made girls more susceptible to such "incentives." In other words, the "trans" explosion was, to a large degree, the creature of social media. Increasingly, however, research showed that the numbers of those regretting their (more or less permanent) surgeries were growing.[406] American teens were facing peer pressure to become a different sex than what they were born, often with devastating results—but in the culture of the twenty-first century, any criticism of such pressure was attacked as "homophobic." Activists infiltrated the institutions, from boardrooms to sports leagues, seizing control often through the human resources departments.

In this, the US had started to diverge in its attitudes about sex change from much of the world. Needless to say, no Muslim nations would even consider such nonsense. Then, in 2020, the National Health Service in Great Britain commissioned the "Cass Review" to examine the increase in patients questioning their sex. The final bombshell review, published in April 2024, shocked the ideological left and the entire homosexual agenda, finding that, to date, the studies that had supposedly supported the entire trans agenda were of "poor quality," meaning that "there is not a reliable evidence base upon which to make clinical decisions" for children and challenging the rationale for early puberty suppression. The study found a complete lack of certainty that children or younger people would even have a so-called trans identity after a few years. Essentially, the study recommended no program of sex change should be applied to anyone under sixteen.[407]

A month later, Peru labeled anyone claiming to be transsexual as having "mental health problems."[408] Uganda likewise enacted tough anti-trans laws in May of 2024. Virtually all of Northern and Eastern Africa labeled homosexuality a crime punishable by prison or a death penalty, with more than half of Africa's countries making it illegal, as did twenty Asian nations. China and Russia both either had no recognition of same-sex couples or had prison sentences. Only Western-influenced nations (such as South Africa) trended in the opposite direction. If there was a "direction" of history, the US was probably on the wrong side of it with this issue.

"WOKEISM"

Feminism and homosexuality, with their victim worldview, fueled another movement by the second decade of the twenty-first century. Broadly speaking, the new term for what had appeared, "woke," infested virtually all of corporate America, culture, and even corporations.[409] Originally intended as "aware" (i.e., you are "woke" if you understood that racism existed), some have defined it as a collection of so-called social justice movements—*all* human mass movements see themselves as "social justice," including the Nazis—or attitudes or customs that emphasized the presumed marginalization of certain groups that required deep reordering of all facets of society.[410] To an extent, the abolitionist movement, Prohibition, and the "flower power" movement of the 1960s were earlier iterations of "woke" movements, except that none of them sought to alter human DNA or reality, only certain practices and behaviors. Moreover, ever since the Slave Power days of the South, no one had argued that merely making an argument against an idea should be deemed illegal. (The slaveholders did not get too far with that notion.) Theodore Kupfer offered the following definition of "woke": "Wokeness, most observers would agree, can be defined as the progressive worldview that views all racial and sexual disparities as proof of discrimination, and rejects liberal procedural traditions in favor of a totalizing politics that seeks to dismantle those disparities and silence dissenters."[411]

Addressing what woke liberals saw as deeply embedded racial and sex discrimination, the new "wokesters" had a weapon no other group in history had: the technology of social media to enforce their views and denounce, or "cancel," opponents. That meant that anyone who disagreed with them could be forced out of jobs, social circles, accessibility to insurance or banking, or, in the case of the Covid vaccine, even food. Thus, attempts to portray the deeply poisonous "woke" movement with earlier American Protestant reform efforts erred: Those groups never sought to change who humans *were* (except by salvation), but rather what they did.[412]

Such pseudo-religious explanations fail (as they always do) by leaving open the question, "If you're so brilliant as to escape these prejudices, why do you think other people aren't as well? Or that they don't exist in the first place?" Perhaps a more persuasive explanation of why "woke" took over, especially at the corporate level, was that activism on social issues was a type of bribe or insurance against the "peasants with pitchforks"—that if enough racial/sexual/cultural sops were distributed to the activists, the CEOs would be immunized against attacks on their own personal positions and fortunes.

In the 1990s, no activist had been better at "shaking down" corporate America than Jesse Jackson, whose Operation PUSH extorted huge sums from companies under the guise of "donations" in return for an unspoken promise by Jackson to keep the companies from boycotts. Since Jackson's time, more corporate boardrooms began to fall from internal pressure rather than outside threats. A new mantra, "diversity, equity, and inclusion" (DEI), had originated in colleges and found its way into human resources divisions and marketing. Ads had to represent "diverse" groups of people. Personnel had to be "inclusive," whether those included were competent or not. (The National Basketball Association, a totally woke institution, nevertheless never saw the hypocrisy that well over 90 percent of its players were black and that the number of Asians could be counted on one hand missing two fingers.) DEI quietly took over many major American companies in a short time, some (Nike) more naturally opened to the leftist concepts than others. DEI's reach, however, Many opine that woke corporations merely copied business peers, even if the arguments underlying the wokeness (that, for example, "diversity" would improve the bottom line) were flat-out wrong. As of the early part of the twenty-first century, explaining the malignant *effects* of "wokeism" remained far easier than finding its major causes and means of transmission.[413]

New woke gatekeepers attempted to control and manipulate information. Wokeness quickly metastasized into not only policing language and dictating behavior but into thought and attitude control straight out of Mao Zedong's reeducation camps. Marketing demanded images of homosexuals. Black people and other minorities had to have representation—to the point that by the early 2020s, a sample of ads on mainstream television networks and cable would be completely devoid of white men, particularly masculine white men. (Indeed, if aliens watched US ads from this period, they would conclude that the American population was 85 percent black, 95 percent female, 30 percent homosexual, and that the only white men who existed were doddering grandpas or inept, incompetent, soft, feminine "soy boys.") With the homosexual movement, it was not sufficient to be "tolerant." One had to approve and participate in the overall practices by sanctioning homosexual marriage or by acceding to banning anti-sodomite sermons in churches.

Sex roles and sexual confusion were only two aspects of "wokeism." Whether it was the leading or trailing edge of the "woke" revolution will require far more study. It was perhaps the only movement that threatened to fracture liberal coalition for it posed a direct and significant threat to women's gains since the 1970s. Homosexuals were hounded if they did not accept surgical transsexuals, and most notably, so-called transgender athletes (almost always men competing in women's events) upended female sports. Born a male, Will Thomas, now called Lia Thomas, changed his sex surgically and competed in women's swimming events from 2017 to 2020, winning several by large margins. According to the *International Journal of Environmental Research and Public Health* in 2022,

> Without the sex division, females would have little chance of winning because males are faster, stronger, and have greater endurance capacity. Male physiology underpins their better athletic performance including increased muscle mass and strength, stronger bones, different skeletal structure, better adapted cardiorespiratory systems, and early developmental effects on brain networks that wires males to be inherently more competitive and aggressive.... Male physiology cannot be reformatted by estrogen therapy in transwoman athletes because testosterone has driven permanent effects through early life exposure.[414]

At one point, the top female tennis player in the world could not compete with any of the top one hundred male players. Men competing in women's events in an education setting threatened to end Title IX protections entirely.

Overall, the trends embodied an assault on masculinity—not just in the US but worldwide. The problem grew so serious that even Communist China found it necessary to teach masculinity to boys.[415] American schools increasingly sought to allow children to "change their gender" while at school without parents' knowledge. Gender ideologues came to see parents and families as a major threat to transgenderism and sought to keep curricula and school events secret from parents.[416] Of course, activists issued calls to "abolish the family."[417]

At its peak, wokeism was predicted by some to be a major American export. Tyler Cowen wrote that "wokeism is an idea that can be adapted to virtually every country: Identify a major form of oppression in a given region or nation, argue that people should be more sensitive to it, add some rhetorical flourishes, purge some wrongdoers (and a few innocents) and voila—you have created another woke movement."[418]

Thankfully, to a large degree by 2024, "wokeism" had begun to fade as corporations backed off. As Anheuser-Busch learned with its campaign for Bud Light beer featuring a man (Dylan Mulvaney) who presented himself as a woman, the public had little tolerance for mainstreaming such messages. Bud Light, the market leader, lost over $1 billion in sales.[419] Anheuser-Busch tried to retreat but without success. State Farm insurance, which had announced a program to distribute homosexual/transsexual materials to teachers, community centers, and libraries, dropped the initiative like a hot potato when a whistleblower revealed it to the public. State Farm abandoned the program immediately.[420] Other companies followed suit. ExxonMobil, which had originally planned to allow a so-called gay rights flag to be flown outside its headquarters, backed off and issued new "guidance."[421]

In entertainment, where wokeness had made major inroads, companies such as Netflix reversed course. Netflix canceled several "justice-oriented projects" and laid off 150 employees associated with that kind of content.[422]

Another indicator that woke had run its course came in the fact that research about race, diversity, and "wokeism" declined. For example, one study found that "prejudice-denoting terms" had fallen, while cable news discourse focusing on "diversity," "sexism," and other work terms had also declined.[423] Climate change doomerism also seemed to peak around 2021. And, as one author put it, by 2023, the "Great Awokening" of higher ed may have started to wind down as well.[424]

A political rebellion to wokeness appeared perhaps first in Virginia, in 2021, where Republican Glenn Youngkin—the underdog—shocked pundits by winning largely on an anti-woke position of ending transexual policies in schools and opposing "critical race theory." Tyler Cowen, who had just a year earlier predicted that wokeism would spread around the world, admitted that the ideology was on the rocks.[425]

To no small degree, "wokeism" also incorporated attitudes about Covid, or, as it was sometimes called, the "China Virus." Wearing a mask became a social symbol of compliance and a statement that the government's "guidance" deserved respect. When it came to the lockdowns, however, the woke movement took the most extreme positions that all schools and public places needed to be closed. With schools, those closures (thanks to teachers' unions) took on near-immortality. Woke lockdown ideology came to a shocking end in San Francisco where a school board election in February 2022 resulted in three members recalled by a margin of more than 70 percent: "Voters were upset that the school board spent time trying to rename some schools in a more politically correct manner, rather than focusing on reopening all the schools."[428]

AMERICA DUMBED DOWN

Education itself constituted a problem not only because of wokeism but also because of rising crime and violence in public schools. The introduction of radical racism in the

SIDEBAR: "Critical Race Theory" vs. the "Four Pillars of American Exceptionalism"

In the early parts of the twenty-first century, the term "American exceptionalism" came into broad use. Radio host Limbaugh used it frequently, though virtually no one explained what it was other than that the US had a government that was (in theory) run by the people. Otherwise, "American exceptionalism," which Obama took time to discredit when he gave a speech to the North Atlantic Treaty Organization in April 2009, was eschewed by the elites and the ruling class. In his speech, Obama said, "I believe in American exceptionalism, just as I suspect that the Brits believe in British exceptionalism and the Greeks believe in Greek exceptionalism"[426] Although he went on to try to play down the comments, the very word "exceptional" means "different from anything else." The fact that large numbers of Americans believed in American exceptionalism became a problem for the left.

To counter it, the left launched the "1619 Project," beginning with a special issue of *The New York Times Magazine*, in which essays argued that since the *founding* of America stemmed from the Jamestown colony and because slavery was introduced in Virginia in 1620, there could be no such thing as American exceptionalism because all of US history was tainted by slavery. Entire curricula were devised and spread to American school systems with this flawed and evil premise.

In fact, while "America" may have been founded at Jamestown

in 1607, American exceptionalism *was not.* In our recent editions of *A Patriot's History of the United States,* Mike Allen and I (with help from Dave Dougherty in our work on *A Patriot's History of the Modern World*) established the "Four Pillars of American Exceptionalism." The first two—the most critical—were missing from Jamestown. All four were present in Plymouth. Those pillars are the following:

1) A Christian, mostly Protestant religious tradition, whose "bottom-up" congregational church government was seen nowhere else in the world.
2) A bottom-up government of the people in which the Pilgrims believed God had put the law in their hearts and minds (Ezekiel 11:19, 36:26; Jeremiah 31:33; Hebrews 8:10). Again, no nation on Earth had ever had a bottom-up government, let alone one combined with a Protestant, bottom-up religion.
3) Private property with written titles and deeds (much of Africa still lacks the latter component).
4) A free market economy (which began in Plymouth with the creation of the mill in 1630).

The Jamestown colonists were *Anglicans* to the extent that they were religious at all, and accepted top-down religious government; their colony was governed not by them, but from England with appointees

form of "critical race theory" and the "1619 Project," not to mention the introduction (as noted above) of homosexual and other sexual-themed concepts as young as first or second grade, contributed to the education crisis. In the name of equity and removing distinctions, schools across the nation had already eliminated such traditional celebrations as naming a valedictorian, honors classes, or handing out "participation trophies" so that no one "loses."

Accordingly, achievement itself came under assault. Many major universities announced they would no longer use standardized tests such as the ACT or SAT test to determine qualifications for admissions. Such anti-education and anti-knowledge practices ensured an increasingly poorly educated citizenry. In Illinois, a report showed that not a single student was proficient in either math or reading at sixty different schools. [429] New York had to lower its math and English proficiency because of terrible test results, rather than improve the proficiency.[430]

Yet despite over fifty years of education "reform," by 2023, the gap between the poorest performers and the best had not closed at all.

A so-called opportunity gap (the relationship between socioeconomic status and achievement) failed to move. As one group of writers glumly reported, "Interventions thus far have been unable to dent the relationship between socioeconomic status and achievement."[431] Critics such as Charles Murray have claimed that many of these differences stemmed from IQ, which could not be made up with various social programs.[432] While many challenge Murray's findings, the programs they have enacted seem to confirm them. (And, in passing, new research has shown that the strongest predictor of authoritarianism was low verbal IQ.)[433]

And DEI, in one form or another, wormed its way into education, particularly with the movement to end testing. Standardized tests had, as Murray showed, long been a target of the left, who saw such measures as inherently racist and unequal. A Brookings article in 2020 insisted "Sat Math Scores Mirror and Maintain Racial Inequality," while "Education Advocates Say the Best Way to Address Racial Bias in Standardized Testing is to Eliminate the Tests Completely" echoed the Brookings's position.[434] In the meantime, widespread use of altering grading standards swept the nation. Maryland's Office of Inspector General for Education reported that more than twelve thousand failing grades in the Baltimore public school system were changed to passing grades in a five-year period.[435] (A subsequent "audit" challenged the results, yet the city reviewed and updated its grading policy nonetheless.)[436] Not one student from Ohio's LeBron James "I Promise Schools" passed the state's math proficiency test since 2019.[437] Western New York reported that students in only nineteen of ninety-nine school districts could read at grade level; statewide barely half could read or do math at grade level; and in New York City, even after a new phonics-based program was rolled out, not even 50 percent of students could achieve grade-level reading.[438]

from the king. And Plymouth did not have a single slave.

When the "pillars" are placed against the "1619 Project," the latter falls apart. While a great adventure, the founding of Virginia did not entail the establishment of American exceptionalism.[427]

A similar story came from Chicago, where only one in six Chicago third graders could read at level.[439]

And it was not just a reluctance to test but to even make an effort to ensure students attended school. In Minnesota, for example, chronic absenteeism nearly doubled between 2019 and 2022, and Minnesota stood out as one of the *better* states for attendance. Matters looked far worse in "the third of districts with the lowest achievement and also the third of districts with the highest rates of poverty [where] chronic absenteeism…[rose to] 37 percent" in that same period.[440] As if to underscore the real problem, such chronic absenteeism was not viewed as a major concern, either for the general population or parents—of which only 5 percent of *each group found it a problem or concern!*[441]

Predictably, much of the criticism was directed at grading, not at failing instruction. Researchers insisted there were deficiencies in traditional grading.[442] California school districts considered eliminating D and F grades as a means to boost students' chances of getting into state colleges.[443] Others moved to pass/fail instead of letter grades.[444] Regardless of the variation, the underlying premise was clear: Schools could no longer teach students in a way that they could reflect achievement as measured by certain standards reflected in the grades and therefore, abolished standards.

The point here is not to debate the usefulness of grade standards that merely had helped make the US the most educated and powerful nation on Earth for much of the time since 1900, but to note that it is just one additional area of culture rot that has contributed to a dégringolade of shocking rapidity. Just forty years ago, the US embarked on a "Morning in America" that saw unemployment fall, military power rise, international respect soar, and America's economy be without parallel.[445]

Academia's problems involved far more than a decline in standards, however. Woke played a key role, not just in manipulating minds and inflaming hatred and distrust but in blasting costs through the atmosphere. Every woke or DEI program needed administrators, to the point that college administrations grew faster than waistlines at an obesity convention. At the University of California, Berkeley, for example, there was *one administrator for every four undergraduates.*[446] Those attended some thirty different DEI programs. (At my own university, a private Midwestern Catholic school, there was one provost and one dean for liberal arts when I was hired in 1985. When I retired in 2016, there were three provosts and five deans—but the student enrollment hadn't increased by more than one thousand in that time.) DEI constituted a petri dish for growing administrators: the more DEI programs, the more $100,000+ salaried administrators. Hence, spreading and promoting DEI and woke constituted job security and growth for the managerial class in universities, while doing nothing for students. It was only when, under Trump in his second term, Elon Musk's Department of Government Efficiency discovered billions of dollars in "aid" going to various colleges through needless and often realistic grants.

As DEI wormed its way into the university systems, America's top knowledge generators devolved into little more than "victimist" propaganda. Egregious violations of basic common sense—not to mention academic rigor and ethical behavior—swept the universities. One college, Oberlin in Ohio, managed not just one, but two major scandals in the course of a few years. In 2016, a student tried to shoplift wine from a local bakery in town. The student and two other black students assaulted a staff member at Gibson's Bakery…but the college's students protested the *bakery*! Gibson's sued the college and Dean Meredith Raimondo for supporting the protests and for defaming the owners and employees as racist. The bakery won its suit in 2019 and was awarded $44 million in damages, which after appeals and adjustments, resulted in the school paying the bakery $36.59 million.[447] Then, in 2007, Oberlin hired a radical Iranian Muslim named Mohammad Mahallati, who had strong ties to the violent ruling elites in Tehran, Iran. Families of those murdered by the mullahs in Iran challenged his appointment, but Mahallati brushed it off, with the administration supporting him. Over the years, he had defended Ayatollah Ruhollah Khomeini's 1989 fatwa to murder novelist Salman Rushdie and labeled the 1988 massacre of over five thousand prisoners as "battlefield casualties."[448] Nothing moved the Oberlin administration—even after proof was offered that Mahallati (contrary to his claims) had indeed been present in Tehran when the orders went out to murder more opposition families. Finally, allegations of sexual harassment—which apparently trumped justice for those killed—did him in, and he quietly was removed.[449]

Oberlin may have condensed more scandal into a shorter period than other universities, but at almost every major academic institution, previously unthinkable behaviors against Jewish students became commonplace after the terrorist organization Hamas used paragliding killers to drop into an Israeli music festival and gun down over one thousand helpless youths and families.[450] Campus-wide anti-Israel protests erupted when Israel *responded* to the attacks. Jewish students were threatened, attacked, and victimized at numerous major universities, particularly in the Ivy League. When called before Congress to explain why no action was taken against the Muslim pro-Hamas attackers, presidents and administrators offered no defense. Columbia did not expel a single student involved in the anti-Jewish attacks.[451] Congresswoman Virginia Foxx who headed the House Committee on Education and the Workforce, blasted the university, saying "By allowing its own disciplinary process to be thwarted by radical students and faculty, Columbia has waved the white flag in surrender while offering a get-out-of-jail-free card to those who participated in [the riots]."[452] Emerson College, which allowed pro-Palestinian protests, saw an immediate decline in enrollment that led to layoffs.[453]

It wasn't alone. In May 2023, Cazenovia College in upstate New York closed due to falling enrollments. Before it did so, administrators gave students a list of comparable schools in the region. One of those on the list, Wells College, shut down a year later. So did Notre Dame College (Ohio), Birmingham-Southern (Alabama), University of Saint Katherine (California), and Hodges University (Florida). Adam Kissel, an expert on education policy at The Heritage Foundation, summed it up: "Many people no longer trust colleges to educate students well."[454] Or at all.

Then there was cost. In 1969, the average cost of annual tuition at a public four-year institution was $558 in 2024 dollars; in 2022, it was $9,349.[455] For a private four-year school—such as those the elites populated—the cost was a stunning $35,000 per year. None of that included boarding, food, books, or supplies. (Food alone accounted for another $5,000 to $7,000 depending on whether the school was public or private.) Each year, both public and private schools had increased tuition, but some schools, such as the University of Pennsylvania, raised tuition by more than 4 percent in 2023. Predictably—and with increasing support from both parties—the answer was not to hold universities accountable but to simply throw additional federal subsidies at the problem. Yet for every dollar sent by the government to a college or university in the form of a federal student loan, schools *increased* tuition by another sixty-seven cents. In other words, far from *assisting* students in completing college, the student loans were driving tuition costs up further.[456]

Government doles to the universities grew exponentially after the CARES Act, or the China Virus relief act of 2020. Federal support for postsecondary education stood at just under $175 billion prior to Covid, but after CARES, it soared to $577 billion. That, of course, only constituted the "on budget" aid: Another $83.6 billion flowed to universities through "off-budget" and nonfederal (i.e., state) support. Consequently, between 2010 and 2022, the total cost of attending college (fees, room, food, etc.) increased over 48 percent, growing annually by more than 5 percent. Since 2000, the cost of attending college skyrocketed by more than 136 percent, and to hide accelerating tuition, schools increasingly hid expenses under "fees."

Politicians rushed to provide student loans to address the problem they had created with subsidies. And predictably, the government solution accomplished nothing except put young people further into debt. For example, after "uncapping" the amount grad students could borrow, more students in fact borrowed but fewer *enrolled or finished their degrees*.[457] Nor did it significantly change the enrollment of minorities. The only net effect the uncapped student loans had? They increased tuition to almost exactly the same amount as the borrowing increased.

In the 1980s, George Gilder wrote about "taxflation," or the notion that businesses will increase prices precisely enough to cover any increases in taxes of government fees. What had happened with the increased student lending was "lendflation," in that universities merely added the new ability to pay onto their existing tuition structures.

Biden attempted to wipe away all student loan debt, first trying to cancel over $400 billion in student loan debt in 2022. That move was invalidated by the Supreme Court in 2023, when, in *Biden v. Nebraska*, the court ruled that a national student loan forgiveness violated individual state's policies in their own lending institutions.[458] Most shockingly, perhaps, polling showed that the public disapproved of canceling the debt and even a higher percentage of those *with* debt disapproved.[459] Public rejection and court rebukes aside, Biden plodded forward to try to cancel yet another $1.2 billion in additional debt, that time for public service employees based on a program Congress created in 2007. Less than a day after the Biden administration unfurled a new debt relief program, another court put it on hold.

A major thorn in the flesh of those seeking to expand government aid for education came from the widespread, and growing, perception that more education paid off. For example, only 25 percent of adults said it was extremely or very important to have a four-year degree in order to obtain a well-paying job. A Pew Research Center survey found that only 22 percent thought the cost of college was worth it, and half said that it was less important to have a four-year degree than it was twenty years ago.[460]

For those, and many other reasons that had become obvious to Americans, college enrollment fell. Although journalists still attempted to blame Covid, the reality was that students did not find university education *or its credentials* to have value any longer. From 1985 to 2011, college enrollments steadily rose by about 2 percent a year, with enrollment peaking in 2010 at about eighteen million students. But since then, enrollments have fallen at 1.5 percent per year, then sank during the China Virus pandemic. Overall, by 2021, enrollment at four-year private colleges fell by over 50 percent, while enrollment at two-year public schools dropped by 38 percent.[461]

Still, however, many analysts ignored one of the leading concerns about people attending college: its bias and leftward dominance. One survey of reasons for enrollment decline included (naturally) the China Virus, but add rising tuition (true), the decline in the birth rate (true), and the dubious value of a college degree (which is not only true, but also encompasses the bias issue, as classes no longer teach actual subjects but propaganda). Increasingly, Gen Z especially (those born after 1997) were becoming the "toolbelt generation," ditching college for trade schools.[462] And with good reason: By June 2025, unemployment among young college grads outpaced the overall jobless rate in the United States.[463] Gallup found that confidence in higher education fell by over twenty points to just 36 percent by 2023.[464] In Utah, for example, enrollment in the state's eight technical colleges rose almost four times faster than at general public universities.[465]

Those pointing to the China Virus complained that the "federal COVID relief money is now gone" but that only avoids the question: Where would the colleges have been anyway?[466] They were still on a trajectory to lose students. Or, as the acting head of a small Minnesota college put it of the universities, "They were holding on, holding on," and were now required to face the music.[467] Internal pathologies of universities related almost as much to an engorged bureaucracy as they did to the poisoned coursework instituted by faculty. At MIT, for example, the staff grew by 1,200, while enrollment barely budged. Much of that stemmed from DEI hires, where MIT hired six new DEI *deans* in a single year.[468]

Covid accelerated many of the negative or disruptive trends in public education. City districts almost universally lost enrollment, while rural, town, and suburban districts grew. Municipal education systems shrunk in forty-one states by nearly 8 percent, even as rural, suburban, and town locales saw enrollments slightly rise during the pandemic.[469] Overall, all states saw significant enrollment declines from pre-panic levels: However, when school districts such as Fort Worth, Texas, added 107 new personnel, virtually none were teachers.[470] New positions included "family community liaisons," "customer service," or "social media management" positions." Similar hiring patterns were seen in Allentown, Pennsylvania, the District of Columbia Public Schools (easily one of the worst school districts in the nation) and Guilford County, North Carolina.

A central challenge to genuine, productive education came from the global shift from books to screens.[471] Newspapers, books, and periodical publishing had trended down since the 1990s, then fell more dramatically after internet publishing gained popularity. Even government employment flattened out. Whatever education American students had received, little of it met with employment needs. Indeed, shockingly, polls showed that college-educated Americans were less happy than high school–educated peers.[472] College grads, simply put, were overeducated for the jobs at hand. In part, that view reflected a fundamental misunderstanding of the nature of work.

An explosion among "soft" college majors (mostly the humanities) from 2000 to about 2015 exacerbated these downward trends and affected real productivity in America.[473] Peter Turchin, among others, postulated that this trend produced "elite overproduction"—that too many highly educated people armed with great expectations both about earnings and job satisfaction ran straight into market realities that did not need so many college-educated employees.[474] Here, the late twentieth century's revolutionary redefinition of work itself came into play. Whereas for most of human existence, work was necessary for survival, the arrival of extraordinary prosperity since World War II introduced new nostrums. American youth had been indoctrinated for decades to think that work should be "fun" or at least "meaningful," failing to understand that the origins of work in the Bible (not to mention the real world!) was the precise opposite of "play." Confronted with jobs in which they "didn't make a difference" or where they were not "making the world a better place," they grew dour and resentful.[475] Not surprisingly, the protests of 2020 disproportionately involved the college educated.

Such attitudes were nothing new, nor were responses to the situation novel: the French Revolution, the Russian Revolution, and many others originated not in "the masses" or the so-called working classes but in disaffected elites. (Miles Kimball and Robert Willis have theorized that "happiness" is the difference between what a person has and what he expected to have.)[476] It was a formula for unrest. No elite enclave was safe. Even in the legal profession, Americans were "over-lawyer-ized," and enrollment in law schools—which had grown for decades—finally fell.[477]

As the education boom that started in the 1950s wound down, the implications for American cities likewise faced new, somewhat dismal, realities. After all, many urban areas—such as Pittsburgh, Pennsylvania; Dayton, Ohio; and Boise, Idaho, to name a few—had repackaged themselves under the banner of "eds, meds, and feds," meaning colleges, hospitals, and federal government bastions (either military or bureaucratic). If higher education fell, or even declined substantially, would that trio stay viable?

One justification or appeal of urban areas, heralded by sociologist Jane Jacobs—who claimed higher densities created better communities—had already started collapsing. Researchers found that for every 10 percent drop in population density, the likelihood of someone talking to a neighbor *increased* by 10 percent, regardless of race, education, or marital status.[478] Certain "hip" cities such as Seattle, Manhattan, and Boston continued to attract younger and richer people capable of paying the skyrocketing housing costs. But more troubling was the decline of cities like Detroit, Cleveland, and Buffalo that maintained anti-family policies and paid the price.

Amid the exposure of wokeness within government education systems and the exodus from public schools came a movement to not only demand various school voucher programs but to expand them. In 2017, Arizona, for example, provided vouchers for any students—including homeschoolers—to attend any institution or to be schooled at home. It encompassed all 1.1 million Arizona students, and by 2022 over eight thousand had signed up. (Many in the homeschool movement still hesitated, thinking that any government program came with strings.) The vouchers gave recipients 90 percent of the amount that the state would have spent on the student, regardless of the status of the institution (i.e., public, charter, or private). Most vouchers amounted to about $7,000 per student, but some ran as high as $30,000 for students with special needs.[479] By 2024, eleven states had universal voucher laws, including Florida, South Carolina, and Iowa.[480]

Predictably, the teachers' unions threw a fit, seeing their funding go out the window. Leftist ProPublica said that the vouchers "blew a massive hole in Arizona's budget."[481] Even if that were true, it suggests that the public schools then were not doing nearly enough to educate students. It also was an interesting charge, given that liberals never were concerned about budgets when their own programs were massively over budget. Rating schools is always a questionable proposition, as the rating agencies have their own biased templates. Consider this oddity: The top five elementary schools in Arizona were all public schools, yet the elites all choose to send their kids to (presumably poorer performing) private schools.

CULTURAL LIGHT IN THE DARKNESS

America's first twenty-five years of the century were not without important cultural contributions. Though perhaps more than in previous eras, the candidates for inclusion in "most important" or "most influential" were more hotly debated.

In literature, J. D. Vance's *Hillbilly Elegy* provoked a sympathy for Appalachia's lower class, ravaged by unemployment and drug addiction. Unlike Barbara Eherenreich's *Nickel and Dimed* (2001), which (at least to many liberal-leaning students) seemed like a long whine, *Hillbilly Elegy* avoided the victimization of its subjects. Suzanne Collins's *The*

Hunger Games trilogy (2008, 2009, and 2010) offered a now-common dystopian landscape, but its female protagonist, Katniss Everdeen, in many ways resembled Dagny Taggart of *Atlas Shrugged.* Both *Hunger Games* and *Atlas Shrugged* were written by women, pitted a strong female against the government/establishment, and identified the class divisions of the "ruling class vs. the country class" who, in the case of Panem (*Hunger Games*'s country), featured an annual child sacrifice for the good of the many. Whether by design or not, *Hunger Games* both was a call to revolution against Washington, DC, (the "Capitol" in the books) and to preserve and celebrate life.

A depressing, postapocalyptic world became the backdrop for a number of influential books, none more than *The Road* (2006) by Cormac McCarthy, which follows a father and son journeying south for survival. A similar survivalist story, set in World War II, *All the Light We Cannot See* (2014) by Anthony Doerr, features a French girl hiding from the Nazis in Paris who encounters a young German soldier.

In areas of nonfiction, William Easterly's *The Tyranny of Experts* (2014) was built from his previous works *The Elusive Quest for Growth* (2001) and *The White Man's Burden* (2006) on the "dev biz" in developing nations. Far from the dystopian messages, Easterly argued that the best hope for escaping poverty worldwide is personal freedom. Closer to home, *American Default* (2018) by Sebastian Edwards detailed the epic battle over the national debt default in 1933 when Franklin Roosevelt depreciated the dollar relative to gold. A significant economics paper by Daron Acemoglu and James Robinson, "The Rise and Decline of General Laws of Capitalism" in the *Journal of Economic Perspectives* (2015), challenged the work of Thomas Piketty's *Capital in the 21st Century* (2013) that presented an "iron law of interest rates" that would lock in inequality inherent in capitalism. Acemoglu and Robinson found better ways to understand inequality, often stemming from government or unequal resources.

Indeed, inequality constituted a major source of literary debate in the early twenty-first century, epitomized by former Senator Phil

Gramm's book *The Myth of American Inequality* (2022) that found that the government measures on inequality (one might add, on all things) were deeply flawed. Income inequality, in fact, was lower in 2022 than in the past.

Supporting that overall notion, if obliquely, was Robert Gordon's masterful *The Rise and Fall of American Growth* (2016). Though Gordon was pessimistic about American growth in the more recent decades, ironically, he proved that statistical measurements of almost all previous eras—especially from 1880 to 1950—were significantly low. Growth measures such as the *quality* of products had virtually been ignored, with one of his best examples being the difference between candle power and electric lights in lighting a room. Not only was electricity cheaper, but it was also hundreds of times more luminescent.

The field of history saw excellent additions with James Oakes's *Freedom National*, a new look at the destruction of slavery that stemmed on the abolitionist movement realizing that "slavery" was not mentioned in the Constitution. Possibly one of the most influential history books of the twenty-first century, Victor Davis Hanson's 2001 *Carnage and Culture* placed Western culture at the center of explanations for the West's (and America's) military success over a two thousand–year period. Hanson offered, for the first time, a non-technological explanation for Western military superiority and badly damaged Jared Diamond's earlier *Guns, Germs, and Steel* (1997).

Indeed, even as the study of military history disappeared from major US college history offerings, several major superb new works on World War II arrived from naval historian Ian Toll. His trilogy on the US Navy in the Pacific in the World War II—*Pacific Crucible* (2011), *The Conquering Tide* (2015), and *Twilight of the Gods* (2020)—will prove difficult to surpass. At the same time, John McManus, in a comparable (though less engaging) trilogy, followed the US Army through the Pacific War in his works, *Fire and Fortitude* (2020), *Island Infernos* (2021), and *To the End of the Earth* (2023). Toll also wrote a prize-winning history of the US Navy in its formative years, *Six Frigates* (2008).

Likewise, whereas academic historians abandoned any topic not dominated by race/class/gender nonsense, some of our best biographies have come from non-academics such as Ron Chernow, whose *Alexander Hamilton* (2005) and *Titan: The Life of John D. Rockefeller* (1998) were masterful. Chernow was joined by another non-academic, David McCullough with his *John Adams* (2001), *The Wright Brothers* (2015), and his Revolutionary War history, *1776* (2005).

Hollywood, despite churning out completely forgettable pap and a fungal-like spread of increasingly woke "girl boss" films and television shows (like where a 120-pound woman beats up 250-pound Navy SEALs), nevertheless reached a few heights that may prove impossible to match. One of those, *The Lord of the Rings* trilogy—*The Fellowship of the Ring* (2001), *The Two Towers* (2002), and *The Return of the King* (2003), totaled more than eleven hours run time, with each film over three hours. Based on J. R. R. Tolkien's novel and directed by Peter Jackson, the breathtaking epic follows a hobbit (Frodo) and his hobbit companions who must return the Ring of Power to Mount Doom to destroy it before any human, elf, dwarf, or orc can claim its power. Frodo is not entirely immune to the ring's allure, but, more than anyone else, he is able to resist it for long periods of time. An intricately woven story sees an outlaw king (Strider/Aragorn) reclaim his crown through faithfulness and heroism; Frodo's best friend, Samwise Gamgee, remains loyal to the point of carrying him the final distance on his back; and two other hobbits who, lacking battle skills, nevertheless hold their own against the evil of the orcs and Saruman. Set against the phenomenal New Zealand scenery (and only deftly enhanced by computer-generated images), the trilogy attained artistic levels likely to never be rivaled.

A close second, from Walt Disney/Marvel Studios came an astounding series of twenty-three films about the comic book heroes, "The Avengers." Unlike *Lord of the Rings*, however, the Avenger series consisted of multiple stand-alone films, such as *Iron Man* (2008), *Thor* (2011), and *Captain America: The First Avenger* (2011), leading up to *The Avengers* movie in 2012, following a story arc revolving around six

"Infinity Stones." It then continues to weave its way through *Guardians of the Galaxy* (2014), *Ant-Man* (2015), *Doctor Strange* (2015), and the sequels to *Thor*, *Iron Man*, and *Captain America*. All those twenty-three storylines (!!) culminated in a 2018–2019 two-film saga, *Avengers: Infinity War* and *Avengers: Endgame*. Due to the incredibly interwoven stories built over a decade and the "power creep" of the villains as each got more unbeatable than the next, most critics maintained that *Avengers* in the broad sense could never be recreated. Or, in short, the first quarter of the twenty-first century produced two massive multi-episode films that likely cannot ever be equaled.

Although, on the whole, movies declined in popularity (in large part due to wokeism and unimaginative writing), new cable networks such as Netflix and HBO (Home Box Office) were turning out arguably some of the best drama and comedy in American entertainment history. Although the opening episode of *The Sopranos* (HBO) aired in 1999, the majority of the series ran in the twenty-first century, ending in 2007. Tony Soprano, a crime boss in *Godfather*-style played by James Gandolfini, showed surprising vulnerability to the point of seeing a therapist. (One can't imagine Al Pacino's *Scarface* visiting a shrink!) HBO's *The Wire*, a gritty five-season police drama, involved the use of wiretaps by Baltimore cops to take down drug dealer Avon Barksdale. A similar tone involving police corruption characterized *The Shield* (2002–2008) on FX, with its antihero Vic Mackey (Michael Chiklis). In *Breaking Bad* (2008–2013), a high school chemistry teacher named Walter White with inoperable cancer turns to methamphetamine manufacturing and sale to provide for his family. *Game of Thrones*, which ran from 2011–2019 on HBO, was a fantasy replete with dragons and ice zombies based on the bestseller by George R. R. Martin.

All of those series pushed the limits in on-screen nudity, profanity, and violence. Nevertheless, all featured extraordinary writing and gripping stories. While few characters were perfect, heroism, loyalty (or lack thereof), and justice remained central themes.

In the realm of comedy, *Friends*, which started in 1994 and ran through 2004, followed six friends as they dealt with daily, often insignificant or trivial problems. It resembled in its style the earlier hit *Seinfeld* (1989–98), which its star, Jerry Seinfeld, often admitted was a "show about nothing."

Wokeism poisoned virtually all film comedy by 2010. Prior to that, however, the Wayans brothers produced an all-time parody on race with their film *White Chicks* (2004), in which two black male undercover FBI agents don extensive costuming to the point of recoloring their skin to appear as two Hamptons debutantes. Their themes borrowed heavily from their 1996 underground hit, *Don't Be a Menace to South Central While Drinking Your Juice in the Hood.* Suffice it to say, such comedy—along with a classic such as *Blazing Saddles* (1974)—would not be permitted in modern-day woke Hollywood.

Culture did not completely drift into a wasteland in the twenty-first century. Finding diamonds in piles of woke dung, however, remained a daunting task.

CHAPTER 5

THE DESTROYER

Except for George Washington, perhaps no other president had entered the office with as much good will as Barack Hussein Obama. To black Americans, he offered fulfillment of Martin Luther King Jr.'s "dream"; to white Americans, he embodied the proof they desperately sought—and which they knew in their hearts to be true—that they were not racist. To Democrats, he was the antithesis of the hated Bush years, a (supposed) noninterventionist who had socially progressive views. To Republicans, he was the grudging apology for the failed Bush presidency. And to the country as a whole, he constituted living proof that, indeed, America had entered a new era of tolerance and openness.

In his presidential campaign, Obama had promised fundamental change and a week before his election he insisted, "We are five days away from fundamentally transforming the United States of America."[482] Americans have always been well meaning and generally unskeptical, and they took Obama's words as a positive sign: The "transformation" was for the better. Few could have guessed how it would work out. Indeed, reality was so shocking and Americans so blindly naive that even after four years of Obama's destruction, many voted for his reelection, essentially saying to themselves, "He really didn't mean it."

Often referred to on the right as a sort of "Manchurian candidate," there was some truth to the claim in that many, if not most, Americans had little idea who Obama really was or what he believed. And the media did its best to keep it that way.

Barack Hussein Obama had been born in 1961 to a radical and groomed by radical leftists all his adult life. His father, Barack Sr. a Kenyan, and his mother, Ann Dunham from Wichita, Kansas, met in Hawaii while students at the state university. Barack Jr.'s parents separated two years later and divorced in 1964, after which his father left Hawaii for Harvard before returning to Kenya to work in government service. Obama only saw his father one more time in 1971. Obama's mother, meanwhile, had married Lolo Soetoro, a surveyor from Indonesia, and the family moved to Jakarta. There, Barack was taught in the highly Islamized Indonesian schools. The family sent him back to Hawaii under the care of grandparents. After Obama graduated high school in Hawaii, he enrolled in Occidental College for two years, then transferred to Columbia University, where he majored in political science.

Oddly, however, no one seemed to remember him. Wayne Allyn Root, who was at Columbia in the political science/pre-law program at the same time as Obama recalled: "[I] never met him in my life, don't know anyone who ever met him. At the class reunion, out 20th reunion five years ago [2003]...who was asked to be the speaker of the class? Me. No one ever *heard* of Barack!"[483]

Root went on to say that the man who took class notes had never found anyone who ever met Obama. Because Obama's grades were sealed, Root offered $1 million in a challenge to prove that he, Root, had better grades than Obama. There were no takers.

Indeed, it was that way in all aspects of Obama's life. One reporter said of the Obama team, "They're terrified of people poking around Obama's life..."[484] Team Obama contacted old friends and Harvard classmates to request no one even speak to the press about Obama without permission.[485]

He attended Harvard Law School and was selected as an editor of the *Harvard Law Review*, then was elected president of the publication. It was that connection that gained him the book contract to *Dreams from My Father*. Offered a position at the University of Chicago Law School, he taught constitutional law for twelve years as a lecturer (not a professor). Obama married Michelle Robinson in 1992, and the couple had two daughters.

Although raised for many years in an Islamic society and by a mother who was, in his words, a secular humanist and a father who was a "confirmed atheist," Obama claimed to be a "Christian by choice" and that he believed in "the redemptive death and resurrection of Jesus Christ. I believe that faith gives me a path to be cleansed of sin and have eternal life."[486] In his 2006 "Call to Renewal" keynote address, Obama reaffirmed his own salvation story.[487]

Long before that, however, Obama had come under the teaching of Trinity United Church of Christ pastor Jeremiah Wright, a "sprawling, profane bear of a preacher."[488] Wright, a fervent racist and anti-American once described the terror attack on the Twin Towers by saying the "chickens are coming home to roost."[489] Wright's "incendiary sermons" contained a doctrine of "Black Liberation Theology [and was] arguably more Afrocentric and Marxist than Biblical in orientation."[490] Wright spoke of the "U.S. of KKK A" and insisted America was founded on racism, despite the fact that there wasn't a single slave (or black person, for that matter) at either Jamestown or Plymouth.[491] Slavery only came to the former in 1619 (hardly the "founding") and never came to Plymouth. Wright spoke favorably of Nation of Islam leader Louis Farrakhan, condemned Israel with regularity, praised Palestine, and said white people's greed ran the world. Obama, who would downplay his exposure to Wright, managed to relate this specific sermon in his book *Dreams from My Father*.[492] The politician Obama, however, insisted that he "hadn't heard" any "such incendiary language" and if he had, he "would have quit."[493]

Obama carried another religion with him, that of anti-imperialist hatred for the "colonial" powers. In his mind, that included at times the US. As much as Obama heard weekly excoriating grievance rhetoric from Wright, he also absorbed a hefty dose of communism from his mentor, Frank Marshall Davis, who literally was a "card carrying Communist" (card number 47544) and who was "the prototype of a dedicated CPUSA [Communist Party USA] foot soldier and loyal Soviet patriot."[494]

Understanding who Obama was suffered from the sharp polarization he relished and featured less-than-stellar biographies from either side. Although David Limbaugh's two books on Obama's administration hammered home the tone of his governments with unrelenting evidence, Limbaugh never delved into the full biography of the president.[495] David Garrow's *Rising Star* was a "work of dreamy literary fiction."[496] As *Tablet's* David Samuels noted of Garrow's book, it highlighted "a remarkable lack of curiosity on the part of mainstream reporters and institutions about a man who almost instantaneously was treated less like a politician and more like the idol of an inter-elite cult."[497] Yet in that, Garrow was hardly alone. Virtually all of the mainstream biographers and critics took the same approach.

Questions about Obama's birth certificate, which some conservatives claimed was fake, or his still-concealed records to college and universities merely fueled the claims that no one knew who he was. What did become clear was that, on one hand, he was extremely lazy, and, on the other hand, was phenomenally narcissistic. As he told talk show host Stephen Colbert in 2015, "If I can make an arrangement where I had a stand-in or a front man or front woman, and they had an earpiece in, and I was just in my basement in my sweats…I could sort of deliver the lines while someone was doing all the talking."[498] Ironically, Obama had described how a substantial minority in America saw him—as someone who delivered someone else's lines and carried out a shadowy figure's agenda.

THE FIRST BLACK PRESIDENT

Obama's candidacy and election were out of time in the sense that neither was expected. Most observers anticipated that New York Senator Hillary Clinton, former president Bill Clinton's wife, would be the nominee. She had moved to New York to establish residence to seek the Senate seat in 1999 held by four-term Senator Daniel Patrick Moynihan. To qualify as residents, the Clintons had purchased a house in Chappaqua, New York, in September 1999, just over a year out from the election. She only defeated Republican Congressman Rick Lazio by twelve points—hardly a landslide in a completely Democratic state. With eight years of being a senator under her belt, Clinton should have been unopposed in 2008. After two terms, it was conceded that the world would be ready for a black president in Obama.

However, two major developments changed that outlook. First, early in her senatorial career, Clinton was forced to back George W. Bush's invasion of Iraq. The evidence at the time was that Saddam Hussein indeed had weapons of mass destruction, the US public was still reeling from the attacks on the Twin Towers, and it was generally thought that a vote against the invasion would be political suicide. A second event occurred at the 2004 Democratic National Convention, where Illinois Senator Obama spoke. Interrupted thirty-three times by applause, when Obama finished his speech, "delegates leapt out of their seats, many in tears. [Many present spoke] about the moment with almost mystical reverence."[499] Television commentator Chris Matthews announced, "We've just seen the first black president."[500] Obama's rhetoric seemed unifying, claiming to worship an awesome God in the so-called blue states and to hint that farmers, single mothers, and military personnel were all on the same page. Whether he actually believed his own words or not, Democrats certainly saw them as the means to win an election.

Four years later, with Bush's approval nearing all-time lows, a host of Democrats, including Obama, lined up for the nomination, including Clinton, Al Gore, John Kerry, and Senator John Edwards. Obama shocked all of them when he won the Iowa caucus: Clinton only came in third! He followed it up with a strong performance in New Hampshire, where Clinton eked out a 2 percent victory. As the race tightened, both candidates landed blows: At one point, Obama reeled off ten straight victories. Only in June did Obama secure enough votes for the nomination. It had stunned Clinton, who saw herself as entitled to the position as Bill's wife and as what she had planned as a campaign to be the "first female president." She had been trumped by someone who could run as the "first black president."

Against Obama, the Republicans—as they had in 1996—nominated someone essentially because it was his turn: Arizona Senator John McCain. Having established good relationships with the media (critics joked that his designation was "R-Media"), McCain promoted the image of himself as a "maverick," a word constantly used to reference his criticism of Bush, the flawed (in his view) Iraq War strategy, and of the inability of Republicans to pass "immigration reform." The latter was a code term for amnesty and had been solidly defeated at the beginning of Bush's second term when radio host Rush Limbaugh, for the only time in his career, urged his army of listeners to flood DC's phone lines with their disapproval. It worked.

McCain, the son of US Admiral John McCain Jr., had (like his opponent) not been born in the continental US but on the Coco Solo Naval Air Station in Panama's Canal Zone. At the time, the zone was under US control and thus an American territory. Bounced around through twenty schools in his military family, McCain managed to enter the US Naval Academy. There, he fostered a reputation of disrespect for authority: "He collected demerits the way some people collect stamps," said one interviewer.[501] He graduated fifth from the bottom of his class in 1958.

Training as a naval airman, he flew A-1 Skyraiders and gained a reputation as a subpar flier: Two of his missions crashed, one cut down power lines. He was also unlucky. While on the deck of the USS *Forrestal* off the coast of Vietnam, a rocket fired from one of the planes on deck hit the aircraft next to McCain. Three months later, his plane was shot down while on a bombing mission over Hanoi. Captured, McCain was dragged from a lake by the North Vietnamese who crushed his shoulder with a rifle butt and bayoneted him before hauling him to the "Hanoi Hilton" (Hoa Lo prison). There, after some time in a hospital, he was tossed into solitary confinement. In mid-1968, when McCain's father was named commander of all US forces in the Vietnam theater, the North Vietnamese sought favorable publicity by offering to let younger McCain go. He refused unless all others taken before him were released.

Tortured daily and forced to make an anti-US "confession," he nevertheless refused to sign further statements and was subjected to more beatings. After five and a half years, he was released. Vietnamese torture left him unable to lift his arms above his head. Serving until 1981, McCain settled in Arizona with his new wife and took a job in her father's company, a beer distributorship. He won a seat in Congress in 1982 and then ran for the Senate in 1986, replacing legendary Arizona Senator Barry Goldwater.

McCain's march up the political ladder hit a pothole in the early 1980s when he was named in the "Keating Five" scandal, where he had received political donations. After the contributions, however, Charles Keating contacted McCain for help in preventing the government from seizing Keating's Lincoln Savings and Loan. Although cleared by an ethics committee, McCain admitted that it reflected a "wrong appearance."[502] He cochaired, with 2004 presidential loser John Kerry, a Senate committee on POW/MIA affairs that found "no compelling evidence that proves that any American remains alive in captivity in Southeast Asia."[503] That conclusion angered many activists who thought Americans were still held by the Vietnamese.

As a "maverick," McCain voted to confirm President Clinton's nominees to the US Supreme Court, Ruth Ginsburg and Stephen Breyer. Ginsburg later proved one of the most liberal appointees in court history. McCain also began a campaign against "soft money," or political action committees. He worked with Wisconsin Democrat Russ Feingold on campaign finance reform, which was filibustered. Passed up for the GOP nomination in 1994 in favor of Kansas Senator Bob Dole (whom insiders thought deserved it because his "time had come"), McCain wasn't even named Dole's vice presidential nominee. He reloaded and planned for the 2000 race.

McCain's opening salvo was a book, *Faith of My Fathers*, which became a bestseller and was made into a film. Lacking the big money of his opponent, Governor George W. Bush of Texas, McCain cultivated a relationship with the media that, in 2008, he badly overestimated. More important, the "soft money" that he had attacked visited revenge on him with blistering ads. Bush aligned with the evangelical Christian wing of the GOP and after McCain lost the South Carolina primary, his campaign was over.

Bush's reelection in 2004 meant that McCain was increasingly running out of time. He continued to rely on his media support, being named as one of America's "10 Best Senators" by *Time* in 2006. He also played up his "maverick" role, questioning the progress in the Iraq War to the point that he forced Bush to adopt the "troop surge" strategy in 2007. Seeing 2008 as his year, he won key primaries and beat the future 2012 GOP loser, Mitt Romney, for the nomination.[504] Stumbling to double-digit deficits in the polls due largely to Republicans' dissatisfaction with his excessive eagerness to work with Democrats, McCain chose firebrand Alaska Governor Sarah Palin as his running mate, which energized the GOP base. Quickly, however, two things became apparent about Palin: First, she was far more popular with the base than he was and second, she was immensely unpopular with McCain's valued media friends. From that point on, the campaign sabotaged Palin and did little to prepare her for key interviews.

On September 24 and in light of the ongoing financial crisis, McCain suspended his campaign to go to DC to help craft a $700 billion bank bailout. If he thought he could distance himself from the unpopular Bush, that action dispelled any such notions. Worse for his image, he was viewed by the once-favorable press as playing an insignificant role. Then, he abruptly decided to participate in the debates on September 26, contributing to his reputation of being erratic. Ultimately worst of all, when the final bailout of the big banks came a few days later, he, Obama, Joe Biden, and Hillary Clinton all voted for it. Consequently, it was difficult for McCain to be a "maverick" if he marched in lockstep with the left.

Obama had to do little to tank McCain with the voters. The Arizona senator was aligned fully with the "Bush bailout" and with the "Bush war." Moreover, dreadfully fearful of being labeled a racist or Islamophobe, McCain repeatedly kneecapped his own supporters who aggressively challenged Obama's anti-war/pro-Islamic positions, ensuring that a Cincinnati radio host who, when he mentioned Obama's full name, strongly emphasized "HUSSEIN," was fired.

For his part, Obama ran rings around McCain when it came to implementing the "new media" of the internet, particularly the dominant platform of the day, Facebook, where Obama had three times more followers, or Twitter, where Obama's followers outnumbered those of McCain more than 20:1.[505] Most of all, Obama took advantage of YouTube for free advertising.[506] And the younger the voters, the more likely they were to turn to social media for their political information: 37 percent of eighteen to twenty-four-year-olds got election news from social media.[507] Not surprisingly, the stodgy and older McCain and the Republican Party he dominated failed miserably to attract younger voters through social media—not that they would have been attracted to his message in the first place.

Obama's tech advantage, however, went far deeper. Scholars Daniel Kreiss and Philip Howard found that in the 2008 campaign, Obama's minions compiled massive data on more than 250 million Americans, including "a vast array of online behavioral and relational data collected from use of the campaign's Web site and *third-party social media sites such as Facebook* [emphasis mine]."[508] Indeed, after the election, Obama's relationship with Google—whose CEO backed him—was called a "love affair" by *Fortune* magazine.[509]

Obama not only had an advantage with social media platforms, but traditional journalists supported him as well. A Pew Research Center poll found that 70 percent of registered voters thought that journalists favored Obama, but only 9 percent thought that the media favored McCain.[510] Already, some of the members of the media had cast off any objectivity when it came to the Illinois senator. Chris Matthews said when he heard Obama speak, "I felt this thrill going up my leg."[511] David Brooks, the supposed "conservative" columnist for *The New York Times*, had interviewed Obama in 2005 and was obsessed with his "perfectly creased pant."[512] Such fawning did not subside when Obama won the presidency. In November 2010, *Newsweek* presented Obama on the cover as the Hindu god Shiva with the headline "God of All Things," as he juggled economy, war, travel, and the globe.[513] If Obama had believed in reincarnation, he would have come back as himself. Aides referred to him as "Black Jesus."[514] Left-wing radio commentator Ed Schultz reported that the West Wing had become a "shrine" to Obama, with pictures of him everywhere.[515]

Certainly, Obama's ego reflected the media views. Even *Rolling Stone* described him as "righteous and cocky."[516] At his speech on Super Tuesday in Chicago in 2008, Obama intoned "change will not come if we wait for some other person.... We are the ones we've been waiting for."[517] He didn't have to wait long. It was a quick concession on election night, when Obama won 365 electoral votes to McCain's 173 and romped to a nearly ten million popular vote majority with a record 131.3 million turnout. Obama then appeared at Chicago's Grant Park in front of reportedly 250,000 to deliver his victory speech.[518] He echoed one of his campaign themes when addressing whether the US could meet a number of challenges: "Yes we can." As might have been expected, Obama won the youth, McCain those over sixty-five. And, as was expected with the first black presidential candidate, black people turned out as a percent of the total vote at a 13 percent rate (vs. 11 percent in 2004) and voted for Obama at a 95 percent majority.

Yet the crucial reality was that most Americans really did not know who they had just elected. Obama's skin color protected him from a variety of genuine criticisms. Probably the greatest of those was that Obama rejected American exceptionalism and said so, repeatedly. This apparently, in part, derived from his view that the US identified with Israel, while he (being the anti-imperialist that he was) consistently sympathized with Arab states.

At any rate, most Americans sincerely believed that electing a black president would end the notion of racism in America once and for all. Instead, Obama exacerbated it. There *was* racism directed at Obama—most of it coming from the Democrats. When Obama ran for president, his own future vice president, Senator Biden, said of him: "I mean, you got the first mainstream African-American who is articulate and bright and clean."[519] A *Los Angeles Times* writer referred to Obama as a "magic negro," whereupon a song parody based on that liberal writer's appellation appeared on *The Rush Limbaugh Show* called "Barack, the Magic Negro," sung to the tune of "Puff, the Magic Dragon." Of course, it was the parody of the liberal writer, not the liberal writer himself, which drew all the "racist" criticism. On numerous occasions, black people whispered about Obama being inauthentic or insufficiently black—a distinction among African Americans that went back to the Civil War era or before, when miscegenation produced lighter-skinned "house" slaves and darker-skinned "field" slaves. Over time, the former dominated the elite eight of black colleges and worked their way into "white" society with much greater ease. In March 2007, for example, the darker-skinned (and, presumably, more "authentic") Al Sharpton criticized Obama and threatened to withhold his support for Obama's campaign. Yet another liberal writer referred to "Sharpton's magic act," referring to Sharpton's claims that Obama was downplaying his race to become acceptable to whites.[520] A *Columbia Journalism Review* article admitted that the most common question for Obama was "When did you decide you were black?" because for most of his life he had navigated white society and had little to do with black causes.[521] After all, he had been raised in Jakarta by a white—if radical—Kansas mother and mostly absent Kenyan father, and as a *New York Daily News* columnist pointed out, "Other than color, Obama did not—does not—share a heritage with the majority of black Americans, who are descendants of plantation slaves."[522]

The entire argument missed the point: It was never about whether Obama was "black enough" for African American voters but whether he was "black enough" for guilty whites. And the answer soon was clear: absolutely. Recall that in 1998 poet Toni Morrison called Bill Clinton "our first black president," by which she referred to how Clinton had been prosecuted during impeachment.[523] In the early months of the 2008 campaign, in fact, black voters supported Hillary Clinton 3:1 until they slowly shifted.

If even Obama's race was in dispute, much of the rest of his life was a cipher, despite publishing a memoir called *Dreams from My Father* in 1995. It did not help that the book was filled with inaccuracies, composite characterizations, and adjusted timelines.

All those influences were minimized, suppressed, or outright ignored by the media as Obama claimed the presidency. They would surface in short order.

As with all presidents in the modern era, Obama's first acts were to issue executive orders undoing many of his predecessor's executive orders. He suspended all ongoing proceedings at Guantanamo Bay and ordered the controversial detention center there shut down in a year. He banned many of the coercive techniques used by the government to obtain information, such as "waterboarding."[524] And, of course, he instantly reversed Bush's federal abortion policy known as the "Mexico City Policy" that banned federal money to international groups that provided abortions.[525]

Most immediately, Obama had to continue cleaning up the wreckage from the subprime mortgage disaster. Most major legislation had already been passed under Bush, and a pre-written $787 billion stimulus bill (called the American Recovery and Reinvestment Act) was enacted in February 2009. Unemployment continued to rise until October 2009 when it reached 10 percent. However, the official unemployment rate did not, as many economists pointed out, account for the millions who had quit looking for work entirely. (The Economic Policy Institute calculated that in 2010 this was at least another 1.1 percent.)[526]

Part of the American Recovery and Reinvestment Act included $48 billion for infrastructure, which, it was assumed, would alleviate some of the unemployment. Obama added to that another $50 billion in the American Jobs Act that the administration described as "shovel-ready jobs."[527]

Programs such as those, as proven in the Great Depression, did almost nothing to affect employment. (In the Great Depression, when there was a much stronger work ethic, they did restore dignity, which may not be the case today.) Economist Martin Feldstein found that each of Obama's "created" jobs cost taxpayers $200,000.[528] More important however, the bloated government—largely but not entirely the fault of the Democrats—meant that, in fact, there was no such thing as a "shovel-ready job." Environmental impact statements, public hearings, and land acquisition alone meant that such jobs couldn't break ground for two to three years. One study of the initial spending of $20 billion on roads and bridges showed that it had no effect on local unemployment rates. Obama was forced to admit, "Shovel-ready wasn't as…uh… shovel-ready as we thought."[529] As soon as it became apparent that the stimulus did not stimulate many jobs, Obama convened a "jobs summit" in which he solicited advice from those who already supported his programs. Businesspeople who disagreed with him and free market economists were excluded.

Most of Obama's actions occurred without any input from Republicans, even after the GOP took control of Congress in 2010.

Left-leaning Reuters news identified Obama's strategy as appealing "to Republicans to make compromises and if they do not, accuse them of obstruction."[530]

THE OBAMACARE DISASTER

For his first two years, Obama didn't need a single Republican vote to pass anything. His affordable medical care legislation, however, would require every Democrat vote he could muster and, even among those, severe arm-twisting. Having run on "affordable medical care" (a code phrase for government health care), Obama began work with Congress on the Affordable Care Act, or what would be colloquially known as "Obamacare." Based on Massachusetts Republican Governor Mitt Romney's plan, it was a general expansion of insurance coverage via an "exchange" that provided insurance at taxpayer expense for low-income residents.

Yet the concept stemmed from a fundamental misunderstanding that the Democrats used routinely to batter Republicans, namely that someone who was uninsured lacked medical care itself. Of course, some people paid cash, but even the poor had access to emergency rooms. What they did not have access to was "preventative care," the in vogue approach to wellness that included routine doctor visits, screenings for high-risk diseases such as diabetes or intestinal cancer, and other doctor visits that would enable physicians to charge higher prices to health insurance companies.

Socialized medicine, or "single payer," sought to address the free-rider problem of people who did not pay for health insurance, which was becoming a drain on the taxpayers who subsidized emergency room care, as hospitals were required by law to treat everyone, whether patients could pay or not. It has been called "one of the great unfunded mandates in American history."[531] Particularly after illegal immigrants began to pour into the country, the hospital system was additionally stressed.

In February 2009, Obama announced his plan to Congress. Republicans eagerly worked with him on it. Quickly the "individual mandate" emerged as the central obstacle. It *required* every American to buy health insurance and threatened to fine them via taxation if they did not. Conservatives steadfastly opposed this. If ordinary people could not afford to buy (even cheaper) insurance, how could they pay a fine or a tax? Moreover, the fine was affixed only if the person *paid* an income tax, leaving out those who worked in black markets. In short, it encouraged criminality and disproportionately harmed the poor it was presumably there to help.

Obama's plan also included federally funded abortion, which ruffled many pro-life Democratic congressmen, including Bart Stupak of Michigan, who threatened to vote against it unless the abortion coverage was removed. Eventually, all the pro-life House Democrats crumbled and on November 7, 2009, the House passed the Affordable Care Act with a mere five-vote margin. The Senate followed. In fact, unconstitutionally, the Senate had worked on its own bill, violating the constitutional requirement that all revenue bills had to originate in the House. To skirt the constitutional language, the Senate repurposed an existing House resolution regarding tax changes for service members.

It was a dishonest and disingenuous tap dance, which became even more corrupt when it came to overcoming the Senate Republicans' vow to filibuster the legislation. A Senate filibuster required sixty votes; Democrats only had fifty-nine, even after Republican Senator Arlen Specter of Pennsylvania switched to the Democratic Party. But a contested Senate race in Minnesota finally resulted in the seat being handed to comedian Al Franken on a tiny margin of just over three hundred votes after multiple counts when Franken trailed. With the filibuster broken, one or two more "conservative Democrats" changed their positions, most notably Ben Nelson of Nebraska, who agreed to back the bill after an amendment (known as the "Cornhusker Kickback") was added, providing a higher rate of Medicaid reimbursement for Nebraska. (After the bill was passed, the "kickback" was removed, allowing Nelson to say that he had fought for Nebraska values but was just outvoted.) Then there was the "Louisiana Purchase," a provision in the bill that was needed to buy the vote of Louisiana Senator Mary Landrieu. It gave extra Medicaid funding to any state in which every county had been declared a "disaster area," which applied to the Pelican State due to Hurricane Katrina.[532] Typically, Obama denied he had crafted the kickbacks or deals ("I didn't make a bunch of deals"), but his top medical adviser, Rahm Emanuel, admitted that "we were involved in the legislation all the way through."[533]

Fewer shady and manipulative bills had ever become law in American history. As Obamacare fraudulently rewriting an unrelated House "tax" bill so as to become the Affordable Care Act, it began in deception. It depended upon one Republican lying to his constituents to run as a Republican so he could change parties after the election and on a razor-thin Minnesota Senate race that may well have involved "inventive" vote counting. Most of all, it required strong-arm bullying of pro-life congressmen, thirteen of whom lost their seats in the next election,

It was a Pyrrhic victory. Over the next fifteen years, the fracture of the modern iteration of the Democratic Party originated with the fissures first cut with Obamacare. Pro-life Democrats who had supported the bill were ousted quickly, to be replaced by either Republicans or more radical Democrats. By 2016, the number of pro-life Democrats had dropped from forty to two.[534] They mostly represented Rust Belt, heavily Catholic districts, and Southern conservative areas. Pro-life groups rightly viewed their collapse on opposition to Obamacare with federally funded abortion as treason. They campaigned against them; then after removing twenty pro-life representatives, more lost their seats to redistricting into districts that were not as conservative as they once were, losing another ten. By 2014, lacking any voice in the pro-abortion Democratic caucus, all but two of the rest retired. On the other hand, by 2016, there were only two pro-choice Republicans in that caucus, making the GOP the inevitable default for pro-life Democrats.

By starting the fracture with the issue of life, Democrats began a decade-long exodus of Catholics from the party. It would spread to economic aspects of politics, but the initial break came when the Democratic Party decided it could ignore and roll over a sizable element of its New Deal coalition with impunity. With that arrogance, the party itself resembled its president.

The long-term and almost inevitable erosion of the Democratic Party started immediately, as did the successful effort to defeat Obamacare in pieces. Within three weeks, polls showed 58 percent of Americans wanted the law repealed. And, as David Limbaugh pointed out, keeping the opposition even that low required misleading the public on the price tag. The administration had juggled the numbers to achieve a passing grade from the Congressional Budget Office and even then, the White House wasn't satisfied. Peter Orszag, the Obama budget director, insisted that the falsified Congressional Budget Office tallies didn't go *far enough* in reflecting the (non-existent) savings.[535]

The lies needed to sell Congress's so-called budget hawks (who almost universally ended up voting for significantly higher budgets on any item) were voluminous. Then–House Budget Committee member Paul Ryan noted that the unrealistic Obamacare cost assumptions revealed a "stark reality": "If these assumed savings are never realized—as is the likely scenario—[the Congressional Budget Office] project that rather than reducing the deficit in the years beyond 2019 the deficit would increase…"around one-quarter percent of GDP"…or about $600 billion."[536]

Over the following years, court suits and legislation chipped away at Obamacare. But the first significant challenge, which came before the US Supreme Court in 2012 (*National Federation of Independent Business v. Sebelius*), challenged Congress's power to enact most of the provisions of the Affordable Care Act, including the penalty to forgo the mandated health insurance that would take effect in 2014. To effect the mandate, the "Obamacare case," as it was called, required the Chief Justice John Roberts to rewrite the legislation by claiming it was a "tax" and fell under Congress's taxing power. Yet in a logic rivaling that of the *Dred Scott* decision, Roberts (and a majority of the justices) admitted that the "individual mandate," though, was *not* constitutional under the Commerce Clause or the Necessary and Proper Clause. The court further ruled that Congress's expansion of Medicaid was not a valid exercise of the congressional spending power. Under the Medicaid mandate, a state would have had to accept the costly expansion of Medicaid or lose all existing Medicaid funding.[537]

Later it was revealed that Roberts had opposed the Obamacare mandate and was prepared to vote with the conservative majority to (rightly) overturn the law, but that "as chief justice [Roberts was] keenly aware of his leadership role on the court and...is also sensitive to how the court is perceived by the public. There were countless news articles...warning of damage to the court—and to Roberts' reputation—if the court were to strike down the mandate."[538]

Oddly, most conservative pundits missed a "poison pill" in Roberts' ruling. Even while upholding Obamacare, Roberts had struck a profound blow against the expansion of the "Deep State" by removing the Commerce Clause as a justification for expansion of federal power. While Obama would ignore this aspect of the ruling, it later further emphasized future courts' rulings that invoked the "Chevron deference" and made it difficult for unelected bureaus to expand at will.[539] Indeed, the initial euphoria—some of which claimed Obamacare would cement Obama's legacy—seemed oblivious to the clause regarding states' rights to withdraw from Medicaid expansion.[540] With the state Medicaid mandate removed, Congress then castrated the original power of the bill by reducing the individual mandate tax to zero dollars in the Tax Cuts and Jobs Act of 2017. Then, after an appeal from Texas, the Supreme Court agreed to hear yet another Obamacare appeal in 2020, which, by 2025, has not yet occurred.[541]

Without the individual mandate or the Medicaid requirement and with the individual "exchanges" closing to the point they were irrelevant, the only thing remaining was for Congress to formally repeal it.

Republicans, however, suffered from the same problem since Obamacare was first passed: a viable alternative. In 2017, after almost all Republicans had campaigned for ten years on repealing Obamacare, a repeal bill (known as a "skinny repeal") was introduced through the Senate first to send the bill back to the House for a final repeal-and-replace that both houses could agree to. At that point, the "maverick" Senator McCain—at the time suffering from brain cancer—delivered a theatrical vote against the repeal when he walked up to the podium and, Caligula-like, gave a "thumbs down."[542] Many observers believed McCain had voted less on the specifics of the bill and more as retribution against President Donald Trump, who had repeatedly made negative references to the Senator as an example of what was wrong with America.

Regardless, Obamacare's death came via a thousand cuts and McCain's theatrics likely actually benefited the GOP from being blamed for an equally unworkable plan. In 2021, the Supreme Court refused to hear an appeal from Texas claiming that the state lacked standing—a convenient dodge the Supreme Court has used for numerous thorny cases. Nevertheless, the appeal meant little, as the entire Obamacare structure had been emasculated and nullified by subsequent laws and rulings. Nothing remained but the name.

FURIOUSLY RUNNING GUNS

Obama's penchant for destruction swept into all aspects of his administration, with none more damaging than the effort of his attorney general, Eric Holder, to launch a war on guns. Holder and Secretary of State Hillary Clinton claimed that 90 percent of guns used in crimes committed by the Mexican drug cartels were sold in America. They intended to reinstitute the Clinton-era ban on so-called assault weapons (an absolutely fraudulent term). That ban had resulted in more of the banned weapons sold than before, as well as a host of other unintended consequences.[543] Against a background of ramped up gun store checks and a propaganda campaign against gun dealers, Holder's Department of Justice (DOJ) tasked the Bureau of Alcohol, Tobacco, Firearms, and Explosives, better known as ATF, to engage in an operation known as "Fast and Furious." ATF agents surveilling gun shops would set up "straw purchases" then (they hoped) track them across the border into the hands of the cartels. John Dodson, a special agent on the case admitted that "allowing loads of weapons that we knew to be destined for criminals, this was the plan."[544] Such stings were not abnormal. What stood out in Fast and Furious is that the majority of those in the upper ranks of the crimes resided in Mexico and could not be "stung" by American law enforcement.

Not only was the scheme a failure—most of the two thousand weapons purchased by straw men disappeared, then later turned up in *Mexican* crimes in which two hundred Mexicans were killed—but a US border patrol agent Brian Terry was also murdered in part of the operation. And while no major cartel arrests in Mexico occurred, there were more than fifty Fast and Furious weapons" that were tied to *American* crimes. Not only did Obama and Holder not apologize or offer an explanation, but they hid Fast and Furious from Congress.[545] Requests from the House Oversight Committee refused to provide documents, and Holder would not answer questions or comply with subpoenas. Congressman Darrell Issa warned Holder, "We're not looking at straw buyers...we're looking at you....[and] your key people who knew or should've known about this."[546] Obama and Holder responded that they preferred an internal investigation by the inspector general within the DOJ. At the same time, in the Senate, a frustrated Charles Grassley of Iowa waited for seventy-four thousand subpoenaed documents that were never delivered.

Meanwhile, as always, Obama tried to pin the fiasco on the Bush administration, claiming it was part of an operation known as "Wide Receiver" (a small-scale operation with about 25 percent of the number of guns involved). In Wide Receiver, however, when guns went missing from their electronic tracking, the operation was terminated. Wide Receiver also took place with the knowledge and aid of the Mexican government, unlike Fast and Furious.

When, in June 2011, Congress produced its report on Fast and Furious, it found, among other issues, that agents knew that large numbers of the trafficked weapons would have "tragic results." Agents were told to stand down when trafficked weapons were being sold, and ATF agents feared that every time law enforcement officials in Arizona (where the operation was based) were shot, the weapon might be traced to Fast and Furious.[547] Worse, after the House report appeared, new evidence surfaced showing that other federal agencies were involved and the DOJ had attempted to muzzle ATF itself as it sought to contain fallout over Terry's death.[548] Whether due to their ineptitude in Fast and Furious or as a reward for keeping silent, three ATF officials involved in the operation were promoted in August 2011.

Slowly, a number of ATF agents blew the whistle on the operation and most faced retaliation from the DOJ, a practice that would become commonplace in Democratic administrations. At the same time, Democrats in Congress tried to use Fast and Furious to expand gun control—which some thought was the point of Fast and Furious all along. After letters from Senator Grassley, Holder's staff insisted that ATF, in fact, made every effort to interdict illegally purchased weapons. That stood completely in contradiction to statements by numerous on-the-ground ATF agents. Congressman Trey Gowdy of South Carolina followed up in December 2011 by asking Holder in open testimony to admit that a DOJ letter to Grassley was demonstrably false. Holder refused, saying that "nobody at Justice has lied."[549] In fact, Holder had clearly lied about when he knew about Fast and Furious, receiving briefings in late December 2010 and early January 2011 that described the specifics months before the date of his stated knowledge (May 3, 2011). As Holder and Obama ducked and dodged, whistleblowers at ATF were demoted, categorized as a "nut job" or "disgruntled," and warned that their careers were in jeopardy.[550]

Ultimately, Congress had enough. In June 2012, the House overwhelmingly voted to hold Eric Holder in contempt, the first time Congress had taken such a dramatic move against a cabinet official.

The charge authorized Republican leaders to seek criminal charges against the attorney general. Holder was also hit with a civil contempt resolution that allowed the House Oversight and Government Reform Committee to sue the DOJ for Fast and Furious documents.[551] When the case came before Obama-appointed judge Amy Berman Jackson in October of 2014, she declined to follow through and had him jailed—quite unlike what happened to Steve Bannon over his refusal to honor a House subpoena.[552]

"WE NEED ANOTHER TEA PARTY"

When Congress introduced Obama's new Homeowner Affordability and Stability Plan in 2010, it came under unusual assault from a normally friendly space, CNBC. There, business reporter Rick Santelli on air accused the government of "promoting bad behavior" and "called for a new tea party."[553] The "rant" (as it was often called) had little, if nothing, to do with Obama specifically but rather with an ongoing escalation of massive government spending programs crafted by a "bipartisan" Congress that spent money like drunken sailors given crypto accounts. Moreover, his rant was unusual because the mainstream media was overwhelmingly positive to Obama.

It caught on like a wildfire, in part reflecting a growing anxiety over bailouts of all sorts. Santelli had turned to the floor traders at the Chicago Mercantile Exchange and asked if they would like to bail out their neighbors who had spent too much on their homes. A resounding "NO!" came back. His reference to a "tea party" quickly morphed into the "TEA party," or "Taxed Enough Already."[554]

Marches and assemblies sprang up across the nation. The number of attendees are nettlesome because almost all Tea Party gatherings involved people coming and going the entire time. In Dayton, Ohio, over eight thousand showed up at city hall; in St. Louis, double that number assembled. Many of those Tea Partyers had not participated in politics before at all. Large numbers hadn't even vote before. Yet they began attending speeches and events, buying books on history and the Constitution, and seeking to run for office. And predictably, the Obama administration labeled them racists. Reporter Kelly O'Donnell dutifully said to one black Tea Partyer, "There aren't a lot of African-Americans at these events. Have you ever felt…uncomfortable?" to which the protester shot back, "No, no, these are my people, Americans."[555] Black Congressman John Lewis said in March that Tea Party protesters yelled racial slurs at black congressmen. Film footage at the time showed that Lewis lied. That did not prevent the predictable claim from the National Association for the Advancement of Colored People that the "tea party is racist" without the slightest hint of proof.[556] Obama's "spiritual adviser" Jim Wallis (having dumped the inflammatory Reverend Wright) claimed that no Tea Party movement would have existed without a black man in the White House.[557] Even Obama himself, who had carefully avoided making public comments, in a private 2010 dinner agreed with a suggestion that there was a racially based "subterranean agenda" afoot.[558]

Such attacks were so predictable that before Obama was sworn in, talk show host Limbaugh said that any criticism of Obama's policies would be labeled as racist. In fact, by mid-2010, only 40 percent thought that Obama had improved race relations, and in 2011, that fell to 35 percent.[559] One columnist wrote that Obama's "reckless" rhetoric fostered civil strife and "racial animosity."[560]

Race aside, the backlash from the administration against the new tea party groups came swiftly as Lois Lerner, Cincinnati, Ohio, head of the Internal Revenue Service (IRS), went on a jihad against members by conducting waves of audits against Tea Partyers. In one Wisconsin tea party group, 90 percent of the members were subjected to IRS audits that year. This author was audited for the first time in forty years. An investigation by Congress indeed found "clear evidence that Tea Party and other conservative organizations were targeted for enhanced scrutiny because their organization's names reflected their conservative beliefs." Additionally, Congress learned that no new "Tea Party" groups had been approved for tax-exempt applications as were other "progressive" groups.[561] As with Holder, Republicans had little follow-through. Lerner resigned but with no criminal charges. A clear message emerged, however; Obama's administration would not tolerate criticism or opposition and would use the levers of government to suppress it.

In the area of foreign policy, particularly in the Middle East, Obama promised during his campaign against McCain that the US would withdraw all forces from Iraq within sixteen months. Some nineteen months later, a "status of forces" agreement resulted in all combat troops removed from the unstable Middle Eastern state. Obama, however, had implied that all US forces would be evacuated from the Middle East. No sooner did he enter office, however, than he announced an increase in US troops in Afghanistan.[562] US forces there would reach one hundred thousand by 2010. By 2012, the US and Afghanistan signed a "strategic partnership agreement" that, in theory, turned over major combat operations to the Afghans and even designated Afghanistan a "major ally." After the election, Obama began withdrawing troops in the twelve-year-old war with a goal of removing most troops by 2016. On January 1, 2015, the US officially ended the Afghan war by ending "Operation Enduring Freedom."

Other aspects of the war dragged on quietly through Obama's first term. His DOJ also issued a court filing saying that there would be no change in the status of detainees at Bagram Airfield in Afghanistan. American drone attacks inside Pakistan, begun under Bush, increased substantially.[563]

An anti-colonialist at heart, Obama sympathized with the Palestinians against Israel. He directed $20 million to Gaza. In his apologetic Cairo speech in June 2009, he begged the Palestinians to abandon violence and to abandon Hamas, saying that the organization did not represent the Palestinians." Hoping for "a new beginning," he implored the students at Cairo University that America and Islam were not exclusive, and, quoting the Koran, he said he would "speak the truth." He then recited "civilization's debt to Islam" and further intoned the dubious proposition that "Islam is a part of America."

His message to Iran, while expressing concerns about the violence following the 2009 election that ran roughshod over the pro-democracy movement, nevertheless suggested that the US would steer clear of getting involved in Iran. He expanded sanctions on Iran in 2010, reducing Iran's oil exports, but continued to allow Iran to develop nuclear weapons. Iran stalled until 2016 when it agreed to refrain from making nuclear weapons (having already conducted much of the research for five years). As part of the arrangement, Obama gave $1.7 billion (literally in palates full of cash) to Iran and shielded Hezbollah from a Drug Enforcement Administration operation that involved drug smuggling by the terrorists.[564]

While tacitly endorsing Iran's nuclear buildup, the Obama administration encouraged the "Arab Spring" protests in the Middle East. A series of anti-government protests broke out in Tunisia, Egypt, Libya, and other Middle Eastern countries, but most notably at Tahrir Square in Cairo on February 9, 2011. Demonstrators were frustrated with stagnant economies, overall backwardness, and government repression. In addition to mass protests, demonstrators responded to government crackdowns with violence. Egypt, in particular, served as a focal point when Mohamed Morsi, who was affiliated with the radical Muslim Brotherhood, was elected. He had Obama's blessing and immediately sought to consolidate power, provoking a coup that removed him from office. A bloodier outcome afflicted Libya, where the Obama administration had supported groups opposing strongman dictator Muammar Gaddafi. Instead of the peaceful democratic "moderate" Islam Obama dreamed possible, Libya got a gruesome battle for Tripoli when Gaddafi fled. Captured, he was beaten on camera then sodomized by a bayonet, bringing howls from Amnesty International. US-backed North Atlantic Treaty Organization aircrafts were involved in destroying parts of the convoy to assist in his capture, and following the public display of Gaddafi's mutilated body, Secretary of State Clinton laughed, "We came. We saw. He died."[565] Libya descended into a constant hell of warring

Islamic groups. Obama admitted his administration's handling of Libya was "the worst mistake" of his presidency.[566]

That was quite an admission, given that he created new tensions with Saudi Arabia because of his coddling of Iran, which had tried to force Syrian President Bashar al-Assad to step aside (like Mohamed Morsi and Gaddafi), and had been helpless to stop the rise of a new al-Qaeda replacement group, ISIS (Islamic State of Iraq and Syria). Indeed, the Obama administration specifically used another term for ISIS, "ISIL" for the "Islamic State of Syria and *the Levant*," which tacitly admitted that Islam had claim to *all territory* in the Middle East, including Israel. ISIS, rather than concealing horrific images of terror, reveled in them. ISIS murders of their opponents in jailed cages dropped into the ocean, set afire, or beheaded in groups were gleefully shared on social media by its perpetrators. Just a few years after Obama had taken office, the entire Middle East had collapsed into chaos and bloodshed.

A DOG ON TOP OF THE CAR

As Obama's 2012 reelection neared, the Republicans had no charismatic figure to counter him. Newt Gingrich, a walking encyclopedia and the former Speaker of the House when the Republican revolution of 1994 finally regained control of Congress after forty years, was a spent force. His humiliation at the hands of Bill Clinton drained much of the leadership mantle from him. Many within the party assumed that the onerous nature of the Obama policies would allow them to run a nondescript moderate who would refrain from attacking Obama directly. Enter Mitt Romney.

A former governor of Massachusetts—itself something of a feat for a Republican to achieve—Romney had introduced a variant of "Obamacare" into that state well before Obama came to the presidency. (Obama's team used "Romneycare" as a model for Obamacare.) Romney's greatest public accomplishment, however, came when he saved the bankrupt Salt Lake City winter Olympics in 2002. A handsome Mormon burnishing a toothpaste-ad smile, the moderate, non-controversial Willard "Mitt" Romney had run a capital fund, which, before he actually ran for office, seemed to be the worst thing opponents could say of him.

Concern about his moderate stances led Romney to pronounce at the Conservative Political Action Conference in February 2012 that he was "severely conservative," a phrase Limbaugh lampooned, saying, "I have never heard anybody say, 'I'm severely conservative.'"[567] Romney, in short, seemed too bland to attack or, in other words, the perfect candidate to face Obama.

No political analysts at the time had yet figured out that as strong and widespread the resistance to Obama's *policies* were, he personally remained untouchable because of his race. Only in the area of foreign affairs and only for a moment, did it seem Romney might have a chance to seriously damage him. Thus, when Romney finally mustered the courage to actually go after Obama—in that case, over Libya in a presidential debate—the *moderator* Candy Crowley intervened and corrected Romney.[568] Crowley's intervention broke Romney's real momentum, which he never regained.

For his part, Obama was vicious in his attacks on the Republican: Romney had said Russia was America's number one enemy, to which Obama said, "The 1980s are now calling to ask for their foreign policy back."[569] Most of the time, Romney volunteered statements that easily provided the Obama team with fodder. At a private fundraiser, which was secretly recorded, Romney said that 47 percent of the public would vote for Obama because they were "dependent upon government."[570] Responding to complaints that he was sexist, Romney said he had "binders full of women," meaning he had binders full of job applications from women.[571] Then Romney admitted that in a 1983 cross-country, twelve-hour trip, the family put their dog Seamus in a carrier on the roof of the family's station wagon, wherein the dog had health problems. A *Time* story called "Romney's Cruel Canine Vacation" was revived.[572]

Obama also had his share of gaffes, particularly a speech in Virginia where he told business owners that they were dependent on government infrastructure to succeed and lectured, "You didn't build that."[573] (Most media of the day, as well as modern Wikipedia references, emphasize *Romney's* use of the term in ads rather than the offensiveness of the comment itself.) But Obama remained largely insulated from criticism by his race. Americans, simply put, were not willing to give up on the "first black president," no matter how much they disliked his policies. And his tech advantage remained: Romney's team relied on a flashy data-driven program called ORCA that flopped miserably, while Obama's team, as they had in 2008, dominated the digital sphere. His campaign knew "every single wavering voter in the country that it needed to persuade to vote for Obama, by name, address, race, sex, and income."[574] Voters gave Obama another four years by a 51 to 47 percent margin and winning 332 electoral votes. It was far less than his first election, where he walloped McCain by 7.2 percent in the popular vote and had 365 electoral votes. Even so, the outcome was not in doubt. Democrats gained two seats in the Senate. While the Democrats managed to gain eight House seats, they still trailed by thirty-three.

THE RACE CARD

Even before he left office, Obama, just as Limbaugh predicted, was using race to explain his failures. He in 2009 told *The New Yorker*, "some folks really dislike me because they don't like the idea of a black President."[575] Then he came close to the truth by admitting, "Some white folks… really like me and give me the benefit of the doubt precisely because I'm a black President."[576] Of course, Obama had a long string of failures or controversial programs that voters of all colors disliked, including Obamacare, unemployment, the failed "shovel-ready" stimulus bill, the "green energy" projects such as Solyndra that went bankrupt, and foreign policy failures.[577]

By 2016, Obama had injected race into everything. His Federal Communications Commission ordered an inquiry into black radio stations whose ratings had declined due to playing more hip-hop. His press secretary complained that criticisms of Supreme Court Justice Sonya Sotomayor were race based. His black attorney general, Eric Holder, cited for contempt of Congress, dismissed a case against the New Black Panther Party for voter intimidation even after the Panthers had won the case. Following the arrest of a black Harvard professor, Henry Gates, for disorderly conduct, Obama accused the Cambridge police of "acting stupidly" and implying race was at the root of their actions. His "green jobs" czar Van Jones said, "You've never seen a Columbine done by a black child," when every month in Chicago a "Columbine" occurred on the streets. Obama's "diversity czar" said in 2009 that there were few things in the American mind "more frightening" than "dark-skinned black men." His DOJ under Holder overruled a decision in the city of Kinston, North Carolina, to do away with party identification in local races, saying that black people could not achieve equal rights without the Democratic Party. After Obama twice insulted the city of Las Vegas and discouraged tourism there, his supporters cried "race" when the mayor defended the city. It was no wonder that Americans thought racism had grown since Obama was elected.[578]

The second term produced more of the same misdirection as the first. Instead of reducing the debt, it nearly doubled since Obama took office. Official unemployment, which stood at 5.8 percent in 2008, had only dropped to 4.9 percent eight years later. GDP growth officially had risen slightly to an anemic 1.7 percent. Yet as always, the official statistics were dubious, as various unemployment measurements did not include those who had dropped out of the work force and entirely quit looking for employment. With those added in, the true unemployment rate still hovered near the double digits.

In his first term, he had signed the repeal of the "Don't Ask, Don't Tell" policy in the US military that prohibited openly homosexual people from serving in the military. His stated views on homosexual marriage before the election—he had opposed—shifted when the case of *Obergefell v. Hodges* came before the Supreme Court.[579] It challenged the prohibition of homosexual marriage in many states, and by his second term, Obama supported the action by filing an amicus brief. The court ruled in favor of homosexual marriage, a ruling that constituted in the minds of many conservatives the thorough betrayal of the court after its previous Obamacare decision. Suddenly Bush's selection of Justice John Roberts as chief justice looked to be a mistake.

Immigration policy had plagued the nation for decades. In 1981, President Ronald Reagan, partly in order to deal with the Haitians and Cubans who were allowed in by President Jimmy Carter, had started to develop a national amnesty that eventually became the Simpson-Mazzoli Act of 1996. Claims that he was fooled by Congress or did not know what was actually in the legislation are refuted by a trove of administration documents showing how Reagan's team created the amnesty plan.[580] Under George W. Bush, attempts at a wider-ranging immigration "reform" failed amid public outrage. Obama tried to nibble around the edges with a policy called "DACA," or Deferred Action for Childhood Arrivals, which protected some seven hundred thousand illegal aliens from deportation.[581] Then, in 2014, through executive order, he added another four million to that number before the Supreme Court blocked it. Nevertheless, by 2015, the percentage of foreign-born living in the US reached an all-time high of 13.7 percent. In addition, Obama sought to resettle ten thousand Syrian "refugees" in America, urging Americans to welcome them as latter-day Pilgrims.[582]

In other areas, Obama's promises seemed hollow: He said he would protect civil liberties—especially when it came to government surveillance—but under his watch, the National Security Agency intercepted the calls of American citizens, including a US congressman.[583] As senator, Obama had complained about Patriot Act abuses; as president, he approved the extension of the act.[584] Of course, it would be the Obama-approved spy network that circulated and enhanced the fake "Russia conspiracy" charges against Trump in the 2016 campaign. Similarly, when it came to issues of transparency, where he promised to run the "most transparent" administration in US history, Obama prosecuted whistleblowers and used secret memos whenever possible. His DOJ charged several people with leak-related provisions of the Espionage Act. The best known of those individuals was Edward Snowden, a National Security Agency contractor who disclosed classified information to journalist Glenn Greenwald. Snowden, who had become disillusioned with domestic spying, leaked a variety of documents whereupon he was threatened by the DOJ. He fled to Russia, obtained asylum status, and eventually became a Russian citizen in 2022.

Republicans surged in the 2014 midterms, taking back thirteen seats in the House (247–188) and nine in the Senate (54–44). Neither constituted a "supermajority," but even without a supermajority, the GOP proved feckless and uncommitted in its willingness to do battle with Obama. For example, at any time the House could have shut down government until it had a reasonable budget. Speaker John Boehner of Ohio had no such inclination. In the Senate, Majority Leader Mitch McConnell could have used the filibuster to stop many of Obama's appointees, particularly judges. He would not. (Later, many of these judges would play crucial roles in persecuting and hounding President Trump.) McConnell had one courageous act in him. When Justice Antonin Scalia suddenly died in February of 2016, Obama quickly selected Merrick Garland to fill the seat. Normally, that would have produced a routine Senate process and a (likely) vote or approval. However, McConnell insisted that the "American people should have a voice in the selection of their next Supreme Court Justice" and that the vacancy should not be filled until there was a presidential election.[585] It was ironic that McConnell and other Republicans cited "the Biden rule" from 1992 when then-Senator Biden said that "once the political season is under way…action on a Supreme Court nomination must be put off until after the election campaign is over."[586] Thus, a rule cooked up by Obama's own vice president more than twenty years earlier denied him a Supreme Court pick. Once Hillary Clinton lost, that once-Democrat-held seat would become a Trump pick. (McConnell certainly did not think Trump would win. Rather, he wanted the moral credit from Republicans for standing firm, even if it didn't matter. Except it did.)

When his second term was up, Obama stayed out of the Democratic primaries as his secretary of state, Hillary Clinton, sought to become the first woman president. Her team was busy feeding information to the effort to link the Republican, Trump, to "Russian collusion." Obama's CIA and FBI both played an active role in the scheme (called "Crossfire Hurricane"): When investigations into the two agencies' participation in the attempted coup were finally raised, they were combining into a special investigation under Robert Mueller. Obama was effectively "fire-walled" off.

On October 30, 2008, Obama told a crowd in Columbia, Missouri that "we are five days away from fundamentally transforming the United States of America."[587] By that, Obama meant much more than merely electing the first black president. His wife, Michelle, said in May 2008 that they were "going to have to change our conversation; we're going to have to change our traditions, our history; we're going to have to move into a different place as a nation."[588] In most measurable ways, he did none of that. In other ways, particularly those affecting the US government, he did all that and more.

Over a five-year period, he purged over 197 military officers (he referred to "my military") who appeared to be of the "warrior" mentality and who had criticized Obama's military policies.[589] He staffed the DOJ with ultra-liberal prosecutors who laid the foundation for the non-prosecution of violent crime in the Biden years. If the nation wasn't fundamentally transformed, at least the bureaucracy was from Obama's point of view.

Legacy building had played a critical role in Obama's presidency. When he stepped down on January 20, 2017, he broke tradition by becoming the first president to maintain a residence in Washington, DC, renting a 6,400 square foot, nine-bedroom house just two miles from DC. One bedroom was reserved for his key adviser, Valerie Jarrett.[590] Reagan couldn't wait to hit the trail for Rancho del Cielo. Obama, however, indicated his intention to play a role in future administrations, either as an adviser/confidant or as gadfly and critic. This seemed all the more odd because he gave the impression that "he'd rather be anywhere other than in Washington."[591]

His library, an architectural monstrosity carved out of the South Side of Chicago by evicting inner-city residents, was resisted by community groups, especially those at Woodlawn. One writer at the *Chicago Tribune* warned of "The Dilemma of Development: Will Obama Center Hurt Those It's Supposed to Help?" (The *Tribune* removed that from the web archive.)[592] An athenaeum to Obama's accomplishments built at a cost of nearly $500 million dollars, drew intense resistance. Obama attempted to squelch opposition by announcing the hiring of a "diversity consultant" (for what was likely the least diverse library in the US presidential library system) to hire "local, diverse residents for construction and subcontracting."[593] When that failed, the library tried to silence opposition with the "Community Benefits Agreement."[594] (One of the "benefits" was an athletic center.) This bribe reflected Obama's view that "communities ha[ve] to be created," as opposed to springing up naturally as they have in the past.[595] Rent increases near the library immediately followed, whereupon public resistance solidified.[596] Obama announced that there would be no Community Benefits Agreement, the center needed to move past the debate stage, and claimed his center would attract over 700,000 annual visitors. (The most-visited presidential library in the nation, the Ronald Reagan Presidential Library, only attracted about 450,000 visitors in its annual, pre-COVID high.)

And Obama's legacy? For all his preparation, grooming, and seeming entitlement, he was "never the leader of anything, neither then nor now."[597] Fixated on "collecting laundered wealth from intermediaries such as Spotify and Netflix, buying luxury properties, and hanging out on private yachts with celebrities," Obama cultivated the image of a popular figure ("the One") who called the shots.[598]

All along, legislatively, Obama had been less than energetic. Having squandered almost the entire first two years with an entirely compliant Congress on Obamacare, the president had to compromise. Obama proved terrible at that. Instead, he bullied, ridiculed, and cajoled.

Nothing to speak of came from the GOP-dominated House. He certainly had a slew of executive orders. Contrasted with the legacies of Ronald Reagan and Donald Trump—let alone that of Lyndon Johnson or Franklin Roosevelt—Obama's record was anemic.

Where he had his greatest impact was in schmoozing with billionaires, particularly in the tech sector. This enabled a Silicon Valley oligarchy populated by Jeff Bezos, Mark Zuckerberg, and Peter Cook as well as big tech companies such as Amazon, Yahoo, and Google to function as a Praetorian Guard for Democrats. It was aided and abetted by the mainstream media he had also wooed. His legacy certainly included a shadow government that would take a decade to root out and purge. And ironically, by his second term, many of those billionaires, including Elon Musk, Jeff Bezos, and Mark Zuckerberg, had decided they liked the Trump agenda and willingly worked with him!

Politically, Obama's legacy was particularly shallow and frail. His biographer, David Garrow, when asked what interested him about Obama five years after he left office was "how completely he's vanished."[599] In 2008, when Obama took office, Democrats held fifty-five seats in the Senate and 256 seats in the House. It constituted the national backlash against George W. Bush's wars, the housing market catastrophe, and ineptitude dealing with Hurricane Katrina. Yet, no one could claim that the Republicans did much with their six years of House control or two years of Senate control or even offered any meaningful resistance. Quite the contrary. From the Clinton years forward, the recurring inability of the House to demand a budget and to refuse to pass a continuing resolution constituted the last vestige of its shrinking power. Despite three consecutive victories in the Obama years, Republicans watched the House drift into irrelevance, unwilling to employ its key constitutional power of the purse.

Republicans proved that once in office, they lacked the will to accomplish anything of significance. Obama, on the other hand, proved unable to get anyone elected except himself or to fundamentally transform anything except a small Chicago neighborhood.

CHAPTER 6
THE ESCALATOR

As the Obama administration came into its twilight, the opportunity for a Republican to win the presidency seemed glowing. After all, Republicans had taken back the House in 2010 and the Senate in 2014. Their field was awash in good candidates—that is, by traditional standards. There were Governors Scott Walker of Wisconsin, Chris Christie of New Jersey, Jeb Bush of Florida, and John Kasich of Ohio; Senators Ted Cruz of Texas and Rand Paul of Kentucky; surgeon Ben Carson; former Arkansas Governor Mike Huckabee and former Virginia Governor Jim Gilmore; former Senator Rick Santorum of Pennsylvania; and Hewlett-Packard exec and California gubernatorial candidate Carly Fiorina.

One stood out as having no chance, completely unconventional, and, to many, unserious: real-estate billionaire and television personality Donald Trump.

The Republicans aligned against Democrat Hillary Clinton, who was the former secretary of state, former New York senator, wife of former president Bill Clinton, and...most important, the expected first female president of the United States. Despite the crowded GOP field, her ascension over any of them was expected. For many, it was considered inevitable. And, as they say in football, that is why you play the game.

THE PERSISTENT THREAT

Since George W. Bush's second term, "immigration reform" (by which Washingtonians almost always meant "amnesty") had persisted as a promise and a threat for American politicians. Bush had to fold on the issue relatively quickly when the so-called Gang of Eight led by Senators John McCain, Lindsey Graham, and a young Marco Rubio triggered such a massive popular backlash that the legislation fizzled out for the lack of votes. That episode, pregnant with lessons about the concerns of the American public, faded into DC's foggy past. Although Obama tiptoed around the edges of immigration with his "DACA" program, he dared not risk a full-scale grassroots rebellion on the issue.

All immigration—and illegal immigration in particular—wove together multiple domestic problems facing America. It touched on the problems of the Rust Belt, with manufacturing moved to Mexico; it touched on Silicon Valley jobs, with H-1B immigrants taking programming work at lower wages; it generated rising crime rates; and it stretched America's thinning "social safety net." Yet for the myriad of problems created by immigration (legal and illegal), no one in either party wanted to address it. Restricting new immigration or stopping the flow of illegals across the border was particularly unpopular among the ruling class.

Ross Perot had run what was termed a "populist" campaign in 1992 and while he netted nearly 19 percent of the vote, he didn't carry a single state in the Electoral College. He won more than enough to derail George H. W. Bush, but his campaign struggled and was even temporarily suspended. Many pundits failed to detect the significant differences between Trump and Perot. Although Trump had been a businessman then a part-time television entertainer all his life, he had nevertheless stayed active in issues, testifying before Congress on housing and construction. For a decade, he had been critical of America's involvement in foreign wars. As illegal immigration increasingly became a problem too big to ignore, he took that on as his major issue. The media and politicians in both parties were shocked at how much the issue resonated with ordinary Americans.

An early lightning rod for his claims about the dangers of unchecked immigration came in February 2015 when Kate Steinle was shot and killed by an illegal immigrant and repeated felon in San Francisco.[600] Immediately, it galvanized Trump's message. In Phoenix, he had been booked at a ballroom at The Phoenician resort that had a capacity of 2,500 and suddenly had to be moved to the Phoenix Convention Center with a capacity several times that. To those paying attention, it should have raised alarms. At the very least, it should have suggested that he was onto something. Instead, critics derided Trump as a racist.

On June 16, 2015, Trump rode down the golden escalator at Trump Tower to announce that he was running for president. The once fawning media—Oprah had him on her show, race bigwigs like Al Sharpton and Jesse Jackson palled around with him, and the who's who of show business had been photographed with him at one time or another—almost immediately went into attack mode. Stories claimed that Trump paid people fifty dollars to "wave signs and make noise" and that he handed out merchandise for his remarkably insightful campaign theme of "Make America Great Again" (MAGA). Within months, the same outlets would be quibbling over whether Trump had ten thousand or fifteen thousand supporters at a rally. Hateful reporters later said of the supporters there that "basically, none of them spoke English."[601] Aware, however, that Trump had tapped into genuine concern about illegal immigration, the media sought to portray him as xenophobic and depicted his (later proven correct) claims that many of the illegals were rapists and murderers as lies. By doing so, they unwittingly made Trump the only Republican candidate who could win.

Other Republicans, even including the Senate firebrand Ted Cruz who once led a filibuster to stop Obamacare, failed to understand the growing weight of the immigration argument. Because it affected jobs, Trump easily connected illegal immigration to the decline of the Rust Belt and appealed to laid-off workers in Michigan, Ohio, and Pennsylvania. Because it affected national defense, Trump defanged the neocon hawks such as Marco Rubio. Because both legal and illegal immigration placed such a monstrous burden on social services and schools, Trump tied it effortlessly to the out-of-control budget and failing education system in America, not to mention making it the enemy of Obamacare. Thus, there were sixteen other candidates at one point or another in the race—and Trump. Only he and Dr. Ben Carson stood out for being "non-politicians" and after Trump won, he was the only president never to have previously either held political office or served in the US military. One month after he came down the escalator, Trump led in his first national poll. Except for a brief stint when Carson topped Trump nationally, the New Yorker maintained his GOP polling lead for the rest of the season.[602]

Despite Trump's astoundingly consistent strength before primary voting began, a strange refrain emerged that the polling leads were vaporous, and that Trump could not win. Breitbart's Jerome Hudson created a list of experts who predicted his defeat:

- Ross Douthat, *The New York Times*: "Donald Trump will not be the Republican Nominee."
- James Downie, *The Washington Post*: "Let's dispense with the notion that Trump has a real shot at winning in November [2016]."
- Hilary Rosen, CNN: Trump lost the election "from the first day he announced."
- *The Huffington Post*: "Donald Trump will not…win the general election."
- Mark Green, *Los Angeles Times*: "Hillary Clinton will beat Donald Trump" by 7 percent with "perhaps a double-digit landslide."
- Karl Rove, MSNBC: "Trump can't win the general election."

- Sean Trende, RealClearPolitics: "There's probably a 90% chance Trump loses."
- Jonathan Bernstein, *Bloomberg*: "Seriously, Trump won't win."
- Jon Weiner, *The Nation*: "Relax, Donald Trump can't win."
- Noah Williams, *Forbes*: "Trump won't win Wisconsin."
- Frank Luntz: "Hillary Clinton will be the next President of the United States."[603]

As noted in my book with Joel Pollack, *How Trump Won*, I not only said that Trump would win the primaries easily but that he would also win the general election with between 300 and 320 electoral votes. (The final was 304.)[604]

One by one, Trump's opponents dropped out, with one of the first being the latest Bush to run, Jeb. Extremely well-funded, Jeb became the target of Trump's satirizing when, during a debate, Trump said he had "low energy." Only Cruz and Ohio's John Kasich remained, eventually attempting a type of state delegate tag team, where each promised not to oppose the other in their most favorable remaining states. None of it worked. After Cruz won the Iowa caucus, Trump racked up victories, interspersed by only a few defeats. His dominance would have caused profound soul-searching in previous decades. In defeating two Florida natives, Bush and Rubio, Trump won every county in the state, every county in Virginia, and every county in New York, save one. Despite a checkered past of two divorces and a persona as a playboy, Trump carried the Bible Belt. Trump won 75 percent of the vote in California and took the college educated as well as blue-collar voters. In May, Trump acquired enough delegates to secure the nomination.

Even then, the members of the establishment in both parties could not believe what they had witnessed. After the 2012 Mitt Romney debacle, the GOP produced a report claiming that it needed to be more diverse, and the field Trump beat was diversity on steroids: an Indian American (Bobby Jindal), a black surgeon (Carson), two Cuban Americans (Rubio and Cruz), and a woman (Fiorina). Yet Trump appealed to diverse *voters* more than any of them. Trump deliberately spoke to the substantially white working class that had seen its wages decline, its jobs disappear, and its cities filled with immigrants receiving welfare. He, not McCain, was popular with the families of those who had overwhelmingly provided the soldiers for the failed expeditions in Afghanistan and Iraq (who were disproportionately Hispanic). And he, not budget balancers like Scott Walker, appealed to the Tea Party conservatives who looked beyond balanced budgets to policies that would truly restore American economic greatness. To apply Amity Shlaes's phrase about those whom the New Deal left behind, Trump appealed to the modern "forgotten man."[605]

As much as anything that accounted for Trump's appeal, people realized "he fights," a phrase that came to dominate their otherwise amorphous source of support. Like Limbaugh, Trump refused to just accept the other side's assumptions. Trump rejected media narratives and told the reporters so to their face, pulling no punches. He would not go along with fallacious assumptions about such things as "global warming" or inherent white racism. Above all, Trump made it clear that he fought for his supporters, not himself. "I always loved to fight," he told one biographer, "all types of fights, including physical."[606] It was no surprise then that after he was wounded in a Pennsylvania assassination attempt, he defiantly stood and as the Secret Service tried to remove him from the stage, raised a fist and shouted to the crowd, "FIGHT! FIGHT."[607]

NOT *THE APPRENTICE*

So, who was Donald John Trump? As of 2015, Trump was one of the most recognized names in America. Ninety-six percent of Americans knew him, at least at a distance. One critical author observed that "in one way or another, Donald Trump has been a topic of conversation in America for almost forty years," and no other businessman since 1950 has been as famous.[608]

While some would place him in the pantheon of high achievers of questionable business ethics (such as John D. Rockefeller or Andrew Carnegie), Trump's businesses never came close to the massive networks of oil and steel wrought by his predecessors. However, Trump easily matched those titans in negotiating ability and vision for an empire—not an empire of product like rails or petroleum but of brand. One court deposition found the brand name "Trump" was worth $3 billion.[609] Trump's empire was ultimately Trump himself. As biographer Michael D'Antonio noted, "Dozens of men and women with several times Trump's holdings are unknown to those outside the world's billionaires."[610] By the 1980s, he was the seventh most admired man on Earth out ranked only by the Pope and presidents. At six foot three and possessing pure blond hair, Trump's physical bearing was more impressive than that of either Bush or Obama. His life story was scarcely less impressive.

Trump's grandparents came from Germany in the 1880s with the name Trumpf. His grandfather soon dropped the *f*. His son, Frederick Trump Sr., resided in the Bronx then moved to Queens, working in home construction before starting a real estate business. Eventually, Frederick Trump built twenty-seven thousand apartments in New York. In 1946, the family had their fourth child, Donald John, born on June 14, 1946. He grew up in a house built by his own father.

Donald disliked school, leading his father to dispatch him to New York Military Academy. That straightened him out, teaching him strict discipline. On top of that, Frederick required all the kids to work.[611] Frederick not only encouraged stiff competition but also total victory: "Be a killer," he instructed them.[612] Young Donald heard his father. In sports at school he told his teammates that their only purpose was to win.

Enrolling in Fordham University in 1964, Trump transferred to the prestigious Wharton School in 1966, majoring in economics. Endued with an Adderall-level of energy, Trump never smoked cigarettes, drank alcohol, or did drugs. He also exercised little, aside from golf. Based on available records, he never suffered any serious illness that debilitated him or took him off the board for long periods of time (as had occurred with John F. Kennedy). Trump boiled with constant energy. He slept only four to six hours a night. In his presidential runs, he would—in his seventies—hold two rallies per day at times where he spoke for over an hour at each. In modern terms, he was an excitement junkie.

Whether his energy level or educational training gave him business advantages, Trump learned the real estate business well from his father. In 1971, Frederick made Donald president of The Trump Organization. Some of his projects were grandiose: He once proposed a castle development for Manhattan, and a 1985 model of the skyline featured a tower that very much resembled the modern World Trade Center replacement, the Freedom Tower.[613] One of his most-noted real estate achievements was the renovation of the Commodore Hotel next to Grand Central Terminal, which Trump reopened as the Grand Hyatt Hotel. This particular project was worth reviewing because it showed Trump's "art of the deal" in real life and at the same time, completely refuted notions that "Trump doesn't read."

> Negotiating simultaneously with Hyatt, the city [New York] and Penn Central, Trump used one to leverage the other. Hyatt's reputation as a hotel developer and operator would reassure [commissioners] that Trump could manage the Commodore project. [The Penn Central] execs gave Trump an informal first position on the property, based on an eventual $10 million purchase price. But they did not sign a binding agreement to do the deal. For Trump, who didn't have the $250,000 required to finalize his option on the property, this was not a real problem. He announced to the press that he had "an option" and a "purchase contract" for the Commodore, and no one contradicted him. When city officials asked for a copy of his agreement with Penn Central, he sent them the paperwork, minus the

> signatures that would have made it binding...[and no one noticed]. [The] bureaucracy continued to move forward, as if the parties had signed, and Trump had actually paid.... The key to it all was the paperwork sleight of hand, which became, years later, a matter of pride for Trump "They only asked to see an agreement," he would say. "They didn't say it had to be signed."[614]

Trump, describing this in *The Art of the Deal*, recalled that the contract copy "was signed only by me, and not the railroad, because I had yet to put down my $250,000. No one even noticed that until almost two years later."[615]

What stands out was that not only did Trump successfully play one participant against another, but also that *only he* had read the paperwork well enough to know that signatures were missing. It illustrated Trump's keen interest in the very process of negotiating itself: "I won't make a deal just to make a profit," he once told one bureaucrat. "It has to have its own excitement. Its own flair."[616]

During his construction career, Trump had a number of bankruptcies—most developers do. He would later point out that of over one hundred construction projects going on around the world, only a few—but high profile—were bankruptcies. One of the largest, the Trump Taj Mahal in Atlantic City, forced Trump to sell his airline, Trump Shuttle, and yacht, *Trump Princess*, to cover his personal debt. His last major construction project was the Trump International Hotel in Chicago.

Along the way, in addition to an airline, Trump purchased a pro football team, the New Jersey Generals, and tried to change the United States Football League to a fall schedule to force the National Football League into a merger because of antitrust violations. He purchased the Miss Universe, Miss USA, and Miss Teen USA pageants and produced the shows. He authored several books, including his number one bestseller, *The Art of the Deal* (1987), as well as subsequent campaign-related books such as *Crippled America* in 2015. As with most books "written" by celebrities, politicians, or preachers, Trump used ghostwriters.

Trump, however, showed extreme wit in his many postings on Twitter (now X). In June 2014, he tweeted, "I hope we never find life on other planets because there's no doubt that the U.S. Government will start sending them money!"[617] In another tweet, he said, "I love Twitter…it's like owning your own newspaper—without the losses."[618]

Already featured in a cameo in *Home Alone 2*, numerous other films, and several television shows, he also produced and hosted *The Apprentice*. It was a reality TV show starting in 2004 about business skills where the contestants attended a boardroom meeting with Trump, who terminated them with "You're fired." The show ran fourteen seasons, but Trump left after three seasons and was awarded a star on Hollywood's Walk of Fame. By appearing in *The Apprentice*, Trump joined President Ronald Reagan as the only two US presidents to be in a labor union (the Screen Actors Guild). Fittingly, he married a star model, and a millionaire in her own right, Melania Knauss.

He had already come to criticize foreign military interventions. Still, he knew intuitively that Mitt Romney would lose and already the seed of running in 2016 had been planted. His 2015 book, *Crippled America*, he intoned "America needs to start winning again…. If I ran my business that way [that America was run], I'd fire myself."[619] In the book, he also dropped hints of how he would run for president, noting how he got the traditional media, despite its bias, to give him free coverage.

Still, whether it was the sometimes-positive media or his various onetime friends, once he was a Republican running for election, the knives came out. By the end of the 2016 campaign, most estimates were that Trump received at least 90 percent negative coverage. Civil rights leaders who just a few years earlier had rushed to have their pictures taken with him now denounced him. In the very first debate, Fox News moderator Megyn Kelly opened up by slamming him about his slurs against women. He retorted, "Only [against] Rosie O'Donnell."[620]

Politically, Trump was not ideological but practical. He made an anemic run for the presidency in 2000 by seeking the nomination of the Reform Party, but followed it extensively, thinking the Republicans had gotten "too crazy." Trump once said, "Non-politicians represent the wave of the future."[621] In that, Trump was getting close to the truth: The Republicans in 1994 had sported a number of nonpoliticians, including former Seattle Seahawks wide receiver Steve Largent; former Oklahoma University quarterback J. C. Watts; former history teacher Newt Gingrich (who became Speaker of the House); Arizona's J. D. Hayworth, who was a radio DJ; former pop star singer Sonny Bono; and in the Senate, heart surgeon Bill Frist. As *The Hill* noted, they "were doctors and farmers, pop stars and football players."[622] And in 2020, just when it appeared that his prophecy might come true with the announcement by rapper Kanye West that he was running for the highest office, Covid hit. Celebrity politics in America suddenly were knocked backward a decade as frightened Americans turned to (ostensibly) pros.

Trump's celebrity status did not change the fact that he depicted himself honestly: "I'm not prepackaged. I'm not plastic. I'm not scripted. And I'm not 'handled.' I'll tell you what I think."[623] Such "plainspeak" drove his 2016 campaign. Radio host Rush Limbaugh—at first skeptical of Trump precisely because the candidate lacked a typical ideological grounding—came to be one of his most vocal supporters. Trump's frankness, however, always contained a pinch of P. T. Barnum's salesmanship. Everything was the biggest, the greatest, the most beautiful. He would frequently insist that his rallies broke attendance records or, after the election, that his inauguration was the biggest. When he introduced projects, they would always be "great" or "the best"—because in Trump's mind they *were* going to be the best. Hyperbole of that type seemed to drive the press insane, leading them to label Trump a liar.

It was just Trump salesmanship. *The Atlantic* correctly noted that the media "takes [Trump] literally, but not seriously; his supporters take him seriously, but not literally."[624] Thus, when Trump first said in 2013 that he'd build a big, beautiful wall to keep out illegal aliens, conference attendees "just went nuts." Trump added, "Nobody...builds like Trump."[625] The media obsessed over the type or even the materials of the wall, while MAGA voters didn't care what it looked like: It was big and beautiful if it worked, sort of like a 1956 Chevy. More important, it came to represent a physical, tangible reality that spoke to his broader policy ends.

"YOU'D BE IN JAIL"

It became clear to Trump before he won the nomination that his campaign manager, Corey Lewandowski, was not skilled or connected enough to nail down the final nomination details. Trump handed control over to a longtime Republican operative Paul Manafort, who, as was later discovered, had businesses steeped in corruption. Manafort really had only one task: Make sure the delegates that Trump won stayed "won." He accomplished that, but the campaign then took on water. In part, Manafort struggled because he surrounded himself with non-MAGA loyalists from the Scott Walker and Chris Christie campaigns, neither of which was viewed as sufficiently loyal to MAGA's core ideas.

By August, some of Trump's chief donors grew antsy, most notably Robert Mercer, who had contributed heavily. After the Democratic convention, when Trump made a series of ill-considered (or badly interpreted) remarks, Mercer's daughter, Rebekah, flew to meet Trump in East Hampton and told him bluntly to find someone more aggressive than Manafort to run the campaign. Her suggestion was Steve Bannon.

Bannon, a gruff ex-Navy officer who had become involved in entertainment financing at Goldman Sachs (including financing the hit television series *Seinfeld*, which provided Bannon with a financial safety net for his entire life), had taken over the conservative news site *Breitbart*. Named after activist Andrew Breitbart, who died of a heart attack in 2012, *Breitbart* news had surpassed all other sites as the leading edgy conservative news site on the web. Bannon pushed it even further. By the time Trump ran for president, *Breitbart* was full MAGA.

As a typical big-picture strategist, Bannon fed off statistics, polling, and intuitive voter sentiment as he felt it. He prioritized the issues that Trump highlighted in his rallies. Bannon benefited from a more traditional cochairman, Kellyanne Conway. She focused on organization and general public relations. A third but largely unseen member of the troika running the Trump campaign was his son-in-law Jared Kushner, who handled the financial side. In the background lurked David Bossie of think tank Citizens United. Bossie had led the charge against the McCain-Feingold Act, seeking to limit "soft money"—and won. Now he, Conway, and Bannon all were involved in a super PAC (political action committee) called "Defeat Crooked Hillary PAC." The genius of the "Defeat Crooked Hillary" committee lay in the fact that it enabled those reluctant to support Trump to nevertheless donate to Clinton's defeat.[626]

Perhaps Bannon's greatest contribution to the campaign involved refocusing it on "crooked Hillary" as the campaign now referred to Clinton. It minimized Trump's own comments and weaknesses and directed Americans to Clinton's multiple problems, including the ongoing FBI investigation of her reckless and immature use of classified emails. Intuitively, Bannon knew that voters just did not like Hillary. Since her White House days, dozens of stories had leaked about her abuse of staff, her overall condescension, and her sense of entitlement. Trump turned people off because of the things he said. Hillary repelled people because of who she was.

Having lost in a shocking primary to Barack Obama, Hillary Clinton was subsequently expected to be Obama successor. She had, by Washington standards, the prototypical résumé. Ambitious for her husband's success, reportedly she brought him literally off the floor in a fetal position after losing the Arkansas governor's race in 1980. Hillary (as she was more commonly known) played a powerful supporting role to Governor Clinton. Once he won the presidency in 1992, Clinton named his wife to head a medical insurance reform effort. Couched in secrecy when

Hillary's bus tour finally rolled the program out, it was repudiated immediately by the public and never got off the ground.

During Bill Clinton's sexual foibles in the 1990s, Hillary (as the song went) stood by her man. Pundits generally agreed that she expected "her turn" when Bill's presidency ended. The family moved to Chappaqua, New York, so that she could run for the New York Senate seat previously held by legendary Daniel Patrick Moynihan. She won easily. Forced by the popular mood to support the invasion in Iraq—which damaged her run against Obama—Hillary took the position of Obama's secretary of state in 2009. Her tenure included such ill-considered policies as undermining established "strongman" governments in the Middle East, funneling money to Iran, and fomenting hostility toward Russia. At one point, concerned that US-Russian relations had deteriorated so much, she pulled out a box with a red "reset" button to urge a do-over.

The bubbling of stories about Clinton's treatment of those working for her seemed to reach a boil by 2016, heated by greater public exposure. Secret Service agents assigned to her detail "considered [it] a form of punishment and the worst assignment in the Secret Service."[627] She told Clinton FBI agent in charge, Gary Aldrich, "Stay the f**k back, stay the f**k away from me! Don't come within ten yards of me!"; she "just let everybody have it" said Bill's chief of staff Leon Panetta; she had "screaming, child-like tantrums that have left staff members in tears and unable to work," said a campaign worker; and so on.[628] Peter Hart, a Democratic pollster, observed that all of Hillary's problems came down to "one thing and one thing only, and that is likeability."[629] Gallup found that some 65 percent of Americans considered her "untrustworthy."

Bill Clinton had almost everything Hillary did not. People liked him. While voters viewed Hillary as radical and far left, they still thought of Bill as moderate. Yet she did not want him as a major component of the campaign, lest she be viewed as reliant on him. Nor did she listen to his recommendations for policy or even tactics. "She resented the fact that Bill was treated like a rock star," one campaign adviser noted.[630]

Her primary campaign in 2016 was supposed to be smooth sailing, but the crotchety socialist senator from Vermont, Bernie Sanders, threatened to throw a wrench into Clinton's Ferrari engine. Sanders unveiled a strong class-warfare message—to some degree a leftist version of MAGA—that oddly, despite his age, resonated well with youth. Sanders exploited big gatherings and large, enthusiastic crowds—something Clinton rarely could do. He seemed authentic in his socialist worldview (at least until he purchased his third house for $600,000, hardly the image a poor socialist would convey). Critics, however, noted that he slinked away quietly after Hillary won the requisite number of delegates, leading to questions of whether the house was a form of payoff for his silence. He had the crowds and notched a few primary victories, but Clinton won just enough to make her real strength felt—that of the superdelegates who were already pledged to her. On the surface, it appeared Sanders might had have a chance. Beneath the surface, it was clear that Clinton had the machinery and the nomination locked up before she started.

In fact, Clinton had more assistance than Democratic voters knew. Leaked emails showed that the DNC was conspiring to secure the nomination for Hillary. Later, when the emails were revealed, the beginnings of the Russia Hoax led the Clinton network to try to portray the operation as a *Russian government effort* to stop Clinton. (In fact, the Russians saw her as less of a threat than Trump.)[631] Later still, under the weight of more evidence becoming public, the chairwoman of the DNC, Debbie Wasserman Schultz, was forced to resign. Another competitor of Clinton's, Senator Elizabeth Warren of Massachusetts, agreed that the DNC had attempted to "rig" the election.

Armed with the nomination, Clinton faced an issue that Sanders refused to raise: She had been reckless if not criminal in her use of unsecured emails. During her tenures at the State Department, she began using a private email server for her public communications. While an initial review concluded that she did not have any classified emails on the server, agencies found that some sixty-five documents should have been labeled "SECRET" and another twenty-two "TOP SECRET." An additional two thousand retroactively were designated classified by the State Department. In July, the director of the FBI, James Comey, issued a statement saying Clinton had been "extremely careless" but because she did not act with "criminal intent," no charges should be filed. (It should be noted that most crimes short of murder do not require "intent" to be proven, only the crime.)[632] Trump, already suspecting that American democracy was being manipulated, simply tweeted: '@realDonaldTrump The system is rigged...."[633] Obama eventually would tell Trump to "stop whining" and that there as "no serious person out there who would suggest somehow that you could even rig America's elections." This was four years before the highly questionable simultaneous shutdowns of five major urban counting centers, massive late vote counting that often ran 90–10 in favor of the Democrats, and more than a third of the public who thought that the 2020 election was illegitimate.[634] It was also before a rash of convictions for election tampering spread across the country. And needless to say, it was before the largest election tampering operation in American history, the Russia Hoax, had started.

Yet it soon became apparent that through a pseudonym Obama himself had been emailing over a nongovernment, nonsecure system.[635] That is, when it "emerged that the White House was refusing to disclose at least 22 communications Obama had exchanged with then-secretary Clinton over the latter's private e-mail account...Obama had knowingly engaged in the same misconduct that was the focus of the Clinton probe: the reckless mishandling of classified information."[636] Not only had Obama "engaged in the same misconduct" as Clinton, he had also engaged in it *with* Clinton. Thus, Comey joined the cover-up by refusing to even demand the documents, let alone act on the results. And thus, Obama himself became a part of the very election fraud he insisted couldn't occur.

In an October debate, Hillary said, "It's just awfully good that someone with the temperament of Donald Trump is not in charge of the law in our country," to which Trump retorted, "Because...you'd be in jail."[637] The email controversy had not ended, but a much different one had begun.

On October 7, word leaked of footage from an NBC show called *Access Hollywood* where Trump supposedly was bragging about the sexual lengths women allowed stars to go with them, saying, "You can do anything"[638]—women would even allow powerful men to grab them by their genitals. (Trump was confirming what two generations of rock stars and movie producers already admitted.)[639] Anti-Trump Republicans saw their chance to boot him from the ticket and suddenly jump in with one of their moderates. High-ranking Senator John Thune said that Trump should quit and "Mike Pence should be our nominee effective immediately."[640] Smelling blood in the water, House Speaker Paul Ryan announced he would no longer "defend" Trump; Republican National Committee chairman Reince Priebus withdrew from his round of Sunday morning shows and went to Trump's penthouse to advise him to quit or "go down with a worse election loss than Barry Goldwater"; and Senator Mike Lee agreed Trump should step down.[641] As Bannon later said, virtually the entire campaign thought Trump had to withdraw—except for Bannon.

Having learned well from Democrats, Bannon knew that a candidate can never apologize and never retreat: attack, attack, attack. He immediately planned a crushing pivot, and one that no other strategist on either side would have dared. Although Trump issued an apologetic statement for his words, he instantly turned to Bill Clinton's *actions* toward women, highlighting his alleged rape of Juanita Broaddrick, his admitted affair with Paula Jones for which he had paid a settlement, and the groping of Kathleen Willey. In addition, Bannon came up with a touch that tied the sexual abuse back to Hillary herself: Kathy Shelton had been twelve years old when then-lawyer Hillary Clinton had defended her accused rapist in court. Bannon, in a jujitsu move that virtually no one would have conceived, brought the four women together at a press conference right before the debate that night and then sat them in the debate audience in clear eyeshot of both Bill and Hillary.

An iconic photo captured Bill wide-eyed staring at the four women. In a single, brilliant political act, Bannon had mostly nullified the impact of the *Access Hollywood* tape and reminded the voters that while Trump had *said* things, Bill Clinton stood accused of actually *doing* them. Many of the squishy Republicans who had just days earlier denounced Trump slithered back to his side.

It would be inaccurate to say that the *Access Hollywood* incident did not permanently scar Trump's campaign. It played a role in making Florida closer; it badly hurt Trump in New Hampshire, which he likely would have won without it. But after a week, most of the damage receded and Trump's polls recovered.[642] Without question, Trump never would have been president without Bannon's aggressive attack dog reversal in that incident.

The Donald (as he was often called) had taken the Deep State's best shot. Hillary's turn came soon after, when on October 28 James Comey resurfaced like the shark from *Jaws* to notify Congress that the FBI had looked into thousands of new emails. Critics claimed that he had violated the DOJ's guidelines against interfering in an election (a concern never raised in 2024 when Attorney Merrick Garland and his minion hordes of prosecutors and lawyers released report after report on Trump in the election). Yet once again, the FBI claimed that it found no evidence of Clinton's criminality. Both sides howled. Democrats were furious that the issue had been raised in the first place; Republicans insisted that for anyone not named "Clinton," the DOJ would have brought charges.

By that point, each campaign had survived a serious setback, and virtually all expert observers thought Clinton had the election in the bag. She had let slip a line in which she referred to Trump voters as "deplorable"—an appellation MAGA supporters wore with pride—but it again illustrated to many the "ruling class vs. country class" division at work in the nation and the scorn with which embedded politicians of both parties viewed ordinary people. Clinton also suffered from health maladies, which even to this date have never been explained. She had bouts of coughing during her speeches. At one point, while getting into her SUV, she completely collapsed and had to be lifted in by Secret Service agents. Whether that played any role in voters' views of her was never polled or tested.

Early ballot returns in Florida especially showed Trump's strength far more potent than pollsters estimated. Clinton had fallen behind Obama's early voting numbers by significant margins. Pollster Richard Baris noted that Clinton lost Florida "before Election Day" and that she had quietly surrendered North Carolina as well.[643] Although the RealClearPolitics' "No Toss-Up States" average had the race a close Clinton victory in the Electoral College, most polling looked hopeless for Trump. Not a single major poll had Trump winning. One pollster, however, found a unique way to measure Trump's hidden support. The Trafalgar Group, like other polling organizations, asked, "Who do you plan to vote for?" or some variation of that question, but then added another question: "Who do you think your neighbor will vote for?" Suddenly, a hidden swell of support surfaced for Trump. A new category, the "shy Trump voter," was born.

Nevertheless, even Trump did not expect to win. Bannon and the rest of the campaign organization gathered around the television monitors at Trump Tower. Baris, long before anyone else, calculated that Trump would win Florida—itself a big blow to Clinton, but not fatal. He made the call at 9:20 p.m. ahead of any network, and then, an hour later, a stunned Megyn Kelly on Fox announced that Trump was projected to win Wisconsin. That alone provided him the electoral votes to win the election. Soon, Pennsylvania and Michigan followed. Baris called the Clinton headquarters for a comment: "They're crying," he said. "They hung up on me…but they know they lost."[644]

Hillary had indeed won the popular vote by two million ballots but lost the Electoral College 304–227, including key states such as Texas, Florida, North Carolina, Ohio, Michigan, Pennsylvania, and Wisconsin. Indeed, Hillary barely even visited Wisconsin. Protests erupted and while Hillary did not want to be seen as contesting the outcome, she fully supported recounts in Wisconsin, Michigan, and Pennsylvania by Green

Party candidate Jill Stein. One by one, those recounts were stopped or allowed to continue with no change in the outcome. Donald Trump was the forty-fifth president of the US.

"RESIST"

To say that Democrats and those on the left were stunned on election night is an understatement. Footage of election night coverage showed Hillary supporters dumbfounded, crying, and even yelling. Although the concept of "manufacturing" votes after most were counted dated back to at least 2000 and the "butterfly" ballots—if not back to Cook County in the 1960 election,[645] when there were widespread allegations of fraud and dead people "voting"—no one had yet attempted a national post–Election Day ballot-stuffing operation. Put another way, the left was unprepared for Donald Trump. It wouldn't happen in 2020.

Caught mostly unawares, Democrats relied on their major activist group, "antifa" (standing for "antifascist"—an odd name for a group that operated much like Benito Mussolini's Brownshirts). Rioters started protests in which fires were started, blocked freeways, and (when city officials decided to enforce the law) battled with police. Democratic leaders such as Senator Chuck Schumer, as liberal writer Camille Paglia observed, "asserted absolutely no moral authority as the party spun out of control in a nationwide orgy of rage and spite."[646] Over two hundred thousand angry women showed up in DC at the "Women's March," with another four million staging protest marches around the country. Women in Washington wore pink "pussy hats" and carried prepared signs funded and fabricated by Clinton staffers.

Celebrities such as Cher, Katy Perry, and Madonna spoke to the crowd, avoiding the fact that Trump had won a decisive victory. "I have thought an awful lot," said Madonna, "of blowing up the White House."[647] Comedian Kathy Griffin posed with the bloody head of Trump as if she had just come from a guillotine.[648] New York's "Shakespeare in the Park" featured a mock assassination of the president, Julius Caesar–style.

Not one was visited by the Secret Service or agents of the DOJ for such comments, whereas four years later, people who simply made comments on Twitter were arrested. At various marches, odd stacks of bricks—with nary a construction site in view—suddenly appeared for protesters to use. Almost every leftist group joined in. Sierra Club's executive director, Michael Brune, said, "We will fight like dogs."[649]

Indeed, they did violently respond. At the Democrat-Republican baseball game in Virginia in 2017, a deranged Sanders supporter shot several GOP congressmen, seriously wounding Republican Congressman Steve Scalise.[650]

Without question the former "mainstream news" media joined into the frenzy. *The Washington Post* put a new byline in its masthead: "Democracy Dies in Darkness" (then proceeded to cover up the FBI's and the Clinton campaign's role in the Russia Hoax). The *Post* alone assigned over fifty reporters and staff just to dig up dirt on Trump. A new name was developed for the level of unhinged rage against Trump: "Trump Derangement Syndrome."[651]

On Inauguration Day, 2017, the aforementioned *Post* announced, "The campaign to impeach President Trump has begun." *Time* echoed the *Post*: "Legal Scholars: Why Congress Should Impeach Donald Trump." *Politico* added, "Trump Impeached? You Can Bet on It."[652] Yet Trump literally had done nothing yet in office. To the left, any fair election that did not yield a victory for its candidate was grounds for impeaching the victor. But not far away was the ever reliable Trump-hater McCain, who insisted (again, with nothing having happened) that the Trump presidency was of "Watergate size and scale."[653]

Both within Congress and within the "Never Trump" Republican Party, there were campaigns to try to convince Trump electors to "vote their conscience." (Those making such appeals never asked if perhaps by voting for Trump the electors *were* voting their conscience.)[654] Colorado's secretary of state fought a clearly unconstitutional ex post facto attempt to pass a law binding the state to the winner of the popular vote. It did not always work out as planned: On December 19, two electors voted against Trump, but five voted against Clinton—expanding Trump's lead. Still, others attempted to vote against Clinton and were replaced or forced to vote again.

Hillary's postmortem, published in her 2017 book *What Happened* (meant as a statement, not a question), constituted a cavalcade of blame (of others) and lack of serious self-reflection or honest assessment of the campaign's history. Claiming she was in constant touch with local leaders, she did not campaign hard at all in Michigan and barely campaigned in Wisconsin. She blamed a "vicious cycle" with the political press, when subsequent analysis found that Trump got 93 percent negative coverage. Her early opinion research correctly noted the "pain points" of economic pressure and political gridlock but entirely ignored two of Trump's most successful issues—stopping illegal immigration and making the US a great power again. She admitted that even as a woman she was unlikely to be viewed as a "transformative figure" and that she had "been on the national stage too long." For half of America, that meant Hillary was part of the swamp that needed draining. She and her team desperately were working on a theme when Trump came down the escalator with one of the greatest elevator pitches ever: "Make America Great Again." Above all, Clinton never seemed to be able to answer the one question that had torpedoed candidates from Ted Kennedy to Mitt Romney: "Why are you running for president?"[655]

Nevertheless, the Democrats weren't quite finished. On January 6, 2017, when the official Electoral College count was held, many Democrats issued objections to the certification. (In 2020, similar attempts by Republicans to challenge Biden's totals were not entertained by the chair.) In fact, a much different, more damaging and utterly despicable resistance campaign had already started, concocted by Hillary's campaign with the help of the FBI and CIA. They all had help from a group of Never Trump Republicans. None of the left's efforts to slow Trump down could have happened without this fifth column, and thus it is important to understand the nature of that group.

The Never Trump Republicans included both former Bush presidents; five GOP presidential nominees, twenty-two former cabinet-level officials, twenty former governors, seventeen former and (at the time) current senators, and over fifty members of the House. Author Ed Klein constructed a long list puzzling why those officials opposed Trump as he stood for almost every single issue they (supposedly) favored.[656] The question mostly unasked was not whether Trump changed his positions on those issues but rather whether the Never Trump group ever truly believed in them in the first place. What happened was that so long as the establishment GOP could "claim" the issue without ever possessing a means to actually address it, its members remained safe. They could fundraise on promises without hardships; they could provide the foil on television panels without ever having to actually envision their purported positions becoming a reality. Trump had no such interest. His only objective was to affect change and to accomplish what he said he would. That posed a grave danger to them.

Ed Klein found an FBI field report on people within the "resist" movement in the government. It stated,

> The Bureau has gotten actionable intelligence that there is, within the federal government, a growing and organized movement to block or interfere with administration policy decisions.... There have been regular organized meetings of large numbers of government workers at a church in the Columbia Heights area of the District [of Columbia] where plans have been discussed to actively sabotage government programs they disagree with.... One management level government employee said, 'Bureaucrats are going to delay, drag their feet and throw roadblocks in the way of unconscionable actions by the Trump White House. It is going to become impossible to get these actions done.'[657]

(The author of the memo was likely stupefied at exactly how much Trump achieved in spite of the author's efforts and those of their fellow cabal members.)

The new resistance began with a hack of the DNC email server, was facilitated by an entirely falsified CIA document attributed to the British MI5, and was accelerated by Never Trumper Senator McCain, who passed along the wholly concocted, false document to the FBI that loaned credibility to the fabrication.[658] The effort eventually became known as the "Russia Hoax."

THE RUSSIA HOAX

It is a matter of argument as to which constricted Trump's achievements more in his first term: an oppositional Congress and Senate—even in Republican hands but, after 2018, with a Democratic House—or the thoroughly corrupt and ungrounded "Russian collusion" investigation that infected every aspect of Trump's presidency. Never in the history of the Republic had anything even remotely close to this occurred, not even with the media's treatment of Watergate. Collusion did exist on a massive scale. But it had not been between Trump and Russia, but between the Democrats, the media, and the intelligence agencies, most notably the FBI.[659] It was none other than Democratic Senator Chuck Schumer of New York who made oblique references to what was coming. In January 2017 he said, referring to Trump, "You take on the intelligence community, they have six ways from Sunday at getting back at you."[660] Newt Gingrich confirmed the existence of the Deep State: "Of course the Deep State exists.... There's a permanent state of massive bureaucracies that do whatever they want and set up deliberate leaks to attack the president."[661] In Trump's case, however, the Deep State did far more than merely "leak."

Unraveling the story—especially due to the obstruction of the mainstream media to admit their errors (which few ever did and some grudgingly and ineffectively)—requires a somewhat detailed examination of the events leading up to the election, beginning with Hillary Clinton's tenure as secretary of state.

Obama was using a pseudonym when communicating with Clinton in her private email account, even when it was not in secure locations. This in itself should have constituted a major scandal forcing Clinton (and, in a just world, Obama as well) from office. It meant that America's secrets were, with the right hack, publicly available and that both officials were mishandling classified information. The House Committee on Benghazi had sought to obtain Clinton's secret server without success. She maintained that "here was no classified material contained in her emails, a statement that was a blatant lie. A staffer, trying to send her a classified document that was proving difficult due to the classification, was instructed by Clinton: "Turn into nonpaper w [*sic*] no identifying heading and send *nonsecure* [italics mine]."[662] FBI investigators later found over 110 classified emails that it rushed to explain as nonclassified.

Clinton's emails may have just fallen off the political globe except for an event on June 15, 2016. And there we have two contrasting stories still disputed some nine years later. The first, and most accepted version of events, was that sometime in early 2016, a cyberhacker named "Guccifer 2.0" had published a trove of emails stolen from the DNC that showed that the DNC had actively conspired to undermine the campaign of Clinton's primary rival, the popular Bernie Sanders of Vermont. (Sanders, for the record, was registered not as a Democrat but as a socialist until the moment came for him to run for the Democratic nomination.) A second, even more sinister analysis of the publication was that there was no "hack" at all—and that someone inside the Clinton campaign had deliberately pilfered the materials and downloaded them. In that version of the story, Seth Rich, an employee of the DNC, had stolen and shared the materials. Typically, the "mainstream" news, including Wikipedia, roundly denounced that version, as Rich was discovered murdered on July 10, 2016, with apparently nothing stolen in the police-designated robbery. Determining which version is true is as much a reflection on actual truth as it is the state of the media in the twenty-first century.

Here is what appears to be the most accurate review of the events. In April 2016, *The Washington Free Beacon*, which had a deal with a company called Fusion GPS to investigate opposition research against Trump, backed out of their agreement. DNC lawyer Marc Elias of the law firm Perkins Coie learned of this opposition research against Trump and hired Fusion GPS for his own research project. (During this time, a background operation under Ukrainian American Democratic operative Alexandra Chalupa was underway, giving the DNC her information that claimed Trump and his campaign manager, Manafort, had ties to Russia. Chalupa was directly coordinating with the Hillary campaign at the time, and it should be noted that she as a Ukrainian was hostile in all ways to Russia.)[663] Another bad actor, Nellie Ohr—wife of DOJ associate deputy attorney general, Bruce Ohr—went on the payroll of Fusion GPS to supply anti-Trump material to the DOJ.

Fusion GPS then hired an ex-British spy Christopher Steele to conduct opposition research on Trump: He used "Russian sources" (which in retrospect were nonexistent) to compile a "dossier" that contained utterly ridiculous claims, including one that when he was in Moscow, Trump paid prostitutes to urinate on a bed that the Obamas had slept in when they visited. "Irregular contacts" with the Russians were also played up in this fictitious "dossier."

In June 2015, the DNC told its employees that its computer system had been hacked again, this time directly blaming Russia. Five days later, "Guccifer 2.0" published a hacked document from the Clinton campaign chairman John Podesta. (It was during this time that former president Bill Clinton met on the tarmac in Phoenix, Arizona, with then–Attorney General Loretta Lynch to try to squelch the Hillary email scandal—an illegal act in itself. Such Clinton illegalities were building up.) Shortly thereafter, Steele, his "dossier" complete, approached the FBI in Rome with all the allegations against Trump. FBI official Peter Strzok, a Trump hater, opened a probe into Trump that day. Three weeks later, Strzok opened a counterintelligence operation—not a criminal prosecution or criminal investigation—called "Crossfire Hurricane" into another Trump associate, George Papadopoulos, but with the ultimate objective of somehow implicating Trump himself.

When Seth Rich was found dead on July 10, it opened the door for allegations that he, not Guccifer, had actually provided the email leaks to various outlets. But the police announced that they could not solve the murder. During that time, one of Trump's young advisers, Carter Page, had been invited to visit Russia to make a speech (highly unusual, given his relative lack of credentials: In retrospect, it was clearly an attempt to entrap Page as a Russian asset). Later, the director of national intelligence would claim that the hack was the work of Russia's military intelligence unit, the GRU, to "undermine public faith in the US democratic process, denigrate Secretary Clinton, and harm her electability."[664] Either way, Trump, joking, said to the FBI that he hoped "you're able to find the 30,000 emails that are missing."[665]

Once again, in retrospect—given the shocking bias of not only the FBI but all government agencies against President Trump and their repeatedly proven record of lying in public documents—it is well within reason to suspect that the entire special counsel investigation of Robert Mueller was itself a giant "cleaning" operation designed to shift the blame from Clinton, eliminate traces to her, and to put the media (which needed little coaxing) onto the Russians. And that all became evident through the revelations of the so-called Steele dossier.

The FBI had no choice but to investigate, but the entire team conducting the investigation was already in Clinton's corner. One agent, Lisa Page, told the agent leading the exam, Peter Strzok (also her lover), that "the last thing you need [is] us going in there loaded for bear."[667] In fact, by that time, the FBI's Clinton team and FBI Deputy Director Andrew McCabe were routinely (and illegally) sharing information with the news media—contrary to a direct lie Comey told Senator Charles Grassley in sworn testimony.[668] Gregg Jarrett's book, *The Russia Hoax*, contains multiple pages of personal text messages from Strzok and Page demonizing Donald Trump and exposing their vile bias, which was beyond question.

All of this took place against the background of *Clinton*'s email investigation, wherein Comey repeatedly lied about every aspect of the FBI's work. For example, he claimed the bureau had "reviewed all of the communications," but researcher Paul Sperry found that only 3,077 of the *694,000* emails were directly reviewed for classified or incriminating information.[669] Even more shocking, the FBI agreed to "destroy records and laptops of Clinton associates after reviewing them," precluding anyone afterwards from doing another examination.[670] Clinton's team used a computer program called BleachBit to wipe clean any once-deleted files to further guard against investigators turning up any nefarious activities. Comey's actions arguably meant that he also was breaking the law and certainly was not observing FBI practices. As President Trump would later say of Hillary, "Comey kept her out of jail."[671] Three years after Comey absolved Clinton, the US State Department admitted that there were at minimum thirty separate security breaches of Clinton's emails. But that was barely the tip of the iceberg.

Comey had appointed McCabe as deputy director of the FBI (whose

SIDEBAR: The NSA, FBI, Mar-a-Lago, and the Russia Hoax

To appreciate how corrupt and criminal the entire investigation of President Trump was, one must understand the complex web of deceit that infected almost every agency, from the National Security Agency (NSA) to the FBI to the CIA to the DOJ itself. Moreover, while complicated, an understanding of the declassification process and snooping process by various agencies is useful.

From 2015 to 2016, the NSA database (which is galactically vast) was being exploited by contractors (some known as "tax-exempt government agencies") and the FBI conducting unauthorized searches. Outside contractors were never identified, though Neustar and CrowdStrike were likely candidates. CrowdStrike would later play a role in developing the fake Steele dossier. Georgia Tech provided resources to Rodney Joffe of Neustar to assemble data for the phony Russia scam. Later, in 2022, it was revealed that the FBI had a workspace and computer portal *inside Hillary Clinton's lawyer's office*, that of Perkins Coie.

During a March 2016 internal review of FBI personnels' access to the system, thousands of unauthorized FBI search queries were discovered about individuals. The FBI alerted NSA Director Mike Rogers, who ordered a review. Rogers didn't like what he found, shutting down all access to contractors to the database. Searches using FISA 702 (Foreign Intelligence Surveillance Act Section 702, which only allowed the US government to collect information on *noncitizens* outside the US) using the words "about" and "to/from" were being conducted without authorization. Of more concern, Rogers found that operators (again, "contractors") were searching for the term "US persons," which was explicitly illegal. Those findings were given to a FISA court, which reported by 2017 that "while the government reports it is unable to *provide a reliable estimate of the non-compliant queries since 2012, there is no apparent reason to believe the November 2015 [to] April 2016 period coincided with an unusually high error rate* [emphasis mine]." (In other words, the "non-compliant"—illegal—rate was a whopping 85 percent or up to forty-two thousand illegal searches.) Obama's NSA and FBI routinely used the database illegally to conduct surveillance. As one researcher concluded, "There is little doubt the NSA database system was used by Obama-era FBI officials and political allies, from 2012 through April 2016, as a way to spy on their political opposition." (Sundance, "Part 2—Why did the DOJ and FBI Execute the Raid on Trump," in sources below.)

Moreover, it ought to be noted that in 2012 the FBI director was Mueller, who would become the special prosecutor into the Trump "collusion" in 2017. At the time, the CIA director, John Brennan, and the director of national intelligence, James Clapper, were later revealed as utter Trump haters who completely bought into the hoax. Mike Rogers wanted all of them fired. It didn't work: They started an effort to get Rogers removed.

wife was a Democrat Virginia state senate candidate). On those grounds alone he should have been disqualified from anything even associated with a political investigation. The same applied to many other agents, especially Page and Strzok. They were busy conducting an inquiry into Manafort (as well as Papadopoulos and Page), and in August 2016, they all met in McCabe's office. Referring to the possibility of Trump wining, Strzok texted his lover Page, "We can't take that risk." He also wrote of an "insurance policy" against a Trump presidency.[672] Approximately during this time, the FBI started to wiretap Manafort.

It was into the hands of this cabal of Trump haters that the Steele dossier would fall in September 2016. (Later, when the Special Counsel Mueller questioned Strzok, he was never asked whether his hate for Trump had influenced his investigation, suggesting Mueller himself was so biased that he didn't even consider raising the question.) No one noted that five Clinton officials had been granted immunity from prosecution for their information, meaning that at least some of the dirt being passed around was coming from the opposing political campaign. Nor did anyone ask about Obama's involvement. In fact, that September, Page and Strzok texted that Obama wanted "to know everything we're doing," as he had just warned Russia not to interfere in the US election.[673]

Of course, the FBI was doing just that—interfering in a US election. On October 3, the FBI seized computers belonging to Anthony Weiner, who was accused of sexually harassing an underage girl and who was married to one of Hillary's top aides, Huma Abedin. Weiner's computers contained many of Hillary's emails. Yet in possession of this damning evidence, the FBI waited *weeks* before even telling Congress and reopening the investigation.

Other departments and anti-Trump actors joined in. James Clapper, the director of national intelligence and homeland security stated that the Russian government was responsible for hacking the Democrat's emails, when no such evidence had yet been proven. Lisa Page at the same time was working on opening a wiretap on Carter Page with the investigation name "Crossfire Hurricane." The FBI then informed Christopher Steele that the agency wanted to see his dossier

Not coincidentally, then, the day after Trump sealed the GOP primary by winning the majority of Super Tuesday states and then five more by March 8, the NSA reported that there was unusual activity in the NSA searches. In April 2017, a FISA judge, Rosemary Collyer, who reviewed these, said that many of the searches used the same identifiers over a different date range. Specifically, they were snooping on Trump as a "US person." Moreover, in her review of the spying, she stated that Obama's DOJ had an "institutional lack of candor" in its responses to the FISA court's review. In layman's terms, Obama's people lied, almost all the time.

When the alerts from the NSA came up on March 9, 2016, those inside the FBI had to find other methods to spy on Trump. The FBI switched to human intel and confidential sources to place inside the Trump campaign, specifically Joseph Mifsud and Stefan Halper. Trump did not help himself when he hired Manafort as his campaign manager on March 28, because Manafort had previously been under investigation by the FBI, which now had a way to legally spy on Trump.

In other words, the Steele dossier in large part was created as a cover-up for the FISA abuse and illegal searches and to find a way to justify further searches on Trump in the future. Seen in that light, Mueller's appointment as special counsel allowed him to sanitize his own role in that weaponized search process and to cover up the potential criminality of others in the FBI.

It also appeared that Obama failed in an earlier dry run at spying using the Internal Revenue Service (IRS) in the "secret research project" under the direction of Lois Lerner. Mueller and the attorney general, Eric Holder, were both involved in this "secret research project," as Holder had *in 2010* requested over one million tax records about tax-exempt organizations he could prosecute. What became known as the "IRS scandal" (with the IRS getting records of conservative tax-exempt organizations) in fact was the DOJ using the IRS as a data collection agency for its planned prosecutions.

After the creation of the Steele dossier, the various agencies were able to continue legally spying on Trump. He, of course, had figured out exactly what was going on and repeatedly sought to declassify the documents that would prove it. In March 2022, Trump filed a civil lawsuit against the Clinton campaign where he accused her and her allies of "maliciously conspiring to weave a false narrative" that Trump was "colluding with a hostile foreign sovereignty" (Sundance, "Part 2"; see the lawsuit in the article). It was this trail of government documents that Trump sought to declassify that would prove his innocence and the Clinton/FBI cabal's guilt.

With the 2020 election ousting Trump, Biden's DOJ quickly appointed Jack Smith as a special counsel to investigate Trump's involvement in the January 6 protests at the US Capitol. But even as he departed, Trump continued to seek the documents' release. Literally on January 20, 2021, as one of his last acts, he advised the DOJ to release the documents that he had personally ordered declassified.

"right away" and offered him $50,000 for the dirt. Steele flew to Rome to meet with FBI agents and offer a full briefing. He could not confirm one single important detail and yet even then the FBI was not discouraged, nor did it second-guess "Crossfire Hurricane."

It was important for the "stop Trump" coup to do more than investigate, however. Ultimately, most knew that there was no "there" there in the Steele dossier. So, it became critical to get the salacious stuff out to the media as soon as possible. Gregg Jarrett explained it this way: "Gradually, Simpson and Steele had discovered the key to spreading the hoax: journalists had trouble reporting out the allegations because they weren't true, but they could report truthfully that the government was looking into something."[674]

Therefore, in September and October, six weeks before the election, Steele and Fusion GPS met with *The New York Times*, *The Washington Post*, Yahoo, CNN, ABC, *Mother Jones*, and *The Guardian* to get the word out. As part of that effort, former CIA director John Brennan, another anti-Trump bureaucrat, had overseen the planting of the idea for "collusion" with the agency. With or without direct instruction from the CIA, Clinton peppered her campaign speeches with sly references to Trump's relationship to Russian president Vladimir Putin.

BuzzFeed, an internet site, was the first to run the whole dossier, saying "These Reports Allege Trump Has Deep Ties to Russia."[675] Just like that, the story was out. An outraged Trump blasted out on Twitter, "FAKE NEWS—A TOTAL POLITICAL WITCH HUNT."[676]

The election drew near, and the cabal grew more agitated, with a key associate writing a second time of the need for an "insurance policy." As Steele told Justice Department official Bruce Ohr, he was willing to falsify or fabricate evidence to stop Trump.[677] Those criminal behaviors did not seem to bother the FBI, but when he leaked his involvement with the bureau to *Mother Jones* magazine, the FBI ended their association. He still, however, continued to "back channel" salacious info to the "get Trump" programs via his relationship with Ohr. *Mother Jones*, who hyped the "Russian collusion" story as much as possible, claimed that David Corn, the editor, had interviewed a

It was that process that confused so many. (See "Why didn't Trump just release the declassified documents?") By 2018, it was clear US agencies were falsely targeting President Trump in the Russia Hoax, and the Mueller investigation reached a conclusion. Once Mueller started his official investigation, Trump was helpless. His Deputy Attorney General Rod Rosenstein (who had taken over most of the DOJ's activities once Attorney General Jeff Sessions recused himself, then became virtually invisible) advised Trump in September 2018 that should Trump personally release any documents that were *then under the purview of Mueller*, it would be considered "obstruction of justice," and he would be charged. Likely, under that scenario, he not only would have been impeached but also convicted by the Senate and removed. Trump tweeted that "key Allies' called to ask not to release [sic]" (Sundance, "Part 3, Why Did the DOJ and FBI Execute the Raid on Trump—a Culmination of Four Years of Threats and Betrayals"). Instead, Trump asked the inspector general (who was part of the cover-up) to review the documents on an expedited basis. *This constituted nothing less than the bureaucracy neutering a president by refusing to follow his orders.* While Trump theoretically had authority to declassify anything, he faced a second investigation, this one over "obstruction" of revealing the catchall "sources and methods" if he did so.

In a routine declassification process, the FBI director, the director of national intelligence, and the attorney general all had to approve or sign off on the release (and the process can also include other agencies such as the CIA). National Intelligence Director Dan Coats certainly was no Trump ally, while Rosenstein and FBI Director Chris Wray were soft enemies. If any of them told Trump a document was not cleared for release, the only way it could be released would be to fire the head of the agency and replace with someone else. Given the depth of the swamp, it was unlikely Trump could fire enough people—which would cause an explosion in Congress—to get to someone who would comply with his orders.

But it got worse for Trump with more deception. Mueller finished his investigation with no charges in April 2019 and the following month, Trump-appointed William Barr as the new attorney general following the resignation of the useless Sessions. Barr requested the authority to oversee the documents' release, and Trump acceded, thinking he had finally found someone loyal. But Barr was as complicit as the others. He named John Durham to look into the entire Russia Hoax affair without telling Trump that now because he was a *victim* of the scheme, he now became part of the universal DOJ/FBI catchall "ongoing criminal investigation," whereby neither Barr nor Durham could…release any documents. Again, they could not release any documents related to the president of the US who ordered them declassified! Durham's investigation lasted from May 13, 2019, to May 15, 2023, when Biden's DOJ did not release any classified

"former senior intelligence officer" who was "credible"—referring to the hoaxer Steele![678]

Conspirators then felt liberated enough to shoot the dossier out in all directions. Ohr's wife, Nellie, sent it to three prosecutors at the DOJ (again, without ever verifying anything). Meanwhile, Steele's handler at the FBI had received the dossier and then took it straight to…*The New York Times*, not the bureau to be verified. Even on its surface and even had it not been entirely made up, the Steele dossier was replete with hearsay from anonymous sources. Nevertheless, the FBI used an unverified document of innuendo and unnamed sources to launch a fully partisan investigation of Trump, and they were joined by members of the Clinton campaign working through Glenn Simpson and his company Fusion GPS.

At that point, Clapper, the director of national intelligence, apparently had seen holes in the dossier, and he publicly said that he was not "ready to make a call" on whether it came from the Russians. But John Brennan, head of the CIA, soon got Clapper's mind straight, and they handpicked a group of analysts to reach a "consensus," code word for "majority rule," on the dossier. It took until January 2017, after Trump was elected, for the consensus to be delivered. Clapper also had a problem in that the CIA could not spy on Americans. For that he needed Comey and the FBI.

Getting the FBI on board did not prove difficult. Already the *unverified* dossier had received verified status to enable Obama's Justice Department and the FBI to get a wiretap on a onetime Trump adviser and to assert without any evidence that he was a Russian spy. To obtain the warrant, not only did the Obama/FBI activists mischaracterize the Steele dossier but to get the wiretaps, they also defrauded FISA judges as to where the so-called actual information came from. This started the counterintelligence (note: not criminal) investigation within the FBI, which landed on a foreign policy adviser to Trump's campaign, Papadopoulos, who on his own initiative had contacted Russian sources to try to broker a meeting between Putin and Trump. By focusing on Papadopoulos, the CIA now could jump in with both feet.

The level of deception was extraordinary. Virtually all of the investigations and "analysis" undertaken was done so because of individual disdain for one man, Trump. On November 9, 2016, an unnamed FBI attorney quoted in a Justice Department inspector general report had texted another FBI agent: "I'm just devastated.... Who knows if the rhetoric about deporting people, walls, and crap is true...there is [sic]

documents, and Trump could no longer force them out.

However, Trump—as was his authority and privilege—*did* take those documents with him to Mar-a-Lago after he left office.

When the DOJ authorized the FBI and Special Counsel Jack Smith to raid Trump's Mar-a-Lago home on August 8, 2022, searching for "classified documents," what specifically were they looking for? It now became clear. Trump had the declassified document trail of the Russia Hoax and the subsequent cover-up through Mueller and Durham, whose report recommended *none* of the key players for prosecution. When Trump again attempted to make public the documents, the Eleventh Circuit Court ruled that any documents defined as "classified" by Biden could not be released. The shell game of "official investigations" had ensured that the deception and criminal behavior of the DOJ, the FBI, and the NSA continued to be covered up.[666]

going to be a lot more gun issues, too, the crazies won finally. This is tea party on steroids."[679]

Top officials, including Strzok and McCabe, engaged in a new mission to review all of Trump's associates looking for "derogatory" information. Obama officials such as Samantha Power (the UN ambassador) and Clapper began searching for ways to "unmask" (i.e., make public) General Mike Flynn's name as having been captured in surveillance, thereby implying that Flynn was engaged in some sort of conspiratorial activity. Another *ten* efforts to unmask Flynn occurred within a month. Finally, frustrated at the lack of progress, Obama's National Security Adviser Susan Rice "secretly" unmasked several names, including those of Flynn, Bannon, and Jared Kushner.

Trump started to suspect that the FBI and other government agencies were not honorable actors and moved his team meetings out of Trump Tower (which was bugged). He also named Gen. Flynn as his national security advisor and, in that role as would normally happen, Flynn met with numerous international leaders. The media, through numerous planted stories—including to such outlets as *The Wall Street Journal*—began a chorus of "investigations" of Flynn over his meeting with Russian Ambassador Sergey Kislyak. Then on January 24, Acting Attorney General Sally Yates sent two FBI agents (including the duplicitous Strzok) to question Flynn, circumventing normal processes. Notes were kept hidden until May 2020, which showed that the FBI agents were discussing whether the goal of the meeting was to "get him to lie" so that he could be prosecuted. Right on schedule, Yates—who still hadn't been replaced yet by Trump—met with White House attorney Don McGahn to tell him that Flynn had lied to Vice President Pence about his talk with the Russian ambassador. Trump finally managed to give Yates the boot by January 31, but the damage to Flynn was done.

While the mainstream media played up Flynn and the Trump-Russia connection (which did not exist), five employees of the Democrats in the House were under investigation for gaining access to the House's IT system without anyone's knowledge.[680] Finally in February, apparently dissatisfied that the FBI was moving too slow to indict Flynn, *The Washington Post* reported the Flynn material, contradicting what Flynn told the FBI. Indeed, National Public Radio reported that "official transcripts" of Flynn's calls showed no wrongdoing. Flynn, thinking he was falling on his sword, resigned. That act only fueled the fire. As one Democratic operative told author Ed Klein, "This isn't about Flynn: this is about getting Trump out."[681] Of course, anyone who had paid attention to the opposition being erected against Trump would have known that instantly.

Trump had named his loyal transition leader, Senator Jeff Sessions of Alabama, as his attorney general. Sessions came highly recommended, having defeated the Ku Klux Klan in Alabama. Once in office, he became the "invisible man." On March 2, he recused himself from all Russia-linked investigations, thereby opening Trump to the full onslaught of the FBI, CIA, and DOJ under another Trump hater, Rod Rosenstein, the deputy attorney general who had already signed off on one of Carter Page's wiretaps.

The trick for the anti-Trump cabal was twofold. First, they had to make it appear that Trump's actions (or those of his subordinates) "caused" the investigations, and second, they had to simultaneously seal off lines of inquiry into the vast, illegal spying on a number of Americans. This was made public on March 10, 2017, when former Democratic Congressman Dennis Kucinich of Ohio revealed that Obama's intel had illegally recorded some of *his* communications. Likewise, the Republican Chairman of the House Intelligence Committee Devin Nunes announced he had evidence of Trump associates being "incidentally" surveilled by Obama's intelligence agencies and their names being unmasked and illegally leaked.[682] For his part, President Trump suspected that "President Obama is behind [these activities]...and some of the leaks possibly come from that group."[683]

Still active on Twitter, one of his major communication sources, Trump tweeted in March "@realDonaldTrump How low has President Obama gone to 'tapp' [sic] my phones during the very sacred election process. This is Nixon/Watergate. Bad (or sick) guy!"[684] (In his use of Twitter, Trump, for reasons not yet known, developed a habit of misspelling key words. It later became clear that this was deliberate, often used to make a point.) Not surprisingly, the mainstream media, who saw it as their job to protect Obama at all costs, did not take any of Trump's alerts seriously. Clapper, who knew about all the wiretaps, flat-out lied on *Meet the Press* when he said, "There was no such wiretap activity mounted against the president, the president-elect, at the time, or as a candidate, or against his campaign." He even denied there had even been a FISA court allowing surveillance of Trump. Clapper was never forced under penalty of perjury to address those lies, and even *The New York Times* had already run a story in January confirming President Trump's claims: "Wiretapped Data Used in Inquiry of Trump Aides."[685]

Trump had distrusted Comey since he found in favor of Hillary not once, but twice. He fired the FBI director in May, but that just allowed another notorious anti-Trump deputy, McCabe, to take over as acting director. (This is what was obliquely referred to as "the swamp" or the "Deep State": Even replacing individuals who clearly did not have the administration's goals in mind accomplished nothing—they were just replaced by someone equally as bad.) One of those who Trump interviewed, but did not hire, was former FBI director Robert Mueller. Trump said he "wanted very badly to have the job...and to return to the FBI. I don't want him. I rejected him."[686] Trump should not have been surprised when shortly thereafter Deputy Attorney General Rod Rosenstein appointed Mueller as a special counsel to head a Russia-Trump probe, all based on either no evidence at all or on wiretaps obtained by illegal means.

The Republican House did what it could to stop the out-of-control crazy train: The House Intelligence Committee subpoenaed material related to the unmaskings by Obama and his officials, including Rice and Brennan. But the House could not compete with a special counsel and ninety-three lawyers, handpicked by Mueller and all of them hostile to Trump. In July, the FBI raided the home of Trump's former campaign manager, Manafort. Mueller, sensing low-hanging fruit, charged Manafort with money laundering in October, but there was no connection to Trump. Legal pressure on other Trump advisers led to a string of plea deals, including that of Papadopoulos, who said he lied about facilitating meetings between Trump officials and the Russians. And in December, Flynn plead guilty to lying to the FBI.

Comey may have been out, but he was hardly down, signing a $2 million book deal. Trump, having scorned Mueller as his replacement, named Christopher Wray as the new director. He proved no better than Comey. One of Wray's first acts was to lie to congress, testifying that there had been no "702" (FISA) surveillance abuses by the government. Many had already repeatedly been proven. Nevertheless, in another example of how deep the Deep State ran, in January 2018, the House approved further 702 wireless surveillance authority, the very authority that had been abused in the effort to "get Trump." Trump, at the urging of his own congressional leaders and Director Wray, signed the six-year extension.

To appreciate the Keystone Cops' level of venality and unprofessionalism at work, in January of 2018, Senator Charles Grassley and Senator Lindsey Graham referred criminal charges against Steele to the FBI—which could not investigate him because the FBI was *using* Steele's fictitious dossier to obtain its illegitimate wiretaps! Mueller, meanwhile, obtained a guilty plea from a Dutch attorney for lying to investigators, but the plea had nothing to do with Trump or the 2016 campaign. By then it was clear that Mueller, finding nothing, was desperately trying to "look busy" and produce charges against anyone he could find. He filed new charges (still unrelated to Trump) against Manafort. Trump's former lawyer, Michael Cohen, pled guilty to eight counts of tax evasion and campaign finance violations—but not anything related to Russia. Mueller got Rick Gates to plead guilty to lying to investigators—yet again, with no connection to Trump or Russia.

Mueller slinked into his final report in March 2019, admitting there was no collusion or coordination between Trump or *any* American and

Russia. He recommended no new charges.[687] But he made a special note of saying that he did not determine whether Trump could be considered guilty of obstruction. This was an absolute abomination of a report by such a special counsel, who is to weigh in on the evidence and simply report the subject for charges, or not. Then-Attorney General Bill Barr, who had replaced the resigned Jeff Sessions, found the "whole passage very bizarre."[688] Mueller's comments proved he had gone the extra mile to try to find anything to pin on Trump—and had failed.

The media published every claim and innuendo of the Mueller investigation for months. Over 8,507 articles mentioning the investigation were identified by the Republican National Committee. Once it had become clear that they had published false information, the news media did everything but step forward and admit their bias. *The New York Times*, rather than admitting error, prohibited its reporters from going on any news shows to discuss the hoax. No one can deny the long list of media errors (most of them deliberate) and the media's complicity in the hoax.[689]

In retrospect, the FBI and Clinton operatives had failed badly at damaging Trump with associations with Russia. As author Lee Smith pointed out, the FBI engaged in seven different instances where the FBI or its lackeys approached the Trump campaign before "Crossfire Hurricane" actually began. One former FBI agent said, "What appear to have been repeated attempts to implicate the Trump campaign, in some sort of quid pro quo arrangement with Russians who claimed to have 'dirt' on Hillary…look like efforts to manufacture evidence against members of the Trump campaign or create pretexts to investigate it."[690]

An inspector general report of December 2019 outlined numerous abuses by the FBI and DOJ in obtaining the wiretaps and found an FBI attorney, Kevin Clinesmith, who had altered a document (at someone else's order, but that person was cleverly hidden). Cleinsmith was the only member of the anti-Trump cabal—which had fraudulently obtained wiretaps, "unmasked" ordinary Americans, spied on members of Congress, and destroyed the lives of a half dozen people—to face any punishment. He was later charged by the John Durham investigation and pled guilty to altering the warrants used to indict many of the above.

One name was missing: Donald Trump. Democrats (and Republicans hostile to Trump) had used the Mueller report to cripple Trump's agenda for two years, with many (including virtually all of the insiders) knowing that the evidence was entirely a hoax. The report by Durham, in May 2023, found there was never any basis to the Steele dossier and that almost all of those involved in pursuing Trump knew it.[691] Specifically, Durham found that the "FBI discounted or willfully ignored material information that did not support the narrative" of the Trump-Russia collusion; the FBI never spoke to the people who provided the information for the "Crossfire Hurricane" investigation that started the collusion hoax; British intelligence found Mueller's case so weak they refused to provide assistance; not only did McCabe terminate any investigations into Hillary Clinton, but he also required his approval to be obtained to engage in any further investigations; the CIA knew about the investigations and knew that Hillary Clinton was using the fake documents as a pretext to vilify Trump; and the FBI knew that the Carter Page FISA warrants were dubious.[692]

Aside from Clinesmith and a peripheral figure, Igor Danchenko, no one of any significance was indicted, let alone convicted of what was nothing less than a Deep State coup attempt to remove Trump. The Durham report, for all its findings of errors, refused to pin the blame on anyone in an infamous "mistakes were made" cover-up that all too often had concealed or excused ongoing malfeasance by individuals.[693] Meanwhile, Trump's entire first term had been consumed with constant distractions of submitting documents and officials appearing for depositions, while individuals such as Papadopoulos, Carter Page, and Michael Flynn had faced bankruptcy or had their lives destroyed by the illegal and illicit FBI/Mueller probes, all without recompense. And the investigation played no small role in the Republicans losing the House in 2018.

RIDING HIGH

Trump's inaugural address was unique in modern history. Few incoming presidents so lambasted not only their predecessors (in both parties) but the leaders of Congress while speaking directly in front of them. He said, "For too long, a small group in our nation's Capital has reaped the rewards of government while the people have borne the cost.... Politicians prospered—but the jobs left, and the factories closed.... *That*...changes—starting right here, and right now because," he directed toward the massive crowd that had gathered, "this moment is your moment."[694]

Trump wasted no time pulling the US out of the North American Free Trade Agreement as he promised after only four days in office. A month later, the US left the "climate change" Paris Accords. Such actions had an immediate impact, as the American manufacturing sector added 314,000 jobs through August of 2018, refuting Obama's claim that manufacturing jobs were the "jobs of the past" and were "just not going to come back."[695] GDP, which languished at 0.6 percent in the first quarter of 2016, rose to 2.3 percent by the first quarter of 2018 and to 4 percent—a number thought impossible to attain—by the second quarter of 2018. Obama, ridiculing Trump's claim that he would restore American manufacturing, asked "How, exactly are you going to do that? ... What magic wand do you have?"[696] Apparently, Trump's "wand" was larger than Gandalf's staff, for the growth rates continued to rise.

Meanwhile, unemployment fell to 3.7 percent, and where Obama had lost 116,000 manufacturing jobs in his last two quarters in office, Trump added 186,000. And by April 2018, manufacturing jobs exceeded 322,000.[697] Some of those jobs came through another promise Trump fulfilled of imposing stiff tariffs on European trading partners and the Chinese, who themselves had significant tariffs on American steel, autos, and farm goods. He renegotiated North American Free Trade Agreement under more favorable terms, renaming it the US-Mexico-Canada Agreement, and America, with its $20 trillion economy, resumed its place as the largest in the world with one quarter of the entire economy of the globe.[698]

Black unemployment reached record lows; overall employment was near record highs. American energy production had achieved a goal previously thought impossible, namely energy independence. With his son-in-law Jared Kushner running point, Trump had made new breakthroughs with Saudi Arabia and had negotiated the Abraham Accords, bringing a temporary truce between Israel and her Muslim neighbors. For the first time in decades, the US was involved in no foreign wars.

The border remained a battle zone, though. For two years, the Republican Congress under Paul Ryan and the recalcitrant Senate under Mitch McConnell had starved Trump's border wall of funding. Ryan claimed that it was too divisive an issue to raise before the 2018 midterms, even as the likelihood grew that Republicans would lose their majority in the 2018 elections. Ryan and McConnell removed funding for the wall in Trump's first budget. They agreed to minimal funding in the second.[699] A frustrated Trump finally pressured Kushner to find the extra wall money in the budget. His team found $600 million in a Treasury forfeiture account, $3.6 billion in an account for overseas military construction, and $6 billion in narco-terrorism funds. These were accessible if Trump declared the border an emergency, which he did. A Kushner put it, "They'd found the government equivalent of nickels and dimes and came up with $11 billion in existing funding" for the wall.[700] When he left office, he had overseen construction of a significant portion of the wall, but many gaps remained.

Trump's tighter border enforcement went well beyond a wall. Apprehensions continued, but leftist media outlets thought they found a chink in Trump's border policy armor. US law did not permit the incarceration of minors for the crimes of their parents, so the border policy of incarcerating illegal aliens required the temporary separation of children from parents. Democrats wailed that Trump was "ripping children from their mothers' arms" and keeping them in "cages."[701] Shortly, however, sources exposed the photos showing "kids in cages" as coming from the Obama years.

Elsewhere in the fight to secure the border, in twelve years, apprehensions rose to their highest level while under Trump, doubling over the previous year in 2019. ICE (Immigration and Customs Enforcement) also rose under Trump after declining steadily under Obama.[702] After the 2018 midterm defeat for Republicans, getting funding from the House for border security vanished.

Trump also had gotten the US nearly to energy independence by restarting the Keystone Pipeline, increasing domestic oil production, issuing new leases for drilling, and opening up the Arctic National Wildlife Refuge. Gas prices fell to roughly $2.50 a gallon for most Americans. Likewise, prior to the pandemic, mortgage rates had fallen into the high 2 percent range. Employment was surging, especially for black and Hispanic Americans.

India had recommitted to friendship with America, as Prime Minister Narendra Modi visited the US to make a campaign appearance with Trump. Saudi Arabia, Trump's first foreign visit, had recommitted as an ally and continued to keep oil prices low. His trip to China saw him welcomed as "Donald the Great." On December 6, 2017, President Trump kept a campaign pledge that many other presidents had made but not fulfilled: He moved the US Embassy in Israel to Jerusalem, officially recognizing Jerusalem as the capital of that nation.[703] As a result, streets in Israel were renamed for Trump.

He also succeeded where Obama had failed in crushing ISIS and doing so in short order. That permitted him to—over objections of his State Department and the secretary of defense—withdraw two thousand American troops from Syria, further minimizing the US military "footprint" around the world.

After warning North Korean dictator Kim Jong Un that unlike his predecessors he was unwilling to tolerate a nuclear North Korea, Kim agreed to end his nuclear program and began talks to normalize relations with South Korea to formally end the sixty-year-old Korean War. Trump and Kim exchanged communications, then met in Singapore, marking the first time a North Korean leader had met with any American president. They signed an accord to release all the remains of dead Americans from the Korean War. North Korea also began to open the demilitarized zone. In one of the most astounding feats of diplomacy in American history, Trump walked into North Korea across the demilitarized zone with Kim, who said to flabbergasted reporters, "I think meeting here, two countries that have a hostile past, we are showcasing to the world that we have a new present and we have a positive meeting going forward."[704]

Throughout all this, Trump was being undercut by members of his own administration, including his first secretary of state, Rex Tillerson, and most important, by his second chief of staff General John Kelly. Trump thought a four-star general would be suitable for organizing and directing the White House. But Kelly immediately tried to carve out turf, excluding Kushner from meetings. He also ignored the National Security Advisor H. R. McMaster who, in Kelly's mind, was "inferior" as holding only a three-star rank to Kelly's four stars, despite the fact that on the organizational chart McMaster was his superior.[705] Kelly went even further—he secretly listened to Trump's phone calls without the president's knowledge![706]

Such examples were the tip of the iceberg. As Mark Moyar noted in his book, *Masters of Corruption*, efforts to resist or undermine the Trump administration operated at every level. First, political appointees who came in—and this was common to many administrations—found themselves short-circuited by career bureaucrats who thought they, not the appointees, ran the agencies. Even before the appointees could even be named, "Jockeying between factions of the Republican Party also impeded prospective appointees."[707] Then, once appointed, they were subjected to an incredible woke "orientation" of pure identity politics. Once in place, however, the appointees found not just traditional bureaucrats desperate to maintain their fiefdoms but an army of Barack Obama's implants who were specifically inserted via a process called "burrowing in."[708] Even if the political appointees genuinely sought change and wanted to implement the Trump agenda, they found themselves undercut by the "burrowed in" troops in the field.

The House, still starving Trump of all the money he requested for the border wall, passed a major tax cut with his blessing. Although it took more than a year, Trump's tax cuts significantly boosted business.[709] Corporate investment leaped 20 percent. Yet by absorbing so much of Trump's time and political capital with standard Republican issues—tax cuts—the Republican swamp had somewhat dodged the voting issues upon which it was elected. Little was done about illegal immigration, infrastructure, or domestic manufacturing. Congressional Republicans left that almost entirely to Trump.

By January 2018, The Heritage Foundation concluded that Trump had managed to enact 64 percent of the foundation's agenda, making him "more conservative" than Reagan.[710] His signature issue of immigration, however, stalled in the Republican House even before the Democrats took over. Amnesty groups had filed suits that stalled construction of the wall, and Honduras began encouraging massive "caravans" to march up through Mexico to illegally enter the US. News of the caravans pushed "immigration" to the top of voter attitudes over "health care" by that time.

THE SWAMP STRIKES BACK

When the Russia Hoax failed, the antifa and Black Lives Matter movements could not stop Trump, and the GOP-controlled House could not stall, the swamp swallowed a suicide pill. One way to slow the president down was to deprive him of a House majority. The easiest way to accomplish that was for Republicans to simply not run—then they wouldn't be held responsible for opposing him (which was what they in reality did from 2017 to 2018). Consequently, forty-three GOP incumbents, including many powerful House chairman, resigned or announced they would not seek reelection in 2018. It was truly an astounding moment in which many House Republicans would rather end their careers rather than assist Trump in rebuilding the country. All total, the GOP lost sixteen House seats but in a first, gained three Senate seats at the same time. And of the House members who departed, many more were "Never Trumpers," such as Arizona's Jeff Flake or the Senate's Bob Corker, who were replaced by pro-Trump Republicans. While the total Republican House number fell, the percentage of Trump loyalists rose. With a Democratic House in place, it was only a matter of time until Trump was impeached for something—or nothing.

Despite all that, and despite losing the House in the 2018 midterms, Trump continued to advance the agenda. An open US Supreme Court seat had been waiting to be filled after the death of Justice Antonin Scalia in February 2016. While Senate Majority/Minority leader (at various times) Mitch McConnell deserved most of the criticism he got as an obstructionist, he held firm in refusing to allow the Senate to consider a replacement to Scalia until after the 2016 elections in November. Thus, Donald Trump had the opportunity to name Scalia's replacement, nominating Neil Gorsuch in his place. While few would suggest Gorsuch was at Scalia's level in jurisprudence, he proved reliable in his decisions. Then came a thunderclap in June 2018: the resignation of Justice Anthony Kennedy, a "swing" justice who had voted to perpetuate abortion in the *Planned Parenthood of Southeastern Pennsylvania v. Casey* abortion case, followed by siding with liberals in the *Obergefell v. Hodges* homosexual rights case.

Trump then had an opportunity to truly change the *direction* of the court, not just its numbers. He nominated Judge Brett Kavanaugh, whose nomination was sailing through until allegations of a high school sexual assault were brought by Christine Ford.[711] Those proved spurious, as she could not remember any details. And in an unusual one-man stand, Senator Lindsey Graham (hardly considered a conservative or even strong Trump supporter) cobbled the votes for Kavanaugh in committee, and he, too, was confirmed to the court. Still, the balance was tenuous. Justice John Roberts had already "gone rogue" on two key decisions, Obamacare and *Obergefell.* With only a 5–4 majority, he would continue to play kingmaker. That changed a year later when Ruth Ginsberg died. Trump quickly named Amy Coney Barrett to the court, and again, McConnell got her confirmed. Trump had his trifecta. Over the subsequent years, the "Trump court" would be a lasting legacy to Trump's positions.

Unable to pass any bills hostile to Trump without the support of the Senate, the House prepared to find some cause for which it could ceremonially impeach Trump. Speaker Nancy Pelosi, a hater of the first order, on national television had torn up the copy of Trump's State of the Union when he finished in 2019. (The House had attempted to pass an impeachment resolution in 2017, which failed by an overwhelming 564–58 vote.) Once Democrats gained control of the House, they launched multiple investigations into Trump's finances and other actions that they characterized as obstruction of justice. (This was essentially defined by Democrats as Trump doing anything he promised to do in his campaign.) In July 2019, they finally settled on a single topic, Trump's efforts to pry information out of Ukraine on Vice President Biden's efforts to squash an investigation there of his son Hunter. Biden had literally bragged on camera about his successful ousting of a Ukraine official for investigating his son. On July 25, Trump conducted a phone call with Ukraine's president Volodymyr Zelenskyy, and following that call, the White House instructed the Pentagon to withhold funding of military aid to Ukraine.[712]

Trump urged Zelenskyy to do him a favor, to "find out what happened with this whole situation with Ukraine, they say CrowdStrike.... The server, they say Ukraine has it.... I would like to have the Attorney General call you or your people and I would like you to get to the bottom of it."[713] Zelenskyy was well aware of the fired prosecutor and vowed to have his new prosecutor look into Hunter Biden's company there. Trump described it as a "perfect" phone call, and indeed as the memorandum shows, there wasn't the slightest illegality or obstruction in the discussion.

Pelosi pounced, leaping to name not one but *six* committees to look into impeaching Trump. She accused him of betraying national security, among other charges. Controlling the majority of the House members, Pelosi easily got her committees to report out resolutions for an impeachment. The Judiciary Committee began drafting articles on December 5, and just five days later, the Democrats levied two articles of impeachment based almost entirely on the phone call, one of abuse of power and one of obstruction of Congress. Both lacked any merit whatsoever. The articles were adopted by the whole House on a 229–198 vote with only two Democrats voting against them.[714] In the Senate, however, Senate Majority Leader McConnell, who strongly disliked Trump's attempts to end lobbying money flowing to the Senate, could have simply dismissed the charges, but did not. He held a hearing, but the Senate found Trump not guilty on both articles (52–48 on abuse of power and 53–47 on obstruction). Pelosi's witch hunt was over for the time being.

Trump continued to fight an obstructionist House, an inactive DOJ, an impotent Senate, and a tsunami of negative press coverage for the remainder of 2020. By then, however, a new peril had arrived on his doorstep—or more appropriately, in New York's airport, that of the Covid epidemic. Most of Trump's final year was taken with dealing with "the China Virus," as many called it. And it is to that we shall turn our attention.

CHAPTER 7
THE PANDEMIC

The Covid pandemic, and enforcement of its "cure," constituted a world-changing event. It affected nearly every nation—some more than others—not just medically but politically and socially. In the United States, it produced a rush to create a cure in the form of a vaccination, an unprecedented level of censorship and throttling of public discussion, and socio-physical changes that included lockdowns and social "spacing." Had that been its only short-term effect, it likely would not have reshaped America the way it did. Instead, Covid—or, as it is also referred to, "the China Virus"—magnified, accelerated, or perversely expanded ongoing trends in science, the media, and society as a whole. To appreciate why the response to Covid grew so tyrannical so fast, why like a lava flow it covered everything, and why it reshaped politics by the counterresponse, a brief review of the growth of the risk-averse environment is needed.

DECLINE OF MEANINGFUL SCIENCE

More than a decade before the China Virus arrived on American shores, the stifling of scientific discussion or inquiry had become a troubling trend. Researchers had noticed a change. They found that over a sixty-year period, an exponential growth in the volume of new scientific and technological papers occurred. That would suggest a climate ripe for technological advance, industrial growth, and major breakthroughs. To their surprise, no such advance occurred: Rather, an examination of nearly forty-five million papers found that research papers and patents proved increasingly less likely to break with significant ideas or understandings of the past. The authors called this a "decline in disruptiveness," and it reflected an growing reluctance to take risks or to stand out in ways that might nevertheless result in negative reactions.[715] Another researcher noted that among his contacts who were senior scientists, "their top priority is in achieving deltas: a physics jargon word that they use here to refer to tiny, incremental advances of their current research."[716] Put another way, they were playing small ball with their research.

Scientific investigation only constituted merely one component of the post-2000s risk-averse climate. That flight to safety and adversity to failure spread through all walks of life. Seat belts, made mandatory in 1968 with little resistance, only constituted the first step in "nanny mobiles"—current cars with multitudes of bells, warnings, alerts, and "assists" (almost all of which, according to *Why We Drive*, actually make drivers worse by lowering their role as a driver, their ability of practice, and their situational awareness.)[717] Soon mandatory airbags and other safety features followed—again with little resistance. Under Joe Biden, an infrastructure bill would install technology in cars to "stop drunk people from driving" by using breath or blood sensors or cameras to examine the driver for impairment.[718] As it is, cars warn you with bells and alarms about leaving something in the back seat, about crossing a solid line without signaling (even if there's no one on the road at two in the morning), and a host of other incredibly annoying "assists." The problem is that people learn specifically by *forgetting* they left something once in a back seat, or that they changed lanes and didn't see the vehicle next to them (which often got you a raucous and not-so-friendly horn and middle finger). People *learned through life experience* not to do those things. They developed habits precisely to ensure against mistakes. Musicians found that it was wise to touch their guitar against a microphone stand to make sure both were grounded before they got a possibly deadly electric shock. Diners knew to test the heat of soup or coffee before shoving a third-degree burn into their mouths.

Understanding a little of pre–twenty-first-century childhood and adolescence is helpful for understanding the dramatic changes in how children grew up. Almost anyone who was under ten in 1970 experienced life moments that would turn modern parents pale. And even then, their experiences weren't that different from boomer children. Gen X, born between 1965 and 1979, received more material abundance than any generation in American history. At the same time, due to the reality of the first working generation of married women, they became a "latchkey" generation. The number of working mothers was over 50 percent by 1972, and from 1952 to 2000 the number of high school seniors who had a mother who worked most or all of the time nearly quadrupled. That meant kids were often on their own. Whereas boomer kids were sent out to play by the mother who was at home cooking, in the 1970s and 1980s, there was no mother to send them anywhere.[719]

Yet when it came to life-learning experiences, they differed dramatically from those born after 2000. In many ways, their comments echoed those of boomer youths. "Parents had literally no idea where their kids were or what they were doing...90% of the time," said one member of that generation. Another added, "We just figured things out. It was both terrifying and exhilarating, the total freedom we had, and the absolute vulnerability we weren't yet aware of."[720] Part of the lack of supervision was that millennial overprotective parents were "constantly googling, 'best parenting strategies for your growing miracle,'" whereas the Gen

Xer parents essentially said, "You can play with a knife in your room just don't smoke weed in the kitchen."[721]

Then came the 2000s, where such stories became the stuff of parent gatherings and campfire legends. Not only did parents seek to halt that trend of "learn by doing" and unfettered freedom, but the iPhone and iPad, introduced toward the end of the first decade of the 2000s, brought about behavioral changes that directly obstructed such life experiences. As generational researcher Jean Twenge found, "The way teens spent their time outside of school fundamentally changed after 2012."[722] They spent far less time with others, and less time sleeping. Most schools simply ceased trying to fight the ubiquitous nature of cell phones and allowed them in school, transforming even the time spent in classrooms. When not in school, they spent far more time on their devices. A standard complaint about boomers and especially Gen Xers was that they spent too much time watching television or gaming (a far more male-dominated activity). Surprisingly, however, research found that television did not in any meaningful way contribute to such pathologies as unhappiness, nor did gaming (unless it reached a threshold of over five hours a day).[723] Twenge and others found the *type of screens* actually mattered, that watching television was a far more interactive activity than once thought, and that social media and internet time were "strongly linked to depression and self-harm behaviors, especially among girls."[724]

It could be argued that from 2000 to 2010, the only significant scientific or technological advance was the iPhone. Certainly, it constituted an expansion of previous cell phones capabilities, but it also represented a fundamental new creation in that it was designed and marketed as a device of multitudinous capabilities that included a phone.

Indeed, the changes wrought by cell phones and the internet were both miraculous and catastrophic. For the first time in history, ordinary people around the world had instantaneous information and answers in their hand. Want to know the population of Helsinki? Google it. Need to see a recipe on curry sauce? Hit the search bar. Want to keep track of your daily caloric expenditure? Use a Fitbit or a pedometer on your phone. Don't have a camera handy? There's one in your phone, and not only that, you have the ability to manipulate ("improve") photos so that if you post them on social media, you look your best.

No invention in human history—save the internet—spread to one-quarter of the US population as fast as cell phones did. Whereas after just thirteen years phones reached 25 percent of the population, the auto required fifty-five years, the old rotary dial phone thirty-five years, and the computer sixteen years to spread as far as fast. Countless other benefits from computer/phone/network advances have improved everything from health and medicine to financial assessments and personal book-keeping. At the same time, at least an identical number of harms also surfaced. Some of them had been reinforced by ongoing social trends discussed by Twenge and others. First, more screen time meant less healthy habits. Kids walked far less, played outside less, and ate more. More than 30 percent of twelfth graders rarely exercised and almost 60 percent of those aged eighteen to twenty-five were medically overweight or obese.[725]

What emerged as a reaction was a near consensus view from anyone who had intensive contact with younger generations, including well-known commentators such as Camille Paglia, raising warning flags at every opportunity. A 2018 British study found "striking" evidence that frequent internet users developed additions and depressions, "over-engaging…to replace normal social function."[726]

How destructive were phones and internet-linked laptops? One study approached the problem from the perspective of "What happens when you take them away?" Researchers found that when employees monitored their email and then abstained from monitoring it at all, even when at work, they spent more time outside, became better employees, switched tasks less frequently, and showed less distraction. They also reported that they were healthier.[727] Facebook, arguably the number one social media site in the world, found that not only were 63 percent of its users checking in daily but that a year later that percentage increased to 70 percent, amounting to almost one hour a day spent checking Facebook alone![728] A survey of Christians found that eight thousand checked their cell phones within minutes of waking up, and most did so before praying.[729]

If the effects of cell phones had been limited to a small number of youths, the social outcomes might have been much different. But by 2004, already the Kaiser Family Foundation found 40 percent of kids had a cell phone, and by 2009, when nearly 80 percent of young people had a cell phone, they consumed over ten hours of media per day.[730] Girls used the devices more than boys, mostly for texting. Whether on their phones, home computers, or iPads, by 2016, 44 percent of youth of all nations said that they were online "constantly." And for protective parents seeking to shield their kids from pornography, bullying, or socially undesirable sites, they were in trouble. A significant majority of children hid their phone usage from their parents, including a subgroup that kept their passwords secret. Some 22 percent used proxy tools to make their activities untraceable and 10 percent routinely wiped their browsing history. They probably didn't need to bother, as nearly two-thirds of parents said that they did not speak regularly with their teenagers about their online activities.[731]

Cyberbullying was common, as one Ohio pastor noted: "Kids are never out of the realm of comparison," while the resulting depression and anxiety from social media had exploded.[732] In 2015, Dr. Kim Khosla, a pediatrician, had a patient a week come in for symptoms of anxiety but five years later saw three or four *a day*, almost all of them young people. Entirely new pathologies emerged: "FOMO" (fear of missing out) or "ghosting" (leaving someone without any phone or text response). Direct connections were difficult to prove, but the correlations were enormous.

Most of these examples involved "protection creep," a form of technological security against unwanted outcomes. And in many cases, they soon went from a small snowball to an avalanche. Phones and electronic devices, which proved entries to identity theft, soon became digital "Fort Knoxes" to access, requiring fingerprints or facial recognition. (Can you imagine explaining to someone from the 1950s why they would need fingerprint identification on their phones?) These examples, however, constituted merely modern (growing) inconveniences that threatened to take over life in twenty-first century America. Far worse, the impact of risk aversion in science disregarded one of the greatest motivators to find the "right" answer: failure.

An equally troubling reading on the research thermometer than the increasing meaninglessness of studies was the falsification of data. Some of the most-noted stars in their fields were implicated. Dan Ariely's book *Predictably Irrational* (2010) contained a *potpourri* of amazing studies that intertwined ethics and behaviors. Subsequently, he coauthored a paper on making people more honest on such things as tax forms or business records.[733] Except that someone—Ariely denied it was him—altered the data after it was collected. The Hartford Insurance company, which worked with Ariely, stated that the data it provided for the study had been altered and was "manipulated inappropriately and supplemented by synthesized or fabricated data."[734] Given his track record, Ariely may indeed have been innocent.

Others, however, did not get off so easily: The president of Stanford University, Marc Tessier-Lavigne, authored a dozen reports (and was the principal author on five) that contained falsified information, including "lab panels that had been stitched together, panel backgrounds that were digitally altered and blot results taken from other research papers."[735] Any falsification or misrepresentation of data is basic fraud, but in that case the research involved neuroscience studies of Alzheimer's, a particularly heinous abuse. Or how about the retraction by *Nature* of a paper on superconducting, requested by eight coauthors who said the work did not "accurately reflect the provenance of the investigated materials, the experimental measurements undertaken and the data-processing protocols applied"?[736] Unlike Ariely, who had a pristine research record, that was the third high-profile article written by Ranga Dias of the University of Rochester and Ashkan Salamat at the University of Nevada, Las

Vegas. Other researchers said that Dias plagiarized portions of his doctoral dissertation.[737]

According to *The Guardian*, these cases didn't begin to cover the scope of the problem: "The number of retractions each year reflects about a tenth of a percent of the papers published in a given year—in other words, one in one thousand. Yet the figure has grown significantly from about 40 retractions in 2000, far outpacing growth in the annual volume of papers published."[738]

Volunteers had increasingly debunked bad research. Some sleuths even made it a cottage industry of their own, but that did not make their work any less valuable. Thanks to the efforts of such internet detectives, retractions rose. Publishers' business models that "made them susceptible to paper mills" or academic equivalents of "chop shops" that sold authorship and even entire research papers began to flag.[739]

Whereas studies that purported to offer new ways of instilling honesty constituted mere fraud, a much worse problem emerged with actual medical research that affected real people. *Science* reported that "hundreds of cancer papers mentioned cell lines that don't seem to exist."[740] Researchers published in the *International Journal of Cancer* found "misspellings or 'miscellings'" of a minimum of seven unverifiable cell lines that suggested the experiments "weren't actually conducted," as summarized by *Science*.[741] Some claimed the cell lines were merely misspelled, but over a course of more than four hundred papers, the problems soon surpassed merely sloppy spelling. And as in any inverted research pyramid, the original paper (containing the unverifiable cell lines) constituted a cornerstone that supported subsequent research that produced dozens of papers.

Those episodes provided merely the warm-up acts to the scandal at science publisher Wiley, which had acquired an Indian imprint in 2021 for $450 million—only to find "the presence [of manipulation] in certain special issues of compromised articles."[742] One was a study of drug resistance in newborns, another, an analysis of MRI scans in the diagnosis of liver disease.[743] Within a few months, Wiley retracted *eight thousand papers* and announced it would close the imprint it just bought for $298 million. The hemorrhaging continued, and by December 2023, Wiley had yanked an astonishing 11,300 scientific papers and shut down almost twenty journals. As the curtain rolled back, a more sinister hand than mere incompetence or inattention surfaced: Organized crime rings had operated research paper mills out of China, India, Iran, and Russia and planted their own editors in charge of journals, giving them kickbacks of up to $20,000 per paper published.[744] One unpublished analysis—which, given the track record of the journals, was probably as valid as most of their papers—found hundreds of thousands of bogus "paper-mill" articles in the literature.[745] One of the favorite tricks involved a "special issue" edited separately from the regular journal.[746]

Why would such "research" be necessary in the first place? Why endanger people's lives with phony findings? As the US university system grew exponentially in the late twentieth and early twenty-first century, "publish or perish" took on added weight. Science and engineering departments, in particular, relied heavily on grant funding to produce research. Faculty needed citations. But more important, they needed them *fast.* With the proliferation of academics and their output, all journals in all disciplines were swamped. As a young historian coming up in the 1980s, I found that one could submit a paper to a reputable journal and get the referees' judgments back within about six months. (The more prestigious, however, the longer it took.) If one could write fast and address all the concerns of a referee—and *none* came back "Yes! Publish this as is!" because it defeated the very need for referees in the first place—a faculty member might get a paper submitted, returned, then resubmitted and approved in a year, and then possibly see it published the following year. By 2024, that timeline had at least tripled for lesser journals, and for the top-of-the-line "name" journals, turnaround was closer to five years. The backlog was that great. Thus, it was incumbent on researchers to get multiple papers out to different journals at the same time, and as fast as possible. Enter the for-hire journal editors.

A fairly common standard for promotion and tenure in universities was at least two (often three) scholarly papers and/or a single book. Based on the 2025 review and acceptance rates, young scholars seeking to take the route of publishing shorter papers had become all but untenable. The alternative, however, was daunting. Turning a dissertation into a book was no easy task, and if the original review came back negative on a book, there was no plan B.

Fraud, plagiarism, and data manipulation offered a way to compress years of waiting and papers being refereed to allow anxious academics to get the results out now! The results were predictable. When some of the authorities and journals caught on, the paper mills shifted their tactics to simply bribing reputable editors. One publisher said it had to fire three hundred editors. With cash available, though, the practice became almost impossible to contain, but as more became aware of the practice, retractions soared, from just over 700 per year in 2009 to almost 4,500 annually in 2021.

Then came artificial intelligence (AI), which could write the fraud for you. AI offered ready-made papers with "100% Acceptance Guarantee."[747] Governments scrambled to catch up. Australia passed a law in 2019 criminalizing any advertising of commercial cheating. But as one observer put it, "The incentives of modern science seem almost designed to encourage widespread fraud."[748] A shift in academia, protected by the tenure system, led researchers to concern themselves less with problems they found challenging (including bigger-picture subjects) and more on problems that were likely to be funded, but which were extremely narrow and less important. That, in turn, transformed the graduate student system from one in which students worked on smaller, less important, but still meaningful topics to engaging in sub-domain work for their advisers. An incremental approach of increasingly smaller areas of study that refined a few areas of existing knowledge by minuscule advances, not only could not be sustained in the long run (as policymakers and taxpayers would lose interest in insignificant discoveries) but would also ensure that all of America's scientific complex would wither.

Two researchers, Didier Sornette and Peter Cauwels, identified five leading factors that fueled the trend toward risk aversion in science: (1) increasing wealth and aging, (2) increasing inequality, (3) the "illusion of control" offered by technology, (4) herding, especially through social media, and (5) management shaped by extremes and overreaction.[749] Much of the pathology of small thinking reverted back to the role of education, where increasingly failure was no longer seen as part of the learning process.

Kids, the argument went, were traumatized by failure and thus needed to be protected against it. British author Tim Gill called this the "shrinking horizons of childhood."[750] In 1971, eight out of ten children went to school by themselves (without an adult), but by 2007 that number had dropped to…one in ten. While by many measures children appeared in the early part of the twenty-first century to have "grown up faster" (largely through access to technology and by mimicking adult behavior), the fact was that children in 2025 reflected far younger behavior than their predecessors from just fifty years earlier. Routine games of the 1960s, such as red rover or kickball, were increasingly banned as too dangerous. Practices such as having valedictorians or awarding trophies for first place ceased as it made those who did not receive such distinctions "feel uncomfortable." Indeed, the infamous participation trophies were nothing new, first appearing in a newspaper in February 1922, but has mostly been identified with millennials.

Structurally and institutionally, risk aversion crept into the national and state bureaucracies. After all, what is a government bureaucrat to do if "public safety" or "children's safety" is part of his job description? The natural inclination was to expand the number of "unsafe" activities over which he had authority. Fear of liability also exacerbated the problem: Playgrounds took on the aura of fun prevention, such as wrap-around swings, soft landing areas under climbing equipment (rubber surfacing), and fewer overall pieces of playground equipment. In Texas in 2003, a host of playground equipment was banned, including seesaws, overhead rings, and parallel bars. Ironically, some studies suggested that the "risk compensation" by kids led to them thinking that the risk was less than if the ground beneath them was cement and engaged in riskier behavior.[751]

This is history, after all, and while this may be anecdotal, it may well resonate as true with most of you readers. I grew up in a small town in the 1960s that was surrounded by farms. Many of my friends lived in the country. It was normal to ride my Sting-Ray bike five miles outside of town to visit a friend, often stay overnight, and in the process set off fireworks or romp through watermelon fields. Occasionally with my friend's parents away, we would shoot shotguns and make our own ammunition. In high school, we would commonly go to the large hydro-electric pumping areas in the canals where the depth was perhaps five feet and repeatedly jump in. Typically, we left after school on bikes—or, later, cars—and didn't return till dinner. In my entire youth, only one child was killed or even seriously injured in any of these activities, when a friend's brother at a public pool with a lifeguard present nevertheless dove in and hit his head on the bottom, drowning before he could be rescued. Whatever incidents and accidents occurred, we learned not to engage in that particular behavior again.

THE NEW PANDEMIC REGIME

No disease in recent memory, not even AIDS, affected America as much as Covid.[v] The epidemic became the first human illness in history deliberately misreported and often medically mistreated. Within the US, medical authorities refused to critically investigate, question, challenge, or even (when they learned they were in error) temper official statements emanating mostly from the Centers for Disease Control and Prevention (CDC) domestically or the World Health Organization internationally. Health authorities with few exceptions fell in line with the official (and wrong) pronouncements, treatments, and policies.[752]

---

v As noted earlier, this is also represented as "COVID-19" or the "China Virus." For purposes here, I will use "Covid" or "China Virus" interchangeably.

Five years after the plague, disagreement about the origins of Covid remain. A commonly used and extremely flawed source, Wikipedia, continued to maintain the possibility of human contraction through wet markets and eating bats. Congressional testimony, however, suggested that the disease was created in a laboratory in Wuhan, China. In 2025, belatedly, the CIA agreed.[753] It emanated from "gain-of-function research" (that is, for potential uses as a weapon), it was released at some level either deliberately or accidentally, and it received funding from Dr. Anthony Fauci and the National Institute of Allergy and Infectious Diseases.[754] One of the doctors who, at an early stage, questioned the protocols, the dismissal of prophylactic treatments, and the efficacy of the vaccine, Dr. Scott Atlas, noted "the pandemic exposed grave problems with the essential functioning of science, research and debate… foster[ing] a climate of fear [that] inhibited other scientists and health experts from contributing to the discussion, effectively inducing self-censorship."[755] However, it also played a political role in helping to unseat then-President Trump. As reporter Mollie Hemingway put it, the China Virus was "so perfectly suited to damaging President Trump's re-election that it almost seemed designed in a laboratory."[756] As indeed it was.

From there, however, questions remain whether the release was deliberate (as an attack on the West or as a test of non-Chinese responses) or accidental. Witnesses to Congress, including Nicholas Wade, the former editor of *Science*, testified that Dr. Fauci and Dr. Francis Collins used unverified data to dismiss the initial lab leak theory. Mainstream scientific journals, such as *Scientific American*, attempted to perpetuate the notion that the lab leak explanation was anything but "insidious" and a "myth" despite that fact that evidence confirmed that Fauci and his cadre of associates had lied and hid or deleted records related to the origins of the China Virus.[757] Researchers who had tried to discredit the lab leak evidence received more money to study viruses.[758] Despite those efforts, a majority of Americans believed the virus leaked from a lab.[759] New evidence not only supports that, but also goes further in arguing that Covid was developed by the "military" at Wuhan. Investigators examining top secret communications and scientific research claim the Chinese were engaged in covert weapon experiments, which leaked.[760]

Major epidemics have hit the US in the past, including the deadliest up to that point, the Spanish Flu, which killed 675,000 Americans. Given the relative population number of 1918 and 2023, Covid killed only about half that number, and in 1918 the nation never locked down, masked up, isolated, or had a vaccine.

Word first surfaced of a pneumonia-like illness in China's Hubei Province at the town of Wuhan where the Communists had a biological laboratory. Whether by accident or design—and many would argue the latter—horrific images equivalent to scenes from the Black Death began to circulate. Rows of Chinese workers in biohazard suits spraying the pavement and health officials chattering frenetically in front of cameras were posted on social media. Then came word that supposedly exposed that Chinese citizens in Wuhan were welded inside their houses and apartments—the equivalent of slamming someone behind a watertight door on the *Titanic*. Indeed, the Chinese locked down entire cities.[761] Whatever the intent, the stories and images had the effect of creating a certain hysteria, making the American public malleable to large-scale government control and enabling authorities to employ isolation and control at levels never before attempted in the US.[762]

It should be noted that the world's news media and most medical professionals enthusiastically joined in the descriptions of the pandemic as an international disaster requiring novel and radical solutions. Simply "riding it out" or letting natural immunity take its course was immediately dismissed. Estimates of twenty million dead in America alone were thrown out with virtually no serious challenges.[763] Those extremely high death rates momentarily seemed possible as Italy showed a "borderline apocalyptic" outbreak, according to Trump's son-in-law Jared Kushner. He recalled, "Patients lined hallways and field hospitals as overwhelmed doctors triaged the sick and were forced to make life-or-death decision about who would receive care."[764]

The World Health Organization declared Covid to be a public health emergency on January 30, by which time it had spread to Italy. Trump issued a nationwide travel ban from China the following day. It took less than a week for leftist groups to call the ban "xenophobic."[765] Former Vice President Biden accused Trump of "fanning the flames" of "hate, fear, and xenophobia" with the restrictions.[766]

Who was really "fanning the flames"? None other than the scientific and medical research establishment, trying to generate hysteria about the China Virus. Neil Ferguson, a British epidemiologist (with a reputation for being grotesquely wrong), predicted that 510,000 would quickly die in Britain and up to 2.2 million in the US.[767] (Three years later, the actual US numbers were only half that.)[768] Other research soon showed that the extreme failures of Ferguson's model were "worse than we knew."[769] Yet at the same time, Dr. Fauci, who by then was the darling of the American media and viewed as trustworthy by nearly 80 percent of the public, had already uncritically embraced Ferguson's egregiously wrong data and, actually, *expanded it* to forty million deaths if the disease was "unchecked."[770]

Fauci, due to his tenure, his (supposed) experience in combating AIDS, and his senior status at the National Institute of Allergy and Infectious Diseases, de facto became the "medical authority" from whom President Trump took advice. As Robert F. Kennedy Jr. in his exposé of Fauci, *The Real Anthony Fauci*, observed, "Due to his vast budgetary discretion, his unique political access, his power over HHS [Department of Health and Human Services] and its various agencies, his moral authority, his moral flexibility, and his bully pulpit, Tony Fauci has more power than any other individual to direct public energies toward solutions."[771] Equally important, over time, Fauci had the ability to rig the critical drug approval panels by appointing primary investigators who were tied to pharmaceutical giants and drug approval panels. He received fifty-eight royalty payments in 2020 and 2021 alone from companies that produce antibodies and from Novartis, a company contracted to develop a bird flu vaccine. It also meant Fauci had a financial interest in stifling the use of any non-vaccine treatment of the China Virus, in particular Ivermectin or hydroxychloroquine.

Not only did no one in a position to do so challenge Fauci, the media also quickly touted him as "America's Doctor," and his approval rating in polls stood at 80 percent.[772] The fawning media coverage stemmed in part, according to researchers who studied the journalism during the China Virus, to the fact that reporters "have historically been ill equipped to report on scientific matters because they so often lack the depth of knowledge to ask the right questions about studies [and] reports."[773] As a consequence, virtually no major news outlets challenged Fauci on his constant flip-flops: Wear masks, don't wear masks, the disease is virulent, the disease is difficult to contract. It was a repeat of Fauci's comments on AIDS, where he warned that "the possibility that routine close contact, as within a family household, can spread the disease" and claimed "non-sexual, non–blood-borne transmission [was] possible."[774]

THE STING

Already the Deep State was laying the groundwork to use the China Virus to weaken—if not remove—Trump. Many had hoped he would not respond at all and thus could be blame for millions of deaths. Indeed, new research on the intelligence agencies showed that it looked "like the disease started spreading in late August, early September, 2019," and was hidden from Trump. "So what we really have here," said Dr. Andrew Huff, who reviewed the process to inform the president, "is a giant scandal to subvert the President of the United States."[775] Trump, however, acted rapidly when he was briefed.

On January 29, Trump named Vice President Mike Pence to head the Coronavirus Task Force that included Dr. Fauci, Dr. Deborah Birx, Dr. Francis Collins, Dr. Robert Redfield (director of the CDC), Jerome Adams (the surgeon general), and heads from the Department of Health and Human Services (Alex Azar), the Department of Housing and

Urban Development (Ben Carson), National Institutes of Health, State Department, and others. (Scott Atlas could not determine how Birx found her way on to the task force, noting only that Pence "inherited her.")[776] Notably absent were dozens of doctors advocating for therapeutic treatments that included hydroxychloroquine or Ivermectin. Atlas was invited to join, but noted that Fauci, Birx, and Redfield dominated the discussions. Most notably, all but a few such as Carson were quite comfortable with "big government" solutions.

At least the task force realized that the first goal was to develop an adequate test. Those tests, however, proved entirely unreliable, telling people they had the virus when they didn't or vice versa. Throughout it all, Fauci and Birx insisted they were *undertesting.*

Robert Kennedy later explained Fauci's strategy to manage Covid: "suppress viral spread by mandatory masking, social distancing, quarantining the healthy (also known as lockdowns), while instructing COVID patients to return home and do nothing—receive no treatment whatsoever—until difficulties breathing sent them back to the hospital" to receive either a ventilator or the intravenous drug remdesivir.[777] Millions could attest to the fact that when calling their family doctor, they were instructed *not* to come to the doctor but go to the hospital, yet if people were not displaying significant difficulty breathing, hospitals sent them home…with nothing. Far from considering temporary treatments that might minimize effects of the virus, such as Ivermectin or hydroxychloroquine, the task force began aligning with Fauci's protocols.

The anti-Trump media descended on the slightest thing the president said, whereas Fauci's self-contradictions were voluminous. (One survey by the National Bureau of Economic Research found that China Virus coverage was overwhelmingly negative—as if designed to induce panic—but that American news coverage was especially so and that if Trump was involved, it was nearly universally so. For example, it noted, "among U.S. major media outlets, stories discussing President Donald Trump and hydroxychloroquine [were] more numerous than *all stories combined that cover companies and individual researchers working on*

COVID-19 vaccines [emphasis mine].")[778] Where there was success, the media only saw death and failure. Meanwhile, Fauci still clung to a "bat" origin of the China Virus, claimed masks worked after first saying they didn't, and ridiculed hydroxychloroquine and Ivermectin, both of which were already proving effective if administered early. Moreover, the initial goal of focusing on testing came with its own problems: The more people who were tested, the more cases that would appear. But cases did not mean people were sick, only that they tested positive for Covid.

From the start, the media had tried to claim that the virus did not originate in a Wuhan lab because that would make China look bad, and that lockdowns, masks, and social distancing constituted effective steps to combat the disease (even though Sweden had not locked down and had a far lower percentage of cases). During a call between Dr. Atlas and President Trump, the president told him, "I'm sure you will teach me many things...But there is only one thing you'll learn from me. Only one. You will learn how vicious, how biased, how unfair the media is."[779] If anything Trump still understated the destructiveness of the media during the China Virus. For example, virtually none of the stories made regular references for comparative purposes to the death levels from the Spanish Flu, where almost twice as many Americans had died.[780] Moreover, through ignorance or design, the media routinely papered over the issue of "comorbidities"—that is, the fact that someone already suffering from diabetes, heart disease, or cancer was more likely to die from Covid than someone without serious comorbidities.[781] In one case, the CDC overstated pediatric deaths alone by seventy-two thousand through a "coding error" (its term for ignoring comorbidities).[782] By 2022, the CDC was removing forty to seventy-five cancer deaths per week and reclassifying them as China Virus deaths, and an investigation showed that *any* unvaccinated person who died of *any* disease was categorized as a Covid death.[783]

Fauci had emphasized getting *cases* down but kept raising the target number as to what percent of cases was acceptable for normal living. (Toward the end, he was almost at 100 percent: The disease—a flu—had to be totally eradicated.) But a positive China Virus test combined with a death, in Fauci's eyes, *had to mean* that Covid was responsible. He even changed the CDC's death certificate protocol to ignore the 84 percent who died with comorbidities to state that only Covid was responsible. In turn, this escalated the number of people who thought the China Virus was deadly. Democrats, especially, were fearmongers, believing that 50 percent of those infected would die of the disease. The number was 1 percent.[784]

It also fed his unstoppable appetite for more testing. Dr. John Ioannidis increasingly challenged the absurd fixation that Fauci and Birx had on the number of cases reported versus the number of actual fatalities. (Astonishingly, by 2022, Birx insisted they had *undertested* and continued to claim that herd immunity was a myth.)[785] Ioannidis did his own study, and concluded that infections were far higher than others projected, meaning that deaths per infection were much lower.[786] Nevertheless, as Kushner warned Atlas, Birx was "easily threatened" and "task force doctors were fixated on a single-minded impossible view that all cases of COVID must be stopped or millions of Americans would die."[787]

White House Cassandras who received backing through false claims from the World Health Organization at one point or another said the following:

- The China Virus was extraordinarily deadly and worse than any other flu by several orders of magnitude.
- Everyone was at risk of dying from it.
- No one had immunity (true at first, but that rapidly changed as people contracted Covid, lived, and developed immunity).
- Everyone spread the infection.
- Masks worked.
- The only hope was a vaccine.
- Quarantines and lockdowns were required.

Based on such hysterical falsehoods, no wonder large numbers thought that contracting the virus would mean hospitalization. (By 2022, even Birx would admit in her book that "the harsh reality was that silent spread could occur even among the vaccinated," but she refused to admit that in fact the vaccines were causing enormous damage. She also admitted that "vaccinated people can infect their loved ones.")[788]

Trump's team rolled out testing in early March—but this even generated more panic for two reasons. First, the tests were not reliable, and second, *inevitably* as more tests were administered, more people would be shown to have Covid. Ultimately, even National Public Radio had to throw in the towel on testing as effective, by which time Dr. Jay Bhattacharya at Stanford found reported fatality rates "were grossly off-base, too high by a factor of fifty."[789]

Another element of Fauci's strategy against the virus was the quarantine or "lockdown." On March 15, 2020, New York City closed all school buildings and shifted to "remote learning."[790] Such actions defied logic, as in the first sixty thousand deaths, only twelve were children, and in New York City, which had 15,756 deaths, only eight were children—but only one lacked an underlying condition. Even the *Journal of the American Medical Association*, which toed the Fauci-Birx line, acknowledged that kids were more at risk of dying from the everyday flu than from the China Virus.[791] Teachers' unions played a key role in shutting down schools.

Trump was largely hoodwinked by the Fauci-Birx lockdown brigade. He had already been browbeaten by White House staff, including his son-in-law, Jared Kushner, into referring to the disease as "Covid" instead of the "China Virus" (which was in keeping with traditional naming, such as the "Spanish Flu"). Trump had also used his presidential leverage against 3M company for not sending the bulk of its masks to the US. He invoked the Defense Production Act, requiring the company to send all of its China-made masks to the US. (Again, at that time, it had not been established that the masks were useless, and Fauci's flip-flops had not yet become a cause for concern.) Birx, meanwhile, insisted even after Covid that the masks were useful. She wrote, "Wearing a mask limited the amount of aerosols or droplets an infected person could spread and reduced the number of these particles others could inhale."[792] That, of course, proved absolutely false. Likewise, the number of ventilators required was outlandishly unrealistic and, in retrospect, unnecessary.

Kushner was receiving panicked calls from New York Governor Andrew Cuomo, who besieged the White House with calls for more ICU beds. Cuomo told Kushner, "This is getting really bad, and I fear we are soon going to run out of ICU beds."[793] Cuomo asked for 150,000 ICU beds. He also begged the White House for more ventilators, all the while hoarding two thousand in his own warehouses. (It was not known then that putting a person on a ventilator dramatically increased the likelihood of dying from the virus.) Kushner was outraged and replied, "We did not send the ventilators from the federal stockpile to sit unused in the New York stockpile."[794]

Fauci was diligently at work trying to institute a national quarantine or lockdown. He told Trump, Kushner, and Vice President Pence who headed the task force, based on Ferguson's outrageously flawed statistics, that there would be 160 million dead worldwide without lockdowns. Pence's task force soon produced "guidelines" (but not mandates) that recommended closing nonessential businesses for two weeks to slow the spread of the virus and ease the (expected) burden on hospital beds and ICUs. (Again, with a few exceptions, this torrent of cases never appeared, and often ICU beds were empty.) Referring to the expected high infection rate, Pence's team called for "two weeks to flatten the curve." They presented their case to Trump, Fauci, and a few others in a briefing, and Trump responded, "That's it?… I thought you were going to ask me to call in the military to make people stay in their homes. We can't do this forever, but people will tolerate this for a few weeks."[795]

On March 16, Trump issued the guidelines that included avoiding discretionary travel, avoiding social gatherings of ten or more people, not to use food courts, bars, or restaurants, and to refrain from visiting nursing homes. Although billed as "15 Days to Slow the Spread," referring to the infection rate to ensure enough hospital beds, the actual guidelines boosted that to thirty days. Nowhere did the federal guidelines require closing down anything.[796] On the other hand, as Birx related in her book, she and her cohorts were pressuring Trump 24/7 to lock down everything and test unceasingly. That Trump resisted as much as he did was a miracle.

Pence already had conceived of a strategy to have the states take the lead in determining how far to go with lockdowns. On the surface, this seemed a legitimate and sensible "states' rights/federalism" approach—but only on the surface. In reality, no state had medical officials capable of challenging the CDC's statistics or recommendations, and few did. Governor Kristi Noem of South Dakota kept her state open, one of the very few. For most, Pence's "states' rights" strategy played into the hands of Dr. Fauci, who became the medical supremo for the nation. Whether Pence knew that at the time remains unresolved.

At the ground level, it was even worse. Governors became hostage to big-city Democratic mayors. How much of their eagerness to shut down the cities came out of genuine concerns for health and how much stemmed from them seeing an opportunity to deeply harm Trump in an election year has yet to be determined. Not one single big-city mayor bucked the trend; all locked down. Trump rejected this approach, agreeing only to federal "recommendations" and insisting that the country needed to reopen by Easter.[797]

Regardless, Trump had had enough by April 15 and said in a meeting that he wanted to reopen the country immediately, adding "I'm not going to preside over the funeral of the greatest country in the world."[798] He had also had enough of Fauci, but discovered that civil service laws prohibited him from firing Fauci, even if he wanted to, and the media portrayed Trump's (correct) position that the nation should open up as a "rejection of science."

One immediate problem with the lockdowns was that shipping had stopped worldwide, yet many of the medical supplies needed came from China. For decades, America had outsourced its critical industries, including computer chip manufacturing and medical technology. Now the US was in thrall to a communist nation. Trump's team wanted China to prioritize deliveries to America, and they agreed but on one condition: Trump stop referring to the Covid virus as the "China Virus." He agreed.[799]

Few at the time, save, perhaps, Robert F. Kennedy Jr., appreciated how deeply intertwined the large pharmaceutical companies were with the CDC and, specifically, Fauci. The CDC itself owned fifty-seven vaccine patents and spent one-third of its annual budget buying and distributing vaccines.[800] Fauci, who influenced everything at the CDC and National Institute of Allergy and Infectious Diseases, stood as the highest-paid employee in the entire federal government. Through the Covid pandemic, Fauci became a virtual health dictator, even stating that attacks on him constituted "attacks on science."[801] His portfolio also leaped.

How, precisely, Fauci got into a position to control the pandemic response, even with his administrative titles, remains shrouded in mystery. If President Trump had maintained control and rejected Pence's federalist approach, the lockdowns would have been over before Easter 2020. (As was later revealed, Pence was Fauci's major support in the administration.)[802] Trump, however, not Fauci, was on the side of "science." Even though his administration would accelerate a vaccine, he predicted the virus would disappear without a vaccine.[803]

Informed by the White House legal counsel that he could not fire Fauci, Trump cut him off from access by June. The president urged therapeutic treatments if infected: Ivermectin and hydroxychloroquine (HCQ), an anti-malarial drug. (Later, it was learned that Africa, which uses HCQ regularly, had an extremely low rate of the China Virus.) Although by July 2021, Trump was calling Fauci an "alarmist," he admitted that the media had insulated the doctor against criticism. By August 2020, Trump had begun to bring in those who had warned against excessive vaccinations and lockdowns all along, including Dr. Atlas.

When Trump announced, "two weeks to flatten the curve," the stock market crashed. But in March Trump rolled out testing for the virus, and the market rallied 1,400 points twenty minutes later. On April 15, Secretary of Health and Human Services Alex Azar proposed a plan to develop a vaccine within six months. The federal government would underwrite the production costs and accelerate the approval process by combining three testing phases simultaneously. He promised it could be done without compromising safety. Several drug companies already had been testing vaccine technology that they thought could work against Covid. One of the conditions, however, was that they could not be held liable for side effects of the vaccines or for lack of effectiveness. It was a one-way street.

Even as he unveiled the "Operation Warp Speed" vaccine program, Trump reminded everyone that "vaccines are only partially effective... what are we doing about therapeutics?"[804] Trump had urged the use of therapeutics such as Ivermectin and HCQ to minimize the impact of the virus, along with sunlight and weight loss. All of these would later prove to be at least partially effective or recommended by mainstream doctors. But Fauci would have none of it: He and the CDC collaborated with the major media and social media outlets to utterly suppress *any* discussion of vaccine dangers or of any alternative treatments besides their vaccines and lockdowns. That included natural immunity, which Birx lampooned. Fauci even reversed his own statements about the ineffectiveness of masks. In his private emails, he correctly stated that masks were of little value against viral infection.[805]

On May 15, 2020, Trump announced "Operation Warp Speed" to deliver a vaccine against Covid by January 2021. That was both good and bad news. Some 82 percent of Americans eventually took the vaccine—many under duress or at risk of losing their jobs if they did not—but industry documents revealed that the drugs did not undergo even normal testing and that numerous side effects, including myocarditis, were possible, even prevalent in certain groups. By January 2021, Fauci was on a vaccine jihad: He not only insisted that all Americans, even infants, be vaccinated, but he also wanted those who already had the disease and now had natural immunity (such as your author) to get the "jab" as well.[806] He ultimately said that all Americans would have to take the vaccine to stop the virus. Some noted that as long as people remained un-vaxxed, there would be a real-world "control sample" to prove the vaccines were dangerous.

TYRANNY OVER EVERYDAY LIFE

Even before the arrival of Biden and the vaccine, the lockdowns and social distancing illustrated the deplorable fact of government control of almost every aspect of life. Churches—probably the most essential aspect of American life—were deemed "non-essential," as were restaurants, theaters, and health clubs, and were closed. Grocery stores and home improvement businesses had to put stickers for "social distancing" on the floors along with arrows directing people which direction to travel to stay away from other people. (With the exception of Covid zealots, these kinds of meaningless markers and requirements were largely ignored, except on airplanes, where the crew patrolled aisles like the cheka.)

Almost everywhere, resistance started against the tyranny over everyday life. Some states saw more resistance—and freedom—than others. Governor Kristi Noem in South Dakota had never locked down (and Biden punished the state by forbidding the annual fireworks at Mt. Rushmore due to "fire danger"), Governor Brian Kemp in Georgia reopened his state on April 20, 2020, Utah followed the same day, and Florida's Governor Ron DeSantis reopened his state in September. The media howled.[807]

Yet officials largely continued to let Fauci's ungrounded edicts rule them. As Dr. Peter McCullough, a critic of the lockdowns and emphasis on vaccines as a cure, noted, "We didn't have a single academic institution come up with a single protocol.... Not a single medical center set up even a tent to try to treat patients and prevent hospitalization."[808] Yet rogue doctors, intervening early before hospitalization, had phenomenal results in which no patients died.[809] Later it was revealed that the CDC tests on early prevention were rigged by ensuring they failed by waiting far too late in the disease process to administer HCQ or other protocols. Robert F. Kennedy Jr.'s book *The Real Anthony Fauci* described in detail about the rigging of tests to be against HCQ and in favor of vaccines.

It was also later revealed that Fauci, obsessed with his vaccine-oriented strategy, had persuaded the CDC to abort its normal three-year clinical trials and instead adopt only a six-month trial period. This was far too short a time to detect numerous side effects. Fauci and the CDC refused to fix the Health and Human Services' Vaccine Adverse Event Reporting System (VAERS), wherein patients who experienced side effects from a vaccine could report it to the CDC. Multiple reports usually triggered a response, if not an entire halt to vaccine delivery. In this case, when the VAERS data started to show dangers, the now-dominant COVID establishment and the media, ignored it. Meanwhile, the original "anti-vax" population (who had concerns about all vaccines and their connection to diseases such as autism) were joined by those who had concerns about the lack of testing in the Covid drugs and about the rapidly spreading word of mouth regarding vaccine side effects and/or death. Shortly after the vaccines were rolled out, news leaked that some of them had DNA-changing properties, causing resistance to shoot up to a whole new level. News from Britain suggested that the vaccines actually enhanced transmission; and Israel, the most vaxxed nation in the world, had some of the highest Covid rates. VAERS data, that Fauci and the CDC for the first time ignored, suggested that "in just eight months, the COVID vaccines have injured and killed far more Americans than all other vaccines combined over three decades."[810] By October 2021, studies appeared in reputable journals such as *The Lancet* showing that the vaccine effectiveness disappeared so rapidly it was ephemeral, falling 88 percent after only a month. Thus, the need for constant new boosters was introduced. At that time, many people grew skeptical, even though between 70 percent and 80 percent of Americans had received at least one vaccine. Many said, "*No más*." Yet at the same time, Fauci and the

CDC continued to press for low-risk people, including children under five, to get the vaccine. As post-pandemic evidence continued to roll in, one by one, major scientific sources were forced to admit that the vaccines either were not effective or were dangerous, or both.[811] The case study fatality rate data from the Pfizer vaccine shoed that recipients were five times more likely to die than un-vaxxed individuals.[812]

Many different social harms surfaced from the effects of the lockdowns.[813] One study found that they, at best, "may" have saved four thousand lives, but they increased Covid morbidity and caused world poverty to soar.[814] After the election in 2021, Biden perpetuated the mask mandates on airplanes, in airports, and on public transportation as long as he could, until the weight of evidence showed that masks were next to useless.[815]

How much of Covid policy was driven by Fauci's personal lust for power, the CDC's view that it alone was the arbiter of all medical issues in America, or the political effort to use the pandemic as a means to undermine President Trump—who in October caught the virus and quickly recovered—remains to be researched. One thing is certain: Even leftist media organizations admitted the pandemic proved excellent cover for the Democrats to "fortify" (many would say, "steal") the 2020 election.

CORONAVIRUS CARNAGE

Trump's stellar economy, his most glowing achievement, came apart with the lockdowns. Not only did they cause massive immediate disruption, but they also produced the "largest upward transfer of wealth in history."[816] Despite the fact that America had thirty million small businesses compared with just twenty thousand big corporations, large companies were deemed "essential" and allowed to stay open during the pandemic when gyms, salons, restaurants, movie theaters, pet stores, and hundreds of other businesses were shuttered.[817] Meanwhile, seven big tech companies alone gained $3.4 trillion in market value as ordinary Americans were losing their lifelong dreams. Supposedly, to help compensate, the government instigated a monetary stimulus and provided loans: The stimulus resulted in inflation (which reached 7 percent by 2023) and getting the loans was time consuming. Even if a business qualified, it might not arrive in time to save the firm. All those horrors were accompanied by clever marketing campaigns telling viewers, "We're all in this together." Any business executive who spoke out against the lockdowns was fired, as described by Levi's executive Jennifer Sey, who resigned over the lockdown politics.

And the pandemic spurred a massive burst of new government spending, perhaps as high as $6 trillion. Congress passed the CARES Act in March 2020, a huge money giveaway to attempt to offset the economic pain of closed businesses and lost income. As Trump's son-in-law, Jared Kushner, who was deeply involved in the China Virus response, said, "We were shooting bullets into a cloud of smoke and hoping enough of them would hit their targets to save an economy veering toward collapse."[818] Personal income, which had soared under Trump by $4.2 trillion, temporarily grew as people banked their "stimulus checks." Savings tripled in the first quarter of 2020, then plummeted.

Incredibly basic health care was denied under the lockdown rules: Teeth cleanings were ruled "nonessential," but to obtain a root canal, a patient first had to have…a cleaning! And Dr. Fauci admitted that he didn't even think about things such as the economic impact of lockdowns.

In addition to the massive shocks brought about by the China Virus and its attendant lockdowns, a large structural change in the American economy was afoot. Baby boomers had changed the economy when they entered the workforce in the early 1960s. Retired during the China Virus period, they may have normally just waited out the epidemic. Sharply rising prices spurred by inflation, however, required them to reenter the workforce. Often, they did so by working for cash. Federal and state welfare also destroyed work and, according to many, affected the marriage rate.[819] College enrollment dipped. There was a decline in the share of college graduates working in so-called creative jobs or web/computer occupations.[820]

To the present, no one has yet fully calculated the damage done by the response to the China Virus. Trust in medical professionals fell dramatically, moving from 71.5 percent in 2020 to 40.1 percent in 2024.[821] Whereas over 80 percent of Americans took the initial China Virus vaccine, 60 percent said they would not take a booster.[822] Perhaps the ultimate rebuke to Dr. Fauci and the pro-vaccine crowd came when, after winning the election in 2024, President Trump named Robert F. Kennedy Jr. as his secretary of health and human services.

Covid and its response also caused trust in the media to fall further. Needless to say, trust in official pronouncements by US government officials fell. Covid wrecked the US economy, severely traumatized a younger generation, and validated anti-social behaviors. Slowly, there were lawsuits against the drug companies over the vaccine; against federal, state, and local governments over wrongful termination; and over religious discrimination. Lawsuits for refusing to accept a vaccine worked their way through the courts. For the most part, decisions sided with individuals against organizations. Even more slowly, nations began to prohibit the vaccine for children. On top of all those harms, the pandemic provided the perfect cover for Democrats to attempt to steal an election through mail-in ballots. After all, what else did locked-in people have to do…except vote?

CHAPTER 8
THE GRAVEYARD

Joe Biden—or his staff—had crafted a plan to defeat Donald Trump that relied heavily on the China Virus. First, they would use the excuse of Covid to keep the aging and decrepit Biden out of the public eye as much as possible. Second, they planned to use, for the first time in American politics, a national mail-in vote campaign as an incubator for fraud. "Ballot harvesting" had worked well for Hillary Clinton in some areas in 2016. Now the Democrats had a plan to take it national. Finally, Americans' dissatisfaction with the lockdowns and a growing number of people concerned about Trump's supposed crowning policy accomplishment, the vaccine from "Operation Warp Speed," gave Biden an opportunity to pretend that he could somehow fight the epidemic more effectively than had Trump.

Still, the Democratic Party that Biden inherited was reeling from his boss's tenure. Barack Obama had overseen a loss of 947 state legislative seats, eleven senators, and thirteen governors.[823] Obama (likely deliberately) never built a bench, and left the Democratic National Convention (DNC) over $2.4 million in debt when he handed over the nomination to Hillary Clinton in 2016. Obama's aides had selected

Debbie Wasserman Schultz to replace Virginia Governor Tim Kaine as DNC head as a means to secure Florida. Instead, Wasserman Schultz (as would her counterpart with the Republicans Ronna Romney McDaniel) used the position as a platform to promote herself.

As the Democratic convention of 2016 approached, internal emails surfaced from leaks that showed she and her staff had sought to tilt the nomination to Clinton over Bernie Sanders. That reality, combined with Clinton's abysmal performance as a candidate, led to Vice President Biden ruminating about how well he might have done in 2016. (His team conveniently sidestepped the reality that the Clinton team would have crushed him in the same way they did Sanders.) Biden himself did not want to risk being humiliated by a Clinton. Indeed, as early as 2014, when Obama "aides were rushing to do one final reboot of his presidency after the Republican rout in the midterms," Clinton's team was already staffing up.[824] Moreover, the inevitability of a "female president" piled on top of other factors to convince Obama that he could not back someone to oppose her in the primaries.

Like everyone else, Obama was stunned at the result on election night in 2016. Large donors had arrived at the Javits Center with their requests for ambassadorships lined up. He quickly recovered, however, avoiding the public "resist" movement while spawning a new, poisonous organization called "Obama for America," whose goal was to keep his reelection campaign intact. It constituted little more than a second Democratic National Committee, but one firmly in Obama's hands. Then, typically, he did nothing. The Organizing for Action organization didn't even hear from him for a year. He spent time on Richard Branson's boat or in his new $12 million fifteen-bedroom mansion on Martha's Vineyard. He charged top-of-the-line speaking fees and jetted about on private planes.[825] The Obamas, all the while speaking of class bias and a two-tiered society, netted a $60 million joint book deal.[826] Within a year, they'd sign an unprecedented agreement with video giant Netflix, whose details are still not fully disclosed: Estimates were that Netflix paid the Obamas between $100 and $250 million for a production contract—all while ridiculing a man who donated his entire salary as president to the country.[827] Most of all, he spent time receiving other politicians who came "to tell him he was the smartest man in the party."[828]

When he did show up at Organizing for Action, his favorite game was "Who will be the Democrat nominee in 2020?" He never expected that it could be Biden whom Obama thought was already too old to run for president. But one thing was clear: Obama was Trump obsessed. He would compare "likes" and "retweets" on Twitter of his and Trump's posts.[829] He could not decide if Trump was a puppet or a Jimmy Carter–style micromanager. Many in his team thought Jared Kushner called the shots.

As with so many before him and after him, Obama failed to understand that voters, indeed, had specifically voted for Donald Trump's policies. As he often did, he cleverly spoke through surrogates, in this case Josh Earnest, his press secretary. Earnest said of Trump's positions, "Those represent the president's actual views and preferences about the direction that he'd like to see the country go…but that's not what the American people voted for."[830]

Most notably, Obama's team worried about whether Trump's aides would sift through emails and find evidence of his own criminality. Obama threw himself even more energetically into the Russia Hoax, terrified that the criminal unmasking of various Americans under his administration would lead to arrests of people such as Susan Rice. Obama tried to convince himself that Team Trump was incompetent—a position from which he was disabused quickly when Trump began a radical restoration of the country, undoing much of Obama's eight years.

As it dawned on Obama that increasingly he was helpless to prevent Trump from undoing his already meager achievement record, candidates lined up to replace him as head of the movement. Perhaps the most underestimated was Obama's vice president, Biden. After all, in 2012, Obama considered the unthinkable: substituting Hillary Clinton for Biden as Obama's poll numbers sank. But the human gaffe machine,

Biden, still made ill-considered remarks. He warned a black audience that Republicans would "put ya'll back in chains."[831]

"DON'T UNDERESTIMATE JOE'S ABILITY TO F**K THINGS UP"

Obama had never held much respect for Joe Biden. During cabinet meetings, Obama's staff would roll their eyes when Biden spoke. Referring to what should have been an easy Iowa caucus win in 2020, Obama said "Don't underestimate Joe's ability to f**k things up."[832] For his part, Biden thought he had performed with 100 percent loyalty to Obama and that his faithfulness was not rewarded.

The track record of vice presidents seeking the presidency was poor, with Al Gore, Walter "Fritz" Mondale, and Richard Nixon some of the most recent veeps to fail. Biden was campaigning for higher office as the ultimate insider at a time when, around the world, electorates were rejecting insider candidates. A former senator, he also had the baggage that few senators had been successful in their quest for the Oval Office.

Born 1942, Joseph Robinette Biden Jr., or "Scranton Joe" as he liked to call himself for his Scranton, Pennsylvania, birth, fancied himself a man of the people. His family only stayed in Pennsylvania for nine years, moving to Delaware. Biden, though a poor student, attended the University of Delaware and Syracuse University, where, in his first year of law school, he plagiarized a law review article. In 1968, Biden began half an unbroken century in politics, moving from the New Castle County Council straight to the US Senate in 1972. He used five student deferments to escape Vietnam, but unlike Trump, did not even attend so much as a military school.

In a marriage with Neilia Hunter, Biden had two sons, Beau and Hunter, and a daughter, Amy. Beau went into the army, became Delaware's attorney general, and then died of cancer in 2015, an event that left an indelible mark on the elder Biden. As his mind began to fail, Joe would routinely have Beau dying in combat in Iraq when in fact he died of brain cancer. Hunter, with no money of his own, became a founding partner in the Chinese investment firm BHR and was on the board of Burisma Holdings, one of the largest natural gas producers in Ukraine. His lobbying efforts came under extreme scrutiny in the 2020 presidential campaign, and his culpability was so great that his father, the president, pardoned him in 2024 to prevent any indictments. Biden's first wife and daughter were killed in an auto accident in 1973. Both his boys were sent to the hospital. He later remarried Jill Jacobs, whom he met on a blind date in 1975. They had another daughter, Ashley.

Biden would later claim that he was a professor, but he only co-taught a single seminar for three years as an adjunct at the Widener University Delaware Law School. By that time, Biden's had become well known for enhancing the truth or even fantasizing to the extreme. For example, he told a story about how he had backed down a swimming pool bully named "Corn Pop." (No witness ever confirmed that story.) He again plagiarized, this time in 1988 from a speech by Robert F. Kennedy and British Labour Party leader Neil Kinnock. He again plagiarized from an article in the *Fordham Law Review*.[833] At various times, Biden claimed he earned three degrees in college, he attended law school on a full scholarship, he graduated in the top half of his class (he was seventy-sixth out of eighty-five), and he marched in the Civil Rights Movement.[834]

Although his embellishments and flat-out lies drove him out of the 1987 presidential race, his Senate career continued uninterrupted. He won six reelections, usually by hewing to the conservative side of the Democratic Party, voting for the Defense of Marriage Act and opposing to allow homosexuals in the US military. He voted "against" Operation Desert Storm in 1991 but then "for" with the wars in Afghanistan and Iraq, before flip-flopping on those. One of his most publicized moments came when he spearheaded a "high-tech lynching" of Supreme Court Justice (then nominee) Clarence Thomas.

Biden made a second stab at the presidency in 2007. He could not raise money, had no attendance at his rallies, and quickly fell behind Hillary Clinton with her (supposed) star power. Never climbing above single digits in the polls and getting spanked in the Iowa caucus, he withdrew. Indeed, Biden's weakness in the primaries proved an advantage for him when it came to the winner, Obama, who considered him for vice president. Obama was the star and wanted no competition—such as might come from Clinton. Biden also had an appeal for middle- and working-class voters, particularly white voters, that Obama did not possess. Obama named Biden his running mate in August 2008.[835] Even then, during the campaign, Biden constantly aggravated Obama with his constant gaffes: "How many times is Biden going to say something stupid?" Obama fumed.[836]

As veep, Biden was compared by Obama to a basketball player "who does a bunch of things that don't show up in the stat sheet."[837] Obama tasked Biden with keeping tabs on Iraq. Also charged with overseeing infrastructure spending, Biden typically found no waste or corruption had occurred, then nevertheless later claimed the administration reduced the number of fraud incidents.[838] Slowly Obama, who had little success with Congress, dispatched Biden to be his negotiator, though he never casted a tie-breaking vote in the Senate, making him the longest-serving vice president with that distinction.

Preparing to run for the presidency in 2016, Biden was coping with the death of his son Beau and concluded that he did not have the energy or attention to seek the presidency at that time. Most thought he was finished, and that he would be too old to run in 2020, regardless of what happened with the eventual nominee, Hillary Clinton.

He took an honorary professor title at the University of Pennsylvania, where he was paid $900,000 since he left the White House—yet taught no regular classes and had no defined role. It was purely a political bribe.[839] Like so many other former big-name politicians, Biden received a book offer from which (along with speaking engagements) he reported earning $15 million.[840]

A MOST UNUSUAL ELECTION

Few predicted that Biden would actually run in 2020. Aside from possibly Abraham Lincoln, who wasn't listed on the party program as a candidate, and, of course, Trump, Biden's journey to the White House was possibly the most surprising and unexpected in American history. For that reason, it bears more attention than typical primary campaigns.

When Biden considered another run, he sat at the end of an extremely weak Democratic bench. None of the other candidates had even the slightest history of appealing to blue-collar, middle-class voters except for Sanders. Among those who threw their hat in the ring was California's Senator Kamala Harris who, on paper, had all the credentials deemed most important in the twenty-first century: She was female and black. That gave her an advantage over Massachusetts Senator Elizabeth Warren or Minnesota Senator Amy Klobuchar, both boring and nondescript outside of their home states. South Bend, Indiana, Mayor Pete Buttigieg checked the DEI box of being a homosexual, which could have been another "first." Vermont Senator Sanders was back for another try, although this time, missing his mojo. The press ignored him.

Biden eventually won on the basis of the complete unacceptability of any other candidate and the knock-out blow provided in South Carolina's primary by Congressman James Clyburn rallying the black voters there. Clearly, it seemed to party insiders, Biden had several advantages no other candidate had, including national name recognition, support from black people, and a tenuous access to the white, blue-collar vote. What Biden had lacked in all his other races was that he "never focused on the basic mechanics and never surrounded himself with the operatives who could."[841] What he had in this race was the perception that out of a stable of entirely radical so-called progressive candidates, he was a "moderate." It was a view he would dispel quickly in his presidency.

Even as the increasingly presumptive nominee, Biden still had serious problems. In March and April of 2019, eight women accused him of inappropriate physical contact, including touching or kissing.[842] One of the eight, Tara Reade, accused him of sexual assault in 1993. The media was uninterested, and he never faced any serious interrogations about it.[843] Most of Biden's personal appearances, unlike Trump's, where fifteen thousand people would whoop it up, "had the feel of a retired ball player waving to the crowd before the national anthem."[844]

Progressive (that is to say, socialist) Democrats lined up behind Warren. Indeed, one "Obamaite" insider even wrote a memo for Warren, assuring her she'd be president, and she was already focused on beating Sanders (her aides described the battle as "Beer Track/Wine Track" in terms of appeal).[845] Then Warren imploded over claims (which got her into Harvard Law School) that she was an American Indian, specifically a Cherokee. But the Cherokee never heard of her. That left Sanders and, shockingly, Biden in the race. Obama continued to shill for generic Democratic candidates without naming a favorite, saying "What we have not seen before, at least in my lifetime, are politicians who are blatantly, repeatedly, baldly, shamelessly lying.... I mean, no shame." It appeared he was speaking of himself.[846]

Others, however, knew the reality. As onetime DNC head Tom Perez said, "We had a fairy dust model of government. All's you had to say was 'Barack Obama' and the fairy dust would come down, and you'd win elections.... That's not how you win elections."[847] Indeed, Obama had *never* won elections for anyone but himself, but in 2020 Democrats were still too cowed by concerns of racism to say so. And meanwhile, Hillary Clinton was still hovering on the outer perimeter of the primary process, hoping for a brokered convention where she'd get another shot.

Harris knocked herself out quickly by demanding Americans do away with their insurance policies. She could never answer the question "Why do you want to be president?" and ended up as "the mascot of the Democratic Party," according to one Democrat author.[848] She left without garnering a single delegate. Biden continued to appear before half-empty venues, including only 250 at one theater. He continued to dismiss the claims of sexual advances toward women by reasoning that of the tens of thousands of women he'd fondled over the years, only a dozen or so were not complaining. Then James Clyburn won South Carolina's primary for Biden—with his primary goal of making sure the socialist Sanders didn't win—and "Scranton Joe" suddenly became unbeatable.

The only serious threat to Biden's nomination came from the continued charges against Hunter, which popped up like Whac-A-Moles. No sooner would the campaign seem to squash one charge than another Hunter escapade with Ukraine or China would pop-up. Biden's team tried to prevent outlets from booking Republican supporters of Trump, who would even bring up the perceive graft, and they complied. Rudy Giuliani, for example, was banned from all networks except Fox. But one warning sign that would follow Biden through his presidency could be discerned in the polling from the failed Harris campaign: Despite being increasingly more "progressive" and tracking further left, her polls didn't move. There was only so much support in America for "progressive" ideas. Warren soon stumbled over the same health care issues that had forced Harris out. The simple fact was that Americans for the most part liked the health insurance they had and wanted nothing to do with a single-payer socialist system as existed in Great Britain or Canada. Sanders, on defense after South Carolina, blamed Warren for not dropping out and endorsing him.

Once armed with the nomination, Biden desperately sought support from Obama, which came only late and lamely. There is little to suggest that the fateful decision Biden made to name Harris as his running mate came from Obama. Quite the contrary, her choice was driven heavily by Biden's previous commitment to name a woman and by the fact that there were few female candidates who would even remotely add to his vote total rather than subtract from it.[849] He had said in March that he would put a woman on the ticket, and most assumed it would be Stacey Abrams, who failed in her Georgia governor's race in 2018. But Michigan's lockdown queen, Governor Gretchen Whitmer, was also considered a candidate. Harris hovered in third place. Again, Clyburn figured prominently in the choice of Harris over Whitmer.

Biden made some token appearances—attacking Trump on his handling of the pandemic without specifically saying he'd try to mandate vaccines and lock the country down again. He referred to Trump as a "fatal" infection.[850] Questions about Hunter's unusual influxes of money continued, forcing Biden to retreat to remote video speeches, as critics would say, from his basement. Typically, Democrats received shockingly bad polling that masked the reality among voters: In one case, Ohio Senator Sherrod Brown told Biden he'd win Ohio and win it early. (Biden lost by more than eight points.) Yet Biden did count on winning by swaying a large number of Trump voters. Whether that happened or not remains undetermined.

Virtually all data, all statistics, about the 2020 election should be affixed with an asterisk such as that is applied to various home run records by players using steroids. Democrats had played up early voting by mail. Using Covid as a smoke screen, and taking advantage of several states' extended vote-by-mail periods due to the China Virus, Democratic operatives had scoured the nation for places where they could request ballots on behalf of real people, but real people who were either dead, had moved, or were non compos mentis. Again, that was made possible only by the extended voting period, which not only allowed for a long period of compiling such voter rolls, but then of acquiring the ballots and voting for such voters fraudulently. Videos of "mules" illegally feeding dozens of mail-in ballots into ballot boxes suggested that totals were enhanced by millions of votes. Hence, the (purported) eighty-one million votes on election night for Biden—who had never been wildly popular, who lost almost every single "bellwether" district in the United States, and who *still* only managed to win the Electoral College by forty-three thousand votes.

Virtually all of the Electoral College margin came from five states: Arizona, Wisconsin, Michigan, Pennsylvania, and Georgia. Those states all had something in common, in that the vote counting—which had

Trump ahead, in some instances, by hundreds of thousands of votes—was abruptly, mysteriously, and simultaneously shut down in Detroit, Atlanta, Phoenix, Madison, and Philadelphia. In Atlanta, Ruby Freeman, a Democrat election worker, told poll workers it was necessary to clear the building due to a water main leak—which turned out to be an overflowing urinal. What happened next was purely criminal:

> Surveillance footage from the tabulation center revealed that once workers who had been sent home were gone, Freeman, her daughter, and a handful of other people resumed counting, pulling large boxes containing thousands of ballots from under a table where they had been hidden since earlier that day. Video confirms that these individuals [illegally—because there were no poll watchers] remained in the office counting ballots for approximately two hours until they left around 1:00 a.m. The camera also captured them running the same ballots through tabulation machines multiple times.[851]

Fulton County, Georgia, was not the only place counting was stopped, and the timing was important. Mysteriously, in Philadelphia—as Trump was leading in Pennsylvania—at 9:30 p.m., counting was also supposedly stopped for the night. Some four hundred thousand mail-in votes, the most ever received in an election, were counted over the next three days. Four other battleground states (Wisconsin, Michigan, Arizona, and Nevada) continued counting under odd circumstances: A white van pulled up at the counting center in Detroit, Michigan, and the driver brought in a suitcase and a large box. Spikes in Biden's vote followed. A truck filled with 250,000 ballots sent from Bethpage, New York, to Lancaster, Pennsylvania, (itself a crime) arrived early on November 4.[852]

Republican observers were kicked out of observing the count in Wayne County, Michigan, (where the last ballot drops shifted heavily to Biden). Cardboard was put up to prevent people from watching the count, and observers complained that counters were being videotaped.[853] Mollie Hemingway detailed the legal hurdles thrown up to stop Republican challenges, apply state laws to counting, and force states and localities to stick to constitutional deadlines—all with no success.[854]

When the counting stopped in Atlanta and Philadelphia, Trump was certainly headed back for the Oval Office. Betting markets had him at 99 percent likelihood. But when counting resumed, the overwhelming number of "new" ballots were for Biden. Trump got the highest number of votes for a Republican ever—seventy-four million—and held every single indicator of victory except one, the forty-three thousand difference in five states that had "late ballots." The Heritage Foundation conducted a compilation of all those *convicted* of election fraud just in the years 2020–2022 and found that ten were convicted, mostly of filing absentee or fraudulent ballots.

Moreover, few outside of conservative media even tried to explain how Biden miraculously generated eighteen *million* more votes than Hillary or how that Trump had expanded his vote total by eleven *million* from 2016 but lost. It became even more puzzling after 2024, when Trump increased his vote total again, this time by another three million, yet Harris's total fell by six million from Biden's. Where did the voters go? Overall turnout was up 6.6 percent more than 2016. Or was it?

Seth Keshel produced an analysis of the election showing "Ten Irrefutable Points":[855]

- Trump won the bellwether counties. Those counties had been perfect predictors of elections since 1980. They included Essex County, Vermont; Cortland County, New York; Vigo County, Indiana; Wood County, Ohio; and fifteen more. Trump won eighteen of them, Biden, one. Reagan, both Bushes, Clinton, Obama, and Trump in 2016 all won all nineteen. Vigo County, Indiana, and Valencia County, New Mexico, had been predictors of the presidential winner since the 1950s.

- Trump won the bellwether states of Ohio, Iowa, Florida, and North Carolina, which had been 100 percent accurate predictors since 1896.
- The primary model, previously always accurate and developed by Helmut Norpoth, relied on primary election numbers and showed Trump with a 91 percent chance of winning. Trump had a higher primary share of the vote (98.9 percent) than did Reagan, Nixon, or Eisenhower—all of whom won reelection.
- Trump had an enormous incumbent vote gain of 11.2 million over 2016.
- Trump's party gained thirteen seats in the House, the first Republican in 148 years to gain such votes and lose an election.
- The shift in voter registration was in the Republican direction, particularly in Pennsylvania, which saw a net four-point shift to Republicans. Trump won the state in 2016 with that additional four-point disadvantage.
- Florida's big 2.2 percent rightward shift since 2016 correlated strongly with similar shifts in Ohio, Michigan, Pennsylvania, Wisconsin, and Minnesota.
- Trump's gains in Georgia and other battleground states were at all-time-record levels, especially in the suburbs, which were apparently his nemesis.
- Trump's gains among minorities in 2020 signaled a landslide for him.
- Far from going away—as one would expect if the claims of illegitimacy were invalid (and as happened after 1876)—evidence that the election lacked integrity not only continued to pile up but was also validated by the media...reluctantly. Robin Vos, an anti-Trump Republican Speaker of the Wisconsin General Assembly, had to admit on camera that there was widespread fraud in a state decided by twenty thousand votes. Arizona Attorney General Mark Brnovich acknowledged in writing that the election in Maricopa County was so tainted that multiple

> reforms and prosecutions were needed to right the ship. The Democrats' efforts to imprison anyone for suggesting that the election was "rigged," to use President Trump's words, further underscored their awareness that the public thought something was fishy.

So, for a second time, we ask, was the election illegitimate?

In a rare admission of guilt, on February 6, 2021, *Time* magazine brazenly admitted that a "shadow campaign" had "fortified" (i.e., stolen) the 2020 election.[856] It used a strategy that had been planned for months to employ business and corporate leaders against Trump, which resulted in Trump saying that "within days after the election, we witnessed an orchestrated effort to anoint the winner, even while many key states were still being counted." *Time* said, "Trump was right."[857] Democrats had organized an "informal alliance" between the Chamber of Commerce (an anti-Trump group because of his tariffs) and the AFL-CIO (traditionally in the pocket of the Democratic Party) to "keep the peace" and "oppose Trump's assault on democracy." In the aftermath of the election, the real "assault" was being led by the Democrats to ram through the certification of Biden's election before anyone could challenge the numbers. In theory, *Time* claimed, the concern was "an election so calamitous that no result could be discerned at all," which was in most ways what the conspirators got. In other words, *Time* admitted that a Trump victory—especially a narrow one—would be "calamitous" and, just as with the Russia Hoax, unconstitutional, and illegal measures had to be used to stop it.

The chief strategist, *Time* admitted, was AFL-CIO adviser Mike Podhorzer, who was convinced that if Trump won, it could only be by "corrupting the voting process in key states." It will be recalled that the voting process was corrupted in five particular counties, four of which were Democratic and one of which (Arizona) was controlled by the forces of John McCain—a hated enemy of Trump. Their effort at what they called "securing the vote" was in fact an effort to secure the fraud from any judicial oversight.

Seldom in human history has a crime been so publicly admitted so soon after its commission. Such was the case precisely because the left believed that not only had it stolen the election, but that with media allies, it would also "stay stolen" in history. And with no prodding, the media jumped in to quickly establish that Biden had won, eking out victories in Arizona, Georgia, and Wisconsin by forty-three thousand votes. And when extremely narrow victories in Michigan, Pennsylvania, and Nevada were included, Biden still only manage 306 electoral votes—essentially getting what Trump had in 2016. In the Senate, Republicans lost three net seats, their majority, and fell into a tie (to be broken by Vice President Harris). One Georgia seat was so close as to require a second special election. Democrats held the House, despite a thirteen-seat gain by Republicans. That would prove crucial in the subsequent second impeachment of President Trump and in the House committee on the January 6 protests, wherein numerous Trump loyalists were dragged in to testify or otherwise were intimidated.

An issue equally as significant as the charges of fraud was the media's collusion in stifling any reporting about the laptop of Biden's son, Hunter. The FBI was in possession of the laptop and knew it contained a treasure trove of documents that would not only implicate Hunter in corruption—including taking bribes from China and Ukraine—but Joe as well, who was present at some of the meetings. Yet the FBI refused to acknowledge that the laptop was real, let alone to release any incriminating material from it (which it would have done if it had been a Trump laptop). For example, an email on the laptop from Hunter to Ye Jianming, the government-approved owner of a Chinese energy company CEFC, showed that Biden demanded $10 million *per year* just "for introductions alone."[858] A photo captured Joe Biden meeting Hunter's alleged business partner from Kazakhstan, and reports showed that both Joe and Hunter golfed with a Ukrainian gas executive while Joe was vice president.[859]

Predictably, the mainstream press circled the wagons and labeled the Hunter Biden laptop story as "Russian disinformation."[860] *The New York Times*, running more blatantly false information, tried to smear Trump's attorney Rudy Giuliani with the same brush.[861] Equally predictable, the same former intelligence officials, including the diabolical James Clapper, who had knowingly run with the Russia Hoax, produced a letter stating that no one knew if the emails were real (precisely because the FBI refused to conduct such an investigation), almost certainly due to orders from those who despised Trump. This was even the same playbook as the Steel dossier/Russia Hoax in reverse: There, a false story involving "Russian disinformation" was pushed into the public sphere via what officials "told" Trump, thus making it fair game for the media to report falsehoods. After all, Comey "told" Trump about some of the Steele dossier, so the reporting that Trump "was told" was in fact true, even though *what was told* was a complete lie. Now, Trump "was told" to beware of Giuliani's emails and other evidence on the (true and factual) contents of the Hunter Biden laptop on the grounds that it "could" be "Russian disinformation." No wonder by then trust in the US media had fallen to record lows.

National Public Radio called it a "waste of time" to investigate the laptop. *The Atlantic* said that anyone not in the Fox News "bubble" didn't need to know what was on the laptop. *Vice* said, "almost none of this actually matters," when in fact it was the largest vice presidential—then presidential—corruption story in American history. Social media, particularly Facebook and Twitter, made it impossible to post articles about the laptop or corruption. Twitter even banned the *New York Post*, which was doing most of the reporting.[862] Friendly interviewers refused to ask Biden a single solid question about the laptop, Hunter's role in making Biden rich, or corruption. Even after one of Hunter's *partners*, Tony Bobulinski, went on record with a *Wall Street Journal* reporter that Biden—called "the Big Guy"—was given a cut of every deal, the *Journal* squelched the story. Trump eventually staged a press conference with Bobulinski before the second debate. When the *Journal* finally did publish the story, the subhead was Biden's denial. Of course, at that point, the *Journal* became a target for the Biden media.

Would simple exposure of the corruption implicated by the laptop have flipped forty-four thousand votes nationally? Almost certainly. Would confirmation of the corruption have flipped more than three states, amounting to about two hundred thousand votes? Most likely. The cover-up of the laptop constituted a case of major election interference by Twitter, Facebook, and the mainstream press. After the election, Twitter's CEO Jack Dorsey said, "We recognize it was a mistake...both in terms of the intention of the policy and also the enforcement action of not allowing people to share it publicly or privately."[863]

FLIGHT OF THE SQUIDPICKLES

Few events in American history have terrified the established elites as that which ensued next: a populist protest against what was perceived to be a stolen election in January 2021. There had been two major issues, which no court had been willing to tackle. First, was the election fair and free of fraud? In addition to courts citing "standing" as a reason for denying fraud cases, other legal hurdles made challenging the election difficult. One thorny problem involved "ripeness," in which a case must have reached the point where it embodies serious harms that have the potential to be proven. Such reasoning, however, largely prevents any preemptive action against fraud, meaning that candidates must wait until elections are over to file suits. Indeed, people bringing suits too early can be sanctioned by courts. This catch-22 was also known as "latches." However, the flawed legal reasoning often has been that once an election—no matter how fraudulent—has taken place, "the people have spoken" and judges have been hesitant to ever overturn such results.[864] (This notion subsequently was overturned in many places, including Bridgeport, Connecticut, when a judge ruled an election invalid due to fraud in 2023.)

Case after case was dismissed—not on the merits—but on standing or latches. Not one single court heard the slightest bit of actual evidence about fraud in the 2020 election in *any* state. Arizona got the closest with a state legislature–mandated audit, but as the auditors got close to their final proof, which required key fobs from Maricopa County commissioners, the commissioners refused to comply and a single vote prevented a subpoena that would have compelled them to provide the information. Over and over—given the massive number of mail-in ballots—strict signature match investigations were struck down and/or disallowed.

By the time of the national reading of the electors in Congress on January 6, it was clear that the fix was in. By that time, the best Trump's supporters could hope for was a challenge within the vote count process itself whereby in the Senate at least (where Republicans held the majority), senators could, within a limited time, get a formal statement of the facts of the fraud on record. As a result, Trump's team sought to bring pressure to bear on Vice President Mike Pence (a thoroughgoing institutionalist who did not think fraud possible) to do what John Adams did in 1796—acknowledge a motion from the floor during the counting by one congressman and one senator. That would have forced both houses to adjourn to their chambers and examine the evidence.

The House, of course, under the grotesquely bitter Nancy Pelosi as Speaker, would not entertain an examination of evidence for a moment. But, supporters had hoped, the Senate would be more calculating and at least *hear* the evidence. Pence, on two occasions, told Turning Point USA crowds that he would indeed allow such a motion, saying "I'll make you a promise. We're going to keep fighting until every legal vote is counted. We're going to keep fighting until every illegal vote is thrown out."[865]

Then, on January 6, Pence delivered a letter to Trump saying that he did not think it within his power to entertain such a motion.[866] (Constitutional scholars have in fact argued otherwise.) By that time, Trump had called for a "day of love" on January 6, inviting crowds to let their voices be "patriotically and peacefully" heard. Over 120,000 showed up, all unarmed. The left, whose "women's march" against Trump four years earlier engaged in a meltdown about the protest, claiming the gathering was unconstitutional and violent. Trump spoke briefly, urging the crowd to "peacefully and patriotically let your voices be heard."[867]

Once again, the story one subscribes to relies largely on what evidence is witnessed, seen, and read. At one point, *before Trump had even started speaking*, various doors to Congress were opened. These included magnetically locked doors that could only have been opened from inside. Videos show countless US Capitol Police removing barriers and waving crowds *into the Capitol*. Hours of Capitol video footage show peaceful and quiet people walking through the rotunda, greeting the police, smiling, and taking selfies. There was no violence at all in that footage. Later, however, outside various rabble-rousers agitated the crowd, even as some tried to point out that the inciters were either federal agents or antifa plants. (Video shows such "protesters" changing clothes out of antifa gear and into clothing that looked more like that worn by MAGA supporters.) Later evidence revealed more than twenty-six FBI agents were in the crowd, acting as provocateurs.[868] Ray Epps, a known FBI accessory, was filmed agitating for violence. The police fired tear gas and rubber bullets into crowds that were just standing around.

Some violent protesters (again, as yet unclear if they were feds inciting a riot or malevolent aspects of the crowd) did break windows and get inside. Several people stood behind the Speaker's lectern. Meanwhile, in the chamber where the vote counting was being conducted, legislators ran for their lives, hid under desks, and fought to get in the elevators, taking them down to the nuclear bunkers. Conveniently, Pelosi's daughter—a filmmaker—had been hired beforehand to catch the action, begging the question of how Pelosi knew there would be anything to film. All in all, America's legislative class looked like utter cowards—I labeled their retreat the "Flight of the Squidpickles" in one article. Not one stood his ground against a single (unarmed) protester or resisted in any way. They all fled.

It is absolutely critical with the jihad-level prosecutions of protesters that followed to understand what was truly at stake and why the notion of an "insurrection" was elevated to a religious-level mantra by the administration and the left. By forcing the legislators—the elites—to flee like frightened animals and to *embarrass* the elites on national television was the unpardonable sin. Far from being courageous or statesmanlike, the senators and representatives alike ran in panic as civilians—citizens—merely walked through what on other occasions the same legislators would call "The People's House." The image of those elites hiding under desks as a guy in a Viking helmet carrying an American flag calmly walked around spoke volumes.

Meanwhile, at one locked door with a small window, Capitol policeman Michael Byrd shot Ashli Babbitt, an unarmed grandmother who was trying to keep people from breaking the window. His shot killed Babbitt. Byrd was behind a metal locked door and faced no imminent threat but was nevertheless cleared by an internal investigation.

When the joint session resumed, Pence did not recognize any challenge from the floor and the final aspects of the "fortification" were complete.

Trump sought to ensure that there wouldn't be the slightest hint of violence. He had suggested bringing in National Guard troops to preserve order and the Pentagon generals dismissed the request. So did Speaker Pelosi, who wanted the "riot" so she could blame Trump.

Pelosi pounced on the opportunity to claim that Trump had engaged in "insurrection" and quickly mobilized Congress. The House formed the January 6th Committee to investigate with only a couple of virulently anti-Trump Republican representatives added (including virulent anti-Trumpers Lynne Cheney and Adam Kinzinger). No opposing voices were allowed. The videos shown to the committee were heavily edited. Only two years later when Republicans regained the House were some of the full videos released to Tucker Carlson, then of Fox News. It was then the public saw for the first time the overwhelmingly peaceful activities, and yet even in 2025 all of the videos have not been released.

Pelosi's radical House impeached Trump a second time within seven days of the January 6 protests. And the Senate refused to convict him a second time. It was an act reeking of pettiness and desperation against Trump, who clearly was not going to be president again…yet.

Trump's travails had only started. In March 2023, the Manhattan district attorney, Alvin Bragg, indicted Trump on thirty-four counts of misfiling business records to a supposed payoff to porn star "Stormy Daniels" to stay quiet about the supposed affair. Most legal analysts thought the attempt to bundle potential misdemeanors into a felony was excessive and completely unprecedented. Even Trump's critics on the left found the indictments weak and unconvincing. Merely the prospect of tying up the front-running candidate of a political party in courts and with suits for over a year of a campaign constituted a shocking, overtly political act that to many suggested that the US had sunk to the level of a banana republic.

It wasn't over for Trump though. On August 6, 2022, Biden's Department of Justice staged a morning raid on Trump's Mar-a-Lago home, supposedly seeking the classified materials that Trump (lawfully) had in his possession. Using the contents seized from that raid, the Attorney General Merrick Garland—who had been blocked from a Supreme Court appointment in Obama's final year by Senate Majority Leader Mitch McConnell—appointed a special counsel, Jack Smith, who then indicted President Trump on thirty-two counts of "national security" violations in June 2023. Then, on July 28, the special counsel added three more charges.[869] And yet another set of criminal charges was levied against President Trump in August 2023 when Fulton County District Attorney Fani Willis issued an indictment accusing him of efforts to overturn the 2020 election.[870]

Even before "Patriots Day" (January 6), Democrats sought to prevent Trump from ever even running for office again—an action not even taken against Confederate officers who fought against the Union if they swore an oath of allegiance. Senator Tim Kaine filed such a resolution, then Democrats, terrified of Trump's legacy, sponsored a bill that would have banned the federal government from naming monuments or buildings for him and preventing him from being buried in Arlington National Cemetery. They even attempted to strip him of his federal pension (which he certainly did not need, being the only American president in memory to serve without pay and leave the presidency poorer than when he went in), office space, and paid staff.[871] These were astoundingly petty actions that, above all, showed how much the Democrats still feared Trump. No American leaders had ever been treated with such angry contempt, including Confederate generals Robert E. Lee and James Longstreet, who led armies in actual violent rebellion against the US, or Aaron Burr, who killed a former secretary of the Treasury.

New President Biden's Department of Justice under Attorney General Garland launched a manhunt for "insurrectionists" not even used against communists in the McCarthy era of the Cold War. As soon as the "violators" could be located, they were arrested, including grandmothers and people who had not even entered the Capitol building itself. Brought before heavily Democrat-dominated Washington, DC, courts, the defendants either were found guilty (most commonly of "parading") or pled guilty to lesser charges. Even so, many, including the "Shaman" Jacob Chansley, who wore a horned American Indian headdress into the Capitol while carrying an American flag, was sentenced to forty-one months in prison for a nonviolent offense.[872] Eventually, over one thousand would be charged and jailed, usually with the maximum sentences, often by adding an "obstruction of justice" charge. In June 2024, the US Supreme Court ruled 6–3 that prosecutors had improperly used a felony charge of obstructing justice.[873]

THE RADICAL JUDICIARY

Any thoughts that Joe Biden as the new president would be the venal but largely "moderate" Democrat that had haunted the halls of the Senate for decades disappeared when immediately his Department of Justice began the January 6 prosecutions. It was an interesting contrast to Trump's

DOJ under Bill Barr. During protests of the Brett Kavanaugh hearings for his spot on the Supreme Court, which indeed delayed proceedings, Barr's DOJ did not arrest a single protester, let alone jail anyone.

Very quickly, a dual standard of law became apparent. Under President Trump, while local prosecutors had, in fact, arrested a few members of so-called antifa or Black Lives Matter in either the inauguration protests or the George Floyd riots, they were quickly released. Virtually none of them served a prison sentence longer than a week. All January 6 protesters faced maximum sentences and were threatened with more charges if they did not plead out. All the trials took place in a kangaroo court setting of the District of Columbia, whose population votes over 90 percent Democrat and where not a single defendant had a true "jury of his peers."

Nor did a single defendant see that footage of the Capitol that showed a largely peaceful protest with police waving protesters in. Nor did juries hear that the FBI had planted at least twenty-six agents, whose purpose it could be argued was solely to incite riots. Nor did juries see what apparently were members of antifa changing from their black garb and masks into "MAGA-type" clothing. Moreover, the conviction rate in federal cases is monumentally on the side of government because of the resources involved. Many January Sixers accepted plea bargains for acts they did not commit because of the threat of longer sentences by the prosecutors.

Convictions in the so-called J6 cases exposed a fundamental weakness in American jurisprudence. While only four of the eleven judges in the DC appellate court system had been appointed by Republicans (one by George H. W. Bush, three by Trump), the overall structural bias of the system was illuminated as seldom before. Contrary to public assumptions, many cases are not decided on a "D/R" basis, but rather the entire judiciary has a predisposed bias in favor of government at any level. Most federal judges come from the ranks of prosecutors. They, therefore, have a "prosecutor's mentality" and overall assumption that the defendants are there for a reason. Above that, very few hold a skepticism of governmental authority at all. The presumption rested with the state, and the January 6 defendants needed a twenty-first century version of a Gerry Spence, the 1960s-era defendants' lawyer who wore buckskin and had a reputation of using extreme tactics for his clients. But none not emerged. (During Trump's tenure, liberal Harvard lawyer Alan Dershowitz repeatedly came to Trump's defense and challenged the pro-state bias, but Dershowitz rarely took cases anymore.) As alluded to earlier, finding a jury of one's peers would be impossible in the District of Columbia: And even if a "Republican" could be placed on a jury, a DC Republican would likely be highly out of touch with populist principles and unfavorable to the role that the US government, through the FBI, planted instigators at the January 6 protests (even though subsequent documents showed there were over twenty-five). Taken together, these factors meant that the January 6 defendants not only would not get a fair trial, but that they could expect the most harsh sentences once convicted.

As the law was unraveling before people's eyes in Washington, DC, across the country it became clear that the strategy mounted by billionaire (and devout anti-American) George Soros to elect local prosecutors and district attorneys had borne fruit. In city after city, violent crimes were not prosecuted; when they were, judges handed down light (if not nonexistent) sentences, usually parole. This was a pivotal development in American history—it was the first time a massive, national effort was undertaken to subvert enforcement of the law. (This was in contrast to Prohibition, where police attempted to enforce the law.) About 90 percent of criminal cases in America were handled by the 2,300 elected district attorneys in the 3,143 counties. A few crimes were prosecuted by US attorneys. As former prosecutor and legal expert Charles "Cully" Stimson noted, for more than one hundred years, the local district attorneys did their jobs, regardless of party affiliation. They "upheld their end of the social contract" by enforcing the laws.[874] Their stiff enforcement played a key role in driving down crime, which had peaked in 1992. But when Soros launched his initiative to place "progressive" prosecutors in office in 2015, the entire structure of America changed.

Soros's extremists believed that the entire criminal justice system is inherently racist and that enforcement of the law had to take a back seat to dismantling the "racist" system. It goes without saying that in the areas where this view prevailed, the victims were overwhelmingly racial minorities who benefited from a police presence and strong law enforcement. Not surprisingly, the entire progressive ideology behind the progressive prosecutors came from '60s radicals such as Angela Davis. Soros and his minions began raising vast amounts of money for local district attorney races, where the conservative opponent had no chance to match the progressive spending. One radical stated the goal as "to reverse-engineer and dismantle the criminal justice infrastructure."[875]

Soros spent $40 million in a ten-year stretch to put rogue prosecutors in power. He wasn't alone. Uber-wealthy progressives such as Mark Zuckerberg also kicked in money. What did it buy?

One of those radicals led the crusade against Trump—New York's Attorney General Letitia James, who admitted she viewed Trump in his first term as an "illegitimate president," said he should have been charged with obstruction of justice, and that he laundered money from foreign sources (describing, ironically, Joe Biden).[876] She also targeted the National Rifle Association, calling it a "terrorist organization."[877]

Other rogue prosecutors simply refused to prosecute actual crimes, particularly those that might be committed disproportionately by minorities. By 2024, citing "prosecutorial discretion," these lawbreaking prosecutors announced in California that they would not prosecute any property crime under $950.00.[878] But that was just the formal announcement of a policy in place in virtually all major cities, where raids of retailers by gangs in broad daylight were common, where chain drug stores and even Walmarts had to put everyday items under lock and key, and where self-checkout had to be ended because of extensive theft. In the last year of available statistics, retailers lost almost $94 billion to theft.[879] Combined with homelessness and drug use—two other areas that were not or only lightly prosecuted—major retailers began to flee the central cities. In downtown San Francisco, Old Navy, Nordstrom, LEGO, Whole Foods, Express, and AT&T were just a few of the major businesses to pull out.[880] Before long, they were followed by one of the leading tech icons, Twitter/X, which relocated to Texas.

One such prosecutor, Rachael Rollins, former district attorney of Suffolk County, Massachusetts, listed fifteen misdemeanors that would not be prosecuted. George Gascón of Los Angeles County likewise sent a formal order to all one thousand prosecutors, outlining thirteen misdemeanors that "shall be declined or dismissed without arraignment" and without conditions.[881] Others, including Kim Foxx of Chicago and Larry Krasner of Philadelphia, followed suit. Their attitude entirely encompassed the warnings of the "broken window syndrome," in which neighborhoods begin to have numerous broken windows, indicating low-level crime would not be prosecuted. Non-prosecution in one area inevitably has led to more crime at all levels.

An obvious result? Crime rates skyrocketed. Prior to Krasner, Philadelphia had an average of 271 homicides per year. That number nearly doubled every year since then. And the obvious victims? Black people accounted for 83 percent of the victims. Nonfatal shootings rose by over 30 percent.[882] But as Brooke Rollins wrote, "We have to understand chaos as a well-honed and deliberately constructed institutional capacity of the American Left." Indeed, it is.[883] This strategy "represents the development of a series of operational capabilities, both physical and ideological: the ability to seize city centers, cut transportation arteries, occupy targeted facilities, combat or deter law enforcement, and psychologically dominate the societal commanding heights in academia, media, and governance. It is all of a piece, and all mutually reinforcing."[884]

However, the left misunderstood (or deliberately ignored) the historical record of responses to this, which isn't *them* getting power but their exact opposite. When the communists created chaos in the Weimar Republic, it led to the Nazis taking power, not socialists.

This decriminalization of genuine crimes as traditionally defined did not take place in a vacuum. It was steeped in a much deeper and more sinister ideology of evil, a spurious, solipsistic fog of contorted law that allowed those in power to punish political opponents. The Cheka of the czar or Napoleon's secret police led by Joseph Fouché defined crime as simply being on the wrong side of power. People who did nothing more than take selfies inside the Capitol rotunda were labeled insurrectionists and terrorists, and for the first time in American history, a duly elected president was tried in multiple venues for seeking to ensure a fair election. One could almost hear Eugene V. Debs, the Socialist candidate in 1920 who ran for president from prison, in the voice of *Die Hard*'s John McClane: "Welcome to the party, pal."

Attorneys were disbarred merely for questioning the machinery of an election that by 2024 was viewed as fraudulent by a majority of Americans. Prosecutors in five states brought legal actions against what they called "fake electors" (there is no such thing) or alternates named if the courts decided Biden had not won the election.[885] Expert in constitutional law John Eastman lost his law license for merely advising President Trump on an alternative understanding and explanation of the elector process. Slates of electors, who voluntarily had signed up in the event that ongoing investigations proved violations in the election process, were charged with crimes. Even in 1876, when Congress found that three states had submitted electoral slates that had been the result of dishonest counts, not a single elector faced jail time. This was entirely the result of a process termed "lawfare" that wielded the legal system as a weapon against political enemies. The very concept assumed that the will of the people could not be trusted (let alone honored), or that the public must not be allowed a free choice. Rather, through sympathetic district attorneys (there they are again!) minor or even frivolous charges could be launched at political opponents in such a way as to prevent them from running, or at the very least, from winning.

"DIMINISHED CAPACITY"

Throughout the campaign, as numerous insiders documented, Biden grew more radical and "progressive." It remains unclear as to how much of this was actually Biden and how much came from his inside staff who took advantage of his obvious dementia. The inside secret—that Americans had supposedly elected a man with dementia and rapidly diminishing mental and physical capabilities—was not fully revealed, or, at least, publicly admitted, until 2024.

For the most part, no public admission of Biden's mental state was allowed for the first three years of his presidency. On March 19, 2021, he fell twice climbing the steps of Air Force One.[886] Two months later, he fell on a stage in June 2021 while participating in a graduation ceremony for the US Air Force Academy.[887] Staff responded by trying to make him look more fit: He jogged to Marine One (for a few steps at a time). The staff had him ride a bike, until in June 2022, he fell off.[888] If he rode again, it was not publicized. Then he stumbled up the stairs to Air Force One, not once, but several times.[889] In his March 2022 State of the Union he said "Iranian" when he meant "Ukrainian," "America" when he meant "Delaware," and "profits" when he meant "prices." At a conference in September 2022, he asked for Jackie Walorski, an Indiana representative: "Jackie, where are you? Jackie?" She couldn't answer because she died in a car accident the previous month. That November, he claimed that inflation was due to a "war in Iraq," when he presumably meant Ukraine, then made it worse by saying "I think of Iraq because that's where my son died," when Beau died in the US of brain cancer, not combat, in 2015.[890] In March 2022, Biden also called for Vladimir Putin to be removed from power; said in a speech "Let me start with two words: 'Made in America;'" called President Yoon Suk Yeol of South Korea "President Loon;" called the prime minister of Great Britain a "president;" called India's Prime Minister Narendra Modi the leader of "a little country" and referred to it as "China;" again confused Iraq and Ukraine; said he visited the 9/11 site the "next day" (he didn't get there for nine days); called his homeland security secretary his "health secretary;" claimed Francois Mitterrand was from Germany (he was from France); mixed up the presidents of Egypt and Mexico (these are not easy things to do!); literally appeared to freeze during a musical performance at the White House; and again forgot the name of his homeland security secretary, Alejandro Mayorkas.[891]

The media treated these as everyday occurrences—which, in fact, they were—but were, in reality, instances of danger to national security. Instead, the media attempted to portray the growing number of incidents as about age, not mental decline. And those incidents were on top of dozens of times Biden slurred words, walked off stage the wrong direction (or not at all and had to be escorted off), or froze on camera. By 2023, his wife Jill had increasingly taken to escorting him via physical contact as he walked, and staff formed a protective shell around him so that observers and media would not see his halting gait (often called the "Alzheimer's gait").

An early public statement on Biden's declining mental health came from Special Counsel Robert Hur, who had been appointed to look into Biden's own classified documents case. In March 2024, Hur told Congress that Biden "willfully" retained classified materials as a private citizen and gave them to the ghostwriter of his $8 million book (itself a form of a bribe, in that no book made back an $8 million advance).[892] Biden angrily insisted, "I did not share classified information.... Guarantee you, I did not." Then he went on to say, "I don't recall" and "I have no god [d**n] idea" over one hundred times.[893] Hur also admitted that Biden broke the law but said that pressing charges would be difficult because Biden would present to the jury "as a sympathetic, well-meaning, elderly man with a poor memory."[894] In front of Hur's questioners, he forgot, for example, when his son Beau died, when Trump was elected, and even when he was vice president.

In December 2024, *The Wall Street Journal* finally broke a story that Biden was diminished from the moment of his election.[895] About the *Journal* story, the UK *Daily Mail* said that his staff engaged in "an extensive, deliberate and years-long cover-up that also saw the administration gaslighting those who dared claim Biden's abilities had deteriorated" since he had been vice president.[896] Speaker Mike Johnson, who was blocked from meeting with Biden for weeks by Biden's staff, finally demanded a conference. He was surprised to see many other cabinet members in the room. Finally, Johnson convinced Biden to talk to him privately, at which point Johnson asked why Biden had paused liquefied natural gas exports to Europe—which he had in an executive order three weeks earlier. First, Biden insisted he had not, and Johnson offered to have the executive order printed and given to him. Even then, Biden insisted he had only signed a "study," at which point Johnson realized that members of Biden's staff were making policy and having Biden unwittingly sign executive orders on a routine basis.[897]

That incident shocked even Johnson, who had said in October 2023 that Biden was in "cognitive decline."[898] If others knew as much at the time, they kept quiet. Biden's own doctors insisted he was sharp. Left-wing talk show host Joe Scarborough, prior to Biden's disastrous debate against Trump, called him the "best Biden ever" and said that he was "better than he's ever been" and "cogent."[899]

Few knew at the time that different cadres of staffers, or cabals, were directing national policy, including an immigration cabal, a Ukrainian war cabal, a green energy cabal, and so on. Contrary to the popular opinion on the right that Obama was "running" Biden, in fact different cadres battled for who was last in his ear or who last controlled his pen. It accounted for one of the reasons that Biden got little done: The cabals could not agree.

HARD LEFT

Biden, having presented himself early as a "moderate" who would bring America together, had veered left during the campaign. After the election, he either willingly became more of a progressive or was led by his staff. At any rate, his policies looked more like those of Alexandria Ocasio-Cortez than those of Bill Clinton.

The first group to seize his attention were those who wanted America out of Afghanistan immediately. In April 2021, Biden reversed Trump's conditions for the withdrawal of US troops and issued a blanket withdrawal order for September 11 of that year, regardless of whether of any of Trump's conditions had been met.[900] Just a week later, the commander of US Central Command said he was concerned about the ability of the Afghan military to hold their ground without American support. Word leaked of Afghan translators who worried they would be killed by the new Taliban government once the US left. A groundswell of voices, including military and members of Congress, pleaded with Biden to begin an orderly evacuation of Afghanistan. The Taliban took Biden's withdrawal date for what it was, capitulation, and ramped up their offensive. Meanwhile, Biden's administration made no effort to expedite the extraction of American civilians or translators.

When the Taliban entered Kabul on August 15, Americans and their allies scrambled to get to the safe area around Kabul International Airport, where many US military forces were quickly and chaotically redeployed. In scenes reminiscent of the helicopters lifting off of the embassy rooftop in Ho Chi Minh City, service members tried to allow Americans to evacuate while pushing back against teeming crowds of terrified Afghans. Over 124,000 escaped, but not before two suicide bombers struck at the airport and the Baron Hotel that left more than a dozen military personnel dead—the deadliest day in Afghanistan for the US since 2011.[901] Images of desperate Afghans pressed against the metal fencing soon gave way to pictures of the more than $7 billion of state-of-the-art military equipment that was just abandoned in the hasty retreat, leaving it to the very enemy the US had sought to defeat.[902]

The Afghan debacle seriously damaged Biden in just his first year, when he was attempting to mobilize the country to hate Trump and the January 6 protesters. Already, Attorney General Garland had announced his plan to go after "white supremacists" and domestic terrorists (of which only Black Lives Matter and antifa had been active in the previous two years—but those groups were off the table).[903] Soon, Catholics were added to the "white supremacist" group to be monitored when a whistleblower revealed the FBI's Richmond, Virginia, office had referred to "radical-traditionalist Catholics…as extremists" and proposed to infiltrate Catholic churches as a form of "threat mitigation."[904]

Biden's hard progressive turn showed up in his environmental policies. Whereas Trump had taken the US out of the Paris Accords, Biden rejoined as quickly as possible and stated that the administration supported "sustainable transport." His tax plan to Congress removed subsidies for fossil fuels and replace them with green incentives. He ordered the amount of energy produced by wind turbines to be doubled by 2030 (of course not appreciating that a government "order" of any type cannot radically increase or decrease anything if the public does not want it or if it is financially unsustainable).

Both his Infrastructure Investment and Jobs Act of 2021 and his Inflation Reduction Act of 2022 were laden with green "climate change" incentives. The Inflation Reduction Act alone (in theory) created $3 *trillion* in climate investments over the subsequent decade—which failed to materialize. Biden's team provided unprecedented funding for energy efficiency implementation and weatherization, but most of that involved "emission trading systems" that showed absolutely no savings of energy between participating and nonparticipating companies in Holland).[905] He also canceled the Keystone XL Pipeline that Trump had restored.

Under Biden in 2021, Congress provided $7.5 billion for electric vehicle charging stations: Two years later, none were built, and by the end of Biden's term, only *eight* had been constructed.[906] Such actions to reduce carbon emissions were exposed as meaningless compared to natural disasters, as when wildfires swept Los Angeles in early 2025 and in a matter of weeks offset *the entire "carbon savings"* in California's history. Meanwhile, Biden could do nothing about China, which built over one hundred new coal plants a year.

"Going green" demanded an even stronger reliance on China. The major component of the electric vehicle batteries, lithium, existed abroad in unfriendly or downright hostile countries. Chile had nationalized its lithium deposits. Worse, Chile had even begun to negotiate with the Communist Chinese about exclusive lithium delivery to them! And if that wasn't enough, by 2020, China made 76 percent of the world's lithium, the US, 8 percent.[907] "Going green" would have placed most of America's transportation network in the hands of a sworn enemy.

Moreover, key elements of America's transportation system were collapsing, despite Biden's promises to build infrastructure. His transportation secretary, Pete Buttigieg, former mayor of South Bend, Indiana, and utterly out of his depth, was perpetually late to the scene of disasters: whether the East Palestine, Ohio, toxic railroad spill or the cargo ship *Dali* that smashed into the Francis Scott Key Bridge in Baltimore, causing it to collapse.[908] Biden showed his disdain for the working-class community by avoiding a visit to East Palestine for a full year, although he made it to Baltimore in ten days.

THE UKRAINE MORASS

Ever since the USSR shattered, elements of the old Communist Party had sought to reconstruct it. Concerns of a new "Cold War" arose in 2000 when Vladimir Putin, a former KGB officer, was elected president of the Russian Federation. Tensions almost immediately ensued with the former Soviet republic of Georgia. Russia claimed areas in Georgia, such as South Ossetia, as vital to its ability to operate on the Black Sea. Rather than invade, however, Putin's government engaged in a form of "illegal immigration" through a process called "passportization" in which it allocated large numbers of passports to Georgia without that state's permission, almost all of them to regions of South Ossetia and Abkhazia. Those regions sought separation from Georgia in 2008; war broke out in August of that year. Shortly, Russia recognized the two breakaway states and maintained a military presence there.[909]

Then, in February 2013, Russia invaded and annexed the Crimean Peninsula, taking it from Ukraine. Removal of Ukrainian president Viktor Yanukovych led to pro-Russian demonstrations there. Ethnic Russians constituted a strong force in Crimea, allowing Putin to once again claim he was just (Anschluss-like) reuniting Russians with their homeland. A more politically realistic reason was that Crimea and Sevastopol constituted important naval bases for the Russian Navy on the Black Sea. It also constituted an important cross-shipping point for Russian oil.

Both acquisitions set the table for conflict with Ukraine's Donbas region, which was heavily Russian and had large contingents of neo-Nazi Ukrainian separatists. Russia claimed that the anti-Russian forces there constituted a threat; Ukraine claimed that the pro-Russian regions were rebellions and needed to be brought under control. Matters were inflamed in 2013 when Yanukovych, who had become popular, was nevertheless seen as corrupt and authoritarian—and definitely pro-Russian. By that time, Ukraine received most of its gas from Russia but sought closer ties with the North Atlantic Treaty Organization. Yanukovych decided not to sign a trade agreement with the European Union and instead chose Russia, sparking major protests. Turmoil continued into 2014 when the Ukrainian parliament voted to remove Yanukovych: Russia denounced that as a coup, and counterprotests started. The European Union exerted pressure, and a new presidential election was scheduled. Tensions with Russia increased. In 2019, a comedian, Volodymyr Zelenskyy, won a landslide victory over the incumbent, Petro Poroshenko.

There were concerns that Ukraine was the site of massive US and European money laundering, that the government was hopelessly corrupt, and even that the CIA had maintained bioweapons labs there. Deterioration of relations with Russia, especially over the pro-Russian areas, was used by Putin to order a "special military operation" in the Kherson and Zaporizhzhia regions to protect native Russians there.[910] The US, Great Britain, France, and Germany denounced the invasion and imposed sanctions against Russia, most notably cutting off all delivery of Russian gas to Europe. This had the effect of depriving Europeans of cheap energy throughout the winter and driving up prices. Western powers also began a steady torrent of weapons deliveries to Ukraine, which temporarily slowed down the Russians, but did not prevent them from taking large sectors of Eastern Ukraine.

By 2022, over $46.6 billion in American and European cash and weapons flowed into Ukraine, while at home in the US the nation struggled with bloated budgets, skyrocketing debt, and inflation—caused, in part, by the bloated budgets and skyrocketing debt![911] Yet by 2023, most members of Biden's party still supported the money shipments, as did many "neo-con" Republicans such as Senators Marco Rubio, John Cornyn, and Lindsey Graham. Donald Trump and Robert F. Kennedy Jr. were alone among the major candidates calling for a negotiated peace in the region. Yet the Ukraine conflict remained a potential powder keg, with Putin making dark references to the use of nuclear weapons if the North Atlantic Treaty Organization formally got involved.[912] (News reports of events in the region were so unreliable with their pro-Ukraine bias—that fighter pilots proclaimed dead appeared later and great Ukrainian "victories" ended up being in reality defeats.) It is true that the Russians paid a price, but so did Ukraine in terms of territory and lives lost. Support for Ukraine remained a dividing line for Trump voters and Democrats, and worked against Biden, then Harris, in the 2024 election.

Already, though, alliances were shifting. Professor Jeffrey Sachs, for example, who had globalist tendencies, admitted that American foreign policy under Biden was a "scam built on corruption."[913] From Afghanistan to Ukraine, Biden's foreign policy increasingly was in shambles.

THE INVASION

Americans, in fact, were much more concerned with another invasion, this one occurring mostly on their southern border with Mexico. By 2023, even the most conservative estimates put the illegal alien population at 11.7 million—but of course counting them proved problematic, and other sources estimated the number was over twenty-two million.[914] A number much higher than eleven million seemed entirely likely, as illegals hid from authorities and census takers.

Under Biden, the problem—which Trump largely had under control and was improving when he left office—exploded into "the worst border crisis in American history."[915] As the retired director of Immigration and Customs Enforcement Tom Homan said, "Biden is the first President to ever un-secure a border on purpose.... For three years, this Administration has directed and overseen the implementation of an open borders agenda."[916] During Trump's last year, total enforcement actions numbered 646,000. That tripled in Biden's first year, then rose to 3.2 million in his third year. Whereas under Trump, in any given month, perhaps twenty thousand people entered the country, under Biden that rose twenty fold.

Biden immediately stopped building Trump's wall, ended the "remain in Mexico" policy (whereby asylum seekers or others had to stay in Mexico until they were processed), and signed over ninety executive orders abolishing the effective Trump policies. That not only encouraged border jumpers but also encouraged the cartels to smuggle more fentanyl through illegal invaders. Many, if not most, of the illegals coming in were military-aged men, not families. Ten former FBI officials called the threat from those young men "new and unfamiliar.... It would be difficult to overstate the danger represented by the presence inside our borders of what is comparatively a multi-division army of young single adult males."[917]

Illegal invaders saw the door swing wide open under Biden. Between 2021 and 2023, illegal immigration reached record highs.[918] Venezuelan gangs took over entire apartment complexes in Aurora, Colorado, other gangs terrified Chicago residents, and the waves of invaders in all major cities displaced citizens from their auditoriums, gyms, and other facilities. A "civil war" broke out in Democratic cities over the new invaders and the inner-city residents (mostly black) whose resources were yanked from them. Mayor Eric Adams of New York was one of the first to break ranks with Biden, insisting that the federal government had caused the problem and now the Biden administration needed to supply some money.

Usually, a single incident would spark national outrage that finally forces policy changes—or personnel changes via elections. In Trump's first presidential campaign, a girl killed by an illegal immigrant in San Francisco—Kate Steinle—helped fuel Trump's support. But in 2024, the murder of Georgia student Laken Riley struck a similar nerve. Eventually, Congress, with strong bipartisan majorities, passed and Trump signed the Laken Riley Act that required the detention of illegal invaders accused of theft and violent crimes. Riley was killed by a Venezuelan illegal immigrant released in New York because of its sanctuary policy.[919]

Even left-leaning *Vox* admitted Biden's border policy was "disastrous."[920] And Biden even loosened policies more just before President Trump took office in 2025, including letting migrants skip Immigration and Customs Enforcement check-ins.[921] In 2022, a judge blocked Biden's attempt to overturn Title 42, which allowed US authorities to turn away most asylum seekers. Biden merely instructed his subordinates to broaden the definition of asylum to include almost anyone who claimed at some time or other they were persecuted.[922]

Biden had given Vice President Harris the role of "border czar." Although she made a trip to the border in June 2021, she never went back until her own campaign in September 2024.[923] Even then, she avoided the high-crossing areas.

No other conclusion could be reached than that the Biden policies were not the result of incompetence but of deliberate action—that Biden wanted the country overrun with illegals. Why? For years, within Democratic circles, it was quietly assumed that Hispanic illegal aliens would eventually be registered to vote and would vote for Democrats. Many argued that the goal was to deliberately and methodically reduce the population of whites by Muslims in Europe or Hispanics in America.

While no one has yet strained out which among Hispanics were here illegally (something very had to do as most would not admit it), by 2025 there was a distinctive shift to Trump specifically and, somewhat less so, to Republicans by Hispanics. Not all estimates agreed, but at minimum, Trump got 42 percent of the Hispanic vote, only less than George W. Bush's total for a Republican candidate since 2004.[924] It looked quite convincing that Democrats had supported illegal immigration, thinking the new arrivals would vote overwhelmingly Democrat. Historical irony thus struck again as it seemed if anything they would be MAGA voters.

If it was a deliberate strategy by Democrats—which again remains to be proven—it would mark it as one of the most astounding political developments in Americans history. Ronald Reagan's Simpson-Mazzoli Act may have temporarily turned California into a Democratic state, although that still is a hotly debated thesis. But given the trajectory of Hispanic voters, it would constitute one of the only instances in American history where one party miscalculated on such a level by consciously allowing a flood of people who voted for the other party.

America's illegal immigration issues also raised concerns about the extensive use of H-1B visas to foreign workers, including many from India. American employees were displaced at high levels. Since the 1960s, nonsupervisory, goods-producing jobs shrank from 42 percent to 17 percent.[925] Much of that could be ascribed to illegal aliens and H-1B visa applicants replacing Americans by accepting lower wages.[926] Not surprisingly, three fifths of H-1B jobs were at the two lowest wage levels. (An interesting argument for more immigration was that the immigrants were sending money home—remittances—and that was making other countries, particularly Mexico, better off so wages would rise there. But as Michael Lind noted, "No country has ever joined the ranks of developed industrial economies on the basis of remittances from the impoverished workers it sends to the low-wage labor markets of industrialized countries.")[927] The H-1B debate would surface strongly in 2025 with the Trump campaign, which had promised to reduce and control the use of H-1Bs.

THIN RED LINES

Between 2021 and 2022, Biden's approval rating had sunk as low as the high twenties in some polls and hovered in the high thirties in most. Inflation had soared to nearly 8 percent, mortgage rates had risen from 2.9 percent under Trump to nearly 5 percent, and little real employment recovery had occurred (new jobs were added, but the number of people working stayed roughly the same). At the same time, backlash had built against the Biden-supported lockdowns and continuing efforts at vaccinating everyone. In short, the 2022 midterms were a recipe for a red wave.

Then it disappeared. Expected to take as many as forty seats, the Republicans succeeded in gaining only nine seats—but nevertheless won control of the chamber. (It must be recalled that in 2020, even with Trump's defeat, the Republicans had also gained nine, making it slightly more difficult to reach the expectations some held.) While most thought the GOP would also win the Senate, several close races went to the Democrats, including another Georgia runoff, giving the Democrats a net gain of one for a 51–49 edge (assuming the "independents" Bernie Sanders of Vermont and Angus King of Maine both continued to vote as they always did with Democrats). Still, almost immediately, there were problems with the Senate majority, as two Democrats (Dianne Feinstein of California and John Fetterman of Pennsylvania) had health problems that either hospitalized them or prevented them from showing up to vote. In addition, the Republican minority leader, Mitch McConnell of Kentucky (a man who according to the polls was the least popular person in Washington), also was absent due to health problems. When two recalcitrant "maverick" Democrats, Joe Manchin of West Virginia and Kyrsten Sinema of Arizona—who had previously bucked many of Biden's agenda items—were tossed into the mix, the Democratic majority all but vanished. Anything Biden wanted to accomplish would have to be done by executive order, not legislation.

This, of course, was a troubling development since the George W. Bush years: Congress in either house had become so ineffective and sclerotic that little serious legislation could pass. While the founders would have celebrated this trend as fostering the balance of power, they would not have approved of the accompanying expansive use of executive orders by presidents. The result was a form of "yo-yo governance," where the executive orders of one president were quickly and overwhelmingly countermanded by the next. That, in turn, empowered the courts even more than ever. After President Trump nominated Amy Coney Barrett to replace the deceased Ruth Ginsberg in September 2020 to howls from the left, the Supreme Court had flipped in reality from a 4–4–1 court (with Chief Justice John Roberts frequently playing the "swing" vote) to a 5–3–1 court, counting Trump's two other conservative nominees, Neil Gorsuch and Brett Kavanaugh. In such a case, to retain influence with the majority, Roberts frequently voted with the majority and/or wrote opinions instead of toothless dissents.

Meanwhile, the Supreme Court continued dismantling as much of Biden's Deep State as possible. In April 2022, a US district judge struck down the federal requirement for wearing a (Covid/China Virus)

surgical mask on an airplane or in other sectors of mass transportation.[928] Later, numerous researchers found that there were genuine harms associated with wearing masks, not to mention employment and lifestyle effects imposed by employers who perpetuated the mask rules.[929] Deaf people, or those hard of hearing—who depended heavily on lip reading to understand conversations—were put at a severe disadvantage.

Those studies began to prove extremely important in unraveling the lies associated with the entirety of Covid regimes, from lockdowns to vaccines to social isolation and masking. Indeed, only in 2023 were studies actually taken seriously about the side effects of the vaccines. Slowly, the extensive harms of *all* of those social distancing and mask policies started to unfold, while what research that was permitted on the vaccines likewise told a dismal tale. Documents showed that Dr. Anthony Fauci had stifled or covered up unfavorable research, and that his adviser hid emails from Freedom of Information Act requests by using a personal account.[930] Other revelations showed that many of the vaccine makers had either done sloppy testing or buried unfavorable results, and most of all, that high numbers of people were dying from myocarditis, which research slowly showed involved a link to the vaccines.[931]

Meanwhile, in two cases involving universities, the Supreme Court ended affirmative action, thus placing significant constraints on federal activities with regards to higher education. The direction of the Supreme Court, and many of the appellate courts, was clearly toward reigning in the administrative state, even without Trump. Trump-appointed judges had proven crucial to limiting the power of the state, and former presidential adviser Steve Bannon stated that their positions on the administrative state had been the determining factor in why President Trump selected them, figuring even more importantly than their stances on social issues.[932]

The *Dobbs v. Jackson Women's Health Organization* decision, in particular, proved a lightning rod in the 2022 midterm elections. While not a universal determinant (in Pennsylvania, for example, pro-life districts voted for the Democrat, John Fetterman, while pro-choice districts went for the Republican, Mehmet Oz), the abortion issue galvanized Democratic voters in several states. Tighter abortion restrictions failed in heavily Republican states such as Kansas and Montana.

SHIFTING ALLIANCES

By 2023, Biden's policies were under attack from all sides. In April, he launched a reelection effort. Wokeism in the military, combined with inept leadership and Biden's recurrent threats to engage the US in the Ukraine War, badly injured military recruiting. The army saw a 6 percent drop in white recruits.[933] Biden's oddball and incompetent appointees, from Pete Buttigieg had massively failed to handle the Francis Scott Key Bridge disaster or the East Palestine, Ohio, train derailment. Several high-profile transsexual appointees (men posing as women) appeared in dresses, and Sam Brinton, a Biden nuclear official, was arrested for luggage theft not once, not twice, but three times.[934] Biden's secretary of defense, Lloyd Austin, initially showed up at troop reviews in full uniform with not only a Covid mask but also a plexiglass facemask and a large medal draped around his neck. Later, he went missing in action twice and didn't tell Congress, saying he underwent an "initial medical procedure."[935]

Against that backdrop, in April 2023, Biden announced his reelection campaign. While there would be a traditional primary process, no one believed that any other Democrat could defeat him. However, Robert F. Kennedy Jr., who had opposed the China Virus vaccine, opposed the war in Ukraine, and stood far from Biden on a host of issues, announced his candidacy six days later. Initially, many experts thought he might take votes from Trump, who had announced his run in November 2022. As matters progressed, polling showed that RFK Jr. took more votes from Biden.

Democrat "lawfare" had made what followed inevitable. In 2023, when, as previously noted, virtually every insider (and most of the public) were fully aware of Biden's growing mental problems, members of the party hierarchy decided to continue to back him because they were absolutely certain Trump would be both indicted and bankrupt, and likely in jail. Further, they were well convinced that even a diminished Biden could swat away either of the two remaining contenders, Governor Ron DeSantis or Nikki Haley. Lawfare ensured not Trump's collapse, but Biden's. Lawfare guaranteed he would be the nominee—or would be for enough of the campaign to cripple the eventual "final" nominee, Kamala Harris—and that Trump would win the election.

What followed had the feeling of a great scene from the movie *Gettysburg*, where Sam Elliott, as Union cavalry general John Buford, describes what would happen if the Yankee forces did not arrive in time to hold the high ground. Speaking to Colonel Thomas Devin, he said:

> Devin, I've led a soldier's life, and I've never seen anything as brutally clear as this. It's as if I can actually see the blue troops in one long, bloody moment, goin' up the long slope to the stony top. As if it were already done…already a memory. An odd…set…stony quality to it. As if tomorrow has already happened and there's nothin' you can do about it. The way you sometimes feel before an ill-considered attack, knowin' it'll fail, but you cannot stop it. You must even take part, and help it fail.[936]

By December of 2023, it was already brutally apparent to some that the most significant parts of lawfare had failed, namely the attempt to label Trump an "insurrectionist" and convict him of federal crimes, likely with jail sentences. The Supreme Court refused Special Counsel Jack Smith's request to "fast track" the immunity case, which Trump's legal team had brought. To those who understood the court system, with its Byzantine calendars, that meant that it would be April 2024 before any cases were even heard, then likely July before the court reached a ruling. And even if favorable, it would be late 2024—right in the apex of the presidential campaign—that any trials would begin. At that point, should the court rule against Trump, it was then highly likely that it would rule in his favor that to hold a trial at that time would involve election interference, and thus would delay it until after the election. In other words, the December 2023 decision meant that the federal cases would be decided by the people in the election.

Yet those realities seemed invisible to both the Democrats' legal drive-by shooters and to the party as a whole, which continued to back Biden. Party leaders had an opportunity in late 2023 to meet with Biden and convince him to announce he would not run, allowing sufficient time to stand up a different competitor to Trump (though, in fairness, no other Democratic candidates polled as well against Trump as did Biden). Of prime importance, more lead time would have allowed a different candidate to assemble the war chest needed. Instead, Biden continued to vacuum up all available money for the Biden-Harris ticket. Thus, even if (as eventually happened), Biden withdrew to support someone else, he was limited to one choice—Harris—because only she could have access to the hundreds of millions of dollars in the campaign fund.

As Buford said, then, it was "as if it were already done." Either a diminished Biden or an extremely unpopular Harris would be the Democratic nominee. The Democrats made the decision easier by agreeing to a debate between Biden and Trump on June 27—quite early for presidential debates. Most assumed this scheduling rested on a view by insiders that Biden had to put up or shut up: He had to dramatically defeat Trump, or the hierarchy would pressure him to drop out.

In fact, the debate could not have gone worse for Biden, who was exposed as forgetful, angry, wandering, mentally diminished, and completely incapable of being the candidate, let alone the president. Trump wisely checked himself and allowed Biden to melt down on national television. Shortly thereafter, when the reviews labeling it as a disaster came in, Biden's fate was all but sealed.

CHAPTER 9
THE RESURRECTION

In the case of President Donald Trump, the entire 2024 election strategy rested entirely on "lawfare." After just two years of Joe Biden's administration, it was clear that while he was only four years older than Trump, his mental condition was that of a person suffering from dementia. A reasonable question to ask was whether Biden could even survive four more years, let alone govern. Unfortunately for the Democrats, polling consistently showed that Biden far outperformed any other potential candidate, including California's Gavin Newsom, Vice President Kamala Harris, or even ex–First Lady Michelle Obama. All trailed Trump, many badly. Biden was the best choice for Democrats, both for his incumbency and for his polling.

Democrat insiders, however, saw that from 2022 on, President Trump consistently was leading. This came as a shock. Trump only led a few times in a few polls in 2016 and didn't lead at all in the 2020 race. For him to be steadily and unrelentingly ahead nationally—as well as in the key "swing state" polls—meant Biden was in trouble. Moreover, the mechanisms by which suspected fraud had entered the electoral process under Covid, namely the lockdowns with months of "ballot harvesting," would not be available in 2024. Thus, with coordination from the White House itself, a "lawfare" offensive was launched against President Trump along multiple lines that will be discussed shortly.[937] This coordinated federal, state, and local attack, Democratic "lawfare" strategists thought, would bankrupt Trump and/or put him in jail. At the very least, they assumed Trump would be incapable of campaigning due to courts requiring his constant presence in the courtroom.

It is critical to understand that *the anticipated success of lawfare explained why Democrats made no effort to replace Biden in 2023.* After all, Biden could certainly beat nobody, which is who the Republicans would have to run if Trump was in jail.

As the primary campaigns unfolded, it became clear a second group besides the Democrats was counting on lawfare removing Trump: a group of non-MAGA GOP. Early in February of 2023, key GOP players who disliked Trump saw an opportunity to beat him at the ballot box by convincing enough voters that he wouldn't be able to run. He would either be in jail or so tied up with constant trials he would have no time or freedom to run.[938] Attendees were the usual suspects in the anti-MAGA movement, including Congressman Chip Roy, David McIntosh of the Club for Growth, and others who were shown purported polls that had Governor Ron DeSantis beating Trump in a head-to-head matchup. Of course, such polls were entirely concocted and had no grounding in reality. Mainstream polls at the time, such as that by Fox News, had Trump up nearly twenty points over DeSantis.[939] Astute insiders could see DeSantis had planned to run: He had a new book (*The Courage to be Free*), engaged on a world tour, and stumped in 2022 for GOP candidates—although his speeches sounded much more like they were tailored to his own campaign and not those of the actual candidates he ostensibly was supporting.

A new word, "hopium," described the DeSantis dalliance. It was simultaneously self-destructive and lacking any reality. It, like the entire "lawfare" strategy of the Democrats, relied entirely on President Trump being removed from the picture through the multiple cases against him.

That made DeSantis's decision entirely treacherous and mercenary. At the time, veteran political observers, including pollster Richard Baris and this author, noted the foolishness of the move, for it likely not only would result in a massive early political defeat for DeSantis (which it did) but would also possibly cripple him from *ever* running for another political office. MAGA has a long memory.

Yet DeSantis wasn't the only one to think an opportunity existed. At almost the same time DeSantis met with donors, former South Carolina Governor Nikki Haley announced that she would also run, and then the anti-woke entrepreneur Vivek Ramaswamy jumped in, as did some others.[940] Given Trump's grip on the Republican Party, these campaigns not only seemed doomed but also suicidal. By nature, Trump, a counterpuncher, was going to begin tearing into them for disloyalty. Yet at first, several rivals had substantial donor support, especially DeSantis and Haley. Donors wanted the excitement and turnout of the dominant MAGA wing of the party but without Trump's foibles and high disapproval numbers. Even the most casual examination, however, should have reminded everyone that "you can't have Falstaff, and have him thin." (The 1988 movie, *Tucker: The Man and His Dream* featured a scene where revolutionary automaker Preston Tucker (Jeff Bridges) fumed at the fact that one of the "Big Three" automakers he had foolishly put on his board betrayed him. The "Big Three' CEO told Tucker that he knew who he was bringing onto his board).

At another level, there was a substantial division among those such as Governor Brian Kemp of Georgia and the old-line McCain campaign managers (who had lost countless campaigns that were actually competitive—as opposed to campaigns in Republican-heavy districts that had virtually no opposition). That was the clique that had pushed Mitt Romney to the nomination in 2012 and constantly supported the candidate of least change. And that certainly was not Donald Trump. This division rested heavily on one's assessment of the 2020 defeat. Many, including the vast majority of the MAGA wing, insisted that the election had been stolen, that Mike Pence had failed in his duty to allow objections to the fraud during the counting process, and that the subsequent January 6 protesters were heroes, not criminals, who had been set up by the "feds." The traditional "don't rock the boat"/"lose with dignity" wing of the party went along with the notion that Joe Biden's eighty-one million votes were legitimate and that the protesters deserved to be locked up for "insurrection."

During the coming primary, those positions quickly and sharply defined the sides. And almost by default, anyone challenging Trump had to accept the view that the election was conducted fairly, that several states shutting down their counting simultaneously was not unusual, that every single major bellwether marker in previous elections (which showed that Trump won) was wrong, and that (conveniently) almost 90 percent of the votes that were tallied *after* Election Day were for Biden. They had to also accept that, therefore, the protesters were violent criminals who deserved jail. And they had to also embrace—if at arm's length—the notion that Trump himself was partially guilty of "insurrection."

That was a tough sell at any time in the post-2020 election cycle, but almost immediately, large numbers of Americans said the Biden election was illegitimate. By January 2024, one-third of adults agree that the election was fraudulent; two-thirds of Republicans thought the election was not legitimately conducted.[941] Even though the media went on a crusade to stamp out the claims of fraud, Americans increasingly embraced the idea. (Google was particularly diligent to list dozens of "debunking" fraud websites in its first pages of results when searching for information about fraud in the election.) In sum, for any candidate to challenge Trump, let alone defeat him, the candidate had to accept that 2020 was a fair election without fraud, that protesters were violent and "stormed" the Capitol (versus being let in and incited by federal plants), that Trump's policies as president had failed, and that they could somehow attract the infamous "white suburban females" without simultaneously losing the working-class Midwestern vote of all colors. Good strategists would have told such candidates that it was impossible.

But, of course, most of the advisers for those campaigns were in it for a paycheck, not to actually win.

Early polls showed DeSantis and Haley alone at the top of the contenders—usually separated by about ten points—while trailing Trump by twenty or more. For their insurrection to work, they had to maintain the illusion that (a) they could beat Trump, and (b) they could then beat Joe Biden. And above all, they had to maintain the illusion that they opposed a "two-tiered justice system" without mentioning Trump by name—the central figure in the entire assault of the two-tiered justice system. The facade of being loyal to Trump's MAGA policies but seeking a different face to present them became difficult to maintain. By early 2024, evidence surfaced that a DeSantis super PAC had funneled money into an anti-Trump group.[942] Indeed, one of DeSantis's initial funders, Ken Griffen, had ties to George Soros. One could not get more anti-MAGA than that!

Things seldom worked out the way the elites planned. DeSantis stumbled frequently in his primary. Some issues were, in the grand scheme of things, silly—yet they were the type of images that shaped voters' opinions permanently. For example, DeSantis had a penchant for wearing cowboy boots with his suit. Perhaps that would have flown with Ted Cruz from Texas, but it looked strange on the Florida governor. He had a personal style described as stiff and awkward, and it soon became apparent that he was genuinely uncomfortable around people. His laugh erupted from an entirely stoic face, and then, after a moment of hilarity, the stone countenance returned. None of those characteristics were fatal, but they opened the door for Trump supporters to label him "weird," before noticing that his boots appeared to have lifts in them. Memes spread across cyberspace, and DeSantis's team failed to counter. It wasn't long before Haley began to overtake him in the polls.[943] Then Haley almost immediately committed seppuku by saying that the United States should drone-bomb Iranian leaders inside Iran, thereby provoking a war![944] In the Iowa GOP caucuses, Trump crushed DeSantis by thirty in what was considered a state where the Florida governor may have actually had a chance. Haley didn't break 20 percent. Then in one of the two states (her home state of South Carolina being the other) where Haley supposedly had a chance to steal one from Trump, he beat her by over 11 percent. Haley then bungled the Nevada primary/caucus system, getting no delegates.

Two factors worked powerfully against both DeSantis and Haley. First, the underlying supposition that they would prove better candidates against Biden than Trump; second, that lawfare would not only occupy Trump's time, but would also result in rulings that would turn voters against him. The polls refused to cooperate. A "stunning" February poll by NBC showed that Trump not only led DeSantis and Haley but also led Biden by six points nationally and lead on "every issue voters care about."[945]

Meanwhile, Trump, realizing that he would vanquish DeSantis and Haley easily, had already turned his attention to revamping the anemic and often incompetent Republican National Committee (RNC). The RNC had utterly failed in its many election appeals during the suspected fraud of the 2020 election, and its chairwoman, Ronna Romney McDaniel, had proven singularly incapable of directing voter turnout. She, instead, managed to balloon the RNC budget for her travel and personal appearance. In early February 2024, Trump met with her and essentially presented her with walking papers.[946]

Indeed, *Politico*—a largely Democrat-front publication—noted that in a "72 hour span, Trump led the charge to crush a painstakingly negotiated border security deal in Congress, pushed the Republican National Committee chair to the exist and, in Nevada, embarrassed his last remaining rival in the presidential primary."[947] To read the virtual screams from *Politico* brought up memories of radio host Rush Limbaugh who always said of liberals, "They will always tell us who they fear most." In fact, the "border security deal" was vehemently opposed by the large majority of the MAGA movement and by Republicans at large. It sent still more money to Ukraine and offered an easy citizenship provision for the millions who already entered. Trump knew that if he was in office, he could get a better deal—one with teeth.

Concerns voiced by *Politico* spoke to other obvious problems with the Republican Party, namely Ronna McDaniel was a favorite of the liberals precisely because she was so ineffective and incompetent. Trump was preparing the GOP for a genuine battle without insiders who believed in the old standby, "lose with dignity," which terrified the left. Then, of course, finally vanquishing the last hope of the neocon right, Haley, was the icing on the cake for MAGA conservatives. Trump's dominance and, with him, MAGA's were reflected in the long list of so-called moderate Republicans who announced their retirement at the end of the term, suggesting they expected Trump to be elected again.[948]

LAME LAWFARE

Keeping track of all of the lawfare launched at President Trump almost required a scorecard. Overall, beginning with the special counsel appointed by Attorney General Merrick Garland in November 2022, Trump faced ninety-one charges in four different criminal cases. Two of those involved the special counsel, Jack Smith.[949]

- In August 2023, Trump was indicted on three criminal conspiracies to defraud the US government by contesting the questionable 2020 presidential election. Smith wanted to start the trial on January 2, 2024, and begin jury selection in December 2022 in the courtroom of Judge Tanya Chutkan. She set a trial date of March 4, 2024.
- In August 2022, the Justice Department had staged a raid of Trump's home in Mar-a-Lago, Florida, searching for "classified documents" that Trump supposedly had (it was almost certainly the proof he had in 2019 that the Foreign Intelligence Surveillance Act Section warrants were based on fraudulent claims from the FBI). Trump was indicted in July 2023. Smith

eventually took over this case as well. A trial in the courtroom of Judge Aileen Cannon in Florida was set for May 20, 2024.

- On August 14, 2023, Trump and eighteen codefendants were indicted by another Democrat, Fani Willis, Fulton County, Georgia's county attorney, on thirteen RICO (Racketeer Influenced and Corrupt Organizations Act) charges for a conspiracy to commit filing of false documents. The trial was to be held in Atlanta.
- Trump was indicted in New York on thirty-four charges of falsifying business records with the intent to hide an unspecified crime. (Note that even after his conviction, no crime has yet been specified.) The trial was to take place in New York under Judge Juan Merchan.
- In October 2023, New York filed a civil fraud lawsuit against Trump and his companies for supposedly overvaluing Trump properties, including Mar-a-Lago. The trial was to be held in New York in the courtroom of Judge Arthur Engoron.
- Finally, author E. Jean Carroll filed two suits against Trump for defamation and sexual abuse. Judge Lewis Kaplan heard the suit in his New York courtroom.

The total was ninety-one felony counts, with not a single one of merit.

Any objective observer would note two things about these actions. First, they only came after President Trump had announced he was running for reelection (strongly suggesting that this was retaliation and a strategy designed to keep him out of office), and second, all but Judge Cannon in Florida were activist Democratic judges, and the venues (except for Florida) were all in deep-blue Democratic strongholds of New York, DC, and Atlanta.

Smith knew just how politically important it was to attach a guilty verdict of "insurrection" (for which Trump was never charged) or other "treason-like" charges that the Democrats could use in the campaign. It demonstrated just how closely the political arm of the Democratic Party and the supposedly "independent" Department of Justice were linked in their lawfare. Smith's job, pure and simple, was to provide a highly significant criminal judgment that would wound Trump. However, given the degree to which Republican primary challengers depended on such a verdict, their involvement in the overall strategy—even at arm's length—must be scrutinized. And it's not just DeSantis and Haley, but virtually all of the primary opponents such as Chris Christie, the anti-Trump, former New Jersey governor who still nursed a grudge when Trump did not offer him a cabinet position. For those campaigns to have had sympathetic ears inside the Democratic strategy meetings would not have been uncommon.

Thus, when Smith filed a petition for certiorari before judgment in December, he sought to goad the Supreme Court into accepting or rejecting Trump's claims of presidential immunity at that time. When the court denied his petition and delayed its ruling until February 28, many legal insiders knew there would be no chance for a conclusion of a Trump federal trial before the election. Smith was furious, as were his fellow liberal bloggers, who understood they had just lost—regardless of what eventually any verdict was, because the real verdict would be rendered by the American public at the polls before any criminal court could get its hands on Trump.

One of the goals of lawfare was not just to hit Trump with criminal charges but to bankrupt him through the E. Jean Carroll case and the New York financial assets case (where he was charged with claiming that his properties were worth more than they were—and in fact, they actually were worth more than even he stated). In January 2024, a jury awarded Carroll $7.3 million in emotional damages, $11 million for damage to her reputation, and $65 million in punitive damages. Then, a month later, Judge Arthur Engoron ruled in the assets trial that Trump and his organization had to pay $355 million in damages and barred Trump from doing business in New York for three years. Trump's legal team immediately filled separate appeals on the amount and on the judgment itself (New York had two different legal systems for such rulings).[950] Most businessmen would have been crushed by cumulative rulings of more than $440 million, but Trump, after some pointed comments, shook it off much the way John D. Rockefeller dusted off the ruling by Judge Kenesaw Landis of $29 million, the largest fine in American history (of which Rockefeller's share was $8 million). At the time, Rockefeller was playing golf with three others when one of the foursome brought up the judgment, asking "How much is it?" Rockefeller replied, "Twenty-nine million, two hundred and forty thousand, the maximum penalty, I believe." Then, pointing to the course, he said, "It is your honor. Will you gentlemen drive?"[951]

One of the greatest ironies of the "Trumpersecutions," going back to his first term, was that Twitter (at the time, not controlled by Elon Musk) had banned Trump. That led him to start his own social media network, Truth Social.[952] MAGA supporters and Trump fans jumped from Twitter and other platforms to join Truth, and over the years, it defied critics and continued in business. In February 2024, which, despite Engoron's ruling, was already a great month for Trump, he merged Truth with Digital World Acquisition Corp. In the merger, he pocketed as much as $4 billion.[953] Taking a long view, the Twitter ban made Trump $4 billion richer, leaving him with a net gain of over $3.5 billion after *or if all of the judgment amounts against him were upheld!* Or, Trump made ten times what the total judgments—even if ultimately upheld—would come to. Some would see that as the fickle finger of fate in an upraised position.

In what were considered to be the most serious and consequential cases, the two federal cases involving the classified documents and the "insurrection" claims, Trump had already won a significant victory in December of 2023. That was when the US Supreme Court did not grant Smith's request for a quick review (a certiorari), setting in play a delay of the court's ruling on immunity for months and likely delaying any trial—no matter how the Supreme Court ruled—until after the election. Likewise, in the Georgia case against Trump and fourteen others, the prosecutor Fani Willis ran into roadblocks when information surfaced that she had had an affair with her lead prosecutor, Nathan Wade, and the state of Georgia put that case on hold while it investigated her! To sum up all these cases: None of the "insurrection" or classified documents cases were going anywhere until after the election, no matter what the Supreme Court said about immunity—it's ruling wouldn't come until July—meaning that politically Trump could not be labeled an "insurrectionist." There was one last shoe to drop, however: In another New York case brought by District Attorney Alvin Bragg, Trump was charged with laundering a "hush money" payment to porn actress Stormy Daniels through the campaign. Regardless of the veracity of Daniels's claims, legal scholars across the board agreed that this was at worst a misdemeanor and would never have been brought against any other person. Normally, such charges were considered misdemeanors. Nevertheless, the jury found Trump guilty of thirty-four counts of "falsifying business records" (even though Daniels wrote that she had never had a sexual affair with Trump).[954] Sentencing was to occur on July 11, but on July 1, the US Supreme Court issued its decision on Trump's appeal for immunity from the prosecution in the federal trials due to his status as president. The court held that he enjoyed limited immunity, but in the context of the Trump charges, the ruling was broad. The most immediate impact of the decision was that the Washington, DC "insurrection" case was remanded back to the lower court to determine what was considered an "official act." Meanwhile, Judge Cannon dismissed the documents case, writing: "The Court is convinced that Special Counsel's Smith's prosecution of this action breaches two structural cornerstones of our constitutional scheme—the role of Congress in the appointment of constitutional officers, and the role of Congress in authorizing expenditures by law."[955]

Smith, in other words, had not been constitutionally appointed.

Biden's mental decline was apparent from his first day in office. Staffers and the media covered it up. The public, however, saw what it saw. Not only were Biden's policies unpopular, but increasingly, he personally became less well liked.

He dropped further in the polls behind Trump (at one point he was within single digits in powerful Democratic strongholds such as Virginia, New York, New Jersey, and even Washington state). Trump had led in a total of only a handful of polls when he won in 2016 and was ahead in virtually none in 2020: Now, he led in most and led safely in most battleground states. Democrats pinned their hopes on the June 27, 2024, debate with Trump. Many on each side speculated that the debate had been scheduled unusually early to either stifle discussion of removing the president or to allow time to replace him. A good performance from Biden might have secured his position as the nominee.

Biden delivered the worst debate performance in history. In his nonsensical rambling, he lost his place, seemed angry yet befuddled, and struggled to finish thoughts. At one point, he announced that he "beat Medicare," to which Trump quipped, "Yeah, you beat the hell out of it."[956] Trump mostly let Biden talk, providing no gaffes or sound bites of his own to negate Biden's onstage implosion. One of Trump's two campaign managers, Chris LaCivita, backstage in the greenroom, turned to comanager Susie Wiles and said, "He's dead. He's not going to stay [in the race]."[957]

One Democrat observer said it was "the worst [debate] that's ever been done."[958] Late night comedy host Stephen Colbert feigned taking a drink before he could talk about it.[959] The Associated Press's Aaron Kall called it the "worst performance of an incumbent candidate ever."[960] Historian Thomas Whalen called it an "unmitigated disaster."[961] CNN's in-house doctor, Sanjay Gupta, admitted it was time for Biden to undergo detailed cognitive and neurological testing and to make the results public.[962] (Within the secretive Biden White House, such an action would never have been taken, let alone made public.)

The Democrats frantically huddled. Speaker Nancy Pelosi and Majority Leader Senator Chuck Schumer now feared Biden would bring the party down nationwide and throw the House and Senate to the Republicans. Several problems confronted them, however, not the least which was that while no polling showed that any of the proposed replacements for Biden could beat Trump, Kamala Harris—the most likely replacement—did worse than Biden. Only the unicorn candidate of Michelle Obama, who repeatedly stated she wasn't interested, came close to beating Trump.

Yet there was another hurdle, perhaps equally large as that of polling: money. According to federal election law, no one other than Harris could "inherit" the war chest (numbers varied from $300 to $400 million) that Biden still had in reserve. As the campaign was labeled the "Biden-Harris Campaign," she could legally still have access to that money, but any other replacement would have to stand up not only an entire campaign structure, with thousands of staff and offices, but also begin anew with fundraising from people who had already given significant amounts to someone who might leave. Thus, the needle increasingly pointed to Harris, and only Harris as the suitable person to step in. Money, from another standpoint, played a further role in shaping the decision. Multiple large donors and political action committee (PAC) bundlers told the DNC they could no longer raise money for Biden.

On July 13, before the disastrous debate, Schumer met with Biden to convince him to drop out. In tears, he told the president that no more than five of the existing senators at that time would support a continued campaign, and that Biden's own pollsters said he only had a 5 percent chance against Trump.[963] It marked a shocking turn when "Schumer and congressional Democrats, who had spent years batting away suggestions that Mr. Biden was too old and mentally frail to be president, ultimately led the effort to pressure him to step aside."[964]

Then lightning struck. The same day as Schumer met with Biden, all attention shifted to an outdoor rally in Butler, Pennsylvania, where an assassin, Thomas Matthew Crooks, managed in broad daylight with Secret Service snipers watching to crawl onto a rooftop and fire a shot from a high-powered rifle at President Trump as he was speaking.[965] Trump, facing forward as he spoke, at the last second, turned his head to the right. High-speed photographic images show the bullet inbound just as he turned, causing the shot to go through his ear but not his head. An audience member, Corey Comperatore, was killed by another shot, and two other attendees were critically injured.[966] The would-be assassin fired eight rounds before the Secret Service's counter sniper team killed him. In a scene for the ages, as the Secret Service agents tried to hustle Trump off the stage, he stopped them and, his face streaming blood, lifted his fist to the crowd and shouted "Fight! Fight!" It became one of the most viral images in internet history.[967]

Trump was treated, then released. Intense criticism was directed at the women in his Secret Service detail who fumbled with their weapons, were too short to block his head from another shot, and in general seemed incompetent. When Trump showed up for his nomination, his detail had only men.

Later, it was learned that Crooks was found with multiple phones. Whether it was divine intervention or whether Trump had a rope around his lucky star, he credited God, who "saved my life for a reason" as he told the GOP convention.[968] Later, he told talk show host Dr. Phil McGraw, "God loves our county and he thinks we're going to bring our country back.... It has to be God."[969] At his first address to the joint session of Congress on March 4, 2025, Trump recalled that event and said again that God had saved him to "Make America Great Again"—to the groans of the Democrats in the gallery. And before he left the podium, he employed Republicans to "Fight! Fight! Fight!" as the audience joined in hysterical applause.

Shortly thereafter, the Secret Service and FBI stopped another attempted assassination of Trump from a shooter who had taken up a firing position near a golf course where Trump was playing. In each case, the security lapses were astonishing to the point of raising questions as to whether there were insiders assisting the attacks. Investigators say Crooks may have had an accomplice.[970] The second would-be assassin, Ryan Routh, escaped initially as multiple shots were fired at him. He eventually was captured and charged.

Trump's iconic image—bloody, with the Secret Service surrounding him, fist upraised—immediately became the young century's most iconic photographs. Once again, he had replaced any of the more mundane pictures of Barack Obama with a scene for the ages.

Trump benefited politically from the attack. Sympathies changed, many pointing to the unceasing characterization of Trump as "Hitler" over the previous years and the violent language of Democrats directed toward him as a motivating factor in the assassin's mind. Nevertheless, newer, more intense security measures attended Trump, including moving his inauguration indoors due to credible threats.

Between the assassination attempt, Trump's remarkable presence after being wounded, and Biden's debate performance, the entire campaign for Biden had gone from bad to worse. He continued to resist calls for him to withdraw from the campaign for weeks, growing more irritated and agitated as former supporters abandoned him. He still held nearly four thousand delegates to the convention, making him unbeatable if they all voted for him as party bylaws required them to do. His wife Jill also insisted he stay, as did the family. By some reports, his wife was negotiating "buy outs" from the Democratic Party in the form of a book deal and other financial and nonfinancial guarantees. (Biden had already received a massive book deal of "at least seven figures" in April 2017.)[971] Finally, on July 21, Biden announced he would drop out of the race and endorse Harris.

Certainly, Trump's team was not taken by surprise: It had been preparing to run against Harris for weeks. Harris failed to win a single Democratic delegate in the primaries and had never been vetted in her California races. Trump, overall, reported being "pretty excited" to run against her.[972] Pollster Richard Baris had been in the field for months by that time. He noted that Harris probably brought a little more strength to the Electoral College—not nearly enough—but likely would lose more of the popular vote.[973] Above all, Harris could not separate herself from Biden's policies. Whenever she criticized a situation or addressed an issue, the bolder questioners retorted, "But weren't you in office then?" That reality outraged the leftist media, who had hoped to cover up Biden's disastrous policies.[974]

She easily received the nomination, whereupon she proceeded to campaign in generic phrases. Her message changed faster than a supermodel donning outfits. In her final week, the Trump team calculated that Harris ran 162 different "creatives" (approaches or messages), which actually appeared to bolster Trump's numbers. Finally pressed to sit for a hostile interview with Fox News's Bret Baier, Harris was grilled and pinned down on the administration's catastrophic immigration policies.[975] But it was in the safest and most favorable of settings—the TV show *The View*—that Harris uttered her most damaging admission. Asked what she would have done differently than Biden, which was a golden opportunity to reject some of his failures, she answered, "There is not a thing that comes to mind."[976]

Harris was already unlikeable—but in previous elections so was Trump. The assassination attempt changed some of that, but so did his discipline on the campaign trail, where he avoided personal spats on X/Twitter and stuck to the issues. Equally important, Trump consistently aligned with Everyman, showing up at a McDonald's not just for a photo opportunity but to work the line and serve fries and malts at the drive-through and appear in a McDonald's apron over his shirt and tie. Then Trump appeared at an event driving a garbage truck. It sent a clear message: Trump, the billionaire, could do the jobs of ordinary people with a smile on his face.

Team Trump, armed with favorable voter registration shifts in Florida, Pennsylvania, Arizona, and Nevada, was confident Trump would win…but would another election drift into a period of extended counting that added more Democratic votes? Working the election night broadcast with Seth Keshel for DecisionUSA2024, we calculated the numbers as each new drop came in from the battleground states. It became clear early that Trump would win Arizona (even though it wouldn't count for days) and Nevada, and that Florida and Texas would be called with double-digit margins for Trump. Just a week earlier, Democratic donors were still being fleeced with stories that Florida and Texas were "in play." Only two states remained to make for an early call for Trump: North Carolina and Pennsylvania—as Georgia had also been called for Trump. As soon as North Carolina's final numbers came in, giving Trump the Tar Heel State, only Pennsylvania really remained as a hope for the Harris campaign. But the massive push for Republican voter registration, led by a volunteer, Scott Presler, had turned so many Democratic counties into Republican majorities that the Keystone State was soon called. Trump finished with 312 electoral votes and a national popular vote margin of 1.5 percent. He had, for a third year in a row, increased his vote total, this time to over seventy-seven million.[977] In June 2025, a review of the election by Nate Cohn said that if more people had voted, Trump would have won by even more, putting to lie the notion that Harris was denied the presidency due to low turnout.[978]

An epiphenomenon of the decades-long war on masculinity surfaced in the 2024 election. Young people, particularly men, swung to Trump, who saw a ten-point jump among youth support overall, but enjoyed a 56 percent share of young men. That same number had voted for Biden just four years earlier.[979] A similar shift in Hispanics, where Trump won 48 percent of Latino men, signaled a crushing rebuke of the Democratic strategy of catering to minorities and the young.

Unlike either 2016, when Hillary Clinton's proxies, such as Jill Stein, protested the election, or afterwards when the "resist" movement took shape, in 2024 no such resistance appeared. As one observer marveled, "That is completely gone. It's completely absent from discourse."[980]Whether the Democrats were truly shocked (later information surfaced that Harris's pollsters never had her ahead) and Trump's victory was unexpected, or whether they concluded the "resist" strategy of 2017 ultimately proved counterproductive, Trump sailed back into office with almost no obstruction.

Concerns about Congress failing to certify the vote vanished and claims that Democrats would somehow hold up the vote in the joint session of Congress on January 6 failed to materialize, although security concerns (officials claimed extreme cold) forced the inauguration indoors into the Capitol rotunda. It was an ironic setting, given that just four years earlier, it was the site of the controversial presidential protests.

Trump swore the oath of office on January 20 with a blistering attack on the status quo. As he did so, growing numbers of media outlets and insiders began to admit they had known about Biden's mental collapse for a long time—some as far back as 2021. It was the "most under-reported story of the Biden presidency."[981] Various left-wing bloggers such as Matthew Yglesias, Josh Barro, and Mehdi Hasan admitted they did not acknowledge his cognitive decline, with *Rolling Stone* calling them "gullible and wrong."[982]

America's 2024 election reflected recent serious frustration with the lack of genuine change in the government. From 2014 to 2024, there were six elections in a row in which the House, Senate, and/or White House changed party control. (The last time even three elections in a row occurred without change was from 2006 to 2010, when the country shifted sharply against the Republicans for the Iraq War and the subprime mortgage crisis.)[983] Nearly three-fourths of those polled said Trump was the "change" candidate, and not surprisingly, the counties with the highest cost-of-living shifted to Trump. And the 2024 election was the third in a row with a single digit margin in the House, suggesting that the public was giving representatives a short leash to perform—or else. Republicans, many of whom still had not learned to embrace MAGA—barely escaped with control.

Much of Trump's MAGA program had been stalled, co-opted, countered, or nullified in his first term by not only Democratic opposition and the "resist" movement, but also by his inexperience with personnel for such tasks. He had dutifully appointed mainstream (non-MAGA) Republicans to multiple offices, thinking they would play ball. He, as a football team might in the draft, reached for a number of unorthodox appointees such as Rex Tillerson, who proved incompetent as a secretary of state. Above all, he came in with almost no genuine behind-the-scenes preparation for his agenda items.

Trump's team in 2025 could not have been more different. Susie Wiles, his chief of staff, streamlined the entire process of presenting ideas to Trump. She ensured no counterproductive anti-MAGA people slipped into the process. Although the Senate dragged its feet some with his cabinet picks, they moved with light speed compared to 2016. He had four cabinet secretaries confirmed in the first week (Obama had twelve). More important, a solid vetting had been done on all. Before hearings even began, Trump's first choice for Attorney General, the congressman from Florida Matt Gaetz, found powerful resistance. He resigned before the hearings started and was replaced by a much more mainstream Pam Bondi, the attorney general from Florida. She, in turn, put on a dazzling display of toughness in front of the Senate, suggesting she would not be the pushover Jeff Sessions was.

Most important, however, was the blizzard of executive orders Trump issued in his first twenty-four hours. Those had all been drawn up over the previous year. They featured careful wording with clear evidence that all the pros and cons had already surfaced internally. Trump also had undersecretaries in place who seamlessly took over enforcing those orders until the secretaries themselves obtained confirmation. That was particularly important at the Department of Justice, where Ed Martin started acting immediately. Thus, even before Trump took office, many agencies had started to reverse previous policies on their own.

A phenomenon known as the "Trump effect," in which Trump's policy outcomes started to materialize before he was sworn in, could be seen across almost all of American society:

- Haitians in Springfield, Ohio, who had become infamous for eating local dogs, fled the city.[984]
- On his way out, Biden, after long delays, finally approved the first antimony mine in America. Antinomy is a key element for battery manufacturing.[985]
- Facebook announced it was ending its fact-checking program for posts, which had been a central tool used against Trump supporters on the site.[986]
- Designers who snubbed Melania Trump in 2017's inauguration begged to dress her in 2025.[987]
- With the likelihood of Robert F. Kennedy Jr. coming in as head of health and human services, the Food and Drug Administration finally banned Red No. 3, a dye, in food and ingested drugs.[988] The Food and Drug Administration also debarred the EcoHealth Alliance that was involved in the Covid gain-of-function research.[989]
- The entry port into El Paso, Texas, from Mexico was closed.[990]
- The Federal Reserve withdrew from a global climate group on January 18.[991]

An astounding 97 percent of the Immigration and Customs Enforcement deportees after just two weeks were shown to have had a removal order under Biden, who did nothing about them.[992] By his March speech to the joint session of Congress, Trump could announce that border crossings had reached a historic low.

Just one week after Trump took office, with his illegal immigrant deportations in full swing, Colombia refused to take a planeload of the migrants. Trump blasted him on his Truth Social platform and threatened at least 50 percent tariffs on all Colombian goods, plus the termination of all Colombian visas. Within ten hours, the Colombian president was on the phone, not only accepting the planeloads of invaders but offering his *presidential plane* to support the effort. This was likely the first ever diplomacy in history conducted by social media.[993] Was it any surprise that belief in miracles among Americans had risen?[994]

Trump's astounding six-day surge caused the left-leaning site *Axios* to marvel: "No modern president has done more—across more areas of American policy, culture and life—than Trump in the past six days. This new operating style and system enabled a strategy of flooding the nation with so many huge moves that it's hard for critics to attack specific ones."[995]

He didn't stop, ordering the Department of Defense to begin work on an American version of Israel's Iron Dome, firing most of the inspectors general who went along with the Russia Hoax, and ordered the Army Corps of Engineers to override California's mindless water policy that was feeding fires in Los Angeles and turn "on the water flowing abundantly from the Pacific Northwest, and beyond. The days of putting a Fake Environmental argument, over the PEOPLE, are OVER."[996] His Justice Department and FBI launched an investigation into where more than $200 billion in State Department and CIA spending went in Ukraine. As mentioned earlier, border crossings dropped to a historic low just one week into Trump's second term.[997]

DOGEBALL

During the campaign, Trump had slowly won over a number of critics or fence-sitters, particularly those in the tech world and among Democratic opponents of Biden. Among the former, tech giant Elon Musk (we will have more to discuss of him in Chapter 10) became friends with Trump. Before the election was over, he had campaigned for Trump. After November 5, Trump announced that Musk and his former primary opponent, tech businessman Vivek Ramaswamy, would head up a new agency called the Department of Government Efficiency, or DOGE, that would look to streamline the government and root out slack (not to mention corruption).[998]

Liberals screamed that this was an unconstitutional agency that Congress had not authorized. But Trump, whose team had spent over two years planning and developing policies to overcome such specific attacks, had cleverly *not* created a new agency that Congress could challenge, but found a somewhat dormant, unknown agency created by Obama "to hire Silicon Valley types exempt from rules" called the United States Digital Service that Trump—under his authority as president—could simply reorganize.[999] The office had helped undermine Trump in his first term, as it was designed to do. But under Trump's control again, it did the opposite. Now simply renamed DOGE and placed under operational control of Musk, the USDS provided the perfect scalpel—or, in some cases, scythe.

Under effective secrecy, Musk assembled over one thousand "nerd" coders who had already been vetted. They were each provided with clear objectives and equipped with appropriate legal authority. President Trump reminded them to move as fast as possible.

At 2:00 a.m. on January 21, 2025, four young coders announced "We're in.... All of it." Using algorithms, the team with an "authorized disruption" got control of agencies' payment systems and could track money going through the US government. "By dawn, they would understand more about [the] Treasury's operations than [the] people who had worked there for decades."[1000] They were inside the Treasury Department so fast that "legal teams had neutralized resistance within hours."[1001] Musk's team had literally shortened the process to acquire key information about government waste and fraud by months, if not years—*if it ever could have been acquired at all!*

DOGE's key finding, according to website RealClearInvestigations, was a "federal budget made into a maze impervious to reform." Total spending across all agencies was 50 percent higher than even the experts thought it was. Almost no one in the government even attempted to get into individual agency budgets, but rather just took "last year's number" and changed it. (This is the essence of "baseline budgeting," whereby Congress just assumed that an agency was worthy of its budget and therefore took the last year's number as a "baseline" on which to add.)[1002] The DOGE team found that programs marked as independent had multiple coordinated funding streams, budgets shrouded in secrecy, and complex networks designed to hide funding. DOGE's most important weapon—besides its unparalleled access—was its speed. Traditional defenses against reform or budget cuts, such as slow-walking decisions, leaking stories on the investigators, or stonewalling requests for information—"proved useless against an opponent moving faster than their systems could react. By the time they drafted their first memo objecting to the breach, three more systems had already been mapped."[1003]

To put it bluntly, Trump kneecapped almost all institutional challenges from the outset. Trump adviser Stephen Miller had spent the better part of a year formulating clever and precise ways to avoid the obstructionist bureaucracy that hamstrung Trump in his first term. Musk quickly—and perhaps, expectedly—took the lead in this telic operation; Ramaswamy resigned to run for the governorship of Ohio.

Almost immediately, Musk began discovering savings, with up to $1 billion saved in the department's first week and over $3.4 billion in the first three weeks.[1004] Unlike government employees, DOGE's young "nerds" worked around the clock.[1005] One of DOGE's most audacious moves was to enter the federal human resources department, the Office of Personnel Management, when the office was empty and changed all computer passwords, locking out the employees. That enabled DOGE to examine all the computers for previous activity, including playing games on the US taxpayers' dollars or watching pornography. It also meant, however, DOGE operatives could see who changed their email comments involving "resist" messages after the election.[1006]

DOGE discovered massive amounts of pure fraud, particularly in the US Agency for International Development (USAID) office. The agency, with a $42 billion budget, was paying billions to utterly ridiculous causes and organizations, including propaganda organs that were designed to keep Trump out of office. USAID paid a terrorist preacher, Anwar al-Awlaki; a week before the heinous October 7 Hamas attack in Israel, USAID gave a Hamas-linked "charity" $900,000; and gave a total of at least $122 million to terror-related groups in the Middle East.[1007] Other expenses for USAID included the following:

- $50 million for condoms in Gaza (liberals complained it was only $46 million)
- $70,000 for a DEI musical in Ireland
- $16 million for institutional contractors in gender development offices
- $6 million in nonemergency funding for the Centers of Excellence
- $37 million to the World Health Organization
- $32,000 to a transgender comedian in Peru[1008]

Often, so-called news outlets claimed the revelations about USAID spending weren't real; for example, $1.5 million went to advance DEI in Serbian workspaces, but only "some" of the money came from USAID. (It was still spent in that amount, often recirculated from USAID to other government entities in a shell game.) It wasn't just USAID: Musk's DOGE team found absurd studies everywhere. One, with news outlet Reuters, involved a $9 million contract with the Department of Defense to study large-scale social deception.[1009] Working with Musk, Trump shuttered USAID, leaving only two hundred active personnel out of ten thousand. DOGE simply began with the money flow, then exposed the networks, and then finally restructured the systems. Whether Congress could stand strong and make the cuts permanent was another matter, but even then, once buildings were closed and employees fired, restarting the program would be a nightmare.

It was telling that even more than the Treasury Department, USAID produced the greatest area of legal resistance. Numerous lawsuits were launched, and a handful of judges tried to block or slow-walk the USAID deconstruction. One judge, in March 2025, ruled that USAID had to pay $1.9 billion on work already performed, and the Supreme Court temporarily upheld that ruling. But in the long haul, most legal experts believed the wall holding back DOGE cuts was thinner than rice paper.

DOGE also found duplication and waste to the tune of tens of millions of dollars in almost every nook and cranny they peered into. At the Department of Education, which Trump announced he would close, the DOGE team terminated eighty-eight contracts totaling $88 million, including one contract for simply observing the "mailing and clerical operations at a mail center.[1010] Another twenty-nine DEI contracts were terminated, saving $101 million. DOGE even recovered $1.9 billion from being "misplaced" in a broken accounting process.[1011]

Democrats took an inordinately long time to respond to the Trump assault, as if mesmerized by his blitzkrieg-level speed. Finally, in mid-February, they launched a series of attacks from liberal judges who, in some cases, issued temporary restraining orders. Nevertheless, the law and the Constitution were completely on Trump's side—the president can hire and fire whom he wants. Of the first six cases brought, two judges reaffirmed DOGE's authority to proceed, two who initially ruled against DOGE slowly backtracked, one was overturned by a federal judge, and one continued in the appeal process presumably to the Supreme Court.

Another focal point of the DOGE investigations involved the post-China Virus "work from home" allowances. At a given time, it was estimated that less than 5 percent of federal employees came into the office. Not only did that prohibit managerial oversight, but it also rendered numerous federal office buildings useless and presented a case for selling them off. Many left the government voluntarily, including the highest-ranking career official at the Treasury, with seventy-five thousand requesting the early buyout deal by February. Those unemployed spots translated into vacant office buildings, which Trump planned to sell off.

As part of this race for efficiency, Trump signed a "ten for one executive order to eliminate federal regulations by requiring that any new federal regulation must be accompanied by ten old regulations to be eliminated before a new one can be imposed. It was a variation of Alexander Hamilton's "sinking fund" to keep the US government out of debt.

ART OF THE DEAL

Looking at Trump's first term and the early parts of his second term, the two were as different as night and day. Obviously in 2025, Trump did not face anywhere near the unified, vicious, unrelenting opposition he encountered in 2017–18. Most of all, he did not have to battle a pre-planned intelligence community coup attempt or the phony Russia Hoax lawfare that the Democrats had concocted. Second, he entered—and enjoyed—much higher public approval. There still existed a large gap between approval for himself personally (in the mid-fifties) to approval for many of his policies (often over 70 percent). Nevertheless, it was more than enough to cement support for his policies and stood far beyond the anemic 35 percent Biden had held. People comparing the two appreciated the difference.

Anything can happen over a year, let alone three. Yet a fascinating look at "Trump One" and "Trump Two" comes from his own words, in his 1987 book, *The Art of the Deal.* From that, an awareness of how Trump intended to run his presidency the first time around and how he changed after 2020, becomes apparent.

In *The Art of the Deal,* Trump described some of his business traits: "I don't carry a briefcase. I try not to schedule too many meetings. I leave my door open. You can't be imaginative or entrepreneurial if you've got too much structure."[1012] Many observers commented in astonishment how *disciplined* and structured Trump's second campaign, than his presidency, was. His chief of staff (and campaign manager) Susie Wiles made it clear that she would act as a rigid gatekeeper to Trump, weeding out all the people who often would sell him on imaginative programs or ideas that had not been vetted.[1013] "I have every hope that the 47 administration will not have the same number of attempts to put sand in the gears," she told *Axios*.[1014]

Trump had outlined his "elements of the deal" as follows:

- "I aim very high, and then I just keep pushing and pushing and pushing to get what I'm after. Sometimes I settle for less...but in most cases I still end up with what I want."
- "Think big."
- "Protect the downside and the upside will take care of itself."
- Maximize the options.
- Know the market.
- "Use your leverage."
- "Fight back."
- "Deliver the goods."
- "Contain the costs."[1015]

Trump noted as to his goal of protecting the downside, "I've never gambled in my life. To me, a gambler is someone who plays slot machines. I prefer to own slot machines."[1016] He noted that in his Atlantic City boardwalk site, Holiday Inn wanted to be a partner, meaning it would get 50 percent of the profits. Trump noted that Holiday Inn offered to pay back the money he already had in the deal, finance all construction, and guarantee him against loss for five years. He could therefore get 50 percent of the profits without putting up any money at all. "It was an easy decision," he recalled.[1017] Viewing himself as "very conservative," Trump always conceived of at least half a dozen different approaches, a bricolage of options, to making his deal work.

However, in 2016, he failed at knowing his market. Instead of the American voters, his immediate market was Congress and the media, both of which were his opponents if not enemies (even though the Congress was in theory a Republican Congress—it was filled with anti-Trump forces). Rush Limbaugh related on his radio show many times how, golfing with Trump, he would find Trump idealistic and even naive about who his enemies were. Trump told him that he assumed they were

Americans and would want what was best for Americans. The reelected Trump did not bring any such utopian notions. In 2025, while working with a Republican Congress, Trump assumed he would not have universal support and set about with a tower of preconceived and drafted executive orders that imposed mass changes on the federal government whether Congress codified them or not.

For example, his DOGE evisceration of USAID was a fait accompli with or without Congress, as Obama had foolishly empowered Trump with a ready-made executive bureau entirely under Trump's authority to strip or even abolish. Likewise, border control lay entirely within Trump's dominion, and he moved astonishingly swiftly to begin shipping illegal aliens out of the country. Congress could do almost nothing, nor could the courts.

Trump largely failed in another, related element of the deal, using leverage. That largely stemmed from the fact that he came in with such a small cadre of loyalists even in the executive branch, and even fewer in the legislative branch. Constant assaults by the Russia Hoax investigations hamstrung him, as no senator wanted to throw his support entirely behind someone whom an investigation would show had worked with Vladimir Putin to swing an election. Not until 2019 did many senators finally conclude that they were better off supporting Trump than opposing him—but that did not extend to Senate Republican leader Mitch McConnell, who had made his bones in the minority and prospered both politically and financially from being a seller of votes rather than an organizer of a majority.

Although in the campaign Trump fought back, especially when prodded by Steve Bannon, he came to Washington, DC the first time with an attitude of glasnost, only to find that he was dealing with a perpetual state of deception. Moreover, Trump tended to fight back against anyone and everyone, including Twitter battles with celebrities. When he returned to DC, whether under the discipline of Wiles or because of his own growth, he shrewdly left the battles to others and instead churned out momentous, nation-changing agenda items.

Containing costs, another stroke in Trump's artwork, was unmatched. No one, not even Warren Harding or Calvin Coolidge came close to Trump's DOGE effort. By the time Trump's second administration concluded, it was well within reason to think that like Harding and Coolidge he could not just balance budgets but actually reduce the national debt. Some estimates by Musk suggested the government could slash the debt by orders of magnitude.

However, when it came to delivering the goods and containing costs, Trump's highly successful first three years crashed into the China Virus. With or without the vaccine, Trump's Covid protocols doomed him to a divided public, half of whom would have claimed he didn't do enough and half who complained he did too much. His second term yielded much different outcomes in its initial stages, with Trump "delivering the goods" on over a dozen campaign promises in less than three weeks! In short, the 2025 Trump embodied every aspect of *The Art of the Deal* that the first-term Trump either did not or could not fulfill.

Meanwhile in his forte—negotiating with foreign leaders—Trump backed down the Canadian Prime Minister Justin Trudeau and Mexico's President Claudia Sheinbaum on border issues through the threat of tariffs (each capitulated within a few days), opened negotiations to end the Ukraine War, warned the European Union that the US was finished carrying the burden of the North Atlantic Treaty Organization; and told Russia's Vladimir Putin and China's Xi Jinping that he wanted deep, three-way cuts in nuclear weapons.

Ukraine's president Zelenskyy resisted peace negotiations—naturally it would involve losing some Ukrainian (but heavily Russified) territory. After an embarrassing Oval Office meeting in which he loudly argued with Trump and Vice President J. D. Vance, Zelenskyy reneged on a peace proposal. Trump shut off his access to long-range rocket codes.

Beyond Ukraine, however, Trump presided over a long-developing geopolitical shift in which Europe was falling into irrelevance. Great Britain, through its immigration policies and unproductive green energy programs, had seen its economy collapse. When, in March 2025, it threatened to send troops to fight in Ukraine, it could at best muster a single actual combat division. Continental Europe—outside of rebel breakaway countries such as Slovakia, Hungary, and even Italy—were tied to the crushing weight of "green energy" that left the Germans literally cutting down forests to put up a coal plant and importing gas from Russia at the very time it was seeking to start a war with Russia over Ukraine.

Trump astutely played on these weaknesses. He pestered Denmark to sell Greenland to the US. He changed the name of the "Gulf of Mexico" to the "Gulf of America." He increasingly ignored the Europeans and placed tariffs on any country that had tariffs on US goods. By the time of his joint session speech, it was clear that there was a new sheriff in town.

Domestically, he issued executive orders to end transsexual policies of allowing men in women's locker rooms and sports: "There are only two genders," he said, "male and female." He promised a program to "Make America Healthy Again" and to once again return to space exploration. His closing stood among the great moments in presidential speeches:

> Despite the best efforts of those who would try to censor us, silence us, break us, destroy us, Americans are today a proud, free, sovereign and independent nation that will always be free, and we will fight for it 'til death.... Now it is our time to take up the righteous cause of American liberty, and it is our turn to take America's destiny into our own hands and begin the most thrilling days in the history of our country.... We are going to create the highest quality of life, build the safest and wealthiest and healthiest and most vital communities anywhere in the world. We are going to conquer the vast frontiers of science, and we are going to lead humanity into space and plant the American flag on the planet Mars, and even far beyond.

Concluding he said, "And through it all, we are going to rediscover the unstoppable power of the American spirit.... Every single day we will stand up and we will fight, fight, fight for the country our citizens believe in and for the country our people deserve."[1018]

As a postscript, an irony of the Trump years, and especially the 2024 election, was that for the liberal hive, Obama was to have been the "Man of the Era." Liberals had expected him to dominate the landscape of the first quarter of the century, just as FDR dominated the first half of the twentieth century. Almost immediately, that fell apart in Obama's third year, when Republicans delivered massive defeats to the Democrats at almost every level. Although Obama won a narrower reelection than his initial race, his influence as a "shot caller" within the party was badly damaged. Individual candidates still sought him, yet no one could provide proof of his electoral value. And by 2024, younger voters had turned on his party. Richard Truesdell and Keith Lehmann expressed it this way: "Obama rose to power in 2008 because the 18- to 25-year-old Millennials believed in his stature as the Black Jesus. In 2024, the 18- to 25-year-old Gen Zs abandoned him because they don't."[1019]

Indeed the "story" from 2008 on was less about the nation's first black president—the novelty of which wore off quickly—than about how Washington as a whole had become unresponsive and even oppressive in its daily functions first under Obama, then under Biden. It was that narrative, not one of race, that became the overarching framework in which the period since 2008 was set.

CHAPTER 10

BRAVE NEW MORNING IN AMERICA

As Donald Trump ushered in a political revolution, his America was undergoing a simultaneous revolution of another sort. Few technologies have brought massive change to humanity—the wheel, the steam engine, and perhaps the cotton gin come to mind. Certainly, the internet, which took off after 1993, has to be counted in this list. That year, various internet providers opened access to new users, followed a year later by AOL and Yahoo. As other large search engines and providers came online, especially Google in 2003, people had access to information and communication via electronic mail (email) as never before in human history. Within seconds, someone could look at the geography of Bolivia, find the population of Sri Lanka, or transmit large data and images to Iceland.

Enhanced by the rise of the iPad, iPhone, and public "social media" sites, such as Facebook, Twitter, Myspace, and Instagram, a less beneficial, dark side of the internet surfaced. Young people found themselves virtually addicted to being online. The internet provided a "temporary escape or a release valve for anyone who didn't quite fit in in the offline world."[1020] At the very time it had come to dominate peoples' lives—particularly those of the young—the internet surprisingly began seeing a decline in relative usage. Sites such as TikTok, Twitter, and Instagram began trending down; even Facebook and Snapchat fell below their earlier highs. Some of this decline was a self-inflicted wound. Sites began to employ ads for more revenue. So-called pop-ups badgered every viewer and obstructed every search. To avoid constant assaults from advertisers, customers employed ad blockers—but that in some ways made the matter worse: Every time a person wanted to look at a specific page, the ad blocker had to be disabled.

Soon, the value of the internet was greatly adumbrated. A search for "drones" on Google could produce a dozen ads for drone manufacturers before linking to sites with information about drones themselves. Algorithmic changes designed to "push" users to certain media also fed disgust. This was especially true if the "push" was toward more established media that younger people had abandoned in droves or toward unwanted dating or sex sites. The once-imaginative internet, full of new possibilities, descended into a carnival of barkers, peddling their games and oddball attractions.

There were more serious concerns about use of the internet. Politics cannot be separated even from the seemingly stark world of digital algorithms. It is worth noting that when Elon Musk took over Twitter (now X) and reinstituted previously banned personalities (including this author), the left began attacking Twitter for the first time in years. New articles in the old media appeared, slanted against Twitter, and its decline was celebrated. But there were definitely harms associated with not just Twitter, but with Facebook, Instagram, TikTok, and any other social media. Those sites all tended to breed isolation and loneliness, encouraged bullying, and fed bad self-image (especially among girls). One study defined social media as "collective traps."[1021] By 2009, kids were consuming ten hours of media per day, but that likely undercounted the total hours, as many "multitasked" by watching a television show while playing a video game.[1022] Although data varied (due to the nature of the collection), between 44 percent and 50 percent of kids told surveys that they were online constantly.

The health effects of social media were apparent not long after young people started getting cell phones from their parents. By 2016, boys' suicide rates had risen by 30 percent and girls' rates 300 percent. In a single year, 2017–2018, emergency room visits for suicidal ideation and/or self-directed harm rose by more than 25 percent, most of it from younger people.[1023] And the Kaspersky Lab survey of over 3,700 families with children eight to sixteen found that 51 percent of those kids in the fourteen to sixteen range hid their online activities from their parents. Worse, about 10 percent of youths deleted their browsing history after each session and double that used anonymous proxy tools to hide.

Jean Twenge, whose book *Generations* constituted the largest single synthesis of millions of surveys ever undertaken, concluded that behavior pathologies correlated strongly with the introduction of the iPhone around 2010. One would have to look far and wide to find a single technology that so negatively affected young people's mental health as much as the cell phone.

AI

Another old phenomena in a new package appeared to threaten the world of work, entertainment, social media, and even the very essence of personhood: AI (artificial intelligence). For business, this was a relatively new term for "robotics," which itself was a highfalutin word for machinery doing the work of people. For many, it was merely automation on steroids. In 2018, a report by Citibank said that 57 percent of jobs in the developed world could be "at risk" of automation (but national researchers in those countries slashed that number to only 14 percent).[1024]

No one doubts that, as they have for over two hundred years, businesses will continue to seek lower prices through the implementation of machinery—in this case, computerization. So far, however, the studies vastly inflated or misclassified the jobs that would be entirely taken over by computers that would, in turn, completely remove a human from the equation. AI, however, threatened much more than traditional job losses. Some ways to consider the impact of AI on humans were the following:

- AI will become Skynet. (In the movie Terminator, AI soon determined humans were the real threat to the world and terminator robots were sent to wipe them out after the AI-controlled Skynet system launched a nuclear war without human approval.)
- AI already is in control, à la The Matrix. In the cult movie The Matrix, the protagonist learns that humanity is already blindly under the control of the Matrix and human decisions don't matter—except for those of a handful of "red-pilled" heroes. For example, this study about ChatGPT says it rewires the brain.[1025] This AI defaulted to blackmail if told it would be removed.[1026]
- One aspect seldom discussed regarding AI is that it could become so self-aware as to know that (a) it isn't God and (b) it isn't and cannot become man, and therefore self-regulates or self-limits. If it's really smart, it could do that, right?
- Ultimately, what most people in business, economics, and sociology envision when they discuss AI is that it can never become "self-aware" and can only do what humans program it to do. It will be used to enhance human activities. Would the reader consider that a reasonable assessment?

A 2023 assessment found that the application of AI could raise American productivity growth by about a percent and a half, increase global GDP by up to $7 trillion, and significantly reverse America's economic downturn. And jobs? Those countries such as Japan, Taiwan, Korea, and China that have in recent years added newer and more computerized manufacturing and assembly plants have seen employment increase. No one whose job was improved through mechanization or computerization would necessarily see that job removed.[1027] Such was not the case in the United States. Meanwhile, those (such as Noah Smith) who argue that AI will produce new jobs, related jobs, and heretofore undiscovered jobs have history on their side with other technologies—but no actual AI-related evidence…so far.[1028]

One development that seems apparent is that AI is following traditional models so that means it is about to hit a "brick wall," a practical limit for its rapid pace.[1029] As of 2024, the costs to train the highest-producing model for AI—not counting a *wide* range of other costs, such as the number of people required, data gathering, learning examples, and others—has reached its practical peak. Or, as one analyst noted, "the industry is already reaching the limits for current hardware with dense models."[1030] To reach the next order of magnitude, scaling would require *hourly* costs of $30 billion. Moreover, others have warned that the very high-quality English language data would be exhausted in a few years.[1031]

As with any new technology, however, AI created unforeseen problems: a tension with "green" energy programs. Simply put, AI was an energy hog. Already by 2024 the US energy grid was taxed by "normal" growth: Adding AI demands would require the electrical grid to grow by several orders of magnitude—a task utterly impossible for green technologies and one setting the stage for a battle to revive nuclear energy programs.

For many, not only was AI inevitable but also highly desirable. By 2025 already an AI tool at Mayo Clinic identified nine dementia types, including Alzheimer's in a single scan.[1032] Certainly, the benefits seemed endless to many in the industry. Google CEO Sundar Pichai insisted "AI is probably the most important thing humanity has ever worked on. I think of it as something more profound than electricity or fire."[1033] The cofounder of Google's AI DeepMind echoed Pichai's sentiments: AI "is going to be the most important technology ever invented."[1034] And of course this embodied the view that it would be good for humanity: Robin Li, cofounder of the Chinese firm Baidu, said, "The intelligent revolution is a benign revolution in production and lifestyle and also a revolution in our way of thinking."[1035] Science fiction writer Ray Kurzweil predicted that AI programs would "surpass human capabilities" in such a way that they would "produce...superhuman capabilities or, more fancifully, that they will merge with humans to create superhumans."[1036]

Or not. In 2015, DeepMind's AI beat one of the two best Go players in the world, and the chess program AlphaZero came a year later—a program capable of defeating any human.

Although a great number of "techno-optimists," such as Noah Smith, maintain that AI will enhance productivity and advance the human condition, others expressed concern. The authors of *Power and Progress*, Daron Acemoglu and Simon Johnson, observed that "AI appears set on a trajectory that will multiply inequalities, not just in industrialized countries but everywhere around the world."[1037] It is, they noted, "stifling democracy and strengthening autocracy...[and] it is profoundly affecting the economy even as, on its current path, it is doing little to improve our productive capabilities." They referred to this as "a new vision oligarchy."[1038] That "new vision oligarchy" consisted of politicians, academicians, and intellectuals—"always at the table and always at the microphone."[1039]

The techno-optimists promised higher productivity with AI, that jobs would not be replaced but retrained and that ordinary people would feel its benefits. That hasn't worked out so far. Labor's share of manufacturing, where automation was highest and the creation of new tasks has been most noticeable, declined by about one-third since the 1980s.[1040] America's auto manufacturers oversaw a 25 percent decline in employment after robotics upgrading. American labor became viewed as something to be eliminated, not improved, retrained, and repositioned as in Germany. And while patents skyrocketed from 62,000 to 285,000, it failed to show up in productivity statistics. US growth since 1980 staggered along at a 0.7 percent rate, whereas if it had merely matched the pre-1980 levels, total factor productivity growth would have been over 2 percent. And that is still nothing to write home about.

How much of this is the kind of mismeasurement highlighted by Robert Gordon in his *The Rise and Fall of American* Growth, where he discovered that US economic growth from 1880 to the 1950s had significantly understated the real levels of economic expansion. Musk's Tesla car plant sought to automate almost every aspect of manufacturing. It didn't work. Musk admitted, "To be precise, my mistake. Humans are underrated."[1041] Yet it must be kept in mind that Gordon himself had dramatically revised *upward* all previous estimates of American economic growth from the 1800s through the mid-twentieth century. Therefore, his own claims that *current* productivity measures are moribund demand skepticism.

And for sheer totalitarian control, nothing is more terrifying than AI. China, which has already imposed a fledgling social credit system, has prevented defaulters from purchasing over twenty-seven million airplane tickets and six million train tickets just since 2019. As Acemoglu and Johnson point out, though, digital censorship has bumped up against some limits. Research into the Chinese Communists' "Great Firewall" against social posts found that most critical posts were not removed—only those highly regionalized that might spark a rebellion.[1042]

As AI has grown, so too has the surveillance capability of the government, and, as one writer noted, "China has a politically weaponized system of censorship" which is "refined, organized, coordinated and supported by the state's resources.... They have a powerful apparatus to construct a narrative and aim it at any target with a huge scale."[1043] And certainly access to foreign media by ordinary Chinese is non-existent. But perhaps the most shocking finding by researchers was that even without the state encouragement, most Chinese students had no interest in visiting foreign websites and did not want virtual private networks, also known as VPNs. Or, as Aldous Huxley had prophesied, banning books would not be necessary in a society in which no one would even want to read a banned book.

Meanwhile, in a development that surprised some, the internet usage appeared to be slowing down. From 2023 to 2024, the usage of apps such as Facebook, Instagram, Snapchat, and Twitter (X) all fell.[1044] Twitter, in particular, took a dive. However, not included in the analysis was the new Truth Social platform from Trump, which for many conservatives had entirely replaced Twitter.

What had not changed was the impact the internet seemed to have on teens, where loneliness rates soared, but other new forces tempered the public's fascination with the internet. For example, ads, which most sites needed to make money, quickly made surfing and visiting sites annoying and time consuming. Whenever sites added access fees to address the customer complaints about the ads, they got more—customer complaints. Google became the poster child for useless ad imposition on a reader. As techie Noah Smith observed, the challenge is "to craft a search query that avoids ad spam and gets you to the well-hidden information that you actually want."[1045]

Enter, again, AI, as the AI-powered Grok search engine vastly outperformed Yahoo, Google, or any other, yet without the ads. Once again—at least in theory—Americans had a "pure" search engine. Until it would be corrupted as well! It is important to remember that AI does not "think"; it "remixes" by reconfiguring old ideas in derivative ways. And that comes with its own dangers, in that if the existing "knowledge" is declining in quality, as we have seen with grotesquely erroneous medical "findings" or the "everybody knows" kinds of fallacies that led to the Russia Hoax, then merely reorganizing wrong answers, stories, "facts," or models will simply produce more corrupted data. And the output would certainly be unoriginal: Already, pop culture was awash in movie sequels, spinoffs, remakes, reboots, or expansions of an existing product. In other words, virtually 90 percent of the existing movies by 2020 were remakes.[1046] Of those movies, the top twenty accounted for 40 percent of all revenue. A similar pattern emerged from television, where by 2020 more than one-third of all shows were, as with movies, spinoffs or remakes. When it came to music, fewer and fewer artists made the top one hundred every year, declining by about 25 percent since 1970. But those fewer musicians accounted for more top one hundred songs than ever. The same trends occurred in publishing, where more and more books in the top ten each year—were written by an author who already had a book in the top ten![1047] So AI drew from an increasingly less inventive and innovative data pool. To make matters worse, that pool was corrupted by increasingly flawed and biased political infiltration.

Already, most platforms—especially Google—used their algorithms not just to spy but to subtly preach. Ask a question about President Trump's legal battles? Chances were that the first ten or more responses would be from left-leaning sites such as CNN, *Newsweek*, or the Associated Press. This quiet censorship or, more appropriately, thought control, extended into the comments sections of articles. In the infancy of the internet, one proven method of ensuring interactions was to allow readers to comment on the articles. But by the late 2010s, it had become clear that in many cases the majority (and occasionally a *big* majority) disagreed with the premises of the articles or their evidence. Well-written comments soon provided powerful alternative data to what was offered. It was a practice known as "ratioing," in which readers added critical comments and in which those criticisms by several orders of magnitude outnumbered the original comment. It didn't take long for individual writers, then entire publications, to shut off all comments. Even Noah Smith, who prided himself on being tech savvy, has banned commentators who disagree with him.

On Twitter, before it became X, the site was a free-for-all and (at first) so long as posters did not make personal threats or propose violence, they "tweeted" whatever they wished. But again, the problem of smart responses forced a policy whereby writers could limit who could comment on their posts. Twitter also had the "mute" button (which allowed people to comment, but whose comments the poster never saw) and the ever popular "block user" feature. The point was that even in highly controlled and monitored platforms, it grew increasingly difficult to silence majorities.

Nevertheless, "the algorithm monster" was impressive indeed. On most sites, algorithms cleverly steered you toward content the algorithms (i.e., the company) decided you needed to see. Or, instead of seeking information on the internet and communicating with others, a growing number of users battled a layer of ads and information, all the while directed in specific directions by a computer. It made using the internet a more passive experience. One of the fastest growing sites, TikTok, utilized short-form videos posted by creators. That, in turn, tacked well with the shorter attention spans of younger people.

While this is a history of the US, clearly what happened elsewhere was bound to bleed into American technological borders. Israel developed spyware called Pegasus that had up to fifty thousand phone numbers of journalists around the globe who reported on political repression. Pegasus was a "zero-click" software that was installed without the user's knowledge.[1048] Mexico likewise systematically used spyware on political opponents. But nothing compared to the horrific cooperation between Facebook and the Democratic Party in 2020 to stifle the campaign of Trump or the revelations that the NSA illegally spied on everyone from Trump and Senator Marco Rubio to millions of Americans...and not a single NSA official has been arrested, let alone jailed.

When Trump could not be denied the 2016 election, the so-called Deep State went to work fabricating the disinformation. As with any good magician, the purveyors of the Russia Hoax generated a smoke screen of "Russian disinformation." Without question, Russia, as well as China, Israel, Great Britain, and virtually every other modern nation, engaged in cyberwarfare. Most of it was common compared to what all the other nations used, and some was specifically directed at the US. Some was malicious, some bordered on genuine aggression, but nothing was new or limited to Russia alone.

Thus, the real "disinformation" came from trying to debunk the Russian (mostly real) claims, posts, videos, and other online stories. For example, the Russians correctly pointed out the impact of immigration. Leftists would say the Russians "misstated" the harms. But many well-sourced American groups would say they *understated* the harms and that it was the "mainstream media" (whose outright lies had gotten so outlandish that they deserved the term "hoax news") that was engaging in misinformation and disinformation. Whose information was real?

Whose was fake? Those seeking more control always sought to limit the outlets of their opponents, while those seeking to reduce levels of government control consistently attempted to open media access for all to judge for themselves.

Or consider China and its one-step-removed affiliate, TikTok. Virtually all anti-communist viewpoints on such things as Hong Kong, Tibet, or the Tiananmen Square massacre were met with muscular censorship.[1049]

There is no question AI permitted the creation of "deep fakes" or placing the faces of real people on other people's bodies or making them appear to engage in acts they did not do. Recorded fakes involved a Slovakian case where a candidate supposedly said he rigged an election.[1050]

Individual states have raced to roll out regulations, and of course the European Union passed an act to not only cover AI itself, but even testing and development.[1051]

An expanded World Wide Web also brought with it a barrage of hacks. In 2021, over 1,800 breaches occurred in the US, up by seven hundred from the previous year. They ranged from infantile and annoying to deadly serious. For example, in December 2022, hackers obtained contact information for more than eighty thousand members of the FBI's threat information sharing program InfraGard, then posted them for sale on a cybercrime forum.[1052] Six months later, Chinese hackers wormed their way inside the US outpost in Guam, and shortly thereafter, US federal agencies, including entities related to the Department of Energy, were breached by Russian hackers. Then in July, Chinese hackers breached the emails of several State Department and Commerce Department employees.[1053]

Attacks on the private sector were almost as frequent, if somewhat less reported: An Illinois hospital became the first health care facility to list a 2021 ransomware attack as a reason for closing. Hackers managed to get X/Twitter offline in the US, UK, and other countries, demanding that Musk, the owner of Twitter, open a Starlink internet satellite service in Sudan, and broke into Microsoft to steal emails from the company's senior leadership in January 2024. Three months later, Microsoft claimed a Russian hacker stole its source code and had access to its internal systems. But one outage, affecting 8.5 million machines in locations such as airlines and hospitals and costing over $5 billion, came from a faulty software update for Microsoft Windows by, of all things, cybersecurity firm CrowdStrike. (It should be recalled that CrowdStrike was deeply involved in the Russia Hoax aimed at President Trump in 2016.) Iranians were blamed for breaking into candidate Trump's presidential campaign system to steal documents, which it offered to the Biden-Harris campaign.

Reports from the Center for Strategic and International Studies, which tracked many—but certainly not all—of the cyber incidents—showed that the major culprits were overwhelmingly America's strategic rivals, including Iran, North Korea, Russia, and China. Incidents greatly ramped up after Russia invaded Ukraine in 2022, with cyberterrorism exploding both from Russia and Ukraine. Likewise, the ongoing virtual state of war between Israel and Iran (along with its proxies in terrorist groups Hamas and Hezbollah) had produced a high level of hacking between those nations.

To date, the largest corporate data breaches in the US included Yahoo (2013–16), which affected over three billion users by retrieving names, emails, and phone numbers; the aforementioned Microsoft breaches as well as an earlier one in 2021 that affected thirty thousand US companies; the Real Estate Wealth Network's leak of a billion and a half records in 2023; First American Financial Corporation's leak of 884 million files in 2019; and even Facebook, one of the world's largest web-based companies, which was struck in 2021 and saw names and passwords of over 530 million people pushed out to the public.[1054]

NO MAN HAS GONE BEFORE

Whatever the promise or threat of cyber intelligence, AI, facial recognition, and all the other digital breakthroughs, perhaps the most pivotal development of the first quarter of the twenty-first century occurred with relatively little public celebration. In the midst of the 2024 presidential campaign, the Boeing Starliner, a spacecraft designed to transport crew to the International Space Station (ISS) developed by Boeing and National Aeronautics and Space Administration (NASA), rocketed Butch Wilmore and Suni Williams to the ISS. Almost as if it were a sitcom like *Gilligan's Island*, an eight-day flight turned into months. Some of the Starliner's thrusters misfired, and the crew could not return. NASA, once the gem of the US government and once heralded as the epitome of federal efficiency, could not get them down. Instead, entrepreneur and overall big thinker Musk redesigned his SpaceX capsule with extra seats and in September docked with ISS and rescued the stranded duo.[1055] It constituted a profound shift in the attitude toward the functions and abilities of government versus the private sector. The Starliner itself, though subsidized by the government, represented a major departure from the decades-old monopoly that NASA had on space travel. Its failure to return the astronauts, only to be rescued by another private rocket service, constituted a breakthrough of immense proportions, akin to that of James J. Hill building transcontinental railroads in the 1800s without federal subsidies.

Musk truly was an Andrew Carnegie for the twenty-first century. Born in Pretoria, South Africa, in 1971 and heir to an emerald mine, Musk shared his father's opposition to apartheid.[1056] Attending various Pretoria schools, Musk was once severely beaten by other boys and hospitalized, after which his father berated him for an hour as worthless. "Adversity shaped me," he later recalled.[1057] Following a cousin to Canada, Musk worked at a farm, then a lumbermill, then entered Queen's University in Ontario before transferring to the University of Pennsylvania's Wharton School. There, he wrote a business plan for a Google Books–type electronic book scanning company.

Musk moved to Silicon Valley in 1994, holding internships where he worked on electrolytic ultracapacitors. A serial entrepreneur, he founded an internet mapping service called Zip2 in 1995. When that was purchased four years later, he founded X.com, a financial services company—essentially an online bank; then Confinity merged with X.com. Its PayPal money transfer service was superior to X.com and Musk soon found himself as CEO. During his stint there, he battled with another tech presence coming on the scene, Peter Thiel, and although Musk won the battle, he lost the war. After resigning, Thiel replaced him as CEO in 2000, and the company focused exclusively on PayPal.[1058]

He had already turned his attention as an investor to an electric vehicle company called Tesla, becoming the majority shareholder and chairman of the board in 2008.[1059] Envisioning the car as something exotic and desirable—instead of affordable and pedestrian—Musk turned out the Tesla Roadster that became a must-have item. (When he divorced his wife, she insisted on one as part of the package.) Tesla fought through numerous challenges, but eventually reached a price where middle-class families could afford it. By that time, the company's stock value had shot up tenfold over its trough of $25 in 2020, hitting $260 a share in 2021 and making Musk the richest man in the world, pushing him past Amazon's Jeff Bezos.

Once Musk had said that his life vision was to do things that would "truly affect humanity" and came up with "the internet, sustainable energy, and space travel."[1060] Already, Musk was gazing at the stars. He began to work with Russia in refurbishing intercontinental ballistic missiles for private space travel. That led him to the decision to build affordable (and reusable) rockets. Using $100 million of his own money, Musk founded SpaceX in May 2002. He said, "I wanted to hold out hope that humans could be a space-faring civilization and be out there among the stars.... And there was no chance of that unless a new company was started to create revolutionary rockets."[1061]

Anyone who had ever been involved in aviation—let alone space—knew what would come next: failure. His first rocket launch in 2006 did not reach orbit. Nor did the two subsequent launches. On the verge of bankruptcy, SpaceX achieved orbital launch with *Falcon 1* in 2008. To put that feat into perspective, Musk, with his own money, had achieved orbital launch in less time than had NASA with all the government's funding in the 1950s. He did so in part because he questioned every assumption. When an engineer said that something was "a requirement," Musk jumped in: Who said so? Who made it a requirement? An answer of "the military" or "the legal department" did not suffice.[1062] On one occasion he and his executives walked through a factory when they found a delay at a workstation where a robotic arm was sticking cells to a tube. It was having difficulty getting aligned. Musk's team did the job manually, then calculated how much time a human could do the job over the robot. The humans won, and Musk brought in people to replace the machines.[1063]

NASA, however, saw an opportunity and signed him up for a commercial resupply services contract for $1.6 billion later that year. SpaceX and the company's *Dragon* spacecraft, replacing the ancient space shuttle, would fly to the ISS. The *Dragon* proceeded to dock with the ISS in 2012.

Musk and Boeing weren't the only players seeking the title of "sachem of space." Billionaire Richard Branson threw his own helmet into the galaxy race when he created his own spacecraft, Virgin Galactic, whose maiden flight occurred in 2018. As with almost any revolutionary technology, Virgin Galactic encountered a setback in October 2014 when the VSS *Enterprise* crashed. In 2018, the project achieved suborbital flight, and in June 2023, it conducted the first ever commercial space tourism flight. Whereas Musk's SpaceX was a traditional rocket with a crew cabin—but one that had mastered reentry and vertical landing (something NASA had not done)—Virgin Galactic was a space plane that was launched by a rocket into sub-orbital space, but which landed like a standard aircraft.

SpaceX's success seemed to expose further the collapse of a major American aerospace brand, Boeing. It was already haunted by the major technological failures of its 737 MAX when two separate crashes in five months (Lion Air in 2018 and Ethiopian Airlines in March 2019) led to the groundings of the fleet and delayed the launch of its supercargo plane 777X until 2026. Meanwhile, Boeing announced it would lay off 10 percent of its workforce.[1064]

Yet in the opposite vein, SpaceX signaled a much broader shift in American business. No longer, it seemed, were companies willing to wait on Uncle Sam to provide needed infrastructure. In 2024, facing the limitations of a national electrical grid that the Biden administration had failed to build, major tech companies Amazon, Google, and Microsoft began buying small nuclear reactors to power their AIs. Not only did that constitute a reversal in direction from the expectation that the federal government would (or could) build a sufficient power grid for AI use, but it also quietly embodied a rejection of the entire green "energy transition" movement.[1065] Thus, in two extraordinarily significant areas, space travel and energy, the private sector had more or less given up on the government.

FROM OUTER SPACE TO TWITTER SPACE

During and after the 2020 election, in which major American (and foreign) so-called news organizations and social media outlets began overtly censoring speech that did not comport with an established central template, the unthinkable happened. Twitter (now X) banned Trump, who just weeks earlier was president of the US. On January 8, 2020, Twitter "permanently suspended" Trump's account due to the insane justification of "the risk of further incitement to violence."[1066]

By then it was well known that Facebook (Meta) for over two years had also engaged in throttling or banning critics of the China Virus vaccine.[1067] Later, in a mea culpa, Mark Zuckerberg, the CEO of Facebook, told podcast host Joe Rogan that Facebook's censorship was "something out of 1984" and that he felt intimidated by the Biden administration. People from the government would "call up the guys on our team and yell at them and cursing and threatening repercussions if we don't take down things that are true."[1068] Zuckerberg's caliginous motives came from a variety of directions, partly to suppress blame and portray himself as a helpless head of a social media company who was bullied by the government. No doubt he also feared government antitrust action, and in January 2025, agreed that Meta would pay President Trump $25 million for suspending his account. (Some $22 million was dedicated to Trump's presidential library.) He also, in the process, admitted that he bought into the fallacious notion that "misinformation spreading on social media swung the 2016 election to Donald Trump."[1069]

Musk, a much more libertarian-minded entrepreneur than Zuckerberg, had observed of the Twitter regime under Jack Dorsey, "What we have now is hidden disruption" and added "Free speech is essential to a functioning democracy." He asked Dorsey if Dorsey believed that Twitter was not free—a view shared by 70 percent of those polled by Twitter. Dorsey said it was. Musk replied he'd like to help and was invited to meet with Twitter officials who wanted to offer him a board seat.[1070]

Instead, what Musk got was an offer that would have limited his ability to make public comments about Twitter. He rejected it, then the board backed down and replied with a more typical board offer. After a month, and meeting with all the board members again, Musk was depressed by their lack of activism: "I began to believe that Twitter was heading off a cliff and that I couldn't save it by just being a board member." So he decided to buy it. In April 2022, he made a generous offer of over fifty-four dollars a share—so generous the Twitter board could not refuse it.[1071] Not long after the board accepted Musks's offer, he released about 75 percent of the staff, many of whom had participated willingly in banning or blocking conservative voices.

Musk then did something few, if any, of the twenty-first century barons would do: He invited in a journalist named Matt Taibbi to investigate Twitter from top to bottom and reports his findings to the public. Taibbi asked incredulously if Musk really wanted him to do a no-holds-barred investigation of Twitter. Indeed Musk did. Taibbi got complete access to interview employees and plow through Twitter's files, emails, or other messages without restrictions. What emerged was something astoundingly new in American business history: a full-disclosure report of what Twitter had done over the past six years. Known as the "Twitter Files," the breadth and depth of Taibbi's report—combined with the irrefutable evidence coming from Twitter's own materials—made it almost impossible for liberals to attack. An incredible compendium showed how Twitter rigged the Covid debate, uncovered Twitter's interaction with "Other Government Agencies," described state governments' censoring of "election misinformation" through the Twitter partner portal, and related how Twitter partnered with the Pentagon for a psyop. Additional files dealt with the removal of President Trump, Twitter's behavior as a subsidiary of the FBI, and Twitter's secret blacklists.[1072]

Taibbi's explosive revelations, combined with the growing pile of reports of Trump supporters or vaccine opponents being banned on Facebook, fed an exploding sense of betrayal of the public by both traditional and social media. After all, social media was touted as the open and honest alternative to the mainstream media's biases. Thus, Musk had not only reopened real, competitive space travel for Americans but had started the process of purging the digital tyranny that had stifled free speech.

While questions about Jeff Bezos's sincerity remain—he had acquired *The Washington Post* in 2013—he had already sensed that the newspaper's bias had reached catastrophic limits. When Trump won in his first campaign, the *Post* assigned over fifty (!!) reporters and staffers to dig up dirt on him full time. The paper affixed on its masthead the phrase, "Democracy Dies in Darkness," a startling and ridiculous line when considering the *Post* did all it could to spread darkness over the next eight years. Finally, in 2024, he'd had enough. Whether as purely a business maneuver or because he actually started reading his own paper, Bezos announced in October 2024 that he wanted more conservative opinion writers.[1073] After the 2024 election, Bezos visited president-elect Trump and contributed significantly to the inauguration festivities.

Born Jeffrey Jorgensen in Albuquerque, New Mexico, in 1964 to a Danish American unicyclist and a high school student (aged seventeen), Bezos was raised with his stepfather, Miguel Bezos. He grew up in

Houston, Texas, attended public schools, and then, after moving to Miami, Florida, he worked at a McDonald's.[1074] (Many American CEOs later in life reported they got their start at the fast food giant, including the CEO of Taylor Morrison, late night comedy host Jay Leno, George W. Bush's Chief of Staff Andrew Card, and Olympic sprinter champion Carl Lewis.) A national merit scholar, Bezos's valedictorian speech at his high school focused on colonizing space. He attended Princeton, where he majored in engineering and computer science.

Bezos got his feet wet at a number of firms, doing everything from customer service to banking, and was a senior vice president at one company by age thirty. In 1994, he became acutely aware of the internet. Though never involved in publishing, Bezos and his wife MacKenzie Scott founded what would become the world's largest book seller, Amazon.com. As did Steve Jobs and Steve Wozniak, Bezos worked out of his garage. Keen attention to business marked every step of the venture, right down to selecting the name Amazon because it began with "A" and would appear earlier in online searches. Yet Bezos knew his strategy was risky. He told investors they had a 70 percent chance that the company would fail, and that he wanted to, in the style of John D. Rockefeller, gain market share at the expense of early profitability. Hence for years market insiders questioned his vision.

Bezos, however, had tapped into a rapidly growing web-based market that quickly put brick-and-mortar competitors, such as B. Dalton and then Borders out of business. Like Musk, he faced several close calls—at the end of 2000, his cash balance stood at only $350 million.[1075] It stood to reason that since books were only the deliverable in Bezos's operation—but the method was the genius—he would soon move into non-book areas. Amazon then offered everything from lawn mowers to cosmetics, wax melts to socks. The company, just as Bezos had envisioned, finally hit critical mass and turned its first profit in history in 2004.[1076]

In 2008, Amazon began to move into direct competition with Hollywood with "Amazon Unbox," then changed to "Amazon Video on

Demand," and then finally, just "Amazon Prime Video," a streaming service. The company started original programming in 2017, and by 2025 offered a wide range of animation, thrillers, crime shows, documentaries, and dramas. Amazon Prime established itself as a legitimate alternative to the Hollywood studios. Already Bezos had snagged the formal designation as the wealthiest person in the world with a net worth of $112 billion, displacing Bill Gates.[1077]

Bezos had actually beaten Musk to the space race by founding Blue Origin, a human spaceflight startup in 2000. Then, he lagged behind, only purchasing land in Texas for a test facility and launch site in 2006. Not until 2015, long after Musk had been building and launching rockets, did Bezos develop a launch vehicle called *New Shepard*, which reached space and executed a vertical landing in Texas. Once again, he came in second as Richard Branson's Virgin Galactic Unity 22 mission carried six people (including Branson) into suborbital space.[1078] Bezos's Blue Origin NS-16 suborbital flight ascended nine days later.

A dizzying space competition of three billionaires had never been seen in history. Even at the peak of their power, the nineteenth century titans—John D. Rockefeller, Andrew Carnegie, James J. Hill, and Henry Clay Frick—never directly swerved into each other's lanes. Indeed, Frick jumped at the chance to work with Carnegie, becoming CEO (during the infamous Homestead strike).

The government had relinquished much of its role with the cancellation of the space program and the final shuttle mission in 2011. All along, the shuttles had proven inadequate to "routine space travel." To return from orbit and land like an airplane, they needed an armored suit of heat-resistant tiles, making them enormously heavy. Returning, however, constituted the relatively easy part. Getting a shuttle up demanded a logistics and launch footprint of titanic capacity, and each launch was treated as a holy miracle. (I once asked students what they noticed when a shuttle was launched. Among other things, they said big crowds. Everyone cheered. Some cried. Then I asked, "How many of you cheer or cry when your car starts?" Actually, every once in a while a hand went up, but I made the point: This was anything but "routine" space travel.) The trick was not *landing* like an airplane but *taking off like one*. From 1988–1995, the US Air Force and NASA worked on a then classified project called the X-30, which went by the somewhat unwieldy name of "NASP" for National Aero-Space Plane. Its approach was radical, much like that of Branson: fly into space without rockets.[1079]

NASP planned to use scramjet engines to achieve hypersonic velocity (3,500 miles per hour) through the atmosphere, long before most people had heard the term "hypersonic." Utilizing slush hydrogen fuel pumped through the entire aircraft—nose first—in order to cool it at incredible temperatures, the aircraft never got off the ground. Indeed, it never got off the computer. But elements of its manufacture and design, including the use of "computational fluid dynamics" or CFD; ultra-advanced, heat-resistant materials; and slush hydrogen, all were advanced forward, and when the program was killed in 1995, it was broken into other NASA/US Air Force programs that specialized in each.[1080]

When NASP shut its doors, the shuttle missions—by then accepted as impractical for real space travel—continued as if by momentum. However, in 1996, the government (largely at the insistence of many of the X-30 leadership) created a prize modeled on the Orteig Prize in 1919: $25,000 offered by hotel owner Raymond Orteig for the first air flight across the Atlantic. Charles Lindbergh won the prize in 1927. A new motivational prize, from entrepreneurs Anousheh Ansari and Amir Ansari, of $10 million was established in 1996: the Ansari Prize or more commonly, the "X Prize." (Musk would have loved that name).

In 2004, pilot Burt Rutan—who had designed the *Voyager*, which, in 1986, was the first plane to fly around the world without refueling, and then the Virgin Atlantic *GlobalFlyer*, which in 2006 flew the globe at the fastest speed without refueling (sixty-seven hours)—took to space. Fueled as it were with funding from Microsoft cofounder Paul Allen, Rutan's *SpaceShipOne* reached suborbital space, thus grasping the X Prize.[1081] Rutan's achievement did not start private space initiatives, but it turned on the money spigots. At least twenty-six teams commenced work on various space-related projects.

Unlike the X-30, *SpaceShipOne*'s design (a mother ship that toted the space aircraft to an air launch position) had the objective of obtaining "single stage to orbit," meaning that like a "jet rocket," it would propel itself into orbit from a standard runway. Rutan's design could land like a traditional jet but still needed the extra boost vehicle to obtain orbit. When Rutan achieved his suborbital flight, he held up a sign that said "SpaceShipOne, GovernmentZero."[1082] The "big two," however—Musk and Bezos—weren't interested in suborbital anything. They wanted the moon and beyond, and by 2024 both men laid plans for lunar missions.

SPY IN THE SKY

When the Deep State spied on Trump in the 2016 election and beyond, evidence surfaced that the National Security Agency had engaged in illegal surveillance of many Americans, including US senators such as Marco Rubio. Nevertheless, the threat of another 9/11 or of Iranian terrorists provided enough constant pressure that Congress (even in Republican hands) continued to reauthorize the FISA courts, which repeatedly approved the snooping even after grotesque abuses were revealed to its members—and even when they were victims themselves!

In 2014, Democratic Senator Dianne Feinstein of California publicly accused the CIA of secretly removing documents from the Senate Intelligence Committee and of searching computers used by the committee. Moreover, she said, the CIA had attempted to intimidate congressional investigators. Then-CIA director John Brennan insisted that the CIA had not snooped on the committee.[1083] After the CIA's inspector general conducted an investigation, he concluded the agency had "improperly" accessed Senate computers. Brennan was forced to apologize for the actions listed in the report.

That, however, begged some even larger questions. Following Inspector General Michael Horowitz's review of the FBI in the Trump spying cases, it was clear that the inspectors general hardly were harsh critics of procedures. (Horowitz did not refer a single agent who broke the law for criminal charges.) Moreover, what the public was allowed to see as "actions by CIA officers *as described in the OIG [Office of Inspector General] Report* [emphasis mine]" were the tip of the iceberg of agency infractions, crimes, and cover-ups.[1084] Nothing more than the apology occurred within the CIA.

In 2022, following more revelations of spying on the Trump team, Senators Ron Wyden and Martin Heinrich alleged that the CIA was again conducting warrantless surveillance through a "newly disclosed programme."[1085] Prism, the spy program, was ruled illegal by a court and was disclosed by Edward Snowden, an NSA-contracted whistle blower. He found that 90 percent of those who were monitored were American citizens, which constituted a clear breach of the CIA's charter. Snowden sent his information to the UK *Guardian*, which published the court order instructing the Verizon telephone company to hand over all telephone data to the NSA on an "ongoing daily basis."[1086] Snowden's materials also showed that the NSA had tapped into the servers of nine internet firms, including Yahoo, Google, Microsoft, and Facebook.

Initially, Snowden tried to raise his concerns to his superiors, but they ignored him. He wisely flew to Hong Kong before releasing the classified documents to select journalists, who them published them in the British paper and *The Washington Post*. Snowden was charged by the Department of Justice in 2013 and fled to Russia, which recognized his revoked passport and gave him both asylum and citizenship. Meanwhile, hiding behind its "sources and methods," the CIA provided one report to the senators, but refused to provide a second.

But the NSA didn't stop its spying on Americans. A surveillance program that was spying on America's allies, including Israel and Great Britain, scooped up intelligence on US citizens, collecting phone records on 151 million Americans.[1087] Instead, unrepentant, the NSA tripled its collection of US phone records by 2018.[1088] And, as noted before, the

FBI engaged in spying on then-candidate Trump using warrants that lacked probable cause.[1089]

A possibly greater concern involved the all-encompassing "data mining" of Americans through their purchases, credit card accounts, and even their listening habits. Any Facebook user knows that video "reels" are all expressly tailored to the user's favorite sports, movies, comedians, and so on.

Interacting on social media, a relatively harmless and unimportant pastime, constituted a testing-the-waters phase for a new, cosmically deeper use of personal information. Driverless cars, next on the agenda for the "edge of tomorrow" afficionados, presented their own spying and consumer behavior modification problems. For example, the mere path an "autonomous" vehicle takes can be programmed based on the data mining of the occupant: it would pass, on a consistent basis, restaurants, retail stores, health clubs, and so on that are subconsciously marketed to the rider. Professor Frank Pasquale expanded upon this "platform capitalism" model in which Americans' movement through space and consumption patterns have become data to be collected and managed by companies. Is "Big Brother" any different from "Big Data" or "Big Google"? All is vacuumed up in "collection," while responsibility for errors remains all but impossible. Put another way, a faceless programmer in a gigantic company writes an algorithm that was supposedly rationally arrived at, with extremely profound consequences on our lives, yet they have no accountability at all to *us*. We don't even see his logic. At least a judge (supposedly) researches the law and provides a "decision" featuring his logic.

Big Data's snooping, whether conducted by for-profit companies or (in theory) "public" agencies, has spread far wider and deeper than most people even dream. In New York City, a Wi-Fi surveillance network of cameras covered virtually everything that happens along a 2.2 mile stretch that is used by 2.7 million people, few of whom ever think about the fact that they are recorded constantly on camera. (Just consider any modern detective novel, where, say, Detective Harry Bosch immediately asks at the crime scene, "Are there any cameras?") Pittsburgh's driverless Ubers don't just ferry people from one spot to the next: The city asked if they could transmit information to "assist" the city in managing its affairs. Publicly, so far, Uber refused to share its data, which the city manager referred to as an "opportunity missed," presumably meaning an opportunity to spy on Pittsburghers.[1090]

Then there were traffic radars that exposed everyone to Big Brother's eye. In 2016, the District of Columbia—one of the biggest violators of personal freedom—raked in over $107 million in photo radar enforcement fines.[1091] When combined with red light cameras and parking tickets, DC collected an astonishing $193 million from drivers. Little did drivers notice that the city had shaved seconds off the yellow lights, making them among the shortest in the nation.[1092] Since most DC drivers came from Maryland or Virginia, the practices lent high irony to the district's current license plates, "End Taxation Without Representation."

Traffic laws, in fact, seemed designed to enhance Big Brother–like tendencies. Engineers from the Federal Highway Administration found that current speed limits "are set too low to be accepted as reasonable by the vast majority of drivers."[1093] Even the Federal Highway Administration itself concluded that raising the speed limit on open highways by fifteen miles per hour, to a speed that 85 percent of the people drove anyway, would then have the total increase in speeds to only one to two miles per hour.[1094] Put another way, the government deliberately set speed limits artificially low for revenue, making a mockery of America's common law tradition where by and large people "know best."

Google made the company's intent clear when founders Larry Page and Sergey Brin said their goal was "getting you exactly what you want, even when you aren't sure what you need."[1095] As car enthusiast Michael Crawford explained it, Google wanted to create a situation where "we will integrate Google's services into our lives so effortlessly, and the guiding presence of this beneficent entity in our lives will be so persuasive and unobtrusive, that *the boundary between self and Google will blur*."[1096] Imagine if "Google" was replaced with "government."

Driverless cars may be an early element, but only one of American surveillance capitalism as Shoshana Zuboff called it. She defined surveillance capitalism as a "new economic order" that "claims human experience as free raw material for hidden commercial practices of extraction, prediction, and sales."[1097] It constituted a "new global architecture of behavioral modification" and sought to "impose a new collective order based on *total certainty* [emphasis mine]."[1098] As discussed in other chapters, "total certainty" was largely a product of fear—the notion that we must avoid pain or hardship in every way, thus all risk must be minimized or even exterminated. That, of course, was the rationale behind the vaccine—that even people who had natural immunity to Covid needed to get the vaccine so that not one other person could catch it. It "claims human experience as free raw material for translation into behavioral data...[fed] into *prediction products* that anticipate what you will do now, soon, and later."[1099]

Not only can surveillance capitalists collect and store private information, but they could also trade it, creating what Zuboff called "behavioral futures markets." Corporations no longer wanted to automate information flows about us, but to automate us.[1100] On the businesses' part, that development was entirely predictable: Anything that could increase certainty, thereby reducing risk, had characterized all major businesses since the "managerial revolution" in the late 1800s. Marketing and advertising, of course, developed entirely around the idea that people have unexpressed desires, and the ad firm can reveal those to you.

In the early 2000s, Google, which nearly ran out of money, stumbled upon this concept by insisting that it, not the advertisers or the users, define search terms. But our "Brave New Digital World" now empowered companies to target individual customers not just on previous purchases, age, or race, but on specific locations while engaged in specific activities and in specific emotional states of mind. We have leaped into the "convince" someone phase almost to the "control" phase. And Google, which led in this arena, soon found itself joined by Amazon,

Apple, and other tech behemoths. Americans increasingly—and without their knowledge or awareness—became the raw materials for the system.

Worse, in previous eras where, with the proper safety clearance, people could visit Andrew Carnegie's steel mill or Henry Ford's auto assembly line, no one had any access to the hidden and mysterious algorithms that shaped and controlled people. In an ironic and mesmerizing way, the "forgotten man" of William Graham Sumner—meaning forgotten by the government—produced a moment when Spaniards actually sued for the right to *be forgotten*. In other words, did people have the right to anonymity?

More transformations swirled around surveillance capitalism. As always, it started innocently, with Apple's iPod. That device, which digitized music, allowed consumers to eliminate (except for the iPod itself) any physical representation of the music itself—packaging, cover art, and discs. iPods also temporarily made consumers king: They could rearrange and restructure their own "albums" or playlists, and no two were ever alike. It constituted a 180-degree reversal of the Ford Model T, where all were alike. Think of the Model T as an elevator that lifted all buyers up to a consumer floor that everyone shared; think of the iPod as a million different staircases leading upward off that floor. People often shared the same "steps" (i.e., songs) but never the same journey. Yet even Ford didn't hold that social position long. As within a decade, General Motors already had introduced different "stairsteps" of its own.

A new feedback loop emerged, however. In order to provide consumers with more products, information, or entertainment *specifically tailored to them*, the more information that corporations needed to suck up; then, in order to ensure that, in fact, they were sweeping up information specific to an individual, they had to *exclude other individuals*, meaning that individual data had to be collated and contrasted. A massive database, with the collapse of the individuality that was originally targeted, emerged. No company could resist getting access to that database for more defined sales.

That returned control to the consumer, for in order to ensure that everyone had the most risk-free experience, perpetual updates were required. Then, as occurred with Apple's iTunes itself, it became imperative to update the applications—and failure to update would cause it not to work at all! Each new iteration was no longer an option, but a mandate.

Yet that's hardly the worst of it. Corporations (for the most part) engage in such activities because they seek to make a profit. Governments—if they are successful in co-opting Google, Yahoo, Amazon, or any other number of product or service providers—in the name of offering "convenience," instead risk falling entirely to the temptation of deciding to co-opt your thermostat because it knows what's "best for you" or for the planet.

Common to all of these developments, a growing separation from both the law and from what constitutes individual autonomy has created a supreme crisis. Those most suspicious of "surveillance capitalism" have sought more regulation: "Old institutions like the law...aren't keeping up with the rate of change that we've caused through technology," argued Google's CEO Larry Page.[1101] Yet that has always been the case and never been the case. While interpretations and specific rulings about the law hardly ever keep pace with technological change (think about the first traffic regulations, which came about long after cars appeared), the *principles,* especially of the Constitution, are always evergreen. A bigger concern than the law not "keeping up" is that the tech giants capture the regulatory state to allow their activities. Once again, the problem isn't too little government but too much.

To avoid such regulation, the surveillance capitalists sought to make themselves available to the Deep State to run its nefarious mercenary spy operations for them. That created a system of exceptions to normal regulation, even to the point that Google and others infringed on private data and information repeatedly in the service of the government. It became both unwise and impossible to regulate Google for doing the work the feds did not want to do, at least not publicly.

Meanwhile, the battle was joined from the other side, namely consumers (especially celebrities) whose images and voices were at risk of being replace by AI. Nothing better encapsulates the "right to life" than the very conception of the specific, individualized traits of a person. Hollywood has found itself in the vanguard of this fight for the rights to one's own image, writing, and voice. It took a 148-day strike for Hollywood's screenwriters to achieve some barriers to AI-originated screenplays.[1102] Actress Scarlett Johansson forced AI chatbot ChatGPT to withdraw use of a "voice" after she declined to sell her voice for a project.[1103] Already AI could regenerate images of any actor or actress, buffed up, slimmed down, and without a single freckle or pimple. The last episodes of the Star Wars series used an CGI version of Grand Moff Tarkin, played by the deceased actor Peter Cushing. Several singers have sung "duets" with other stars who have passed away (such as Natalie Cole with her deceased father, Nat King Cole). The Las Vegas show *Michael Jackson ONE* used a Michael Jackson hologram, as does the Ronald Reagan Presidential Library with its introductory speech by "the Gipper."

Digital behavior modification posed enough threats by itself. However, a new wave of chemical and pharmaceutical behavior modification had also appeared. Known as "neuromodulation," or altering the brain's electrical circuits, these drugs, according to one writer had the "potential to be a delicate scalpel."[1104] Drugs such as Ozempic fooled the brain into suppressing appetite and showed positive results initially, until a raft of side effects were announced. More drastic neuromodulation has come in the form of implants into the human brain. Once again, Musk stood at the forefront with his Neuralink, a brain device that allowed quadriplegics to operate computers with their brain.[1105]

Yet it was ironic that perhaps the best behavior modification that anyone could achieve involved less interaction with the digital world. Several studies have shown that heavy social media use led to feelings of despair and impending doom. One, in particular, cited Twitter.[1106] Another study of Iranians and Americans found that "doomscrolling," or prolonged exposure to negative news (which was to say, news), evoked anxiety and fostered pessimism about human nature.[1107] Another article confirmed the old saw, "If it bleeds, it leads": Each added negative word in a headline increased the click-through rate by 2.3 percent, while each positive word decreased the rate by 1 percent.[1108] Thus an ironic circle emerged: As people ate more because they were depressed, the fatter they got and the less they could engage in outdoor activities, so then non-sedentary activities such as reading phones and computer screens increased—which made them more depressed.

DIRECTIONLESS

Surveillance of consumers, stealth marketing plans to sell to them, and chemical or digital behavior modification not only was considered unsurprising but was also accepted by corporate America as the natural next step in the evolution of the managerial hierarchies. Another troubling element, however, overlaid that "natural" evolution. Traditional politics in the US since the 1990s—but then accelerating rapidly under Obama—had departed from traditional "left/right" or even "conservative/liberal" moorings. Much of that came by design with the long march of the so-called Frankfurt School of communism, which constituted a Maoist, decades-long burrowing in of virtually every aspect of American life. That included, obviously, entertainment and the universities but also, to the surprise of some, the corporate structure as well. While everyone debated the impact of AI on capabilities, few bothered to delve into the ideological damage an unleashed AI might cause.

America's corporate structure since the 1950s, as noted in chapter three, had steadily seen entrepreneurs and founders (outside of some Silicon Valley firms, which, for their own idiosyncrasies, ended up in the same place) cede operational control to CEOs from a finance background. Or, to reiterate a major theme from that chapter, the "finance men" (think Robert McNamara) replaced the "production men" (think Henry Ford). No question that many of the latter could be quirky, ungenerous, occasionally racist or anti-Semitic, and often "class" directed. At the same time, most did what no one else could: build remarkable products with almost no help from the government.

Beginning with the so-called climate change movement in the 1990s, however, US corporations increasingly found themselves pummeled by the left to "think globally," which was a euphemism for the one-world government control of business. With racism largely defeated, however, the left needed another wedge issue with which they could charge conservatives as bigots. That issue was homosexual marriage, which the Supreme Court upheld in the *Obergefell v. Hodges* decision in 2015. Many (including this writer) warned that the decision would open the door to polygamy. In fact, the left blew right past polygamy and went immediately to transsexualism and sex change "rights." Somehow, the philosophical and legal leap went from "homosexuals have the right to marry" to "people shouldn't be governed by their DNA or blood, but rather by their preferences."

Rhetoric and attitudes surrounding all of these issues—sexuality, climate control, and so-called white privilege—congealed into a single rubric of "woke." In 2016, Obama's Justice Department attacked North Carolina, which had passed a law requiring people to use bathrooms based on their sex when born. "Wokesters" went into action, launching a boycott by the National Basketball Association, the National Collegiate Athletic Association, and many other corporations. Then and only then did it become clear to many "normies" (as ordinary, nonconfrontational people were labeled) how deep the woke movement went.

How did it get so far, particularly among America's corporate leaders who (in theory) should have been concerned with profits and therefore should have stayed out of divisive political battles? As Michael Lind explained, "In isolation, the transgender controversy might have been viewed as a strange aftershock of the gay rights movement, which had achieved its more moderate goals of civil and marriage equality."[1109] In fact, transgender ideology was imposed through economic compulsion and by the federal government, joined by CRT (critical race theory) and DEI (diversity, equity, and inclusion), to form a collective hive of nonexistent oppressions. That had been the ultimate objective of the Frankfurt School: destroy American capitalist society from within.

Not only did universities have to comply by hiring incapable and incompetent teachers solely based on a criterion of sex or race, but so did banks, corporations, government agencies, and even the military. Almost without a debate, major corporations flew the rainbow flag of homosexual rights, posted the Black Lives Matter logos and (of course) donated heavily to the organization, and above all enthusiastically jumped onto the "climate change" bandwagon. How did that happen?

When CEOs increasingly came from ranks of the "finance men," they not only separated themselves from their products but also their customers. Few "finance men" even knew the basics of how their products were made or sold; almost none had ever worked a line. It was thus a sad commentary that when candidate and former president Donald Trump donned the McDonald's apron to deliver food at the drive through window, he was doing what many company executives had never done—interacting directly with customers. Increasingly, the new CEOs found themselves under the influence, and even control, of human resources (HR) and marketing departments. Armed with layers of data that most CEOs never see and possessed of "new woke" as well as DEI imperatives to hire and advertise in certain ways, the HR and marketing departments had newfound power they had never experienced in previous iterations of the corporation. HR could apply DEI at almost every level short of the boardroom—and then use shame and embarrassment to even shape that. CEOs proved wobbly if not spineless against the slightest charge of racism or "homophobia." It seemed (for a moment) to make sense to acquiesce to calls for support of marketing campaigns that supported "Pride week" or utilized androgynous celebrities.

These new gatekeepers, giddy with their power, took on the characteristics of Protestant evangelists, except that those missionaries sought "voluntary and whole-hearted conversion [whereas] the new activists seek submission, imposed on penalty of ostracism."[1110] Woke's earlier iteration, "political correctness," died and became the object of ridicule and derision. Instead, a new wave of censorship swept over America (and much of the world). [1111]

What changed with woke? Lind noted that the three gateways of college education, professional accreditation, and commercial online service platforms such as PayPal, Amazon, and Twitter all used a newfound power of exclusion to achieve success. Such exclusion constituted more than keeping someone out of an online "club." It entailed de-banking people or groups for even having the word "patriot" in their name. Credentialism in corporations thus landed in human resources; in law, it landed in the bar association; in medicine, certifying boards, and so on.

A shocking example of the near-totalitarian control of woke credentialism came in two 2020 events. First, with the China Virus, doctors who resisted the "official" and "correct" responses to Covid found themselves denied medical licenses in short order. Needless to say, "acceptable" government authorities, including Dr. Anthony Fauci and members of the World Health Organization, National Institute of Allergy and Infectious Diseases, and Centers for Disease Control and Prevention established what would and would not be tolerated as acceptable treatment protocols. When the vaccine was available, questioning any of the various Covid vaccines was not permitted. To ensure that the information all remained on the "right side," the government and its pro-vaccine "vaxiopaths" completely ignored a long-standing indicator of treatment red flags—the Vaccine Adverse Event Reporting System, or VAERS, reports. Indeed, only later was it learned that government disinformation about the China Virus made it worse.[1112] Researchers found "government-sponsored disinformation was positively associated with the incidence of COVID-19." Disinformation—lying—by government health authorities had become so recognized that by April 22, 76 percent of unvaccinated adults said they would never take a China Virus vaccine.

Then came the false reports about the integrity of the election. Suddenly, the political and the scientific met in the boardroom of government and media disinformation. When Trump challenged the election fraud that seemingly afflicted the 2020 election, lawyers who argued his cases ended up disbarred. Again, "the gatekeepers" were hard at work. Without realizing it, however, they had transferred skepticism over an area where Americans had still maintained fairly high levels of trust—the medical profession—into the political realm. People made the connection: "If they lied about the vaccine and the China Virus, why wouldn't they lie about elections?"

Woke may have been "a vanguard movement that seized control of a new technology and used it as a force multiplier to discipline and terrorize," but it would have had minimum impact had the educational and credential gatekeepers not aided and abetted their crimes.[1113] America's growing consolidation and combination of key sectors, such as social media, meant that search engines such as Google and Yahoo or social media platforms such as Twitter or Facebook could and did "deplatform" people who had joined the "new economy" by marketing online. It constituted a removal from the public realm reminiscent of anti-Jewish laws in medieval Europe. The US government enhanced those gatekeeper positions by exempting them from regulation. And boards, such as Facebook's, include officers of the so-called libertarian think tank, the Cato Institute, which is funded by corporations to justify despotic power grabs in the name of liberty.

Providing a steady stream of indoctrinated employees to the modern woke corporation, universities enforced their own rigid discipline on anyone foolish enough to dissent. No better example could be found than that of the Duke lacrosse team. In 2006, members of the Duke University lacrosse team were falsely accused of rape by a professional hoaxer and stripper, Crystal Mangum. She accused three team members of rape. Without waiting for the slightest actual evidence to be presented, Duke faculty known as the "Group of 88" submitted an ad to the Duke *Chronicle* called "What Does a Social Disaster Sound Like?"[1114]

The scandal provided a perfect window into the intersection between woke universities, woke law, and woke media. Initially, the template was that a group of rich, white boys raped a black dancer at a party, and racial justice would be imposed by radical woke Durham County prosecutor,

Mike Nifong. Seeing faculty and a university administration leap to accuse white players surprised no one, but possibly for the first time in the history of woke actions, a prosecutor disregarded all evidence and lied about sharing DNA tests, which showed no evidence from any of the Duke students. Meanwhile, the entire Durham Police Department violated its own policies to go along with the hoax.

It took the mothers of the accused to unite and launch a civil lawsuit against Duke, which paid out $20 million to each claimant, and they also sued the City of Durham and the police department. Nifong resigned in disgrace. However, no charges for defamation were brought, nor any penalties levied, against the racially motivated woke faculty who signed the letter. Lessons took some time to learn, however.

In 2019, a group of young people from Covington Catholic High School in Kentucky participated in the March for Life rally in Washington, DC, when one of the students, Nicholas Sandmann, was approached aggressively by an American Indian literally beating a drum in his face. Sandmann stood his ground and did nothing but smile. The so-called mainstream news (labeled in the 1990s by Rush Limbaugh as the "drive-by media" for their nanosecond attention to a crisis) by that time was in full woke mode, and they labeled Sandmann's smile a "smirk," accused him of being an "entitled brat," and otherwise defamed the students. As *Reason* magazine put it, the "media's reckless mishandling of the story" stood as a warning against the ideological cancel culture.[1115] Outlets such as CNN claimed that Sandmann and his fellow students engaged in "blocking" and "harassing" the activist, and Sandmann sued CNN for $275 million. CNN settled for an undisclosed amount.[1116] Major outlets, such as the *Detroit Free Press*, simply lied about the events, claiming Nathan Phillips—the American Indian banging his drum—was "peacefully drumming and singing," when in fact he was aggressively challenging the kids.[1117] Leftist voices from *Vox* to NBC News all the way to so-called comedians slandered the Covington boys. In the end, $275 million would have been appropriate if *every single outlet and commentator* who defamed the boys had been forced to pay.

Even if Sandmann and the Duke players had received actual settlements anywhere near what they had asked for, the major media outlets paid such large settlements out of their insurance. Then, if more remained to be covered, their corporate owners and sponsors—Time Warner, General Electric, Microsoft, and so on—made up the difference. For them, it was about getting the proper woke story out, not about profits from their media arm. However, what Trump's DOGE proved in the US Agency for International Development (USAID) revelations was that even some of the better-heeled organizations derived a lot of their revenue from USAID, including *Politico* and *The Washington Post*. (Even George Soros didn't spend his own money when he could siphon funds from USAID—using the taxpayers' own money against them.) When USAID closed up shop, as well as many other liberal funding troughs, suddenly the woke media took steps to regain customers. Facebook's head honcho, Mark Zuckerberg, met with President Trump to grovel and then enact several policies to enhance "conservative voices. In one of the few settlements where a public dollar figure was released, Facebook/Meta agreed to pay Trump $25 million to settle the lawsuit over the suspension of his Facebook account in the 2020 aftermath.[1118] Already ABC had settled a defamation suit for $15 million with Trump for a segment in which an anchor said he "raped" E. Jean Carroll.[1119]

Cumulatively, especially without a stealth USAID gravy train to backstop losses, the woke media suddenly confronted the realities of alienating half the American viewers. In January 2023, CNN's new chief Mark Thompson promised to reinvent the sagging network by remaking the work force, while *The Washington Post's* owner Jeff Bezos said he wanted more conservative voices at his newspaper and sacked several of the unpopular and seldom-read liberal hacks.[1120] By 2025, Warner Bros. Discovery had decided to split off CNN and other divisions from the Warner Bros. label itself.

Regardless, two major problems confronted any moves to the political middle by corporate media. First, once virtue is gone, it's nearly impossible to restore. Readers and viewers had abandoned the mainstream media after its horrid anti-Trump performance in 2016. Even Fox News, considered a "conservative site," lost nearly one-third of its viewers permanently—and half immediately—after it parted ways with its number one journalist Tucker Carlson.[1121] The company also lost $800 million in market share. Carlson's departure marked another critical challenge for the old establishment newspapers and cable television news: younger people absorbed most of their news from podcasts and blogs. Only the oldest cohorts stayed with CBS and Fox.

For almost a decade, Andrew Breitbart's maxim that "politics is downstream of culture" had remained sacrosanct. However, in the latter part of the twenty-tens, a new maxim seemed to be taking hold, namely that "culture is downstream of economics," meaning that finally CEOs and other gatekeepers had to pay attention to a bottom line. As early as 2024, companies began backing away from DEI as "ineffective corporate window dressing."[1122]

Multiple factors had led to a public distaste for "big business," including wokeness, DEI, responses to the Covid virus, and reports of snooping. On top of that, much damage had been done to America's economy since 2000. Bill Clinton had the wisdom not to tinker with the Reagan-era tax cuts, and the absence of any large-scale wars kept optimism high. Clinton finished with the last balanced budget since the year 2000.

Ongoing structural change in business had removed innovators and founders from the driver's seat in most corporations, leading to managers running the companies. They, in turn, largely unwittingly turned that same control over to marketing and HR departments. A few spots seemed to be impervious to the larger trends, including Silicon Valley, which had provided a dividend of sorts until Taiwan, China, and Japan caught up. Then some of that edge disappeared.

Government funding of electric vehicles and a temporary burst of chip investment suggested a factory boom was underway after 2022.[1123] However, electric vehicles could not survive forever on subsidies, and many of the factories built with government cash vanished when the companies went bankrupt.[1124] Stellantis, which closed an electric vehicle factory, only reopened it when Trump won.[1125] Trump made it clear the "green transition" had ended and the subsidy gravy train was pulling into the station.

Stagnation in productivity growth set in. As Biden increasingly attempted to direct American investment and production, America's productivity bogged down. (It did rise in the service sector—cooks, drivers, cleaners, and so on.)[1126] America's main opponent—or, more appropriately, enemy—China had gone on a production rampage (which greatly accelerated its steel industry) that saw "ghost cities" built, the Chinese military (especially navy) expanded, and an electric car industry started. Reports out of China always contained levels of padding and fraud, and as such, they showed mixed results. The best that could be said was that China definitely had expanded rapidly, that its expansion had slowed down equally rapidly, that its real estate sector faced a massive collapse, and that under the correct pressure, American firms might start removing themselves from the Chinese market. Economically, then, the old adage applied to Russia was appropriate: "China is never as weak as she looks. China is never as strong as she looks." Most of America's issues with Chinese competition could be remedied by implementing tariffs, reshoring incentives, and creating reliance on the US's number one advantage: its unmatched energy production capabilities.

Trump rejected the entire "degrowth" notion embraced by many of the Europeans. He knew it not only would not be tolerated in the US by citizens but that for it to "work" (which it would not), developing countries would have to stay poor. Nevertheless, Europe, to a large degree, had committed itself well down the degrowth road, creating an almost clownish situation where they refused to develop or supply their own energy while increasing their imports from the US—all at the same time criticizing America for not following their model![1127]

Europe's slow retreat constituted just more evidence that the era of Bretton Woods had ended and the world economic order was changing rapidly.[1128] Globalism, as many called it, had collapsed of its own weight. Financial and human pressures from wars in Afghanistan, Iraq, and elsewhere in the Middle East had soured the American public on the Bretton Woods model where the US stood as the world's policeman. Across the free world, citizens had rejected globalist programs in elections—Italy, El Salvador, Hungary, Slovakia, Portugal, Argentina, and, of course, America. When delegates met in Davos, Switzerland, at the World Economic Forum in 2024, few of the world's leaders even showed up. President of Argentia Javier Milei did, only to lecture the globalists on their failing policies! Indeed, the World Economic Forum itself knew its time was short: Its theme was "Restoring Trust."[1129]

America, nevertheless, faced some issues outside of the control of any politician, suggesting that austerity was unavoidable, particularly because the cost of borrowing was set to rise.[1130] Trump's radical programs of slashing waste and finding more assets to flow into America upset that analysis. By early 2025, many were wondering if Musk's Department of Government Efficiency (DOGE) could shave trillions of dollars off the national debt, and already Trump had brought in over $1 trillion in new investments. A look at Argentina, which had instituted a very DOGE-ian approach in 2023 when its new President Javier Milei began chopping down the size of that country's government, saw the country get its first balanced budget in years and witnessed inflation collapse there. A similar outcome could be predicted in the far wealthier US.

Biden had presided over falling wages in 2021 and 2022 and had used statistical chicanery to show improved employment. That, in part, resulted in Trump's 2024 victory. And while there was no question that, like Ronald Reagan in 1981, Donald Trump's economic plan would work, it also would take at least a few months to produce results.[1131] For one thing, the massive number of federal employees fired, which likely would end up in the hundreds of thousands, would jar the unemployment rate and produce serious—but temporary—dislocations. For another, the benefit of massively lower government spending would take a while to percolate into the financial markets and lower interest rates. Near-term results, however, were on the horizon for energy prices, which looked to fall dramatically, bringing other prices with them. Trump's tariffs, based on the first few months after being enacted, brought in startling new sums. Whether they can completely replace the income tax—which some think is Trump's long-term goal, remains to be seen, but tariff revenues have not been at the 2025 level since the early twentieth century.

Like Reagan, Trump intended to stick it out and not abandon his Make America Great Again program or adopt temporary fixes. The DOGE cuts had just started, and many arrangements, such as the World Health Organization agreement, had to finish out a fiscal year, and so on. Trump found himself in a race against inflation, trying to boost energy production and reduce the size of government before higher prices kicked in. And the DOGE impact on unemployment, while minimal, still would be felt.

Reagan was able to ride it out, even knowing he was up for reelection. Trump's position was much stronger as he did not have to worry about reelection. As of early 2025, the Democrats—completely out of ideas and issues—briefly veered toward running on the issue of inflation. But they had to almost immediately abandon that when food and gas prices fell, and the overall inflation rate dropped to half of what it was under Biden.

In a legal version of the 2017 "resist" movement, Democrats attempted to stop Trump's policies through restraining orders issued by pre-selected Democrat-friendly judges. A rash of these ensued—over 150—with the subjects of the restraining orders ranging from blocking Trump's efforts to deport various illegal aliens to rolling back the administration's new rules affecting transsexuals in the military to the most basic of administrative powers, including hiring and firing personnel. One of the worst judicial offenders, Judge James Boasberg of the District of Columbia (a George W. Bush appointee) issued a number of rulings related to illegal aliens deemed gang members being deported under the Alien Enemies Act.[1132] The Trump administration could have ignored those restraining orders and fought it out in the battlefield of public opinion, but instead chose to honor them and fight the cases in the courts. Slowly but surely, Trump won almost every case, either at the appellate level or at the Supreme Court. A key breakthrough came in June 2025 when the Court, weighing in on a case of birthright citizenship, dealt a serious blow to the power of district judges to issue national injunctions. The decision, written by Justice Amy Coney Barrett, was so scathing and sweeping that the liberal *Nation* called it a "5-Alarm Catastrophe."[1133] In its 2025 spring term, the Court went on to rule that parents could allow their children to opt out of LGBT classes in public schools and continued to support the ability of private companies to escape undo regulatory burdens.

Since his first term, Trump had repeatedly insisted that he would not allow Iran to have nuclear weapons. His administration engaged in ongoing negotiations, but ultimately, on June 22 after the Iranians refused all carrots, Trump applied the stick. Following a series of raids by the Israel Air Force, which destroyed most Iranian air defenses and command and control networks, the US launched operation Midnight Hammer, which saw seven B-2 bombers attack three major Iranian nuclear facilities, including the uranium enrichment bunkers at Fordow. All were reported heavily damaged, as even the Iranians admitted.[1134]

Congress dug its heels on enacting many of the DOGE cuts, and in the first big funding bill (labeled by Trump the "Big Beautiful Bill") most of the DOGE-recommended cuts were not included. But the House had already received "recission" packages of individual program cuts to be enacted after the Big Beautiful Bill passed. By 2025, however, no plan existed yet to take on the two main drivers of US debt: Medicare and Social Security.

Meanwhile, the Democrats appeared headed for a lengthy time in the desert, as voter registration trends continued in the Republicans' favor after the election. In the year following June 2024, of the 29 states where voter registration was measured by party, every state saw a shift to the Republicans and a decline in Democrat strength. Some of the changes were shocking: In North Carolina, Democrats saw a 175,000 voter registration edge in 2020 plunge to just over 20,000 by June 2025; and Pennsylvania was even more astounding, dropping from a 1.1 *million* advantage in 2016—when Trump carried the state—to an active voter edge of only 83,000 eight years later. But an even more concerning harbinger for Democratic performance came in the ongoing deportations—which took tens of thousands of illegal aliens off voter rolls, with the likelihood that those numbers would reach over one million by 2026—and a court-required voter roll purge by California counties. As of June 2025, that purge had removed more than one million off the voter rolls of the Golden State even without Orange County and Los Angeles County reporting in. The upshot of all those changes was that even in heavily Democratic states such as California, the party's lead was rapidly disappearing, and with no end in sight. Those changes portended another decade of Republican governance as the Democrats continued to struggle with an identity that appealed to Middle America or to find candidates who could carry the so-called "battleground states."

One thing seemed certain, however: barring a China Virus–type economic meltdown, Trump was slated to become the most transformational figure in American politics since Franklin D. Roosevelt.

CONCLUSION
DAY OF THE EAGLE

In a quarter century filled with ironies, perhaps it was fitting that the era that commenced with a near hysteria over the computer-based threat of Y2K would end with a whimper, while the more sinister and genuine cloud of digital control in the form of AI took root with little public concern.

Responding to the terrorist al-Qaeda threat—which in its most virulent form could not match that of the Soviet Union in the Reagan years—George W. Bush oversaw the construction of a national security state (or, better, a national *surveillance* state) that would have been anathema just fifteen years earlier. At that time, both Democrats and Republicans alike would have rejected such intrusions as a danger to individual liberty and, indeed, the rule of law. They would have been right to do so.

Bush's Patriot Act indeed helped squelch the temporary threat of Muslim terrorists only by expanding and normalizing a much greater evil in the permanent, nearly unchecked snooping on ordinary Americans. It was a development that would have greatly satisfied J. Edgar Hoover. Yet at first, it passed seamlessly into the new Obama administration because of the more immediate concern with an economic crisis in the subprime mortgage meltdown, and because Barack Obama and his cabal of spies proved adept at keeping their clandestine efforts secret and beyond the eyes of the American public.

To be sure, aspects of that new quasi-legal and often outright criminal beast surfaced from time to time. The IRS scandal popped up above the water, only to disappear into the depths again when Obama's Justice Department dropped it. Illegal targeting of conservatives using the IRS and other agencies stood little chance of gaining public awareness with a fawning but declining legacy news complex. The fight over Obamacare obscured much of the other illegality churning below the surface.

Where Bush had, for a short time, benefited from an American economy that seemed well past its prime, he nevertheless presented the public image of someone who still cared about stopping its decline. Yet that, too, faded into the dust of Iraq, before the subprime mortgage crisis delivered the coup de grâce. Bush, who had insisted he stood for free markets, echoed the Vietnam-era rationalization that "we had to destroy the village in order to save it," and promptly strong-armed America's top bankers into accepting government bailouts. To save capitalism, he argued, he had to abandon it.

Obama slid into the vacancy Bush left with gusto. He wanted to manage America's decline. The United States stood where it did in the world because of its previous centuries of imperialism and theft. America did not deserve whatever status and wealth it had, and he intended to share it with the rest of the world by cutting the nation down to size. His initial victory in 2008, easily explained by John McCain's incompetence, Bush's pitiful record, and a campaign to elect the "first black president," was succeeded by a much weaker campaign—against an equally weak and unexceptional Mitt Romney—that urged Americans not to give up on the "first black president," regardless of his failures. They did not, electing him a second time by a smaller margin.

During those years, a cultural rot set into the American fabric. Planted and cultivated by schools and universities, watered by Hollywood and entertainment, and explained away by intellectuals, a true malaise swept the country that dwarfed the crisis of confidence of which Jimmy Carter had spoken decades earlier. Not only was America unexceptional, she was also evil. Not only was science to be dismissed because it came to uncomfortable conclusions, but also now because it was racist, it was not even allowed to come to uncomfortable conclusions. Not only were men and boys to be equaled by women and girls, but they were also to be demonized for their "toxic masculinity." No effort was made at any level—in the churches, in entertainment, in culture, and certainly not in politics—to reverse those fatal trends.

Added to that, a new technological element, the iPhone, caused those malignant tumors to spread throughout the American body. The mental and emotional conditions of young people particularly suffered from the damaging effects of being constantly online. Fear of being left out carried damaging, even suicidal, messages. Religion proved incapable of stopping anything: In the first decade, the Christian churches had methodically refrained from opposing homosexual marriage, then slowly adopted and celebrated it. Of course, that was only a first step, with the transsexual movement already waiting in the wings to step onto center stage.

That rot, to a large degree, had engendered the weakness of the politicians of the early twenty-first century. It meant, first and foremost, that doing those things that were hard or difficult was perpetually delayed and deferred, shifted to another generation. That weakness enabled and shaped the subprime mortgage crisis as traditional notions of thrift, savings, responsibility, and diligence by individuals gave way to student loans, government-backed mortgages, and Obamacare, all of which promised something for nothing. Few politicians could have resisted that, but fewer still when appellations of "racist" or "homophobe" accompanied them—all fueled and fanned by an ignorant, hateful, and superficial media and entertainment class. One could hardly blame the country for producing a Bush, McCain, Obama, or Romney. Moreover, that same culture ensured that over the course of thirty years, Congress increasingly could do nothing of significance. It could not address the Social Security or Medicaid entitlement crises; it could not produce budgets; it could not (with few exceptions such as Obamacare) even draft meaningful legislation without an overwhelming majority of one party or the other.

Politicians had grown incapable of carrying out some of the most basic review and reform functions of government. While some of this inability could be traced to pure partisanship, even more originated in the 1990s when the Republican House backed down in the face of Bill Clinton's government shutdown. Republicans grew inordinately fearful of the mainstream media, and individual politicians sought the approval of the media at every occasion. Thus, when Donald Trump—who did not care about what the largely liberal media said about him—came along, he was seen as crude, wild, and revolutionary. Yet he was only doing in most ways what Ronald Reagan did in the 1980s, if, perhaps, with less refinement.

Until that point, however, the invasion of illegal aliens liberally in massive columns coming from Latin America, the hollowing out of the major manufacturing centers, the homelessness and crime that drowned the cities, and the seeming shoulder-shrugging of the ruling elites to these maladies created an unrest in the country bordering that of the 1960s.

Taken together, all those factors created among Americans a sense of *saudade*, as the Portuguese would say: homesickness in your own home. Majorities increasingly wondered, "Where did my country go?" That question involved far more than leftist-imagined yearning for a "white, old-fashioned" country. Who in the world could be happy with spikes in suicide rates among teens or tens of trillions of dollars in US debt?

Donald Trump, in his first iteration, emerged as a populist hero because, unlike any of the rest, he seemed to actually seek to make America home again. He focused on solutions to problems, not continuation of the status quo for the sake of securing government jobs for friends. What his first term would have been if "the swamp" had treated him like any other president, no one knows. It's highly likely, though, that barring the Russia Hoax, he may have lost reelection anyway due to the China Virus. On the one hand, he was blamed for not doing enough—there were still deaths—and on the other hand, those who suffered from the vaccine also blamed him for introducing the vaccine and for temporarily going along with Dr. Fauci and permitting lockdowns. It is likely he would have gotten more done in the traditional sense—finishing the wall, improving the economy—but that is unprovable because of Covid. But such an outcome likely would have meant he got very little done in terms of a true populist revolution.

A larger issue is that Trump both benefited from, and was damaged by, the investigations. Slowly, he took on the mantle of a martyr, which looked more like reality the minute he left office and was hounded by the Biden administration and lawfare. On the other hand, there is little doubt that the media's perpetual (and fraudulent) hype about the Russia Hoax damaged him in the eyes of many, some of whom still have not arrived at the truth: It was fraud designed to cripple him.

What is certain is that the combination of the Russia Hoax and the Covid lies perpetuated by the government and the medical community ("trust the science") accelerated a growing skepticism among the public, and particularly for younger people, about anything coming from "the establishment" (to use a '60s phrase). Whether it was doctors, scientists, teachers, or religious leaders—all of whom enjoyed a higher level of public trust and confidence before 2020 than after—those with the greatest influence over American behavior lost credibility.

All of that worked to Trump's benefit in his reelection bid when it was clear to many that, in fact, he had been the victim of a once-thought impossible claim that the entire government was, well, "out to get him." When combined with real-life incompetence and downright maliciousness of the Biden administration, and the economic realities for many younger people and minorities, Trump's second election was all but assured. Again, the irony: If they'd left him alone, he might have been a two-term president, but a more traditional two-term president. Their attacks through Lawfare and the (at least) two attempts to kill him, turned him into a political version of Captain America. He was (as Admiral Isoroku Yamamoto is misquoted as saying) "filled with a terrible resolve." When he told a group in February 2025 that his decision to run again was "dangerous" because if he lost he faced jail or worse, he was not exaggerating. And yet at the same time, a somewhat more mellowed, controlled, and determined Trump returned to the White House in 2025. Some attributed the change to his chief of staff Susie Wiles; others to the assassination attempts. Regardless of the cause, it was as if the Trump of 2017 had ingested the political equivalent of an energy drink in 2025.

Thus, in a final irony of the twenty-first century, the excessiveness and vile hatred of Donald Trump led the Deep State to empower the one creature capable of bringing it all down. When Trump waded into the bureaucracy wielding Elon Musk as a human battle-ax, it dawned on many that not only had they gone too far, but there was no turning back. They had sown the wind and were reaping the whirlwind.

How long can Trump and his "Mighty Men" keep it up? Can the courts stop or derail him? Can his health hold up? One certainty is that early in Trump's second term, J. D. Vance has proven to be a deep thinking, fearless warrior—the exact opposite of Mike Pence. Even when Trump leaves office in 2028, it will be unlikely his successor would take the foot off the gas. And to accomplish all of that, Trump had brought along one of the geniuses of the twenty-first century, Elon Musk, who stood as a doer, a creator, and a finisher. That seems especially true when compared against his counterpart from Microsoft, Bill Gates, who despite the success of his company, had developed a reputation as a meddler, a do-gooder (in the worst sense of the term), and even a threat to humanity. That Gates stood on the outside looking in constituted perhaps the second bullet dodged in the second decade of the twenty-first century.

NOTES

INTRODUCTION: THE DISASTER THAT WASN'T

1 Francine Uenuma, "20 Years Later, the Y2K Bug Seems like a Joke—Because Those Behind the Scenes Took it Seriously," *Time*, December 30, 2019, https://time.com/5752129/y2k-bug-history/.

2 "Visa Debits the Vendors," *Information Week*, September 15, 1997.

3 Microsoft, "Excel Incorrectly Assumes That the Year 1900 Is a Leap Year," *Microsoft Learn*, June 25, 2025, https://docs.microsoft.com/en-US/office/troubleshoot/excel/wrongly-assumes-1900-is-leap-year.

4 Francine Uenuma, "20 Years Later, the Y2K Bug Seems like a Joke—Because Those Behind the Scenes Took it Seriously," *Time*, December 30, 2019, https://time.com/5752129/y2k-bug-history/.

5 US House of Representatives, *The Year 2000 Problem: Fourth Report by the Committee on Government Reform and Oversight*, October 26, 1998, https://www.congress.gov/congressional-report/105th-congress/house-report/827/1.

6 Francine Uenuma, "20 Years Later, the Y2K Bug Seems like a Joke—Because Those Behind the Scenes Took it Seriously," *Time*, December 30, 2019, https://time.com/5752129/y2k-bug-history/.

7 John Maynard Keynes, *The Economic Consequences of the Peace* (1920), quoted in the Online Library of Liberty, https://oll.libertyfund.org/quote/j-m-keynes-reflected-on-that-happy-age-of-international-commerce-and-freedom-of-travel-that-was-destroyed-by-the-cataclysm-of-the-first-world-war-1920.

8 Drudge Report, "Newsweek Kills Story on White House Intern," *Drudge Report*, January 17, 1998, https://australianpolitics.com/1998/01/17/original-drudge-reports-lewinsky-scandal.html.

9 Toby Harnden, "Matt Drudge: World's Most Powerful Journalist," *UK Daily Telegraph*, January 3, 2008, https://web.archive.org/web/20080527022920/http://www.telegraph.co.uk/news/worldnews/1580164/Matt-Drudge-world%27s-most-powerful-journalist.html.

10 Caleb Howe, "Mueller Redactions Include Claim Russia Secretly Taped Bill Clinton Having Phone Sex with Lewinsky: Report," *Mediaite*, April 23, 2019, https://www.mediaite.com/news/mueller-redactions-include-claim-russia-secretly-taped-bill-clinton-having-phone-sex-with-lewinsky-report/.

11 Department of Defense, Memo, *Detainee Assessment: Khalid Shaykh Muhammad*, December 8, 2006, https://int.nyt.com/data/documenttools/82528-isn-10024-khalid-shaikh-mohammed-jtf-gtmo/c629488fa6d90379/full.pdf; Lawrence Wright, *The Looming Tower: Al-Qaeda and the Road to 9/11* (New York: Knopf, 2006), 235–6.

12 Richard C. Paddock and Josh Meyer, "Suspect's Role in '95 Plot Detailed," *Los Angeles Times*, June 7, 2002, https://www.latimes.com/archives/la-xpm-2002-jun-07-fg-khalid7-story.html.

13 "Clinton Passed on Killing bin Laden?" *Factcheck.org*, January 18, 2008, https://www.factcheck.org/2008/01/clinton-passed-on-killing-bin-laden/; *The 9/11 Commission Report: Final Report of the National Commission on Terrorist Attacks Upon the United States* (New York: W. W. Norton, 2004), 110; Lawrence Wright, *The Looming Tower: Al-Qaeda and the Road to 9/11* (New York: Knopf, 2006), 220.

Wright states that Erwa communicated to CIA operatives that Sudan wanted off the "excrement list" as radio host Rush Limbaugh put it, and that if the US wanted to press charges, "We are ready to hand him to you."

14 Penelope Muse Abernathy, *The Expanding News Desert* (Chapel Hill: University of North Carolina Press, 2018), https://www.usnewsdeserts.com/reports/expanding-news-desert/loss-of-local-news/bigger-and-bigger-they-grow/#:~:text=4-,The%20most%20active%20purchasers%20of%20newspapers%20in%20recent%20years%20have,th%2D%20largest%20with%2050%20papers.

CHAPTER 1: A RAZOR-THIN ELECTION

15 Rush Limbaugh, "Rush Reads the Stitches on the Fastball: Socialism Disguised as Stimulus," *The Rush Limbaugh Show*, March 29, 2021, accessed July 1, 2025, https://www.rushlimbaugh.com/daily/2021/03/29/rush-reads-the-stitches-on-the-fastball-socialism-disguised-as-stimulus/.

16 Rush Limbaugh, "What's the Drive-By Angle on the Marco/Hillary Matchup?" *The Rush Limbaugh Show*, April 14, 2015, accessed July 1, 2025, https://www.rushlimbaugh.com/daily/2015/04/14/what_s_the_drive_by_angle_on_the_marco_hillary_matchup/.

17 Kenneth Baer, *Reinventing Democrats: The Politics of Liberalism from Reagan to Clinton* (Lawrence, KS: University Press of Kansas, 2000); Jon Hale, "The Making of the New Democrats," *Political Science Quarterly* 110 (1995): 207–232.

18 Jimmy Carter, *Keeping the Faith: Memoirs of a President* (New York: Bantam, 1982); Peter Bourne, *Jimmy Carter: A Comprehensive Biography from Plains to Postpresidency* (New York: Lisa Drew, 1997).

19 Donald Critchlow and W. J. Rorabaugh, *Takeover: How the Left's Quest for Social Justice Corrupted Liberalism* (Wilmington, DE: ISI Books, 2012).

20 David Horowitz, *Radical Son: A Generational Odyssey* (Brentwood, TN: Bombardier Books, 2020).

21 Donald Critchlow and W. J. Rorabaugh, *Takeover: How the Left's Quest for Social Justice Corrupted Liberalism* (Wilmington, DE: ISI Books, 2012), 27.

22 "Democrats: Humphrey's Bandwagon," *Newsweek*, June 10, 1968; "Nation: Democratic Countdown," *Time*, June 7, 1968, https://time.com/archive/6635394/nation-democratic-countdown/; "After Oregon—HHH and Nixon?" *U.S. News & World Report*, June 10, 1968.

23 Adam Cohen and Elizabeth Taylor, *American Pharaoh: Mayor Richard Daley: His Battle for Chicago and the Nation* (Boston: Little, Brown, 2000), 462–63.

24 Paul Johnson, *Modern Times: A History of the World from the Twenties to the Nineties*, revised ed. (New York: HarperCollins, 1991), 644.

25 Richard Craig, *Polls, Expectations, and Elections: TV News Making in U.S. Presidential Elections* (Latham, MD: Lexington Books, 2015), 36.

26 Larry Schweikart and Michael Allen, *A Patriot's History of the United States*, 15th Anniversary Edition (New York: Sentinel, 2019), 731.

27 Joseph C. Keeley, *The Left-Leaning Antenna: Political Bias in Television* (New Rochelle, NY: Arlington House, 1971), 109.

28 Saul Alinsky, *Rules for Radicals: A Practical Primer for Realistic Radicals* (New York: Vintage, 1989).

29 Larry Schweikart, *Seven Events That Made America America* (New York: Sentinel, 2010), 5–33.

30 Richard Brown, "The Missouri Crisis, Slavery, and the Politics of Jacksonianism," in *New Perspectives on the American Past*, ed. Stanley N. Katz and Stanley I. Kutler, vol. 1, 1607–1877 (Boston: Little, Brown, 1969), 241–55.

31 Paul Ehrlich, *The Population Bomb* (New York: Ballantine, 1968).

See the famous bet between Ehrlich and economist Julian Simon: that Ehrlich pick any five raw materials and select any date more than a year away, and Simon predicted the commodity's price would be lower than at the time of the wager. Although the Earth's population grew by more than 800 million, all five of Ehrlich's selected metals fell in inflation-adjusted terms, and three actually fell in nominal terms. Simon even offered to raise the bet. Ehrlich tried to wiggle out by changing the issue to "global warming," a process thousands, if not millions, of years old with no connection to human activity. But the embarrassment for Ehrlich—such that any liberal can ever be embarrassed—was powerful.

Julian Simon, *The Ultimate Resource* (Princeton, NJ: Princeton University Press, 1981); Marian Tupy, "Julian Simon Was Right: A Half-Century of Population Growth, Increasing Prosperity, and Falling Commodity Prices," *Cato Institute Economic Development Bulletin* no. 29, February 16, 2018, https://www.cato.org/economic-development-bulletin/julian-simon-was-right-half-century-population-growth-increasing#findings.

32 Bill Turque, *Inventing Al Gore: A Biography* (Boston: Houghton Mifflin, 2000), 83.

Turque's chapter discussing Gore's very short tour of duty is entitled "Saving Private Gore."

33 Myra MacPherson, "Al Gore and the Window of Certainty," *Washington Post*, February 2, 1988, https://www.washingtonpost.com/archive/lifestyle/1988/02/03/al-gore-and-the-window-of-certainty/b50fef61-3ad9-4953-bb1e-a2d5cd35b2e9/.

34 Bill Turque, *Inventing Al Gore: A Biography* (Boston: Houghton Mifflin, 2000), 118.

35 "Gore Abortion Rights at Issue," *Nashville Banner*, July 28, 1976; Bill Turque, *Inventing Al Gore: A Biography* (Boston: Houghton Mifflin, 2000), 120–21.

36 "Did Gore Hatch Horton?" *Slate*, November 1, 1999, https://slate.com/news-and-politics/1999/11/did-gore-hatch-horton.html#:~:text=Gore%20did%20ask%20Dukakis%2C%20in%20a%20debate,wrote%20it%20up%20a%20few%20months%20later:&text=Gore%20never%20mentioned%20that%20Horton%20was%20black;%20indeed%2C%20he%20nev.

37 Bill Turque, *Inventing Al Gore: A Biography* (Boston: Houghton Mifflin, 2000), 247.

38 Al Gore, Jr., *Earth in the Balance: Ecology and the Human Spirit* (Boston: Houghton Mifflin, 1992).

39 Paul Richter, "COLUMN ONE: Gore May Be Dull, but to His Party He Shines: Suddenly, His Solid Image and Moderate Views Are Attracting Attention—From Democrats Scrambling to Recover From the November Landslide," *Los Angeles Times*, January 15, 1995, https://www.latimes.com/archives/la-xpm-1995-01-15-mn-20305-story.html/.

40 Jacob Weisberg, "Why Gore (Probably) Lost," *Slate*, November 8, 2000, https://slate.com/news-and-politics/2000/11/why-gore-probably-lost.html.

41 Michael Duffy and Karen Tumulty, "Campaign 2000: Gore's Secret Guru," *Time*, November 8, 1999, https://time.com/archive/6736857/campaign-2000-gores-secret-guru.

42 Ibid.; Bill Turque, *Inventing Al Gore: A Biography* (Boston: Houghton Mifflin, 2000), 359.

43 *Washington Post*, March 16, 1999.

44 The Commission on Presidential Debates, *The Second Gore-Bush Presidential Debate*, October 11, 2000, https://www.debates.org/voter-education/debate-transcripts/october-11-2000-debate-transcript/.

45 George W. Bush, *Decision Points* (New York: Crown, 2010), 41.

46 Ibid., 44.

This was an astounding accusation to make against George H. W. Bush. In World War II, he enlisted as soon as he turned 18; flew Avenger dive bombers; and was in a raid on Chi-Chi Jima, where his engine was shot and on fire. He not only completed the bombing run on fire, but also got the aircraft to an area where he and his gunner could be rescued. (His gunner's parachute did not open, and he died.) Bush spent four hours in a life raft before being picked up by a submarine. He was awarded the Navy's highest honor for heroism, the Distinguished Flying Cross. Some wimp!

47 Larry Schweikart, *Reagan: The American President* (Nashville, TN: Post Hill Press, 2019), passim.

48 Ibid., 68.

49 Donald Critchlow and W. J. Rorabaugh, *Takeover: How the Left's Quest for Social Justice Corrupted Liberalism* (Wilmington, DE: ISI Books, 2012), 109.

50 Matthew Connelly, *Fatal Misconception: The Struggle to Control World Population* (Cambridge, MA: Harvard University Press, 2008), 276–326.

51 George W. Bush, *Decision Points* (New York: Crown, 2010), 74.

52 Troy Gipson, *From Carthage to Oslo: A Biography of Al Gore* (Charleston, SC: Clearspace Publishing, 2012), 139.

53 "Historical Polling for U.S. Presidential Elections," *Wikipedia*, https://en.wikipedia.org/wiki/Historical_polling_for_United_States_presidential_elections#2000_United_States_presidential_election.

54 George W. Bush, *Decision Points* (New York: Crown, 2010), 76.

55 "Bush Acknowledges 1976 DUI Charge," *CNN.com*, November 2, 2000, https://www.cnn.com/2000/ALLPOLITICS/stories/11/02/bush.dui/.

56 Exit polling would prove consistently wrong, most notably in 2004 when exit polls had John Kerry winning multiple states he lost.

57 George W. Bush, *Decision Points* (New York: Crown, 2010), 77.

58 Stephen Hayward, *The Age of Reagan: The Fall of the Old Liberal Order, 1964–1980* (New York: Three Rivers Press, 2001), 712; Larry Schweikart, *Reagan: The American President* (Nashville, TN: Post Hill Press, 2019), 185.

It was argued that Jimmy Carter's early concession in 1980 caused California voters to turn around and cost not only Carter votes in the popular election but also local and statewide Democratic candidates their races.

Ibid., 712.

When NBC projected that Ronald Reagan would become the 40th President, less than 4% of the national vote had been counted.

59 George W. Bush, *Decision Points* (New York: Crown, 2010), 77.

60 Bill Sammon, *At Any Cost: How Al Gore Tried to Steal the Election* (Washington, DC: Regnery Publishing, 2001).

61 Troy Gipson, *From Carthage to Oslo: A Biography of Al Gore* (Charleston, SC: Clearspace Publishing, 2012), 143.

62 "The Election of 2000," *Wikipedia*, https://en.wikipedia.org/wiki/2000_United_States_presidential_election#:~:text=The%202000%20United%20States%20presidential,incumbent%20Vice%20President%20Al%20Gore.

63 Troy Gipson, *From Carthage to Oslo: A Biography of Al Gore* (Charleston, SC: Clearspace Publishing, 2012), 143.

64 Sammon, *At Any Cost*, 78; "Feeding the Media Beast: Leaks, Rats, and Black Berrys," *Washington Post*, December 17, 2000; "Ballot Probably Not the Wisest Thing," *Palm Beach Post*, December 16, 2000.

65 *USA Today*, "Five Weeks of History," December 14, 2000.

66 James V. Grimaldi and Roberto Suro, "Risky Bush Legal Strategy Paid Off," *Washington Post*, December 17, 2000, https://www.washingtonpost.com/archive/politics/2000/12/17/risky-bush-legal-strategy-paid-off/8fd75e3a-6c96-4cb7-bb5d-0e03dd149485.

67 James Ceaser and Andrew Busch, *The Perfect Tie: The True Story of the 2000 Presidential Election* (Lanham, MD: Rowman & Littlefield, 2001), 188.

68 *Bush v. Gore*, 531 U.S. 98 (2000), https://www.law.cornell.edu/supct/html/00-949.ZPC.html.

69 James Ceaser and Andrew Busch, *The Perfect Tie: The True Story of the 2000 Presidential Election* (Lanham, MD: Rowman & Littlefield, 2001), 210.

70 Michael Holt, *By One Vote: The Disputed Presidential Election of 1876* (Lawrence, KS: University of Kansas Press, 2008); Mark Summers, *The Era of Good Stealings* (New York: Oxford University Press, 1993); C. Vann Woodward, *Reunion and Reaction: The Compromise of 1877 and the End of Reconstruction* (Boston: Little, Brown, 1951).

71 James Ceaser and Andrew Busch, *The Perfect Tie: The True Story of the 2000 Presidential Election* (Lanham, MD: Rowman & Littlefield, 2001).

72 Ibid., 160.

73 Ibid.

74 Ibid., 27.

75 Larry Schweikart and Michael Allen, *A Patriot's History of the United States: From Columbus's Great Discovery to the Age of Entitlement*, 15th Anniversary Edition (New York: Sentinel, 2019), 834.

CHAPTER 2: THE GREAT SATAN

76 Larry Schweikart, *Reagan: The American President* (Nashville, TN: Post Hill Press, 2018), 451–2.

77 George W. Bush, *Decision Points* (New York: Crown, 2010), 111.

78 Ibid., 121.

79 Ibid., 121.

80 Paul Johnson, *Modern Times: A History of the World from the Twenties to the Nineties*, rev. ed. (New York: HarperCollins, 1991), 636.

81 Rush Limbaugh, "The Host's Take on Trey Gowdy and George W. Bush," February 9, 2018, https://www.rushlimbaugh.com/daily/2018/02/09/the-hosts-take-on-trey-gowdy-and-george-w-bush/.

82 Carlton Sherwood, *Inquisition: The Persecution and Prosecution of the Reverend Sun Myung Moon* (Washington, DC: Regnery Gateway, 1991); George Chryssides, *The Advent of Sun Myung Moon: The Origins, Beliefs, and Practices of the Unification Church* (London: Macmillan Professional and Academic, 1991).

83 Lisa Napoli, *Up All Night: Ted Turner, CNN, and the Birth of 24-Hour News* (New York: Harry N. Abrams, 2021).

84 *Press Bias and Politics: How the Media Frame Controversial Issues* (Westport, CT: Praeger, 2002); Jim Kuyperes, *Bush's War: Media Bias and Justifications for War in a Terrorist Age (Communication, Media, and Politics)* (Lanham, MD: Rowman & Littlefield).

85 Bill Sammon, *Fighting Back: The War on Terrorism—from Inside the Bush White House* (Washington, DC: Regnery Publishing, 2002), 43, 62, 83–107.

86 George W. Bush, *Decision Points* (New York: Crown, 2010), 121.

87 Ibid., 83–84.

88 Ibid., 91.

89 Tom Junod, "The Falling Man: An Unforgettable Story," *Esquire*, September 9, 2021, https://www.esquire.com/news-politics/a48031/the-falling-man-tom-junod/.

90 Dan Balz and Bob Woodward, "America's Chaotic Road to War," *Washington Post*, January 27, 2002.

91 Ibid.

92 Popular Mechanics Editors, *Popular Mechanics*, "Debunking the 9/11 Conspiracy Theories: Special Report–the World Trade Center," September 8, 2021, updated September 10, 2024, https://www.popularmechanics.com/military/a6384/debunking-911-myths-world-trade-center/. Olson was on the phone to her husband, Solicitor General Ted Olson, at the time the plane entered its final descent. I have also personally spoken to an eyewitness who was outside the Pentagon and was on his way into work, when he saw the plane come in at a shockingly low level. He said its wings clipped some light poles on the way in.

93 Bill Sammon, *Fighting Back: The War on Terrorism—from Inside the Bush White House* (Washington, DC: Regnery Publishing, 2002), 97.

94 Ibid., 102.

95 George W. Bush, *Decision Points* (New York: Crown, 2010), 130.

96 *Clear the Skies*, directed by Peter Molloy, 2002, https://www.imdb.com/title/tt7874798/?ref_=fn_al_tt_1.

97 "George W. Bush's National Cathedral Speech," 2001, in Larry Schweikart, David Dougherty, and Michael Allen, *The Patriot's History Reader* (New York: Sentinel, 2011), 407–09.

98 Bill Sammon, *Fighting Back: The War on Terrorism from Inside the Bush White House* (Washington, DC: Regnery Publishing, 2002), 189.

99 "Bush: 'You Are Either With Us, or With the Terrorist'," *VOA*, September 9, 2021, https://www.voanews.com/a/a-13-a-2001-09-21-14-bush-66411197/549664.html.

100 Anne Rogers, "KC's Swanee recalls Bush's 1st Pitch after 9/11," *MLB.com*, September 11, 2021, https://www.mlb.com/news/mike-swanson-saw-george-bush-s-1st-pitch-after-9-11#:~:text=Bush%20threw%20out%20the%20ceremonial,deadly%20terrorist%20attacks%20of%20Sept.

101 Baseball Quotes (@BaseballQuotes1), "Don't bounce it…," *X* (formerly Twitter), September 10, 2021, https://twitter.com/baseballquotes1/status/1436684150866595849?lang=en. The Kansas City Royals' Director of Public Relations recalled, "I'm not sure there was a dry eye in the place when [he] let that thing go."

Anne Rogers, "KC's Swanee Recalls Bush's 1st Pitch after 9/11," *MLB.com*, September 11, 2021, https://www.mlb.com/news/mike-swanson-saw-george-bush-s-1st-pitch-after-9-11.

102 George W. Bush, Address to a Joint Session of Congress and the American People, Office of the Press Secretary, White House, September 20, 2001, https://georgewbush-whitehouse.archives.gov/news/releases/2001/09/20010920-8.html.

103 Ibid.

104 Sandy Gail, *Afghan Napoleon: The Life of Ahmad Shah Massoud* (London: Haus Publishing, 2021); "He Would Have Found Bin Laden," *CNN*, May 27, 2009, https://edition.cnn.com/2009/WORLD/asiapcf/05/27/massoud.afghanistan/; "Rebel Leader Warns Europe and US About Large-Scale Imminent Al-Qaeda Attacks," April 6, 2001, *History Commons*, https://web.archive.org/web/20161220142831/http://www.historycommons.org/context.jsp?item=a040601massoudspeech&scale=0.

105 Barbara Grewe, "Legal Barriers to Information Sharing: Erection of a Wall between Intelligence and Law Enforcement Investigations," August 20, 2004, Commission on Terrorist Attacks Upon the United States Staff Monograph, https://irp.fas.org/eprint/wall.pdf.

106 Molly Riley, "Ashcroft Blames Clinton-era FBI, CIA," *NBC News*, April 12, 2004, https://www.nbcnews.com/id/wbna4721976.

107 Lawrence Wright, *The Looming Tower: Al-Qaeda and the Road to 9/11* (New York: Alfred A. Knopf, 2006), 343.

108 Ibid., 342.

109 Ibid., 350.

110 Ibid., 351.

111 George Tenet, *At the Center of the Storm: My Years at the CIA* (New York: HarperCollins, 2007), 196.

112 Ibid., 296–298

113 Jerry Markon and Timothy Dwyer, "Damning Evidence Highlights FBI Bungles," *Sydney Morning World Herald*, March 22, 2006.

114 George Tenet, *At the Center of the Storm: My Years at the CIA* (New York: HarperCollins, 2007), 191–204.

115 Ibid., 192.

Evan Thomas, the senior writer, was asked how the magazine's relationship was with the FBI. He replied, "Well, it was pretty good since we did their bidding."

116 Marie Brenner, "American Nightmare: The Ballad of Richard Jewell," *Vanity Fair*, February 1997; Eric Lichtblau, "Scientist Officially Exonerated in Anthrax Attacks," *The New York Times*, August 8, 2008, https://www.nytimes.com/2008/08/09/washington/09anthrax.html#:~:text=WASHINGTON%20%E2%80%94%20Six%20years%20after%20labeling,involved%20in%20the%20anthrax%20mailings.%E2%80%9D; Scott Shane and Eric Lichtblau, "Scientist is Paid Millions by U.S. in Anthrax Suit," *The New York Times*, June 28, 2008, https://www.nytimes.com/2008/06/28/washington/28hatfill.html.

117 George Tenet, *At the Center of the Storm: My Years at the CIA* (New York: HarperCollins, 2007), 191–204.

Instead, the CIA in July briefed Bush's National Security Advisor Condoleezza Rice, the counterterrorism agents said, "There will be a significant terrorist attack in the coming weeks or months" (Ibid., 151), and that "multiple and simultaneous attacks are possible and they will occur with little or no warning" (Ibid., 152). These incredibly vague warnings could have been produced by almost anyone outside the agency with little more information than the CIA had.

118 Ibid., 207.

119 "President Holds Prime Time News Conference," Office of the Press Secretary, White House, October 2001, https://georgewbush-whitehouse.archives.gov/news/releases/2001/10/20011011-7.html#:~:text=I%20was%20struck%20by%20this,evil%20and%20murder%20and%20prejudice.

120 George Tenet, *At the Center of the Storm: My Years at the CIA* (New York: HarperCollins, 2007), 208.

121 Michael Morell with Bill Harlow, *The Great War of Our Time: The CIA's Fight Against Terrorism from al Qa'ida to ISIS* (New York: Twelve, 2015), 91.

122 Ibid., 96.

123 Ibid., 99.

124 George Tenet, *At the Center of the Storm: My Years at the CIA* (New York: HarperCollins, 2007), 362.

125 Douglas Feith, *War and Decision: Inside the Pentagon at the Dawn of the War on Terrorism* (New York: Harper, 2008), 181.

126 Ibid., 182.

127 General Norman Schwartzkopf, who had allowed Saddam to keep the gunships as a goodwill gesture, claimed he had been tricked by Saddam's generals, who used them to kill Shi'ite civilians.

Rick Atkinson, *Crusade* (New York: Houghton Mifflin, 1993), 489–90; General Norman Schwartzkopf with Peter Petre, *It Doesn't Take a Hero* (New York: Bantam Books, 1992), 48889.

The supporting documentation for the reluctance to remove Saddam at that time is extensive. Kevin Woods, et al., *Iraqi Perspective Project: A View of Operation Iraqi Freedom From Saddam's Senior Leadership* (Joint Center for Operational Analysis, U.S. Joint Forces Command, March 2006), viii, 14–16, http://www.jfcom.mil/newslink/storyarchive/2006/ipp.pdf.

128 US Senate, *Select Committee on Intelligence, Report on the U.S. Intelligence Community's Prewar Intelligence Assessments on Iraq*, 108th Cong., 2nd sess., ordered reported July 7, 2004, 314, https://irp.fas.org/congress/2004_rpt/ssci_iraq.pdf; US Department of State, *A Decade of Deception and Defiance*, background paper, September 12, 2002, https://2001-2009.state.gov/p/nea/rls/13456.htm; U.S. Department of State, *Patterns of Global Terrorism 2002*, report released April 30, 2003, https://2009-2017.state.gov/j/ct/rls/crt/2002/index.htm.

129 Douglas J. Feith, *War and Decision: Inside the Pentagon at the Dawn of the War on Terrorism* (New York: HarperCollins, 2008), 188.

130 United Nations Security Council, Security Council Resolution 688, adopted April 5, 1991, https://digitallibrary.un.org/record/110659.

131 Charle Duelfer, *Comprehensive Report of the Special Advisor to the DCI on Iraq's Weapons of Mass Destruction*, vol. IIIB, "Biological Warfare," September 30, 2004, 11, 13, 27, https://www.cia.gov/readingroom/docs/DOC_0001156478.pdf.

132 "Open Letter to President Clinton," Committee for Peace and Security in the Gulf, February 19, 1998, https://www.iraqwatch.org/perspectives/rumsfeld-openletter.htm.

133 Paul Johnson, *Modern Times: A History of the World from the Twenties to the Nineties*, rev. ed. (New York: HarperCollins, 1991), 450.

134 Ibid., 450.

135 Hans Blix, *Disarming Iraq* (New York: Pantheon, 2004), 54.

136 George W. Bush, *Speech to United Nations General Assembly*, September 12, 2002, https://georgewbush-whitehouse.archives.gov/news/releases/2002/09/20020912-1.html.

137 Douglas J. Feith, *War and Decision: Inside the Pentagon at the Dawn of the War on Terrorism* (New York: HarperCollins, 2008), 203.

138 George W. Bush, *Press Conference*, October 11, 2001, https://www.johnstonsarchive.net/terrorism/bush911e.html.

139 Douglas J. Feith, *War and Decision: Inside the Pentagon at the Dawn of the War on Terrorism* (New York: HarperCollins, 2008), 215.

140 Ibid., 220–21.

Feith strongly rejected several basic criticisms of the decision to go to war. First, he claimed that, contrary to some claims, Bush was not tied to deposing Saddam and that he evaluated numerous options to resolve the problem short of war. Another is that officials lied about the facts to ensure a war. "The assertion that officials lied about the war's rationale is false. In the many thousands of official comments on the matter, there were some sloppy formulations, ill-chosen phrases, and outright errors" (Ibid., 221). He noted that many intelligence reports about the WMDs "later proved faulty." But he also contended that the war was not only about WMDs, but also about a wider range of goals centered on preventing another terrorist attack.

141 George W. Bush, *Decision Points* (New York: Crown, 2010), 232.

142 Ibid., 232.

143 Douglas J. Feith, *War and Decision: Inside the Pentagon at the Dawn of the War on Terrorism* (New York: HarperCollins, 2008), 228.

144 Michael Morell, *The Great War of Our Time: The CIA's Fight Against Terrorism—From al Qa'ida to ISIS* (New York: Twelve, 2015), 100.

145 Ibid., 100.

146 George Tenet, *At the Center of the Storm: My Years at the CIA* (New York: HarperCollins, 2007), 362.

147 Later, the pop journalist Bob Woodward, who had made a career of his book on Watergate, *All the President's Men*, enhanced the "slam dunk" story even further, claiming Tenet leaped into the air and simulated a slam dunk, not once but twice. "This basketball pantomime never happened," wrote Tenet (Ibid., 362). Tenet also admitted in his book that his language was not exact, and that, he thought, had led to the CIA receiving much of the blame for WMDs. But he also "strongly believed" Saddam had WMDs (Ibid., 364).

Bob Woodward, *Veil: The Secret Wars of the CIA, 1981–1987* (New York: Simon & Schuster, 2005).

Woodward had gone on to write about Bob Casey and the CIA in *Veil: The Secret Wars of the CIA*. He claimed to have interviewed Casey—who was in a coma and/or incapable of speech.

It wouldn't be the first time Woodward was accused of fabricating evidence or supporting false narratives. He claimed Mark Felt was "Deep Throat," the Watergate informant, but multiple other insiders claimed "Deep Throat" was a composite. As assistant managing editor of the *Washington Post*, Woodward approved a purely fictional story by reporter Janet Cooke called "Jimmy's World," then submitted it to the Pulitzer Prize committee. Ironically, however, Woodward supported the claims of WMDs in Iraq in his books *Bush at War* (New York: Simon & Schuster, 2002); *Plan of Attack* (New York: Simon & Schuster, 2004); *State of Denial* (New York: Simon & Schuster, 2006); and *The War Within: A Secret White House History, 2005–2008* New York: Simon & Schuster, 2008).

148 Michael Morell, *The Great War of Our Time: The CIA's Fight Against Terrorism—From al Qa'ida to ISIS* (New York: Twelve, 2015), 106.

149 Georges Sada, *Military History Fandom Interview on Fox News*, January 25, 2006, https://military-history.fandom.com/wiki/Georges_Sada; Georges Sada, *Saddam's Secrets: How an Iraqi General Defied and Survived Saddam Hussein* (Nashville: Integrity Publishers, 2006).

150 Snopes.com, *Yellowcake Uranium Removed from Iraq*, last modified July 8, 2008, https://www.snopes.com/fact-check/have-your-yellowcake/.

151 Donald Rumsfeld, *Known and Unknown: A Memoir* (New York: Sentinel, 2011), 432.

152 Ibid., 433.

153 George W. Bush, *Decision Points* (New York: Crown, 2010), 236.

154 Hillary Rodham Clinton, "Iraq War Vote Speech," Archives of Women's Political Communication, October 10, 2002, https://awpc.cattcenter.iastate.edu/2017/03/09/hillary-clinton-iraq-war-vote-speech-oct-10-2002/.

155 Joe Biden, Interview on *Meet the Press*, NBC News, August 4, 2002; Hillary Rodham Clinton, "Authorization of the Use of United States Armed Forces against Iraq," speech, Congressional Record 148, no. 132 (October 9, 2002): S10174; John Kerry, "Authorization of the Use of United States Armed Forces Against Iraq," speech, Congressional Record 148, no. 132 (October 9, 2002): S10174; Al Gore, "Iraq and the War on Terrorism," speech to the Commonwealth Club of California, September 23, 2002.

156 George W. Bush, *Decision Points* (New York: Crown, 2010), 242.

157 Ibid., 242.

158 Ibid., 242.

159 Colin Powell, *Address to the United Nations Security Council*, February 5, 2003, https://www.theguardian.com/world/2003/feb/05/iraq.usa.

160 George W. Bush, *Decision Points* (New York: Crown, 2010), 247.

161 Ibid., 233.

162 Ibid., 234.

163 Tommy Franks, *American Soldier* (New York: HarperCollins, 2004); Peter Bergen, "The Battle for Tora Bora: How Osama Bin Laden Slipped From Our Grasp," *New Republic*, December 29, 2009, https://newrepublic.com/article/72086/the-battle-tora-bora.

164 Donald Rumsfeld, *Known and Unknown: A Memoir* (New York: Sentinel, 2011), 448.

165 Larry Schweikart, *America's Victories: How the U.S. Wins Wars and Will Win the War on Terror* (New York: Sentinel, 2006), 98–131; David Zucchino, *Thunder Run: The Armored Strike to Capture Baghdad* (New York: Bantam, 2003); Williamson Murray and Robert Scales, *The Iraq War: A Military History* (Cambridge, MA: Belknap Press, 2003); Gregory Fontenot, et al., *On Point: The United States Army in Operation Iraqi Freedom* (Washington, DC: US Army Chief of Staff, 2004); Rick Atkinson, *In the Company of Soldiers: A Chronicle of Combat* (New York: Henry Holt, 2004); Karl Zinsmeister, *Boots on the Ground: A Month with the 82nd Airborne in the Battle for Iraq* (New York: Truman Talley Books, 2003).

166 George W. Bush, *Decision Points* (New York: Crown, 2010), 238.

167 ABC News Staff, "Blast Rips U.N. Building in Baghdad," *ABC News*, August 19, 2003, https://abcnews.go.com/International/story?id=79424&page=1.

168 Madelyln Hsiao-Rei Hicks et al., "Casualties in Civilians and coalition Soldiers From Suicide Bombings in Iraq, 2003–10: A Descriptive Study," *The Lancet* 378, no. 9794 (September 3, 2011): 906–914, https://doi.org/10.1016/S0140-6736(11)61023-4.

169 Bruce Pirnie and Edward O'Connell, "Counterinsurgency in Iraq (2003–2006)," RAND Counterinsurgency Study, vol. 2 (Santa Monica, CA: RAND Corporation, 2008), https://www.rand.org/pubs/monographs/MG595z3.html.

170 George W. Bush, *Address to the United Nations General Assembly*, September 23, 2003, https://georgewbush-whitehouse.archives.gov/news/releases/2003/09/20030923-4.html.

171 Central Intelligence Agency, "Comprehensive Report of the Special Advisor to the DCI on Iraq's WMD," September 30, 2004, https://web.archive.org/web/20131002011819/https://www.cia.gov/library/reports/general-reports-1/iraq_wmd_2004/.

172 Seymour M. Hersh, "Torture at Abu Ghraib," *The New Yorker*, May 10, 2004, https://www.newyorker.com/magazine/2004/05/10/torture-at-abu-ghraib.

173 CNN Staff, "Congress Forms Panel to Study Iraq War," *CNN*, March 15, 2006, https://www.cnn.com/2006/POLITICS/03/15/iraq.study/; Ray Suarez, interview with Ann Scott Tyson, *PBS NewsHour*, "Attacks in Iraq at All-Time High, Pentagon Report Says," broadcast December 19, 2006, https://www.pbs.org/newshour/show/attacks-in-iraq-at-all-time-high-pentagon-report-says.

174 John O'Neill and Jerome Corsi, *Unfit for Command: Swift Boat Veterans Speak Out Against John Kerry* (Washington, DC: Regnery Publishing, 2004).

175 CBS News Staff, "Report: Bush Short on Guard Duty," *CBS News*, September 8, 2004, https://www.cbsnews.com/news/report-bush-short-on-guard-duty/.

176 BBC News Staff, "US 'Spying' on Iraqi Leadership," *BBC News*, September 5, 2008, http://news.bbc.co.uk/2/hi/7600077.stm.

177 Associated Press, "U.S. General Says Iraq Violence Down," *Fox News*, December 17, 2007, https://www.foxnews.com/story/u-s-general-says-iraq-violence-at-lowest-levels-since-2004.

178 Larry Schweikart, "The Real Body Count," *FrontPageMagazine*, August 18, 2006, www.frontpagemagazine.com.

Even using a more conservative seventy-five insurgents killed per day, the US had eliminated over thirty-six thousand fighters by 2007.

179 Larry Schweikart, *America's Victories: How the U.S. Wins Wars and Will Win the War on Terror*, rev. ed. (Point Pleasant, NJ: The Knox Press, 2015), 253.

180 Ibid., 254.

181 Michael E. O'Hanlon and Sam Gollob, *Iraq Index: Tracking Variables of Reconstruction and Security in Post-Saddam Iraq*, Brookings Institution, August 2020, https://www.brookings.edu/wp-content/uploads/2020/08/FP_20200825_iraq_index.pdf.

182 "Petraeus Urges 45-Day Halt in Weighing New Iraq Troop Cuts," *New York* Times, April 9, 2008, https://www.nytimes.com/2008/04/09/world/middleeast/08cnd-petraeus.html

183 Barack Obama, "Remarks at Camp Lejeune, North Carolina," *PBS NewsHour*, February 27, 2009, https://www.pbs.org/newshour/nation/military-jan-june09-obama-speech_02-27; Staff Writers, "Iraq Not Fazed by Pending US Pullout: Maliki," *SpaceWar*, February 26, 2009, https://www.spacewar.com/reports/Iraq_not_fazed_by_pending_US_pullout_Maliki_999.html.

CHAPTER 3: *LENT DECLIN*

184 Peter Zeihan, *The Accidental Superpower* (New York: Hanchette, 2014), 91.

185 *Guardian*, "India Overtakes China to Become the World's Most Populous Country," April 24, 2023.

186 Peter Zeihan, *The Accidental Superpower* (New York: Hanchette, 2014), 115.

187 David Halberstam, *The Reckoning* (New York: William Morrow & Co., 1986), passim.

188 Paul Johnson, *Modern Times: A History of the World from the Twenties to the Nineties*, rev. ed. (New York: HarperCollins, 1991), 584.

189 Peter Zeihan, *The Accidental Superpower* (New York: Hanchette, 2014), 138.

190 Thomas Piketty and Emmanuel Saez, "Income Inequality in the United States, 1912–1998," *Quarterly Journal of Economics*, 118 (2003): 1–39; Joseph Stiglitz, *The Price of Inequality: How Today's Divided Society Endangers Our Future* (New York: W. W. Norton, 2012).

191 Gerald Auten and David Splinter, "Income Inequality in the United States: Using Tax Data to Measure Long-Term Trends," *Journal of Political Economy* 132, no. 7 (July 2024), electronically published June 10, 2024, https://doi.org/10.1086/728741.
192 Charles Murray, *Coming Apart: The State of White America, 1960–2010* (New York: Crown, 2012), 26.
193 Ibid., 27.
194 Ibid., 28.
195 Mark Moyar, *Masters of Corruption* (New York: Encounter, 2024), 62.
196 Ibid., 63.
197 J. D. Vance, *Hillbilly Elegy: A Memoir of a Family and Culture in Crisis* (New York: Harper, 2018).
198 Charles Murray, *Coming Apart: The State of White America, 1960–2010* (New York: Crown, 2012), 27.
199 Noah Smith, "Conceiving the 2000s," *Noahpinion* (Substack), March 4, 2023; Noah Smith, "Many Americans Still Feel the Sting of Lost Wealth," *Bloomberg Opinion*, August 8, 2018, https://www.bloomberg.com/opinion/articles/2018-08-08/many-americans-still-feel-the-sting-of-lost-wealth.
200 Smith, "Conceiving" and "Many Americans," passim.
201 Charles Calomiris and Stephen Haber, *Fragile By Design: the Political Origins of Banking Crises & Scarce Credit* (Princeton, NJ: Princeton University Press, 2014), 206.
202 Gary Gordon, "Slapped in the Face by the Invisible Hand: Banking and the Panic of 2007," Yale University and National Bureau of Economic Research, May 9, 2009, https://web.archive.org/web/20140620164026/http://www.frbatlanta.org/news/CONFEREN/09fmc/gorton.pdf.
203 Timothy Geithener, "Reducing Systematic Risk in a Dynamic Financial System," Remarks at the Economic Club of New York, June 8, 2008, https://www.newyorkfed.org/newsevents/speeches/2008/tfg080609.html.
204 Ibid.
205 Charles Calomiris and Stephen Haber, *Fragile By Design: the Political Origins of Banking Crises & Scarce Credit* (Princeton, NJ: Princeton University Press, 2014), 204.
206 Ibid., 204.
207 Ibid., 205.
208 Larry Schweikart, *Banking in the American South From the Age of Jackson to Reconstruction* (Baton Rouge, LA: Louisiana State University Press, 1987).
209 Charles Calomiris and Larry Schweikart, "The Panic of 1857: Origins, Transmission, Containment," *Journal of Economic History* 51, no. 4 (1991): 801–34.
210 Ibid., 208.
211 Ibid., 223.
212 Ibid., 210.
213 Ibid., 209.
214 *The Big Short*. Directed by Adam McKay. Los Angeles: Paramount Pictures, 2015.
215 U.S. Department of Housing and Urban Development, "HUD Announces New Regulations to Provide $2.4 Trillion in Mortgages for Affordable Housing for 28.1 Million Families," October 31, 2000, https://archives.hud.gov/news/2000/pr00-317.html.
216 *Rocket Mortgage*, "Fannie Mae Vs. Freddie Mac: What's the Difference?" April 17, 2023, https://www.rocketmortgage.com/learn/fannie-mae-vs-freddie-mac.
217 Charles Calomiris and Stephen Haber, *Fragile By Design: the Political Origins of Banking Crises & Scarce Credit* (Princeton, NJ: Princeton University Press, 2014), 211.
218 Gary Gordon, "Slapped in the Face by the Invisible Hand: Banking and the Panic of 2007," Yale University and National Bureau of Economic Research, May 9, 2009,

https://web.archive.org/web/20140620164026/http://www.frbatlanta.org/news/CONFEREN/09fmc/gorton.pdf.

219 Michael Lewis, *The Big Short* (New York: W. W. Norton & Company, 2011), 23.

220 Ibid., 25.

221 Ibid., 9.

222 National Commission on the Causes of the Financial and Economic Crisis in the United States, *The Financial Crisis Inquiry Report*, January 2011, https://www.govinfo.gov/content/pkg/GPO-FCIC/pdf/GPO-FCIC.pdf.

223 Thomas Sowell, *The Housing Boom and Bust* (New York: Basic Books, 2009), 33.

224 Ibid., 42.

225 The Economist, "Can't Pay or Won't Pay?" *The Economist*, February 21, 2009, https://www.economist.com/united-states/2009/02/19/cant-pay-or-wont-pay.

226 Thomas Sowell, *The Housing Boom and Bust* (New York: Basic Books, 2009), 46.

227 Ibid., 48.

228 Ibid., 48.

229 Ibid., 50.

230 National Commission on the Causes of the Financial and Economic Crisis in the United States, *The Financial Crisis Inquiry Report*, January 2011, xvii, https://www.govinfo.gov/content/pkg/GPO-FCIC/pdf/GPO-FCIC.pdf.

231 Thomas Sowell, *The Housing Boom and Bust* (New York: Basic Books, 2009), 13.

232 Rupert Neate, "Ratings Agencies Suffer 'Conflict of Interest,' Says Former Moody's Boss," *The Guardian*, August 22, 2011, https://www.theguardian.com/business/2011/aug/22/ratings-agencies-conflict-of-interest.

233 Local10 Staff, "Miami's Changing Skyline: Boom or Bust?" Local10.com, May 11, 2005, https://web.archive.org/web/20110926235236/http://www.local10.com/news/4277615/detail.html; Michael Lewis, *The Big Short: Inside the Doomsday Machine* (New York: W. W. Norton & Company, 2010).

234 Robert J. Samuelson, "Reckless Optimism," *Claremont Review of Books*, 13 (2011), https://web.archive.org/web/20131224113222/http://www.claremont.org/publications/crb/id.1916/article_detail.asp.

235 Ibid.

236 The Associated Press Staff, "Brokers, Bankers Play Subprime Blame Game," *NBC News*, May 22, 2007, https://www.nbcnews.com/id/wbna18804054.

237 Ibid.

238 Gary Gordon, "Slapped in the Face by the Invisible Hand: Banking and the Panic of 2007," Yale University and National Bureau of Economic Research, May 9, 2009, https://web.archive.org/web/20140620164026/http://www.frbatlanta.org/news/CONFEREN/09fmc/gorton.pdf.

239 Charles Calomiris and Stephen Haber, *Fragile By Design: the Political Origins of Banking Crises & Scarce Credit* (Princeton, NJ: Princeton University Press, 2014), 264.

240 Ibid., 272.

241 Ibid., 272.

242 National Commission on the Causes of the Financial and Economic Crisis in the United States, *The Financial Crisis Inquiry Report*, January 2011, xvi, https://www.govinfo.gov/content/pkg/GPO-FCIC/pdf/GPO-FCIC.pdf.

There is some evidence that Henry Paulsen, the Secretary of the Treasury, had a personal grudge against Lehman Bros. for not taking his recommendations to recapitalize sooner. Paulsen later claimed the government didn't have the power to save Lehman, a questionable position given that not long afterwards the government saved AIG and Bear Starns, ostensibly according to Paulsen because they had better balance sheets. But there is some evidence that Paulsen torpedoed acquisition attempts by Bank of America and Barclays to obtain Lehman.

ProPublica, "Why Did Treasury Allow Lehman to Fail?" October 23, 2008, https://www.propublica.org/article/why-did-treasury-allow-lehman-to-fail.

Charles W. Calomiris, email to Larry Schweikart, July 29, 2023.

Charles Calomiris rejects that and said that both "a Korean bank and Met Life had examined [Lehman] earlier and passed on it."

243 NBC News Staff, "New Home Sales Fell by Record Amount in 2007," *NBCNews.com*, January 28, 2008, https://www.nbcnews.com/id/wbna22880294.

244 Kimberly Amadeo, "AIG Bailout, Cost, Timeline, Bonuses, Causes, Effects," *The Balance*, November 16, 2020, https://www.thebalancemoney.com/aig-bailout-cost-timeline-bonuses-causes-effects-3305693.

245 Roger C. Altman, "The Great Crash, 2008," *Foreign Affairs* 88, no. 1 (January/February 2009), https://web.archive.org/web/20090223132656/http://www.foreignaffairs.org/20090101faessay88101/roger-c-altman/the-great-crash-2008.html.

246 George W. Bush, *Decision Points* (New York: Crown, 2010), 440.

247 Ibid., 440.

248 Andrew Roberts, *Churchill: Walking with Destiny* (New York: Viking, 2018).

249 Thomas Sowell, *The Housing Boom and Bust* (New York: Basic Books, 2009), 80.

250 Ibid., 87.

251 Matthew Kuzma, email to author, September 8, 2024.

252 Anonymous, email to author, September 14, 2024.

253 rockit454, "Elder Millennials of Reddit: How Did the Great Recession of 2007–2009ish Impact How you Manage Your Finances Today?" *Reddit*, r/Millennials, https://www.reddit.com/r/Millennials/comments/1ad3k4a/elder_millennials_of_reddit_how_did_the_great.

254 cavaismylife, "It's Shocking How Many People Downplay the Great Recession of the Late 2000s and Early 2010s," *Reddit*, r/Millennials, accessed July 26, 2025, https://www.reddit.com/r/Millennials/comments/1adt5mq/it_is_shocking_how_many_people_downplay_the_great.

255 Ibid.

256 Jason Mick, "Group Wants $7B USD from Apple, Steve Jobs, Executives over Securities Fraud," *DailyTech*, July 2, 2008, https://web.archive.org/web/20120201113415/http://www.dailytech.com/Group+Wants+7B+USD+From+Apple+Steve+Jobs+Executives+Over+Securities+Fraud+/article12258.htm.

257 Walter Isaacson, *Steve Jobs* (New York: Simon & Schuster, 2011), 1–4.

258 Ibid., 5–6.

259 Ibid., 15.

260 Robert Iger, "'We Could Say Anything to Each Other': Bob Iger Remembers Steve Jobs," *Vanity Fair*, September 18, 2019, https://www.vanityfair.com/news/2019/09/bob-iger-remembers-steve-jobs.

261 Robert Gordon, *Rise and Fall of American Growth* (Princeton, NJ.: Princeton University Press, 2016), 326–328

262 Ibid., 384.

263 Ibid., 539.

264 Arjun Ramani (@arjun_ramani3), "Firm boundaries are blurring. Remote work changes the calculus of what to do—and what not to do," *X*, January 14, 2023, https://x.com/arjun_ramani3/status/1614328591478562819.

However, that argument alone may call into question the improvements in the *American* economy, for as more international employees do the work, it reduces the number of employed Americans.

265 Noah Smith, "Repost: Distributed Service-Sector Productivity," *Noahpinion* (Substack), January 15, 2023, https://www.noahpinion.blog/p/repost-distributed-service-sector.

266 McKinsey Global Institute, "Will Productivity and Growth Return After the COVID-19 Crisis?" *McKinsey & Company*, March 30, 2021, https://www.mckinsey.com/industries/public-sector/our-insights/will-productivity-and-growth-return-after-the-covid-19-crisis.

267 Larry Schweikart and Lynne Pierson Doti, *American Entrepreneur* (New York: AMACOM, 2010), 389; Irwin Garfinkle and Robert Haveman, *Earnings Capacity, Poverty, and Inequality*, U.S. Department of Health, Education and Welfare, Institute for Research on Poverty Monograph Series (New York: Academic Press, 1977).

268 George Gilder, *Wealth & Poverty* (New York: Bantam, 1981), 87

269 Peter Zeihan, *Absent Superpower: The Shale Revolution and a World Without America* (Austin, TX: Zeihan Books, 2016), 113.

270 Paul Beaudry, David A. Green, and Benjamin M. Sand, "The Great Reversal in the Demand for Skill and Cognitive Tasks," *National Bureau of Economic Research Working Paper* No. 18901, March 2013, https://www.nber.org/papers/w18901.

271 Damon Linker, "Sorry, Obama, but America Is in Decline—and That Might Not Be Such a Bad Thing," *The Week*, January 10, 2015, https://theweek.com/articles/446473/sorry-obama-but-america-decline--that-might-not-such-bad-thing.

272 The Sunday Times Staff, "US Can No Longer Be World's Only Superpower, Says Clinton," *The Sunday Times*, January 27, 2011, https://www.thetimes.com/article/us-can-no-longer-be-worlds-only-superpower-says-clinton-2zn8gxq39w3.

What was most interesting about Clinton's comment is that at that very time, Obama was allowing NATO allies to avoid paying their fair share of NATO's bills, which, in fact, weakened the US by forcing Americans to pay more for Europe's defense.

273 Peter Zeihan, *Absent Superpower: The Shale Revolution and a World Without America* (Austin, TX: Zeihan Books, 2016), 57.

274 Ibid., 73.

275 Ibid., 93.

276 *Daily Tech*, "Cracking the Bitcoin: Digging Into a $131m USD Virtual Currency," June 12, 2011; Satoshi Nakamoto, "Bitcoin: A Peer-to-Peer Electronic Cash System," October 31, 2008, https://bitcoin.org/bitcoin.pdf; Paul Vigna and Michael Casey, *The Age of Cryptocurrency: How Bitcoin and Digital Money are Challenging the Global Economic Order* (New York: St. Martin's Press, 2015); Alan Sherman et al., "On the Origins and Variations of Blockchain Technologies," *IEEE Security & Piracy*, March 2019, https://ieeexplore.ieee.org/document/8674176; Ritchie King, et al., "By Reading this Article, You're Mining Bitcoins," *Quartz*, December 17, 2013, https://qz.com/154877/by-reading-this-page-you-are-mining-bitcoins#Correction; The Economist Staff, "Bitcoin" and Other Cryptocurrencies are Useless," *The Economist*, August 20, 2018, https://www.economist.com/leaders/2018/08/30/bitcoin-and-other-cryptocurrencies-are-useless; Lily Katz, "Bitcoin Acceptance Among Retailers Is Low and Getting Lower," *Bloomberg*, July 12, 2017, https://www.bloomberg.com/news/articles/2017-07-12/bitcoin-acceptance-among-retailers-is-low-and-getting-lower.

277 Aaron Pellish and Steve Contorno, "Trump Pledges to Fire SEC Chair and Previews Cryptocurrency-Friendly Policies," *CNN*, July 27, 2024, https://www.cnn.com/politics/live-news/kamala-harris-trump-election-07-27-24#h_385f60f5752de1771ecf5b4b0a38d04b.

278 Jennifer Conrad, "Donald Trump Supports a U.S. Bitcoin Stockpile. Economists Aren't Convinced," *Inc.*, August 2, 2024, https://www.inc.com/jennifer-conrad/donald-trump-supports-a-us-bitcoin-stockpile-economists-arent-convinced.html.

279 Mireya Solís, "Trump Withdrawing from the Trans-Pacific Partnership," *Brookings Institution*, March 24, 2017, https://www.brookings.edu/blog/unpacked/2017/03/24/trump-withdrawing-from-the-trans-pacific-partnership; Barnini Chakraborty, "Paris Agreement on Climate Change: US Withdraws as Trump Calls It 'Unfair'," *Fox News*, June 1, 2017, https://www.foxnews.com/politics/paris-agreement-on-climate-change-us-withdraws-as-trump-calls-it-unfair.

280 Peter Zeihan, *Absent Superpower: The Shale Revolution and a World Without America* (Austin, TX: Zeihan Books, 2016), 330.

281 J.R. Wu, "Foxconn CEO Says Investment for Display Plant in U.S. Would Exceed $7 Billion," *Reuters*, January 22, 2017, https://www.reuters.com/article/us-taiwan-foxconn-idUSKBN1560JP.

282 Pete Evans, "Trump Pushes Big 3 Automakers to Build More Cars in the U.S.," *CBC News*, January 24, 2017, https://www.cbc.ca/news/business/trump-auto-ceos-1.3949517.

283 Scott Horsley, "Trump Formally Orders Tariffs on Steel, Aluminum Imports," *NPR*, March 8, 2018, https://www.npr.org/2018/03/08/591744195/trump-expected-to-formally-order-tariffs-on-steel-aluminum-imports; Simon Denyer, "As Trump's Trade War Starts, China Vows Retaliation," *The Washington Post*, July 6, 2018, https://www.washingtonpost.com/world/china-fires-back-at-us-tariffs-vows-to-defend-its-core-interests/2018/07/06/f42fc812-8091-11e8-a63f-7b5d2aba7ac5_story.html.

284 Noah Smith, "The Build-Nothing Country," *Noahpinion* (Substack), February 27, 2023, https://noahpinion.substack.com/p/the-build-nothing-country.

285 David Blackmon, "Energy Absurdity of the Week," *Energy Transition Absurdities* (Substack), April 23, 2023, https://blackmon.substack.com/p/the-energy-absurdity-of-the-week-9cb.

286 Jennifer Sey, "The Predictable Economic Fallout of Lockdown Policy," *Sey Everything* (Substack), March 13, 2023, https://jennifersey.substack.com/p/the-predictable-economic-fallout.

287 Carol Roth, "We're Living Through the Greatest Transfer of Wealth From the Middle Class to the Elites in History," *Newsweek*, October 24, 2021, https://www.newsweek.com/were-living-through-greatest-transfer-wealth-middle-class-elites-history-opinion-1641614.

288 Jeffrey A. Tucker, "The Economic Disaster of the Pandemic Response," *Imprimis*, October 2022, https://imprimis.hillsdale.edu/the-economic-disaster-of-the-pandemic-response.

289 Ibid.; Jared Kushner, *Breaking History: A White House Memoir* (New York: Broadside Books, 2022).

290 *National Federation of Independent Business v. Department of Labor, Occupational Safety and Health Administration*, 595 U.S. (2022), https://www.supremecourt.gov/opinions/21pdf/21a244_hgci.pdf.

291 Monica Torres, "In Defense of 'Coffee Badging,' the Controversial New Office Trend," *MSN*, September 15, 2024, https://www.msn.com/en-us/lifestyle/career/in-defense-of-coffee-badging-the-controversial-new-office-trend/ar-AA1qBpST.

292 Paul Beaudry, David A. Green, and Benjamin M. Sand, "The Great Reversal in the Demand for Skill and Cognitive Tasks," *National Bureau of Economic Research Working Paper* No. 18901, March 2013, https://www.nber.org/papers/w18901.

293 Jeremy Horpedahl, "Who is the Wealthiest Generation?" *Economist Writing Every Day* (blog), September 1, 2021, https://economistwritingeveryday.com/2021/09/01/who-is-the-wealthiest-generation/.

294 Noah Smith, "Will there Be a Millennial Big Chill?" *Noahpinion* (Substack), April 22, 2023, https://economistwritingeveryday.com/2021/09/01/who-is-the-wealthiest-generation/.

295 Dana Anderson and Sheharyar Bokhari, "The Race to Homeownership: Gen Z Tracking Ahead of their Parents' Generation, Millennials Tracking Behind," *Redfin News*, April 21, 2023, https://www.redfin.com/news/gen-z-millennial-homeownership-rate-home-purchases/.

296 Information Station Staff, "How can the Unemployment Rate Rise While Jobs are Created?" *Information Station*, May 10, 2021, https://informationstation.org/kitchen_table_econ/how-can-the-unemployment-rate-rise-while-jobs-are-created/; Trading Economics Staff, "United States Labor Force Participation Rate, 2018–2023," *Trading Economics*, April 2023, https://tradingeconomics.com/united-states/labor-force-participation-rate.

297 David Winston, "Introducing the 'Presidential Inflation Rate': Biden Trails Only Carter," *Roll Call*, March 15, 2023, https://rollcall.com/2023/03/15/introducing-the-presidential-inflation-rate-biden-trails-only-carter.

298 Prof. St. Onge (@profstonge), "UMich Inflation Expectations Haven't Been Higher Since 2008," *Twitter*, May 12, 2023, https://twitter.com/profstonge/status/1657076258147008525.

299 Òscar Jordà, Celeste Liu, Fernanda Nechio, and Fabián Rivera-Reyes, "Why Is U.S. Inflation Higher than Other Countries?" *FRBSF Economic Letter*, Federal Reserve Bank of San Francisco, March 28, 2022, https://www.frbsf.org/wp-content/uploads/sites/4/el2022-07.pdf.

300 Post Editorial Board, "New Fed Study Shows Biden Owns Our Economic Disaster," *New York Post*, April 4, 2022, 8:04 p.m. ET, https://nypost.com/2022/04/04/new-fed-study-shows-biden-owns-our-economic-disaster.

301 "Wasting Away Again in Bidenville! Umich Consumer Confidence Falls to 57.7 …," *Confounded Interest*, May 12, 2023, https://confoundedinterest.net/2023/05/12/wasting-away-again-in-bidenville-umich-consumer-confidence-falls-to-57-7-100-before-covid-housing-seniment-sinks-to-34.

302 Noah Smith, "At Least Five Interesting Things to Start Your Week," *Noahpinion* (Substack), June 5, 2023, https://www.noahpinion.blog/p/at-least-five-interesting-things-5b3.

CHAPTER 4: THE ROT

303 Martin Gurri, "The Elite Panic of 2022," *City Journal*, Summer 2022, https://www.city-journal.org/the-elite-panic-of-2022.

304 Sapna Maheshwari, "Topics Suppressed in China are Underrepresented on Tik Tok," *The New York Times*, December 21, 2023, https://www.nytimes.com/2024/01/08/business/media/tiktok-data-tool-israel-hamas-war.html; David Leonhardt, "Tik Tok's Pro-China Tilt," *The New York Times*, April 24, 2024, https://www.nytimes.com/2024/04/24/briefing/tiktok-ban-bill-congress.html; *Associated Press*, "TikTok Restricts Tool Used by Researcher—and Its Critics—to Assess Content on Its Platform," January 8, 2024.

305 Angelo Codevilla, *The Ruling Class: How They Corrupted America and What We Can Do About it* (New York: Beaufort Books, 2010).

306 Angelo Codevilla, "America's Ruling Class and the Period of Revolution," *American Spectator*, July 16, 2010, https://spectator.org/americas-ruling-class/.

307 Ibid.

308 Eugyppius, "The Administrative Man," *Eugyppius: a Plague Chronicle*, June 21, 2023, https://www.eugyppius.com/p/the-administrative-man.

309 Alfred D. Chandler Jr., *The Visible Hand: The Managerial Revolution in American Business* (Cambridge, MA: Belknap Press of Harvard University Press, 1977).

310 Burton Klein, *Dynamic Economics* (Cambridge, MA: Harvard University Press, 1977).

311 Michael Park, Erin Leahey, and Russell J. Funk, "Papers and Patents Are Becoming Less Disruptive Over Time," *Nature* 613 (2023): 138–144, https://www.nature.com/articles/s4186-22-05543-x.

312 John P. A. Ioannidis, "Why Most Published Research Findings Are False," *PLOS Medicine* 2, no. 8 (August 2005): 696–701, https://journals.plos.org/plosmedicine/article?id=10.1371/journal.pmed.0020124; Philip Magness, "The Failure of Imperial College Modeling is Far Worse than We Knew," *American Institute for Economic Research*, April 22, 2021, https://www.aier.ortg/article/the-failure-of-imperial-college-modeling-is-far-worse-than-we-knew/.

313 That practice dates back to John F. Kennedy, who had his prize-winning book *Profiles in Courage* researched and written for him by Ivy League academics.

314 Charles Murray, *Coming Apart: The State of White America, 1960–2010* (New York: Crown, 2012), 25–26.

315 Larry Schweikart, *Seven Events That Made America America* (New York: Sentinel, 2010), 95–116.

316 Charles Murray, *Coming Apart: The State of White America, 1960–2010* (New York: Crown, 2012), 49–51.

317 Charles Murray, "How Thick Is Your Bubble?" in *Coming Apart: The State of White America, 1960–2010* (New York: Crown, 2012), 103–115.

318 Geoffrey C. Layman, *The Great Divide: Religious and Cultural Conflict in American Party Politics* (New York: Columbia University Press, 2001).

319 Robert D. Putnam and David E. Campbell, *American Grace: How Religion Divides and Unites Us* (New York: Simon & Schuster, 2010).

320 Ryan Burge, "The God Gap in American Politics," *Graphs about Religion* (Substack), September 9, 2024, https://www.graphsaboutreligion.com/p/the-god-gap-in-american-politics.

321 Ibid.

322 Jean M. Twenge, *Generations: The Real Differences Between Gen Z, Millennials, Gen X, Boomers, and Silents—and What They Mean for America's Future* (New York: Atria Books, 2023), 295–301.

323 Ryan Burge, "The Religiosity of High School Seniors, 1976–2022," *Graphs about Religion* (Substack), May 28, 2024, https://www.graphsaboutreligion.com/p/the-religiosity-of-high-school-seniors-1976-2022.

324 Ryan Burge, "The Religion of America's Young Adults," *Graphs about Religion* (Substack), September 25, 2024, https://www.graphsaboutreligion.com/p/the-religion-of-americas-young-adults.

325 Springtide Research Institute, *The State of Religion and Young People 2020: Relational Authority* (Winona, MN: Springtide Research Institute, 2020), 23, 33, 39.

326 Ibid., 27, 40.

327 Ryan Burge, "Where Have Churches Disappeared?" *Graphs about Religion* (Substack), August 29, 2024, https://www.graphsaboutreligion.com/p/where-have-churches-disappeared.

328 Paul Kleppner, *The Cross of Culture: A Social Analysis of Midwestern Politics, 1850–1900* (New York: Free Press, 1970).

329 Ryan Burge, "Where Have Churches Disappeared?" *Graphs about Religion* (Substack), August 29, 2024, https://www.graphsaboutreligion.com/p/where-have-churches-disappeared.

330 Ryan Burge, "Just How Bad Is Denominational Decline?" *Graphs about Religion* (Substack), June 12, 2023, https://www.graphsaboutreligion.com/p/just-how-bad-is-denominational-decline.

331 Jean M. Twenge, *Generations: The Real Differences Between Gen Z, Millennials, Gen X, Boomers, and Silents—and What They Mean for America's Future* (New York: Atria Books, 2023).

332 Ibid., 393–5.

333 Billie Eilish and Finneas O'Connell, "Bury a Friend," *Genius Lyrics*, January 30, 2019, https://genius.com/Billie-eilish-bury-a-friend-lyrics.

334 Jean M. Twenge, *Generations: The Real Differences Between Gen Z, Millennials, Gen X, Boomers, and Silents—and What They Mean for America's Future* (New York: Atria Books, 2023), 396.

335 Olivia Rodrigo and Dan Nigro, "Brutal," *SOUR*, Geffen Records, 2021, lyric video, https://www.youtube.com/watch?v=hM2U8cb8lhI.

336 Jean M. Twenge, *Generations: The Real Differences Between Gen Z, Millennials, Gen X, Boomers, and Silents—and What They Mean for America's Future* (New York: Atria Books, 2023), 401.

337 Ibid., 405.

338 Ibid., 420.

339 Jean M. Twenge, *iGen: Why Today's Super-Connected Kids Are Growing Up Less Rebellious, More Tolerant, Less Happy—and Completely Unprepared for Adulthood* (New York: Atria Books, 2017), 108.

340 Ibid., 109.

341 Springtide Research Institute, *The State of Religion and Young People 2020: Relational Authority* (Winona, MN: Springtide Research Institute, 2020), 15.

342 Noah Smith, "Conceiving the 2000s," *Noahpinion* (Substack), March 5, 2023, https://www.noahpinion.blog/p/conceiving-the-2000s.

343 Ibid.

344 Jean M. Twenge, *iGen: Why Today's Super-Connected Kids Are Growing Up Less Rebellious, More Tolerant, Less Happy—and Completely Unprepared for Adulthood* (New York: Atria Books, 2017), 115.

345 Anne Morris and Debra L. Katzman, "The Impact of Media on Eating Disorders in Children and Adolescents," *Paediatrics & Child Health* 8, no. 5 (May–June 2003): 287–289, https://www.ncbi.nlm.nih.gov/pmc/articles/PMC2792687.

346 Jennifer Sey, "What Happened to Body Positivity?" *Sey Everything* (Substack), October 20, 2024, https://jennifersey.substack.com/p/what-happened-to-body-positivity.

347 Ibid.

348 Caroline Hopkins, "Eating Disorders Among Teens More Severe than Ever," *NBC News*, April 29, 2023, https://www.nbcnews.com/health/health-news/eating-disorders-anorexia-bulimia-are-severe-ever-rcna80745.

349 Larry Schweikart, *Seven Events that Made America America* (New York: Sentinel, 2010), 95–116.

350 Jonathan Engel, *Fat Nation: A History of Obesity in America* (Lanham, MD. Rowman & Littlefield, 2018), 1; Laura Dawes, *Childhood Obesity in America: Biography of an Epidemic* (Cambridge, MA: Harvard University Press, 2014).

351 Jonathan Engel, *Fat Nation: A History of Obesity in America* (Lanham, MD. Rowman & Littlefield, 2018), 2.

352 . Ibid., 3.

Engel blames the design of cities ("unwalkable landscape") and fast food. But Americans were eating fast food at considerably high levels since the 1960s. Obesity did not become as big a problem until the anti-meat/anti-fat propaganda associated with the "population explosion" that took root.

353 Gary Taubes, *Good Calories, Bad Calories* (New York: Knopf, 2007), xvi–xvii.

354 Ibid., xvii.

355 Ibid., xviii.

356 "Taking Exercise to Heart," *The New York Times*, March 27, 1977; "Passion to Keep Fit: 100 Million Americans Exercising," *Washington Post*, August 31, 1980.

357 Kelly Brownell and K. B. Hogan, *Food Fight: The Inside Story of the Food Industry, America's Obesity Crisis, and What We Can Do About It* (New York: McGraw Hill, 2004), 8.

358 Dr. Farah Husain, interview by author, October 15, 2024.

359 Ibid.

360 Husain, like other obesity doctors, noted that the majority of morbidly obese people have suffered from childhood trauma, including beatings. Thus, diets or even surgery alone will not work.

361 David Pimentel and Marcia Pimentel, "Sustainability of Meat-Based and Plant-Based Diets and the Environment," *American Journal of Clinical Nutrition* 78, no. 3, suppl. (September 2003): 660S–663S, https://ajcn.nutrition.org/article/S0002-9165%2822%2903370-6/ppt.

362 Nathan Fiala, "How Meat Contributes to Global Warming," *Scientific American* 300, no. 2 (February 2009): 72–75, https://www.scientificamerican.com/article/how-meat-contributes-to-global-warming.

363 David Krayden, "NPR Blames Men Who Eat Beef for Climate Change," *The Post Millennial*, September 29, 2024, https://thepostmillennial.com/npr-blames-men-who-eat-beef-for-climate-change.

364 Constance Russell, Erin Cameron, Teresa Socha, and Hannah McNinch, "Fatties Cause Global Warming": Fat Pedagogy and Environmental Education, *Canadian Journal of Environmental Education* 18 (2013): 27–45, https://files.eric.ed.gov/fulltext/EJ1061815.pdf.

365 New York Daily News Staff, "Scientists: Fat People Make Global Warming a Lot Worse," *New York Daily News*, April 21, 2009, https://www.nydailynews.com/2009/04/21/scientists-fat-people-make-global-warming-a-lot-worse/.

366 Timothy A. Wise, *Eating Tomorrow: Agribusiness, Family Farmers, and the Battle for the Future of Food*, introduction by Raj Patel (New York: New Press, 2019), vii.

367 Jennifer Sey, "What Happened to Body Positivity?" *Sey Everything* (Substack), October 20, 2024, https://jennifersey.substack.com/p/what-happened-to-body-positivity.

368 Rachel Cohen et al., "The Case for Body Positivity on Social Media: Perspectives on Current Advances and Future Directions," *Journal of Health Psychology* 26 (2021): 2365–2373, https://journals.sagepub.com/doi/10.1177/1359105321 1024521; Alexandra Sastre, "Towards a Radical Body Positive: Reading the online 'Body Positive' Movement, *Feminist Media Studies* 14, no. 6 (2014): 929–943, https://www.tandfonline.com/doi/abs/10.1080/14680777.2014.951605; Celene Leboeuf, "What Is Body Positivity?: The Path from Shame to Pride," *Philosophical Topics* 47, no. 2 (2019): 113–127, https://www.pdcnet.org/philtopics/content/philosophical-topics_2019_0047_0002_0113_0127.

369 Jennifer Sey, "What Happened to Body Positivity?" *Sey Everything* (Substack), October 20, 2024, https://jennifersey.substack.com/p/what-happened-to-body-positivity.

370 Sophia Dorris, "Many Advertising Agencies Use Thin Models in 'Fat Suits' to Sell Plus Size Fashions, Continuing Trend of Fat Shaming," *The Torch*, May 3, 2022, https://

ohtorch.com/6663/features/many-advertising-agencies-use-thin-models-in-fat-suits-to-sell-plus-size-fashions-continuing-trend-of-fat-shaming.

371 Ibid.

372 Ibid.

373 Chrissy Callahan, "Lizzo Addresses Ozempic Rumors and Reveals Her 2 Main Weight Loss Strategies," *Today*, August 30, 2024, https://www.today.com/health/diet-fitness/lizzo-weight-loss-rcna168539.

374 Noah Smith, "At Least Five Interesting Things to Start Your Week," *Noahpinion* (Substack), October 13, 2024, https://www.noahpinion.blog/p/at-least-five-interesting-things-eea.

375 Dr. Farah Husain, interview by author, October 15, 2024.

Another problem with the data is that it relied on doctor's examination reports. However, increasingly (partly due to body-positivity pressure), doctors have ceased even weighing patients. Thus an "examination" could be as little as visual assessment, which could be prejudiced by the common encounters with overweight Americans, normalizing obesity. In 2024, at a routine physical exam, I nudged my doctor. "Obesity is a problem, right?" I asked. He said, "Yes." I pointed toward his nursing and office staff, of which 90% were seriously obese. He sighed. "It's a problem."

376 Katherine Fung, "Amish Farmer Turned Republican Hero Becomes Flash Point in Culture War," *Newsweek*, February 23, 2024, https://www.newsweek.com/amish-farmer-turned-republican-hero-becomes-flash-point-culture-war-1872374.

377 "Barnes and Baris Episode 70: What Are the Odds?" *The People's Pundit* (YouTube), streamed live May 28, 2024, https://www.youtube.com/watch?v=VU2-GIagnJ8.

378 "Why We Need to Give Insects the Role They Deserve in Our Food Systems," *World Economic Forum*, July 12, 2021, https://www.weforum.org/agenda/2021/07/why-we-need-to-give-insects-the-role-they-deserve-in-our-food-systems/.

379 Hillary Hoffower, "The U.S. Birth Rate Hit Another Record Low in 2019," *Business Insider India*, October 9, 2020, https://www.businessinsider.in/science/health/news/the-us-birth-rate-hit-another-record-low-in-2019-experts-fear-were-facing-a-demographic-time-bomb-that-could-be-fast-tracked-by-the-pandemic-/articleshow/78577430.cms.

380 *The Press Democrat* Editorial Board, "California's Baby Bust Has Long Term Consequences," *The Press Democrat*, March 5, 2023, https://www.pressdemocrat.com/article/opinion/pd-editorial-californias-baby-bust-has-long-term-consequences.

381 Rebecca Traister, "Single Women are the Most Potent Political Force in America," *The Cut*, February 21, 2016, https://www.thecut.com/2016/02/political-power-single-women-c-v-r.html.

382 Carolina Aragão, "Among Young Adults Without Children, Men Are More Likely Than Women to Say They Want to Be Parents Someday," *Pew Research Center*, February 15, 2024, https://www.pewresearch.org/short-reads/2024/02/15/among-young-adults-without-children-men-are-more-likely-than-women-to-say-they-want-to-be-parents-someday.

383 Richard Fry, "A Growing Share of U.S. Husbands and Wives Are Roughly the Same Age," *Pew Research Center*, August 15, 2024, https://www.pewresearch.org/short-reads/2024/08/15/a-growing-share-of-us-husbands-and-wives-are-roughly-the-same-age/.

384 Eric Levitz, "David Shor's Unified Theory of American Politics," *Intelligencer*, July 17, 2020, https://nymag.com/intelligencer/2020/07/david-shor-cancel-culture-2020-election-theory-polls.html.

385 Rod Dreher, "No Families, No Children, No Future," *The American Conservative*, October 22, 2020, https://www.theamericanconservative.com/no-families-no-children-no-future-lgbt-30-percent-carle-c-zimmerman/.

386 Joel Kotkin and Wendell Cox, "The Unexpected Future: We Need to Consider Ways to Reverse or at Least Slow Rapid Depopulation," *Quilette*, August 20, 2022, https://quillette.com/2022/08/20/the-unexpected-future/.

387 William R. Emmons, "U.S. Population Growth Slowing to a Crawl," Federal Reserve Bank of St. Louis, February 10, 2020, https://www.stlouisfed.org/on-the-economy/2020/february/us-population-growth-slowing-crawl.

388 Kevin O'Connor, "America's Public Pension System remains Mired in Crisis," *Morning Consult*, January 28, 2021, https://morningconsult.com/opinions/americas-public-pension-system-remains-mired-in-crisis/.

389 Gary Becker and Richard Posner, "Low Birth Rates: Causes, Consequences, and Remedies—Becker," *The Becker-Posner Blog*, August 18, 2013, https://www.becker-posner-blog.com/2013/08/low-birth-rates-causes-consequences-and-remedies-becker.html.

390 Ali Modarres and Joel Kotkin, "The Childless City," *City Journal*, Summer 2013, https://www.city-journal.org/html/childless-city-13577.html.

391 Rod Dreher, "No Families, No Children, No Future," *The American Conservative*, October 22, 2020, https://www.theamericanconservative.com/no-families-no-children-no-future-lgbt-30-percent-carle-c-zimmerman/.

392 Jon Marcus, "Why Men Are the New College Minority," *The Atlantic*, August 8, 2017, https://www.theatlantic.com/education/archive/2017/08/why-men-are-the-new-college-minority/536103.

393 Robert Wagner, *The New War Against Men: The Emasculation of Western Males and What It Portends for Global Society* (Independently published, 2019), https://www.amazon.com/NEW-WAR-AGAINST-MEN-Emasculation/dp/169658132X.

394 Heather MacDonald, "In Loco Masculi: The Feminization of the American University Is All but Complete," *City Journal*, March 5, 2023, https://www.city-journal.org/the-great-feminization-of-the-american-university.

395 Ibid.

396 Ibid.

397 Rollo Tomassi, *The Rational Male* (CreateSpace Independent Publishing Platform, 2013).

398 George Gilder, *Men and Marriage* (Gretna, LA: Pelican Publishing, 1986).

399 Morgan Stanley Research, "Rise of the SHEconomy," *Morgan Stanley*, September 23, 2019, https://www.morganstanley.com/ideas/womens-impact-on-the-economy.

400 *Obergefell v. Hodges*, 576 U.S. 644 (2015).

401 Lillian Faderman, *The Gay Revolution: The Story of the Struggle* (New York: Simon & Schuster, 2016); Don Romesburg, ed., *The Routledge History of Queer America* (London: Routledge, 2019).

402 Michael Lind, "The New Gatekeepers," Tablet Magazine, October 26, 2022, https://www.tabletmag.com/sections/news/articles/new-gatekeepers-woke-michael-lind.

403 Joseph K. Canner et al., "Temporal Trends in Gender-Affirming Surgery Among Transgender Patients in the United States," *JAMA Surgery* 153, no. 7 (July 2018): 609–619, https://jamanetwork.com/journals/jamasurgery/fullarticle/2673384.

The numbers of actual transgender people has varied widely, especially since it became a political issue, with some putting the number of men who wished to be women at one in 14, 705, and women who "identified" as men at one in 38,461.

David Geary, "Understanding the Rise of Transgender Identities," *Quillette*, February 10, 2023, https://quillette.com/2023/02/10/social-contagion-and-transgender-identities.

404 Lisa Littman, "Parent Reports of Adolescents and Young Adults Perceived to Show Signs of a Rapid Onset of Gender Dysphoria," *PLOS One* 13, no. 8 (August 16, 2018): e0202330, https://journals.plos.org/plosone/article?id=10.1371/journal.pone.0202330.

405 David Geary, "Understanding the Rise of Transgender Identities," *Quillette*, February 10, 2023, https://quillette.com/2023/02/10/social-contagion-and-transgender-identities.

406 Michael Irwig, "Detransition Among Transgender and Gender-Diverse People—an Increasing and Increasingly Complex Phenomenon," *The Journal of Clinical Endocrinology and Metabolism* 107, no. 10 (October 2022): e4261–e4262, https://academic.oup.com/jcem/article/107/10/e4261/6652194.

407 Hilary Cass, *The Cass Review: Final Report* (Independent Review of Gender Identity Services for Children and Young People, April 2024), https://cass.independent-review.uk/home/publications/final-report.

408 Joe Kottke, "Peru Classifies Transgender Identities as 'Mental Health Problems' in New Law," *NBC News*, May 20, 2024, https://www.nbcnews.com/nbc-out/out-news/peru-classifies-transgender-identities-mental-health-problems-new-law-rcna152936.

409 "How has the Meaning of the Word 'Woke' Evolved?" *The Economist*, July 30, 2021, https://www.economist.com/the-economist-explains/2021/07/30/how-has-the-meaning-of-the-word-woke-evolved.

410 Noah Smith, "The Wokeness Series," *Noahpinion* (Substack), March 17, 2023, https://noahpinion.substack.com/p/the-wokeness-series.

411 Theodore Kupfer, "Where Did Wokeness Come From? Evaluating the Theories," *City Journal*, August 19, 2022, https://www.city-journal.org/article/where-did-wokeness-come-from.

Wokeness, most observers would agree, can be defined as the progressive worldview that views all racial and sexual disparities as proof of discrimination, and rejects liberal procedural traditions in favor of a totalizing politics that seeks to dismantle those disparities and silence dissenters.

412 Noah Smith, "Who Can Push Back When Wokeness Overreaches?" *Noahpinion* (Substack), June 23, 2021, https://noahpinion.substack.com/p/who-can-push-back-when-wokeness-overreaches.

413 Christopher F. Rufo, "The Universal N-Word," *Christopher F. Rufo* (Substack), April 12, 2022, https://rufo.substack.com/p/the-universal-n-word.

What has become clear is that hiding behind vaporous definitions and an undetermined intellectual family tree, the left has attempted to maintain that "since you can't define it, there's no such thing." Then, using that argument leftists tried to claim the very word and concept of wokeism itself is only a "dog whistle" for conservative attacks. In fact, such maneuvers were merely a means to all speech suppression.

414 Alison Heather, "Transwoman Elite Athletes: their Extra Percentage Relative to Female Physiology," *International Journal of Environmental Research and Public Health* 19, no. 15 (August 2022): 9331831, https://www.ncbi.nlm.nih.gov/pmc/articles/PMC9331831.

415 Zixu Wang, Xin Chen, and Caroline Radnofsky, "China Proposes Teaching Masculinity to Boys as State Is Alarmed by Changing Gender Roles," *NBC News*, March 6, 2021, https://www.nbcnews.com/news/world/china-proposes-teaching-masculinity-boys-state-alarmed-changing-gender-roles-n1258939.

416 Josie Appleton, "The Trans War on the Family," *Spiked*, January 29, 2023, https://www.spiked-online.com/2023/01/29/the-trans-war-on-the-family/.

417 Sophie Lewis, *Abolish the Family: A Manifesto for Care and Liberation* (New York: Verso, 2022).

418 Tyler Cowen, "Why Wokeism Will Rule the World," *Bloomberg*, September 19, 2021, https://www.bloomberg.com/opinion/articles/2021-09-19/woke-movement-is-global-and-america-should-be-mostly-proud.

419 Nathaniel Meyersohn, "Bud Light Boycott Likely Cost Anheuser-Busch InBev over $1 Billion in Lost Sales," *CNN*,

February 29, 2024, https://www.cnn.com/2024/02/29/business/bud-light-boycott-ab-inbev-sales/index.html.

420 Nate Hochman, "Woke Capital Blinks," *National Review*, May 24, 2022, https://www.nationalreview.com/corner/woke-capital-blinks/.

421 Ibid.

422 Caroline Downey, "Netflix Takes Aim at Wokeness, *National Review*, May 20, 2022, https://www.nationalreview.com/news/netflix-takes-aim-at-wokeness/.

423 Musa al-Gharbi, "The 'Great Awokening' is Winding Down," *Symbolic Capitalism* (Substack), February 8, 2023, https://musaalgharbi.com/2023/02/08/great-awokening-ending/.

424 Ibid.

425 Tyler Cowen, "Wokism Has Peaked," *Bloomberg*, February 18, 2022, https://www.bloomberg.com/opinion/articles/2022-02-18/wokeism-has-peaked-in-america-but-is-still-globally-influential.

426 Robert Farley, "Obama and 'American Exceptionalism'," FactCheck.Org, February 12, 2015, https://www.factcheck.org/2015/02/obama-and-american-exceptionalism/.

427 Larry Schweikart and Michael Allen, *A Patriot's History of the United States, 15th Anniversary Edition* (New York: Sentinel, 2019); Larry Schweikart and Dave Dougherty, *A Patriot's History of the Modern World, vol. 1: From America's Exceptional Ascent to the Atomic Bomb, 1898–1945* (New York: Sentinel, 2012); Schweikart and Dougherty, *A Patriot's History of the Modern World, vol. 2: From the Cold War to the Age of Entitlement, 1945–2012* (New York: Sentinel, 2013).

428 Tyler Cowen, "Wokism Has Peaked," *Bloomberg*, February 18, 2022, https://www.bloomberg.com/opinion/articles/2022-02-18/wokeism-has-peaked-in-america-but-is-still-globally-influential.

429 Keith Griffith, "Damning Report Reveals There Are No Students Proficient in Either Math or Reading at 60 Different Public Schools in Illinois," *Daily Mail (UK)*, February 20, 2023, https://www.dailymail.co.uk/news/article-11774133/Report-reveals-no-students-proficient-math-reading-60-Illinois-schools.html.

Chris Papst, "23 Baltimore Schools have Zero Students Proficient in Math, Per State Test Results," *Fox News*, February 6, 2023, https://foxbaltimore.com/news/project-baltimore/state-test-results-23-baltimore-schools-have-zero-students-proficient-in-math-jovani-patterson-maryland-comprehensive-assessment-program-maryland-governor-wes-moore.

430 Jonathan Turley, "'The New Normal': New York to Lower Math and English Proficiency Standards Due to Poor Test Results," *Jonathan Turley Blog*, March 17, 2023, https://jonathanturley.org/2023/03/17/the-new-normal-new-york-to-lower-math-and-english-proficiency-standards-due-to-poor-test-results/.

431 Eric A. Hanushek, Paul E. Peterson, Laura M. Talpey, and Ludger Woessmann, "The Achievement Gap Fails to Close," *Education Next*, Spring 2023, https://www.educationnext.org/achievement-gap-fails-close-half-century-testing-shows-persistent-divide/.

432 Charles Murray, *Losing Ground: American Social Policy, 1950–1980* (New York: Basic Books, 2015).

433 John Leake, "Low Verbal IQ Predictor of Politically Correct Authoritarianism," *Courageous Discourse (Substack)*, June 12, 2024, https://petermcculloughmd.substack.com/p/low-verbal-iq-predictor-of-politically.

434 Ember Smith and Richard V. Reeves, "SAT Math Scores Mirror and Maintain Racial Inequality," *Brookings*, December 1, 2020, https://www.brookings.edu/articles/sat-math-scores-mirror-and-maintain-racial-inequity; Tina Vásquez, "Education Advocates Say the Best Way to Address Racial Bias in Standardized Testing Is to Eliminate the Tests Completely," *Prism*, January 31, 2022, https://prismreports.org/2022/01/31/education-advocates-say-the-best-way-to-address-racial-bias-in-standardized-testing-is-to-eliminate-the-tests-completely.

Murray would absolutely agree that standardized testing "mirrors" racial inequality because, in his view, IQ is already set before the testing. Tests *reflect* IQ differences. They don't cause them.

435 WMAR Staff, "Report: Baltimore City Public Schools Changed More Than 12,000 Grades From Failing to Passing," *WMAR-2 News*, June 7, 2022, https://www.wmar2news.com/news/local-news/report-baltimore-city-public-schools-changed-more-than-12-000-grades-from-failing-to-passing.

436 Bri Hatch, "Audit of Baltimore City Schools Finds No Evidence of Grade Manipulation Last Year," *WYPR*, March 13, 2024, https://www.wypr.org/wypr-news/2024-03-13/audit-of-baltimore-city-schools-finds-no-evidence-of-grade-manipulation-last-year.

437 Seamus Othot, "No 8th Grader at LeBron James' Ohio School Has Passed State Math Test Since 2019," *The Maine Wire*, June 26, 2024, https://www.themainewire.com/2024/06/not-one-8th-grader-at-an-ohio-school-founded-by-liberal-activist-and-basketball-legend-lebron-james-has-passed-math-tests-since-2019.

438 Garrett Looker, "Reading Scores Lag Across WNY," *Investigative Post*, April 25, 2024, https://www.investigativepost.org/2024/04/25/western-new-york-reading-scores; The Education Trust–New York, "Warning Bells: The Growing Proficiency Crisis Among New York Students," *EdTrust–NY Report*, May 2024, https://newyork.edtrust.org/wp-content/uploads/2024/05/The-State-of-Annual-3-8-Assessments_May-2024.pdf; Jillian Jorgensen, "Reading Scores Drop After First Year of New Literacy Curriculum," *Spectrum News NY1*, August 21, 2024, https://ny1.com/nyc/all-boroughs/news/2024/08/21/nyc-reading-scores-drop-after-first-year-of-new-literacy-curriculum.

439 Hannah Schmid, "1 in 6 Chicago Third Graders Can Read at Level, Signaling Dismal Futures," *Illinois Policy*, October 4, 2023, https://www.illinoispolicy.org/1-in-6-chicago-third-graders-can-read-at-level-signaling-dismal-futures.

440 Nat Malkus, "Long COVID for Public Schools: Chronic Absenteeism Before and After the Pandemic," *AEI*, January 31, 2024, https://www.aei.org/research-products/report/long-covid-for-public-schools-chronic-absenteeism-before-and-after-the-pandemic/; Catrin Wigfall, "Minnesota's Chronic Absenteeism Rate Has More than Doubled Since 2017," *Center of the American Experiment*, February 27, 2024, https://www.americanexperiment.org/minnesotas-chronic-absenteeism-rate-has-more-than-doubled-since-2017.

441 Catrin Wigfall, "Chronic Absenteeism Not Viewed as a Major Concern," *American* Experiment, June 20, 2024, https://www.americanexperiment.org/chronic-absenteeism-not-viewed-as-major-concern/.

442 Jeff Cain, Bridget Paravattil, and colleagues, "Deficiencies of Traditional Grading Systems and Recommendations for the Future," *American Journal of Pharmaceutical Education*, October 2022, https://www.ncbi.nlm.nih.gov/pmc/articles/PMC10159463; Rachel Burstein, "Stanford Studies Show Benefits of Forgoing Traditional Grading During Pandemic," *Stanford Digital Education*, n.d., https://

digitaleducation.stanford.edu/stanford-studies-show-benefits-forgoing-traditional-grading-during-pandemic.

443 Carolyn Jones and John Fensterwald, "Why Some California School Districts Are Changing How Students Earn Grades," *EdSource*, December 3, 2021, https://edsource.org/2021/why-some-california-school-districts-are-changing-how-students-earn-grades/664226.

444 Laura Meckler, "Why One School District Says It's 'Most Appropriate' to Stop Giving Kids A-F Grades and Move to Pass/Fail," *The Washington Post*, April 2, 2020, https://www.washingtonpost.com/education/2020/04/02/why-one-school-district-says-its-most-appropriate-stop-giving-kids-a-f-grades-move-passfail/.

445 Larry Schweikart, *Reagan: The American President* (New York: Post Hill Press, 2019); Larry Schweikart and Michael Allen, *A Patriot's History of the United States: Fifteenth Anniversary Edition, From Columbus's Great Discovery to the Age of Entitlement* (New York: Sentinel, 2019), 746–91.

446 Emily Fowler, "At UC Berkeley, There Is One Administrator for Every Four Undergraduates," *Minding the Campus*, March 19, 2024, https://www.mindingthe-campus.org/2024/03/19/at-uc-berkeley-there-is-one-administrator-for-every-four-undergrads/.

447 Keith Allen, "Oberlin College to Pay $36.59M to Bakery Owners Who Claim They Were Falsely Accused of Racism," *CNN*, September 9, 2022, https://www.cnn.com/2022/09/09/us/oberlin-college-bakery-lawsuit-payment-reaj/index.html.

448 Roya Hakakian, "The Professor, His Nemesis, and a Scandal at Oberlin," *Quillete*, August 8, 2024, https://quillette.com/2024/08/08/the-professor-his-nemesis-and-a-scandal-at-oberlin-mohammad-jafar-mahallati-iran-islamism/.

449 Ibid.

450 Barron's Staff, "New Tally Puts Oct 7 Attack Death Toll in Israel at 1,189," *Barron's*, May 28, 2024, https://www.barrons.com/news/new-tally-puts-oct-7-attack-death-toll-in-israel-at-1-189-3e038de6.

451 Samuel Chamberlain, "Columbia Has 'Waved the White Flag' by Failing to Expel Even One Student Who Occupied Campus Building: House Report," *New York Post*, August 19, 2024, https://nypost.com/2024/08/19/us-news/not-one-columbia-student-nabbed-in-campus-occupation-has-been-expelled-house-report-says-disgraceful/.

452 Ibid.

453 Beth Treffeisen, "Emerson College Announces Layoffs Amidst Enrollment Decline Linked to Campus Protests," *Boston.com*, June 19, 2024, https://www.boston.com/news/local-news/2024/06/19/emerson-college-announces-layoffs-amidst-enrollment-decline-linked-to-campus-protests/.

454 Aaron Gifford, "Enrollment Loss, Financial Woes an Increasing Problem at US Colleges," *The Epoch Times*, June 27, 2024, https://www.theepochtimes.com/us/enrollment-loss-financial-woes-an-increasing-problem-at-us-colleges-5675821.

455 Education Data Initiative, "Average Cost of College by Year," educationaldata.org, September 9, 2024, https://educationdata.org/average-cost-of-college-by-year.

456 Ibid.

457 Sandra E. Black, Lesley J. Turner, and Jeffrey T. Denning, "PLUS or Minus? The Effect of Graduate School Loans on Access, Attainment, and Prices," *National Bureau of Economic Research*, Working Paper No. 31291, May 2023, https://www.nber.org/papers/w31291.

458 Amy Howe, "Supreme Court Strikes Down Biden Student-Loan Forgiveness Program," SCOTUSBlog, January 20, 2023, https://www.scotusblog.com/2023/06/supreme-court-strikes-down-biden-student-loan-forgiveness-program/.

459 AP-NORC Center for Public Affairs Research, "Biden's Student Loan Work Gets Tepid Reviews—Even Among Those with Debt, an AP-NORC Poll Finds," *Associated Press*, June 11, 2024.

460 Richard Fry, Dana Braga, and Kim Parker, "Is College Worth It?" *Pew Research Center*, May 23, 2024, https://www.pewresearch.org/social-trends/2024/05/23/is-college-worth-it-2.

461 College Transitions Staff, "US College Enrollment Decline—2024 Facts and Figures," *College Transitions*, April 22, 2024, https://www.collegetransitions.com/blog/college-enrollment-decline/.

462 Te-Ping Chen, "America Needs More Tradespeople. Gen Z Is Answering the Call," *Wall Street Journal*, April 14, 2024, https://www.wsj.com/story/america-needs-more-tradespeople-gen-z-is-answering-the-call-ad2bf68d.

463 AP Staff, "Unemployment Among Young College Graduates Outpaces Overall US Joblessness Rate," *Associated Press*, June 26, 2025, https://apnews.com/article/college-graduates-job-market-unemployment-c5e881d0a5c069de08085a47fa58f90f.

464 Megan Brenan, "Americans' Confidence in Higher Education Down Sharply," *Gallup*, July 11, 2023, https://news.gallup.com/poll/508352/americans-confidence-higher-education-down-sharply.aspx.

Typically, Democrats cared more about the costs of college, whereas Republicans cared more about the political bias.

465 Christine Cooke Fairbanks, "Gen Z Has Been Named the 'Toolbelt Generation.' Is that a Good Thing?" *Sutherland Institute*, May 16, 2024, https://sutherlandinstitute.org/gen-z-has-been-named-the-toolbelt-generation-is-that-a-good-thing/.

466 Collin Binkley, "US Colleges Are Cutting Majors and Slashing Programs After Years of Putting It Off," *Associated Press*, August 21, 2024, https://apnews.com/article/college-degree-programs-cuts-music-f0c271f6d61a13404f93688fcc6c589b#.

467 Ibid.

468 College Fix Staff, "MIT Grew Staff Size by 1,200 While Enrollment Barely Budged," *The College Fix*, July 30, 2024, https://www.thecollegefix.com/mit-adds-12-staff-for-every-1-undergrad-over-past-decade/.

469 Justin Hart, "Public School Enrollment; Abandoning the Cities," *CovidReason* (Substack), April 11, 2022, https://covidreason.substack.com/p/public-school-enrollment-abandoning.

470 Ibid.

471 Noah Smith, "Honestly, It's Probably the Phones," *Noahpinion* (Substack), May 13, 2024, https://noahpinion.substack.com/p/honestly-its-probably-the-phones.

472 Medical Daily Staff, "College Grads Are More Unhappy at Work Than Less Educated," *Medical Daily*, July 19, 2013, https://www.medicaldaily.com/college-grads-are-more-unhappy-work-less-educated-according-new-gallup-poll-understanding-why-key.

473 Ben Schmidt (@benmschmidt), "Here's the raw size of all the fields (just BAs)... sharper-than-normal drops in English, Comp Lit, languages," *Twitter*, August 23, 2022, 11:02 p.m., https://twitter.com/benmschmidt/status/1562213619915493376.

474 Peter Turchin, "Blame Rich, Overeducated Elites as Society Frays," *Bloomberg*, November 12, 2016, https://www.bloomberg.com/opinion/articles/2016-11-12/blame-rich-overeducated-elites-as-society-frays.

475 Noah Smith, "The Elite Overproduction Hypothesis: Did America Produce Too Many Frustrated College Graduates in the 2000s and 2010s?" *Noahpinion* (Substack), March 27, 2023, https://noahpinion.substack.com/p/the-elite-overproduction-hypothesis.

476 Miles Kimball and Robert Willis," Utility and Happiness," Yale University Department of Economics, October 30, 2006, http://www.econ.yale.edu/~shiller/behmacro/2006-11/kimball-willis.pdf.

477 Jordan Weissmann, "Pop! Goes the Law School Bubble," *The Atlantic*, March 20, 2012, https://www.theatlantic.com/business/archive/2012/03/pop-goes-the-law-school-bubble/254792/.

478 Ali Modarres and Joel Kotkin, "The Childless City," *City Journal*, Summer 2013, https://www.city-journal.org/html/childless-city-13577.html.

479 Education Forward Arizona Staff, "Arizona School Vouchers," September 14, 2022, https://educationforwardarizona.org/school-vouchers-explained/.

480 Libby Stanford, "6 More States Will Soon Let Almost All Students Attend Private School With Public Funds," *EducationWeek*, June 15, 2023, https://www.edweek.org/policy-politics/6-more-states-will-soon-let-almost-all-students-attend-private-school-with-public-money/2023/06.

481 Eli Hager, "School Vouchers Were Supposed to Save Taxpayer Money. Instead They Blew a Massive Hole in Arizona's Budget," *ProPublica*, July 16, 2024, https://www.propublica.org/article/arizona-school-vouchers-budget-meltdown.

CHAPTER 5: THE DESTROYER

482 David Limbaugh, *Crimes Against Liberty: An Indictment of President Barack Obama* (Washington, DC: Regnery Publishing, 2010), 1.

483 Matt Welch, "Wayne Allyn Root's Million-Dollar Challenge," *Reason*, September 4, 2009, https://reason.com/2008/09/05/wayne-allyn-roots-million-doll/.

484 David Limbaugh, *Crimes Against Liberty: An Indictment of President Barack Obama* (Washington, DC: Regnery Publishing, 2010), 28.

485 Gabriel Sherman, "End of the Affair," *The New Republic*, August 12, 2008, https://newrepublic.com/article/62381/end-the-affair.

486 Barack Obama, *The Audacity of Hope: Thoughts on Reclaiming the American Dream* (New York: Crown, 2006), 202–206.

487 Barack Obama, "'Call to Renewal,' Keynote Address," Obama.Senate.gov (Archived), June 28, 2006, https://web.archive.org/web/20090104231501/http://obama.senate.gov/speech/060628-call_to_renewal/.

488 Ben Wallace-Wells, "The Radical Roots of Barack Obama," *Rolling Stone*, February 22, 2008, https://www.rollingstone.com/politics/politics-features/obama-radical-roots-ben-wallace-wells-2007-1105526/.

489 Jim Geraghty, "Obama's Pastor After 9/11: 'America's Chickens Are Coming Home to Roost,'" *National Review*, March 13, 2008, https://www.nationalreview.com/the-campaign-spot/obamas-pastor-after-911-americas-chickens-are-coming-home-roost-jim-geraghty/.

490 David Limbaugh, *Crimes Against Liberty: An Indictment of President Barack Obama* (Washington, DC: Regnery Publishing, 2010), 324.

491 Mark Finkelstein, "Obama's Spiritual Guide: God Damn America," *NewsBusters*, March 13, 2008, http://newsbusters.org/blogs/mark-finkelstein/2008/03/13/.

492 David Limbaugh, *Crimes Against Liberty: An Indictment of President Barack Obama* (Washington, DC: Regnery Publishing, 2010), 326.

493 Ibid., 326.

494 Paul Kengor, *The Communist: Frank Marshall Davis, The Untold Story of Barack Obama's Mentor* (New York: Threshold Editions, 2012), 4–5.

Kengor lists 15 specific ideas, proposals, or word usages that found their way regularly into Obama's speeches. A plethora of biographies and biographical sketches, cited by Kengor, show the extent of Davis's influence on Obama.

495 David Limbaugh, *Crimes Against Liberty: An Indictment of President Barack Obama* (Washington, DC: Regnery, 2010); David Limbaugh, *The Great Destroyer: Barack Obama's War on the Republic* (Washington, DC: Regnery Publishing, 2012).

496 David Samuels, "The Obama Factor," *Tablet*, August 2, 2023, https://www.tabletmag.com/sections/arts-letters/articles/david-garrow-interview-obama.

497 Ibid.

498 Ibid.

499 Calder McHugh, "Obama's 2004 Convention Speech Made Him a Star. History Proved Him Wrong," *Politico*, August 20, 2024, https://www.politico.com/news/magazine/2024/08/20/obama-2004-convention-speech-history-00175156.

500 Ibid.

501 Anthony Zurcher, "The Key Moments in John McCain's Life," *BBC News*, August 26, 2018, https://www.bbc.com/news/world-us-canada-44009916.

502 Arizona Republic Staff, "John McCain Report: the Keating Five," *Arizona Republic*, March 1, 2007, https://www.azcentral.com/news/articles/2007/03/01/20070301keating-main.html.

503 U.S. Senate Select Committee on POW/MIA Affairs, *Report of the Select Committee on POW/MIA Affairs*, January 13, 1993, https://irp.fas.org/congress/1993_rpt/pow-exec.html.

504 By losing the presidential election, McCain avoided a Constitutional battle over his status as a "natural-born citizen," because he was not, according to a group of legal scholars, a natural-born citizen because the 1937 law that made him a citizen was passed after his birth. McCain's status would take pressure off his 2008 opponent, Obama, whose birth in the United States at the time of the election was also questioned.

505 Soumitra Dutta and Matthew Fraser, "Barack Obama and the Facebook Election," *U.S. News & World Report*, November 19, 2008, https://www.usnews.com/opinion/articles/2008/11/19/barack-obama-and-the-facebook-election.

506 Claire Cain Miller, "How Obama's Internet Campaign Changed Politics," *The New York Times*, November 7, 2008, https://archive.nytimes.com/bits.blogs.nytimes.com/2008/11/07/how-obamas-internet-campaign-changed-politics/.

Academic studies disputed the impact of the internet, but academics still claimed they could not find evidence that social media "actually drove discussion, participation, or outcomes," but this seems a testimony of the weakness or un-inventiveness of academia's measurement abilities, not of social media's impact.

Albert Maruggi and Emely Metzgar, "Social Media and the 2008 U.S. Presidential Election," *The Conference Board*, July 31, 2009, https://www.conference-board.org/publications/publicationdetail.cfm?publicationid=7078¢erid=1.

This same study admitted that 35% of Americans relied on online video for election news, while 10% used social network sites for news.

507 Albert Maruggi and Emely Metzgar, "Social Media and the 2008 U.S. Presidential Election," *The Conference Board*, July 31, 2009, https://www.conference-board.org/publications/publicationdetail.cfm?publicationid=7078¢erid=1.

508 Daniel Kreiss and Philip N. Howard, "New Challenges to Political Privacy: Lessons from the First U.S. Presidential Race in the Web 2.0 Era," *International Journal of Communications* 4 (2010): 1032–1050, https://ijoc.org/index.php/ijoc/article/viewFile/870/473; Sasha Issenberg, "The Romney Campaign's Data Strategy," *Slate*, July 17, 2012, http://www.slate.com/articles/news_and_politics/victoroy_lab_2012/07the_romney_campaign_s_data_strategy_they_re_outsourcing_.single.html.

509 David Kirkpatrick, "Diary of a Love Affair: Obama-and Google (Obama@Google)," *Fortune*, November 13, 2007, https://archive.fortune.com/galleries/2009/fortune/0910/gallery.obama_google.fortune.2.html.

510 Pew Research Center, "Section 5: The Press and the Campaign 2008," *Pew Research Center*, November 13,2008, https://www.pewresearch.org/politics/2008/11/13/section-5-the-press-and-campaign-2008/.

511 Danny Shea, "Chris Matthews: 'I Felt this Thrill Going Up My Leg' as Obama Spoke," *Huffpost*, March 28, 2008, https://www.huffpost.com/entry/chris-matthews-i-felt-thi_n_86449.

512 NPR Staff, "The New Republic: Obama's Bromance," *NPR*, August 31, 2008, https://www.npr.org/2009/08/31/112399581/the-new-republic-obamas-bromance.

513 Fox News Staff, "*Newsweek* Depiction of Obama as Lord Shiva Upsets Some Indian-Americans," *Fox News*, November 21, 2010, https://www.foxnews.com/politics/newsweek-depiction-of-obama-as-lord-shiva-upsets-some-indian-americans.

514 David Limbaugh, *Crimes Against Liberty: An Indictment of President Barack Obama* (Washington, DC: Regnery Publishing, 2010), 23.

515 Freedom Lighthouse Staff, "MSNBC's Ed Schultz Says the West Wing of the White House is a 'Shrine' to Obama—Audio," *Freedom Lighthouse*, February 4, 2010, http://www.freedomlighthouse.com/2010_02_04_archive.html.

516 Ben Wallace-Wells," The Radical Roots of Barack Obama," *Rolling Stone*, February 22, 2008, https://www.rollingstone.com/politics/politics-features/obama-radical-roots-ben-wallace-wells-2007-1105526/.

517 Barack Obama, "We Are the Ones We Have Been Waiting For," *YouTube video*, posted by wearetheones0, February 5, 2008, https://www.youtube.com/watch?v=molWTfv8TYw.

518 ABC 7 Eyewitness News Staff, "Chicago Could Benefit from Obama Election," *ABC 7 Eyewitness News*, November 6, 2008, https://abc7chicago.com/archive/6490862.

519 Time Staff, "A Dubious Compliment—Top 10 Joe Biden Gaffes," *Time*, n.d., https://content.time.com/time/specials/packages/article/0,28804,1895156_1894977_1644536,00.html.

520 Kathleen Parker, "As Sharpton Slips, He isn't Grabbing Onto Obama," March 18, 2007, *The Record*, https://www.recordnet.com/story/opinion/columns/2007/03/18/as-sharpton-slips-he-isn/52948888007/.

521 Satta Sarmah, "Is Obama Black Enough?" *Columbia Journalism Review*, February 15, 2007, https://www.cjr.org/politics/is_obama_black_enough.php.

522 Ibid.

523 Gary Younge, "Is Obama Black Enough?" *The Guardian*, March 1, 2007, https://www.theguardian.com/world/2007/mar/01/usa.uselections2008.

524 Sheryl Gay Stolberg, "Obama Reverses Key Bush Security Policies," *The New York Times*, January 23, 2009, https://www.nytimes.com/2009/01/23/us/politics/23obama.html.

525 ABC News Staff, "Obama Overturns Mexico City Policy Implemented by Reagan," *ABC News*, January 23, 2009, https://abcnews.go.com/Politics/International/obama-overturns-mexico-city-policy-implemented-reagan/story?id=6716958.

526 Economic Policy Institute, "Missing Workers: the Missing Part of the Unemployment Story," *Economic Policy Institute*, July 7, 2017, https://www.epi.org/publication/missing-workers/.

527 PJ Austin, "The Shovel-Ready Jobs Swindle," *Citizens Against Government Waste*, October 14, 2011, https://www.cagw.org/thewastewatcher/shovel-ready-jobs-swindle.

528 Ibid.

529 Ibid.

530 Steve Holland, "Obama's 2010 Strategy Taking Shape," *Reuters*, February 7, 2010, https://www.reuters.com/article/economy/obamas-2010-strategy-taking-shape-idUSNAHO33333/.

531 Avik Roy, "The Tortuous History of Conservatives and the Individual Mandate," *Forbes*, February 7, 2012, https://www.forbes.com/sites/theapothecary/2012/02/07/the-tortuous-conservative-history-of-the-individual-mandate/.

532 Eric Zimmermann, Obama Defends 'Louisiana Purchase,'" *The Hill*, March 17, 2010, https://thehill.com/blogs/blog-briefing-room/news/64416-obama-defends-louisiana-purchase/.

533 ABC News Staff, "Transcript: Diane Sawyer Interviews Obama," *ABC News*, January 25, 2010, https://abcnews.go.com/WN/Obama/abc-world-news-diane-sawyer-diane-sawyer-interviews/story?id=9659064; Katie Couric, "Rahm Emanuel on the State of the Union," *CBS News*, January 27, 2010, https://www.cbsnews.com/news/rahm-emanuel-on-the-state-of-the-union.

534 Tobin Grant, "Why Pro-Life Democrats Are Disappearing," *Religion News Service*, May 10, 2016, https://religionnews.com/2016/05/10/why-pro-life-democrats-are-disappearing/.

535 David Limbaugh, *Crimes Against Liberty: An Indictment of President Barack Obama* (Washington, DC: Regnery Publishing, 2010), 163.

536 Paul Ryan, "New CBO Analysis: Health Legislation Increases Deficits," *Republican Caucus Committee on the Budget*, March 19, 2010.

537 *National Federation of Independent Business v. Sebelius*, 567 U.S. 519 (2012), https://tile.loc.gov/storage-services/service/ll/usrep/usrep567/usrep567519/usrep567519.pdf.

538 Jan Crawford, "Roberts Switched News to Uphold Health Care Law," CBS News, July 1, 2012, https://www.cbsnews.com/news/roberts-switched-views-to-uphold-health-care-law.

539 Charlie Savage, "For Attorneys General, Long Shot Brings Payoffs," *The New York Times*, June 20, 2012; Editors, "Victory in Defeat: The Supreme Court's Health-Care Ruling Reaffirmed Limits to Congress's Authority," *National Review Online*, June 29, 2023.

540 Kevin Russell, "Court Holds That States Have Choice Whether to Join Medicaid Expansion," *SCOTUSblog*, June 28, 2012, https://www.scotusblog.com/2012/06/court-holds-that-states-have-choice-whether-to-join-medicaid-expansion/.

541 Adam Liptak and Abby Goodnough, "Supreme Court to Hear Obamacare Appeal," *The New York Times*, March 3, 2020, https://www.nytimes.com/2020/03/02/us/supreme-court-obamacare-appeal.html.

542 NPR Staff, "McCain Votes No, Dealing Potential Death Blow to Republican Health Care Efforts," *NPR*, July 27, 2017, https://www.npr.org/2017/07/27/539907467/senate-careens-toward-high-drama-midnight-health-care-vote.

In fact, McCain was joined by two other perpetually Democrat-voting Republicans, Susan Collins of Maine and Lisa Murkowski of Alaska.

543 David Limbaugh, *The Great Destroyer: Barack Obama's War on the Republic* (Washington: Regnery Publishing, 2012), 348.

544 Katie Pavlich, "Obama Administration to Implement More Gun Control Without Congress," Townhall.com, July 8, 2017.

545 David Limbaugh, *The Great Destroyer: Barack Obama's War on the Republic* (Washington: Regnery Publishing, 2012), 346–47.

546 Fox News Staff, "Friction Grows Between Lawmakers and DOJ over 'Project Gunrunner' Probe," *Fox News*, May 4, 2011.

547 Joint Staff Report, *The Department of Justice's Operation Fast and Furious: Accounts of ATF Agents*, United States House of Representatives, Committee on Oversight and

Government Reform, June 14, 2011, https://oversight.house.gov/wp-content/uploads/2012/02/ATF_Report.pdf.

548 "Fast & Furious Was Much Broader, Issa Charges," *U.S. News & World Report*, July 6, 2011.

549 GOP Oversight, "Gowdy Questions AG Holder on Key Players Involved with Fast & Furious," *YouTube video*, December 8, 2011, https://www.youtube.com/watch?v=lbTP7AHLW28.

550 David Limbaugh, *The Great Destroyer: Barack Obama's War on the Republic* (Washington: Regnery Publishing, 2012), 359.

551 John Bresnahan and Seung Min Kim, "Holder Held in Contempt," *Politico*, June 28, 2012, https://www.politico.com/story/2012/06/holder-held-in-contempt-of-congress-077988.

552 Josh Gerstein, "Judge Declines to Hold Holder in Contempt," *Politico*, October 6, 2014, https://www.politico.com/blogs/under-the-radar/2014/10/judge-declines-to-hold-holder-in-contempt-196650; U.S. Attorney's Office, District of Columbia, "Stephen K. Bannon Sentenced to Four Months in Prison on Two Counts of Contempt of Congress," *United States Department of Justice*, October 21, 2022, https://www.justice.gov/usao-dc/pr/stephen-k-bannon-sentenced-four-months-prison-two-counts-contempt-congress.

553 Eric Etheridge, "Rick Santelli: Tea Party Time," *The New York Times*, February 20, 2009, https://archive.nytimes.com/opinionator.blogs.nytimes.com/2009/02/20/rick-santelli-tea-party-time/.

554 Jeff Cox, "Five Years Later, Rick Santelli 'Tea Party' Rant Revisited," *CNBC*, February 4, 2014, https://www.cnbc.com/2014/02/24/5-years-later-rick-santelli-tea-party-rant-revisited.html.

555 David Limbaugh, *The Great Destroyer: Barack Obama's War on the Republic* (Washington: Regnery Publishing, 2012), 52.

556 Fox News Staff, "NAACP Resolution Calls on Tea Party to Repudiate 'Racist Elements' in Movement," Fox News, July 14, 2010.

557 Dana Loesch, "Jim Wallis: Fox, Conservatives Behind Assassination of Obama's Religion," *Breitbart*, November 30, 2010.

558 U.S. News Staff, "Obama Says Race a Key Component in Tea Party Protests," *U.S. News & World Report*, March 20, 2011.

559 David Limbaugh, *The Great Destroyer: Barack Obama's War on the Republic* (Washington: Regnery Publishing, 2012), 57.

560 Jeffrey T. Kuhner, "Is Obama Fomenting a Race War?" *Washington Times*, April 30, 2010, https://www.washingtontimes.com/news/2010/apr/30/is-obama-fomenting-a-race-war/.

561 House Committee on Oversight and Government Reform, "FACT SHEET: Lois Lerner and the Oversight Committee Investigation of the IRS Targeting Scandal," *United States House of Representatives*, March 4, 2014, https://oversight.house.gov/release/fact-sheet-lois-lerner-oversight-committee-investigation-irs-targeting-scandal.

562 Peter Wilson, "Obama Launches Afghanistan Surge," *The Australian*, February 18, 2009, https://web.archive.org/web/20090219134205/http://www.theaustralian.news.com.au/story/0,25197,25074581-2703,00.html.

563 Mark Mazzetti and David E. Sanger, "Obama Expands Missile Strikes Inside Pakistan," *The New York Times*, February 20, 2009, https://www.nytimes.com/2009/02/21/washington/21policy.html.

564 Tracy Wilkinson, "$1.7-Billion Payment to Iran Was All in Cash Due to Effectiveness of Sanctions, White House Says," *Los Angeles Times*, September 16, 2016, https://www.latimes.com/nation/nationnow/la-na-iran-payment-cash-20160907-snap-story.html;

Haaretz Staff, "Obama Administration Reportedly Shielded Hezbollah from DEA and CIA to Save Iran Nuclear Deal," *Haaretz*, December 18, 2017, https://www.haaretz.com/us-news/2017-12-18/ty-article/report-obama-admin-protected-hezbollah-to-save-iran-deal/0000017f-f403-d223-a97f-fddf744c0000.

565 CBS News, "Clinton on Qaddafi: We Came, We Saw, He Died," *YouTube video*, October 20, 2011, https://www.youtube.com/watch?v=6DXDU48RHLU.

566 BBC News Staff, "President Obama: Libya Aftermath 'Worst Mistake' of Presidency," *BBC News*, April 11, 2016, https://www.bbc.com/news/world-us-canada-36013703.

567 Daily Rushbo Staff, "Rush on Romney @ CPAC: I Have Never Heard Anybody Say 'I'm Severely Conservative,'" *Daily Rushbo*, February 10, 2012, https://web.archive.org/web/20150402072945/http://dailyrushbo.com/rush-on-romney-cpac-i-have-never-heard-anybody-say-im-severely-conservative.

The term sounded like a John Lenonism, when he reportedly likened Senator Strom Thurmond's name to a disease: "I've got Strom Thurmond in me arm!"

568 Christian Science Monitor Staff, "Candy Crowley: How Did She Do as Moderator of the Presidential Debate?" *Christian Science Monitor*, October 17, 2012, https://www.csmonitor.com/USA/Latest-News-Wires/2012/1017/Candy-Crowley-How-did-she-do-as-moderator-of-the-presidential-debate.

569 Jillian Rayfield, "Obama: The '80s Called, They Want Their Foreign Policy Back," *Salon*, October 23, 2012, https://www.salon.com/2012/10/23/obama_the_80s_called_they_want_their_foreign_policy_back.

570 David Corn, "Romney '47 Percent' Fundraiser Host: Hedge Fund Manager Who Likes Sex Parties," *Mother Jones*, September 18, 2012, https://www.motherjones.com/politics/2012/09/romney-secret-video-marc-leder-sex-parties.

571 Raul A. Reyes, "Romney's Empty 'Binders Full of Women,'" *CNN*, October 18, 2012, https://www.cnn.com/2012/10/17/opinion/cardona-binders-women/index.html.

572 Ana Marie Cox, "Romney's Cruel Canine Vacation," *Time*, June 27, 2007, https://time.com/archive/6922325/romneys-cruel-canine-vacation/.

573 Fox News Staff, "Romney Hammers 'You Didn't Build That' in New Web Ad," *Fox News*, updated December 23, 2015, https://www.foxnews.com/politics/romney-hammers-you-didnt-build-that-in-new-web-ad/.

574 Jim Rutenberg, "Data You Can Believe In: The Obama Campaign's Digital Masterminds Cash In," *The New York Times*, June 23, 2013, https://www.nytimes.com/2013/06/23/magazine/the-obama-campaigns-digital-masterminds-cash-in.html.

575 David Remnick, "Going the Distance," *The New Yorker*, January 27, 2014, https://www.newyorker.com/magazine/2014/01/27/going-the-distance-david-remnick; Charles Laurence, "Obama Accused of 'Playing Race Card to Explain His Failures,'" *The Week*, January 22, 2014, https://theweek.com/us/56979/obama-accused-playing-race-card-explain-his-failures.

576 Charles Laurence, "Obama Accused of 'Playing Race Card to Explain His Failures,'" *The Week*, January 22, 2014, https://theweek.com/us/56979/obama-accused-playing-race-card-explain-his-failures.

577 Ibid.

578 David Limbaugh, "Obama, Not the 'Post-' but the 'Most' Racial President," *Creators Syndicate*, July 15, 2010, https://www.creators.com/read/david-limbaugh/07/10/obama-not-the-post-but-the-most-racial-president.

579 *Obergefell v. Hodges*, 576 U.S. 644 (2015).

580 Larry Schweikart, *Reagan: The American President* (Nashville, TN: Post Hill Press, 2019), 366–70.

See, for example, Memorandum to the President from Craig L. Fuller, July 1, 1981, in Martin Anderson Files, Series 1, Subject File H Issue (2)_Immigration and Refugee

Policy, Box 19, folder "Illegal Aliens" (1 of 2), Ronald Reagan Presidential Library and Archives.

581 Washington Post Staff, "Obama's 2012 DACA Move Offers a Window into Pros and Cons of Executive Action," *Washington Post*, November 30, 2014, https://www.washingtonpost.com/politics/obamas-2012-daca-move-offers-a-window-into-pros-and-cons-of-executive-action/2014/11/30/88be7a36-7188-11e4-893f-86bd390a3340_story.html.

582 Reuters in Washington, "Obama Calls on Americans to Welcome Syrian Refugees as Latter-Day Pilgrims," *The Guardian*, November 26, 2015, https://www.theguardian.com/us-news/2015/nov/26/obama-americans-welcome-syrian-refugees-pilgrims.

583 Eric Lichtblau and James Risen, "N.S.A.'s Intercepts Exceed Limits Set by Congress," *The New York Times*, April 15, 2009, https://www.nytimes.com/2009/04/16/us/16nsa.html.

584 Timothy B. Lee, "Sen. Obama Warned About Patriot Act Abuses. President Obama Proved Him Right," *The Washington Post*, August 2, 2013, https://www.washingtonpost.com/news/the-switch/wp/2013/08/02/sen-obama-warned-about-patriot-act-abuses-president-obama-proved-him-right; Tom Cohen, "Obama Approves Extension of Expiring Patriot Act Provisions," *CNN*, May 27, 2011, https://www.cnn.com/2011/POLITICS/05/27/congress.patriot.act/index.html; James Sensenbrenner, "How Obama Has Abused the Patriot Act," *Los Angeles Times*, April 19, 2013, https://www.latimes.com/opinion/op-ed/la-oe-sensenbrenner-data-patriot-act-obama-20130819-story.html.

585 Eric Bradner, "Here's What Happened When Senate Republicans Refused to Vote on Merrick Garland's Supreme Court Nomination," *CNN*, September 19, 2020, https://www.cnn.com/2020/09/18/politics/merrick-garland-senate-republicans-timeline/index.html.

586 Ibid.

587 Victor Davis Hanson, "Obama: Transforming America," *National Review*, October 1, 2013, https://www.nationalreview.com/2013/10/obama-transforming-america-victor-davis-hanson/.

588 Ibid.

589 Investor's Business Daily Staff, "Obama's Military Coup Purges 197 Officers in Five Years," *Investor's Business Daily*, October 28, 2013, https://www.investors.com/politics/editorials/197-military-officers-purged-by-obama/.

590 Edward Klein, *All Out War: The Plot to Destroy Trump* (Washington, DC: Regnery Publishing, 2017), 156.

591 Ben Wallace-Wells, "The Radical Roots of Barack Obama," *Rolling Stone*, February 22, 2008, https://www.rollingstone.com/politics/politics-features/obama-radical-roots-ben-wallace-wells-2007-1105526/.

592 Blair Kamin, "The Dilemma of Development: Will Obama Center Hurt Those It's Supposed to Help?" *Chicago Tribune*, March 3, 2018, https://www.chicagotribune.com/2018/03/03/the-dilemma-of-development-will-obama-center-hurt-those-its-supposed-to-help.

593 Obama Foundation Staff, "Obama Foundation Issues Request for Diversity Consultant for the Obama Presidential Center," press release, September 29, 2017, https://www.obama.org/press-releases/obama-foundation-diversity-consultant/.

594 Obama CBA Coalition, "Community Benefits Agreement (CBA) for the Obama Library," *Obama CBA Coalition*, April 2018, http://www.obamacba.org/

595 Ibid.

596 Elaine Chen, "CBA Coalition Protests Rent Increase, Hairston Warns It Not to 'Deceive the Public,'" *Chicago Maroon*, March 29, 2018, https://chicagomaroon.com/25683/news/cba-coalition-protests-rent-increase-hairston-warn/.

597 Richard Truesdell and Keith Lehmann, "Barack Obama: The Political Genius That Wasn't," *American Greatness*, November 14, 2024, https://amgreatness.com/2024/11/14/barack-obama-the-political-genius-that-wasnt/?utm_medium=email&utm_source=act_eng&seyid=33471.

598 Ibid.

599 David Samuels, "The Obama Factor," *Tablet*, August 2, 2023, https://www.tabletmag.com/sections/arts-letters/articles/david-garrow-interview-obama.

CHAPTER 6: THE ESCALATOR

600 Los Angeles Times Staff, "Fatal Shooting in San Francisco Ignites Immigration Debate," *Los Angeles Times*, July 4, 2015, https://www.latimes.com/local/california/la-me-0705-sf-shooting-20150705-story.html.

601 Michael Kruse, "The Escalator Ride that Changed America," *Politico*, June 14, 2019, https://www.politico.com/magazine/story/2019/06/14/donald-trump-campaign-announcement-tower-escalator-oral-history-227148/.

602 "Nationwide Opinion Polling for the 2016 Republican Party Primaries," *Wikipedia*, last modified May 8, 2016, https://en.wikipedia.org/wiki/Nationwide_opinion_polling_for_the_2016_Republican_Party_presidential_primaries.

603 Jerome Hudson, "32 Times Establishment Media and Pollsters Assured the People of Donald Trump's Defeat," *Breitbart News*, November 23, 2016, http://www.breitbart.com/2016-presidential-race/2016/11/23/32-times-establishment-media-pollsters.

604 Joel Pollack and Larry Schweikart, *How Trump Won: The Inside Story of a Revolution* (Washington, DC: Regnery Publishing, 2017), 252–53.

605 Amity Shlaes, The Forgotten Man: A New History of the Great Depression, (New York: Harper, 2007).

606 Michael D'Antonio, *Never Enough: Donald Trump and the Pursuit of Success* (New York: Thomas Dunne Books, 2015) 11.

607 RSBN, "President Trump Live in Butler, PA," *YouTube video*, October 5, 2024, https://www.youtube.com/watch?v=IdO-elq4GaA.

608 Michael D'Antonio, *Never Enough: Donald Trump and the Pursuit of Success* (New York: Thomas Dunne Books, 2015), 2–3.

609 Ibid; Edward Klein, *Guilty as Sin: Uncovering New Evidence of Corruption and How Hillary Clinton and the Democrats Derailed the FBI Investigation* (Washington, DC: Regnery Publishing, 2016).

At the same time, Hillary could not align more closely with Obama because she and Bill believed he was behind the e-mail "crap" (Klein, 2016, 43). In fact, Obama preferred Joe Biden to be the candidate.

610 Michael D'Antonio, *Never Enough: Donald Trump and the Pursuit of Success* (New York: Thomas Dunne Books, 2015), 9.

611 Michael Kranish and Marc Fisher, *Trump Revealed: the Definitive Biography of the 45th President* (New York: Simon & Schuster, 2016), 38.

612 Harry Hurt, *The Lost Tycoon: The Many Lives of Donald J. Trump* (New York: W. W. Norton, 1993), 13.

613 Bruce Handy, "Trump Once Proposed Building a Castle on Madison Avenue," *The Atlantic*, April 2019, https://www.theatlantic.com/magazine/archive/2019/04/trump-tower-real-estate-projects/583243.

614 Michael D'Antonio, *Never Enough: Donald Trump and the Pursuit of Success* (New York: Thomas Dunne Books, 2015), 101.

615 Donald Trump, *The Art of the Deal* (New York: Ballantine, 1987), 134.

616 Michael D'Antonio, *Never Enough: Donald Trump and the Pursuit of Success* (New York: Thomas Dunne Books, 2015), 145.

617 Donald J. Trump (@realDonaldTrump), "I hope we never have a president who starts a war to win an election," *X (formerly Twitter)*, June 3, 2014, https://x.com/DefiantLs/status/1871695449574527076.

618 Donald J. Trump (@realDonaldTrump), "We can't let this happen. We should march on Washington and stop this travesty. Our nation is totally divided!" *X (formerly Twitter)*, November 10, 2012, https://x.com/DefiantLs/status/1871695449574527076.

619 Donald J. Trump, *Crippled America: How to Make America Great Again* (New York Threshold Editions, 2015), 1.

620 Fox News, "Donald Trump Disses Rosie O'Donnell During Republican Debate," *YouTube video*, August 3, 2015, https://www.youtube.com/watch?v=ASd4-Vo7RAU.

621 Edward Helmore, "How Trump's Political Playbook Evolved Since He First Ran for President in 2000," *The Guardian*, February 7, 2017, https://www.theguardian.com/us-news/2017/feb/05/donald-trump-reform-party-2000-president.

622 Reid Wilson, "Consequential GOP Class of 1994 All But Disappears," *The Hill*, September24,2019,https://thehill.com/homenews/house/462705-consequential-gop-class-of-1994-all-but-disappears/.

The Hill all but ignored the fact that many, including Largent, voluntarily stepped down because they had run on the concept of term limits.

623 Edward Helmore, "How Trump's Political Playbook Evolved Since He First Ran for President in 2000," *The Guardian*, February 7, 2017, https://www.theguardian.com/us-news/2017/feb/05/donald-trump-reform-party-2000-president.

624 Jon Allsop, "Taking Trump at His Word," *Columbia Journalism Review*, August 3, 2020, https://www.cjr.org/the_media_today/trump_election_delayed_seriously_not_literally.php.

625 Joshua Green, *Devil's Bargain: Steve Bannon, Donald Trump, and the Storming of the Presidency* (New York: Penguin, 2017), 111.

626 Ibid., 200.

627 Edward Klein, *Guilty as Sin: Uncovering New Evidence of Corruption and How Hillary Clinton and the Democrats Derailed the FBI Investigation* (Washington, DC: Regnery Publishing, 2016), 4.

628 Ibid., 4–6.

629 Ibid., 13.

630 Ibid., 37.

631 Chris Cillizza, "Here Are the Latest, Most Damaging Things in the DNC's Leaked Emails," *Washington Post*, July 25, 2016, https://www.washingtonpost.com/news/the-fix/wp/2016/07/24/here-are-the-latest-most-damaging-things-in-the-dncs-leaked-emails; Nicholas Confessore and David E. Sanger, "Released Emails Suggest the D.N.C. Derided the Sanders Campaign," *The New York Times*, July 23, 2016, https://www.nytimes.com/2016/07/23/us/politics/dnc-emails-sanders-clinton.html; BBC News Staff, "Elizabeth Warren Agrees Democratic Race 'Rigged' for Clinton," *BBC News*, November 3, 2017, https://www.bbc.com/news/world-us-canada-41850798.

632 Massimo Calabresi, "Why the FBI Let Hillary Clinton Off the Hook," *Time*, July 5, 2016, https://time.com/4394178/hillary-clinton-email-fbi-investigation.

633 Edward Klein, *Guilty as Sin: Uncovering New Evidence of Corruption and How Hillary Clinton and the Democrats Derailed the FBI Investigation* (Washington, DC: Regnery Publishing, 2016), xxi.

While a source such as Wikipedia blew the affair off with a couple of exculpatory sentences, Edward Klein listed no fewer than eleven separate violations of federal law in which Clinton engaged (Klein, *Guilty as Sin*, 34).

634 Sharyl Attkisson, "Collusion Against Trump Timeline," *Sharyl Attkisson*, June 2023, https://sharylattkisson.com/2023/06/collusion-against-trump-timeline; Sarah Fortinsky, "One-third of Adults in New Poll Say Biden's Election Was Illegitimate," *Yahoo News*, January 2, 2024, https://www.yahoo.com/news/one-third-adults-poll-biden-135411950.html.

635 Andrew C. McCarthy, "Obama's Conflict Tanked the E-mail Investigation—as Predicted," *National Review*, September 26, 2016, https://www.nationalreview.com/2016/09/obama-email-alias-clinton-why-fbi-didnt-prosecute-hillary/.

636 Ibid.

637 The New York Times Editorial Board, "What We Saw in the Second Debate," *The New York Times*, October 9, 2016, https://www.nytimes.com/interactive/projects/cp/opinion/clinton-trump-second-debate-election-2016/because-youd-be-in-jail.

638 Michael D. Shear and Maggie Haberman, "Transcript: Donald Trump's Taped Comments About Women," *The New York Times*, October 8, 2016, https://www.nytimes.com/2016/10/08/us/politics/donald-trump-women.html.

639 Ibid.

640 Joshua Green, *Devil's Bargain: Steve Bannon, Donald Trump, and the Storming of the Presidency* (New York: Penguin, 2017), 215.

641 Ibid., 215; Joel Pollack and Larry Schweikart, *How Trump Won: The Inside Story of a Revolution* (Washington, DC: Regnery Publishing, 2017, 183–4.

642 Interviews with Steve Bannon, various dates, 2017; Interviews with Richard Baris, various dates, 2017; CNN Politics Staff, "Can Donald Trump Recover from This?" *CNN Politics*, October 8, 2016, https://www.cnn.com/2016/10/07/politics/donal-trump-campaign-crisis/index.html.

643 Richard Baris, "Clinton Lost Florida and the Election because She Lost the Argument," *People's Pundit Daily*, December 7, 2016, https://www.peoplespunditdaily.com/news/elections/2016/12/07/hillary-clinton-lost-florida-before-eleciton-day/; Joel Pollack and Larry Schweikart, *How Trump Won: The Inside Story of a Revolution* (Washington, DC: Regnery Publishing, 2017), 189–90.

644 Joel Pollack and Larry Schweikart, *How Trump Won: The Inside Story of a Revolution* (Washington, DC: Regnery Publishing, 2017), 198.

645 Irwin Gellman, *Campaign of the Century: Kennedy, Nixon, and the Election of 1960* (New Haven, CT: Yale University Press, 2021), 270-294.

646 Edward Klein, *All Out War: The Plot to Destroy Trump* (Washington, DC: Regnery Publishing, 2017), 112.

647 Ibid., 116.

648 Chancellor Agard, "Kathy Griffin Bloody Trump Pic Defended by Photographer," *Entertainment Weekly*, May 30, 2017, https://ew.com/news/2017/05/30/kathy-griffin-trump-head-photo-tyler-shields.

649 Edward Klein, *All Out War: The Plot to Destroy Trump* (Washington, DC: Regnery Publishing, 2017), 131.

650 Daniel Street, "This Is Not Your Grandpa's Democrat Party," *Fake News Exposed* (Substack), June 17, 2025, https://danielrstreet.substack.com/p/this-is-not-your-grandpas-democrat.

651 Edward Klein, *All Out War: The Plot to Destroy Trump* (Washington, DC: Regnery Publishing, 2017), 119.

652 Ibid., 137.

653 Ibid., 144.

654 Bill Dentzer, "Electoral College: Are Idaho's 4 Electors Being Pressured to Dump Trump, or Harassed?" *Idaho Statesman*, November 15, 2016, https://www.idahostatesman.com/news/politics-government/election/article114786018.html; Alexandra King, "Electoral College Voter: I'm Getting Death Threats," *CNN*, November 30, 2016, https://www.cnn.com/2016/11/30/politics/banerian-death-threats-cnntv.

655 Hillary Clinton, *What Happened* (New York: Simon & Schuster, 2017), passim.

656 Edward Klein, *All Out War: The Plot to Destroy the President* (Washington, DC: Regnery Publishing, 2017), 9–10.

657 Ibid., 128.

658 Ibid., 104.

659 Gregg Jarrett, *The Russia Hoax: The Illicit Scheme to Clear Hillary Clinton and Frame Donald Trump* (New York: Broadside Books, 2018); Gregg Jarrett, *Witch Hunt: The Story of the Greatest Mass Delusion in American Political History* (New York: Broadside Books, 2019).

660 Edward Klein, *All Out War: The Plot to Destroy Trump* (Washington, DC: Regnery Publishing, 2017), 127.

661 Ibid., 127.

662 Michael Doran, "The Real Collusion Story," *National Review*, March 13, 2018, https://www.nationalreview.com/2018/03/russia-collusion-real-story-hillary-clinton-dnc-fbi-media.

663 Sharyl Attkisson, "Collusion Against Trump Timeline," *Sharyl Attkisson*, June 2023, https://sharylattkisson.com/2023/06/collusion-against-trump-timeline.

664 Office of the Director of National Intelligence, "Background to 'Assessing Russian Activities and Intentions in Recent U.S. Elections': The Analysis Process and Cyber Incident Attributions," January 6, 2017, https://www.dni.gov/files/documents/ICA_2017_01.pdf.

665 Erica R. Hendry, "Trump Asked Russia to Find Clinton's Emails. On or Around the Same Day, Russians Targeted Her Accounts," *Politico*, July 13, 2018, https://www.pbs.org/newshour/politics/trump-asked-russia-to-find-clintons-emails-on-or-around-the-same-day-russians-targeted-her-accounts.

Typically, Trump was joking, and the media, which was completely unable to process humor, took it seriously.

666 "Sundance," "Part 2—Why did the DOJ and FBI Execute the Raid on Trump—the Evidence Within the Documents," *The Last Refuge*, August 11, 2022, https://theconservativetreehouse.com/blog/2022/08/11/part-2-why-did-the-doj-and-fbi-execute-the-raid-on-trump-the-evidence-within-the-documents/; "Sundance," "Part 3, Why Did the DOJ and FBI Execute the Raid on Trump—a Culmination of Four Years of Threats and Betrayals," *The Last Refuge*, August 11, 2022, https://theconservativetreehouse.com/blog/2022/08/11/part-3-why-did-the-doj-and-fbi-execute-the-raid-on-trump-a-culmination-of-four-years-of-threats-and-betrayals/#more-236402.

667 Michael Doran, "The Real Collusion Story," *National Review*, March 13, 2018, https://www.nationalreview.com/2018/03/russia-collusion-real-story-hillary-clinton-dnc-fbi-media.

668 Gregg Jarrett, *The Russia Hoax: The Illicit Scheme to Clear Hillary Clinton and Frame Donald Trump* (New York: Broadside Books, 2018), 55.

669 Gregg Jarrett, *Witch Hunt: The Story of the Greatest Mass Delusion in American Political History* (New York: Broadside Books, 2019); Paul Sperry, "Despite Comey Assurances, Vast Bulk of Weiner Laptop Emails Were Never Examined," *RealClearInvestigations*, August 23, 2018, https://www.realclearinvestigations.com/articles/2018/08/22/despite_comey_assurance_vast_bulk_of_weiner_laptop_emails_never_examined.html.

670 Charles Grassley, "Grassley on Investigation: Let's Be Transparent," *Grassley Senate Website*, April 8, 2019, https://www.grassley.senate.gov/news/news-releases/grassley-investigation-transparency-lets-be-consistent.

671 Gregg Jarrett, *Witch Hunt: The Story of the Greatest Mass Delusion in American Political History* (New York: Broadside Books, 2019), 10.

672 Sharyl Attkisson, "Collusion Against Trump Timeline," *Sharyl Attkisson*, June 2023, https://sharylattkisson.com/2023/06/collusion-against-trump-timeline.

673 Ibid.

674 Gregg Jarrett, *Witch Hunt: The Story of the Greatest Mass Delusion in American Political History* (New York: Broadside Books, 2019), 252.

675 Ibid., 255.

676 Ibid., 255.

677 Ibid., xiv.

678 David Corn, "A Veteran Spy Has Given FBI Information Alleging a Russian Operation to Cultivate Donald Trump," *Mother Jones*, October 31, 2016, https://www.motherjones.com/politics/2016/10/veteran-spy-gave-fbi-info-alleging-russian-operation-cultivate-donald-trump.

679 Sharyl Attkisson, "Collusion Against Trump Timeline," *Sharyl Attkisson*, June 2023, https://sharylattkisson.com/2023/06/collusion-against-trump-timeline.

680 Ibid.

681 Edward Klein, *All Out War: The Plot to Destroy Trump* (Washington, DC: Regnery Publishing, 2017), 161.

682 Sharyl Attkisson, "Collusion Against Trump Timeline," *Sharyl Attkisson*, June 2023, https://sharylattkisson.com/2023/06/collusion-against-trump-timeline.

The former Deputy Assistant Secretary of Defense Evelyn Farkas admitted she encouraged Obama to "get as much information as they can" about Russia and the Trump officials before the inauguration. Moreover, in April it was learned that Obama's National Security Adviser Susan Rice had requested "unmasked" intelligence on Trump associates.

683 Edward Klein, *All Out War: The Plot to Destroy Trump* (Washington, DC: Regnery Publishing, 2017), 167.

684 Ibid., 169.

685 Ibid., 170.

686 Gregg Jarrett, *Witch Hunt: The Story of the Greatest Mass Delusion in American Political History* (New York: Broadside Books, 2019), 198.

687 Robert S. Mueller, *The Mueller Report: The Final Report of the Special Counsel Into Donald Trump, Russia, and Collusion as Issued by the Department of Justice* (New York: Skyhorse Publishing, 2019).

688 Gregg Jarrett, *Witch Hunt: The Story of the Greatest Mass Delusion in American Political History* (New York: Broadside Books, 2019), 188.

Barr did not prosecute a single FBI agent for lying, for obstruction, or for any of the other multiple nefarious crimes that were committed against President Trump.

[689] Amber Athey, "The Definitive List of Media Screw-Ups on the Trump-Russia Story," *Daily Caller*, May 3, 2018, https://dailycaller.com/2018/05/03/media-failure-russia-trump-story/.

[690] Lee Smith, "Seven Mysterious Preludes to the FBI's Trump-Russia Probe," *RealClearInvestigations*, June 25, 2018, https://www.realclearinvestigations.com/articles/2018/06/25/the_mysterious_seven_preludes_of_the_fbis_trump-russia_probe.html.

[691] Special Counsel John H. Durham, *Report on Matters Related to Intelligence Activities and Investigations Arising Out of the 2016 Presidential Campaigns* (Washington, DC: Government Printing Office, 2023), https://www.justice.gov/storage/durhamreport.pdf.

[692] Techno Fog, "The Durham Report," *Techno Fog* (Substack), May 15, 2023, https://technofog.substack.com/p/the-durham-report.

[693] John Solomon, "Did FBI Get Bamboozled by Multiple Versions of Trump Dossier?" *The Hill*, July 10, 2018, https://thehill.com/hilltv/rising/396307- Did-FBI-get-bamboozled-by-multiple-versions-of-Trump-dossier%3F/.

In the aftermath, the media attempted numerous cover-up methods, rather than simply admitting that its own reporters had run news stories based on lies.

[694] Donald Trump, "Inaugural Address," *The White House*, January 20, 2017, https://trumpwhitehouse.archives.gov/briefings-statements/the-inaugural-address.

[695] "Obama: Some Jobs 'Are Just Not Going to Come Back,'" youtube, https://www.youtube.com/watch?v=CKpso3vhZtw.

[696] Rebecca Savransky, "Obama to Trump: 'What Magic Wand Do You Have?'" *The Hill*, June 1, 2016, http://thehill.com/blogs/blog-briefing-room/news/281936-obama-to-trump-what-magic-wand-do-you-have.

[697] Terence P. Jeffrey, "Manufacturing Jobs UP 18,000 in May, 322,000 under Trump," *CNS News*, June 1, 2018, https://www.cnsnews.com/new/article/terence-p-jeffrey/manufacutinr-jobs-18000-may-322000-under-trump.

[698] Larry Schweikart and Michael Allen, *A Patriot's History of the United States: From Columbus's Great Discovery to America's Age of Entitlement*, 15th Anniversary Edition (New York: Sentinel, 2014).

[699] Lisa Mascaro, "Ryan Says 'Big Fight' Coming over Border Wall After Election," *AP News*, October 8, 2018, https://apnews.com/article/north-america-donald-trump-elections-legislation-wi-state-wire-aa50fbcc11ae44a-89849baa78a732e00.

[700] Jared Kushner, *Breaking History: A White House Memoir* (New York: Broadside Books, 2022), 223; Brakkton Booker, "Trump Administration Diverts $3.8 Billion in Pentagon Funding to Border Wall," *NPR*, February 13, 2020, https://www.npr.org/2020/02/13/805796618/trump-administration-diverts-3-8-billion-in-pentagon-funding-to-border-wall.

[701] Sheryl Gay Stolberg, "Ocasio-Cortez Calls Migrant Detention Centers 'Concentration Camps,' Eliciting Backlash," *The New York Times*, June 18, 2019, https://www.nytimes.com/2019/06/18/us/politics/ocasio-cortez-cheney-detention-centers.html.

[702] John Gramlich, "How Border Apprehensions, ICE Arrests and Deportations Have Changed Under Trump," *Pew Research Center*, March 2, 2020, https://www.pewresearch.org/short-reads/2020/03/02/how-border-apprehensions-ice-arrests-and-deportations-have-changed-under-trump.

[703] Donald J. Trump, *Proclamation 9683 of December 6, 2017: Recognizing Jerusalem as the Capital of the State of Israel and Relocating the United States Embassy to Israel to Jerusalem, U.S. Presidential Documents*, Federal Register 82, no. 236 (December 11,

2017): 58331–58332, https://web.archive.org/web/20171213142840/https://www.gpo.gov/fdsys/pkg/FR-2017-12-11/pdf/2017-26832.pdf#page=1.

704 Kevin Liptak, "Trump Takes 20 Steps Into North Korea, Making History as the First Sitting US Leader to Enter the Hermit Nation," *CNN*, June 30, 2019, https://www.cnn.com/2019/06/29/politics/kim-jong-un-donald-trump-dmz-north-korea/index.html.

705 Jared Kushner, *Breaking History: A White House Memoir* (New York: Broadside Books, 2022), 169–70.

Contacted by Steve Bannon's team, I was one of many who recommended McMaster to the position.

706 Ibid., 221.

707 Mark Moyar, *Masters of Corruption: How the Federal Bureaucracy Sabotaged the Trump Presidency* (New York: Encounter Books, 2024), 56.

708 Ibid., 73.

709 Gabriel Chodorow-Reich, Matthew Smith, Owen M. Zidar, and Eric Zwick, *Tax Policy and Investment in a Global Economy*, National Bureau of Economic Research, Working Paper 32180, March 2024, https://www.nber.org/papers/w32180; Noah Smith, "At Least Five Interesting Things for Your Weekend (#41)," *Noahpinion* (Substack), June 21, 2024, https://www.noahpinion.blog/p/at-least-five-interesting-things-84f.

710 Heritage Foundation Staff, "Trump Administration Embraces Heritage Foundation Policy Recommendations," *The Heritage Foundation*, January 23, 2018.

711 Terry Gross, "Reporters Dig Into Justice Kavanaugh's Past, Allegations of Misconduct Against Him," *Fresh Air*, NPR, podcast audio, September 16, 2019, https://www.npr.org/2019/09/16/761191576/reporters-dig-into-justice-kavanaughs-past-allegations-of-misconduct-against-him.

712 Donald J. Trump, *Memorandum of Telephone Conversation With President Zelenskyy of Ukraine*, July 25, 2019, *The White House Archives*, https://trumpwhitehouse.archives.gov/wp-content/uploads/2019/09/Unclassified09.2019.pdf.

713 Ibid.

714 U.S. House of Representatives, *Congressional Record: Proceedings and Debates of the 116th Congress, Second Session*, February 5, 2020, https://www.govinfo.gov/content/pkg/CREC-2020-02-05/pdf/CREC-2020-02-05.pdf; Michael D. Shear and Peter Baker, "Trump Acquitted of Two Impeachment Charges in Near Party-Line Vote," *The New York Times*, February 5, 2020, https://www.nytimes.com/2020/02/05/us/politics/trump-acquitted-impeachment.html.

CHAPTER 7: THE PANDEMIC

715 Michael Park, et al., "Papers and Patents are Becoming Less Disruptive Over Time," *Nature*, 613, 2023, 138–44, https://www.nature.com/articles/s41586-022-05543-x.

716 Paul Sutter, "Risk Aversion Is Ruining Science," *Undark*, August 27, 2022, https://undark.org/2022/04/27/risk-aversion-is-ruining-science/.

717 Matthew Crawford, *Why We Drive: Toward a Philosophy of the Open Road* (New York: Custom House, 2020).

718 "The Perils of a Risk-Averse Society," *The Week*, November 12, 2021, https://theweek.com/us/1007037/the-perils-of-the-risk-averse-society.

719 Jean M. Twenge, *Generations: The Real Differences Between Gen Z, Millennials, Gen X, Boomers, and Silents—and What They Mean for America's Future* (New York: Atria Books, 2023), 164.

720 Ibid., 162.

721 Ibid., 164.

722 Ibid., 411.

723 Jean Twenge and Eric Farlely, "Not All Screen Time is Created Equal: Associations With Mental Health Vary by Activity and Gender," *Social Psychiatry and Psychiatric Epidemiology*, February 2021, 207–17; Cooper McAlister, et al., "Associations between Adolescent Depression and Self-Harm Behaviors and Screen Media Use in a Nationally Representative Time-Diary Study," *Research on Child and Adolescent Psychopathology*, December 2021, 1623–34.

724 Ibid., 415.

725 Ibid., 417. Twenge, *Generations*

726 John Grohol, "Internet Addiction and Depression," *PsychCentral*, July 8, 2018, https://psychcentral.com/blog/internet-addiction-and-depression/; Catriona M. Morrison and Helen Gore, "The Relationship Between Excessive Internet Use and Depression: A Questionnaire-Based Study of 1,319 Young People and Adults," *Psychopathology* 43 (2010): 121–126, https://www.karger.com/Article/Abstract/277001.

These and many other studies are discussed in Larry Schweikart, *All Thumbs: How Our Obsession with Phones and Devices is Damaging Our Children and Restructuring Their Lives* (Phoenix, AZ: Larry Schweikart/Wild World of History, 2020).

727 Larry Schweikart, *All Thumbs: How Our Obsession with Phones and Devices is Damaging Our Children and Restructuring Their Lives* (Phoenix, AZ: Larry Schweikart/Wild World of History, 2020), 10–11.

728 Mike Isaac, "Facebook Has 50 Minutes of Your Time Each Day. It Wants More," *The New York Times*, May 5, 2016, https://www.nytimes.com/2016/05/06/technology/facebook-has-50-minutes-of-your-time-each-day-it-wants-more.html.

729 This author is guilty as charged, but I prefer to have a clear mind and focused attitude when I approach God. That is surely not the case when I first wake up!

730 Larry Schweikart, *All Thumbs: How Our Obsession With Phones and Devices is Damaging Our Children and Restructuring Their Lives* (Phoenix, AZ: Larry Schweikart/Wild World of History, 2020), 13.

It is important to note that due to "multi-tasking," some surveys double counted media usage.

731 The literature on kids and cell phone/internet use is voluminous. See Amanda Lenhart, "Teens, Social Media & Technology Overview, 2015," *Pew Research Center*, April 9, 2015, https://www.pewresearch.org/internet/2015/04/09/teens-social-media-technology-2015; Hans Geser, "Are Girls (Even) More Addicted? Some Gender Patterns of Cell Phone Usage," *Soziologisches Institut der University of Zurich Online Publications*, 2006, http://socio.ch/movile/t_geser3.htm; Larry Schweikart, *All Thumbs: How Our Obsession with Phones and Devices Is Damaging Our Children and Restructuring Their Lives* (Phoenix, AZ: Larry Schweikart/Wild World of History, 2020), chap. 2, passim.

732 Pastor Charles McMahan, interview by author, Dayton, Ohio, various dates, 2020; Larry Schweikart, *All Thumbs: How Our Obsession with Phones and Devices is Damaging Our Children and Restructuring Their Lives* (Phoenix, AZ: Larry Schweikart/Wild World of History, 2020), 15.

733 NPR Staff, "Tweak the World: Episode 638," *Planet Money*, podcast audio, July 15, 2015, https://www.npr.org/sections/money/2015/07/15/423282438/episode-638-tweak-the-world.

734 Hartford Statement Authors, *Hartford Statement to NPR*, circa July 2023, https://apps.npr.org/documents/document.html?id=23888902-the-hartford-statement-to-nick-fountai; Nick Fountain, Jeff Guo, Keith Romer, and Emma Peaslee, "Fabricated Data in Research About Honesty. You Can't Make This Stuff Up. Or Can You?" *Planet Money*, podcast audio, July 28, 2023, https://www.npr.org/2023/07/27/1190568472/dan-ariely-francesca-gino-harvard-dishonesty-fabricated-data.

735 Ayana Archie, "Stanford President Resigns after Fallout from Falsified Data in His Research," *NPR*, July 20, 2023, https://www.npr.org/2023/07/19/1188828810/stanford-university-president-resigns.

736 Dan Garisto, "Nature Retracts Controversial Room-Temperature Superconductor Study," *Scientific American*, November 8, 2023, https://www.scientificamerican.com/article/nature-retracts-controversial-room-temperature-superconductor-study; Linton Besser, "Wiley's 'Fake Science' Scandal Is Just the Latest Chapter in a Broader Crisis of Trust Universities Must Address," *ABC News*, May 20, 2024, https://www.abc.net.au/news/2024-05-21/wiley-hindawi-articles-scandal-broader-crisis-trust-universities/103868662.

737 Dan Garisto, "Plagiarism Allegations Pursue Physicist Behind Stunning Superconductivity Claims," *Science*, April 13, 2023, https://www.science.org/content/article/plagiarism-allegations-pursue-physicist-behind-stunning-superconductivity-claims.

738 Ivan Oransky and Adam Marcus, "Scientific Misconduct Is a Growing Problem. Retraction Watch Is Trying to Fix It," *The Guardian*, August 9, 2023, https://www.theguardian.com/commentisfree/2023/aug/09/scientific-misconduct-retraction-watch.

739 Ibid.

740 Meredith Wadman, "Hundreds of Cancer Papers Mention Cell Lines That Don't Seem to Exist," *Science*, May 21, 2024, https://www.science.org/content/article/hundreds-cancer-papers-mention-cell-lines-don-t-seem-exist.

741 Daniel Oste, et al., "Misspellings or 'Miscellings'—Non-verifiable and Unknown Cell Lines in Cancer Research Publications," *International Journal of Cancer*, February 29, 2024, 1278–1288; Meredith Wadman, "Hundreds of Cancer Papers Mention Cell Lines That Don't Seem to Exist," *Science*, May 21, 2024, https://www.science.org/content/article/hundreds-cancer-papers-mention-cell-lines-don-t-seem-exist.

742 Linton Besser, "Wiley's 'Fake Science' Scandal Is Just the Latest Chapter in a Broader Crisis of Trust Universities Must Address," *ABC News*, May 20, 2024, https://www.abc.net.au/news/2024-05-21/wiley-hindawi-articles-scandal-broader-crisis-trust-universities/103868662.

743 Xueping Dong, et al., "Common Pathogens and Drug Resistance of Neonatal Pneumonia with Multichannel Sensor," [retracted], *Contrast Media & Molecular Imaging*, August 8, 2022, https://onlinelibrary.wiley.com/doi/10.1155/2022/2208636; Zhogjing Kang, et al., "The Value of MRI Combined with AFP, AFP-L3, GP73, and DCP in the Diagnosis of Early Primary Liver Cancer," [Retracted] *Disease Markers*, October 13, 2022, https://onlinelibrary.wiley.com/doi/10.1155/2022/8640999.

744 Frederik Joelving, "Paper Trail," *Science*, January 18, 2024, https://www.science.org/content/article/paper-mills-bribing-editors-scholarly-journals-science-investigation-finds.

745 Richard Van Noorden, "How Big is Science's Fake-Paper Problem?" *Nature*, November 6, 2023, https://www.nature.com/articles/d41586-023-03464-x.

746 Frederik Joelving, "Paper Trail," *Science*, January 18, 2024, https://www.science.org/content/article/paper-mills-bribing-editors-scholarly-journals-science-investigation-finds.

747 Ibid.

748 Noah Smith, "At Least Five Interesting Things to Start Your Week (#38)," *Noahpinion* (Slack), May 27, 2024, https://www.noahpinion.blog/p/at-least-five-interesting-things-f84.

749 Didier Sornette and Peter Cauwels, "Trapped in the 'Zero-Risk' Society and How to Break Free," *Swiss Finance Institute Research Paper No. 20–78*, September 1, 2020, https://papers.ssrn.com/sol3/papers.cfm?abstract_id=3684550.

750 Tim Gill, *No Fear: Growing up in a Risk Averse Society* (London: Calouste Gulbenkian Foundation, 2007), 12.

751 Ibid., 30.

752 Scott Atlas, *A Plague Upon Our House: My Fight at the Trump White House to Stop COVID from Destroying America* (New York: Liberty Protocol, 2021); C. H. Klotz, ed., *Canary in a COVID World: How Propaganda and Censorship Changed Our (My) World* (Las Vegas: Canary House Publishing, 2023).

753 Eva Fu, "CIA Says COVID-19 'More Likely' Came From Chinese Lab," *Epoch Times*, January25,2025,https://www.theepochtimes.com/article/cia-says-covid-19-more-likely-came-from-chinese-lab-5798864.

754 Nicholson Baker, "The Lab-Leak Hypothesis," *Intelligencer*, January 4, 2021, https://nymag.com/intelligencer/article/coronavirus-lab-escape-theory.html; Nicholas Wade, "Origin of Covid—Following the Clues," *Substack*, May 2, 2021, https://nicholaswade.medium.com/origin-of-covid-following-the-clues-6f03564c038; Rowan Jacobsen, "How Amateur Sleuths Broke the Wuhan Lab Story and Embarrassed the Media," *Newsweek*, June 23, 2021, https://www.newsweek.com/exclusive-how-amateur-sleuths-broke-wuhan-lab-story-embarrassed-media-1596958; Daniel Funke, "Archived Fact-Check: Tucker Carlson Guest Airs Debunked Conspiracy Theory that COVID-19 Was Created in a Lab," *PolitiFact*, May 17, 2021, https://www.politifact.com/li-meng-yan-fact-check.

755 Scott Atlas, *A Plague Upon Our House: My Fight at the Trump White House to Stop COVID from Destroying America* (New York: Liberty Protocol, 2021), 5.

756 Mollie Hemmingway, *Rigged: How the Media, Big tech, and the Democrats Seized Our Elections* (Washington, DC: Regnery Publishing, 2021), 61.

757 Tanya Lewis, "Eight Persistent COVID-19 Myths and Why People Believe Them," *Scientific American* October 12, 2020, https://www.scientificamerican.com/article/eight-persistent-covid-19-myths-and-why-people-believe-them.

758 Caitlin Doornbos and Samuel Chamberlain, "Scientist Who Tried to Squash Wuhan Lab Leak Theory Gets More Cash to Study Viruses," *New York Post*, October 3, 2022, https://nypost.com/2022/10/03/non-profit-tied-to-wuhan-lab-gets-650k-more-to-study-coronaviruses/.

759 Alice Miranda Ollstein, "POLITICO-Harvard Poll: Most Americans Believe Covid Leaked from Lab," *Politico*, July 9, 2021, https://www.politico.com/news/2021/07/09/poll-covid-wuhan-lab-leak-498847.

760 Didi Tang, "What Really Went On Inside the Wuhan Lab Weeks Before Covid Erupted," *The Times*, June 10, 2023, https://www.thetimes.co.uk/article/inside-wuhan-lab-covid-pandemic-china-america-qhjwwwvm0.

761 Q. Chen Wang et al., "Early Containment Strategies and Core Measures for Prevention and Control of Most Coronavirus Pneumonia in China," *Zhonghua Yu Fang Yi Xue Za Zhi* 54, no. 20 (2020): 1–5, https://www.ncbi.nlm.nih.gov/pmc/articles/PMC7163529.

762 Larry Schweikart, *A Patriot's History of Globalism: Its Decline and Fall* (New York: Skyhorse, 2024), 131–170.

763 Alan Reynolds, "How One Model Simulated 2.2 Million U.S. Deaths From COVID-19," CATO at Liberty Blog, April 21, 2020, https://www.cato.org/blog/

how-one-model-simulated-22-million-us-deaths-covid-19; Neil Ferguson, et al, "Report 8: Impact of Non-Pharmaceutical Interventions (NPIs) to Reduce COVID-19 Mortality and Healthcare Demand," *Imperial College COVID-19 Response Team*, March 16,2020, https://www.imperial.ac.uk/media/imperial-college/medicine/sph/ide/gida-fellowships/Imperial-College-COVID19-NPI-modelling-16-03-2020.pdf.

764 Jared Kushner, *Breaking History: A White House Memoir* (New York: Broadside Books, 2022), 335.

765 Silvia Martelli, "Trump's Travel Ban is Islamophobic and Xenophobic, Civil Rights Groups Say," *Medill News Service*, February 4, 2020, https://dc.medill.northwestern.edu/blog/2020/02/04/trumps-travel-ban-is-islamophobic-and-xenophobic-civil-rights-groups-say/.

766 Jonathan Easley, "Biden: Trump's Coronavirus Response Has Been 'Nakedly Xenophobic,'" *The Hill*, March 18, 2020, https://thehill.com/homenews/campaign/498350-biden-trumps-coronavirus-response-has-been-nakedly-xenophobic/.

What was "naked" was the transparency of the politicized attack: had Trump done nothing, Biden and his ilk would have accused him of placing millions of Americans in harm's way and being "uncaring."

767 Alan Reynolds, "How One Model Simulated 2.2 Million U.S. Deaths From COVID-19," *CATO at Liberty Blog*, April 21, 2020, https://www.cato.org/blog/how-one-model-simulated-22-million-us-deaths-covid-19; Neil Ferguson et al., "Report 8: Impact of Non-Pharmaceutical Interventions (NPIs) to Reduce COVID-19 Mortality and Healthcare Demand," *Imperial College COVID-19 Response Team*, March 16, 2020, https://www.imperial.ac.uk/media/imperial-college/medicine/sph/ide/gida-fellowships/Imperial-College-COVID19-NPI-modelling-16-03-2020.pdf.

768 Centers for Disease Control and Prevention, *COVID Data Tracker*, August 5, 2023, https://covid.cdc.gov/covid-data-tracker/#datatracker-home.

769 Phillip Magness, "The Failure of Imperial College Modeling is Far Worse Than We Knew," *American Institute for Economic Research*, April 22, 2021, https://www.aier.org/article/the-failure-of-imperial-college-modeling-is-far-worse-than-we-knew/.

It is worth noting that many of the most damning challenges to China Virus *medical* research came from economic journals. Economists, it seemed—with the exception of the economic charlatan Paul Krugman—were somewhat more honest and accurate in their reporting even about medical issues than medical researchers.

770 Sabine van Elsland and Ryan O'Hare, "Coronavirus Pandemic Could Have Caused 40 Million Deaths if Left Unchecked," *Imperial College London*, March 26, 2020, https://www.imperial.ac.uk/news/196496/coronavirus-pandemic-could-have-caused-40/.

771 Robert F. Kennedy Jr., *The Real Anthony Fauci* (New York: Skyhorse, 2021), xxii.

772 Michael Specter, "How Anthony Fauci Became America's Doctor," *New Yorker*, April 10, 2020, https://newyorker.com/magaine/2020/04/20/how-anthony-fauci-became-americas-doctor. Within a year, there would be those calling Fauci an American version of Dr. Josef Mengele.

Martin Pengelly, "Outrage as Fox News Commentator Likens Anthony Fauci to Nazi Doctor," *The Guardian*, November 30, 2021, https://www.theguardian.com/us-news/2021/nov/30/anthony-fauci-josef-mengele-fox-news.

773 Jim Kuypers, ed., *Public Communications in the Time of COVID-19: Perspectives From the Communication Discipline on the Pandemic* (Lanham, MD: Lexington Books, 2022), 23.

774 Robert F. Kennedy Jr., *The Real Anthony Fauci* (New York: Skyhorse Publishing, 2021), 151; Larry Keen, *HIV & AIDS: Fauci's First Fraud*, documentary film, September 6, 2020, https://www.youtube.com/watch?v=wy3frBacd2k.

775 Hannah Knudsen, "Exclusive—Dr. Andrew Huff: Coronavirus Timeline 'Giant Scandal to Subvert Trump,'" *Breitbart*, January 4, 2025, https://www.breitbart.com/radio/2025/01/04/exclusive-dr-andrew-huff-coronavirus-timeline-giant-scandal-to-subvert-trump.

776 Scott Atlas, *A Plague Upon Our House: My Fight at the Trump White House to Stop COVID From Destroying America* (New York: Liberty Protocol, 2021), 64.

777 Robert F. Kennedy Jr., *The Real Anthony Fauci* (New York: Skyhorse Publishing, 2021), 1.

778 Bruce Sacerdote, Ranjan Sehgal, and Molly Cook, "Why Is All COVID-19 News Bad News?" *National Bureau of Economic Research Working Paper* No. 28110, November 2020, https://www.nber.org/papers/w28110.

779 Scott Atlas, *A Plague Upon Our House: My Fight at the Trump White House to Stop COVID from Destroying America* (New York: Liberty Protocol, 2021), 62.

780 Sara Francis Fujimura, "Purple Death: The Great Flu of 1918," *Perspectives in Health* 8, no. 3 (2003), https://www.paho.org/en/who-we-are/history-paho/purple-death-great-flu-1918.

781 Centers for Disease Control and Prevention, "2020 Final Death Statistics: COVID-19 as an Underlying Cause of Death vs. Contributing Cause," *CDC NCHS Podcast*, January 7, 2022, https://blogs.cdc.gov/nchs/2022/01/07/6291.

782 Mrinalika Roy, "CDC Reports Fewer COVID-19 Pediatric Deaths After Data Correction," *Reuters*, edited by Arun Koyyur, March 18, 2022, https://www.reuters.com/business/healthcare-pharmaceuticals/cdc-reports-fewer-covid-19-pediatric-deaths-after-data-correction-2022-03-18.

783 Leana S. Wen, "We Are Overcounting Covid Deaths and Hospitalizations and That's a Problem," *Washington Post*, January 13, 2023, https://www.washingtonpost.com/opinions/2023/01/13/covid-pandemic-deaths-hospitalizations-overcounting; *The Ethical Skeptic*, "Houston, the CDC Has a Problem (Part 2 of 3)," *The Ethical Skeptic (Substack)*, October 24, 2022, https://theethicalskeptic.substack.com/p/houston-the-cdc-has-a-problem-part.

784 Franklin D. Gilliam Jr., "U.S. Adults' Estimates of COVID-19 Hospitalizations Risk," *Gallup Polls*, September 27, 2021, https://news.gallup.com/opinion/gallup/354938/adults-estimates-covid-hospitalization-risk.aspx.

785 Deborah Birx, *Silent Invasion* (New York: Harper, 2022), 441.

786 John Ioannidis, "A Fiasco in the Making? As the Coronavirus Pandemic Takes Hold, We Are Making Decisions Without Reliable Data," *STAT*, March 17, 2020, https://www.statnews.com/2020/03/17/a-fiasco-in-the-making-as-the-coronavirus-pandemic-takes-hold-we-are-making-decisions-without-reliable-data/.

787 Larry Schweikart, *A Patriot's History of Globalism: Its Rise and Decline*, (New York: Skyhorse, 2024), 143.

788 Deborah Birx, *Silent Invasion* (New York: Harper, 2022), 446.

789 "Is It Time for a Reality Check on Rapid COVID Tests?" *NPR*, January 19, 2023, https://www.npr.org/sections/health-shots/2023/01/19/1149672577/is-it-time-for-a-reality-check-on-rapid-covid-tests.

790 Office of the Mayor, "New York City to Close All School Buildings and Transition to Remote Learning," *City of New York*, March 15, 2020, https://www.nyc.gov/office-of-the-mayor/news/151-20/new-york-city-close-all-school-buildings-transition-remote-learning.

791 Scott Atlas, *A Plague Upon Our House: My Fight at the Trump White House to Stop COVID From Destroying America* (New York: Liberty Protocol, 2021), 35–36.

792 Deborah Birx, *Silent Invasion* (New York: Harper, 2022), 36.

793 Jared Kushner, *Breaking History: A White House Memoir* (New York: Broadside Books, 2022), 346.
794 Ibid., 365.
795 Ibid., 350.
796 White House Coronavirus Task Force, "15 Days to Slow the Spread," *White House Archives*, March 16, 2020, https://trumpwhitehouse.archives.gov/articles/15-days-slow-spread.
797 Stephen Collinson, "Trump's Rebuke of Fauci Encapsulates the Rejection of Science in Virus Fight," *CNN*, May 14, 2020, https://www.cnn.com/us/live-news/us-coronavirus-update-05-14-20/h_9417808495504c7fc8cbadba4128c4d3.
798 Jared Kushner, *Breaking History: A White House Memoir* (New York: Broadside Books, 2022), 373.

In conversations with Steve Bannon, he said when the Trump team came in 2017 they were instructed (he did not say by whom, but the implication was by Mitch McConnell) that they could not touch Fauci or Francis Collins. The further inference was that not only were they protected by civil service laws but also that many members of the Senate, at least, received some sort of kickback from Fauci's deals with Big Pharma. Bannon did not elaborate further.

799 Ibid., 355.
800 Robert F. Kennedy, Jr., *The Real Anthony Fauci: Bill Gates, Big Pharma, and the Global War on Democracy and Public Health* (New York: Skyhorse, 2021), sv.
801 Stephen Collinson, "Fauci: Attacks on Me are Really Also 'Attacks on Science,'" *The Hill*, June 9, 2021, https://thehill.com/policy/healthcare/557602-fauci-attacks-on-me-are-really-also-attacks-on-science/.

Robert F. Kennedy, Jr., *The Real Anthony Fauci: Bill Gates, Big Pharma, and the Global War on Democracy and Public Health* (New York: Skyhorse, 2021), xvii.

One of his toadies, Dr. Peter Hotez, wrote in a scientific journal that Congress should pass hate crime legislation making it a felony to criticize Dr. Fauci.

802 Brett Samuels, "Trump Knocks Fauci: 'I Inherited Him,'" *The Hill*, August 31, 2020, https://thehill.com/homenews/administration/514523-trump-knocks-fauci-i-inherited-him.
803 Philip Bump, "Trump Says Coronavirus Will Disappear Without a Vaccine. Fauci Says the Opposite," *Washington Post*, May 8, 2020, https://www.washingtonpost.com/politics/2020/05/08/trump-says-coronavirus-will-disappear-without-vaccine-fauci-has-said-opposite/.
804 Jared Kushner, *Breaking History: A White House Memoir* (New York: Broadside Books, 2022), 379.
805 Robert F. Kennedy, Jr., *The Real Anthony Fauci: Bill Gates, Big Pharma, and the Global War on Democracy and Public Health* (New York: Skyhorse, 2021), 1.
806 Ibid., 4.
807 Bobby Caina Calvan, "Florida Reopens State's Economy Despite Ongoing Pandemic," *AP*, September 25, 2020, https://apnews.com/article/virus-outbreak-florida-business-ron-desantis-donald-trump-e64376aba8306681b53d52956d15bcd7.
808 Robert F. Kennedy, Jr., *The Real Anthony Fauci: Bill Gates, Big Pharma, and the Global War on Democracy and Public Health* (New York: Skyhorse, 2021), 16.
809 Ibid., 17.
810 Ibid., 88.
811 "The Lancet Concedes: Vaccines are NOT More Effective than Natural Immunity," *The National Pulse*, June 30, 2023, https://thenationalpulse.com/archive-post/the-lancet-concedes-vaccines-are-not-more-effective-than-natural-immunity/.

812 Steve Kirsch, "The CFR from the Pfizer Trial Show the Vaccines Make You 5x More Likely to Die from COVID," *Steve Kirsch's Newsletter*, December 24, 2024, https://kirschsubstack.com/p/the-cfr-from-the-pfizer-trial-show; Nicolas Hulscher, "COVID-19 'Vaccination' Linked to a 141% Increased Risk of Transverse Myelitis Within 42 Days of Injection," *Courageous Discourse* (Peter McCullough Substack), January 2, 2025, https://petermcculloughmd.substack.com/p/covid-19-vaccination-linked-to-a.

813 David Hundeyin, "The World's COVID-19 Response Is a Shocking Farce: Time to Bell the Cat," *Business Day*, April 24, 2020, https://businessday.ng/columnist/article/the-worlds-covid-19-response-is-a-shocking-farce-time-to-bell-the-cat; Jeffrey Tucker, "Twenty Grim Realities Unearthed by Lockdowns," *Brownstone Institute*, June 5, 2023, https://brownstone.org/articles/twenty-grim-realities-unearthed-by-lockdowns.

814 Jonas Herby, Lars Jonung, and Steve H. Hanke, *Did Lockdowns Work? The Verdict on Covid Restrictions* (London: Institute of Economic Affairs, June 5, 2023), https://iea.org.uk/publications/did-lockdowns-work-the-verdict-on-covid-restrictions.

815 Tom Jefferson et al., *Physical Interventions to Interrupt or Reduce the Spread of Respiratory Viruses*, Cochrane Database of Systematic Reviews, January 30, 2023, https://doi.org/10.1002/14651858.CD006207.pub6.

816 Jennifer Sey, "The Predictable Economic Fallout of Lockdown Policy," *Jennifer Sey* (Substack), March 13, 2023, https://jennifersey.substack.com/p/the-predictable-economic-fallout.

817 Carol Roth, "We're Living Through the Greatest Transfer of Wealth From the Middle Class to the Elites in History," *Newsweek*, October 24, 2021, https://www.newsweek.com/were-living-through-greatest-transfer-wealth-middle-class-elites-history-opinion-1641614.

818 Jared Kushner, *Breaking History: A White House Memoir* (New York: Broadside Books, 2022), 368.

819 Larry Schweikart and Lynne Pierson Doti, *American Entrepreneur* (New York: AMACOM, 2010), 389; Irwin Garfinkle and Robert Haveman, *Earnings Capacity, Poverty, and Inequality*, U.S. Department of Health, Education and Welfare, Institute for Research on Poverty Monograph Series (New York: Academic Press, 1977).

820 Paul Beaudry, David A. Green, and Benjamin M. Sand, *The Great Reversal in the Demand for Skill and Cognitive Tasks*, National Bureau of Economic Research Working Paper No. 18901 (Cambridge, MA: NBER, March 2013), https://www.nber.org/papers/w18901.

821 Cynthia McCormick Hibbert, "Trust in Physicians and Hospitals Plummeted Since the COVID Pandemic, Northeastern Research Says," *Northeastern Global News*, August 7, 2024, https://news.northeastern.edu/2024/08/07/trust-in-physicians-hospitals-research.

822 Alec Tyson and Giancarlo Pasquini, "60% of Americans Say They Probably Won't Get an Updated COVID-19 Vaccine," *Pew Research Center*, November 19, 2024, https://www.pewresearch.org/short-reads/2024/11/19/60-of-americans-say-they-probably-wont-get-an-updated-covid-19-vaccine; Mary Van Beusekom, "US Survey Reveals Growing Distrust of Vaccines, Embrace of Untruths," *CIDRAP*, November 1, 2023, https://www.cidrap.umn.edu/anti-science/us-survey-reveals-growing-distrust-vaccines-embrace-untruths.

CHAPTER 8: THE GRAVEYARD

823 Edward-Isaac Dovere, *Battle for the Soul: Inside the Democrats' Campaigns to Defeat Trump* (New York: Viking, 2021), 15.

824 Ibid., 20.

825 Robert Booth, "Obama and Branson Kitesurfing Trip Branded Huge Publicity Stunt," *The Guardian*, February 8, 2017, https://www.theguardian.com/us-news/2017/feb/08/barack-obama-richard-branson-kitesurfing-trip-necker-island.

826 Jessica Roy, "Obamas Sign Rumored $60-million Book Deal with Penguin Random House," *Los Angeles Times*, February 28, 2017, https://www.latimes.com/books/jacketcopy/la-et-jc-obama-book-deal-bidding-20170228-story.html.

827 Daniel Holloway, "Barack and Michelle Obama Sign Netflix Production Deal," *Variety*, May 21, 2018, https://variety.com/2018/digital/news/barack-michelle-obama-netflix-deal-1202817723.

828 Edward-Isaac Dovere, *Battle for the Soul: Inside the Democrats' Campaigns to Defeat Trump* (New York: Viking, 2021), 66–7.

829 Ibid., 64.

830 Ibid., 53.

831 David Von Drehle, "Let There Be Joe," *Time*, September 10, 2012, https://time.com/archive/6642393/let-there-be-joe.

832 Alex Thompson, "'The President Was Not Encouraging': What Obama Really Thought About Biden," *Politico*, August 14, 2020, https://www.politico.com/news/magazine/2020/08/14/obama-biden-relationship-393570.

833 E. J. Dionne Jr., "Biden Admits Plagiarism in School But Says It Was Not 'Malevolent,'" *The New York Times*, September 18, 1987, https://www.nytimes.com/1987/09/18/us/biden-admits-plagiarism-in-school-but-says-it-was-not-malevolent.html; Domenico Montanaro, "Fact Check: Biden's Too Tall Football Tale," *NBC News*, October 16, 2012, https://www.nbcnews.com/news/world/fact-check-bidens-too-tall-football-tale-flna1c6504609; Maureen Dowd, "Biden Is Facing Growing Debate on His Speeches," *The New York Times*, September 16, 1987, https://www.nytimes.com/1987/09/16/us/biden-is-facing-growing-debate-on-his-speeches.html; E. J. Dionne Jr., "Biden Admits Errors and Criticizes Latest Report," *The New York Times*, September 22, 1987, https://www.nytimes.com/1987/09/22/us/biden-admits-errors-and-criticizes-latest-report.html; David Smith, "Neil Kinnock on Biden's Plagiarism 'Scandal' and Why He Deserves to Win: 'Joe's an Honest Guy,'" *The Guardian*, September 7, 2020, https://www.theguardian.com/us-news/2020/sep/07/neil-kinnock-joe-biden-1987-scandal; Robert Shogan and James Risen, "Differing Versions Cited on Source of Passages: Biden Facing New Flap Over Speeches," *Los Angeles Times*, September 16, 1987, https://www.latimes.com/archives/la-xpm-1987-09-16-mn-5412-story.html.

834 Matt Flegenheimer, "Biden's First Run for President Was a Calamity. Some Missteps Still Resonate," *The New York Times*, June 3, 2019, https://www.nytimes.com/2019/06/03/us/politics/biden-1988-presidential-campaign.html.

835 Adam Nagourney and Jeff Zeleny, "Obama Chooses Biden as Running Mate," *The New York Times*, August 23, 2008, https://www.nytimes.com/2008/08/24/us/politics/24biden.html.

836 John Heileman and Mark Halperin, *Game Change: Obama and the Clintons, McCain, Palin, and the Race of a Lifetime* (New York: HarperCollins, 2010), 411–414.

837 Mark Leibovich, "Speaking Freely, Biden Finds Influential Role," *The New York Times*, March 28, 2009, https://www.nytimes.com/2009/03/29/us/politics/29biden.html.

838 Jake Tapper, "Political Punch: 'Sheriff Joe' Biden Touts Recovery Act Succes—and Hands over His Badge" *ABC News*, February 17, 2011, https://blogs.abcnews.com/politicalpunch/2011/02/sheriff-joe-biden-touts-recovery-act-success-and-hands-over-his-badge.html.

839 Anna Orso, "Penn Has Paid Joe Biden More than $900k Since He Left the White House. What Did He Do to Earn the Money?" *The Philadelphia Inquirer*, July 12, 2019, https://www.inquirer.com/news/joe-biden-penn-salary-lectures-20190712.html.

840 Thomas Kaplan, "Joe Biden's Tax Returns Show More than $15 Million in Income After 2016," *The New York Times*, July 9, 2019, https://www.nytimes.com/2019/07/09/us/politics/joe-biden-net-worth.html.

841 Edward-Isaac Dovere, *Battle for the Soul: Inside the Democrats' Campaigns to Defeat Trump* (New York: Viking, 2021), 84.

842 Amanda Arnold and Claire Lampen, "All the Women who Have Spoken Out Against Joe Biden," *The Cut*, April 12, 2020, https://www.thecut.com/2020/04/joe-biden-accuser-accusations-allegations.html.

843 Laura McGann, "The Agonizing Story of Tara Reade," *Vox*, May 7, 2020, https://www.vox.com/2020/5/7/21248713/tara-reade-joe-biden-sexual-assault-accusation; Lisa Lerer and Sydney Ember, "Examining Tara Reade's Sexual Assault Allegation Against Joe Biden," *The New York Times*, April 12, 2020, https://www.nytimes.com/2020/04/12/us/politics/joe-biden-tara-reade-sexual-assault-complaint.html.

It was ironic that just as with Bill Clinton, Biden was accused of *physical* assaults on women while Trump was accused of verbal assaults. The E. Jean Carroll case against Trump was specifically resolved with a "not guilty" verdict on the rape charge.

844 Edward-Isaac Dovere, *Battle for the Soul: Inside the Democrats' Campaigns to Defeat Trump* (New York: Viking, 2021), 89.

845 Ibid., 101–2.

846 Ibid., 121.

847 Ibid., 141.

848 Ibid., 224.

849 Anthony Zurcher, "Biden VP Pick: Kamala Harris Chosen as Running Mate," *BBC*, August 12, 2020, https://www.bbc.com/news/world-us-canada-53739323.

850 Edward-Isaac Dovere, *Battle for the Soul: Inside the Democrats' Campaigns to Defeat Trump* (New York: Viking, 2021), 422.

851 Timothy Corder, *The Big Steal: How An Army of Criminals Rigged the 2020 Election Against President Trump* (Las Vegas, NV: n.p., 2021), 10.

852 "Whistleblowers: Postal Service Labeled Trump Mail 'Undeliverable,' 388,000 Ballots Backdated 'Disappear,' *Washington Examinter*, December 1, 2020; https://www.washingtonexaminer.com/washington-secrets/whistleblowers-post-office-labeled-trump-mail-undeliverable-388,000-ballots-backdated-disappear.

853 Paul Bedard, "'Get to TCF': What Really Happened Inside Detroit's Ballot Counting Center," *Detroit Free Press*, November 6, 2020, https://www.freep.com/story/news/local/michigan/detroit/2020/11/06/tcf-center-detroit-ballot-counting/6173577002/.

It is important to understand that the mainstream media, aided by Wikipedia, was almost entirely Democrat in its leanings and deliberately misled or misrepresented stories in their discussions of what occurred.

854 Mollie Hemingway, *Rigged: How the Media, Big Tech, and the Democrats Seized Our Elections* (Washington, DC: Regnery Publishing, 2021).

855 Seth Keshel, "The Ten Irrefutable Points of 2020: An Epilogue," *Captain K's Corner (Substack)*, April 18, 2022, https://skeshel.substack.com/p/the-ten-irrefutable-points-of-2020.

856 Molly Ball, "The Secret History of the Shadow Campaign that Saved the 2020 Election," *Time*, February 6, 2021, https://time.com/5936036/secret-2020-election-campaign/.

857 Molly Ball, "The Secret History of the Shadow Campaign That Saved the 2020 Election," *Time*, February 6, 2021, https://time.com/5936036/secret-2020-election-campaign; Joe Hoft, *The Steal—Vol. I: Setting the Stage: The Deep State, Big Tech, Big Media, China, Absentee Ballots, the USPS, Non-Profits, and Rallies* (n.p., 2022); Joe Hoft, *The Steal—Vol. II: The Impossible Occurs: Access Denied, Impossible Results, The Drop and Roll, Chain of Custody, Authenticity, System Compliance, System Issues, and Collusion* (n.p., 2022), 53.

For example, as Hoft showed, in Michigan with 91% of the vote counted, Biden suddenly took the lead, and with the exception of a couple of districts with large Biden leads, "every entry was reported at 50 percent for Biden to 489% for President Trump," which Hoft called "completely inconceivable statistically" (*The Steal: Volume II*, 53).

858 Emma-Jo Morris and Gabrielle Fonrouge, "Smoking-Gun Email Reveals How Hunter Biden Introduced Ukrainian Businessman to VP Dad," *New York Post*, October 14, 2020, https://nypost.com/2020/10/14/email-reveals-how-hunter-biden-introduced-ukrainian-biz-man-to-dad; Miranda Devine, "Emails Reveal How Hunter Biden Tried to Cash in Big on Behalf of Family with Chinese Firm," *New York Post*, October 15, 2020, https://nypost.com/2020/10/15/emails-reveal-how-hunter-biden-tried-to-cash-in-big-with-chinese-firm.

A good overall survey of Biden's corruption is in Mollie Hemingway, *Rigged: How the Media, Big Tech, and the Democrats Seized Our Elections* (Washington, DC: Regnery Publishing, 225–248.

Joe Hoft, *The Steal—Vol. II: The Impossible Occurs: Access Denied, Impossible Results, The Drop and Roll, Chain of Custody, Authenticity, System Compliance, System Issues, and Collusion* (n.p., 2022), 51.

Moreover, in Pennsylvania, twice during the night there were large entries (favoring Trump) that were reversed. It is unheard of to deliver votes already "on the board."

859 Isabel Vincent, "Joe and Hunter Biden Golfed with Ukraine Gas Executive in 2014," *New York Post*, October 1, 2019, https://nypost.com/2019/10/01/joe-and-hunter-biden-golfed-with-ukraine-gas-executive-in-2014; Peter Schweizer, *Secret Empires: How the American Political Class Hides Corruption and Enriches Family and Friends* (New York: Harper, 2018), 396.

860 Natasha Bertrand, "Hunter Biden Story is Russian Disinfo, Dozens of Former Intel Officials Say," *Politico*, October 19, 2020, https://www.politico.com/news/2020/10/19/hunter-biden-story-russian-disinfo-430276.

861 Julian E. Barnes and Matthew Rosenberg, "Trump Said to Be Warned That Giuliani Was Conveying Russian Disinformation," *The New York Times*, October 15, 2020, https://www.nytimes.com/2020/10/15/us/politics/giuliani-russian-disiofrmation.html.

862 Mollie Hemmingway, *Rigged: How the Media, Big Tech, and the Democrats Seized Our Elections* (Washington, DC: Regnery Publishing, 2021), 243.

863 Ibid., 248.

864 Josh Kraushaar and Manu Raju, "Coleman Concedes Race to Franken," *Politico*, June 30, 2009, https://www.politico.com/story/2009/06/coleman-concedes-race-to-franken-024383.

In Minnesota's senate race in 2008, Democrat Al Franken defeated Republican Norm Coleman by fewer than 350 votes (with 15% of the vote going to an independent candidate) after an eight-month legal challenge.

Andrew Brown and Dave Altimari, "Bridgeport Primary Election Overturned; New Vote Ordered," *CT Mirror*, November 1, 2023, https://ctmirror.org/2023/11/01/bridgeport-primary-election-ruling-ganim-gomes/.

More recently, courts and election officials have been more discerning of questionable results. In Connecticut, for example, a primary election was overturned by a judge due to fraud.

865 Mike Pence, "Mike Pence Speech at Turning Point USA Event Transcript December 22," *Rev*, December 22, 2020, https://www.rev.com/blog/transcripts/mike-pence-speech-at-turning-point-usa-event-transcript-december-22.

866 "Read Pence's Full Letter Saying He Can't Claim 'Unilateral Authority' to Reject Electoral Votes," *PBS News Hour*, January 6, 2021, https://www.pbs.org/newshour/politics/read-pences-full-letter-saying-he-cant-claim-unilateral-authority-to-reject-electoral-votes35.

867 "Read Trump's Jan. 6 Speech, A Key Part of Impeachment Trial," *NPR*, February 10, 2021, https://www.npr.org/2021/02/10/966396848/read-trumps-jan-6-speech-a-key-part-of-impeachment-trial.

868 Steven Nelson, "FBI Had 26 Informants at Jan. 6 Capitol Riots—And Most Were Involved, Bombshell DOJ Report Confirms," *New York Post*, December 12, 2024, https://nypost.com/2024/12/12/us-news/doj-watchdog-says-fbi-had-26-confidential-sources-in-dc-for-jan-6-riot-but-no-evidence-of-undercover-agents.

869 Eric Tucker, "With Trump Newly Indicted, Here's What to Know About the Documents Case and What's Next," *Associated Press*, June 28, 2023, https://apnews.com/article/donald-trump-new-indictment-classified-documents-81b982b8195dcfb85b7ae8789f108b0b.

870 Andy Sullivan, Joseph Ax, and Sarah N. Lynch, "Georgia Charges Trump, Former Advisers in 2020 Election Case," *Reuters*, August 15, 2023, https://www.reuters.com/legal/us-state-georgia-appears-set-file-charges-against-donald-trump-court-document-2023-08-14/.

871 Valerie Richardson, "Democrats Bill Would Ban Trump's Name on US Buildings," *Washington Times*, February 18, 2021, https://www.washingtontimes.com/news/2021/feb/18/democrats-bill-would-ban-trumps-name-us-buildings-/.

872 Hannah Rabinowitz and Katelyn Polantz, "'QAnon Shaman' Jacob Chansley Sentenced to 41 Months in Prison for Role in U.S. Capitol Riot," *CNN*, November 17, 2021, https://www.cnn.com/2021/11/17/politics/jacob-chansley-qanon-shaman-january-6-sentencing/index.html.

Larry Schweikart, "Flight of the Squidpickles," *UncoverDC*, January 11, 2021, https://uncoverdc.com/2021/01/11/flight-of-the-squidpickles.

It is important to understand that having ordinary people who opposed their views inside the Capitol was nothing new. Protestors had occupied the Capitol on numerous times. The difference on January 6 was that for the first time it was a cause with which the officials themselves did not sympathize; indeed, whether real or not, many felt terrified of the ordinary Americans intruding on their space. I wrote about this at the time in an article called "Flight of the Squidpickles," in which I argued that the embarrassment and humiliation of the congressmen and senators fleeing in terror was caught on film and camera, and that as much as anything motivated their obsession with striking back at the Trump supporters.

873 *Fischer v. United States*, 603 U.S. (2024). AGAIN, left blank on court doc itself on web.

874 Cully Stimson, "Rogue Prosecutors and the Rise of Crime," *Imprimis*, March 2024, https://imprimis.hillsdale.edu/rogue-prosecutors-and-the-rise-of-crime.

875 Ibid.

876 Jeffery C. Mays, "N.Y.'s New Attorney General Is Targeting Trump. Will Judges See a 'Political Vendetta?'" *The New York Times*, December 31, 2018, https://www.nytimes.com/2018/12/31/nyregion/tish-james-attorney-general-trump.html.

877 Jon Campbell, "NY AG Letitia James Called the NRA a 'Terrorist Organization.' Will It Hurt Her Case?" *USA Today*, August 19, 2020, https://www.usatoday.com/story/news/politics/2020/08/19/nra-lawsuit-ny-ag-letitia-james-past-comments/5606437002.

878 Marisa Lagos, "Proposition 47's Impact on California's Criminal Justice System," *KQED*, February 13, 2024, https://www.kqed.org/news/11975692/prop-47s-impact-on-californias-criminal-justice-system.

879 "Retail Theft (Shoplifting) Statistics," *Capital One Shopping*, April 9, 2024, https://capitaloneshopping.com/research/shoplifting-statistics.

880 Aaron Tolentino, "San Francisco Centre: Stores Closing to Begin 2024," *KRON*, January 19, 2024, https://www.kron4.com/news/bay-area/san-francisco-centre-stores-closing-to-begin-2024.

881 ABC7.com Staff, "New DA Gascon to Decline Prosecution on Range of Low-level Crimes," *Eyewitness News (ABC7)*, December 10, 2020, https://abc7.com/george-gascon-los-angeles-district-attorney-lada-misdemeanor-crimes/8674095/.

882 Cully Stimson, "Rogue Prosecutors and the Rise of Crime," *Imprimis*, March 2024, https://imprimis.hillsdale.edu/rogue-prosecutors-and-the-rise-of-crime.

883 Broke Rollins, "Political Violence in America," *The American Mind*, May 7, 2024, https://americanmind.org/salvo/political-violence-in-america/.

884 Ibid.

885 Margot Cleveland, "The Left's 2020 'Fake Electors' Narrative is Fake News," *The Federalist*, May 15, 2023, https://thefederalist.com/2023/05/15/the-lefts-2020-fake-electors-narrative-is-fake-news.

886 "President Biden Falls on Air Force One Stairs," *Sky News*, March 19, 2021, https://www.youtube.com/watch?v=U5Mwc12LtRY.

887 Eli Stokols and Jonathan Lemire, "Biden Falls on State at Air Force Graduation but Is 'Fine,' According to a Spokesperson," *Politico*, June 1, 2023, https://www.politico.com/news/2023/06/01/biden-falls-on-stage-is-fine-00099730.

888 Michael D. Shear, "Biden Takes Tumble During Bike Ride in Delaware," *The New York Times*, June 18, 2022, https://www.nytimes.com/2022/06/18/us/politics/biden-falls-bike-rehoboth-beach.html.

889 Sara Dorn, "Biden Slips On Air Force One Stairs After Staff Try to Prevent Major Falls—As Gaffes Raise Concerns About His Age," *Forbes*, September 26, 2023, https://www.forbes.com/sites/saradorn/2023/09/26/biden-slips-on-air-force-one-stairs-as-his-team-tries-to-prevent-major-falls-as-trips-and-gaffes-raise-concerns-about-his-age; Emily Crane, "President Biden Stumbles—Twice—Boarding Air Force One Despite Using Short Stairs to Avoid Tripping," *New York Post*, February 21, 2024, https://nypost.com/2024/02/21/us-news/president-biden-trips-again-boarding-air-force-one.

890 David Smith, "Warning Signs: A History of Joe Biden's Verbal Slips," *The Guardian*, July 5, 2024, https://www.theguardian.com/us-news/article/2024/jul/05/joe-biden-verbal-decline-warning-signs.

891 Ibid.

892 Morgan Phillips and Kelly Laco, "Robert Hur Admits 'Forgetful' Biden Read ALOUD Classified Files to Ghost Writer of His $8 Million Book—Who Then Tried to 'DESTROY the Evidence'; Special Counsel Confirms President Wanted to Keep Documents for 'Pride and Money,'" *UK Daily Mail*, March 12, 2024, https://www.dailymail.co.uk/news/article-13187601/special-counsel-robert-hur-biden-classified-documents-capitol-hill.html.

893 Ibid.

894 Jackson Richman, "Special Counsel Does Not Charge Biden in Classified Documents Probe, Finds He 'Willfully Retained' Materials," *The Epoch Times*, February 8, 2024, https://www.theepochtimes.com/us/special-counsel-does-not-charge-biden-in-classified-documents-probe-finds-he-willfully-retained-materials-5583539; Robert K. Hur, *Report From the Special Counsel on the Investigation into Unauthorized Removal, Retention, and Disclosure of Classified Documents Discovered at Locations Including the Penn Biden Center and the Delaware Private Residence of President Joseph R. Biden, Jr.*, U.S. Department of Justice, February 2024, https://www.justice.gov/storage/report-from-special-counsel-robert-k-hur-february-2024.pdf.

895 Rebecca Ballhaus, "How the White House Functioned With a Diminished Biden in Charge," *The Wall Street Journal*, December 19, 2024, https://www.wsj.com/podcasts/whats-news/how-bidens-white-house-functioned-with-a-diminished-president/c10e61d7-784e-4089-acd7-28081a3bd9f2.

896 Katelyn Caralle and Charlie Spiering, "White House Biden Health Cover-up Blown Wide Open in Bombshell Report: Joe Was Senile from Day One of His Presidency," *UK Daily Mail*, December 19, 2024, https://www.dailymail.co.uk/news/article-14210053/white-house-conceal-joe-biden-decline-hired-voice-coach.html.

897 Olivia Reingold, "WATCH: When Mike Johnson Knew Joe Biden Was Not in Charge," *The Free Press*, January 7, 2025, https://www.thefp.com/p/when-mike-johnson-knew-joe-biden-not-in-charge.

898 Steven Nelson, "House Speaker Mike Johnson Says Biden Has Cognitive Decline: 'It's Just Reality,'" *New York Post*, October 27, 2023, https://nypost.com/2023/10/27/news/house-speaker-mike-johnson-says-biden-has-cognitive-decline-its-just-reality.

899 Byron York, "'The Best Biden Ever,'" *Washington Examiner*, March 7, 2024, https://www.washingtonexaminer.com/daily-memo/2909317/the-best-biden-ever/.

900 Jim Inhofe, "Afghanistan Was a Predictable, Preventable Disaster," *Foreign Policy*, August15,2022,https://foreignpolicy.com/2022/08/15/afghanistan-withdrawal-pullout-military-taliban-chaos-evacuation-biden-inhofe/.

901 Chuck Ross, "Deadliest Day for Troops in Afghanistan Since 2011," *Washington Free Beacon*, August 26, 2021, https://freebeacon.com/national-security/four-marines-killed-in-afghan-airport-bombing.

902 Ellie Kaufman, "First on CNN: US Left Behind $7 Billion of Military Equipment in Afghanistan after 2021 Withdrawal, Pentagon Report Says," *CNN*, April 28, 2022, https://www.cnn.com/2022/04/27/politics/afghan-weapons-left-behind/index.html.

903 Kate Sullivan, Maegan Vazquez, and Christina Carrega, "Garland Announces National Strategy to Combat Domestic Terrorism, Invoking US Capitol Riot," *CNN*, June 15, 2021, https://www.cnn.com/2021/06/15/politics/white-house-strategy-domestic-terrorism/index.html.

904 U.S. House of Representatives, Committee on the Judiciary and the Select Subcommittee on the Weaponization of Government, *The FBI's Breach of Religious Freedom: The Weaponization of Law Enforcement Against Catholic Americans*, December 4, 2023, https://judiciary.house.gov/sites/evo-subsites/republicans-judiciary.house.gov/files/evo-media-document/2023-12-04-the-fbis-breach-of-religious-freedom-the-weaponization-of-law-enforcement-against-catholic-americans.pdf.

905 Christiann Abeelen et al., "Implementation of Energy Efficiency Projects by Dutch Industry," *Energy Policy* 63 (2013): 408–418, https://www.sciencedirect.com/science/article/abs/pii/S0301421513009725.

906 James Bikales, "Congress Provided $7.5 Billion for Electric Vehicle Chargers. Built So Far: Zero," *Politico*, December 5, 2023, https://www.politico.com/news/2023/12/05/congress-ev-chargers-billions-00129996.

907 Lili Pike, "China Is Owning the Global Battery Race. That Could Be a Problem for the U.S.," *Grid*, December 28, 2021, https://www.grid.news/story/global/2021/12/28/china-is-owning-the-global-battery-race-that-could-be-a-problem-for-the-u-s/.

908 "Container Ship Removed 8 Weeks After Francis Scott Key Bridge Crash in Baltimore," *NBC News*, May 20, 2024, https://www.nbcnews.com/news/us-news/container-ship-set-removed-8-weeks-francis-scott-key-bridge-crash-rcna153005.

909 Ronald Asmus, *A Little War that Shook the World: Georgia, Russia and the Future of the West* (New York: Palgrave, 2010).

910 United Nations, *Russian Federation Announces 'Special Military Operation' in Ukraine as Security Council Meets in Eleventh-Hour Effort to Avoid Full-Scale Conflict*, Meetings Coverage and Press Releases, February 23, 2022, https://press.un.org/en/2022/sc14803.doc.htm.

911 Jonathan Masters and Will Merrow, "Here's How Much Aid the United States Has Sent Ukraine," *Council on Foreign Relations*, July 15, 2025, https://www.cfr.org/article/how-much-us-aid-going-ukraine.

912 CBS News, "As U.S. and Allies Arm Ukraine, Russia Warns That Losing a Conventional War 'Can Trigger a Nuclear War,'" *CBS News*, January 19, 2023, https://www.cbsnews.com/news/ukraine-russia-nuclear-war-threat-us-nato-weapons-tanks/.

913 Jeffrey Sachs, "A Scam Built on Corruption," *Common Dreams*, December 26, 2023, https://www.commondreams.org/opinion/corruption-of-us-foreign-policy.

914 Center for Migration Studies, *US Undocumented Population Increased to 11.7 Million in July 2023: Provisional CMS Estimates Derived from CPS Data*, September 5, 2024, https://cmsny.org/us-undocumented-population-increased-in-july-2023-warren-090624; Mohammad Fazel Zarandi, Jonathan S. Feinstein, and Edward H. Kaplan, "Yale Study Finds Twice as Many Undocumented Immigrants as Previous Estimates," *Yale Insights*, September 21, 2018, https://insights.som.yale.edu/insights/yale-study-finds-twice-as-many-undocumented-immigrants-as-previous-estimates.

915 U.S. Congress, Committee on Oversight and Accountability, "Wrap Up: Biden Administration's Policies Have Fueled the Worst Border Crisis in U.S. History," *U.S. House of Representatives*, January 17, 2024, https://oversight.house.gov/release/wrap-up-biden-administrations-policies-have-fueled-worst-border-crisis-in-u-s-history.

916 Ibid.

917 FBI agents to Members of Congress, "The United States Is Facing a New and Imminent Danger," January 17, 2024, https://justthenews.com/sites/default/files/2024-01/Scan%20Jan%2024%2C%202024%20at%203.43%20PM.pdf.

918 John Gramlich, "Migrant Encounters at U.S.-Mexico Border Have Fallen Sharply in 2024," *Pew Research Center*, October 1, 2024, https://www.pewresearch.org/short-reads/2024/10/01/migrant-encounters-at-u-s-mexico-border-have-fallen-sharply-in-2024.

919 Stephen Groves, "House Passes Immigrant Detention Bill That Would Be Trump's First Law to Sign," *AP News*, January 22, 2025, https://apnews.com/article/congress-immigration-crackdown-laken-riley-act-trump-a3e52af60b6b952f487e-4ae03ebfacde.

920 Nicole Narea, "What Democrats Must Learn from Biden's Disastrous Immigration Record," *Vox*, January 17, 2025, https://www.vox.com/politics/395339/biden-border-immigration-record-legacy.

921 Jennie Taer, "Biden Admin Quietly Loosening Immigration Policies Before Trump Takes Office—Including Letting Migrants Skip ICE Check-Ins in NYC," *New York Post*, November 21, 2024, https://nypost.com/2024/11/21/us-news/biden-admin-to-let-illegal-migrants-skip-nyc-ice-appointments.

922 Al Jazeera Staff, "US Judge Blocks Biden's Plan to End Title 42 Border Expulsions," *Al Jazeera*, May 20, 2022, https://www.aljazeera.com/news/2022/5/20/us-judge-blocks-bidens-plan-to-end-title-42-border-expulsions.

923 Fritz Farrow, Gabriella Abdul-Hakim, and Will McDuffie, "Harris Criticizes Trump in Her 1st Visit to the Border in More than 3 Years," *ABC News*, September 27, 2024, https://abcnews.go.com/Politics/harris-criticize-trump-1st-visit-border-3-years/story?id=114245136.

924 Fritz Farrow, Gabriella Abdul-Hakim, and Will McDuffie, "Harris Criticizes Trump in Her 1st Visit to the Border in More than 3 Years," *ABC News*, September 27, 2024, https://abcnews.go.com/Politics/harris-criticize-trump-1st-visit-border-3-years/story?id=114245136; Gladys Gerbaud, Chase Harrison, and Khalea Robertson, "How Latinos Voted in the 2024 U.S. Presidential Election," *AS/COA*, November 6, 2024, https://www.as-coa.org/articles/how-latinos-voted-2024-us-presidential-election; Geoff Bennett, Shrai Popat, and Saher Khan, "Exploring Why More Latinos Voted for Trump and What it Means for Future Elections," *PBS NewsHour*, November 13, 2024, https://www.pbs.org/newshour/show/exploring-why-more-latinos-voted-for-trump-and-what-it-means-for-future-elections; Jason Lange and Iris Lee, "Trump's Return to Power Fueled by Hispanic, Working-Class Voter Support," *Reuters*, November 7, 2024, https://www.reuters.com/world/us/trumps-return-power-fueled-by-hispanic-working-class-voter-support-2024-11-06/.

925 Michael Lind, *Hell to Pay: How the Suppression of Wages Is Destroying America* (New York: Portfolio, 2023), xvii.

926 Ibid., 57.

927 Ibid., 61.

928 Martin Gurri, "The Elite Panic of 2022," *City Journal*, Summer 2022, https://www.city-journal.org/the-elite-panic-of-2022.

929 Jennifer Sey, "The Harms of Masking-Part 1," Substack, March 29, 2023, https://jennifersey.substack.com/p/the-harms-of-masking-part-1; "CDC Used Journal to Promote Masks Despite 'Unreliable' and 'Unsupported Data': New Analysis," *Epoch Times*, July 14, 2023.

930 Josh Christenson "Fauci Adviser Hid Emails From FOIA Requests by Using Personal Account: Records," *New York Post*, June 29, 2023, https://nypost.com/2023/06/29/fauci-adviser-hid-nih-emails-from-foia-requests-during-covid/.

931 The growing list was extensive, much of it cited in Kennedy, *Real Anthony Fauci*, passim. NO, the reader can do a little work once in a while.

Peter McCullough, "Toxicity of SARS-CoV-2 Spike Protein from the Virus and from COVID-19 mRNA or Adenoviral DNA Vaccines," *Substack*, July 31, 2023, https://petermcculloughmd.substack.com/p/toxicity-of-sars-cov-2-spike-protein; "Subclinical Heart Damage More Prevalent Than Thought After Moderna Vaccination: Study, *Epoch Times*, July 26, 2023; "US Military Confirms Myocarditis Spike After COVID Vaccine Introduction," *Epoch Times*, July 20, 2023; Fadi Nahab et al., "Factors Associated with Stroke After COVID-19 Vaccination: A Statewide [Georgia] Analysis," *Frontiers in Neurology*, February 5, 2023; "IgG4 Antibodies Induced by Repeated Vaccination May Generate Immune Tolerance to the SARS-CoV-2 Spike Protein," *Vaccines*, May 17, 2023, https://www.mdpi.com/2076-393X/11/5/991; "IgG4 Antibodies Induced by repeated Vaccination May Generate Immune tolerance to the SARS-CoV-2 Spike Protein," *Vaccines*, May 17, 2023;

Wendi Mahoney, "Moderna Spikevax Trial Data Show Serious Adverse Events and Death," www.uncoverdec.com, July 24, 2023, *Substack*, July 18, 2023; Steve Kirsch, "COVID Vaccines Increase Risk of Serious Cardiac Events by 18x," https://kirschsubstack.com/p/covid-vaccines-increase-risk-of-serious;

Both disabilities in the US and Britain soared after the vaccines were introduced (Steve Kirsch, "Can Anyone Explain the Alarming Rise in Disability in Both the US and UK?"https://kirschsubstack.com/p/can-anyone-explain-the-alarming-rise?utm_source=post-email-title&publication_id=548354&post_id=135232788&isFreemail=true&utm_medium=email); "Significant COVID-19 Vaccine Study Censored by Medical Journal Within 24 Hours," *Epoch Times*, July 19, 2023; Though not a scientific study, a survey done with Steve Kirsh of 5,684 children found almost a 9:1 ratio of those vaxxed who reported cardiac arrest or Myo/Pericardial disease vs. those who were unvaxxed. (Steve Kirsch, "COVID vaccines increase risk of serious cardiac events by 18," Substack, July 30, 2023); "CDC Removed 'COVID Vaccine' as Cause of Death on Death Certificates," *The DailyFetched*, July 5, 2023, https://www.dailyfetched.com/cdc-removed-covid-vaccine-as-cause-of-death-on-death-certificates/.

In addition to these sources, Robert Kennedy's book, *The Real Anthony Fauci* is exhaustively resourced with hundreds of studies, and my column, "Today's News: The News of Today is the History of Tomorrow" on www.uncoverdc.com contains an almost-daily section on "China Virus News" that includes hundreds of articles and studies.

Peter McCullough, "Toxicity of SARS-CoV-2 Spike Protein from the Virus and from COVID-19 mRNA or Adenoviral DNA Vaccines," *Substack*, July 31, 2023, https://petermcculloughmd.substack.com/p/toxicity-of-sars-cov-2-spike-protein; Zachary Stieber, "Subclinical Heart Damage More Prevalent Than Thought After Moderna Vaccination: Study," *Epoch Times*, July 26, 2023, https://www.theepochtimes.com/health/subclinical-heart-damage-more-prevalent-than-thought-after-moderna-vaccination-study-5440992; Zachary Stieber, "US Military Confirms Myocarditis Spike After COVID Vaccine Introduction," *Epoch Times*, July 20, 2023, https://www.theepochtimes.com/article/us-military-confirms-myocarditis-spike-after-covid-vaccine-introduction-5434223; Fadi Nahab et al., "Factors Associated with Stroke After COVID-19 Vaccination: A Statewide Analysis," *Frontiers in Neurology*, February 5, 2023, https://www.frontiersin.org/articles/10.3389/fneur.2023.1199745/full; Vladimir N. Uversky et al., "IgG4 Antibodies Induced by Repeated Vaccination May Generate Immune Tolerance to the SARS-CoV-2 Spike Protein," *Vaccines*, May 17, 2023, https://www.mdpi.com/2076-393X/11/5/991.

932 Larry Schweikart, interviews with Steve Bannon, *War Room*, various dates, 2022, https://warroom.org.

933 "Army Sees 6 Percent Drop in White Recruits," *Newsmax*, January 11, 2024, https://www.newsmax.com/newsfront/army-drop-white/2024/01/11/id/1149223/.

934 Graig Graziosi, "Former DOE Official Arrested for Third Time for Allegedly Stealing Luggage at Airport," *The Independent*, May 18, 2023, https://www.the-independent.com/news/world/americas/crime/sam-brinton-luggage-theft-arrest-doe-b2341647.html.

935 Shawn Fleetwood, "Report: Defense Secretary Lloyd Austin Went MIA Twice Last Year and Didn't Tell Congress," *Federalist*, January 16, 2025, https://thefederalist.com/2025/01/16/report-defense-secretary-lloyd-austin-went-mia-twice-last-year-and-didnt-tell-congress/.

936 IMDb, "Gettysburg Quotes," *IMDb*, accessed July 24, 2025, https://www.imdb.com/title/tt0107007/quotes/?item=qt2229144.

CHAPTER 9: THE RESURRECTION

[937] David A. Graham, "The Cases Against Trump: A Guide," *The Atlantic*, May 8, 2024, https://www.theatlantic.com/ideas/archive/2024/05/donald-trump-legal-cases-charges/675531/.

[938] Aaron Navarro, "DeSantis Gathers Donors, GOP Politicians at Event as He Considers 2024 Presidential Run," *CBS News*, February 27,2023, https://www.cbsnews.com/news/desantis-donors-gop-retreat-considers-2024-presidential-run/.

[939] Ibid.

[940] Meg Kinnard, "Nikki Haley Announces Run for President, Challenging Trump," *Associated Press*, February 14, 2023; Sam Stein, "Vivek Ramaswamy Announces He Will Run for President," *Politico*, February 21, 2023, https://www.politico.com/news/2023/02/21/vivek-ramaswamy-president-2024-00083903.

[941] Sarah Fortinsky, "One-third of Adults in New Poll Say Biden's Election Was Illegitimate," *The Hill*, January 2, 2024, https://thehill.com/homenews/campaign/4384619-one-third-of-americans-say-biden-election-illegitimate/.

[942] Jessica Piper, "DeSantis Super PAC Quietly Funnelled [sic] Money Into Anti-Trump Group," *Politico*, January 30, 2024, https://www.politico.com/news/2024/01/30/desantis-pac-anti-trump-00138630.

[943] Hannah Knowles, "Nikki Haley Tops DeSantis for the First Time in Iowa Poll," *Washington Post*, January 11, 2024," https://www.washingtonpost.com/politics/2024/01/11/iowa-poll-nikki-haley-ron-desantis/.

[944] Jim Hoft, "'We've Got to Do This Immediately!' Warhawk Nikki Haley Says US Should Strike and Kill Iranian Leaders Inside Their Country," *The Gateway Pundit*, January 30, 2024, https://www.thegatewaypundit.com/2024/01/weve-got-do-this-immediately-warhawk-nikki-haley/.

[945] "NBC News Poll: Biden Trails Trump by 20 Points on the Economy as His Approval Ratings Plummet," *NBC News*, February 4, 2024, https://www.nbcnews.com/meet-the-press/video/biden-trails-trump-by-20-points-on-the-economy-as-his-approval-ratings-plummet-nbc-news-poll-203574341540.

[946] Jack Posobiec (@JackPosobiec), "Trump Meets With Ronna McDaniel…Then Says He'll Be Recommending RNC Changes," *X*, February 6, 2024, https://x.com/JackPosobiec/status/1754838379189989870; Nikki Schwab and Katelyn Caralle, "Ronna McDaniel Tells Trump She Will Resign as Republican National Committee Chair…," *Daily Mail*, February 6, 2024, https://www.dailymail.co.uk/news/article-13054259/ronna-mcdaniel-tells-rrump-resign-RNC.html.

[947] "'It's Devastating': Trump Seizes Unmatched Control over the GOP," *Politico*, n.d. (Circa February 2024), https://www.msn.com/en-us/news/politics/the-week-trump-seized-unmatched-control-over-the-gop/ar-BB1i1uML.

[948] Vince Quill, "Here's a List of ALL the GOP Reps Who Won't Be Seeking Re-Election in 2024," *WLT Report*, February 12, 2024, https://wltreport.com/2024/02/12/heres-list-all-gop-reps-who-wont-be; Stuart Rothenberg, "The Wrong People Are Retiring from Congress," *Roll Call*, February 12, 2024, https://rollcall.com/2024/02/12/the-wrong-people-are-retiring-from-congress/.

[949] Epoch Times Contributor, "INFOGRAPHIC: Key Updates in Trump's Legal Battles," *Epoch Times*, August 4, 2023, https://www.theepochtimes.com/article/infographic-key-updates-in-trumps-legal-battles-2-post-2-post-5444441.

[950] Catherine Yang, "Judge Orders Trump, Executives to Pay More than $350 Million," *Epoch Times*, February 16, 2024, https://www.theepochtimes.com/us/judge-orders-trump-organization-executives-to-pay-more-than-350-million-5575864.

[951] Ron Chernow, *Titan: The Life of John D. Rockefeller* (New York: Vintage, 1998), 541.

952 Matt Egan, "Trump's Truth Social Is Now a Public Company. Experts Warn Its Multibillion-Dollar Valuation Defies Logic," *CNN Business*, March 26, 2024, https://www.cnn.com/2024/03/26/markets/trump-media-stock-truth-social/index.html.

953 Aimee Picchi, "Trump Media's Merger With DWAC Gets Regulatory Nod. Trump Could Get a Stake Worth $4 Billion," *CBS News*, February 16, 2024, https://www.cbsnews.com/news/trump-media-dwac-sec-approval-spac/.

954 Adam Reiss et al., "Donald Trump Found Guilty in Historic New York Hush Money Case," *NBC News*, May 30, 2024, https://www.nbcnews.com/politics/donald-trump/donald-trump-verdict-hush-money-trial-rcna152492.

955 Kyle Cheney, Josh Gerstein, and Betsy Woodruff Swan, "Judge Dismisses Trump's Mar-a-Lago Classified Docs Criminal Case," *Politico*, July 15, 2024, https://www.politico.com/news/2024/07/15/judge-dismisses-trumps-mar-a-lago-classified-docs-criminal-case-00168231.

956 "Full Debate: Biden and Trump in the First 2024 Presidential Debate | WSJ," YouTube video, 1:38:18, posted by The Wall Street Journal, streamed live June 27, 2024, https://www.youtube.com/watch?v=qqG96G8YdcE.

957 "Trump's Campaign, LaCivita, Fabrizio," *Politico*, December 19, 2024, https://www.politico.com/news/magazine/2024/12/19/trump-campaign-lacivita-fabrizio-qa-00195206.

958 "Chris Stirewalt on Biden's Debate Performance," YouTube video, 6:34, posted by NewsNation, June 28, 2024, https://www.youtube.com/watch?v=Qq4kAICt418.

959 "Stephen Colbert Reacts to the First Presidential Debate," YouTube video, 9:12, posted by The Late Show with Stephen Colbert, June 28, 2024, https://www.youtube.com/watch?v=MF5pcrdvnSQ.

960 "Aaron Kall on Biden's Debate Performance," YouTube video, 1:25, posted by AP Archive, June 28, 2024, https://www.youtube.com/watch?v=9kXiJE3aTqc.

961 "Thomas Whalen Calls Biden Debate an 'Unmitigated Disaster,'" YouTube video, 2:21, posted by WCVB Channel 5 Boston, June 28, 2024, https://www.youtube.com/watch?v=Puo-7a6UrH8.

962 Dr. Sanjay Gupta, "Dr. Sanjay Gupta: It's Time for President Biden to Undergo Detailed Cognitive and Neurological Testing and Share His Results," *CNN*, July 5, 2024, https://www.cnn.com/2024/07/05/health/gupta-biden-cognitive-testing-analysis/index.html.

963 Bryan Chai, "Crucial Meeting with Biden Caused Chuck Schumer to Break Down in Tears: Report," *Western Journal*, January 17, 2025, https://www.westernjournal.com/crucial-meeting-biden-caused-chuck-schumer-break-tears-report.

964 Ibid.

965 Meridith McGraw and Natalie Allison, "Trump 'Felt the Bullet Ripping Through the Skin' During Apparent [sic] Assassination Attempt," *Politico*, July 13, 2024, 6:34 p.m. EDT, updated July 14, 2024, 1:47 a.m. EDT, https://www.politico.com/news/2024/07/13/trump-rushed-off-stage-at-pennsylvania-rally-after-possible-gunfire-00167977.

Use of the term "apparent" was dishonest and erroneous. It was a clear assassination attempt.

966 "Trump Safe After Assassination Attempt," *The New York Times*, live coverage, July 13, 2024, https://www.nytimes.com/live/2024/07/13/us/biden-trump-election.

967 Dave Andrusko, "Trump's Campaign Strategists Explain His Amazing Victory," *National Right to Life News Today*, December 27, 2024, https://nrlc.org/nrlnewstoday/2024/12/trumps-campaign-strategists-explain-his-amazing-victory/.

One of Trump's campaign managers, Chris LaCivita, said, "I don't think people give enough credit to the fact that the world has a visual [with Trump pumping his fist in the air]. It's an iconic visual.... And what that visual conveys. Not only about him, but the country as a whole. Americans get knocked down, but they always fight back"

968 "RNC 2024 Donald Trump Full Speech," *PBS NewsHour*, live coverage, July 19, 2024, https://www.pbs.org/newshour/politics/watch-live-donald-trump-speaks-at-2024-republican-national-convention.

969 "Dr. Phil's One-on-One Interview With Donald Trump," YouTube video, 1:00:46, posted by Merit Street Media, June 6, 2024, https://www.youtube.com/watch?v=sVGg90hukLI.

970 Dana Kennedy, "Would-Be Trump Assassin Thomas Crooks May Have Had an Accomplice, as Investigators say FBI is Suppressing Info," *New York Post*, https://nypost.com/2025/02/27/us-news/would-be-trump-assassin-thomas-matthew-crooks-may-have-had-accomplice-data-shows/.

971 Associated Press and Zoe Szathmary, "First the Obamas, Now the Bidens: Joe and Jill Sign Multi-Book Deal With Former Veep Focusing on Year He Lost Son Beau and Decided Not to Run for President," *U.K. Daily Mail*, April 5, 2017, 11:10 a.m. EDT, updated November 9, 2020, 1:38 p.m. EST, https://www.dailymail.co.uk/news/article-4383290/AP-NewsBreak-Joe-Jill-Biden-multi-book-deal.html.

972 Matt Dixon, Allan Smith, and Henry J. Gomez, "Trump World Has Been Preparing to Run Against Kamala Harris for Weeks," *NBC News*, July 21, 2024, https://www.nbcnews.com/politics/2024-election/trump-world-preparing-run-kamala-harris-weeks-rcna162929.

973 Richard Baris, personal communication with the author, various dates in 2024.

974 Kelsey Walsh, Soo Rin Kim, and Lalee Ibssa, "Trump is Running Against Harris, But he Can't Seem to Stop Attacking Biden," *ABC News*, August 13, 2024, https://abcnews.go.com/Politics/trump-running-harris-stop-attacking-biden/story?id=112806452.

975 "Vice President Kamala Harris Interviewed by Bret Baier," YouTube video, 29:36, posted by Fox News, October 17, 2024, https://www.youtube.com/watch?v=80DaR2CVNNk.

976 "'The View' Host Asks Harris What She Would have Done Differently than Biden," *CNN*, October 8, 2024, https://www.cnn.com/2024/10/08/politics/video/kamala-harris-the-view-interview-ana-navarro-digvid.

977 In multiple places over the summer, including Twitter/X, I predicted Trump would win the electoral college with 312 electoral votes, just as in 2016 I predicted in October he would win with "between 300 and 320 electoral votes" (the final was 304). In October, I also predicted Trump would win the popular vote by 1.5% and that Republicans would win a net three seats in the Senate (the Senate final was a net four).

978 Nate Cohn, "The Tilt: Nate Cohn, the Times's Chief Political Analyst, Makes Sense of the Latest Political Data," *The New York Times*, June 27, 2025, https://www.nytimes.com/newsletters/the-tilt.

979 TuftsNow News Staff, "Young Voters Shifted Toward Trump but Still Favored Harris Overall," *TuftsNow*, November 12, 2024, https://now.tufts.edu/2024/11/12/young-voters-shifted-toward-trump-still-favored-harris-overall.

980 Lomez, interviewed by Christopher F. Rufo, "Trump's Extraordinary Opening Moves," podcast audio and transcript, *Christopher Rufo Substack*, January 31, 2025, https://christopherrufo.com/p/trumps-extraordinary-opening-moves.

981 Francis Menton, "The Most Under-Reported Story of the Biden Presidency," *Manhattan Contrarian*, January 7, 2025, https://www.manhattancontrarian.com/blog/2025-1-7-the-most-under-reported-story-of-the-biden-presidency.

982 Naomi LaChance, "'Gullible and Wrong': Journalists Lament Missing Joe Biden's Decline," *Rolling Stone*, December 30, 2024, https://www.rollingstone.com/politics/politics-news/joe-biden-decline-journalists-media-1235221753/.

983 Bruce Mehlman, "The Morning After," *Bruce Mehlman Substack*, November 6, 2024, https://brucemehlman.substack.com/p/the-morning-after.

984 Benedict Smith, "Trump Accused Them of Eating Cats and Dogs. Now Springfield's Haitian Migrants Are Fleeing," *Yahoo News*, January 4, 2026, https://www.yahoo.com/news/town-dead-haitian-migrants-flee-165314310.html.

985 David Blackmon, "Idaho Antimony Mine Finally Receives Final Permit," *David Blackmon Substack*, January 6, 2025, https://blackmon.substack.com/p/idaho-antimony-mine-finally-receives.

986 Zachary Stieber, "Meta Ends Fact-Checking Program in US, Introduces X-Style Community Notes," *Epoch Times*, January 7, 2025, https://www.theepochtimes.com/us/meta-ends-fact-checking-program-in-us-introduces-x-style-community-notes-5787499.

987 Caroline Graham and Sharon Churcher, "She Was Shunned for Donald Trump's Inauguration 2017…but Now Fashion Giants Are Begging to Dress Melania on Her Husband's Big Day," *U.K. Daily Mail*, January 11, 2025, https://www.dailymail.co.uk/tvshowbiz/article-14274329/Donald-Trump-inauguration-2017-fashion-giants-begging-dress-Melania.html.

988 Chase Smith, "FDA Bans Use of Red No. 3 in Food, Ingested Drugs," *Epoch Times*, January 15, 2025, https://www.theepochtimes.com/us/fda-bans-use-of-red-no-3-in-food-ingested-drugs-5792573.

989 John Leake, John Leake, "BREAKING: HHS Formally Debars EcoHealth Alliance, President Peter Daszak Fired," *Courageous Discourse Substack*, January 19, 2025, https://petermcculloughmd.substack.com/p/breaking-hhs-formally-debars-ecohealth.

990 Calvin Coolidge Project X (@TheCalvinCooli1), "BREAKING NEWS: The Port of Entry in EL Paso was Shut Down after Trump Sworn in as President," *X*, January 20, 2025, https://x.com/TheCalvinCooli1/status/1881426450571739164.

991 Naveen Athrappully, "Federal Reserve Withdraws From Global Climate Group as Trump Set to Assume Office," *Epoch Times*, January 18, 2025, https://www.theepochtimes.com/business/federal-reserve-withdraws-from-global-climate-group-as-trump-set-to-assume-power-5794554.

992 Jackson Richman, "97 Percent of ICE Deportees Had Removal Order Under Biden Admin: White House," *America First Report*, February 1, 2025, https://americafirstreport.com/97-percent-of-ice-deportees-had-removal-order-under-biden-admin-white-house/.

993 Isabel Vincent, "Colombia's President Gustavo Petro Buckles Under Trump's Trade War Threat—Offers Presidential Plane for Deportation Flights," *New York Post*, January 26, 2025, https://nypost.com/2025/01/26/us-news/colombias-president-gustavo-petro-buckles-under-trumps-trade-war-threat-offers-presidential-plane-for-deportation-flights/; Cynical Publius (@CynicalPublius), "BREAKING: Colombia's President Gustavo Petro buckles under Trump's trade war threat—offers presidential plane for deportation flights," *X*, January 26, 2025, https://x.com/CynicalPublius/status/1883609921197060262.

994 Ryan Burge (@ryanburge), post on *X*, January 7, 2026, https://x.com/ryanburge/status/1837127432060453088.

995 Marc Caputo, "Scoop: Trump's Black Box," *Axios*, January 26, 2025, https://www.axios.com/2025/01/26/trump-white-house-inner-circle-influence.

996 Donald J. Trump (@realDonaldTrump), post on *Truth Social*, January 27, 2025. Archived image via *X*, https://x.com/AwakenedOutlaw/status/1884128095436955730/photo/1.

997 Kaley, "Border Crossings Drop to HISTORIC LOW Just One Week Into President Trump's Second Term," *WLT Report*, January 28, 2025, https://wltreport.com/2025/01/28/border-crossings-drop-historic-low-just-one-week.

998 Marc Caputo, "Trump Taps Musk to Lead a 'Department of Government Efficiency' with Ramaswamy," *NPR*, November 12, 2024, https://www.npr.org/2024/11/12/g-s1-33972/trump-elon-musk-vivek-ramaswamy-doge-government-efficiency-deep-state.

999 Tom Renz (@RenzTom), "The White House: Executive Order establishing the Department of Government Efficiency," *X*, 2021. Image via https://x.com/RenzTom/status/1887038847629877714/photo/2; Luke Rosiak (@lukerosiak), "HOW DEMS BUILT THE WORLD'S BIGGEST RAKE, THEN STOMPED ON THE DOGE ORIGIN STORY," *X*, February 6, 2025, https://x.com/lukerosiak/status/1887747888630976597.

1000 Ekol Loves You (@EkoLovesYou), "Override: Inside the Revolution Rewiring American Power," *X*, https://x.com/EkoLovesYou/status/1887301698814988567.

1001 Ibid.

1002 James Varney, "DOGE's Key Revelation: A Federal Budget Made Into a Maze Impervious to Reform," *RealClearInvestigations*, March 3, 2025, https://www.realclearinvestigations.com/articles/2025/03/03/doges_key_revelation_a_federal_budget_made_into_a_maze_impervious_to_reform_1093963.html.

1003 Ekol Loves You (@EkoLovesYou), "Override: Inside the Revolution Rewiring American Power," *X*, https://x.com/EkoLovesYou/status/1887301698814988567.

1004 "Just In: DOGE Releases Incredible Progress report After Its First 10 Days," Trendingpoliticalnews.com, January 31, 2025, https://trendingpoliticsnews.com/just-in-doge-releases-incredible-progress-report-after-its-first-10-days-mace.

1005 "DOGE's 120-Hour Grind vs. Bureaucracy's 9-to-5: Elon Musk Claims DOGE Is Shaping the Future of Work," *The Economic Times*, February 2, 2025, https://economictimes.indiatimes.com/news/international/global-trends/doges-120-hour-grind-vs-bureaucracys-9-to-5-elon-musk-claims-doge-is-shaping-the-future-of-work/articleshow/117857199.cms.

1006 Brett T., "DOGE Locks Out OPM Officials by Changing Their Passwords," *Twitchy*, February 1, 2025, https://twitchy.com/brettt/2025/02/01/doge-locks-out-opm-officials-by-changing-their-passwords-n2407700.

1007 Post Editorial Board, "College for Terrorists Is Just One USAID Funding Folly—Trump's Right to Bring the Pain," *New York Post*, February 11, 2025, https://nypost.com/2025/02/11/opinion/college-for-terrorists-is-just-one-usaid-funding-follies-trumps-right-to-bring-the-pain/.

1008 Taylor Fishman, "LIST: 'Insane Priorities' of USAID Spending During Biden Administration," *KUTV*, February 4, 2025, https://kutv.com/news/nation-world/list-insane-priorities-of-usaid-spending-during-biden-administration-foreign-assistance-president-donald-trump-karoline-leavitt-condoms-in-gaza-elon-musk-department-of-government-efficiency.

1009 Kenneth Li, "Thomson Reuters' $9M Contract with US Defense Department Draws Ire from Trump, Musk," *Reuters*, February 13, 2025, https://www.aa.com.tr/en/world/thomson-reuters-9m-contract-with-us-defense-department-draws-ire-from-trump-musk/3481308.

1010 Techno Fog, "An Impressive Start," *The Reactionary*, February 14, 2025, https://technofog.substack.com/p/an-impressive-start.

[1011] Department of Government Efficiency (@DOGE), X post, July 19, 2025, https://x.com/DOGE/status/1890507556033876142.

[1012] Donald Trump, *The Art of the Deal* (New York: Ballantine Books, 1987), 1.

[1013] Marc Caputo, "Axios Interview: Susie Wiles Vows to Block West Wing Troublemakers," *Axios*, January 6, 2025, https://www.axios.com/2025/01/06/axios-interview-susie-wiles-trump.

[1014] Ibid.

[1015] Donald Trump, *The Art of the Deal* (New York: Ballantine Books, 1987), 45–59.

[1016] Ibid., 48.

[1017] Ibid., 39

[1018] Associated Press, "Transcript of President Donald Trump's Speech to a Joint Session of Congress," *U.S. News & World Report*, March 5, 2025, https://www.usnews.com/news/us/articles/2025-03-05/transcript-of-president-donald-trumps-speech-to-a-joint-session-of-congress.

[1019] Richard Truesdell and Keith Lehmann, "Barack Obama: The Political Genius That Wasn't," *American Greatness*, November 14, 2024, https://amgreatness.com/2024/11/14/barack-obama-the-political-genius-that-wasnt.

CHAPTER 10: BRAVE NEW MORNING IN AMERICA

[1020] Noah Smith, "The Death (Again) of the Internet as We Know It," *Noahpinion* (Substack), May 11, 2024, https://www.noahpinion.blog/p/the-death-again-of-the-internet-as.

[1021] Leonardo Bursztyn, et al., "When Product Markets Become Collective Traps: The Case of Social Media," *Becker Friedman Institute for Economics*, October 12, 2023, https://bfi.uchicago.edu/insight/research-summary/when-product-markets-become-collective-traps-the-case-of-social-media/.

[1022] *Larry Schweikart, All Thumbs: How Our Obsession With Phones and Devices Is Damaging Our Kids and Restructuring Our Lives* (Phoenix, AZ: Wild World of History, 2020), 17; James B. Stewart, "Facebook Has 50 Minutes of Your Time Each Day. It Wants More," *The New York Times*, May 5, 2016; Amanda Lenhart, "Teens, Social Media & Technology Overview, 2015," *Pew Research Center*, April 9, 2015, https://www.pewresearch.org/internet/2015/04/09/teens-social-media-technology-2015/; Adam Alter, *Irresistible: The Rise of Addictive Technology and the Business of Keeping Us Hooked* (New York: Penguin, 2017), 78–79; Stanton Peele, *The Truth About Addiction and Recovery: The Life Process Program for Outgrowing Destructive Habits* (New York: Fireside, 1991); Stanton Peele and Archie Brodsky, *Love and Addiction* (New York: Taplinger, 1975); Stanton Peele, *The Meaning of Addiction: An Unconventional View* (Lexington, MA: Lexington Books, 1985); Isaac Marks, "Behavioural (Non-chemical) Addictions," *British Journal of Addiction* 85, no. 11 (November 1990): 1389–94.

[1023] Rachel Simmons, *Odd Girl Out: The Hidden Culture of Aggression in Girls* (New York: Mariner, 2003); Sabrina Tavernise, "Young Adolescents as Likely to Die from Suicide as From Traffic Accidents," *The New York Times*, November 3, 2016; "ED Visits for Suicidal Ideation and Self-Harm on the Rise," *Medpage Today*, January 30, 2020, https://www.medpagetoday.com/publichealthpolicy/publichealth/84633; "Growing Up Online: What Kids Conceal," *Kaspersky Labs Report*, 2016, https://kids.kaspersky.com/wpcontent/uploads/2016/04/KL_Report_GUO_What_Kids_Conceal.pdf.

1024 Noah Smith, "Nobody Knows How Many Jobs Will 'Be Automated,'" *Noahpinion* (Substack), April 10, 2023, https://noahpinion.substack.com/p/nobody-knows-how-many-jobs-will-be.

1025 Nataliya Kosmyna et al., "Your Brain on ChatGPT: Accumulation of Cognitive Debt When Using an AI Assistant for Essay Writing Task," *arXiv* 2506.08872 [cs.AI], June 10, 2025, https://doi.org/10.48550/arXiv.2506.08872.

1026 Liv McMahon, "AI System Resorts to Blackmail if Told it Will be Removed," *BBC*, May 23, 2025, https://www.bbc.com/news/articles/cpqeng9d20go.

1027 James Pethokoukis, "Why Generative AI Could Have a Huge Impact on Economic Growth and Productivity," *American Enterprise Institute* (AEI), March 27, 2023, https://www.aei.org/articles/why-goldman-sachs-thinks-generative-ai-could-have-a-huge-impact-on-economic-growth-and-productivity/.

1028 Noah Smith, "What if Everyone Is Wrong About What AI Does?" *Noahpinion* (Substack), October 7, 2024, https://substack.com/home/post/p-149881887.

1029 Dylan Patel, "The AI Brick Wall—A Practical Limit for Scaling Dense Transformer Models, and How GPT 4 Will Break Past It," *SemiAnalysis*, January 24, 2023, https://www.semianalysis.com/p/the-ai-brick-wall-a-practical-limit.

1030 Ibid.

1031 Pablo Villalobos et al., "Will We Run Out of Data? Limits of LLM Scaling Based on Human-Generated Data," *arXiv* 2211.04325 [cs.LG], October 26, 2022, https://doi.org/10.48550/arXiv.2211.04325.

1032 Susan Murphy, "Mayo Clinic's AI Tool Identifies 9 Dementia Types, Including Alzheimer's, With One Scan," *Mayo Clinic*, June 27, 2025, https://newsnetwork.mayoclinic.org/discussion/mayo-clinics-ai-tool-identifies-9-dementia-types-including-alzheimers-with-one-scan/.

1033 Daron Acemoglu and Simon Johnson, *Power and Progress: Our Thousand-Year Struggle Over Technology and Prosperity* (New York: PublicAffairs, 2023), 30.

1034 Ibid., 32.

1035 Ibid., 32.

1036 Ibid., 32.

1037 Ibid., 31.

1038 Ibid., 31–33.

1039 Ibid., 34.

1040 Ibid., 259.

It is important to note that Germany, whose auto industry has a different union structure with employees having seats on the boards, saw employment in the auto industry rise after the introduction of robotics.

1041 Ibid., 294.

1042 Beina Xu and Eleanor Albert, "Media Censorship in China," *Council on Foreign Relations*, February 17, 2017, https://www.cfr.org/backgrounder/media-censorship-china; Gary King, Jennifer Pan, and Margaret E. Roberts, "How Censorship in China Allows Government Criticism but Silences Collective Expression," *American Political Science Review* 107, no. 2 (May 2013): 326–43, https://doi.org/10.1017/S0003055413000014.

1043 Raymond Zhong, Paul Mozur, Aaron Krolik, and Jeff Kao, "Leaked Documents Show How China's Army of Paid Internet Trolls Helped Censor the Coronavirus," *ProPublica*, December 19, 2020, https://www.propublica.org/article/leaked-documents-show-how-chinas-army-of-paid-internet-trolls-helped-censor-the-coronavirus.

1044 Noah Smith, "The Death (Again) of the Internet as We Know it," *Noahpinion* (Substack), May 11, 2024, https://www.noahpinion.blog/p/the-death-again-of-the-internet-as.

1045 Ibid.

1046 Adam Mastroianni, "Pop Culture has Become an Oligopoly," Adam Mastroianni, "Pop Culture Has Become an Oligopoly," *Experimental History* (Substack), May 2, 2022, https://www.experimental-history.com/p/pop-culture-has-become-an-oligopoly.

1047 Ibid.

1048 Craig Timberg et al., "Private Israeli Spyware Used to Hack Cellphones of Journalists, Activists Worldwide," *The Washington Post*, July 19, 2021, https://www.washington-post.com/investigations/interactive/2021/nso-spyware-pegasus.

1049 Ibid.

1050 Curt Devine, Donie O'Sullivan, and Sean Lyngaas, "A Fake Recording of a Candidate Saying He'd Rigged the Election Went Viral," *CNN*, February 1, 2024, https://www.cnn.com/2024/02/01/politics/election-deepfake-threats-invs/index.html.

1051 Charlie Guo and Timothy Lee, "States Are Racing Ahead of Congress to Regulate Deepfakes," *Understanding AI* (Substack), March 20, 2024, https://www.understandin-gai.org/p/states-are-racing-ahead-of-congress.

1052 "Significant Cyber Incidents," *Center for Strategic International Studies*, September 2024, https://www.csis.org/programs/strategic-technologies-program/significant-cyber-incidents.

1053 Ibid.

1054 Kyle Chin, "Biggest Data Breaches in U.S. History (Updated 2024)," *UpGuard*, September 16, 2024, https://www.upguard.com/blog/biggest-data-breaches-us.

1055 Jeffrey Kluger, "NASA Has Some Bad News for Its Stranded Astronauts," *Time*, August 5, 2024, https://time.com/7011415/nasa-boeing-starliner-astro-nauts-press-conference/; Loren Grush, "Stranded Astronauts Set to Come Home After SpaceX With Extra Seats Reaches ISS," *Time*, September 30, 2024, https://time.com/7026608/stranded-astronauts-spacex-rescue-iss/.

1056 Declan Walsh and Lynsey Chutel, "Elon Musk Left a South Africa That Was Rife With Misinformation and White Privilege," *The New York Times*, May 5, 2022, https://www.nytimes.com/2022/05/05/world/africa/elon-musk-south-africa.html.

1057 Walter Isaacson, *Elon Musk* (New York: Simon & Schuster, 2023), 5.

1058 Ashlee Vance, *Elon Musk: Tesla, SpaceX, and the Quest for a Fantastic Future*, 2nd ed. (New York: Ecco, 2017), 26–30.

1059 John Markoff, "Elon Musk Steps in as CEO at Tesla, Lays Off Staff," *The New York Times*, October 15, 2008, https://www.nytimes.com/2008/10/15/technology/15tesla.html.

1060 Walter Isaacson, *Elon Musk* (New York: Simon & Schuster, 2023), 58.

1061 Ibid., 100.

1062 Ibid., 113.

1063 Ibid., 274.

1064 Tom Ozimek, "Boeing to Slash 17,000 Jobs, End 767 Cargo Plane Production," *The Epoch Times*, October 11, 2024, https://www.theepochtimes.com/business/boeing-to-slash-17000-jobs-end-767-cargo-plane-production-5740135.

1065 Jo Nova, "Google, Amazon, Give Up on National Grid, Ignore Renewables, and Buy Their Own Nuclear Plants," *JoNova*, October 2024, https://joannenova.com.au/2024/10/google-amazon-give-up-on-national-grid-ignore-renewables-and-buy-their-own-nuclear-plants/.

1066 "Twitter 'Permanently Suspends' Trump's Account," *BBC*, January 8, 2021, https://www.bbc.com/news/world-us-canada-55597840.

1067 Shannon Bond, "Facebook Bans Ads Discouraging Vaccines, in Latest Misinformation Crackdown," *NPR*, October 13, 2020, https://www.npr.org/sections/coronavirus-live-updates/2020/10/13/923331982/facebook-bans-ads-discouraging-vaccines-in-latest-misinformation-crackdown.

It should be noted that it was NPR that was engaging in "misinformation" about the vaccines, from "effective" (they weren't) to safe (they definitely weren't).

1068 Angrej Singh, "Zuckerberg on Rogan: Facebook's Censorship was 'Something Out of 1984,'" *Axios*, January 10, 2025, https://www.axios.com/2025/01/10/mark-zuckerberg-joe-rogan-facebook-censorship-biden.

1069 Ibid.

1070 Walter Isaacson, *Elon Musk* (New York: Simon & Schuster, 2021), 444.

1071 Ibid., 451-53.

1072 "Q-Trust Trump's Plan—12/20/2022 Vol. 442, Q Day 1879, Post 1469 Has the Complete, Indexed Twitter Files," *Free Republic*, December 20, 2022, https://freerepublic.com/focus/chat/4117830/posts; "The Twitter Files," *The Epoch Times*, January 17, 2023, https://www.theepochtimes.com/us/infographic-key-revelations-of-the-twitter-files-4986669.

1073 Ariel Zilber, "Washington Post Owner Jeff Bezos Wants More Conservative Opinion Writers at Paper: Report," *New York Post*, October 28, 2024, https://nypost.com/2024/10/28/media/washington-post-owner-jeff-bezos-wants-conservative-writers/.

1074 Charles Fishman, "Face Time With Jeff Bezos," *Fast Company*, January 31, 2001, https://www.fastcompany.com/42412/face-time-jeff-bezos; "Biography of Jeffrey P. Bezos," Academy of Achievement, https://achievement.org/achiever/jeffrey-p-bezos/.

1075 Gary Rivlin, "A Retail Revolution Turns 10," *The New York Times*, July 10, 2005, https://www.nytimes.com/2005/07/10/business/yourmoney/a-retail-revolution-turns-10.html.

1076 Juan Carlos Perez, "Amazon Records First Profitable Year in History," *Computerworld*, January 28, 2004, https://www.computerworld.com/article/1325643/amazon-records-first-profitable-year-in-its-history.html.

As an author, I am acutely aware of the "Amazon number." While publishing still first and foremost focuses on what Barnes & Noble orders, the second most important order now is that of Amazon.

1077 Lauren Debter, "Jeff Bezos Is $1.8 Billion Richer as Amazon's Market Cap Briefly Hits $1 Trillion," *Forbes*, September 4, 2018, https://www.forbes.com/sites/billions/2018/09/04/jeff-bezos-is-18-billion-richer-as-amazons-market-cap-briefly-hits-1-trillion/.

1078 Virgin Galactic, Press Release: "Virgin Galactic Announces First Fully Crewed Spaceflight," July 1, 2021, https://www.virgingalactic.com/news/virgin-galactic-announces-first-fully-crewed-spaceflight.

1079 Larry Schweikart, *The Hypersonic Revolution, Case Studies in the History of Hypersonic Technology: Volume III, The Quest for the Orbital Jet: The National Aero-Space Plane Program (1983–1995)* (Washington, DC: CreateSpace Independent Publishing Platform, 2012).

1080 Ibid.

1081 Christian Davenport, *The Space Barons: Elon Musk, Jeff Bezos, and the Quest to Colonize the Cosmos* (New York: Public Affairs, 2018), 79–97.

1082 Ibid., 91.

1083 Electronic Privacy Information Center (EPIC), Press Release: "EPIC v. CIA – CIA Spying on Congress," 2014, https://epic.org/documents/epic-v-cia-cia-spying-on-congress/.

1084 Ibid.

1085 BBC News, "Lawmakers Allege 'Secret' CIA Spying on Unwitting Americans," *BBC*, February 11, 2022, https://www.bbc.com/news/world-us-canada-60351768.

1086 BBC News, "Edward Snowden: Leaks That Exposed US Spy Programme," *BBC*, January 7, 2024, https://www.bbc.com/news/world-us-canada-23123964.

1087 Charlie Savage, "Reined-in N.S.A. Still Collected 151 Million Phone Records in '16," *The New York Times*, May 2, 2017, https://www.nytimes.com/2017/05/02/us/politics/nsa-phone-records.html.

1088 Dustin Volz, "Spy Agency NSA Triples Collection of U.S. Phone Records: Official Report," *Reuters*, May 8, 2018, https://www.yahoo.com/news/spy-agency-nsa-triples-collection-u-phone-records-150539607.html.

1089 Charles "Cully" Stimson and Stephanie Neville, "Warrants to Spy on Trump Campaign Lacked Probable Cause, DOJ Admits," *Heritage Foundation*, January 30, 2020, https://www.heritage.org/crime-and-justice/commentary/warrants-spy-trump-campaign-lacked-probable-cause-doj-admits.

1090 Matthew Crawford, *Why We Drive: Toward a Philosophy of the Open Road* (New York: Custom House, 2020), 289.

1091 Ibid., 218.

1092 Ibid., 218.

1093 Matt Labash, "The Safety Myth," *The Weekly Standard*, April 2, 2002, http://www.weeklystandard.com/the-safety-myth/article/2375.

1094 Matthew Crawford, *Why We Drive: Toward a Philosophy of the Open Road* (New York: Custom House, 2020), 223.

1095 Ibid., 292.

1096 Ibid., 292.

1097 Shoshanna Zuboff, The Age of Surveillance Capitalism: The Fight for a Human Future at the New Frontier of Power (New York Public Affairs, 2019), "The Definition," frontpiece.

1098 Ibid., "Definition."

1099 Ibid., 8,146–50.

1100 Ibid., 8, 303.

1101 Ibid., 105.

1102 Jake Coyle, "In Hollywood Writers' Battle Against AI, Humans Win (for Now)," *AP*, September 27, 2023, https://apnews.com/article/hollywood-ai-strike-wga-artificial-intelligence-39ab72582c3a15f77510c9c30a45ffc8.

1103 Jennifer Saba, "Hollywood is First and Lat Defense in AI War," *Reuters*, May 21, 2024, https://www.reuters.com/breakingviews/hollywood-is-first-last-defense-ai-war-2024-05-21/.

1104 Noah Smith, "At Least Five Interesting Things to Start Your Week (#38)," *Noahpinion* (Substack), March 27, 2024, https://www.noahpinion.blog/p/at-least-five-interesting-things-f84.

1105 Laura Ungar, "Elon Musk Says a Third Patient Got a Neuralink Brain Implant. The Work Is Part of a Booming Field," *Associated Press*, January 13, 2025, https://apnews.com/article/elon-musk-neuralink-brain-computer-interface-9dbc92206389f27fd032825cf1597ee5.

1106 Victoria Oldemburgo de Mello, Felix Cheung, and Michael Inzlicht, "Twitter (X) Use Predicts Substantial Changes in Well-Being, Polarization, Sense of Belonging, and Outrage," *Nature Communications Psychology* 15 (2024): 1–11, https://www.nature.com/articles/s44271-024-00062-z.pdf.

1107 Reza Shabahang et al., "Doomscrolling Evokes Existential Anxiety and Fosters Pessimism About Human Nature? Evidence from Iran and the United States,"

Computers in Human Behavior Reports 15 (August 2024): 100438, https://www.sciencedirect.com/science/article/pii/S245195882400071X.

1108 Claire E. Robertson et al., "Negativity Drives Online News Consumption," *Nature Human Behaviour* 7, no. 5 (2023): 812–822, https://www.nature.com/articles/s41562-023-01538-4.

1109 Michael Lind, "The New Gatekeepers," *Tablet*, October 26, 2022, https://www.tabletmag.com/sections/news/articles/new-gatekeepers-woke-michael-lind.

1110 Ibid.

1111 Armando Simon, "A Blanket of Darkness is Falling Over the West," *Issues and Insights*, September 19, 2024, https://issuesinsights.com/2024/09/19/a-blanket-of-darkness-is-falling-over-the-west/.

1112 Thung-Hong Lin et al., "Government-Sponsored Disinformation and the Severity of Respiratory Infection Epidemics Including COVID-19: A Global Analysis, 2001–2020," *Social Science & Medicine* 296 (March 2022): 114744, https://www.sciencedirect.com/science/article/pii/S245195882400071X.

1113 Michael Lind, "The New Gatekeepers," *Tablet*, October 26, 2022, https://www.tabletmag.com/sections/news/articles/new-gatekeepers-woke-michael-lind.

1114 Duke University, "What Does a Social Disaster Sound Like?" *African & African American Studies Program*, 2006, https://today.duke.edu/showcase/mmedia/pdf/socialdisasterad.pdf; Don Yaeger and Mike Pressler, *It's Not About the Truth: The Untold Story of the Duke Lacrosse Case and the Lives It Shattered* (New York: Threshold Editions, 2007); K.C. Johnson and Stuart Taylor Jr., *Until Proven Innocent: Political Correctness and the Shameful Injustices of the Duke Lacrosse Rape Case* (New York: Macmillan, Kindle Edition, 2010).

1115 Robby Soave, "A Year Ago, the Media Mangled the Covington Catholic Story. What Happened Next Was Even Worse," *Reason*, January 21, 2020, https://reason.com/2020/01/21/covington-catholic-media-nick-sandmann-lincoln-memorial/.

1116 National Trial Lawyers, "CNN Confirms Settlement After $275 Million Lawsuit With Nick Sandmann," *National Trial Lawyers*, https://thenationaltriallawyers.org/article/cnn-confirms-settlement-after-275-million-lawsuit-with-nick-sandmann/; Daily Wire, "Nick Sandmann's Lawyers Respond to CNN Settling in $275 Million Lawsuit," *Daily Wire*, accessed July 26, 2025, https://www.dailywire.com/news/nick-sandmanns-lawyers-respond-to-cnn-settling-in-275-million-lawsuit-cnn-confirms-settlement.

1117 Robby Soave, "A Year Ago, the Media Mangled the Covington Catholic Story. What Happened Next Was Even Worse," *Reason*, January 21, 2020, https://reason.com/2020/01/21/covington-catholic-media-nick-sandmann-lincoln-memorial/.

1118 Bobby Allyn, "Meta Agrees to Pay Trump $25 million to Settle Lawsuit Over Facebook and Instagram Suspensions," *NPR*, January 29, 2025, https://www.npr.org/2025/01/29/nx-s1-5279570/meta-trump-settlement-facebook-instagram-suspensions.

1119 Paula Reid and Katelyn Polantz, "ABC News Settles Defamation Suit With Trump for $15 Million," *CNN*, December 14, 2024, https://www.cnn.com/2024/12/14/politics/trump-abc-news-defamation-lawsuit-settle/index.html.

1120 Benjamin Mullin and Michael M. Grynbaum, "CNN Plots Major Overhaul as It Enters A New Trump Era," *The New York Times*, January 1, 2023, https://www.nytimes.com; Ariel Zilber, "Washington Post Owner Jeff Bezos Wants More Conservative Opinion Writers at Paper: Report," *New York Post*, October 28, 2024, https://nypost.com.

1121 Aleks Phillips, "Fox News Ratings Fall Off a Cliff After Tucker Carlson's Departure," *Newsweek*, May 9, 2023, https://www.newsweek.com/tucker-carlson-departure-fox-news-ratings-msnbc-1799153.

1122 Emily Peck, "Companies are Backing Away from 'DEI'," *Axios*, January 4, 2024, https://www.axios.com/2024/01/04/dei-jobs-diversity-corporate.

1123 Noah Smith, "At Least Five Interesting Things to Start Your Week (#2)," *Noahpinion* (Substack), June 5, 2023, https://www.noahpinion.blog/p/at-least-five-interesting-things-5b3.

1124 David Blackmon, "Ho, Hum: Another Year, Another $5 Billion EV Loss at Ford Motor Co.," *Energy Transition Absurdities*, February 6, 2025, https://blackmon.substack.com/p/ho-hum-another-year-another-5-billion.

1125 M. Winger, "President Trump Gets Giant Automaker to Return, Nearly 1500 UAW Jobs," *WLT Report*, January 22, 2025, https://wltreport.com/2025/01/22/president-trump-gets-giant-automaker-return-1500-uaw.

1126 Joseph Politano, "America's Productivity Boom," *Apricitas Economics* (Substack), November 25, 2024, https://www.apricitas.io/p/americas-productivity-boom.

1127 Noah Smith, "Degrowth: We Can't Let it Happen Here!" *Noahpinion* (Substack), May 23, 2023, https://www.noahpinion.blog/p/degrowth-we-cant-let-it-happen-here.

Even as he wrote that column, Smith, a rabid Democrat, supported Joe Biden and his degrowth policies.

1128 The Economist, "The World's Economic Order is Breaking Down," *The Economist*, May 9, 2024, https://www.economist.com/briefing/2024/05/09/the-worlds-economic-order-is-breaking-down.

1129 Larry Schweikart, *A Patriot's History of Globalism: Its Rise and Decline* (New York: Skyhorse, 2024).

1130 Noah Smith, "An Age of Austerity is Probably on the Way," *Noahpinion* (Substack), September 18, 2023, https://www.noahpinion.blog/p/an-age-of-austerity-is-probably-on.

1131 Larry Schweikart, *Reagan: The American President* (Post Hill Press, 2019).

1132 Rebecca Beitsch and Zach Schonfeld, "Judge Boasberg Rules Migrants at Salvadoran Megaprison Can Contest Gang Accusations," *The Hill*, June 3, 2025, https://thehill.com/regulation/court-battles/5333555-venezuelans-deported-prison-judge-ruling/.

1133 Elie Mystal, "The Supreme Court's Birthright Citizenship Ruling is a 5-Alarm Catastrophe," *The Nation*, June 27, 2025, https://www.thenation.com/article/society/supreme-court-birthright-citizenship-ruling-trump-v-casa/; *Trump v. CASA, Inc.*, 606 U.S. (2025).Same as earlier cases.

1134 Jon Dougherty, "Hegseth, Joint Chiefs Chairman Reveal Details of Iran Strike," *The Conservative Brief*, June 23, 2025, https://conservativebrief.com/hegseth-reveal-92514; Jim Hoft, "Iranian Foreign Minister Refutes Fake News CNN and NYT: 'Our Nuclear Installations Have Been Badly Damaged,'" *Gateway Pundit*, June 25, 2025, https://www.thegatewaypundit.com/2025/06/iranian-foreign-minister-refutes-fake-news-cnn-nyt/.

ACKNOWLEDGMENTS

To David Bernstein and the team at Post Hill Press. Thanks also to those who provided such great insight and influence through my career, even if you don't know or don't want to claim me, especially Robert Loewenberg, W. Ellot Brownlee, Paul Johnson, Rush Limbaugh, Frederick K. C. Price, David Dougherty, Steve Bannon, and my wife, Dee, who understood there were times when I had to be alone to wrestle with the past.